THE

FRENCH

SECRET

SERVICES

THE

FRENCH

SECRET

SERVICES

*From the Dreyfus Affair
to the Gulf War*

D O U G L A S   P O R C H

Farrar, Straus and Giroux
New York

Library of Congress Cataloging-in-Publication Data
Porch, Douglas.
The French secret services : from the Dreyfus Affair to the Gulf
War / Douglas Porch.
p.   cm.
Includes bibliographical references and index.
1. Intelligence service—France—History.   2. Secret service—
France—History.   3. France—Politics and government.   I. Title.
JN2738.I58P67   1995   327.1244'09'04—dc20   94-46833 CIP

CONTENTS

TERMS AND ABBREVIATIONS

Abwehr German military intelligence.

ALN Armée de Libération Nationale   Military wing of the Algerian FLN.

AS Armée Secrète   Amalgamated Resistance military forces.

BCRA Bureau Central de Renseignements et d'Action   Gaullist intelligence service, became the DGSS in 1944.

BMA Bureau des Menées Anti-nationales   Camouflaged sections of SR under Vichy until abolished August 1942.

BTLC Bureau Technique de Liaison et de Coordination   Colonial Ministry security service.

cabinet noir Black chamber charged with reading mail and breaking codes.

CFLN Comité Français de Libération nationale.

Chiffrierstelle German cipher bureau.

CNR Conseil National de la Résistance.

Deuxième Bureau G2: intelligence section of the general staff.

DGER Direction Générale des Etudes et Recherches   Responsible for foreign intelligence from November 1944 to January 1946.

DGSE Direction Générale de la Sécurité Extérieure   Heir of SDECE, responsible for foreign intelligence since 1981.

DGSS Direction Générale des Services Spéciaux   Heir of BCRA, which became DGER in 1944 and eventually the SDECE in 1946. Responsible for foreign intelligence.

DPSD Direction de la Protection de la Sécurité de la Défense   Heir of Sécurité Militaire since 1981.

DST Direction de la Surveillance du Territoire   Created in 1944 from the old ST, responsible for internal security.

FLN Front de Libération Nationale   Algerian liberation organization.

FTP Franc-tireurs et Partisans   Communist-led resistance movement.

Gestapo A branch of the German secret political police.

GIGN Groupement d'Intervention de la Gendarmerie Nationale Elite force of gendarmes.

GQG Grand Quartier Général GHQ.

humint Human- or agent-generated intelligence.

katiba ALN company.

maquis Resistance forces in World War II. The term was later applied to the French-led Montagnard forces in Indochina.

Milice The paramilitary Vichy police.

OAS Organisation Armée Secrète Pro-*Algérie française* organization opposed to de Gaulle.

11ème Choc Special operations parachute commando regiment.

ORA Organisation de Résistance de l'Armée A resistance movement made up of army officers.

OSS Office of Strategic Services.

pieds noirs Algerians of European extraction.

PTT Postes, Télégraphes, Téléphone French postal and telephone services.

Quai d'Orsay French Foreign Office.

RG Renseignements Généraux.

RGPP Renseignements Généraux de la Préfecture de Paris.

SAC Service d'Action Civique Gaullist "security service."

SD Sicherheitsdienst Nazi Party security service under Himmler.

SDECE Service de Documentation Extérieure et de Contre-espionnage Created in January 1946 from the DGER. Responsible for foreign intelligence.

Section du Chiffre Cipher Bureau.

Service Action Operational section of the SDECE.

SHAEF Supreme Headquarters Allied Expeditionary Force.

sigint Signals intelligence.

SIS British Secret Intelligence Service.

SM Sécurité Militaire Keeps watch on subversion in the ranks and at defense installations. In 1981, became the DPSD.

SR Service de Renseignements Under the Deuxième Bureau, responsible for collating intelligence from several sources, as well as counterintelligence, the running of agents, spies, telephone taps, and the analysis of foreign newspapers and periodicals.

ST   Surveillance du Territoire   Intelligence section of the Sûreté or Special Branch, forerunner of the DST.

STO   Service du Travail Obligatoire   Forced labor in Germany.

Sûreté   Special Branch.

TR   Travaux Ruraux   Camouflaged counterintelligence section under Vichy.

wilaya   Military division of the ALN.

ZL   Zone libre   Zone of southern France left unoccupied by the Germans June 1940–November 1942.

ZO   Zone occupée   Zone under direct German administration.

PREFACE

Initial credit—or blame—for this book must go to Michael Handel and Christopher Andrew, who encouraged me to expand a paper on French intelligence and the Fall of France in 1940, written for a 1986 conference at the U.S. Army War College at Carlisle, Pennsylvania, into a larger study of the modern French secret services. The idea simmered as I completed my book on the French Foreign Legion, until it was taken up with enthusiasm by my agents, Michael Congdon and Jill Coleridge, and subsequently by John Glusman at Farrar, Straus & Giroux. The topic seemed ideal.

Since the revelation in the mid-1970s of the Ultra secret made intelligence studies a subject for serious inquiry, works on the CIA, KGB, MI5, or Mossad have proliferated. Those on the French remained fragmented, largely the province of investigative journalists in France, who, though apparently privy to "insider" information, lurch between what Wesley Wark, a Canadian historian of intelligence organizations, has identified as two opposing interpretations: either the secret service-induced scandals which they investigate represent the pathetic intrigues of marginal functionaries, or, conversely, they reveal the tip of a vast, criminal, and ceaseless conspiracy against the state whose potential for damage is incalculable.

Of course, many countries endure an ambiguous relationship with their secret services—fascinated, dependent, yet disapproving, perhaps repelled, even made fearful by the very character of their charter, the occult range of their preoccupations. That said, however, secret service relations in France have offered an arena of more than ordinary turmoil. France's history of war and invasion in the twentieth century, its politically fragmented society which has presented secret service organizations with extraordinary opportunities for partisan activity, and a tradition of governments and police spying on their own citizens have made this so. For these reasons, there is obviously room for a study of the French secret services which attempts to chronicle their development in the modern era, which asks basic questions about what France expected and expects from its secret services, and which attempts to strike a balanced assessment of their role and influence in the state and the military.

As I subsequently plunged into my research, however, the elusiveness of the subject was brought home full force. Archives were seized, scattered, or destroyed during World War II, or, though listed and summarized in inventories, remained closed by France's restrictive sixty-year rule on intelligence documents. On one occasion, a young French archivist returned from her lunch break to discover that, in her absence, a dossier entitled "telephone taps on the Japanese embassy, 1939" had been "communicated" to me. She galloped across the room screaming, "Monsieur, you have no right to see that!," swooped on the documents spread across my desk, and, clutching them tight to her breasts, clattered back across the hardwood floor to her work station. It was the high point of the day for the other readers in the archives, and for the first time in my life I came to appreciate the benefits of a French two-hour lunch break to which I had not been invited, because in this instance it allowed me to consult the documents at leisure.

But these restrictions obviously pose a problem for serious scholars. The difficulties experienced by all historians of intelligence in trying to determine how far policy or command decisions are influenced by information acquired through clandestine means become especially acute in France. Such restrictive laws tell us far more about France's ambiguous attitudes toward its secret services than about any actual benefits France thinks it reaps from a prolonged concealment. Because the French services have a long history of spying on their own people, especially their political leaders, do those who pass these laws actually do so out of self-interest rather than state interests? A potential treasure trove of French intelligence documents seized during the Nazi occupation and subsequently captured by the Soviets in 1945 survives in Moscow. However, at the time of writing, French archivists have assured me that, despite agreement to repatriate these documents to Paris, the Russian government so far has declined to do so. Should these documents ever see the light of day, then obviously the work of

French secret services at least in the pre-1940 period might have to be reevaluated. In the meantime, the task of this book is to ask pertinent questions about the role of the secret services over the last century or so of French history, when possible to fill gaps in our historical knowledge, and, finally, supply what I hope is a resilient framework for the analysis of any new material which may appear in the future.

I have tried to compensate for the limitations of archival access by means of other sources. Published works on the secret services are surprisingly plentiful, not the least because a number of former French agents have rushed boldly into print. While these memoirs or historical studies by ex-officers of the Deuxième Bureau, SDECE, DST, or one of a number of smaller, sometimes transient, services can be useful, they often—indeed, usually—advance claims for the value or influence of their intelligence activity which can appear boastful, inflated, or skewed because the writer has some ax to grind or grudge to settle. Some French intelligence operations, like the 1985 sinking of the *Rainbow Warrior* in Auckland harbor, appear so poorly conceived, almost clownish, that it would be deceptively easy to write a history of the secret services in a vaudevillian mode.

Since 1894, when the French Statistical Section discovered the *bordereau* in the wastebasket of the Prussian military attaché which launched the notorious Dreyfus Affair, the role of the French services has been too important to dismiss as irrelevant to the history of France in the twentieth century. The problem for the historian is to trace that influence, to delineate the relationship between France and her secret services, no easy task for organizations which work in the shadows, whose activities often seem more suitable subjects for writers of fiction than for scholars. Truth is further obscured by polemics which revolve around France's perpetual "war of the secret services," a struggle fought on many fronts between Vichyites and Gaullists, between "technicians" and "political" operatives, between regular services and parallel organizations, among the DST, RG, RGPP, and the SDECE/DGSE, between those who see intelligence as the collection of information and those who prefer a more "operational" approach. A study of intelligence invariably must confront one of the central myths of modern French history—the importance of the World War II French Resistance as an intelligence and "action" organization and its legacy to the world of postwar French intelligence. To sift the debris of these struggles and arrive at something resembling accuracy makes for a bewildering challenge. The author can only come as close to the truth as his sources and his judgment can lead him.

I am grateful to former intelligence officers who consented to interviews, especially Admiral Pierre Lacoste, Paul Paillole, and Roger Joint-Daguenet, and to CIA officials with names like Bob, Fred, and Jim, who generously offered their observations on the French services. That most of their conclusions agreed with mine should comprise, I suppose, a source of some comfort to a historian who hopes to have "got it right." Christopher Andrew, Michael Handel and David Kahn have remained unstintingly helpful in suggesting new avenues of approach, including guidance through a growing theoretical literature which seeks to explain how intelligence organizations interact with politicians and commanders. The appendix on code breaking is largely the work of Commander Robert Godwin. The Citadel Development Foundation provided generous grants which allowed me to complete my research, while the Strategy Department of the Naval War College invited me to serve as a Secretary of the Navy Fellow while I completed the manuscript. Last, I should like to thank my wife, Françoise, and children Charles and Olivia, constant reminders of what is really valuable in life.

Naval War College
Newport, Rhode Island

THE

FRENCH

SECRET

SERVICES

ONE

THE BIRTH OF THE
MODERN FRENCH
SECRET SERVICES

—"Our emissary has been warned."

Nothing in the background of Captain Alfred Dreyfus singled him out as a spy. The son of a family of wealthy Alsatian Jews who had spurned the offer of German citizenship when their native province was annexed by Berlin in 1871, Alfred had been cast by his German-speaking father into the pressure cooker of schools and *lycées* which fashioned France's educated elite, a path which carried Alfred into the prestigious Ecole Polytechnique. Upon graduation in 1880, Alfred Dreyfus had rejected an obvious road to preferment in his family's textile empire and instead chose to make his life in the French army. Patriotism played a major role in this decision. Nothing so symbolized France's sense of damaged pride, her unity in the face of the German menace, her desire to avenge her defeat in the Franco-Prussian War of 1870–71 and reclaim her amputated provinces of Alsace and Lorraine than did the French army. For a son of Alsace, a military career offered ennoblement, a high calling, a statement of devotion to France.

Besides, the army appeared to offer a natural outlet for Dreyfus' considerable talent. His sense of purpose focused and honed by years of exam taking combined with his intellectual brilliance to earn for him a place in the French army staff college, whose students were recruited by competitive examination among senior captains. He had completed the two-year course near the top of his class, virtually a passport to high military rank, especially when complemented by the laudatory service reports of his superiors. More to the point, his own wealth, combined with that of his wife, Lucie, daughter of Paris' leading diamond merchant, insulated him against financial embarrassment, the more usual condition of army households. In short, Dreyfus, who with his wife and two young children led an existence of bourgeois, even almost dreary, respectability, hardly fit the popular image of a spy. In retrospect, Dreyfus counted only two liabilities— his Jewishness and an emotional personality, which he disguised with such success that those who met him came away with the impression of a man of aloof, almost arrogant, detachment.

So, when at 8 a.m. on Monday, 15 October 1894, Captain Dreyfus walked from his sumptuous apartments on Paris' Right Bank along the Seine and across the Pont de l'Alma to the War Ministry on the rue Saint-Dominique in answer to a strange summons that he arrive at work early and in civilian clothes, the fact that he was about to be charged with spying for Germany would have struck him as preposterous. Even after he had been seated by Major Mercier du Paty de Clam and asked to take a dictation, at the end of which the major clamped his hand on Dreyfus' shoulder and announced in a sententious voice, "I arrest you in the name of the law. You are accused of the crime of high treason," the captain was at a loss to discover why suspicion had fallen on him. Patriotic, rich, happily married, obviously destined for career success, why should Dreyfus have felt compelled to pass French secrets to the German military attaché in Paris?

The consequences for France of Dreyfus' twelve-year calvary of court-martial, incarceration on Devil's Island, retrial, presidential pardon, and eventual rehabilitation were profound. The anti-Semitic passions it aroused, the attacks on the honor of the army, precipitated a political realignment which shaped French politics for much of the twentieth century.

That an affair so heavy with consequence could be touched off by the Statistical Section, the French general staff's secret service, was no mere accident. The defeat of France in the Franco-Prussian War of 1870–71, and the unification of "the Germanys" into a single empire dominated by Prussia on 18 January 1871, had tilted the balance of power in Europe irrevocably against France. In the quarter century since that defeat, France's predicament had only grown worse. Though France had created a modern conscript army to replace the small professional force which had been shredded in the debacle of 1870–71, it matched German forces neither in size nor in reputation for efficiency. Since the war, Germany's population and industrial growth had exceeded that of France by a wide margin, while the skillful diplomacy of German Chancellor Otto von Bismarck, which had locked Germany, Russia, and Austria-Hungary into an alliance, conspired with Anglo-French imperial rivalry in Africa to keep France friendless. Bereft of allies as France was, in relative decline vis-à-vis her principal adversary, the perception that the Hun could steal yet more advantage through espionage or subversion was extremely damaging to French notions of security and amour propre. For this reason, the uniquely important mission to act as the sentinels of France devolved upon the general staff and its Statistical Section. Alas, the question raised by the Dreyfus Affair from a secret service perspective was: "Who guards the guards?" This was to pose the great dilemma for France in the twentieth century.

France required an efficient secret service as the sine qua non of her security. Yet the Dreyfus Affair, which envenomed French politics at the turn of the century, was a clear indication to France that she could never be certain of the loyalties of her secret services, convinced of their objectivity, persuaded that their competence and integrity were absolute. In short, France required efficient secret services, yet she was to remain skeptical of their motives, distrustful of their product.

The *pièce à conviction* upon which the Statistical Section suspended their case against Dreyfus was an unsigned note which contained information on maneuvers and artillery. That an affair of such magnitude should have begun with a piece of intercepted correspondence was hardly surprising, for in France the practice of reading other people's mail was practically as old as the nation itself.

The creation by the first Bourbon king, Henri IV, of the Poste aux Lettres in 1590, offered government ministers regular access to the private affairs of the nation. Letter-opening services known at various periods in the *ancien régime* as the *cabinet noir* (black chamber), the Bureau du Secret, or even the Bureau du Dedans (Inside Bureau) intercepted mail usually out of "an unhealthy desire to learn family secrets."[1] Indeed, the use of agents to supply kings and ministers with salacious information on the sexual escapades of courtiers was practically a secret service industry under the Bourbons. Richelieu and Mazarin regularly appropriated letters, a practice adopted by their successors under Louis XIV, Colbert, Louvois, and Le Tellier, who especially targeted the correspondence of the powerful Jesuits to gain information during the Sun King's many wars.

The knowledge that correspondence was being read encouraged the development of codes and ciphers, many of them sophisticated enough to stump twentieth-century experts. It also offered new opportunities for deception—for instance, during the siege of Hesdin in 1639, the French intercepted an appeal for Spanish assistance from the town, which allowed them to fabricate an encoded reply from the Cardinal Infante announcing that relief was impossible and ordering the garrison to surrender. But none of this came cheaply. Expert code breakers like Rossignol, Pajot, and Rouillé, who served the Bourbons, were able to command significant wages, as were the squads of technicians who concealed any hint of tampering by the reconstruction of broken seals. The revolutionaries of 1789 published documents showing that the later Bourbons were spending 300,000 livres a year on the black chamber. Protests over the interception of correspondence figured prominently in the *cahiers de doléances*, lists of popular grievances drawn up in 1789 from which the Estates General was to compose an agenda for reform. Both the Legislative Assembly and its successor, the Constituent Assembly, declared tampering with the mail to be illegal.[2]

But espionage proved a hearty shrub, especially in the atmosphere of invasion and civil war spawned by the Revolution. Local *comités de surveillance* began to open the letters of those suspected of royalist sentiments, so that not a few *ci-devants* mounted the scaffolds of the Year II on the basis of evidence gleaned from the intercepted letters of émigré nobles or priests. Paris considered correspondence to and from regions in rebellion against the central government or from the regime's opponents fair game, and a special office in the *bureau de police générale* was created to filter this correspondence. The Quai d'Orsay, the French Foreign Office, established a *bureau statistique* where "one brought, copied, falsified, destroyed for the needs of all surprise dispatches."[3]

It was Napoleon, however, who elevated espionage into an efficiently run, centrally directed state enterprise. At first glance this may appear surprising; the Emperor said little about intelligence when he dictated his maxims on St. Helena near the end of his life. But in fact he made extensive use of intelligence, both for purposes of internal security and for making war.

The task of regulating internal security fell to the Emperor's redoubtable Prefect of Police, Joseph Fouché. Fouché's character blended that lethal mixture of ambition and conspiracy which so few are able successfully to manipulate. Son of a sea captain from a small village near Nantes in the heart of staunchly pro-Catholic and pro-royalist France, Fouché felt early in the French Revolution the requirement to establish his impeccably Jacobin credentials. A disciple of Robespierre, Citizen Fouché sat with the radical "Mountain" in the Convention and voted for the death in 1792 of the hapless Louis XVI. Fouché's "regicide" past combined with his obvious opportunism to make him forever suspect among the more conservative elements of Napoleon's entourage. And this despite, or even because, he had been a prime player in the conspiracies to overthrow Robespierre in 1794 and, as Minister of Police under the Directory, in the 1799 coup d'état of 18 Brumaire which elevated Napoleon to First Consul. His drooping eyelids, long nose, and small, tight mouth etched across his features the chilling reminder that this was a man for whom secrecy had become part of his psychological makeup. The braided and bemedaled uniform accorded Fouché as Duc d'Otrante badly disguised the reek of intrigue, the odor of treachery and the guillotine which hovered about him.

Thus, while it falls to all spymasters to frequent people of doubtful character and questionable morals, Fouché appears to have been drawn quite naturally to his vocation. The truth was that Napoleon needed Fouché's contacts, skills, and police experience built up during the decade of revolution to help him impose his authority over a murderously riven nation. This point was emphatically pushed home in 1804 when police failed to detect a royalist plot against Napoleon's life.

Alerted to the conspiracy by one of his agents in London, Méhée de la Touche, Napoleon ordered the arrest of the chief conspirators, as well as a few who had nothing to do with the assassination plot. He then reestablished the Ministry of General Police under Fouché in July 1804. Fouché's spy network informed the Emperor of the activities of his enemies and even of his own administrators at home and abroad, working on Napoleon's premise that "a leader has the right to be beaten, but never the right to be surprised."

The most important office in Fouché's Ministry of General Police was the Sûreté, or secret police, which from 1800 to 1814 was run by Pierre-Marie Desmarest. In the imperial league table, Desmarest ranked as the "third most powerful man in France," bare fractions of percentages behind Napoleon and Fouché. Fouché called Desmarest "my trusted ferret," whose skills at interrogation he particularly admired.[4]

Most of Desmarest's ferreting was done by a *cabinet noir*, which in this era was a sophisticated collection of code breakers, technicians, linguists, and men knowledgeable about "foreign habits," under the direct authority of the Postmaster General, Antoine Lavalette. A voracious reader, Lavalette was destined for the priesthood. But the Revolution deflected Lavalette's path toward the army, where good fortune caused him to be appointed to Napoleon's staff during the 1796 Italian campaign. Barely five feet tall, Lavalette hardly cut a dashing figure in the Army of Italy—Madame Junot, the wife of one of Napoleon's marshals, described his appearance as practically comical: "He had this burlesque appearance," she remembered. "Built like a Bacchus, with short legs holding up a promising paunch, and a comical face because of his tiny eyes, a pea-sized nose between two fat cheeks, all this surrounded by hair which you could count not in curls but singly." Napoleon, however, recognized in Lavalette an intelligent and devoted servant, and dispatched him to Paris, Vienna, Venice, and eventually Dresden on political and espionage missions. Indeed, so devoted was Lavalette that he even consented to marry Emilie de Beauharnais, the niece of Napoleon's wife, Josephine, whose lack of dowry, partial disfigurement by smallpox, not to mention the eccentric behavior of her divorced parents (her father remarried a nun, her mother a black man), had combined to make her marriage prospects uniquely bleak.

In 1800, Lavalette was appointed Commissioner General of the Post Office, which required him to oversee the *cabinet noir*. Though he claimed in his memoirs to be disgusted with the idea of reading other people's mail, the task appears to have supplied him with an arsenal of witty gossip which made him a sought-after guest at fashionable Parisian dinner parties.

Through Lavalette, the Emperor could keep track not only of the plans of his enemies but more importantly the activities of his own ministers, marshals, and even the Bonaparte family, all in all an excellent return on its 600,000-franc annual budget. This black chamber also exercised postal censorship, stopping letters which brought news of French reverses in Spain so as not to demoralize the population.[5] As the Empire expanded, black chambers were created in provincial France, and eventually extended to European centers in Italy, Amsterdam, and Hamburg. Letters were intercepted through the regular post, but also through agents working in various parts of Europe. But French mail was also being read—in December 1811, for instance, Napoleon ordered Lavalette to stop letters between his brother Louis Bonaparte to Princess Pauline because "these letters are read abroad, and it is putting Europe into the family secrets."

Lavalette rallied to Napoleon during the Hundred Days, a crime for which he was sentenced to death in the aftermath of Waterloo. However, whatever burdens his marriage to the unfortunate Emilie de Beauharnais may have imposed proved well worth the years of agony—the night before his execution, Emilie, with the connivance of two bribed prison wardens, substituted herself for her husband, who was spirited out of the country into a Bavarian exile by British officers incensed over the execution of Marshal Ney. When given news of the escape, Louis XVIII, who in 1820 was to issue Lavalette the pardon which allowed him to die in Paris in 1830, sighed that Emilie appeared to be the only one of his subjects prepared to do her duty.

The problem for the Emperor, as for his successors, was how far to trust his own intelligence services? The knowledge which made Talleyrand and Fouché such valuable servants also opened to them the perspective of initiatives independent of higher authority. When combined with Fouché's naturally conspiratorial disposition, it was a recipe for deception, even disloyalty. One consequence was that, if Napoleon was eager to avoid the "surprises" of his enemies, he also took out insurance against the possible treachery of those around him. On St.

Helena, Napoleon insisted that the most valuable service provided by Lavalette's black chamber, which was presented to him each morning in a red morocco briefcase marked "foreign gazettes," was to open the letters of those close to Talleyrand and Fouché, so that he could follow their activities and know their intentions. Napoleon especially distrusted Fouché, and required Paris Police Prefect Louis Dubois to supply him with a confidential daily report on Fouché's activities.[6] It proved a wise precaution—in 1810, Fouché was replaced by René Savary, Duc de Rovigo, after the Emperor discovered that his Prefect of Police was dealing secretly with the English. Fouché bore his disgrace badly, and destroyed, lost, or otherwise disorganized a significant portion of the police archives, in particular his extensive file index, on his departure. As a consequence of Fouché's disgruntled behavior, Savary had to rebuild portions of the intelligence services virtually from scratch. He was well placed to do so. First of all, Napoleon's ex-bodyguard enjoyed the Emperor's complete confidence—"If I ordered Savary to do away with his wife and children," Napoleon is alleged to have said, "I am sure that he would not hesitate."[7] Fortunately for Madame and the kids, it was not they but the Duc d'Enghien, son of Napoleon's royalist opponent the Prince de Condé, whom Savary had been ordered to "do away with." In 1804, agents under Savary's direction kidnapped Enghien in Baden. The seizure of a royal prince on foreign territory was regarded at the time as a criminal defiance of international convention, all the more so as, following the merest pretense of a court-martial, the unfortunate Enghien was executed by firing squad in the moat of the Château de Vincennes just east of Paris. Savary's loyalty assured, Napoleon had given him a certain latitude in foreign espionage duties alongside Fouché as an extra check on his Police Minister. In this office, Savary had proved to be no deskbound bureaucrat, but one willing, for instance, to travel incognito into Austria to scout out enemy positions prior to Napoleon's 1805 campaign which terminated with his stunning victory at Austerlitz. Loyalty to the Emperor preempted any residual notions of morality or even political justice which might have survived, admittedly against the odds, Savary's upbringing. Brutal, lacking tact, "a thug without finesse," he suppressed reports, detained agents, and generally conspired to undermine Fouché's authority.

After 1810, Savary rebuilt Fouché's organization into an even more repressive machine which tightened press censorship, disseminated false information through the press and double agents, and sealed frontiers and ports prior to a campaign. He also struggled to limit the damage caused by Russian-, Austrian-, and especially English-directed agents, often émigré aristocrats well supplied with "St. George's Cavalry," as English gold came to be called, eager to gain an early warning of Napoleon's offensives. As a consequence, Napoleon and his closely watched Imperial Guard rushed from Paris for the front only at the last possible moment.

In 1812, Savary had two clerks in the French War Ministry shot for passing information to one of the Czar's aides-de-camp. So detested was Savary that, when he died in 1833 while occupying the post of governor general of the "French possessions in Africa," as Algeria was then called, as a result of a hideously disfiguring mouth cancer triggered by his excessive cigar smoking, the Arabs insisted that God had stricken him for his mendacity.

Napoleon's extensive use of intelligence on campaign is all the more intriguing in view of the fact that the two men who most closely studied Napoleon's wars to extract lessons and principles from them, Clausewitz and Jomini, accorded little importance to military intelligence in the preindustrial age. Unlike Sun Tzu, who built an entire philosophy of military operations around intelligence, surprise, and deception, Clausewitz believed "many intelligence reports in war are contradictory, even more are false, and most are uncertain . . ." For Clausewitz, war, like no other human activity, dwelled in the realm of chance, uncertainty, and complexity. Rather than reduce the "fog" of war, intelligence was a "flimsy structure" upon which to build a vision of victory, simply another element of "friction"—those factors which erode and eventually destroy the most calculated of plans. Strategic surprise was virtually impossible to achieve, because a good commander should intuitively know his enemy's objective and keep his forces concentrated to deny it to him. Deception, or "cunning" as he calls it, "should not be considered as a significant independent field of action at the disposal of the commander."[8] For Clausewitz, Napoleon's success lay with his ability to concentrate maximum force at the decisive point. The huge armies of the French Revolution were too large and ponderous to make dispersion of forces to deceive the enemy anything more than an exercise in futility which made concentration more difficult to achieve. One of the great ironies of the dismissal of intelligence by Clausewitz is that he believed deception and surprise were impossible precisely because preparations would be quickly discovered by the enemy's diplomats, spies, and outposts.[9]

Perhaps because he served on Napoleon's staff and because he lived into the age of the telegraph, Jomini had a better feel for the value of intelligence than did Clausewitz. Jomini argued that a general should take steps to gain intelligence on the enemy. And while he acknowledged that accurate information was difficult to come by because "the truth may often be sifted" from the best reports, a commander should be able to make "hypotheses" about enemy intentions on the basis of intelligence. He agreed with Clausewitz that "the surprise of an army is now next to an impossibility . . . because in order to plan one it becomes necessary to have an accurate knowledge of the enemy's camp." And while Jomini did not "despise" surprise, he believed it "less brilliant than a great strategic combination which renders victory certain even before the battle is fought."[10]

It is a credit to the power Napoleon exercised over his age that even his most ardent pupils chose to diminish the importance of the elaborate intelligence structure in place in the Napoleonic armies and to regard it as marginal or even detrimental to victory, which was attributed almost exclusively to the Emperor's genius and his ability to read the chaos of the battlefield. But by the standards of the time, that structure was elaborate indeed.

The Bureau de Renseignements formed one of the three divisions of Napoleon's Grand Quartier Général under Marshal Louis Berthier. Berthier's personal military cabinet was also divided into troop movements, personnel, and intelligence. The latter, under Engineer Colonel Blein, was especially concerned with tactical intelligence gleaned from the swarms of spies which screened Napoleon's armies. Many of these were professional agents, and it appears that French intelligence had evolved fairly sophisticated techniques to control them based on their character, motivations for spying for the French, and the quality of the information they provided.[11] Index cards were kept on foreign armies down to battalion level, and updated daily on campaign.

Napoleon was especially concerned to have detailed knowledge of his routes of march, transport, and supplies he might acquire along the way, the nature of the roads and the fords. Even generals like Murat and Bertrand were not above undertaking these missions, sometimes disguised as peasants or sutlers infiltrated into the moving cities of camp followers which accompanied the armies of this period. Cavalry patrols, interrogation of prisoners of war, and local inhabitants also provided significant information.

Mapping offered one of the most valuable forms of intelligence, and Napoleonic armies placed great emphasis on it, either sending out scouts to sketch the land which lay on the route of march or ransacking newly liberated towns to locate maps. Sometimes local inhabitants actively collaborated in intelligence collection—national minorities, itinerant Jewish merchants in Eastern Europe, or Freemasons in Spain opposed to the priest-ridden resistance to the French were especially valuable. Others might have to be coerced by kidnapping or have property seized to be returned only on receipt of useful information. Local particulars gained in this way were corroborated with summaries of strategic intelligence provided by the Bureau de Renseignements from reports of spies and agents, translations of foreign newspapers, reports from other French commanders, or from the *cabinet noir* in Paris, which read up to two hundred agent letters or diplomatic messages a day.

The Quai d'Orsay also sent a small staff under Hugues Maret into the field to supply the Emperor with news gathered by spy networks and from foreign press reviews organized by French diplomats. This would include political information such as reports of secret negotiations between England and Prussia in 1806 to bring Prussia into the Third Coalition. Court intrigues and commercial and financial relationships were also reported on. Information could be conveyed by the Chiappe telegraph, which made possible communication over long distances through a primitive semaphore system installed on towers. On the basis of this intelligence, Berthier's staff maintained up-to-date battle cards on the location, strength, and distinctive uniform characteristics of each enemy regiment.[12]

How important were Napoleon's intelligence services to his success? One may safely conclude that, if no effective opposition to the Empire emerged in France, it was not entirely due to the Emperor's popularity. Fouché was particularly effective in containing the pro-royalist Chouan uprising in western France by obtaining precise details on places of refuges, travel routes, and lines of communication, as well as setting up an elaborate file system of known English agents and suspects.

Royalist émigrés abroad appear to have been especially gullible and easy targets for Fouché's agents, who infiltrated and ultimately betrayed their conspiracies, which were invariably backed by England. But Fouché was notably reluctant to carry the persecution of many of the Emperor's political enemies, like Madame de Staël, to the point of exile, which was one reason for his ultimate destitution in 1810. Savary was less efficient and imaginative than his predecessor, which helps to account for the near-success of General Claude-François Malet's attempted coup d'état while Napoleon was preoccupied in Russia in 1812.[13]

In the military sphere, deception, combined with the incompetence of enemy services or possibly refusal by foreign governments to heed their warnings, contributed to the strategic surprise achieved by Napoleon's campaigns of 1805, 1806, 1813, and 1815. French agents like Méhée de la Touche, supported by unorthodox tactics like kidnapping British agents and even diplomats on neutral territory, appeared to have successfully compromised English spy networks in Germany in 1804.[14]

Napoleon's most celebrated secret agent was Karl Schulmeister, son of a Lutheran pastor who, behind the cover of a modest shop in his native Strasbourg, operated a successful smuggling business. A solid build, a mind capable of storing vast quantities of information, almost reckless bravery, a talent for disguise, and fluency in both German and French were the basic ingredients of Schulmeister's success. His smuggling activities along the Rhine gave him useful contacts on both sides of the frontier and a knowledge which brought him to the attention of Colonel Savary when he plotted to kidnap the Duc d'Enghien in Baden in 1804.

The following year, Schulmeister disguised himself as a Hungarian nobleman and, with funds supplied by Savary, bribed his way into the staff of Austrian general Karl Mack, whose confidence he gained with bogus intelligence on the French order of battle, Napoleon's line of approach, and a planned coup d'état against the Emperor in Paris, all supplied by Savary. This information is credited with luring Mack to destruction at Ulm.

So impressed was Napoleon with the intelligence supplied by Schulmeister that he rewarded him with a large estate in Alsace and briefly gave him police duties in Vienna. Quite naturally, all this made Schulmeister persona non grata among the Austrians, so that he was retired from government service at Vienna's request when Napoleon threw over Josephine to marry the Austrian princess Marie Louise in 1809. By that time, however, Schulmeister and Savary had made a substantial fortune selling state gambling concessions and investing in a wide variety of commercial ventures. When the Austrians invaded Alsace in 1814, they took care to reduce Schulmeister's estates there to rubble.[15]

Certainly, rivalry between Fouché and Savary helped to compromise French espionage activity in Germany, in particular when Savary intentionally exposed the activities of Edouard Fetny, a former Austrian officer whom Fouché successfully introduced into French émigré and Austrian military circles in 1804.[16] But political intelligence, supplied mainly by diplomats, possibly bribed by Schulmeister, who continued to run networks in Prussian and Russian courtly circles, appears to have been fairly complete, especially that which predicted Austrian belligerence in 1809. Fouché warned Napoleon of the unsuccessful British landings in the Netherlands planned to coincide with his 1809 Wagram campaign.

However, intelligence is a two-way game, one in which Napoleon was not always able to protect his own secrets. French correspondence and dispatches were vulnerable to interception, especially in Spain, where guerrillas regularly captured French couriers, and even peasants paid to deliver messages written on thin paper and concealed in their clothing. The substitution codes used by the French might have posed a problem had the French proved more security-conscious. But messages like that sent Marshal A. F. L. V. Marmont by King Joseph which read: "I have ordered General Trelliard to 117.8.7 the valley of 1383 before marching to 498," seldom baffled men like Captain George Scovell, chief of Wellington's communications in Spain.

Given the military situation, 117.8.9 must certainly mean "evacuate," 1383 "Tagus," and 498 some large city. It appears that both the Austrians and the Russians had success in breaking the French codes. After the fall of Napoleon, Czar Alexander boasted to French marshal Etienne Macdonald that he regularly read encoded French dispatches during the 1812 campaign. This might help to explain the Russian leader's refusal to concede defeat, which ultimately forced Napoleon's catastrophic retreat.

Napoleonic scholar John Elting declares the achievements of French intelligence during the Russian campaign of 1812 "a tantalizing mystery," but points out that Napoleon's movements up to Moscow at least unsettled the Russians significantly by giving the impression that he knew their plans and the whereabouts of their armies.[17] But either Napoleon was not informed or he chose to disbelieve reports that the Czar was resolved to fight on even after his capital had been occupied and partially destroyed. Indeed, the Russian campaign, like that of Spain, illustrates the problem of a leader on the offensive, determined to push on despite intelligence on the climate, population, or political disposition of either nation which might have induced caution.

Whether the Russian campaign may be considered a failure of intelligence or a failure of the leader to heed his intelligence, it did bequeath one enduring legacy in the form of the "Testament of Peter the Great." It is unclear if the "Testament" was a product of the French secret services or a private effort of one of Napoleon's subordinates to manufacture propaganda for the 1812 invasion. But the forgery, which laid out a master blueprint for Russian expansion into Poland, Scandinavia, the Balkans, Turkey, Persia, and the Far East and the desire to secure a warm-water port, must rank with Prester John and the "Protocols of the Elders of Zion" as among the most influential deceptions in history. Despite obvious geographical inaccuracies—like locating Archangel on the Baltic rather than on the Barents Sea—which should have raised immediate questions about its authenticity, the "Testament" was revived by British propagandists in the Crimean War of 1854–56 and the Russo-Turkish War of 1877, conjured up by Anglo-American geopoliticians at the turn of the century as a rationale for Russian strategy, by Hitler, and even in the 1980s by Pakistan to explain the Russian invasion of Afghanistan.[18]

The Post-Napoleonic Services

By general agreement, the quality of French intelligence services declined rapidly when liberated from Napoleonic control. This was resoundingly demonstrated as early as the Hundred Days, when Napoleon's return from Elba took the restored Bourbons utterly by surprise. The *cabinet noir* later noted that they had intercepted only one letter from Elba, written to a correspondent in Grenoble, which said that Napoleon was seeking the first favorable opportunity to escape his exile and requested information on the state of opinion in French regiments stationed in the South of France. The Prefecture of Police in Paris had been alerted, but had taken no action.[19]

After Waterloo, the *cabinet noir* in the Quai d'Orsay was kept busy reading the correspondence of the Bonaparte family in exile and that dealing with the activities of the Congress of Vienna called to establish a new balance of power in Europe. But with the easing of international tensions, the main concern of the restored Bourbons, and consequently the main activity of the *cabinet noir* located in the Post Office, focused on the loyalty of the population, especially the large numbers of civil servants and officers whom they had inherited from the Empire. The *cabinet noir* reported on public reaction to some of the main events of the time, such as the assassination of the Duc de Berry, heir to the throne, in 1820, and the death of Napoleon the following year.

As opposition to the Restoration grew in 1828, the *cabinet noir* became a focus of discontent. After a parliamentary debate on the activities of the *cabinet noir*, prompted in part by the claims of a French journalist that these postal spies had placed a letter destined for someone else in an envelope addressed to him, the government declared black chambers abolished. However, it appears that for the Quai d'Orsay's *cabinet noir* it was business as usual, while that in the Bureau de Poste sought a discreet refuge in the offices of the Sûreté Générale of the Interior Ministry.

The Revolution of July 1830, which toppled the Bourbon monarchy and brought a member of the Orléans family, Louis Philippe, to the throne, declared the *cabinets noirs* abolished once again. And even if this proved yet another administrative fiction, it does appear at least as if they had their budgets slashed from 600,000 francs under the Restoration to a modest 60,000 to 80,000 francs annually by the July Monarchy.[20] French police made aggressive use of spies and agents provocateurs to disrupt the revolutionary groups which threatened the regime. This was necessary in great part because the July Monarchy had no strong ideology, offered no focus of loyalty beyond the challenge to "get rich!"

For the police, and more especially for those portions of it which dealt with intelligence, the realization that this parade of mid-nineteenth-century French regimes—Bourbon Restoration, July Monarchy, Second Republic, Second Empire—formed a fragile basis for personal and professional survival, was an important step in the professionalization of attitudes toward intelligence and the adaptation of the counterintelligence services to an increasingly democratic culture. What cynical outsiders condemned as opportunism, policemen and letter openers viewed as a perfectly logical response to political reality—why chain their careers to a regime which tomorrow might fall victim to popular wrath? Therefore, like military officers in this period, they began to adopt the more detached view that they served the French state, not the particular regime, that their task was to preserve order, not political orthodoxy. As historian of the European police Hsi-Huey Liang has noted, this offers a partial explanation why the French Sûreté did not descend to the depths of suspicion, persecution, even torture that was to characterize the Czarist secret police.[21]

In the long term, however, one consequence of this bureaucratization of a police and with it a counterintelligence culture is the view that efficiency, even bureaucratic survival, requires a freedom from political control. From this, it is but a short step to the development of a negative, even hostile attitude toward politicians and political groups.[22]

The Revolution of 1848 eliminated *cabinets noirs,* and this time they apparently meant it, especially after the Quai d'Orsay's letter openers caused substantial embarrassment by replacing the dispatches meant for one Paris embassy in the envelope of another. But as if playing out a parody of the Christian story, death proved merely a prelude to resurrection. Many of the same agents who had spied on Louis Napoleon Bonaparte when he had plotted to overthrow the July

Monarchy went to work for him when he became Napoleon III. Like his uncle, Louis Napoleon demonstrated a deep interest in the political opinions of the French people. "Given the current state of things," Louis Napoleon wrote to his Police Minister on 22 January 1852, "the President of the Republic can only understand imperfectly the general state of the country. . . . There is no organization which reports rapidly and with certainty the state of public opinion . . . which, disinterested, has the power to be impartial, to tell the truth and to transmit it."[23]

Under the Second Empire, Louis Napoleon built up a permanent secret police organization which included the *"police du château"* directly answerable to the Emperor.[24] In 1855, the *commissaires spéciaux*, a new category of police, were created to keep watch on the railway stations along the frontiers and in larger cities, on the theory that it was in the surveillance of the major routes of communication that much vital intelligence could be gleaned. The following year, three *brigades politiques*, comprising a total staff of sixty-three officials, were established in Paris to keep watch on political malcontents.[25]

The *cabinets noirs* which existed in both the Interior Ministry and the Post Office, as well as in the Quai, reached standards of efficiency hitherto unmatched, at least in France, claiming to be able to open the most complicated diplomatic pouches and envelopes, copy the letters, reconstruct the seals, and have the originals on their way within two hours.[26] Agents working for the Interior Ministry made a specialty of bribing the concierges and domestic servants of important people to have a peek at their employers' mail. Victor Hugo, whose opposition to Louis Napoleon forced him into exile in Guernsey, became so exasperated with the tampering with his letters that he had the article of the penal code forbidding such acts printed on his envelopes, or would write on the back flap: "family affairs, of no interest." When this also failed to deter, at least he was able to make significant economies by placing several letters in a single envelope with instructions to the *cabinet noir* to forward them to the addresses indicated, which they invariably did.[27] Louis Napoleon was regularly shown letters written by his wife, Eugénie, to the Spanish court, which he destroyed if they were not to his taste. He also opened the private correspondence of his generals in Mexico because he was suspicious of their official reports. One of these generals reportedly became so upset by this that he included a note in a letter to his wife addressed to *"Monsieur le chef du cabinet noir"* threatening "to cut off his ears" if he persisted in opening his mail.[28] How far these activities benefited the state is unclear, but at least one *cabinet noir* supervisor is alleged to have supplemented his already generous income by intercepting the letters of bankers and financiers and then using the information thus gained to play the stock market.[29]

British historian Christopher Andrew has concluded that the *cabinets noirs* between the fall of Napoleon I and the advent of the Third Republic in 1870 were employed more in the role of domestic surveillance than in foreign affairs.[30] There are two reasons for this, which helps to explain why counterintelligence was bureaucratized in France far earlier than foreign intelligence. The first is that, in France, domestic surveillance was the foundation stone of foreign intelligence. When, in 1876, Georges Clemenceau, who as Prime Minister in 1918 would lead France to victory in World War I, spoke of the role of the police, and with it the panoply of intelligence organizations which it encompassed, as the *"défense du territoire,"* he was creating a conceptual framework for intelligence work which already had become internalized in the French police.

As the homeland of the Revolution and the "capital" of European culture, France and especially Paris had traditionally offered asylum to large numbers of foreigners, many of revolutionary persuasion. These people posed a latent threat to French security, especially if they allied with homegrown opponents of the regime. There was also the residual fear after 1871 that the conservative states of Europe, led by Berlin, would use the issue of large numbers of their political refugees in Paris as an excuse to make demands on the French government. In Clemenceau's view, strict controls must be set on foreigners, to be complemented with offensive intelligence actions to collect information on them abroad. In this way, France could build her democratic institutions free from unwanted influence from the outside.[31] Therefore, the view based on the Anglo-Saxon model that assigns domestic surveillance to the realm of police work rather than "intelligence" in the pure sense of a group or bureaucracy which informs government of external threat, fits badly into the French historical experience. In France, the fear of internal subversion, aided by outside influence, was the first preoccupation of intelligence. This also helps to explain why the frontier between intelligence, domestic surveillance, and counterintelligence has always been more difficult to define in France than in Great Britain or the United States.

The second reason for the tardy bureaucratization of foreign intelligence, a corollary of the first, was that, until 1866, there was no power large enough to threaten the supposed preeminence of the French army. French military intelligence actually appears to have operated less efficiently in the mid-nineteenth century than it had a century earlier.[32] Specialized military publications like the *Spectateur militaire* printed articles on developments in foreign armies, usually on the technical level. The Section Statistique du Dépôt de la Guerre was responsible for intelligence gathering, as well as serving as a historical and geographical bureau for the army. It read foreign military publications, received reports from military attachés, who had become a regular addition to diplomatic embassies from the 1830s, and on occasion dispatched officers on special missions abroad. But it ran no spies,[33] reflecting a prejudice common in official circles that the mere fact of associating with such people threatened to taint the character of any officer who dared undertake such work.

French cryptographic skills, already a significant intelligence weakness under Napoleon I, had declined further after 1815. There were two reasons for this: First, French intelligence was concerned primarily with domestic documents, which seldom required cryptanalytic skills to read. Second, the cryptographic skills of rival foreign services also appear to have declined, which produced a lower level of expertise generally—for instance, the Deciphering Branch of the British Foreign Office was disbanded in 1844 following parliamentary protests,[34] while the Austrian *cabinet noir* had also been disbanded with the overthrow of Metternich in 1848.

More damaging than the absence of intelligence was the fact that the army had no way to digest this information efficiently and make it part of the decision-making process. For instance, Louis Napoleon's ultimately disastrous decision in 1862 to send an expeditionary force to Mexico was based in part on highly optimistic reports, from French nationals with vested interests in French intervention, that the Juarista government was so unpopular that the people would welcome a French invasion. There appears to have been no attempt to assess the military problems of subduing a vast country with a force which numbered no more than 37,000 troops. Once in Mexico, the French discovered that the intelligence situation favored the Mexican insurgents. Lack of intelligence did not lose Mexico for the French. But it certainly compounded a problem composed of strategic and operational overstretch and desperately bad political decisions, the most egregious of which were to create a throne for Maximilian of Austria and to bet on a Southern victory in the American Civil War. In 1867, his Mexican policies in tatters and the situation deteriorating in Europe as a result of the Prussian triumph in the Prusso-Austria War of 1866, Louis Napoleon ordered his troops home.

How far the Prussians profited from lax French counterintelligence in the years preceding the outbreak of the Franco-Prussian War in July 1870 is unclear. If one is prepared to believe Wilhelm Stieber, Berlin's former chief of police, who was ordered by Bismarck to turn the attentions of his espionage service from Vienna to Paris in 1866, they profited immensely.

Stieber claimed that he could penetrate France at virtually no risk and at remarkably little cost. The favoritism practiced by the Second Empire had created a class of bypassed officers and aggrieved functionaries, some of whom were also ideological opponents of the Bonapartists, disgruntled enough to help the Prussians. "The impression of betrayal was weak," Stieber remembered of his French recruits, "and they believed rather that they were acting to liberate their country from the yoke of an execrable prince. Each one was therefore proud of his acts, without asking for the slightest remuneration in exchange . . . I was particularly proud to count an informer in all of the important civil and military services of the country, without having one discovered or relieved of his post." Stieber even claimed to have suborned Louis Napoleon's valet. The range of political, military, and economic intelligence which he presented to Bismarck was greeted by the Iron Chancellor as "an invitation to march for the German soldier!"

It is certainly possible that intelligence helped to convince Bismarck that Napoleon III's government could not survive military defeat.[35] Once war broke out, Stieber's costs increased, largely because to keep track of French military movements he now had to rely on "spies coming from the lowest social classes," who nevertheless worked for the relatively modest sum of five francs per day. In this he was also aided by the French press, "incorrigibly talkative," by intercepted French telegrams which demonstrated beyond doubt the utter confusion of French mobilization and logistics, and by a spy on Marshal Patrice MacMahon's staff who informed him of the retreating marshal's decision to march to Metz, where he was entrapped, rather than fall back on Paris. Stieber suffered no undue modesty. He claimed that Bismarck boasted that no other country had benefited from so much intelligence in wartime.[36]

At least some of Stieber's boasts have a ring of truth. That the French army only slipped into a wartime organization once hostilities began baffled the more methodical Germans, who initially were unable to deduce the configuration of their enemy based on his regional peacetime commands. To solve this puzzle, the German general staff does appear to have used newspaper reports of French troop movements to build up an order of battle as the scattered French regiments pulled together into brigades, divisions, corps, and armies on the outbreak of war. For their part, the French appear to have been remarkably uninformed of their adversaries. In 1868 and 1869, some staff studies were carried out on the roads from Strasbourg to Berlin. But these appear to have done little to alleviate the insecurity of General Auguste Alexandre Ducrot, the commander at Strasbourg, who lamented, "It is really a pity that we have no means for watching what is done or being prepared by our too active neighbors." Of course, this was not altogether accurate, as the French military attaché in Berlin, Baron Eugène Georges von Stoffel, had dispatched detailed and perceptive assessments of Prussian military preparations for war. Obviously, these reports failed to find their way into the hands of commanders most in need of that knowledge.

The approach of the Franco-Prussian War found the French remarkably ignorant of their Prussian enemy, or even about parts of their own country, for that matter. One of the unfortunate ironies for the French army of 1870 was that Algeria, where the French had campaigned since 1830, was far better mapped than eastern France, where most of the fighting took place. When war broke out in 1870, the armies of Napoleon III attempted to fight the Franco-Prussian War virtually blind, and so stumbled from defeat to defeat. Charles de Freycinet, who took over defense duties in the Government of National Defense which was proclaimed on 4 September 1870, following the French defeat at Sedan two days earlier, discovered that the French army had no intelligence service. "The ideas on this point were so far opposed to this kind of investigation that it was one of our greatest difficulties to get the generals to spend the secret funds allowed them for this purpose," Freycinet wrote, noting that he was able to disburse only 300,000 of the 750,000 francs allocated to pay agents and spies.

Freycinet created an Intelligence Office under the direction of a military engineer named Cuvinot, divided into a spy service, a bureau to translate captured German documents, and one to interrogate POWs, run by an ex-judge and a gendarme. According to Freycinet:

> With relatively straitened means and a quite recent organization [Cuvinot] managed to obtain important results. He placed himself in constant communication with the corps commanders and had come to furnish them every evening with a circular, showing the positions of the enemy, and often even with the number of the regiments. He had some very able agents; one of them lived, for two months, in the midst of the Prussian headquarters, and from time to time brought us back most detailed information . . . It was an agent of Monsieur Cuvinot who, in the month of December, obtained for us a plan of the works of investment round Paris, stolen at Versailles from an officer of von Moltke's staff.[37]

Intelligence in the Third Republic

One might imagine that the French defeat in 1870–71, which resulted in German unification and a decided tilt in the European balance of power against Paris, would have stimulated France as the weaker power to create an efficient intelligence organization to keep watch on its major enemy. In fact, this did not happen, at least not immediately. In defense of the French, the institutionalization of military and foreign intelligence services in European countries took hold only slowly in the years preceding the Great War of 1914–18. In the meantime, domestic surveillance, counterintelligence, and foreign intelligence continued to be concentrated in the hands of a relatively small number of diplomats, soldiers, and policemen. The Sûreté reported on the activities of high-profile French politicians like the leader of the Republican opposition Léon Gambetta and radical General Georges Boulanger, as well as carried out surveillance of Bonapartists, ex-Communards (survivors of the rebellion of Paris against the government in 1871, some of whom continued to be active in revolutionary movements), and German spies in France—hardly an onerous assignment; the numbers and ability of all three categories to disturb the public order or peer into the secret recesses of French decision making or military capabilities were fairly limited. It was believed that Bismarck's agents were best represented in the business and financial world, and in journalism, where they both collected information and planted articles in a French press which was easily corrupted and in which news was seldom distinguished from editorial comment. In the mid-1870s, the Prefecture of Police estimated that 165 German agents were active in Paris.[38]

This activity was not without implications for foreign policy and foreign intelligence. A major concern of all European governments was to keep an eye on revolutionary socialist and anarchist movements. The Sûreté maintained agents in Geneva, Berlin, and elsewhere in Europe, including St. Petersburg, and there was even a degree of collaboration between them and their German and Russian counterparts, who exchanged files on men considered dangerous subversives. In 1887, for example, the Russian government formally asked the French not to expel Russian Nihilists from French territory because they would simply drift to Switzerland or England, where the police were less cooperative in tracking them. This cooperation was considered a major selling point in France's courtship of a Russian alliance to break out of its Bismarck-imposed isolation. Without this cooperation, St. Petersburg might be tempted for internal political reasons to make common cause with the conservative monarchies of Germany and Austria, eager to portray France's generous asylum as evidence of the subversive intentions of the French Republic. Indeed, the crackdown of the French police on Russian Nihilist exiles in Paris in 1890, after they foiled a plot on the life of Alexander III, earned the Czar's deep gratitude and helped to pave the way for the Franco-Russian alliance of 1894.

Once that alliance was consummated, the French police took the job of hunting down Russian dissidents in Europe very seriously as a way of consolidating the Czarist regime, to the point that it tolerated a good deal of Czarist police activity among Russian exiles on French soil. Unfortunately for the police, this was to put them at odds with French public opinion, increasingly agitated after 1900 by Czarist oppression and in fundamental sympathy with the Russian dissidents.

In 1909, Okhrana—Czarist secret police—activity in France exploded as a political issue when the socialist leader Jean Jaurès, reacting to the deportation of a Russian dissident long resident in France, denounced it in the French Chamber of Deputies as "a standing disgrace. I personally know French citizens who, on French soil, have been subjected to investigation and frisking by Russian police agents!" Despite pallid denials by Interior Minister Clemenceau, the Sûreté conceded in private that Okhrana activity surpassed its ability to monitor it. Operating out of their embassy, the Russians ran extensive networks of Russian and French informers. Nor were they above bribing French police to turn a blind eye.[39]

French police also maintained networks in Alsace-Lorraine, where they kept an eye on German police measures against German socialist refugees in France and Switzerland, followed the evolution of public opinion in Alsace-Lorraine, and took steps to prepare clandestine operations there in the event of mobilization. But they retained enough realism to report that the inhabitants had accepted the inevitability of German administration.

Nevertheless, when in 1887 the jingoistic War Minister, General Georges Boulanger, ordered espionage activities in Alsace-Lorraine stepped up, German police responded by luring the police superintendent of Pagny-sur-Moselle, Charles Schnaebelé, over the border and arresting him. Bismarck deflated the subsequent diplomatic crisis by releasing Schnaebelé, while pointing out to the French ambassador in Berlin that the Emperor's gesture of magnanimity undoubtedly had spared the French superintendent the most severe penalties in a German court for "seeking to incite German nationals to commit crimes against their fatherland for money . . . even if he acted on higher orders."[40]

Foreign intelligence was also supplied by the *cabinet noir*, which continued to intercept mail, targeting the correspondence of important people like Gladstone and Leopold II during their frequent and lengthy visits to the Riviera. However, it is unlikely that this form of espionage paid more than moderate dividends for the French.

In the first place, most people with secrets to divulge were well aware that their mail was being read, and therefore unlikely to place information of importance within reach of the *cabinet noir*. In one well-publicized incident, Leopold II summoned the postal inspector of Cap Ferrat on the Côte d'Azur to demand that his employees at least put the pages of his correspondence back in order once they had been read.[41] Nor were foreign diplomats above including information designed to deceive the French, as when during the Agadir crisis of 1911 German Foreign Minister Alfred von Kiderlen-Waechter wrote letters to his mistress at Chamonix promising severe consequences if the French government refused to make concessions.[42] However, the best-known case of deception played on the *cabinet noir* was by an aristocratic Frenchwoman married to a foreigner. "Here are three violets which I have just picked in my garden," she wrote in a letter which she anticipated would be intercepted. "They are the first of spring." When the letter arrived, it actually contained three violets—the *cabinet noir*, fearing that they had lost the flowers, actually placed three violets into the envelope which had contained none.[43]

Because internal police surveillance remained efficient, and because it served as a tool of French foreign policy, a solid structure specializing in foreign intelligence, especially foreign military intelligence, evolved only slowly. The Franco-Prussian War had served as a serious wake-up call for the French. The days when Clausewitz could dismiss intelligence as unimportant were well and truly consigned to the preindustrial age. With the expansion of railways, the telegraph, rapid changes in weapons technology, and the enormous economic power now placed behind the organization and mobilization of armies, war slipped into high gear. Communications were far more rapid, huge armies could be shifted more quickly to strike with weapons of great lethality. Strategic surprise was now possible, as was technological surprise. Warning became vital if a nation, especially one which dwelled in the shadow of a powerful neighbor, was to survive. The strength of enemy forces, their war plans, mobilization schedules, and numbers and quality of their armaments were things which France could no longer afford to ignore, any more than she could ignore the intentions or inclinations of allies and enemies alike.

Given these obvious trends, why, then, did it take the French intelligence services in the Third Republic so long to shed the haphazard, slightly ad hoc character of earlier decades to meet the challenges of war and diplomacy in the technological age? The most obvious explanation is political. Because of a historical accident, the Third Republic in its first decade was dominated by monarchists who hedged on reforms, especially military ones, which might strengthen the institutions of a regime which they hoped to sweep away. Only in the 1880s, when the republicans finally gained control of the Republic, could the work of institutional construction really begin. But throughout its life, the Third Republic was plagued by ministerial instability. This had two consequences: First, it compromised the ability to initiate and sustain institutional reform. Second, it encouraged the natural tendency of the ministries of the Interior, War, and Foreign Affairs to gather intelligence in isolation.

Military intelligence would prove especially critical, as the French army was forced to acknowledge that it had been outperformed in almost every category by the Prussians in 1870–71, including that of intelligence. The French general staff was reformed along Prussian lines to include a Deuxième Bureau which had a Section de Statistiques et de Reconnaissances Militaires, located on the rue de Lille near the German embassy, which appears to have been directly answerable to the deputy chief of the French general staff.

One of the subsequent ironies of the Dreyfus Affair was that the Statistical Section, denounced as a hotbed of anti-Semitism, had been constructed out of the ashes of defeat primarily by a Jewish officer, Major Samuel. Samuel established a *bureau de première ligne* at Nancy, from which he began to establish spy rings in Alsace and Berlin, although it is not clear how many of these were his own and how many reported to the Sûreté.[44] In any case, it serves once again to underline the close links in France between foreign intelligence and counterintelligence. The Statistical Section also sponsored the *Revue militaire de l'étranger*, a digest of developments in foreign armies which was distributed to French regimental libraries.

The Dreyfus Affair, which was to have such a serious impact on the future of civil intelligence, as well as civil-military relations in France, had its origins in two developments within the French intelligence community in the 1880s—the emergence of counterintelligence as a primary concern of the Statistical Section and the progress of French code-breaking capabilities. Espionage and counterintelligence were given a boost when the flamboyant Georges Boulanger, whose popular nickname was "Général Revanche" (General Revenge), took over the Ministry of War in 1886. As has been seen, one result of this new emphasis on espionage was the Schnaebelé incident, an example when an *excès de zèle* on the part of intelligence operatives was the cause of a serious diplomatic incident between the two nations. Boulanger also sought to ferret out traitors in France with an 1886 law which toughened the penalties for espionage and treason.

Primary responsibility for tightening military security fell to Samuel's successor, Colonel Jean Sandherr. Like Dreyfus, Sandherr was a native of Mulhouse in Alsace and had established his expertise in the problems of security in frontier areas. Frustrated by the lack of counterintelligence cooperation from the Interior Ministry, Sandherr threw his small five-man section, housed in a few rooms of the War Ministry on Paris' rue Saint-Dominique, into the work of protecting French security. Sandherr ran agents throughout Europe, but especially in France, Alsace, and Germany, who specialized in surveillance and theft of documents. One of the agents employed by Sandherr was a Madame Bastian, the wife of a soldier of the Republican Guard, who was hired as a cleaner by the German embassy in 1889. Described by Sandherr as "a vulgar, stupid, completely illiterate woman about forty years in age,"[45] she was given the task of bringing the contents of her employers' wastepaper baskets to a rendezvous which invariably took place at the Church of Sainte-Clotilde or the Church of Saint-François-Xavier to be handed over to Major Hubert Henry of the Statistical Section. So poor was security in the German embassy that the embassy's chief "spymaster," Colonel Maximilian von Schwartzkoppen, regularly discarded compromising personal and secret documents into his office dustbin, and continued to hire Madame Bastian until 1897, fully three years after Dreyfus' conviction based on evidence taken from his office.[46]

It is not difficult to trace how the problems of external espionage and internal subversion became mixed in the minds of the officers of the Statistical Section. Military attachés were closely watched by the Statistical Section because one of their functions was to gather intelligence on France by recruiting their own agents. Foreigners were particularly suspect. When Boulanger ordered a census of foreigners of military age living in France, Sandherr prepared a list of those to be interned in the event of war; this was called the *Carnet* A. A *Carnet* B listed those, French or foreign, suspected of spying and who were automatically to be rounded up in the event of a crisis. Among those were members of France's growing anarchist, socialist, and trade union movements whose reverence for revolutionary ideals was thought to supersede their patriotism. Sandherr's procedures were adopted in a secret 1889 session of the Supreme War Council made up of France's senior corps commanders. One of Boulanger's successors, Charles de Freycinet, confided these lists to the Interior Ministry, which in 1892 began to make plans for the internment or arrest of 100,000 persons in the event of war under conditions which would permit virtually no appeal.

In the meantime, the Statistical Section threw itself into the counterintelligence business. The result was such a rash of treason cases in the French army in the late 1880s that the *Daily Telegraph* could write in 1888: "Traitors seem to abound in the French army . . . the War Office authorities are almost at their wits' end."[47] The vigilance continued. In 1890, an archivist employed in the technical division of the French artillery was convicted of passing on plans to the German military attaché. Four others, military or civilian personnel employed by the French army or navy, were found to have passed plans to the German military attaché between 1888 and 1890.

But the Statistical Section could not rest on its laurels, because despite these arrests and convictions, plans of frontier and coastal fortifications continued to disappear. Spies were everywhere, and none appeared more intriguing than one designated by the initial D., which appeared in a piece of correspondence between Schwartzkoppen and the Italian military attaché Alessandro Panizzardi, duly recovered by the indefatigable Madame Bastian. "Attached are 12 master plans of Nice which that scoundrel D. gave me in the hope of restoring relations," a note of April 1894 read. Two suspects named Dacher and Dubois were cleared of suspicion.

The classic interpretation of the origins of the Dreyfus Affair has been that, by the 1890s, the Statistical Section had become the preserve of confirmed anti-Semites eager to persecute a Jewish officer who fell into their midst, Alfred Dreyfus. While some of the officers of the Statistical Section were certainly anti-Semitic, the origins of the Dreyfus affair can be found rather in a weakness common to counterintelligence officers.

Those whose job it is to search for spies begin to see them everywhere. Paranoia becomes an occupational hazard in counterintelligence. The Statistical Section was suffused with an atmosphere of exaggerated spy mania, where "vigilance was the rule," wrote French historian Jean-Denis Bredin. "Treason seemed to permeate the very air one breathed."[48] Its imperfections were those of the men who determined its direction. An air of patriotic righteousness lingered like a *déformation professionelle*. Their task was to shield France from foreigners, miscreants, and miserable opportunists. This mission required them, in their view, to compile *carnets* of suspects in which the legal rights of those detained were extremely circumscribed. American historian Allan Mitchell has suggested that in the minds of these officers the mere fact of arrest implied guilt and conviction no matter how flimsy the evidence. A deep suspicion of foreigners was directed particularly at Alsatians, German speakers like Dreyfus who had opted for French nationality in 1871. In fact, the Statistical Section had well-defined notions of what constituted French citizenship. Even though recovery of the "Amputated Provinces" of Alsace and Lorraine remained a prominent political slogan until the Versailles Conference of 1919, the citizens of those provinces, even those who had elected often at great personal sacrifice to remain French—especially those who had chosen French nationality—continued to be suspect in the minds of the Statistical Section officers, because they were not altogether French. The result was that Alsatians figured prominently in Sandherr's *Carnet B.*[49]

A second intelligence development which would play a role in the Dreyfus affair was the advancement of French code-breaking capabilities. In many respects, this was forced upon the French, as on all governments, by the development of the telegraph from the mid-nineteenth century.

By the last decades of the nineteenth century, foreign governments increasingly relied on the telegram for important communications. Because they were easily accessible, telegrams solved the problem of access to communications which had bedeviled black chambers in the past. Unfortunately, the accessibility of communications was offset by the increasing use of codes. Black chambers had to develop expertise in code breaking or condemn themselves to ignorance. Of course, codes were nothing new, and had been used since antiquity. France of the *ancien régime* and Napoleon had used simple substitution codes—that is, lists of numbers substituted for place names—which had sufficed for the low volume of correspondence and the specific geographical areas or campaigns for which they were used. But after 1815, the Service du Chiffre in the Dépôt de Guerre was directed by a civilian, an unmistakable indication that the military considered it of secondary importance. Indeed, French officers appear to have adopted a very casual attitude toward security—for instance, the military codes used by the French for the 1859 Italian campaign were the same ones which had already served in the Crimea in 1854–56. In fact, many important orders like troop designations were sent *en clair* because, incredibly, French generals considered them of little importance to the enemy. During the Franco-Prussian War of 1870–71, French commander-in-chief Marshal Achille Bazaine felt moved to cite the inadequacies of his code system, whose vocabulary omitted such essential words as "artillery" and "infantry."[50]

Fortunately, French intelligence was well placed to take a lead in the expanding field of cryptology in the 1880s. The primary quality possessed by the French was motivation. A sense of vulnerability, weakness, and fear combined to cause France to rely on intelligence which otherwise would be ignored. They developed an acute sensitivity to the superiority of German power, in itself a product of changes in intelligence gathering which after 1870 focused increasingly on enumerating the military resources available to foreign countries on mobilization.[51]

The French sought any advantage which might be obtained through code breaking. This created an atmosphere receptive to a new generation of cryptographers which began to emerge in 1883 when Auguste Kerckhoffs, a Dutch schoolteacher and linguist living in France, published *La Cryptographie militaire*. Kerckhoffs' work revolutionized cryptography by adapting it to the telegraph. Kerckhoffs recognized that, unlike "a momentary exchange of letters between several isolated individuals," modern military communications required a system which would work over time, which was simple, reliable, and rapid. For the first time, Kerckhoffs made a distinction between a general system, which the enemy may know, and a specific key changed constantly to baffle the adversary. (See Appendix.)

One of the great virtues of Kerckhoffs' work was that it was comprehensible. The War Ministry bought three hundred copies of *La Cryptographie militaire*, which Kerckhoffs had condensed into sixty-four pages, and published excerpts in the prestigious *Journal des sciences militaires*. Kerckhoffs developed a cryptographic slide which allowed the rapid superimposition of plain and cipher alphabets, which he named the St.-Cyr system because it was used to train cadets at the French military academy. As American historian of code breaking David Kahn put it, what followed was a "cryptologic renaissance" in France which witnessed the publication of two dozen significant works on cryptography, and a number of minor ones, between 1883 and the outbreak of World War I. By comparison, a half dozen third-rate tracts appeared in Germany. A Commission du Chiffre de l'Armée de Terre was created in 1889, and made concerted, although not entirely successful, attempts to establish liaisons with cryptanalysts working for the Quai d'Orsay and the Ministry of the Interior. Other French writers, like the Marquis Gaetan de Viaris, a graduate of the Ecole Polytechnique and a former naval officer, who developed a code system based on mathematical formulae, refined and extended Kerckhoffs' work, so that, on the eve of World War I, French military cryptanalysis was light-years ahead of that of Germany.[52]

France's enhanced cryptanalytic capabilities, combined with a long tradition of intercepting diplomatic messages, was an open invitation to attack the codes of other nations. Some codes, like those of the American State Department, which used such oblique references as "Mars" and "Neptune" to designate the Secretary of the Army and the Secretary of the Navy respectively, could be broken by teams of schoolboys. The Belgian ABC Viaris codes held few mysteries for the Quai d'Orsay because Gaetan de Viaris was employed by them.

Translations of diplomatic telegrams found in the French archives suggest that few diplomatic codes around the turn of the century resisted French code breakers.[53] In this task, the *cabinet noir* was often aided by French espionage, which could reconstruct the British code through copies of the telegrams of the British ambassador, Lord Lytton, furnished by his valet. In 1896, a French agent copied part of the Italian diplomatic code book in the office of the Italian consul general at Marseille. It was an important coup since the previous year the indiscretions of a French newspaper had alerted the Italians that their codes were being read by the *cabinet noir,* which caused them to be changed. The German codes were probably furnished by a double agent, Jules de Balasy-Belvata, well paid by both sides for his information.[54]

But much of this progress was the work of French code breakers of the 1890s, the most notable of whom was Eugène Bazeries. Nothing in Bazeries' background appeared to destine him for the cryptological preeminence which he eventually achieved.

The son of a Pyrenean peasant family, Bazeries enlisted in the French army's Supply Corps at the age of seventeen to escape the tedium of rural life. The transformation of the French army after 1871 from a small professional force to a broad-based conscript army created a need for experienced officers. In 1874, after more than a decade as a common soldier, during which time he served in the Franco-Prussian War, Bazeries became a sublieutenant. But little changed as he followed a routine career of garrison assignments in France and Algeria.

When Bazeries first became interested in cryptography is uncertain, but he clearly developed a talent for entertaining his messmates by translating cryptograms, some of them sordid invitations to adulterous rendezvous, in the personal columns of local newspapers. In 1890, the forty-four-year-old Captain Bazeries came to the notice of the commander of the XI Army Corps at Nantes after he had boasted in the mess that he could break the French military cipher without a key. When he succeeded, the general then gave him messages in the new French code, which had yet to enter service, which Bazeries also cracked. After other demonstrations of cryptanalytic skills, word of Bazeries' talents reached Paris, and within a year he had been seconded to the Quai d'Orsay's *cabinet noir.*

Through the 1890s, Bazeries became such a successful code breaker that he was known variously as the "Lynx of the Quai d'Orsay," the "Napoleon of Ciphers," and the "Magician." In 1892, he distinguished himself by shattering the codes of a group of anarchists who communicated in sequences of numbers. Bazeries calculated that the numbers were alphabet counts. So once he determined the first letter, by counting past these he could reconstruct the messages. The codes of royalist conspirators against the Republic which he was called in to solve in 1899 were more difficult to crack. Although they resembled those of the anarchists in that they, too, communicated in sequences of numbers, each letter was assigned a number which was not repeated sequentially. So, while 11 might designate the letter A the first time it was used, in subsequent usages A would be assigned a different number. Bazeries' task was complicated by the fact that the conspirators themselves manipulated the codes with difficulty, so that the messages were full of errors—so full, in fact, that the pretender to the throne, the Duc d'Orléans, could not read the messages sent him by his own supporters. After sitting up all night working on a message which had been dispatched by the Duc, Bazeries discovered that it consisted of a date and a single word—"Merde!"[55]

Despite the prestige he acquired as the government's star witness in the trial of the royalist conspirators, Bazeries' warnings that French military ciphers were desperately insecure, and his proposals for new systems, fell on deaf ears. In 1899, Bazeries retired from the army and lashed out at both his former employers and his cryptographic enemies—including Viaris—in a book entitled *Chiffres Secrets dévoilés* (*Secret Ciphers Revealed*). Despite its polemical tone, it remains one of the most articulate explanations of the subject. Bazeries spent the remainder of his active career, which lasted until 1924, alternately working for the Quai and for the Prefecture of Police.[56]

While the Statistical Section determined Dreyfus' guilt by methods altogether peculiar to itself, code breaking was to contribute decisively to the confirmation of that conclusion. On 1 November 1894, French newspapers broke the story that Dreyfus had been arrested for spying for either Germany or Italy. On the following day, the Italian military attaché, Colonel Alessandro Panizzardi, wired Rome a message which concluded: "If Captain Dreyfus has not had relations with you, it would be wise to have the ambassador deny it officially, to avoid press comment." When the Post Office took the wire to the Quai d'Orsay for translation, the Bureau du Chiffre recognized that it had been composed in a new key. On 6 November, they returned to Sandherr a provisional decryptment which read: "If Captain Dreyfus has not had relations with you, it would be wise to have the ambassador deny it officially. Our emissary is warned." This appeared to confirm Dreyfus' guilt, a conclusion which Sandherr refused to abandon even when on 10 November he was brought the correct decryptment.

To overcome Sandherr's doubt, Major Pierre Maton, the army liaison officer with the Quai d'Orsay, composed a message with some easily recognizable proper names and had a double agent slip it to Panizzardi, who obligingly encoded the message verbatim and sent it to Rome. When the *cabinet noir* at the Quai, unaware of the ruse played on Panizzardi, intercepted the message and correctly deciphered it, Maton produced the original dispatch, thereby proving that the code breakers had now mastered the new key and that the second version of the telegram, which did not support the theory of Dreyfus' guilt, was the correct one.

At this point, however, a third development, which had gained ground in the Statistical Section, kicked in—deception. With bureaucratization, intelligence had become, in Kipling's words, a "Great Game," one in which points must be scored, victories carried. In this way, the Statistical Section validated its own function, raised its prestige, proved its worth to itself and to those who subscribed to its services. In such an atmosphere, it became very difficult to keep a clear mind and view events with detachment. More, to admit a mistake could only weaken the position of the Statistical Section and the general staff to which it answered. From this perspective, it was but one easy step to the fabrication of evidence. If one possessed the certainty of guilt, then morality was not compromised; it was not an issue. Besides, the good of the secret service required it. So Dreyfus' prosecutors in the Statistical Section were acting in a way entirely faithful to their vocation when Major du Paty de Clam manufactured a completely fictitious version of the telegram, which he placed in the so-called Secret File of evidence against Dreyfus: "Captain Dreyfus arrested," it read. "The Minister of War has proofs of his relations with Germany. Parties informed in the greatest secrecy. My emissary is warned." "This telegram," du Paty de Clam proclaimed, "is, for me, the pivot of the affair." Only in April 1899 during Dreyfus' retrial was the correct version entered into evidence.

This attempt to deceive not only the French courts but also the French government was to have baleful consequences for civil-intelligence relations in France. When Dreyfusards exposed the Statistical Section as no more than "a common fake factory,"[57] ready to commit any act, however despicable, in support of its own twisted notions of patriotic mission or to further its own interests, it would become an object of controversy within the state. In the end, the government did not so much solve the problem as slam the door on it. This was because the appearance of secret service competence was as important politically to Frenchmen as was the "honor of the army." Therefore, in the aftermath of the exposure of the transgressions of the Statistical Service, the President of the Republic pardoned Dreyfus in September 1899. The War Minister, General Gaston de Galliffet, issued an order to the army which announced that henceforth "the affair is closed!" The future Naval Minister Camille Pelletan believed that it was not so easy to wipe the slate clean: " 'Attention! On my command, by the left flank, Forget!' That is what was missing from the military regulations," he noted sarcastically.[58]

The Dreyfus Affair had bathed in an atmosphere of spy fever and intrigue which conjured up fantastic theories about conspiracies by a "Dreyfus syndicate," veiled ladies procuring secret documents from dashing army officers, even speculation about an elaborate deception operation run by the Statistical Section against the Germans to which Dreyfus fell unfortunate victim.[59] But while a thirst for conspiracy theories, fed by a sensationalist press, linked the secret services in the popular mind with treason and mystery, the reality is more often far less romantic. Where did the end of the Dreyfus Affair leave the French secret services?

The three decades between the end of the Franco-Prussian War and the new century had witnessed the construction of a French intelligence edifice virtually from nothing. But even as the modern French intelligence community entered into its institutional adolescence, certain of its character traits had already begun to emerge. It had a number of strengths, which included a staff of trained cryptographers who supplied France with a definite superiority over her German rival in that art, a superiority which would grow more pronounced as radios replaced land lines as a major means of field communications. But the French intelligence community also betrayed weaknesses. The confusion over the Panizzardi telegram was simply one of several examples which demonstrated that cryptography still owed as much to divination as to mathematics. But more important than its technical lapses, the Dreyfus Affair had revealed an emerging character, one might even say a "culture," of French intelligence which would become increasingly defined in the twentieth century. A primary characteristic of French intelligence culture would be poor civil-intelligence relations. Of what use was intelligence, even the most accurate intelligence, in the hands of men whose preconceptions or prejudices predisposed them to distort, ignore, or misuse information?

It escaped the attention of no one that the French intelligence community had provoked the most significant political scandal in modern French history. This was a heavy legacy from which it was never fully to recover. The secret services' confusion of their own success and parochial interests with their mission to protect the state from enemies both within and without would time and again defy the government's best efforts to bring them under firm control. The result was that governments, especially left-wing governments, would live in an uneasy and ambiguous relationship with their secret services, upon whom they depended, but which they never were fully to trust. This distrust would be perpetuated by the continued domination of foreign intelligence by the French military, a group which appeared to place loyalty and obedience above independence of mind, skepticism, and pursuit of "truth."

If the role of intelligence is to "reduce uncertainty," poor civil-intelligence relations would make it difficult for France to use its intelligence services to construct a rational response to the greatest threat to national survival in the first half of the twentieth century—the German menace.

TWO

SUCCESS AND SCANDAL, 1900—14

The outbreak of war in 1914 came as no surprise to Europeans. For over a decade, European politics and diplomacy had contained with difficulty Franco-German disputes over Morocco, Anglo-German tensions caused by Germany's questionable decision to build a fleet to challenge Great Britain's primacy on the seas, and a festering situation in the Balkans which pitted Russian influence against that of Austria-Hungary in that cauldron of feuding nationalities. Increasingly conscious that war lay on the horizon, European countries tightened their alliances with military conventions and war plans. For France, whose weakness in the face of her Teutonic rival could escape no one, an effective intelligence service could prove a particularly valuable asset, what a modern military analyst would call a "force multiplier." An ability to read the enemy's mind, to divine his intentions, should permit one to devise countermoves, to ferret out, even deceive, his spies, to confound his intentions.

French intelligence did make qualitative improvements in this period, especially in the field of cryptanalysis. This was the result of both a strong tradition in this field and the initiatives of some quite remarkable men able to build upon the work of Bazeries and adapt it to radiotelegraphy. Nevertheless, though the craft of intelligence made notable strides in this period, it suffered from two defects: The first defect of intelligence in France was that it was fed into a political system which misused, even compromised it. Second, intelligence, especially military intelligence, was still very much a poor relation. It lacked the resources, prestige, and ultimately the ability to penetrate the plans of the enemy.

One obvious lesson to draw from the Dreyfus experience was that cryptanalysis by itself offers an inadequate foundation upon which to establish policy. The inaccurate decipherment on 6 November 1894 of the Panizzardi telegram caused no end of mischief because it fixed in the minds of the Statistical Section the certainty of Dreyfus' guilt. It should have been clear to even the least reflective of observers that the artfulness of the cryptographers in this period depended as much upon inspiration as craftsmanship. Yet the French government was more likely than, say, the British to continue to refer to intercepted diplomatic correspondence.

For starters, French politicians remained untouched by notions of gentlemanly fair play which induced at least discretion among Anglo-Saxon politicians over the interception of foreign diplomatic messages. Even after World War I, British intelligence chiefs feared a widespread public reaction if news leaked that diplomatic correspondence was monitored. The French population, on the other hand, while they might grumble about the eavesdropping habits of the Sûreté and the Quai, when push came to shove accepted it as a necessary requirement of security. These attitudes translated into law: The French government had the legal right to intercept telegrams, whereas the British government had no warrant to do so in peacetime, which stunted the development of cryptanalysis in Britain.[1]

The Fashoda crisis of 1898 supplied a thumping demonstration that the French had not fully realized the limitations of early cryptanalysis. The origins of the Fashoda crisis reached back to 1896, when Captain Jean-Baptiste Marchand set out from the mouth of the Congo River to march across Africa. His goal was the upper Nile, which he reached in the summer of 1898, planting the French tricolor on a malarial island covered with maize fields and an abandoned Egyptian fort called Fashoda.

This was quite unacceptable to London, which regarded the upper Nile as part of the Egyptian hinterland, even though it was controlled by Muslim fanatics who, under the leadership of the Mahdi, had submerged the Anglo-Egyptian garrison at Khartoum in 1885. To challenge the French initiative, in 1898 a large British army under Lord Kitchener steamed up the Nile to defeat the Mahdi's army at Omdurman across the river from Khartoum, and then close in on Marchand's beleaguered sandbank. London and Paris were on the brink of war.

On 30 September 1898, only four days after the celebrated meeting between Kitchener and Marchand during which the two men decided to allow their governments to sort out the issue, the *cabinet noir* deciphered a telegram from the Italian ambassador in Paris to his government stating that the British ambassador, Sir Charles Monson, was to deliver an ultimatum to the French government to pull out of Fashoda or face war with Great Britain. When, a few hours later, Monson appeared before Théophile Delcassé, before he could open his mouth the French minister began to plead with great passion that London not force France to sacrifice her honor. When Monson, rather startled by Delcassé's impassioned plea, failed to pronounce the ultimatum which he did not possess, Delcassé became convinced that his fervent appeal had persuaded Monson to rethink his demands.

To his wife, Delcassé wrote that 30 September 1898 was "perhaps a historical day . . . It is in these times that one feels fully what patriotism is." The conviction, based on an erroneous decrypt, that he had forced Britain to modify her policy placed Delcassé on the road to compromise.[2] This episode might have been merely amusing, except that it helped to persuade Delcassé—and several of his successors— that decrypts were an essential element of diplomatic action, perhaps *the* foundation stone of policy planning, often to the exclusion of others. Indeed, in 1912, one of the Quai d'Orsay's leading diplomats complained that the habit of reading other people's mail had completely skewed French policy planning. "We base all our policies on *les verts* [Quai decrypts, so called because they were written on green paper]," he wrote. "The ambassadors' reports count for nothing."[3]

If intelligence gathering remained in favor at the Quai, the same cannot be said of military intelligence. Indeed, the Dreyfus Affair harmed the cause of military intelligence by deepening the prejudices against it in an organization already unpersuaded of its value. In the case of humint—that is, "human" or agent intelligence—part of the explanation for this bias was social. As people of dubious character, spies were not only unreliable. Worse, the mere act of frequenting this espionage demimonde of marginal characters like Major Esterhazy, homosexuals, blackmailers, liars, and sneaks was thought to place the integrity and moral rectitude of the intelligence officer in great danger.[4] Indeed, the career of an intelligence officer who operated in the shadows, who bathed in an atmosphere of intrigue and duplicity, suggested the very antithesis of the military ideals of inspirational leadership, openness, and the prospect of heroic demise on some distant *champ d'honneur.* Furthermore, as the fate of the officers of the Statistical Section testified, to pursue a career in intelligence was to play Russian roulette with one's future.

The value of sigint—signals intelligence—in the early years of the twentieth century remained unproven. The first problem was access. Although telegraph traffic had been tapped in the American Civil War, and some officers like British general Garnet Wolseley realized the possibilities of infiltrating men armed "with a small pocket instrument" behind lines to intercept enemy wires, communications intelligence was not considered a way to achieve significant advantage—for several reasons. Tactical and operational intelligence was of fleeting value and must be acted upon rapidly. To collect and transmit that intelligence in a timely way depended on a fluid battlefield, one on which chance would play an enormous role. Besides, the assumption was that the use of ciphers which would take weeks, perhaps months, to crack would foil attempts to eavesdrop. Even a message intercepted *en clair* was assumed to be of only limited value to an enemy only dimly aware of its context.

Only gradually did commanders begin to wake up to the intelligence possibilities offered by the increasing use of radios for military communications as war approached in 1914. But as Canadian historian John Ferris has noted for the British case, "few officers were interested in either signals or intelligence, let alone in an amalgam of the two. Their appreciation of these possibilities was uneven. Their understanding of those techniques was low." As a consequence, although the Royal Navy proved to be relatively open-minded, interest in signals intelligence in the British army was severely limited.[5] As will be seen, the same could be said of the French army.

Military intelligence bore the brunt of a post-Dreyfus reorganization which aggravated rather than resolved two long-standing problems of French intelligence—its fragmentation and its politicization. The Statistical Section was dissolved, its officers scattered or retired, and its counterespionage functions delegated to the Sûreté Général of the Interior Ministry.

The Deuxième Bureau maintained a diminished Service de Renseignements whose officers were prohibited foreign travel. Five officers at headquarters ran frontier posts at Chambéry, Briançon, and Nice to collect intelligence on Italy and Austria, and ones at Nancy, Remiremont, Epinal, and Belfort to keep an eye on Germany. No officer was tasked with gathering intelligence on Belgium, a rather unfortunate oversight, as the Germans intended to march to Paris via that route in 1914.

From 1912, the French moved toward fewer but better-manned posts—intelligence collection on Germany was centered on Belfort, Nancy, and, from 1913, Mézières on the Belgian frontier, created in response to increasing certainty that the Germans intended to march through Belgium, while Grenoble and Nice continued to look to Italy and Austria. These posts cost the French army 535,000 francs a year, at least 10,000 of which was spent on the War Ministry's annual Bastille Day luncheon, until the practice ceased in 1911. Eighteen Sûreté agents in frontier regions were to coordinate with military intelligence, while the Sûreté also picked up some foreign intelligence through its counterespionage activities and contacts with foreign police. For instance, during the Russo-Japanese War of 1904–5, the Sûreté obtained the Japanese diplomatic codes by means which are still unclear. The Deuxième Bureau also received reports from military attachés, while the Naval Ministry ran its own intelligence operation on a budget of 100,000 francs a year.[6]

While cooperation between the Sûreté and the Deuxième Bureau was assured in part by their fairly well-delineated functions of espionage and counterintelligence, the Quai d'Orsay adopted an attitude of Olympian contempt for the other secret services. This attitude sprang from a reluctance to permit other services to trespass upon its unique preserve of foreign affairs, fortified by the Quai's aristocratic self-image, maintained with refined tenacity against the Republic's egalitarian ideology. As in Napoleonic times, French diplomats were accorded fairly lavish sums to recruit local agents and bribe journalists to support French policy. However, a 1913 parliamentary report complained that France received a poor return on the Quai's million-franc annual intelligence investment—unreliable or stale information which was often no more than common gossip, paying for articles praising a particular minister rather than supporting French national interests, or serving as a slush fund to meet nonintelligence expenses, like disaster relief or even the salary of the French provost in Andorra.[7]

A major problem with this system was that no centralized organization existed to coordinate, evaluate, and assimilate this cacophony of intelligence pouring in from ambassadors and attachés, the views of the various desks at the Quai, and the War Ministry. The differences between ambassadors and desk officers meant that the Quai d'Orsay did not always speak with a single voice. The Foreign and War Ministries might squirrel away vital information.[8] The instability of French cabinets, whose average life span was nine months before 1914, and a tradition according to which foreign policy was run as a President of the Republic/Foreign Minister condominium discouraged coordination of foreign intelligence by the cabinet. In one respect, this was just as well; the Third Republic contained its fair share of garrulous, indiscreet, and sometimes unscrupulous politicians who, as will be seen, were quite prepared to employ intelligence in their personal interests, even when these might conflict with those of the nation. But the French "system" was badly placed to construct a coherent intelligence picture and then fold it smoothly into a more or less rational decision-making process. The Agadir crisis of 1911, during which Berlin threatened war over the French army's march on Fez, jolted the government into forming a Conseil Supérieur de la Défense Nationale in July 1911 to coordinate defense and foreign policy strategy. But the main responsibility for assessing Germany fell on the War Ministry. The shortcomings of the army's ability to assimilate intelligence into a coherent and accurate view of the enemy will be discussed later. Suffice it to note here that the lack of coordination of foreign and defense policy made for a fragmented intelligence world, a compartmentalization of information where assumptions or attitudes too often did duty for hard fact. One of the consequences was an antagonism and mutual suspicion among France's various intelligence bureaucracies, which caused delays in the transmission of intelligence and a certain amount of confusion in its assessment during the critical July crisis of 1914.

The fragmentation of the intelligence services both encouraged and was the consequence of the second problem of prewar French intelligence—its politicization. While politicization, like bureaucratic rivalry, was not a uniquely French problem, its development in France was closely linked to the progress of French code-breaking capabilities.

The cryptographic skills of French code breakers should have been a strength. But in the hands of Third Republic politicians, intelligence vital to French security too often became a liability. One of the problems which Octave Homberg set out to correct when he joined the staff of Foreign Minister Delcassé in 1903 was to impose a rigor on the code breakers of the Quai so that erroneous or preliminary decrypts like that of the Panizzardi telegram would no longer be sent forward. In dealing with Bazeries, he had his work cut out for him.

Homberg found that the Quai's chief code breaker was "remarkably bohemian" for a former army officer. "A passionate gambler, always short of cash, an alcoholic besides," Bazeries nevertheless behaved "like a marvelous hunting dog" before an enciphered telegram. "He scented, sniffed the ciphers, sized up rapidly the repetitions, the 'frequencies' of the same cipher, and if one gave him a vague indication of the probable subject of the message, he piled up with vertiginous speed hypothesis upon hypothesis." Soon, with the aid of several telegrams used to cross-check, "the mysterious cipher emerged with a blinding clarity, like a photo plate during the developing process." But if Bazeries had enormous flair, Homberg recognized that his lack of foreign languages and "general culture" meant that he found it difficult to situate a telegram in context and that he was quick to jump to summary conclusions. As a consequence, although a remarkably gifted cryptanalyst, Bazeries "was incapable of working alone . . . he needed guidance."[9]

With the fall of Delcassé in the wake of the 1905 Tangier crisis and the assignment of Homberg to other diplomatic duties, the quality of French code breaking may have declined somewhat. But the decline probably was not too dramatic, for at least two reasons. First, a second generation of code breakers was coming into its own, more systematic, more professional than the mercurial Bazeries. One of those was Commissaire Haverna of the Sûreté, who asked to be assigned Japanese diplomatic codes, possibly acquired in the Netherlands, after Bazeries failed to crack them in 1904. Working with an assistant, Haverna was able in two months to reconstruct "almost the totality of the Japanese cipher made up of 1,600 pages of 100 lines a page." With uncharacteristic administrative generosity, the Sûreté surrendered the codes to Delcassé, who was now able to read the wires between Paris and other embassies and Tokyo, which, among other things, alerted him to the Japanese reaction to Russia's secret request for mediation beginning in the spring of 1905. But the importance for French cryptanalysis was that Haverna's success, for which he was awarded the Légion d'Honneur, ended the quasi-monopoly which Bazeries had hitherto held over French code breaking.

The creation of two skillful black chambers in the Interior and Foreign Ministries established France, if not as the clear leader of European cryptanalysis, at least as the equal of Russia and Austria-Hungary. Unfortunately, the potential advantages which fell to the front-runner in this field were squandered to a degree by a failing altogether typical of French politics—ministerial rivalries. The incident which smashed any hope of cooperation between the black chambers of the Interior Ministry and the Quai d'Orsay brewed up out of an unfortunate but altogether characteristic misunderstanding.

In 1905, the German Emperor, Kaiser Wilhelm II, sailed his yacht to the Moroccan port of Tangier, rowed ashore, uttered a pronouncement about Germany standing behind Moroccan independence, got back on his boat, and sailed away. The Kaiser's words caused an international crisis because France, with the blessing of Great Britain, was poised to absorb Morocco into her North African empire.

During what came to be known as the Tangier crisis, the decipherment of the telegrams between Germany's Paris embassy and Berlin gave French Foreign Minister Delcassé a critical insight into German policy. However, on 26 April, the French Foreign Minister was handed a deciphered wire which revealed that French Prime Minister Paul Rouvier had paid a secret visit to the German ambassador to denounce Delcassé as a "Germanophobe" and to ask the Germans for the eight days' grace he required to ditch his Foreign Minister.

According to Homberg, Delcassé photographed the decrypt with the intention of revealing Rouvier's treacherous contacts with the enemy behind the backs of his colleagues.[10] But rather than confront the Prime Minister head-on, Delcassé sought to convince Rouvier that his experience was vital as a mediator between the Russians and the Japanese. This could only postpone, rather than suspend, Delcassé's execution, however. The simple fact was that the Germans did not like him, and certainly had no desire to stand on the sidelines and watch him increase his prestige, and that of France, as the mediator of the Russo-Japanese War. Consequently, German patience with Rouvier snapped on 16 June 1905, when the French Prime Minister received an ultimatum to fire his Foreign Minister or face the consequences. By way of revenge, upon his departure Delcassé showed Rouvier the sheaf of decrypts which contained the Prime Minister's secret dealings with the Germans.[11]

In this case, French interests were preserved even if relations between ministers were spoiled. But the practice of interministerial spying was a bomb requiring the merest tremor to detonate. It also served as notice that it would become very difficult for intelligence services to maintain a posture of professional detachment so long as their decrypts were used, not to inform the government on foreign relations, but as ammunition shot off by politicians out to settle scores with their rivals.

Relations between the *cabinets noirs* of the Sûreté and the Quai d'Orsay, already strained by the Rouvier-Delcassé confrontation, and by the rivalry between Haverna and Bazeries, who now worked permanently for the Quai, completely broke down in October 1905. Again, the culprit was Rouvier.

The Russian ambassador brought Rouvier a copy of a German telegram deciphered by the Russian black chamber, which had deciphered German diplomatic correspondence since the end of the nineteenth century. To repay the favor, Rouvier ordered the Sûreté to deliver to the Russians the Japanese wires which they had decoded in the course of the Russo-Japanese War. Unaware of the Prime Minister's order, in October the *cabinet noir* at the Quai, as usual monitoring the traffic out of the Russian embassy, discovered to their horror that the head of the Russian secret police in Paris was dispatching to St. Petersburg the contents of the Japanese wires deciphered by Haverna. Quite naturally, they concluded that a serious security leak had occurred at the Sûreté, and sent Bazeries to confront Cavard, the head of the Sûreté, about a mole in his service. For his part, Cavard felt unauthorized to reveal to Bazeries the Prime Minister's order, and merely insisted that his service was secure. Unsatisfied with this explanation, and no doubt reinforced by Bazeries' jealousy of Haverna's success with the Japanese codes, the Quai ordered its code breakers to break off all contact with their colleagues at the Sûreté.[12]

This ushered in what Christopher Andrew has called the era of "waste" in French pre-1914 cryptanalysis, when the two code-breaking services worked in isolation. Waste, perhaps, but not stagnation. Though they alone had access to German diplomatic correspondence, the cryptanalysts at the Quai were the real losers in this refusal to cooperate with the Sûreté, for at least two reasons.

First, the Sûreté team appears to have been the more skillful. According to Lieutenant Marcel Givierge, who was loaned to the Sûreté from the Military Government of Paris from 1907 to the outbreak of World War I, the cryptanalysts at the Quai, though deeply resentful of their colleagues at the Sûreté, on occasion swallowed their pride and brought over a diplomatic wire which had defied their best cryptanalytic efforts.[13] The second benefit which accrued to the Sûreté stemmed from the fact that French Prime Ministers between 1906 and 1912 also doubled as Interior Ministers. Georges Clemenceau, who served as Prime Minister and Minister of the Interior between 1906 and 1909, was so impressed with Haverna's success in helping the Sûreté smash a German espionage ring in Marseille in 1906, in breaking codes of left-wing revolutionaries, and in reconstructing the codes of the Russian secret police in France, that he tasked the commissioner with creating a Photographic Service at the Interior Ministry. The boycott by the Quai's code breakers of Haverna did not deprive the Sûreté of access to diplomatic traffic of several countries. On the contrary, in 1909 the Sûreté extended surveillance of diplomatic telegrams to Lyon, Lille, and Nice because foreign governments were sending messages there to evade surveillance at the Paris Post Office.[14]

Therefore, despite fairly slender resources, the successes of French cryptographers, and of French intelligence generally, were considerable. During six years of close surveillance of the Post Office wire services, Haverna's cryptographers in the Photographic Service were able to reconstruct the diplomatic ciphers of Turkey, Spain, Italy, and Monaco, as well as of Russian, Serbian, and Rumanian financiers operating in Paris. Spanish intercepts, as well as wires from the British ambassador in Madrid, helped the French to assess Spanish policy on staking out its zone in northern Morocco and revealed which French newspapers the Spanish were bribing to support their policies. Italian and Vatican codes were regularly read, but the diplomatic ciphers of Russia and Austria remained immune, at least in the Sûreté.[15] From 1907, the Sûreté began to cooperate with the War Ministry, which had formed its own Cipher Bureau in 1906. In 1909, a Commission Interministérielle de Cryptographie was formed from representatives of the ministries of the Interior, War, Navy, Post Office, and the Colonies. Characteristically, the Quai maintained its splendid isolation.[16]

In the absence of archives, the full success of the Deuxième Bureau against Germany may never be known. Not surprisingly, the primary French concern was to acquire advance warning of German plans of attack. Indeed, as American historian Denis Showalter has noted, "War plans became the nineteenth-century intelligence equivalent of the medieval knight's Holy Grail."[17] The metaphor is not altogether apt, as knowledge of the enemy's war plans was now a *real* problem, although it might prove as elusive as the original medieval article.

Perhaps the greatest, and most controversial, success of pre-1914 French intelligence was the acquisition in 1904 of a German plan to attack with twenty-six army corps through Belgium. The French diplomat Maurice Paléologue noted in his diary that on 25 April 1904 the chief of the French general staff reported to him how a German officer, believed to be a general on the German headquarters staff, had contacted the Service de Renseignements in the War Ministry to offer the German plan of attack on France. An intelligence officer contacted him three times in luxurious hotels in Liège, Paris, and Nice, to find a man whom he was unable to identify because only a "Prussian mustache" protruded from a mass of bandages which swathed his head, as if he had just undergone an operation. Although the man claimed that revenge was his motive and even signed his letters "Le Vengeur," this did not prevent him from placing a price tag of 60,000 francs on his documents.[18] Needless to say, although the plan described by Paléologue seems to fit the Schlieffen Plan, which served as the basis for the German offensive against France in August 1914, the bizarre descriptions of "Le Vengeur" and the fact that the Schlieffen Plan was not finalized until 1906 have caused historians to cast doubt on Paléologue's story.[19] If "Le Vengeur" was a complete imposter, as appears likely, this must count as one of the few times in history when bogus intelligence actually led toward the right conclusions.

Though the possibility of a German thrust through Belgium had been discussed in French military circles, the Germans had no such plan before 1906. What "Le Vengeur" actually did was to stimulate French intelligence and military attachés to study German railway construction along the Belgian frontier, the theories of German military theorist Friedrich von Bernhardi, and German annual maneuvers in which the virtues of flanking movements were stressed over those of frontal assault. French Plan XV bis, completed in December 1906, was based on the assumption that German forces would come through Belgium, rather than launch a frontal attack on French defenses in Lorraine.[20]

The problem, of course, was that though the French expected a German offensive through Belgium, the Deuxième Bureau underestimated the numbers of troops and the western axis of the sweep which Schlieffen intended to make. General Henri Navarre defends the performance of the Service de Renseignements, arguing that, together with the "Vengeur" documents, in 1908 French intelligence acquired a mobilization plan drawn up by Ludendorff, as well as a second plan on the very eve of war which showed that the Germans planned to march on Paris via Belgium, with the axis of advance on the Oise.[21]

Other historians have indicated that, while certain Deuxième Bureau and military attaché reports discuss issues like the configuration of German railway networks, German operational doctrine which emphasized broad flanking movements, or the ability of the Belgian forts at Namur and Liège to withstand a German onslaught, nothing clearly indicated a wide German sweep through Belgium. But this was the problem which affected French intelligence, as it does all other intelligence services—namely, how to distinguish "signals" from "noise." Intelligence seldom provides a clear-cut answer. Therefore, the tendency of all "deciders" is to fit intelligence into one's own assumptions.

———

In peacetime, there is no way to disprove those assumptions. Any intelligence which seemed to indicate the true scope of the Schlieffen Plan could be dismissed as bogus intelligence, which in the time-honored manner mixed the accurate and the fanciful.[22] In any case, military intelligence can be useful only if the commander takes counsel of it, which, as will be seen, Joffre clearly did not do before he drew up his infamous Plan XVII for the defense of France in 1911. The rather dismal conclusion is that strategic intelligence in peacetime is virtually useless, because it is bound to be filtered by one's own assumptions and expectations.

French intelligence also suffered a serious blow on the very eve of war, one which helped to compromise any advantages, actual or potential, it might have given France on the outbreak of hostilities in 1914. Once again, the culprits were politicians who placed personal interests above those of the nation. The Agadir crisis of 1911 offered virtually a rerun of the Delcassé-Rouvier clash of 1905. Through decrypts of German diplomatic wires, in July of that year French Foreign Minister Justin de Selves discovered that his Prime Minister, Joseph Caillaux, was meeting secretly with the German ambassador. Furious at the revelation of this back-channel diplomacy, Selves threatened to reveal the deciphered German wires and thus expose Caillaux's duplicitous relations with the enemy. Although Selves never carried out his threat, the incident became the subject of common diplomatic gossip.

Meanwhile, Caillaux, fully expecting that Selves's promised revelations would show him in the worst possible light, called on the startled German ambassador, von Lancken, to ask for original copies of the telegrams so that he could verify the accuracy of the Quai's decrypts. Alerted, the Germans changed their codes. For this unbelievable indiscretion, Caillaux was carpeted by French President Raymond Poincaré and admonished for his "inexcusable" conduct. "I was wrong," Caillaux replied, "but I had to defend myself."[23]

A second incident which compromised French code breaking occurred in early May 1913, when the Sûreté decoded two wires which revealed that President Poincaré and Foreign Minister Stephen Pichon had opened secret negotiations with the Vatican, with which France had severed diplomatic relations in July 1904 at the height of church-state tensions brought to the surface by the Dreyfus Affair. The separation of church and state in 1905, and government-ordered inventories of church property the following year, which had sparked riots of the faithful, had divided France into pro- and anticlerical camps. Given the volcanic eruptions which inevitably would have followed a revelation from these secret conclaves, a furious Interior Minister, Louis-Lucien Klotz, produced the wires in a 6 May 1913 cabinet meeting and demanded an explanation. Klotz's ploy to discredit Pichon and end the secret talks with the Vatican backfired, however. Enraged, the Foreign Minister threatened to resign if the Sûreté continued to read diplomatic wires, and won his argument in cabinet. From May 1913 to the outbreak of war, no more diplomatic wires were sent to the Sûreté. Pichon's victory proved a Pyrrhic one as far as French code breaking was concerned, especially when coupled with a December 1913 order which terminated the deciphering of secret financial correspondence which he regularly sent to the Finance Ministry. On 27 July 1914, the Quai returned hat in hand to Haverna for help in reading diplomatic telegrams. The Sûreté obliged, but after a fifteen-month exile from diplomatic ciphers, it took Haverna almost two months to get back up to speed—two critical months during which the French armies came within an ace of defeat.[24]

The reason why the Quai d'Orsay's black chamber was virtually paralyzed on the very eve of war can again be traced to yet another damaging case of ministerial indiscretion. On the afternoon of 16 March 1914 the wife of former Prime Minister Joseph Caillaux, unsettled by a campaign of defamation against her husband led by the newspaper *Le Figaro*, walked into the office of the editor-in-chief, Gaston Calmette, pulled out a pistol, and shot him dead. Madame Caillaux's concern was that Calmette intended to publish excerpts from her love letters written to Caillaux during his previous marriage. But public rumor held that the real purpose of Madame Caillaux's assassination of Calmette was to prevent the publication of the two copies of the 1911 decrypts in the editor's possession which revealed that, during the Agadir crisis which had brought the two countries to the brink of war, Caillaux had maintained secret contacts with the Germans. As enormous public attention focused on Madame Caillaux's trial in July, the German ambassador threatened the Quai that "a bomb will explode" if the decrypts were revealed.

The cunning Caillaux had been careful to amass a stock of weapons with which to retaliate. In January 1914, Haverna had been visited in his office by the personnel director of the Interior Ministry, who asked to see the decrypts for the first six months of 1913. Haverna thought nothing more of it, until March 1914, when Foreign Minister Louis Barthou accused Caillaux of stealing decrypts to use against him.[25] In fact, Caillaux made a habit of collecting decrypts to use against many people, including President Poincaré. He also possessed decoded Spanish diplomatic telegrams proving that Calmette had accepted "subsidies" from Madrid. Caillaux's blackmail worked. So desperate was French Prime Minister René Viviani to avoid scandal that he issued a public declaration denying that the German decrypts existed in return for Caillaux's silence.

But the damage had been done. Madame Caillaux's trial, which swallowed oceans of newsprint, was to have two unfortunate consequences for France. First, the potential scandal which would have resulted from Caillaux's revelations so worried French politicians that their attention was drawn away from the crisis rapidly brewing into a tempest which resulted from the assassination of Archduke Ferdinand in Sarajevo. The French government was more preoccupied with preventing a diplomatic crisis over the Caillaux affair in July 1914 than with the possibility of war with Germany. Second, the scandal placed embassies doing business in Paris on alert, so that most of the major foreign powers changed their codes just days before the war began, blinding French cryptographers at a critical moment in the international crisis. One result, already noted, was that Haverna was reassigned to the business of diplomatic cryptanalysis. In the meantime, a gallant all-male jury acquitted Madame Caillaux.

Christopher Andrew concluded of the Caillaux episode that "those who cannot handle secret intelligence are better off without it."[26] The advantages which the proficiency in code breaking might have afforded French policy makers were compromised by ministerial rivalries and by the indiscretions of politicians. Worse, these advantages actually harmed French interests, for two reasons. First, the availability of decrypts sharpened the atmosphere of mistrust among politicians, which contributed to ministerial instability. Second, it actually distorted French diplomacy because some politicians believed decrypts a more reliable guide to foreign policies of other nations than were the reports of French ambassadors. One of the disadvantages for the smooth process of diplomacy of this surreptitious reading of foreign telegrams was that the decrypts could expose unflattering opinions of French politicians held by foreign officials. This could instill distrust in French negotiators, who assumed that foreign diplomats negotiated in bad faith.[27] The Caillaux affair confirmed the volatile effect of intelligence in the context of a suspicious and divided French political system. It also placed French intelligence at a severe disadvantage in 1914, as it confronted the supreme challenge of its modern existence—the Schlieffen Plan.

THREE

THE FAILED MIRACLE

French military intelligence entered World War I with several assets. By 1914, the French had recognized the potential of aircraft to serve as the "eyes" of the army. Sports aviation had been popular in France for a decade, which had produced large numbers of qualified pilots, engineers, and an innovative aircraft industry. Invariably, this fascination with flying had spilled over into the military field. Air reconnaissance had played a role in French campaigns in Morocco prior to the outbreak of war. Each side had been given air reconnaissance units during the 1912 annual maneuvers. The following year, the pilots were assigned observers supplied with notebooks containing silhouettes to aid in recognizing the enemy. And although the experiment was regarded as a great success, when war broke out in August 1914, much progress remained to be made. Radios, first installed in a plane in 1911, were regarded as too heavy and complex to become standard equipment. A camera developed by the army's Telephotography Laboratory remained untested because the War Ministry believed it impossible for observers also to be trained photographers.

To place the French development in perspective, in 1914 the first British military aircraft were only just beginning to come on-line, while the U.S. Army counted only twenty-eight planes. Germany, which had invested heavily in zeppelins and kite balloons, carried out a crash program from 1913 to get their air inventory on a par with that of France.

In August 1914, the French army counted 650 qualified pilots for twenty-three six-plane squadrons. Attached to each squadron was a fast car and a motorcyclist to rush intelligence to headquarters. Yet, as the French air inventory included ten different types of aircraft, it took some time to shake these out into homogeneous squadrons. Their underpowered Gnome, Renault, and Canton-Unné engines gave them a very slow rate of climb. As a result of the prewar maneuvers, French commanders had concluded that above 1,000 meters air observation was unreliable. Yet this low ceiling made the planes vulnerable to ground fire from front-line troops. Therefore, in common with air doctrine in other armies, planes were assigned the task of scouting rear areas, while observation of the sharp end of enemy armies fell, as tradition demanded, to the cavalry.[1] This was just as well because Colonel E. L. Spears, the British liaison officer with the French in 1914, noted that for French soldiers "the temptation to let fly at anything that appeared over their heads," including their own pilots, "was overwhelming. The Staff were in despair at the reports they received on this subject, and simply did not know what steps to take to educate the troops."[2]

A second source of intelligence potentially even more accurate and valuable than air reconnaissance was electronic. As war approached, a smattering of farsighted French officers began to realize the potential intelligence harvest to be gathered by eavesdropping on the growing networks of radio communications. With the increased use of radios for military communications, the French might receive German orders at the same time as the enemy. As has been seen, in 1909 a Commission Interministérielle de Cryptographie was established to study German military codes and in 1912 a Cryptological Section was created at the War Ministry. In 1913, a course on cryptography was offered every Monday afternoon at the French war college, while encoding exercises were carried out during the 1913 autumn maneuvers and in the first six months of 1914.[3] When war broke out, the French, led by Major François Cartier, had a thorough grasp of the organization of German radios,[4] and had created eight stations to intercept foreign radio transmissions, all linked to his office in the War Ministry. And while cryptographers complained of understaffing and a lack of en-

thusiasm for their activities in the ministry, even these modest preparations put the French substantially ahead of their major rivals and
allies on the Western Front.[5]

But while both these sources of intelligence would prove valuable
once war broke out, the more immediate problem for the high command was to determine the scope and direction of the opening German
offensive against France. The problem for French intelligence, as for
all intelligence services, is that while it is easy enough to chart enemy
capabilities in peacetime—that is, the numbers of men and weapons
at his disposal—his intentions during war are much more difficult to
predict.[6] German intentions could only be divined by studying the
reports of agents, observers, and attachés. As has been seen, the "Vengeur" documents of 1904 had indicated a German attack on France
through Belgium. But for a variety of reasons, not the least of which
were the bizarre circumstances of their acquisition, serious doubt was
cast on their authenticity. Nevertheless, as war approached, indications
that the main thrust of a German attack could come through Belgium
became too numerous to dismiss out of hand.

Students of German military doctrine noted as early as 1904 that
envelopment, as opposed to frontal assault, was increasingly in fashion
east of the Rhine. By 1906, French observers at the German army's
autumn exercises noted that flanking movements and encirclement
had moved out of staff college lecture halls and onto the fields of
maneuver.[7] By 1909, the Deuxième Bureau of the general staff "was
thoroughly convinced," according to American historian Jan Karl Tanenbaum, that the construction of an extensive rail network in the region
of Aix-la-Chapelle indicated that a German attack would cut the southeastern corner of Belgium, while the following year they suggested that
a German swing as far west as Brussels was a possibility.[8] In March
1911, the French military attaché in Berlin, Colonel Maurice Pellé,
reported himself much impressed by the arguments of Britain's Director
of Military Operations, General Henry Wilson, that the Germans
would overwhelm the Belgian fortresses of Namur and Liège with forty
divisions which included reservists. These troops would then roll
through Belgium and into France.[9] Wilson appears to have defined a
vision of German strategy which had become accepted wisdom in the
highest echelons of the British government.[10]

However, despite these intelligence advantages, the strength and direction of the German offensive of 1914 caught the French high command, led by General Joseph Joffre, completely by surprise. Why was this so? Was this surprise caused by a failure of intelligence, a failure of the high command to heed intelligence warnings, or something else—a complicity of wishful thinking on the part of the high command to which French intelligence acquiesced?

General Henri Navarre, who spent much of his career in military intelligence, was in no doubt that it was Joffre, not French intelligence, who must shoulder responsibility for the strategic surprise of 1914. Navarre offered an impressive list of intelligence warnings before 1914, which included the number of reserve units which the Germans planned to use in their opening offensives, reports on the crushing superiority of German heavy artillery, the introduction of new weapons like mortars and *Minenwerfer*, and experiments with toxic gases.

The Schlieffen Plan, the opening German offensive through Belgium designed by the chief of the German general staff, Count Alfred von Schlieffen, and adopted as the German war plan in 1906, "had been known for a long time," Navarre wrote. "And on the eve of war our general staff possessed the 'Plan of Concentration of the German Army in the West,' which revealed the intention to march on Paris by the shortest route: Belgium and the axis of the Oise [River]." Navarre argued that generals refused to give intelligence warnings any credence because they clashed with their preconceived ideas of what the enemy was likely to do.[11]

Preconceived ideas and wishful thinking certainly abounded in the French high command. But, Navarre's defense aside, French intelligence warnings served as much to bolster as to dispel those preconceptions. For starters, French "intelligence" did not speak with a unified voice. If some reports warned of the true intentions of the Germans, others suggested different conclusions. In short, there was a cacophony of information—"noise" mixed with signals. The intelligence selected out by the war planners depended very much on their "preconceived notions," which were not uniformly hostile to the hypothesis of a wide sweep through Belgium. In fact, intelligence reports set off an intense debate in the French high command over strategic options. But while intelligence reports did much to stoke that debate, they were unable to decide it. That the debate over strategic options was won by Joffre depended less on rejecting good or "correct" intelligence than on the political, intellectual, and psychological environment into which those reports were fed: political constraints placed on Joffre's options; the strategic risks posed by rival strategies; operational and tactical theories in vogue in the French army, which reflected both the French army's institutional disarray and a sense of inferiority; and power struggles within the French high command. The combination of these factors enticed Joffre to the brink of disaster in August–September 1914.

Rather than taking place in an intelligence vacuum, French war planning to counter the German invasion was very much influenced by intelligence reports. While early reports of a possible German offensive through Belgium had been dismissed or explained away, by 1909 General Henri de Lacroix, the generalissimo-designate in wartime, felt obliged to make at least some concessions to the mounting evidence. His Plan XVI shifted several French divisions westward to deal with German forces which might choose to cut the southeastern corner of Belgium east of the Meuse River. However, his successor, General Victor Michel, was haunted by a vision of a massive German pivot through Belgium. Michel's fears were not founded exclusively or even primarily on intelligence reports. Rather, Michel reasoned correctly that Belgium was the only place where the Germans could intervene massively in the hope of gaining the rapid decision which the high commands of all armies—prisoners of the "short-war illusion"—believed would come in the opening battles.[12]

In 1911, Michel presented to the Conseil Supérieur de la Guerre, France's highest military body, composed of her most senior generals, a strategy to counter it. Michel's plan contained two very radical features. First, it placed a mere holding force on France's frontiers with Alsace and Lorraine, and shifted the bulk of the French army westward, concentrating the largest portion of 500,000 men at Lille, supported by a reserve army 200,000 strong near Paris ready to reinforce endangered portions of the front. The second feature which immediately caught the attention of Michel's colleagues was that his plan required 1,300,000 men, which would mean that French reservists would have to be thrown into the front lines from the first day of combat.

With the benefits of hindsight, Michel's plan, had it been adopted, would have placed French troops in a far better position to thwart the

Schlieffen Plan than did the French counterplan—Plan XVII—which
in 1914 launched French armies northeastward into Alsace and Lorraine as German armies swung through Belgium to curl around the
French left flank. But in 1911 there appeared to be at least four
excellent reasons to reject it.

The first was that Michel's plan contained serious strategic risks.
Michel assumed that the Germans would not exercise their option to
change their minds, jettison plans for an attack in Belgium, and launch
an assault elsewhere, like Alsace-Lorraine. In that case, argued the
Troisième Bureau (Operations) under the aggressive Colonel (later
General) François de Grandmaison, 700,000 French troops would
languish as distant spectators to the great Teutonic dagger thrust into
the French heartland. If Plan XVII was condemned as a strategic
gamble, so in the eyes of the French general staff was that of Michel.

Michel's second problem was that his plan posed what a war college
would term a strategic/operational and strategic/tactical mismatch.
Strategically, Michel imposed a defensive posture on the French army,
at a time when the French army, in common with other armies in
Europe, increasingly placed its faith in the value of offensive operations. An offensive was mandated by several factors, the most powerful
of which was the generally accepted faith in a short, sharp war. One
did not win wars in which the opening battles would largely dictate
the outcome by allowing the Hun to run amok through Belgium and
slam virtually unmolested into northern France. The French army
had been trained in offensive operations. Its main artillery piece, the
75 mm cannon, was designed for mobility. Above all, how could one
encourage allies, especially Russia, to join in the conflict if French
armies squatted on their own frontiers?

Michel's third problem was organizational. If the Germans were to
make a wide sweep through Belgium, they must integrate their reserve
formations into their battle lines from day one of the campaign. The
logical corollary was that France must do the same, or condemn itself
to numerical inferiority. The question of whether or not the Germans
planned to integrate their reserve forces into their front-line troops
from day one, therefore, became the critical intelligence puzzle of the
prewar period. The answer would give a strong indication of German
intentions, as well as dictate the French response.

French intelligence had received a 1908 German staff paper which stated that the German army "will not always be made up exclusively of active corps, but can include active . . . and reserve corps."[13] If these reports were true, then it caused a real dilemma for the French. French officers believed, with some justification, that their reservists were poorly trained and led, and that their wholesale integration into active units without a period of training and acclimatization to military life would place the fragile cohesion and untested combat qualities of the French army at risk.[14]

When Michel offered his plan for adoption by the Conseil Supérieur de la Guerre on 19 July 1911, it was rejected outright. Michel's strongest argument should have been that intelligence reports indicated at least the possibility of a massive German sweep through Belgium. But the intelligence reports were far from conclusive. For instance, Colonel Pellé, the French attaché in Berlin, who in 1911 had reported Wilson's fears of a massive sweep via Brussels, in subsequent 1912 reports suggested that the Germans could adopt a defensive posture on the Belgian border. The French attaché in Brussels was of the opinion that any German attack through Belgium would remain east of the Meuse, the view adopted by Joffre. Even the Deuxième Bureau dismissed reports that the Germans would integrate active and reserve divisions in the opening offensive.[15]

In the end, if Michel lost the prewar strategic debate, it was not because intelligence reports which supported his strategic options were accorded a low priority, as Navarre claimed, but because he lacked the political clout to have his views adopted. Michel's ouster was part of a palace coup which initiated a period known as the "Nationalist Revival" in France, a series of governments led by men determined to give the appearance, at least, that they sought to bolster French defense. The man selected to sweep away the shards of Michel's plan was General Joseph Joffre.

Joffre's nomination as commander-in-chief came as a surprise to many. His main qualification for the job was that the front-runners had all been eliminated for reasons of age or politics, while nothing in his career automatically eliminated Joffre from consideration. A native of Rivesaltes, a small Mediterranean town near the Spanish frontier, Joffre had posted a fairly mediocre record at the Ecole Polytechnique before his commissioning in the military engineers. Most of his career had been spent in the French colonies designing fortifications. In 1910, he returned to France as "Director of the Rear," a position which required him to make the logistical arrangements for mobilization. Corpulent and easygoing, Joffre had limited staff experience, had circumvented the two-year course at the French war college, an almost obligatory rite of passage for high command, and, his critics charged, possessed a mind which was a strategic tabula rasa. As a consequence, he allowed himself to be dominated by a clique of Young Turks led by Colonel de Grandmaison, and staff officers determined that French war plans reflect the spirit of the offensive with which they hoped to infuse the entire army.

Joffre's Plan XVII, which became operational in the spring of 1914, reflected this commitment to the offensive spirit. One of its consequences was that intelligence on German intentions was shaded and shaped to conform to Joffre's intentions. "Joffre, for his part, continued to pay little attention to intelligence which failed to conform to his war plan," Christopher Andrew has pointed out.[16]

To be fair to him, Joffre was not hostile to intelligence—for instance, French officers insisted that it was through Joffre's protection that the Section du Chiffre survived and prospered between 1912 and 1914.[17] It was simply that he operated in a political and strategic straitjacket which offered him little room for maneuver, and thus in a situation in which intelligence that contradicted his intentions could only place him before an insoluble dilemma.

Joffre accepted intelligence reports that the Germans would come through Belgium. He requested permission from the Poincaré government in February 1912 to march into Belgium as far as Namur to counter an expected German thrust through the Ardennes, only to be refused on the grounds that a French violation of Belgian neutrality risked forfeiting English assistance.[18] While this refusal made political sense, militarily it severely curtailed Joffre's options. The Belgian offensive closed to him, and a defensive strategy unthinkable, Joffre had no choice but to point his offensive elsewhere.[19]

The simple truth was that the 1911 dismissal of Michel confirmed the ascendancy of the offensive mentality in the French army. The result was to strip French commanders of their ability to view intelligence objectively. The French army was not so much hostile to intelligence as close-minded. Intelligence spread before them like a *buffet campagnard* from which officers selected delicacies suited to their tastes, items least likely to cause indigestion. But this was not an exclusively, even a primarily, French failing.

The belief that offensive operations were the sine qua non of victory meant that intelligence was either ignored, as in Germany, or mustered to support plans which were largely inflexible because they had been locked into mobilization schedules and railway timetables. Information which appeared to contradict offensive intentions was culled out or discarded as deception, leaving a residue of "solid" intelligence which supported the ideas of the high command. Although Joffre went to great pains in his memoirs to point out that Plan XVII contained an elaborate "Intelligence Plan" which demanded detailed information on German military movements on the outbreak of hostilities,[20] there is no indication that he allowed German actions to interfere in any way with his scheme. After all, why should attacking generals worry overmuch about the intentions of an enemy condemned merely to parry the thrusts of an aggressive opponent?

But while this state of mind might be common to all armies, in France intelligence estimates—even correct ones—mounted a particularly frail challenge to the prevailing orthodoxy of the offensive. An offensive was irresistibly attractive to the French in 1914 for both political and military reasons. Because the French were acutely aware of the superiority of the German army, and because they realized that the Germans would direct the massive weight of that army westward at the war's outset to achieve a rapid decision over France, they especially wanted Russia to attack Germany from the east. President Raymond Poincaré was at the forefront of those who argued that Russia would be less inclined to launch a lifesaving offensive into East Prussia if France cowered behind her frontiers. And while an offensive strategy per se did not affect the chances of British intervention one way or the other, its direction was critical to the British attitude. With the Belgian option closed to him, and having rejected a defensive strategy, Joffre was left with no choice but to aim his thrust at the German heartland across the French border.

Besides, he could justify this decision in military terms. If the Germans planned to attack through Belgium, Joffre argued, then so much the better! Belgian fortresses at Liège would hold up their advance, while a French attack on a weakened German center and left in Lorraine and Alsace would dislocate the German right wing.[21] Of course, this proved to be sheer fantasy. Joffre, like his counterparts in other armies, grossly overestimated the offensive power of the armies of 1914, and desperately underestimated the strength which modern artillery, machine guns, and barbed wire bestowed upon the defensive.

But intelligence reports which outlined the growing military power of Germany[22] could do little to rattle the faith which Joffre and other French commanders placed in the power of offensive warfare. On the contrary, while they should have induced caution, they aroused a gambler's mentality in men whose nerves were made taut by what they saw as increasingly long odds. Nor was this inversion of reality confined to the French. In Germany, whose army was daily growing stronger in relation to her major rivals, fear of encirclement encouraged planners and politicians to strike their enemies piecemeal before they could unite and crush her.[23]

It was in France, however, that the conflict between the reality of weakness as laid out in intelligence reports and the requirements of offensive warfare produced the greatest distortions in war planning. With the military gap between France and Germany growing every year, with the certainty that France would have to bear the brunt of the initial German offensive probably for six weeks before Russian mobilization could draw off German troops, with little faith in the training and discipline of French troops, especially of the reserves, French officers grasped at a doctrine which minimized the objectivity with which intelligence reports were viewed.[24]

French reliance on the offensive and a set plan certainly helped to create an atmosphere which stimulated wishful thinking and discouraged giving credence to intelligence reports which tended to puncture prevailing orthodoxy. In 1912 and 1913, the military governor of Lille, the French attaché in Brussels, and Allied sources reported the disturbing extension of rail networks near Aix-la-Chapelle, maneuvers emphasizing flanking movements, and predictions of reservists in the front lines, which would allow the Germans to throw divisions west of the Meuse. Unfortunately, this accurate intelligence was mixed in with reports rejecting the idea that the Germans intended to use their reserves. In 1913, the French attaché in Berlin predicted an opening German assault in Lorraine, while in that year even General Henry Wilson retreated from his earlier assurances that the Germans would cross the Meuse, and snuggled closer to Joffre's conception. The result was that the Deuxième Bureau retreated into neutrality, threw up its hands, and reported in 1913 that it did "not possess any really reliable information concerning the operational plans of our adversaries."[25]

Of course, it did possess reliable information about, or reliable indications of, German intentions. Either intelligence officers were unable to formulate a clear assessment of this information or, as good soldiers, they were reluctant to promote "accurate" intelligence which would challenge the prevailing prejudices and dispositions of their leaders for reasons of bureaucratic politics or to salvage their careers. So they retreated into noncommittal assessments which left their views intentionally vague.

It was clear that an offensive strategy and Plan XVII had found favor with Joffre, his chief of staff, General Edouard de Castelnau, and the powerful Troisième Bureau under the direction of Colonel François de Grandmaison, the French army's "Monsieur Offensive." In these conditions, few intelligence officers were willing to stake their career on an unpopular version of possible future German operations. Better just report the information and leave it at that.

As the final months of peace ticked away, at least some senior officers, including Joseph Gallieni, Fifth Army commander Charles Lanrezac, and Third Army commander Pierre Ruffey, began to have serious doubts about German willingness to remain east and south of the Meuse. But their doubts appear to have been induced more by a rationalization of French frontier weaknesses and German options than by intelligence reports per se. Significantly, two of the three commanders were assigned armies designated to cover the French left wing, which would absorb the brunt of the German onslaught, so their concerns might be dismissed as the special pleading of commanders concerned that they were "covered" in the event of unforeseen circumstances.[26] It seemed very much a case of "where you sit is where you stand."

Joffre simply had too much political and personal capital invested in Plan XVII to reopen the issue of French strategic choices, even when German mobilization plans obtained by French intelligence in April 1914 gave strong indications that reservists would play a front-line role.[27] In fact, one can only conclude that had Moltke walked into the French War Ministry and dropped the Schlieffen Plan on Joffre's desk, it would have made little difference. Intelligence in French war planning was simply irrelevant.

With the outbreak of war, however, intelligence ceased to be irrelevant, although it continued to be distorted by wishful thinking and "preconceived ideas" almost down to the battle of the Marne in early September 1914. The share of responsibility laid at the door of the French for the outbreak of war in 1914 has been that they exercised little of their considerable influence with Russia, which forced the pace of the July crisis with its early mobilization activities.[28] One reason for this was that intelligence reports caused Joffre to overestimate the state of German war preparations. In his memoirs, Joffre claimed that the alarmist reports of German mobilization, at least some of them provided by the Russians, filed by French intelligence helped to convince him at least by 27 July if not earlier that war was inevitable.[29]

From late July 1914, French intelligence began to follow the progress of German mobilization, much of it through French agents, while the German press, unlike that of France, which published lists of railway lines and bridges scheduled to be guarded, appears to have been generally security-conscious.[30] Like most agents, those working for France proved reluctant to admit that they had nothing to report; only on July 29 did the Germans move troops out of training camps and begin to guard railway lines and reinforce border fortresses. Even then, the German Chancellor, Theobald von Bethmann-Hollweg, refused to issue *Kriegsgefahr* or premobilization orders on 29 or 30 July.[31] Yet at 3:40 a.m. on 30 July, a wire arrived at the Quai d'Orsay from the French ambassador in St. Petersburg, Maurice Paléologue, stating that Russian sources predicted a German general mobilization order for that very day. At the French War Ministry, reports that German troop trains were moving toward the frontier poured in. These helped bolster Joffre's request of 29 July to order his frontier "cover" forces into their positions, which was granted on 30 July, with the proviso that they would remain ten kilometers behind the frontier to avoid incidents.[32] Despite the certainty in French intelligence circles that their German counterparts closely followed French mobilization through the loquacious French press, the Germans appear to have been unaware of measures taken by the French in late July and were predicting as late as July 29 that the period of tension would last for weeks. If the German commander-in-chief, the younger Moltke, pressed for quick mobilization, he staked his case on his own anxieties rather than on the reports of his intelligence services.[33] French preparations for war ran significantly ahead of those of the Germans, although Joffre told the Council of Ministers the exact opposite on 31 July when he demanded that a general mobilization order be issued. The question was: Why did he choose to believe these reports? The basic reason was fear—fear for the solidity of the alliance with Russia, whose prompt military action was vital for French survival, and fear that the slower French mobilization time would hand the Germans devastating advantages in the opening battles.

The accuracy of intelligence reports appears to have been one of the primary casualties of the confusion which reigned in European capitals. The Deuxième Bureau reported on 1 August that in the preceding days the Germans had secretly called up the five most recent reserve classes and would be on a war footing by 4 August.[34] The danger of this sort of report was that, rather than breaking down the "preconceived ideas" of the French high command, it tended to reinforce Joffre's fear that the Germans were discreetly topping up their active forces with the most recently released reservists behind the cover of diplomatic negotiations before launching a surprise attack.[35] This stood in stark contrast to the Germans, who appear to have been in possession both of Joffre's mobilization schedule and of at least the general outline of Plan XVII.[36]

It took some time before the Deuxième Bureau developed the skills to separate rumor from fact. When E. L. Spears arrived at French headquarters early in August, he noted that the Deuxième Bureau was in the grip of an atmosphere of irrational optimism, and that the wildest rumors circulated that German armies were almost on the verge of physical and moral collapse. Still, he noted, the chief of the Deuxième Bureau, the levelheaded Lieutenant Colonel Zopf, held most of these rumors in check.[37] It is clear, however, that many of these rumors found their way into French intelligence bulletins and that they influenced Joffre's conduct in the early days of the conflict.

Following the German attacks on the Liège fortresses which began on the night of 5–6 August, the Deuxième Bureau reported that the forts "were in an excellent state of defense and promise to hold out for a long time," especially as the German attackers were "very tired and demoralized." The intelligence bulletin for 8 August stated confidently that German artillery fire was inaccurate while German soldiers had revealed a "great fear of the bayonet,"[38] even though the main fortress had surrendered on the morning of 7 August. In this way, intelligence was misled as to the strength of the Belgian resistance and the objectives of the German attack. Joffre declared himself happy to receive these "reassuring" intelligence reports which, combined with others indicating large-scale troop movements in Lorraine, appeared to confirm the soundness of Plan XVII. As late as 10 August, Joffre insisted that the Liège forts were holding out nicely and that intelligence reported that the Germans appeared to have reconciled themselves to a lengthy siege.[39]

The two great intelligence problems of the first month of the war were to detect the direction and strength of the German offensive and to determine whether they intended to use the reserves in the front lines. As already noted, these two problems were linked, for the enemy could not do one without the other. "One has to admit," Joffre confessed, "the use made by the Germans of their reserve corps in August 1914 came as a surprise for us, and this surprise is at the origins of the errors of appreciation which we committed, especially that concerning the extent of their maneuver to the north."[40] But Joffre's surprise is difficult to credit entirely. One of the arguments which he had used in 1913 to defend the extension of military service in the French army from two to three years was that the German military expansion had strengthened the enemy's ability to use reservists.[41] Nevertheless, the least that one can say is that, in 1914, Joffre refused to keep an open mind. By 8 August, the Deuxième Bureau had located fifteen or sixteen of the twenty-six German army corps, only five or six of which, they believed, were opposite Belgium. Joffre assumed that the ten missing corps were forming "in all likelihood behind the impenetrable Metz-Thionville curtain"—that is, in Lorraine![42]

In his defense, an open mind was a luxury which Joffre could ill afford. In 1911, in the wake of the Michel crisis, Joffre was faced with the task of restoring harmony to a divided high command, a charge which today might be compared to concocting peace in the Balkans. The French army in 1914, as in 1940, was an army which ran very much by committee. All senior generals in the French army held the rank of major general, so that Joffre was merely the primus inter pares rather than the undisputed generalissimo. In the turbulent world of the Third Republic, where a cabinet's survival was computed in months rather than years, and where generals assiduously cultivated their own political contacts, Joffre's political position was insecure. Having marshaled the support of his commanders behind Plan XVII, it would have been bureaucratic folly to throw over his war plan merely because of something the Germans might do. This could splinter the fragile harmony of the French high command and expose his plan to attack from politicians with a sure nose for the most hairline of fissures in military solidarity.[43] Besides, Joffre had convinced himself that a German invasion of Belgium would actually work to his benefit, for it would weaken the enemy center and contribute to the success of Plan XVII. So why worry?

By 12 August, the concentration of the German army was complete, apparently twenty-four hours earlier than predicted by the Deuxième Bureau. The Belgians petitioned Joffre for help, while French intelligence counted eight German corps and four cavalry divisions opposite Belgium, at least two corps stronger than previously thought.[44] Still, Joffre continued to ignore the growing threat on his left wing. In part this was because he was distracted by the fighting in Alsace, where the French had penetrated well into German-held territory. He was also able to soothe his conscience somewhat by assigning four British and two North African divisions to his left wing, which he ordered to link up with the Belgians. This, he reasoned as late as 14 August, when evidence of a German advance became unmistakable, could deal with the situation on his left. He convinced himself also that German cavalry launched into Belgium were not the outriders of a general advance because they were unsupported by infantry. He then stuck his head further into the tightening German noose by setting in motion a French attack in Lorraine.[45]

By 15 August, reports of German troop movements into Belgium, and the insistence of his Fifth Army commander, General Charles Lanrezac, that he was confronted by vastly superior forces, began to lay claims even on Joffre's limited attention. The significance of the German advance remained an open question, however. The answer hinged on whether the Germans would combine active and reserve units. Here, Joffre confessed that his prejudices crowded out his common sense. When on 14 August French intelligence reported German reserve units moving north of Liège, the French commander believed them destined for siege operations around Liège rather than an indication of the beginning of a German advance, "because of the ideas that we had concerning the employment of reserve troops by the Germans . . ."[46] In other words, Joffre was guilty of mirror-imaging— that is, assuming that the enemy could or would do what he would do in their place.

Certainly, Joffre was predisposed to dismiss the front-line use of reservists by his adversaries. But how strongly did French intelligence challenge his view? On the face of it, with nothing short of a sledgehammer. On 16 August, the Deuxième Bureau issued a report stating categorically that the Germans were camouflaging their reservists by assigning identical numbers to active, reserve, and Landwehr (for older reservists) formations. Therefore, where the French believed they were dealing with one active regiment, they might in fact be confronting two or even three regiments.[47] Unfortunately, as was often the case, the Deuxième Bureau almost immediately undermined the credibility of their own conclusions by complaining that French soldiers neglected to give the units of captured Germans in their POW reports, or failed to distinguish between active, reserve, and Landwehr formations.[48] This permitted the French commander-in-chief to play out his preconceptions, to linger in his biases for a few hours longer. Joffre remembered telling the commander of the BEF, Sir John French, on 16 August that he was "rather badly informed" about the German forces in front of the Belgians, but suspected that they were "only cavalry," a view which his intelligence had done nothing to demolish on the 18th.[49]

Finally, on 25 August, in a stunning reversal of what they had said on the 16th, Joffre's Deuxième Bureau declared: "In certain armies one has concluded from prisoner interrogations that each active German army corps is followed by a reserve corps with the same number. This conclusion is erroneous." This judgment was based both on a remarkable ability to explain away hard evidence and on what might be called a primitive version of operational analysis.

If regular soldiers, reservists, and members of the Landwehr all wore the same unit numbers, the Deuxième Bureau maintained, this was not by design, but because in their haste to kit out their army, the Germans simply doled out what came to hand. This conclusion betrayed an inflated optimism and confidence in the inefficiency of the German army which Spears had noted permeated the Deuxième Bureau in the early phase of the war. The operational-analysis part of the equation came from counting up the number of officers available to staff these units and the amount of artillery available to support it. If these reserve corps existed, the report concluded, "there are few of them, a maximum of twelve . . . composed of heterogeneous elements, weak in artillery . . ."[50] On the basis of this report, Joffre informed his army commanders that they were not to believe their own eyes, that the Germans were not matching active and reserve corps, and that there could be no more than twenty-eight German reserve divisions scattered across the French front.[51] All of which suggests that French intelligence was not immune to drawing conclusions which reflected the views of their superiors.

Because of this miscalculation, Joffre directed ten divisions of his Fifth Army and four divisions of the BEF into the maw of thirty-four German divisions massed before his left flank.

These opening battles were extremely costly for the French, both in casualties and in ground surrendered. Certainly, intelligence cannot be given all the blame for Joffre's miscalculations. But neither are they excused from responsibility. The sad fact was that in 1914 the French army, like those of the other powers, had little experience or training in intelligence functions, either strategic or tactical. Many of these opening battles are described as "encounter battles," a euphemism for armies blinded by lack of intelligence lurching into head-on collisions. For instance, the French Third and Fourth armies attacked into Lorraine practically without any tactical reconnaissance of the German positions, and their soldiers fell in heaps.[52] Likewise, French cavalry failed to discover the magnitude or locations of the German armies enveloping the French left wing in August.[53]

Of course, intelligence was shamefully neglected by all the armies in these early battles, not the least in Alexander von Kluck's army, which remained ignorant of the whereabouts of the British and French to its front. But intelligence should especially find more favor among the weak, because it is for them that it is a greater force multiplier. With a superior concentration of forces at the decisive point, Kluck had less cause for concern than did his opponents.

However, if French intelligence must bear a portion of blame for the August reverses, so too must they be accorded partial credit for the September revival of French fortunes on the Marne. There are several reasons for this.

The first is that Joffre, with his Plan XVII and his illusions that the Germans would not use their reserves in the front lines in tatters, at last sobered to the realization that his intelligence must be allowed, indeed required, to sketch a credible picture of the enemy. The second point is that the Deuxième Bureau, which had sputtered for nearly a month, at last summoned up the capacity to do just that. This was largely because three important elements of intelligence gathering— the airplane, radio intercepts, and cryptography—at last began to function smoothly nearly a month into the conflict.

The French did not initially wring all of the advantage which they might have from air reconnaissance. The main problem was that, although the French had considerable air resources, pilots were trained to fly, not to scout, and so had difficulty deciphering what they saw as they overflew the apparent confusion which reigns in the rear area of any army.[54] Still, no French pilot recorded an error as egregious as that of the German aviator who reported British troops running about in utter panic and disorder, only to have it pointed out to him that he had just delivered an accurate description of a football (soccer) match.[55]

But such stories made it easy for army staffs to dismiss airmen as "undisciplined acrobats not worth wasting time on."[56] Even Joffre rationalized pilot reports of strong German troop movements into Belgium on 18 August by deciding either that they were inaccurate or that, if true, they could have only been accomplished at the expense of a weakened German center. Therefore, he should attack in Lorraine.[57] The result was that some excellent intelligence was squandered in the early days of the war.

This began to change as the French introduced staff officers into rear seats of aircraft, so that assessments of enemy movements reached the high command which were less easily dismissed. Among these reports which arrived from 31 August were those which indicated that Kluck's army had shifted its direction of march toward the southeast, which meant that it would swing north of Paris, dangerously exposing its right flank. While they made a believer out of Gallieni, recalled from retirement and appointed Military Governor of the French capital, the same could not be said of the Deuxième Bureau of the Sixth Army, which had in its possession an earlier version of Kluck's order captured on 27 August. However, air reconnaissance on 2 and 3 September confirmed that Kluck's army had swung north of Paris, exposing his right flank. Not without some difficulty, Gallieni overcame the skepticism of the Sixth Army intelligence chief to convince Joffre to issue the critical orders from 4 September which allowed the French to prevail on the Marne and turn back the German thrust.[58]

In August 1914, the French also had reason to wish that they had invested more heavily in electronic intelligence, as the small number of listening stations and cryptographers were utterly swamped by the volume of enemy radio traffic. What became clear as French cryptanalysts struggled to decipher these messages was that by studying the volume and pattern of traffic, as well as recording the call signs, they could build up a picture of the German forces. This early version of traffic analysis was rather primitive, as attempts to adopt radio direction finders had foundered on the opposition in 1913 of the Directeur de Télégraphie Militaire, who was upset that Major Cartier preferred a Marconi set to his own invention.

In the absence of such equipment, the French had to guess at the location of the German stations by the strength of their signals, separate out the fast-moving cavalry radios from the more plodding infantry and headquarters ones, and distinguish keys and call signs which indicated different combat groups.

But it was in their naive use of call signs that the Germans presented the French with a potential intelligence bonanza. All radio stations of a German army were given call signs that began with the same letter. Divisional stations of each corps had call signs beginning with "S" if they operated in Belgium, "G" in Luxembourg, "L" on the Woevre Plain, and "D" in Lorraine. From his office in the War Ministry, Cartier detected strong elements of German cavalry invading Belgium. His first serious crisis came on 19 August, when he warned the French command that he had noted at least five different call signs on the Lorraine front used by German army corps, indicating that German forces there were far stronger than Joffre believed. However, a combination of incredulity, the late arrival of this information, and jammed phone lines meant that the French attacks into Lorraine went ahead, at enormous expense to the French.

Reading French intelligence reports preserved in the war archives, it is obvious that by late August radio intercepts had become a principal source of intelligence on German movements. This was largely due, in the words of one German signals officer, to "the astonishing lack of discipline in [German] radio operation . . ."[59] Radio intercepts had also become a principal source of information on Russian movements as well; Joffre learned of the crushing defeat suffered by the Russians at Tannenberg through a German intercept. But he also found out that the Germans had begun to shift troops from west to east to deal with the unexpected Russian invasion of East Prussia.[60] An intercepted message of 26 August confirmed the existence of Kluck's First Army, until then camouflaged as part of Karl von Bülow's Second Army, a sure indication of the growing strength of the German right wing.[61] But the best source of radio intelligence was the abundant number of messages in plaintext giving locations, troop designation, movements, plans, orders, and commands supplied by General Georg von der Marwitz's cavalry corps, which screened the terrain between the First and Second German armies.[62]

French listening services were disrupted on 2 September, when the government evacuated to Bordeaux. However, Cartier claimed that on 3 September he intercepted a message to Kluck sent in the clear, ordering him to swing north of Paris, a change of direction already detected by air reconnaissance.[63] Deuxième Bureau reports for 3 September declared: "One is not certain of the general direction of movement of the German First Army . . ." But by five o'clock on the evening of 4 September, it confirmed: "The German First Army, neglecting Paris and our Sixth Army, before which nothing has shown itself, continues its march toward the Marne." Radio intercepts also noted the increasing logistical difficulties and fatigue of the troops on the German right wing, who had outrun their supplies and especially their heavy artillery. The Deuxième Bureau was also able to determine how the Germans evaluated French strength because the German cavalry scouts broadcast their reports in the clear.[64] On 7 September, it reported a gap opening between the First and Second German armies, one "probably filled by important cavalry forces [probably four divisions]."

One of the great ironies of the German radio traffic in 1914 was that it helped the French far more than the unfortunate Moltke, who, despite his radio networks, was unable to keep track of his own troops from headquarters in Luxembourg. As a result, on 8 September he dispatched Lieutenant Colonel Richard Hentsch from his staff, who, on the basis of his authority as Moltke's representative, ordered a German retreat, thus forfeiting any hope of victory on the Marne. On 10 September, the Deuxième Bureau reported that Kluck had ordered his radios to withdraw, a sure sign that the retreat had begun.[65]

The German withdrawal on the Marne began a phase of the war known as the Race to the Sea. Opposing armies attempted to outflank each other, and in the process created a network of trenches which ran from Switzerland to the North Sea. Radio intercepts allowed the French to track German units as they were pulled from the Vosges or the Lorraine front on the German left wing and transferred to the Aisne. They could also follow the formation of the German Fourth Army, created out of the units which had successfully besieged Antwerp and moved down the Channel coast.[66]

In this phase, code breaking also came to play a significant role in the direction of French operations. On the outbreak of war, Cartier remained with the cryptologic section at the War Ministry, while his assistant, Major Marcel Givierge, established a six-man section at Joffre's headquarters. The sheer volume of German messages, the absence of any classification system, the fact that the small teams had to handle both naval messages and some diplomatic traffic, and, finally, the inability to read the German Ubchi codes limited the influence of the code breakers during the August–September battles.

This began to change on 1 October, when Cartier's team broke the primary Ubchi code, helped by a code book captured from a downed zeppelin. The Ubchi codes were based on a double-columnar transposition. As David Kahn explains, the high command supplied a key word or key phrase, like "Die Wacht am Rhein." This was transformed into a numerical sequence with each letter assigned a number according to its place in the alphabet. With the numerical sequence written across the top of the page, a plaintext message—"Tenth Division to attack Montigny sector at daylight"—was written horizontally into a block beneath the numerical sequence. The message was transcribed vertically by columns in order of the key numbers. Then they were transferred horizontally onto another block by key numbers. Then the result was again inscribed vertically in key order. The message was then sent out in five-letter groups. The receiver simply reversed the process to reconstruct the original message.

Breaking the codes required the French to find messages of the same length in the same keys. The two messages are written out on strips of paper and placed one beneath the other. Then, by using a multiple-anagramming technique, the cryptanalyst tries to reconstruct it on a word-by-word basis.[67] On 17 October, the Germans again changed their key, but now more experienced, Cartier's team broke it in four days. Two other key changes were quickly broken. So successful had the French become that they were able to capitalize on a German message announcing the visit of the Kaiser to the town of Thielt by sending a plane on a bombing run to enliven the festivities.

Unfortunately, this episode, leaked to a French press desperate to report any French success, alerted the Germans that their codes were being read and caused them to institute an entirely new system in mid-November. But while apparently more complex than the Ubchi, it used single-columnar transposition, with ciphertext equivalents two places away from the plaintext in the normal alphabet. Growing French expertise in code breaking combined with mistakes made by German cipher clerks allowed Lieutenant Colonel Anatole Thévenin, a member of the Commission of Military Cryptography, to crack it on 10 December.[68]

For French intelligence, August and September 1914 had presented a war of missed opportunities, a potential miracle which failed due to the absence of a saint powerful enough to achieve it. Cartier lamented that "with a radio direction-finding network, I could have located on a map the headquarters whose messages I was intercepting." This would have allowed him to perform the "miracle" of divining the intentions of the invaders.[69]

Givierge noted that French cryptanalysts, who were translating between thirty and sixty German intercepts a day by October, played an important role in the Race to the Sea by alerting French commanders to movements of troops, armaments, or supplies which could indicate German intentions, and occasionally an operations order for an attack, withdrawal, or flanking movement.[70]

But to be useful to a commander, intelligence had to be sifted, categorized, analyzed, and interpreted in time, a slow, painstaking process of building up a picture of the enemy by a critical and organized staff. One of the effects of the opening battles was to raise the prestige of intelligence, especially of code breaking, in the French command. This proved an important conquest. While it was clear that intelligence alone certainly could not win the war for the French, or anyone for that matter, the lack of a sound intelligence organization would certainly imperil any hope of victory.

The French response to the German threat defined another characteristic of the relationship between intelligence and decision-making in twentieth-century France. Intelligence reports which underscored France's relative weakness vis-à-vis its German adversary only invited demoralization and despair. This did not encourage the French high command to adopt rational strategies tailored to French means. On the contrary, the disparity of the odds against him drove Joffre to take excessive risks, to adopt offensive strategies beyond the capabilities of his armies.

This posed a dilemma for French intelligence. If they continued to supply information on the enemy which challenged Joffre's strategic assumptions, then the French commander would see intelligence, especially accurate intelligence, as a threat, and the Deuxième Bureau would be reduced to irrelevancy. Better "go with the flow," tailor intelligence to Joffre's strategic vision, and retain influence and resources by settling into a tactical and operational role. The stalemate on the Western Front allowed French intelligence to do just that.

FOUR

THE TRENCH DEADLOCK

World War I was to revolutionize French military intelligence in ways completely unforeseen. The battle of the Marne had demonstrated that air reconnaissance, the radio, and the telephone had made "real time" intelligence not only possible but even a critical factor in the outcome of a battle. But in the early battles, the use of intelligence had been very much ad hoc, largely because intelligence organization in the army had been rudimentary. While the army corps had intelligence officers designated on their organizational tables, they had been given no instruction in their craft. Plans to assemble them on the eve of the war at GHQ for a crash course were adjourned for obvious reasons, leaving them with little to fall back on except a small orange pamphlet entitled *What You Need to Know About the German Army*, and a few directives about how to organize the service, interrogate POWs, and transmit information to army level to be "exploited."[1] The increasingly technical nature and sheer diversity of intelligence sources and the need to analyze, synthesize, and interpret the staggering volume of information now available for the command meant that all armies had to invest manpower and equipment in the creation of intelligence bureaucracies which demanded ever higher levels of expertise. But the ability of intelligence to reduce the uncertainty of war proved to be limited. Commanders and staff officers little experienced with intelligence were often skeptical of its value, refused to draw up an "intelligence plan" to orientate subordinate units toward the sort of information they required, or knew how to integrate intelligence into operational plans.[2]

To be fair to them, all commanders were learning to fight a war of unprecedented dimensions and complexity. With the failure of the Schlieffen Plan and the coagulation of the Western Front into trench deadlock, the Germans turned their attention to the East to try to get a decision over the Russians in 1915. In the West, the French could not accept the occupation by the Germans of 10 percent of their territory, including some of its most productive industrial regions. Therefore, Joffre organized massive offensives in the Artois in May–June 1915 and in Champagne in September. They were bloody failures, as waves of attacking Frenchmen perished in a maelstrom of fire.

Planning attacks by hundreds of thousands of men, massing munitions and matériel on a scale hitherto unimaginable, and coordinating artillery barrages with infantry assaults required new skills which were only slowly mastered. In this context, it is hardly surprising that it took until 1916 for the French army to develop an intelligence system which worked from a single doctrine, able to integrate the various sources of intelligence into a coherent picture of the enemy.[3] But in a command committed to breakthrough, which remained convinced that trench deadlock was a product of a lack of courage in the troops, rather than one of technical and tactical shortcomings, impediments to effective integration of intelligence into French strategic and operational calculations remained. The risks were that "wishful thinking" would cause intelligence to be ignored, marginalized, or twisted to fit a commander's operational goals. Likewise, all armies, aware that they were being spied upon, resorted to dispersion of forces, camouflage, and secrecy to make information more difficult to obtain. So at a time when intelligence would become vital to achieve tactical and operational advantage, it became more difficult to pierce the screen of secrecy thrown up by the enemy and interpret the evidence in time for the commander to use it.

The French were well positioned to take advantage of the intelligence revolution which occurred in World War I. Even before the war, soldiers of several nations had realized that the extensive use of the radio for military communications offered the possibility of a remarkable harvest of information on the enemy. Messages reaped from the air were useless if one could not understand them, however. In this domain, the prewar vision of Cartier paid off in spades for the French, who had assembled a small but highly competent team of code breakers able to attack German code and cipher systems as soon as they appeared on the Western Front.

The Germans, who entered the war with no military cryptanalytic service, took almost two years to fashion one virtually from scratch.[4] The cause of Teutonic sluggishness came as no mystery to Marcel Givierge, who believed two years to be the minimum to recruit and train a good cryptanalyst. The apprentice code breaker required some remarkable personal characteristics—a "spirit of intuition" combined with a scientific approach based on hypothesis, experimentation, and observation. Order and method must rule his approach, while perseverance would steel him against the inevitable disappointments and failures. Individual genius was essential. But the most gifted cryptanalyst could not flourish in a vacuum. Givierge believed a developed cryptographic tradition to be a critical element for intelligence success. This cryptographic tradition guaranteed the continuity and the stability of an organization, even a faith in ultimate success, without which the desperate challenges of the submarine codes and especially those provided by the fiendishly complex systems introduced by the Germans in 1918 might never have been surmounted.[5]

The performance of the cryptanalysts during the Marne and the Race to the Sea had served to convince several top generals, including Joffre, of their value. Indeed, Givierge complained that Joffre's GHQ became so enthusiastic in October 1914 during the Race to the Sea, when they realized that French code breakers had cracked the German radio codes, that only with difficulty could they be dissuaded from deceiving the Germans with bogus messages.[6] This command enthusiasm for signals intelligence, once brought under control, allowed the French to build up a team of cryptanalysts who ran from very competent to quite remarkable. Of these, certainly the most talented proved to be Georges Painvin.

Like many cryptographers, Painvin came to his profession—albeit temporary—quite by accident. A brilliant graduate of the Ecole Polytechnique, the tall, dark-eyed Painvin exhibited the fragile appearance which years of study and exam taking impart to so many survivors of the French educational system. Painvin seemed destined for a successful, even brilliant, academic career when the war plucked the twenty-nine-year-old from his job as professor of paleontology at Paris' Ecole des Mines and deposited him into a staff position with the Sixth Army. There he met cryptanalyst Captain Victor Paulier, who initiated Painvin into the mysteries of his craft. For French cryptanalysis, this proved one of the happiest coincidences of the war. In a very brief time, the novice code breaker demonstrated his skill by breaking several German keys. Painvin's success earned him a transfer, initially under protest, to Cartier's Bureau du Chiffre in the War Ministry, where a dozen or so people maintained a surveillance of enemy and Allied communications, and provided methods and keys to Givierge's Service du Chiffre, whose fifteen officers solved German army codes and ciphers for GHQ. From September 1914, the Service du Chiffre had created three-man sections which included a cryptanalyst in each army and army group to enforce the security of French radio communications. These sections eventually began to break tactical codes on their own.[7] The artillery was the first arm to be given radios, and these could be used to listen to German communications, but only when they were not needed for air-ground liaison.[8]

The success of cryptanalysis, the field in which Painvin was to emerge as the star pupil, required the development of radiogoniometry and traffic analysis. The inability to locate the German radios had been one of the great French deficiencies of 1914. One advantage the French derived from being driven well back into their own territory by the early battles was that they depended mainly on telephones for communication, so that their radios could be used for listening to German radio communications rather than transmitting.[9]

In the early days of the war, radio direction finding was made possible largely through cooperation with the French navy, whose coastal listening stations helped to locate German posts. Two or more stations would locate a signal along a straight azimuth. The point at which the azimuths crossed would fix the position of the station. By 1916, when the Germans began to rely heavily on radio communications, the French investment in direction finding began to pay off. By October 1916, GHQ published lists of locations of German radios updated every ten days, associated them with units, recorded changes in volume of traffic from week to week, and changes in call signs, all in an attempt to chart movements and changes in German forces. Order of battle based on analysis of this traffic provided perhaps the single most important source of operational intelligence on the Western Front.

One of the first tips that the Germans were planning an offensive against Verdun in 1916 was the appearance of more radio stations in that sector. Likewise, in the autumn of 1918 the pullback of meteorological and antiaircraft radios not only offered an early warning that the Germans had begun a strategic retreat but also indicated to the French the probable path of the German withdrawal. Although German deception techniques improved dramatically by 1918, Givierge believed that by the war's end direction finding, a crude and inexact science in 1914, had matured into one of the French army's most valuable intelligence sources as more listening stations and mobile direction-finding units came on-line, with better equipment and a more rapid reaction time.[10]

But no single intelligence source was sufficient in itself. Direction finding had to be combined with translations of texts and knowledge of the enemy order of battle. What was required was that all services—direction finding, ciphers, listening services, and the Deuxième Bureau—function within a single organization so that intelligence gleaned from all sources could be evaluated and collated. American officers visiting the Western Front in 1917 reported that, on the division level at least, the French had succeeded very well in pulling together a coordinated intelligence structure. The chief of the Deuxième Bureau presided over a daily—or in calm periods a weekly—intelligence meeting with the intelligence officers of the artillery, the Air Corps, and radiotelegraphical units, and the corps radio officers, sometimes the chief of the Troisième Bureau, to keep their maps and dossiers on enemy order of battle, defensive organization, artillery, aviation, and mines up to date.[11]

But this organization was in the future. In the early days, Givierge complained that his listening services were sometimes sloppy, sending "absolutely defective texts" to GHQ for analysis or flaunting their indolence by forwarding only those messages which had been broadcast in clear (plaintext). Listening services were not combined with direction finding, which for some reason did not fall under the jurisdiction of the Deuxième Bureau in all armies. Only gradually did the listening services acquire enough cryptanalysts and antennae and mobile direction-finding units to function effectively. Nor was Cartier, a mother hen to his cryptanalysts, sufficiently attentive to his translation service. Personality conflicts, bureaucratic turf battles, and sheer indifference abounded. American officers noted that the chief of the Deuxième Bureau in division headquarters was "not entirely absorbed in this duty. He may be employed by the chief of staff in the other departments of staff work," a practice which they attributed to "his special acquaintance with the situation of the enemy."[12]

Givierge complained, however, that assignment to other duties occurred because intelligence was not always taken seriously. For instance, in some armies, staff officers who were given no training in the importance of codes and ciphers continued to treat cryptanalysts as *embusqués*—shirkers—assigning them extra duties which interfered with their work. This was perhaps because cryptanalysts handled the thankless task of imposing security discipline on French wireless and field telephone operators. By 1916 the system had surmounted many of its earlier difficulties. However, whatever advantages France and her army reaped from Joffre's departure as commander-in-chief in December of that year—and they were significant—were not shared by intelligence. Until the end of the war, changes of command produced a general sweep-out of headquarters staff, whose replacements had to be educated in the importance of security and ciphers. According to Givierge, many of the new men proved to be slow and reluctant learners.[13]

While the Germans made considerable progress against Russian radio codes, their success against French codes was limited. Nevertheless, Cartier complained that the lack of security discipline in the French army, not to mention leaks to the press by indiscreet staff officers, alerted the Germans to the insecurity of their radio codes. The result was that in 1915 the Germans clamped down severely on their radio broadcasts, especially in headquarters sections, which made it very difficult for French intelligence to divine their order of battle until January 1916, when the Germans again began to use radios extensively for communications largely because heavy artillery barrages during the battles of Verdun and the Somme had severed phone lines.[14]

This change did not leave French cryptanalysts unemployed, however, for together with developing codes for pigeon-carried messages, they were assigned the task of listening in to trench telephones. One did not necessarily have to tap the line directly, although this was certainly done; during one front-line visit, Givierge deplored the profusion of telephone wires running no one knew where, perhaps even to enemy listening posts.[15] More common were devices which amplified conversations on the one-way trench wires, allowing German-speaking French teams to eavesdrop on enemy telephone conversations. The listening devices were comprised of a series of insulated wires which radiated out from a switchboard placed in the front lines. Each sought to pick up the currents of a telephone line passing through the soil from a specific "search ground." When amplified, the conversations would become audible. The Germans called these listening stations "Arendt Stations" or "Polyps." They proved a valuable source of tactical intelligence—advance warning of trench raids and artillery bombardments, the location of enemy batteries—much appreciated in the armies even if GHQ found it uninteresting.[16] But this sort of front-line intelligence could prove of immense value. The Deuxième Bureau captured a German document in February 1916 which claimed that half of their knowledge of the French order of battle was gleaned from listening to French trench telephones. And no wonder—as late as August 1916, a French staff officer was disciplined for giving the name of his unit and his command post over the phone.[17] German interception of French phone conversations served to confirm predictions of French offensives in the Artois in May–June 1915 and in Champagne in September of that year.

To counter this hemorrhage of information and to supplement telephones whose wires were increasingly vulnerable to artillery fire, both sides developed ground telegraphy instruments which sent buzzer currents in Morse into the earth. Both these instruments and the regular telephones required trench codes to be secure. The French developed them from 1916 and the Germans later that year. Fully thirty German trench codes fell to French cryptanalysts in the course of the war, a tribute to the persistence of French code breakers. But this success was due in part to very sloppy security at the front. Code books were easily captured, often with encoded and deciphered messages scribbled on the jackets. At Verdun, the French captured German enciphering grilles (*cadrans mobiles*) with frequently used abbreviations and names. Unfortunately, the importance of these prizes escaped the average poilu, who too often neglected to pass them up to intelligence.[18] As with radios, those using telephone codes on both sides persisted in repeating formal phrases such as "I have the honor to inform you," "*Bonjour, mes amis*," or "Night calm, nothing to report," which provided key words from which others might be deciphered. Artillery barrages might be laid down on German lines to feign an attack, and then the German radio and telephone response monitored to record the fairly predictable phrases.

Radios continued to be used. Painvin cracked one code during the battle of Verdun in April 1916 because a Bavarian prince was imprudent enough to radio his royal parents, the king and queen of Bavaria, that he had been wounded.[19] A weather report sent out in clear could be compared with one which had been broadcast in code by another radio or phone. In some sectors of the front, the same word—a position or geographical feature—might occur repeatedly. Frequent references in German messages to Deutschland, Vaterland, and the Kaiser were perhaps great morale boosts, but they were pernicious security practices.

The greatest enemy of codes, whether radio or telephone, was to mix clear and code in the same message, an all too frequent occurrence on both sides. Even when a code could not be broken, the sector limits of divisions or armies might be determined by the frontiers at which one trench code stopped and another began, although by 1918 the Germans had developed lateral broadcasting techniques or invented phony units which camouflaged sector limits.

While French telephone discipline improved during the war, the same could not be said of French radio operators. German signals officer Wilhelm Flicke claimed that the Germans learned of French plans to attack on the Somme in 1917 through garrulous and undisciplined operators. Potentially more fatal for the French, however, was news of the French army mutinies in the spring of 1917 which followed the failure of the Nivelle offensive. News of these mutinies, he claimed, was spread across the lines by French radio operators. Flicke's explanation for the failure of the German army to attack while one-third of the French units were in mutinous disarray was that the high command assumed that the French, like the Russians, would collapse without encouragement from the German army.[20] More likely, the Germans were in no position to take advantage of this situation even had they wanted to—their own army had been badly beat up, and offensive operations in this period required lengthy preparations. German Eighth Army documents captured in the summer of 1918 revealed that the French had virtually offered up their order of battle to the Germans on a platter, not because the Germans had enjoyed much success in breaking French codes, but through poor French radio discipline—indiscretions, reports at regular hours, formal salutations, and the like.[21]

Until the war was well advanced, however, codes seem to have been little respected by local units on either side, especially in the heat of a battle like Verdun. The first problem was to strike the right balance between a code that was secure and at the same time user-friendly. Otherwise, as in the Russian army, which developed fiendishly complicated trench codes in the wake of the Russo-Japanese War, their very complexity made them virtually unusable.

"It took a long time, despite the warnings of technicians, to get the message through that the telephone was not a secure means of communications," Givierge remembered. "But after some cruel experiences, where it was obvious that the enemy had been alerted to the arrival of a relief or a raid through an intercepted phone call, one looked for a means to hide the meaning of the messages."[22]

Unfortunately, those attempts might fool no one. Units developed their own code words, which were easily deciphered, as was the case of the French officer who shouted down the line: "*Dimanche* [Sunday], *grand match basque.*" Even the slow-witted Hun could figure out that his was to be the home team in this sporting event. Such indiscretions often brought down a German gas attack, artillery bombardment, or preemptive strike. Some officers did not even display this degree of subtlety, reflecting the collective trench wisdom that Germans were too busy to eavesdrop. Givierge reported that the intelligence officer of the French Third Army phoned the Troisième Bureau to announce: " 'Pay attention, I am going to give you a report in code.' Then, inspiration probably having failed him, he shouted, 'Well, we're attacking at eleven o'clock!' "[23] As late as 22 October 1917, French radio intercepts revealed that the Germans, alerted by indiscretions on French telephones, had prepared a heavy counterbarrage to disrupt a planned French attack at Malmaison, forcing the French to advance their attack by an hour to escape devastation.[24]

Once the war had settled down to stalemate, the problem for commanders on both sides became that of devising a method to break through the crust of trenches and into open country. Any chance of doing this hinged on the achievement of operational and tactical surprise. But in the conditions of trench deadlock, surprise was a commodity in desperately short supply. Between December 1914 and the opening of the Michael offensives, the massive German attacks launched in the spring of 1918, the massing of large numbers of troops and matériel behind a sector of front selected for assault usually gave away the game. The best that one could hope for was partial surprise—that is, attack preparations could be disguised until it was too late for the enemy to organize villages into strong points, dig reserve trenches, bury their phone lines, pull many batteries out of range, and lay new railway lines to bring in reserves before the attack broke upon them. Both French and Germans achieved partial surprise in 1916 on the Somme and at Verdun when the enemy was alerted, but had to receive the attack while units were rotating and with the resources of "a quiet sector" of the front. The Germans came closest to achieving complete surprise with the Michael offensives in 1918.

To guard against surprise, or monitor whether one was achieving it, Deuxièmes Bureaux on division, corps, and army level maintained four different kinds of maps which showed enemy order of battle, artillery emplacements, defensive positions with an assessment of their strengths, and important points in rear areas like hospitals, airstrips, or supply depots.[25] During a battle, these maps were updated daily with intelligence gained from a variety of sources—escalating radio traffic, telephone taps, air reconnaissance, POW interrogations, documents or badges captured at the front. American officers noted that "a book is kept with a page for every German division on which is noted a succinct account of everything referring to the division that appears in French GQG [GHQ] bulletins with data, information and source." Much of that information was credited to a "Captain Ale-meda," head of the Service de Documentation in Paris, who was said to possess "an encyclopedic knowledge of the German regiments" built up from captured pay books, which allowed him to suggest conditions in the German army by charting the dates of call-up.[26]

In 1917, American officers found that low troop strength had caused the French to reduce the size of their tactical reconnaissance forma-tions, although this was offset by the fact that any diligent Deuxième Bureau officer could learn much by interviewing ordinary front-line troops.[27] By general agreement, French intelligence was considered to have honed POW interrogation to a fine art by 1918. This was not achieved overnight, however. French intelligence specialist Colonel Charles Paquet complained that much good information went to waste in 1914 because French interrogators were more interested in con-firming their belief in "misery and the lack of food" in Germany than in collecting intelligence which might help to win the battle. As many French interrogators were schoolteachers chosen for their linguistic skills rather than their knowledge of the military, they frequently did not know what questions to ask. Intelligence from POWs appears to have been taken seriously because it was least subject to deception, especially on order of battle.[28]

Initially, POWs were given a *tourniquet* or "turnstile" interrogation at division level, where their ranks and units were listed and phoned in to headquarters. At first, only officers were searched for documents. But the fact that officers often had orders, maps, or code books carried by soldiers, and the recognition that even things like pay books could yield valuable information, caused the French to create a *service spécial de dépouillement* in the summer of 1916. These German-speaking specialists would tie together all documents taken from a soldier, in-cluding his pay book, with his name, unit, and date of capture, and send them up to the interrogator, while keeping an eye out for papers of special interest to headquarters. One favorite technique was to ex-plain to the German that French policy was to place men from the same village or region in the same POW camp and to give them notepaper so they could write home and tell their families they were safe. They were also given forms to fill out which listed most of the basic information sought in this initial interview. Interrogated POWs were never allowed to mix with those awaiting interrogation. In theory, tracking which armies were being stripped of reserves to shore up sectors under assault gave intelligence an insight into the mind-set of the enemy command. For instance, five days into the Somme offensive of July 1916, no soldiers from the German Second Army had been captured, an indication, according to Colonel Paquet, that the Germans anticipated an attack on the Second Army front between the Somme and the Oise and refused to strip it.[29] This opened an excellent avenue to work deception on the enemy, although it appears that in this case the French made no attempt to lock those soldiers in place by false preparations, as the Allies did so successfully prior to the Normandy invasion of June 1944.

Two or three POWs from various specialties—machine gunner, telephonist, artillery spotter, electrician, etc.—were chosen and sent to the rear, in the company of a German-speaking NCO with instructions to be friendly to them, to interrogators at army level who specialized in armament, combat strength, training, liaison and air observation, artillery, and propaganda/morale/economic situation, although none remained strictly within his specialty. Specialists might also be asked to perform test demonstrations of captured equipment.

The interrogation team periodically met to determine lines of questioning or identify specific intelligence required by the command. The manner of the interrogators during the interviews, which lasted between fifteen and forty-five minutes, was always calm, never threatening. On the contrary, their technique was to sympathize with the unfortunate captive, listen to his tales of woe, gain his confidence. Then the POW might be shown a map or aerial photograph and asked to show where he was captured. American colonel Denis E. Nolan witnessed an argument that broke out between a clever interrogator and his German captive, who, when shown a French map of the German positions, insisted that the French had left out a railway line and a trench. Nor must an interrogator display exhilaration at a particular piece of intelligence which a POW let drop, treating everything in a particularly matter-of-fact manner.

Privates were more likely to talk than NCOs. Most POWs were too scared to lie, especially in the disorienting first hours of capture. "It requires pretty straight thinking to lie straight," American captain James R. Sloane was told by his French counterparts. "Most of the prisoners strove for accuracy." Recalcitrant POWs were given what American observers referred to as the "mutton treatment"—that is, a *mouton* or sheep in the form of a German-speaking Alsatian disguised as a newly captured POW was placed in the cell with the German and by sharing his troubles gradually induced him to talk. [30] Unfortunately, the art of POW interrogation appears to have vanished in the French army after the war, which led to the dreadful scandals of POW torture during the Indochina and Algeria conflicts.

Front-line intelligence was collated with intelligence gleaned the old-fashioned way—through spies. Agents proved to be a surprisingly valuable source of intelligence—surprising because traditionally human intelligence has proved notoriously vulnerable to distortion, inaccuracy, and even fraud. The problem for World War I intelligence organizations was that, while an inventory of front-line units was relatively simple to construct, the location of reserve forces which might launch or stanch an offensive was less easily determined. Even if intelligence "lost" only 20 percent of enemy forces, the results might be disastrous, especially in 1916 or 1918, when the Germans were on the offensive. Therefore "deep" intelligence was required, and agents offered an obvious way to acquire it. An early source of agent intelligence was supplied by Belgian refugees who escaped through Holland. By the spring of 1915, for example, the British ran two separate spy networks, mostly of train watchers, in Belgium and occupied northern France, the most celebrated of which became La Dame Blanche, named after the White Lady of the Hohenzollerns, whose manifestation, legend held, would signal the downfall of the dynasty.

In early 1915, French aircraft began to land agents trained in espionage behind German lines. In 1918, Ralph H. Van Deman, an American officer, visited the espionage school, created in a wing of the Invalides, "run by two rather ancient professors from the Sorbonne." Instruction consisted of learning the uniforms of the Central Powers, how to identify aircraft, and how to estimate the number of troops or amount of matériel a train might carry, "as well as the various methods utilized by them in securing information in enemy territory."[31] From very early in the war, Allied train watchers were able

to detect with fair accuracy German troop movements between the
Eastern and Western Fronts, as well as pinpoint areas of troop concentrations, although this never told Allied intelligence precisely where
they might anticipate a German blow. These networks required constant attention, as they were frequently destroyed by German counterintelligence. Such was the case in the autumn of 1915 when the
French ordered agents to blow up key railway bridges behind German
lines with explosives smuggled into Belgium in false-bottomed trunks
and diplomatic pouches. The purpose was to disrupt an expected German offensive against the British sector, but the operation only succeeded in alerting the Germans, who cracked down on Allied agents.[32]
Nolan claimed that the French services never completely recovered
from this destruction, and as a consequence never equaled in quality
those established by the British.[33]

Agents had their limitations, the most inconvenient of which was
that their reports took up to ten days to reach military intelligence in
France via the circuitous cross-Channel route or through Annemasse
or Belfort, where the French maintained a "control group" of Alsatians
on French leave from the German army. As a result, reports could be
irrelevant on arrival.

The problems of timely agent intelligence increased after 1915 when
the Germans stretched electrified fences across the Belgium-Holland
border. Though daring rubber-booted and gloved *passeurs* continued
to challenge the electrified barrier, and boxcars served to smuggle
messages across the frontier, carrier pigeons offered the best, if only a
partial, solution to the problem. Life for a pigeon on the Western
Front was no bed of roses, however, as front-line soldiers throughout
the war displayed an obstinate inability to distinguish between friendly
and enemy pigeons, and so blasted away at anything with feathers. At
least the birds proved more reliable than the balloons furnished to the
occupied population in 1917 which could be inflated by mixing pre-
supplied chemicals and, in theory, floated back over the lines. In fact,
none ever arrived, and the experiment was abandoned after one intelligence officer noted that the process of mixing the chemicals appeared to be "too complicated for the average peasant." By 1917,
parachutes floated both agents and baskets of pigeons to the people
with instructions on how to send back messages. The British discovered

that almost 40 percent of the pigeons dropped behind the lines returned with messages written by the inhabitants. Both British and French intelligence, who shared information gathered by their agents, established quite extensive networks in Switzerland. Toward the end of the war, some agents were even broadcasting by radio.[34]

The value of agent intelligence is difficult to assess with accuracy, although both contemporaries and modern writers have advanced great claims for the importance of their information.[35] Nolan reported that the head of French intelligence in GQG, Colonel de Cointet, assigned agent intelligence a low value of only 2 on a scale of 1 to 10.[36] Nolan believed the French had an agent highly placed in the German general staff who gave the French advance warning of the Chemin des Dames offensive which fell on French lines on 27 May 1918. Unfortunately, the report arrived on 29 May. The German attack on 15 July was preceded by agent warnings, which helped to confirm reports arriving from other sources. The French also appear to have maintained a large section in Paris to track the fortunes of the German economy. But there is no record of how much agent intelligence helped in this task.[37]

Another obvious source of tactical intelligence was air reconnaissance. At the beginning of the war, all the aircraft of both sides were used for reconnaissance. If the Marne confirmed the value of air reconnaissance, it also demonstrated that it must be well organized to be effective. But the command, and pilots themselves, soon began to find other missions for the planes. As the battle of the Marne was winding down, the top priority for Joffre was artillery spotting, a combination of prewar experiments and some spontaneous air-artillery cooperation against German batteries in September 1914. It took some time to put in place, however. In one celebrated incident during the Artois offensive of May 1915, the French artillery continued to shell a section of the line for three days, ignoring reports from spotter planes that it was held by their own troops. At this stage of the war especially, tactical reporting which uncovered situations unanticipated by staffs upset their prearranged timetables of attack which leapfrogged waves of infantry forward behind set barrages. And while radio communications between batteries and spotter planes or captive balloons eventually offered another source of tactical intelligence once air-ground Morse sets became more sophisticated, as well as opportunities for deception by broadcasting bogus targets, they reduced in the short run the numbers of planes available for tactical reconnaissance.

As early as 14 August 1914, a French pilot carried out a bombing raid on a dirigible hangar near Metz. On 5 October 1914, a French Voisin equipped with a machine gun succeeded in destroying a German two-seater. Gradually, air services evolved specialized functions as bombers, fighters, artillery spotters, and reconnaissance aircraft, although all pilots were expected to keep their eyes open, especially as they returned from a mission. Well into 1916, the principal French reconnaissance planes were the Caudron G 4 twin-engine plane with front turret and the Maurice Farman XI, both of which were easy to pilot and gave the observer excellent visibility. From late 1914, air reconnaissance was aided by the camera, an improvement which emerged out of disputes between airmen and staff officers over what had actually been seen, and because artillery bombardments had so churned the face of the land that conventional maps were virtually useless for operations. As the war progressed, intense antiaircraft fire and German pursuit of reconnaissance aircraft forced pilots to altitudes above 10,000 feet, where the naked eye was useless for reconnaissance purposes. And while by the end of the war air photography became quite sophisticated, with cameras able to pick out details as small as a footprint from 15,000 feet, this required the development of sensitive film and highly trained interpreters able to make sense of what the pilots brought back. By 1916, blanket photographs of sectors were the most critical part of intelligence assessments and even of tactical operations, although interpreters appear to have been in short supply. Paquet noted that during the Somme offensive of July 1916 the Deuxième Bureau of the French Sixth Army counted a mere two photo specialists and that a Service de Renseignements Aériens (SRA) had to be created to deal with the increasingly technical nature of air reconnaissance. Sections of the front were systematically filmed, and officers from the SRA, the Deuxième Bureau, and the artillery met each night to identify enemy batteries, assess the strengths of strong points, and assign calibers of weapons to deal with each.[38] Air photos also charted the effects of artillery bombardments (an Artillery Intelligence Section was created in October 1916) and eventually found their way down to the trench commands so that soldiers could get a better idea of what lay to their front. In 1918, French air reconnaissance produced 675,000 photographs of the front, compared with only 48,000 in 1914 and 1915, and had perfected a distribution system which sped the pictures to front-line units in a matter of hours.

Paquet called photo reconnaissance *"la plus précieuse"* of intelligence sources.[39] The Americans found that air reconnaissance formed the major building block of the French front-line intelligence system. "I got the impression that information on the battlefront from other sources was considered unreliable unless it could be verified by photographs," Major Kerr T. Riggs reported in early 1918, after a visit to the French First Army. "The study of photographs was considered all-important, not only for information concerning defensive works, but also for information on the enemy's intentions, as deduced from indications of routes of circulation, new camps, etc., in the rear."[40]

Although losses of pilots and observers in reconnaissance sections never equaled those of bomber and fighter pilots, this information was not acquired without risks.[41] Lingering over the front lines was not every pilot's idea of a routine day at the office, especially from 1916, when enemy fighters sent to shoot him out of the sky joined a list of predators which included artillery shells and small-arms fire, even from his own troops, who tended to lump spotter planes into the same category as carrier pigeons. In the first two years of the war before reconnaissance became a specialty on its own, pilots might be assigned ancillary missions to drop bombs or leaflets or land agents, or more risky "deep" missions to observe railway or port activity, count bivouac fires, or spot night-firing artillery batteries. Attempts to produce a reconnaissance aircraft which either was fast enough or carried enough firepower to defend itself against fighters failed. The spectacle of a spotter plane sliding earthward, a sliver of oily smoke trailing from its fuselage, remained a poignant war memory for front-line troops, who briefly suspended their own struggles for survival to watch as seconds of life ticked away for the terrified pilot. In the winter of 1917–18, "independent" combat groups of fighters were assigned the duty of protecting reconnaissance missions. But French air reconnaissance really came into its own in 1918 with the introduction of the two-seater Salmson Sal 2 A2. It was well armed, equipped with a radio, and its 260-horsepower engine made it almost as agile as a fighter.

In 1911, the French army had declared captive balloons obsolete, disbanded their balloon companies, and assigned their personnel to dirigibles. But two factors led to the reintroduction of captive balloons on the French front. The first was the disappointing performance of France's six—eventually ten—dirigibles in air observation. With a ceiling of only 2,000 feet, attempts by these swollen behemoths to fly over the front were suicidal, especially as the poilu considered every dirigible to be a zeppelin and thereby fair game. Dirigibles were assigned night reconnaissance missions, then night bombing missions, and finally, in 1917, the army's four remaining dirigibles were given to the navy for anti-U-boat patrols.

The second factor which stimulated the reintroduction of balloons was the surprise appearance in 1914 on the enemy front of the *Drachen*, called a kite balloon because its bag—shaped rather like that of a dirigible or World War II barrage balloon—was equipped with fins which filled with air to stabilize it and maintain it aloft in high winds. In October 1914, ten balloon companies were organized in the French army, which had expanded to seventy-five by the end of 1915. Most were equipped with spherical balloons until 1916, when the "Caquot" balloon, a superior version of the *Drachen* subsequently copied by the Germans, was introduced. Aerostation was employed on a large scale by the French for the first time in the Artois offensive of May 1915. In Champagne in September of that year, each army and corps headquarters was given a "command balloon" to report directly to the corps or division commander on the progress of attacks. From a point of ascension normally five kilometers behind and up to 1,500 meters above the lines, observers equipped with telephone headsets and binoculars were able to record changes in enemy dispositions, and corrected the fire of heavy-artillery batteries up to five kilometers behind enemy lines.

For the first year and a half of the war, the only discomfort a balloon observer was likely to experience was numbing cold caused by spending up to seventy-two hours in a nacelle. But this changed at Verdun in 1916 as German planes attacked the balloons while air observers directed hidden guns which worked in pairs, one to fire time-fused shells at French observation balloons aloft while the other lobbed percussion shells at their winches on the ground. At first, balloonists responded with an evasive movement called the "Cartesian diver," a rapid raising or lowering of the balloon which caused the shell to burst too low or too high. Balloons were also withdrawn up to ten kilometers behind the front and assigned fighter cover. But it soon became apparent that to hover beneath a bag of gas which a tracer bullet could ignite into an exploding fireball required a special degree of lunacy. Although parachutes were introduced in 1916, the altitude and the headsets often meant that the observers failed to hear the distress horn on the ground. Parachutes became entangled in phone lines, or the balloon plummeted too quickly to give the hapless observer time to jerk his rip cord. That said, however, the balloon corps was one of the safest units in the army—of 10,000 personnel who served in it during the war, only 128 were killed, about half of whom were observers—compared with the 30 percent death rate of pilots and observers serving in the French air force.[42]

Bad weather compromised the usefulness of balloons, as did enemy action. But balloons continued to serve as artillery spotters, especially after 1917, when they were equipped with radios, which allowed them to cooperate with passing aircraft. Balloons organized in depth, and able to shift position rapidly, proved very useful in the mobile warfare of 1918, both in artillery spotting and in keeping track of convoys and troop movements. But it was becoming clear that the increasing range of artillery fire meant that the balloon was reaching the limits of its military utility.[43]

From their perspective high over the lines, it would seem impossible for anything to escape the notice of air observation. Incredibly, however, as the French came to rely on air reconnaissance, the Germans demonstrated enormous proficiency at concealing their intentions even from men suspended only a few thousand feet above them. The German attack on Verdun which opened in February 1916 demonstrated the importance that the enemy attached to blinding French air observation. From 1916, the Germans developed fighters with a ceiling high enough to challenge spotter planes, and then massed them against dispersed French flights at critical points to sweep French air observers from the sky.

Camouflage and deception became weapons in the German arsenal. As late as 18 February 1916, only three days before the Germans launched their offensive, French spotter planes sent to confirm growing evidence of a German attack reported great activity far to the rear, but no evidence that the Germans had modified their front lines. Air photos eventually confirmed POW reports that the Germans had disguised preparations for their assault through the construction of *Stollen,* or tunnels, which secretly conveyed their troops to the jump-off point.

French spotter planes did not really return to the sky over Verdun until April 1916, after the French had reestablished air superiority by forming elite fighter squadrons from among their best pilots. But French air reconnaissance continued to suffer through the autumn of 1917 because of the superiority of German fighters and the tardiness of the French aircraft industry in developing a spotter aircraft that could both conduct observations and protect itself. The introduction of the Salmson Sal 2 A2, together with the advancement of photographic techniques and the creation of photo sections in the air wings which allowed for rapid dissemination of air photos, restored faith in the value of the "eye in the sky" as the best guarantee against surprise. Unfortunately for the French, although German intentions to launch a massive, war-winning offensive in the spring of 1918 was common gossip among front-line troops, no intelligence source, including air reconnaissance, was able to name the place and date of the Michael offensives which fractured Allied lines in Picardy on 21 March 1918.[44]

French intelligence was not limited to supplying information on the enemy. Allies, too, became the subject of investigation. Early in 1915, Givierge was given the wires of the Russian and Italian *chefs de missions* in France to decipher, which he was able to do by first locating and translating the French names. He also resorted to the old trick of giving the Russian ambassador intelligence reports on German units on the Eastern Front. When the ambassador sent them to Petrograd without alteration, the French were thereby handed the means to crack the Russian code.[45] Communications intelligence played an important counterintelligence role. German radio broadcasts at regular intervals to U-boats in the Mediterranean alerted the French to the presence of spies at Marseille and Algiers who informed Berlin of the time of departure and itinerary of French ships. A spy ring run by a "neutral" consul was unmasked, and the spies arrested.[46] The French station on the Eiffel Tower eavesdropped on Madrid's radio traffic with Vienna,

Berlin, and Spanish Morocco, a practice which revealed the most celebrated case of World War I espionage.

In December 1917, the Eiffel Tower began to intercept messages between the German military attaché in Madrid and Berlin on the subject of remuneration for agent H-21, who had arrived in Madrid from Paris.[47] These were the intercepts which became the *pièces à conviction* of Margarete Zelle MacLeod, alias Mata Hari. A Dutch national who had abandoned an unhappy marriage to an officer in the Dutch colonial army for a career as an "exotic dancer" and high-class courtesan before the war, in 1916 the middle-aged Mata Hari placed her fading charms at the service of German intelligence. Her calculation was that the spying business would prove sufficiently lucrative to allow her to retire in great comfort with her young Russian lover, who was serving on the Western Front. The Germans trained her in the rudiments of the spying trade and dispatched her to France.[48] They got little return on their money, however. Once in Paris, Mata Hari demonstrated her usual entrepreneurial spirit by contacting French counterintelligence to offer to work for them as well. She was signed up by the director of the French Section de Centralisation des Renseignements, Captain Georges Ladoux, and dispatched to report on the activities of German agents in Spain.

Playing a double-agent game is a risky business for even the most devious and intelligent character. It was one in which Mata Hari proved to be completely out of her depth. In Madrid, her greed and inexperience got the better of her caution when she approached the German military attaché, Major Albert Kalle, to demand more money.[49] Alerted by the Eiffel Tower intercepts of her requests, French counterintelligence interrogated and eventually arrested her on her return to Paris in December 1916. The fact that her client list read like a Who's Who of France's senior diplomats and politicians guaranteed that her trial in the summer of 1917 would attract prurient public interest. The judicial proceedings revealed a woman who was stupid rather than dangerous. However, in the dark days of 1917 following the French army mutinies, when American troops had yet to arrive and those of Russia were deserting in droves, Prime Minister Georges Clemenceau was determined to boost sagging public morale by a show of firm resolve. In October, Mata Hari put on her final performance, and by all accounts it was her best. The spy was awakened before dawn and taken from her prison cell to a muddy field used for cavalry maneuvers at Vincennes. Wearing a pearl-gray dress, long buttoned gloves, ankle boots, and a tricornered felt hat, a cheerful blue coat draped over her shoulders, she was marched out before the firing squad, but refused to be tied to the stake or blindfolded. Between the commands of "Aim!" and "Fire!" she blew kisses to the priest and nuns who had accompanied her, before she crumpled under a hail of bullets. A sergeant came forward and delivered the coup de grace, a single shot to the temple. After a pro forma burial during which her remains were symbolically lowered into a grave, her bullet-riddled body was donated to the University of Paris medical faculty for dissection.[50]

Mata Hari's conviction gave the impression that France was rotten with treason. In fact, German spymaster Walter Nicholai confessed that he got little useful information out of his spies in France.[51] Germany's most able spy, Baron August Schluga, a native of the Austro-Hungarian Empire and a Paris resident, did provide Berlin with some interesting information in 1914 on the disposition of French forces on the fifth day of mobilization. After that, however, he was restricted to reports of legislative and ministry gossip, most of it uninformed because Joffre refused to admit politicians into his military secrets or even into the zone des armées. Ill health forced Schluga out of the spy business in March 1916. And although the Germans subsequently praised his usefulness, like all businessmen Schluga sought to satisfy his customers by offering a salable product. His reports on French lack of resolve reinforced German stereotypes of Parisian decadence, to the point that General Erich von Falkenhayn actually bought Schluga's assessment of France's incapacity to mount an offensive in the Artois in 1915.[52] Nolan, too, believed French counterintelligence—a combined operation of the Cinquième Bureau under Captain Ladoux, a Centre de Recherches which answered to the Prefecture of Police, and the Sûreté—too efficient to allow German spies much latitude for espionage, and suggested that poor agent intelligence actually caused Ludendorff to underestimate the rate of arrival of American troops in 1918.[53] It is unlikely, however, that Ludendorff, any more than Hitler, cared a fig for intelligence estimates of American capabilities.

In fact, French counterespionage does not appear to have functioned particularly well under Ladoux. An Interior Ministry report of 8 June 1918 complained of "the inactivity of our [counterespionage] services, and especially of Captain Ladoux," who allowed German spies to flourish in France.[54] By the time this report was written, however, Ladoux was cooling his heels in jail. Arrested in October 1917, only four days after Mata Hari's execution, Ladoux had been denounced by Pierre Lenoir, a newspaper owner detained as a German agent. Acquitted by a court-martial in May 1919, Ladoux became an inspector of casinos and profited from writing highly sensationalized accounts of his contacts with spies, including Mata Hari.

—

The last two and a half years of the war offered a desperate test of wits between German forces, who worked to improve the sophistication and stealth of their attack methods, and the Deuxième Bureau, which strained to divine German intentions. The first test came at Verdun. In 1915, the French had exhausted themselves in futile thrusts in Artois and Champagne, while the Germans appeared content to hold in the West while attempting to achieve victory against Russia in the East. The costs of these French offensives in manpower and matériel had caused Joffre to strip Verdun bare of both. Alerted to the precarious state of Verdun's defenses by Lieutenant Colonel Emile Driant, whose relatively junior rank belied important political connections, an official delegation of the Army Commission paid the garrison a visit in December 1915. The subsequent report, which echoed Driant's concerns, relayed to the commander-in-chief through the War Minister, threw Joffre into a rage about Driant's insubordination. But according to a British historian of the battle, Alistair Horne, Joffre saw no reason to take action on it, in part because he had no intelligence warnings of German preparations for an attack.[55]

Even though after the war there was no shortage of those who claimed to have given advance warning of the German offensive against Verdun as early as September 1915,[56] the accuracy of these reports is open to question for the simple reason that the decision to attack had yet to be taken. About the time the French Army Commission was touring Verdun, the German commander-in-chief, General Falkenhayn, composed a memorandum to the Kaiser suggesting a strategy to "bleed to death . . . the forces of France" by attacking either Verdun or Belfort. Falkenhayn preferred Verdun, not because his intelligence told him that it had been desperately weakened, but because in his view the salient in the German lines formed by Verdun might provide an excellent springboard for a future French offensive. That the Kaiser's son, the Crown Prince, commanded the German Fifth Army opposite Verdun also heightened the chances of approval, which was given by the Kaiser around 20 December.

Although intelligence played no part in Falkenhayn's choice of Verdun as an objective, he appeared keen to disguise preparations for his attack as long as possible through elaborate security and deception which included false rumors spread by agents in neutral countries and intense military activity in other theaters, including preparations for an attack on Belfort. New army corps began to move toward Verdun from 27 December. But Operation Gericht was kept a secret from many on Falkenhayn's own staff.

In early January 1916 the Deuxième Bureau began to pick up indications that the Germans planned to carry out an offensive somewhere on the Western Front. Poor weather, the heavily wooded terrain of the Meuse foothills, the timidity of French air and tactical reconnaissance, and the absence of enough photo interpreters kept enemy intentions a mystery. The Germans also shattered an Allied intelligence ring behind the lines in the autumn of 1915. However, they failed to arrest all those involved in it, for early in the new year agents reported that a new corps, which turned out to be two new corps, had entrained at Valenciennes for a destination near the Meuse. Still, according to Colonel Charles Paquet, the Deuxième Bureau had listed Verdun as a "probable" target by early January. [57]

By the second half of January, both British and French intelligence had noted that at least four corps had been transported from Belgium to the Meuse. Movements of great quantities of artillery and shells and the construction of hospitals were reported in mid-January, while gossip among German soldiers indicated Verdun as a possible objective. On 20 January, "refugees" reported that two corps headquarters had been shifted north of Verdun. These reports caught everyone's attention, and produced visits from General Edouard de Castelnau, dispatched by Joffre to oversee the strengthening of Verdun's defenses,

French President Raymond Poincaré, and finally from Joffre himself.

Still, although increased German activity was detected near Verdun, what they actually had up their sleeve was not entirely clear. French intelligence admitted that the "alarm" was not sounded until between 6 and 9 February 1916, when deserters—usually men from Alsace-Lorraine or Poles—coming into French lines from a variety of army corps indicated a "concentration of troops" which could only have "a pronounced offensive intention." These reported the stocking of gas shells (first used at Verdun) and flamethrowers, as well as *Stollen*, whose construction was concealed from air reconnaissance by having the soldiers labor at night and carry away the earth in sacks. The Germans brought their assault troops into the front lines only at the last minute so that the French would not detect a swelling population there. And because the *Stollen* proved larger and as a consequence able to conceal more troops than French intelligence predicted, the scale of the German attack surpassed anything the French believed possible. Only on 10 February, however, did a report from "an excellent agent" specify an attack in "the region of Verdun" directed by the Crown Prince in person. A report of 11 February pinpointed Fort Douaumont, which was to become one of the most highly contested defenses of Verdun, as a primary objective. On 12 February, the day when the German artillery preparation for the attack was scheduled to start, two divisions of French reinforcements arrived at Verdun. Radio and telephone intercepts in mid-February revealed the presence of other regiments. When, on 14 February, deserters confirmed the arrival of XV Corps before Verdun with massive quantities of artillery, then *"the attack could no longer be in doubt."* Alistair Horne argues that had the German attack begun on schedule, the French would have faced "hideous disaster," although had Falkenhayn stuck to his original plan to force the French to defend Verdun rather than attempt to seize the fortress, this need not have been so. As it was, when the German guns opened up on 20 February, the Germans had achieved a partial surprise by the massing of 850 German guns against 270 French ones, and 72 elite German battalions to attack 34 French ones burrowed into hastily dug and half-completed defensive positions.[58]

In a report written on 29 February, only eight days after the beginning of the German offensive, French intelligence not surprisingly gave themselves quite high marks for predicting the attack on Verdun. On the face of it, they appear to have a strong case, as their warnings had been precise enough even to shake the complacency of Joffre, who, as in 1914, was still more intent on planning his next offensive than in worrying about the plans of the enemy. To be fair to Joffre, the German decision to attack in the West made little strategic sense, and marked a radical departure from their overall strategy of trying to achieve victory in the East. All the more reason, then, to credit French intelligence for discarding much false information mingled with the good, such as strong rumors of an offensive into Alsace. Nevertheless, Joffre's Deuxième Bureau conceded that the Germans had concealed their intentions with skill.

Until Verdun, the surest indication of a coming attack was a large increase in the number of troops on the front lines. However, the construction of *Stollen* had deceived the French, including air reconnaissance. It took intelligence quite a while to locate these sites which were constructed at night, and camouflaged from air reconnaissance during the day. They were eventually discovered after deserters and POWs indicated their presence. Headquarters had argued initially that *Stollen* were defensive works. [59]

Once more, intelligence had not spoken with a common voice, and those sections of it closest to the commander-in-chief were more likely to promote command preconceptions than challenge them. "Besides," wrote Colonel Paquet of these reports, "one must take note of the very human reflex which wishes to warn without being wrong, and to this end writes reports in which vague formulas and dubious expressions are substituted for clear conclusions." [60]

Until the final hours these camouflaged tunnels gave the French few indications about the actual location of the attack. Intelligence had been able to track the transfer of artillery regiments and matériel from the Eastern Front, "without being able to establish exactly the point where the matériel arrived." The same was true of the troops, whose appearance in the region was recorded. But as the Germans sent only a few workers and reconnaissance parties to the front lines, "one looked to dissimulate their presence for as long as possible . . . Everything was done to obtain the maximum surprise effect." [61] Still, it is hard to escape the conclusion that more aggressive French patrolling, both on land and in the air, would have given the French a clearer and more timely picture of German intentions. Paquet was especially critical of the timidity exhibited by the infantry, which "allowed the Germans to organize at leisure a jump-off point only 300 meters from our lines, without bothering to find out about the works which we were signaling daily, and which the front lines were in a position to check out."[62]

For French intelligence, there were at least two consequences of Verdun. The first and most ominous was that German techniques of concealment were improving. A second, more positive result was that the advances in radio and telephone communication, including trench-to-air radio links to regulate artillery, convinced previously skeptical army staffs of the value of code-breaking intelligence. The demand for code breakers to listen to German radio and telephone traffic in the armies quickly outran the supply.[63] Nevertheless, the increased prestige of intelligence placed them in a strong position to confront the major intelligence challenges of 1917—the German withdrawal to the Hindenburg Line, the collapse of the Eastern Front, and the evolution of German tactics. Unfortunately, the very achievements of French intelligence as Allied fortunes were sagging demonstrated that intelligence was neither a panacea nor a sufficient, at times not even a necessary, condition for success.

From October 1916, the French had made great advances in direction finding and traffic analysis. GHQ began to publish lists, updated every ten days, of German radio stations, link them to command posts, and measure the volume of traffic. By tracking command-post radios, the French were alerted when the Germans began their withdrawal to the Hindenburg Line in March 1917.[64] In fact, intelligence had reported from 23 February that the Germans had begun to evacuate French civilians, destroy houses, and poison wells as part of a plan to shorten their lines between Laon and La Fère on the Aisne.[65] But this intelligence did nothing to cause Nivelle to call off his spring 1917 offensive.

Nor did the weaknesses of France's Russian ally escape the notice of French intelligence. As early as September 1915, the Deuxième Bureau was predicting that "serious internal troubles" were bound to follow from "the notorious insufficiency of war preparation" in Russia. While the morale of the Russian army remained "admirable," war industries were corrupt and inefficient, and in the absence of a high command which never visited the front or issued clear orders, local commanders "are taking a dangerous liberty of action . . ." It was especially worried by the personal assumption of command by the Czar, whom it believed "a weak and impressionable character who can change his mind with dizzying rapidity." While the country in general stood behind the war, "the mentality in Petrograd is detestable," it warned.[66]

In 1916, General Pierre de Laguiche, French military attaché in Petrograd, bombarded Paris with reports on the inadequacies of the Russian armaments industry, the effects of the strikes, the general "lethargy" which seemed to paralyze Russia and her army from top to bottom. While he believed that popular and military morale remained strong, inefficiency was simply too deeply ingrained in the system. "These people are absolutely different from us," he wrote on 16 April 1916, at the conclusion of a particularly bleak report. "None of our conceptions, none of our principles, no dogma as absolute as it might appear applies in Russia."[67] On 29 March 1917, Laguiche predicted that Russia's continued participation in the war "will depend on po- litical events," and held out some faint hope that the Russian people might respond to war and invasion as did the French of 1792, with the enthusiasm of a *levée en masse!*[68]

A third area which French intelligence followed closely was the development of German tactics. Colonel Paquet watched German defensive tactics evolve before his very eyes on the Somme in July 1916, not as the result of any logically derived doctrine, but under the pressure of French attack. One of the effects of the partial surprise achieved by the French was that the Germans were desperately trying to shore up their trench lines when the preliminary artillery barrages broke over them. As a result, the Germans were obliged to establish their solid defensive works beyond artillery range, leaving a mesh of machine-gun nests and isolated strong points to slow up the French assault waves. The Deuxième Bureau of the Sixth Army pointed out that these individual positions were more difficult to take than a con- tinuous defense line, while they economized manpower for the enemy and saved casualties by moving the main defensive positions beyond the range of all but the most powerful French artillery.[69]

The development of offensive infiltration tactics which very nearly split the Western Front wide open in the spring and summer of 1918 was closely followed by intelligence. The classic Allied response to the trench deadlock was to lay massive and prolonged artillery barrages on enemy lines and then leapfrog waves of infantry forward according to a prearranged schedule of attack. Ludendorff and Hindenburg, prompted by some of their front-line commanders, concluded that these tactics were ponderous, inflexible, and provided little hope of breakthrough. Instead, they pioneered tactics based on surprise "hurricane" barrages followed by a single wave of troops armed with grenades and submachine guns. The task of these "storm troopers" was to overrun the front lines rapidly, bypassing strongly held defensive positions to arrive as quickly as possible in the enemy rear.

As these tactics were first tested at the battle of Riga in 1916, it was the French attaché in Petrograd who appears to have alerted the high command to these new methods.[70] An analysis of a German attack of 31 July 1917 on the Plateau de Cerny explained that rather than long artillery preparation, as was the case in Allied attacks, German artillery sought to achieve "the maximum effect of violence and . . . surprise: the assailants arrive in the position before the defenders had hardly begun to seek shelter." These *Stosstrupps*, operating in groups of ten to twenty men, "arrive with the last shell . . . [They] play the double role of leader and scout . . . are given only two minutes in each trench, and leave the job of combat to successive waves . . . its mission is to open the way; one relies on maneuver, *outflanking and bypassing* to reduce resistance points."[71]

Thus, intelligence was available to the French high command on the tactics that would be used against them in the Michael offensives of 1918. But there were limits to the usefulness of intelligence, even good intelligence, in an army which lacked the operational and tactical flexibility to take advantage of it. As the Deuxième Bureau had observed on the Somme, the obvious counter to infiltration tactics was to thin out the front lines and create defensive positions further to the rear. This would nullify the effects of the hurricane barrages and cause the storm troopers to exhaust themselves in the initial assaults before they reached the main defensive positions. General Philippe Pétain, French commander-in-chief from May 1917, did attempt to implement this more flexible defensive system in the French army. However, not all commanders adopted his approach, including the powerful Ferdinand Foch, who denounced it as timorous and passive.

When these three areas of French intelligence success are combined with the ongoing feats of French code breakers, then one might conclude that French intelligence performed extremely well in 1917. The daily intelligence bulletins do not unequivocally sustain this conclusion. These bulletins tracked the locations of German units by sector, reported logistical movements, new German armaments or tactics, classifying its source as *"très sérieuse,"* *"sérieuse,"* or *"sous réserve."* And while there is much accurate information, the signals vs. noise problem afflicted the French as it did all intelligence services.

Intelligence bulletins which offered an assortment of options were of little help in solving the great puzzle of 1918—when and where the German offensives would fall. That the Germans would strike was common gossip among even the most junior privates. The Russian collapse liberated hundreds of thousands of German soldiers for service on the Western Front. The U-boat campaign of 1917 had failed to strangle Great Britain, and instead had succeeded in precipitating the entry of the United States into the war. So the exhausted Germans had a brief opportunity to snatch victory before the arrival of the bulk of the American forces nudged that prospect beyond reach.

The sad fact for Allied intelligence was that by 1918 the Germans had succeeded brilliantly in blinding them. Allied intelligence tracked 190 German divisions in France, as well as vast quantities of matériel shifted from the East to the West. Many of these troops were concentrated in the Hirson–Mézières region. But Hirson was a long way from the front, and French intelligence, which had done a thorough study of the battle of Riga, knew that in that battle the Germans had concentrated fully 140 kilometers behind the front. Air reconnaissance detected new railway lines leading toward the British sector. But new lines also appeared in Champagne and in Alsace.[72] The Germans moved largely at night, and camouflaged their forces by day, thereby diminishing the value of air reconnaissance. The quality of their Morse operators was first-class, so that unlike in 1916, when French listeners could immediately identify the "signature" of an operator, by 1918 "we could not distinguish between two operators chosen by lot in the German army." German signals created a phantom army on the

French front, while imitating preparations for an offensive against the British in Flanders. By limiting communications to short messages, the Germans offered French direction finding as little as possible to work with to establish an order of battle. From 10 March, they began to change their call signs daily, while on the following day a new mode of encipherment went into service, a sure indication that the offensive was imminent.[73] German artillery barrages and raids probed the French and British lines, but it was impossible to tell if these were preparing the great blow or were simply feints.[74]

Deuxième Bureau bulletins proved notably unhelpful in solving the puzzle. The section of the bulletin entitled *"Intentions de l'Ennemi"* offered the usual menu based upon *"source généralement bonne,"* POW interrogations, captured documents, and so on. On 7 March, the Deuxième Bureau reported that sources in Alsace predicted that the offensive would seek to separate the British and French armies. This was certainly the correct conclusion. Unfortunately, it was buried in reports of offensives planned for Champagne, Alsace, and Verdun. This caused the commander of the French Sixth Army to insist that the attack would fall on his portion of the front.[75]

In the predawn hours of 21 March 1918, 6,000 German guns opened an artillery barrage along almost fifty miles of front between Arras and La Fère on the Somme which was held principally by the British Fifth Army and the French First Army. Storm troopers armed with light machine guns followed on the heels of the dying artillery bursts, pouncing upon dazed defenders, bypassing strong points as they slipped like mercury through the previously inviolate front lines. Within a week they had driven the Allies back almost thirty-eight miles to Amiens. French intelligence was as stunned as the rest of the Allied command: "By virtue of my job, I am the best-informed man in France, and at this moment I no longer know where the Germans are," the head of GHQ's Deuxième Bureau declared. "If we're captured in an hour, it wouldn't surprise me"—a *cri de coeur* echoed by British intelligence.[76] But intelligence was able to harvest a bumper crop of information from these Allied reverses. As German storm troopers multiplied their requests for artillery barrages, or for reinforcements to exploit gaps in the Allied defenses, so too did the probability of finding two messages with identical beginnings and endings. This surge in the volume of radio traffic provided the vital ingredient which allowed Georges Pain-vin to crack the new German code on 4 April. By working through old messages in April and May, he was able to solve many of the keys used during the March offensive. By late May, he was able to apply this knowledge of the German keys to break the previous day's codes.

Though the initial enemy offensives had been contained, extensive activity well to the German rear left the Allied command in no doubt that Ludendorff would strike again. But the Germans' skill at disguising their intentions encouraged French intelligence to hypothesize that the blow would fall in Picardy or Artois. Nevertheless, when persistent reports, "less numerous but hardly negligible," most of which were collected from POWs, suggested German activity on the Chemin des Dames west of Reims, none of it could be confirmed by other sources.

When on 26 May a POW reported that a German attack was imminent within the next forty-eight hours, the Sixth Army was placed on alert and began to withdraw some of its batteries beyond the range of German counterbattery fire. The warning came too late, especially for the Sixth Army, whose commander believed in defending from the front lines rather than in the doctrines of elastic defense in depth espoused by Pétain. Therefore, when the German barrage lashed the French positions to a depth of twelve kilometers on 27 May, his troops were submerged by storm troopers, who in three days had hammered thirty miles to Château-Thierry, barely forty-five miles from Paris.[77] By that time, General Ferdinand Foch, the Allied commander-in-chief, had managed to stanch Ludendorff's offensive. But the question of where he would next strike had become one of quiet desperation for the French.

This proved a prediction especially difficult for French intelligence to make, because the military setback on the Chemin des Dames had been compounded by a cryptographic one. In March 1918, the Germans had introduced the ADFGX system, which David Kahn calls "probably the most famous field cipher in all cryptology." These particular letters were chosen because in the Morse alphabet they shared the fewest characteristics and therefore were least likely to be confused in conditions of poor transmission. The message was cut into five-letter word groupings and sent as jumbled repetitions of ADFGX. The receiver, armed with the key phrase, was able to reconstruct his messages on his grid.

The advantage of the ADFGX system for the Germans was that, although the messages now became twice as long, they used only five letters, which made them easier to send. The disadvantage for the French was that it doubled the combinations of letters. The Allies never developed a general solution for the ADFGX. The best they could do was to find two identical, usually brief, messages, which was more likely to happen during days of heavy traffic. The cryptanalyst then checked the time and location of the sender, from which he made certain assumptions about their meaning. If he assigned a meaning to the message, then, working backward, he might be able to construct the key word or phrase. With the key word or phrase in place, then the sequence of letters on the grid might be deduced, which allowed him to read other messages.[78] (See Appendix.)

Through these methods, Painvin had broken the German keys used on 28 and 30 May in quick order. On 1 June, however, it was discovered that the Germans had added a sixth letter to their code groupings, so that they became the ADFGVX system. Within twenty-four hours, Painvin had discovered the solution to this new complication. The problem now became that of finding a message which might give an indication, however minute, of the path of Ludendorff's next lunge. This was not obvious.

In his memoirs, Ludendorff insisted that the Chemin des Dames offensive had been carried out merely to divert French reserves away from Flanders and his real objective—the Channel ports. But the very success of his thrust created a dilemma. His troops had hollowed out an abscess thirty miles deep and thirty-five miles wide in the French lines, enormous by Western Front standards. His efforts after 30 May to widen a salient which was too narrow for its depth had failed. So he had three choices: either surrender much of his hard-won ground and pursue his original plans in Flanders; explode out from the base of his pocket, damn the danger to his flanks; or, finally, widen the salient with a blow so powerful that the French would be unable to resist.

The answer to this puzzle was provided on 3 June. At around nine o'clock in the evening, the listening post at Mont-Valérien intercepted a message which direction finders confirmed had been sent by German headquarters to the staff of the German Eighteenth Corps. The translated message, subsequently celebrated by French intelligence as the "Radiogramme de la Victoire," read: "Rush munitions Stop Even by day if not seen." The munitions, destined to nourish the usual German hurricane barrage, were ordered to Remaugies, which suggested strongly that Ludendorff would try to salvage his salient by attacking southward on a line between Montdidier and Noyon toward Compiègne. Once this "hypothesis" was established, air reconnaissance and POW interrogations came to reinforce it, so that by 8 June there could be no doubt.[79] The onslaught on 9 June by fifteen German divisions advanced only six miles before a spirited counterattack led by five French divisions under General Charles Mangin began to reverse them into stubborn withdrawal.

While this was hardly the final German offensive, it did prove to be Ludendorff's last chance to achieve decisive strategic results. There are many reasons for this. The Germans were running out of steam, while the French had learned a hard lesson on the Chemin des Dames and now organized their defenses in depth. But also, the security which had concealed Ludendorff's early blows was a thing of the past. Ludendorff's offensive, Operation Friedensturm, launched on 15 July toward Reims and Epernay, had been detected by the French, in part because it was logical for Ludendorff to attack east out of his salient. Trench works were also more difficult to conceal in the chalk soil of Champagne. But attack preparations had also been betrayed by bivouac fires, the construction of hospitals and airfields, poorly camouflaged munitions depots, road traffic, and garrulous POWs. German intelligence also found it increasingly difficult to maintain signals deception. Allied intelligence had learned that when German radios fell silent after a flurry of changing call signs and codes, an assault was imminent. The French were able to establish the presence of twenty-three German divisions in the Reims sector, and by calculating the length of front each could cover, the amount of artillery, and size of the munitions depots backing them up, were able to estimate with great accuracy the strength and the location, even the precise time, of the offensive.[80] In fact, French intelligence had expected the attack from 8 July. When a trench raid on the night of 14–15 July netted twenty-seven German POWs who told of the attack slated for dawn, the French opened a fierce artillery barrage on the German lines.[81] Foch's counterattacks near Villers-Cotterets on 18 July were guided by intercepts which located German units.[82] The Michael offensives eventually sputtered to a standstill before Amiens on 8 August 1918, the date which Ludendorff subsequently designated as the "Black Day of the German Army."

The French intelligence community had justifiable cause to look back on their performance in World War I with great pride. They had managed to adapt to, and even pioneer, intelligence devices and techniques of immense sophistication in a period which had witnessed the greatest intelligence explosion in history. Its code breakers proved second to none, including the redoubtable team built up by the British in Room 40 in the Admiralty. Furthermore, the French realized the interdependence of all sources of intelligence: a piece of intelligence is worthless outside its context. The Deuxième Bureau had groped to unify air reconnaissance, cryptanalysis, radiogoniometry (direction finding), POW interrogations, captured documents and equipment, postal control, and traffic analysis into a single intelligence picture with a remarkable degree of success. Nolan, who witnessed the performance of GHQ's Deuxième Bureau during the battle of Malmaison in 1917, declared it "nearly perfect."[83] Furthermore, the vast manpower and energy committed to collection had established intelligence as an indispensable element in warfare, one which provided critical tactical and operational information which commanders ignored at their own risk.

On the other hand, French intelligence had also exhibited its limitations during World War I. In one sense, it is unfair to single out specific failures of French intelligence, for intelligence effectiveness depends to an enormous degree on the system it serves. Thus, while one may cite the failure of French intelligence to divine the scope of the German thrust through Belgium in 1914, it is equally true that Joffre would only take notice of good intelligence once his own Plan XVII had collapsed in a heap. Nothing intelligence could do, even had it been so inclined, could have dissuaded Allied commanders determined to "nibble away" at the Germans from undertaking their offensives in 1915–17. If French deputies like Abel Ferry were making the argument as early as 1915 that Joffre's strategy of attrition was actually working against the Allies, they certainly did not base their views on French intelligence studies, because the Deuxième Bureau was not providing this sort of long-range strategic assessment. Nor is it likely that any military intelligence would rush to criticize the strategy, plans, and beliefs which unite its own forces.

Nor did French intelligence possess the power to make these offensives much less murderous or futile. The French operational and tactical systems were too inflexible to take advantage of knowledge of developments in German attack methods. The French command proved unable to develop techniques of camouflage and deception which equaled those applied by German forces, including their intelligence services, in the spring and summer of 1918.[84] This was because the surprise achieved by Ludendorff during his Michael offensives of 1918 depended on the cooperation of *all* of his forces in a coherent conspiracy of deception. French intelligence, even had it proved capable of developing a similar scheme, was condemned to admire the excellence of Teutonic organization from a distance. The French military system simply could not have duplicated the techniques of operational and tactical shock or logistical and communications concealment mastered by its enemy. And while the revelation by French cryptanalysts of the German offensive on the Chemin des Dames in June 1918 was a considerable technical achievement, its importance must not be overstated. No army, including that of Germany, retained the offensive capacity to smash through to a decisive victory in 1918 so long as the enemy's will to resist remained intact. The "Radiogramme de la Victoire" certainly saved French lives, as timely intelligence warnings did for all armies in World War I, and helped to slow considerably the momentum of the Michael offensives. Deception also helped to mask the French order of battle, although it is unclear how adept French signals became at this skill.[85] Intelligence gave the French useful advantages in halting the Michael offensives of 1918. But it did not supply the critical difference between victory and defeat for the Allies.

In retrospect, World War I was something of a golden era for French intelligence, especially military intelligence. It never again achieved such influence. This was in part because, as David Kahn has noted,

World War I marked, not a beginning, but the end of an era, one in which a lone cryptanalyst like Georges Painvin, no matter how brilliant, could single-handedly smash a code. Hardly had the ink dried on the Versailles Treaty than the age of the mechanical encoder was launched.[86] The challenge for French intelligence was to maintain its prestige, integrity, and technical competence in the postwar years.

FIVE

TRACKING THE
RED MENACE

World War I had converted the secret services from a marginal organization into a solid bureaucratic presence. The postwar era would help to politicize those services in at least two ways. First, as guardians of French security, intelligence officers became increasingly distressed by what they perceived as the *laisser-aller* atmosphere of the interwar years—the decline of patriotism, a diminished sense of duty, the decay of values which had sustained the generation of 1914. This impression was reinforced as sections of the population openly adopted ideologies espoused by foreign powers. With the rise of communism and fascism, foreign issues spilled over into domestic politics. The frontier which normally divided intelligence and police surveillance, even repression, increasingly disappeared as the intelligence services adopted a domestic political role.

Second, frustration with government decisions and policies which appeared to fly in the face of intelligence warnings grew as World War II approached. The intelligence community, they believed, had been marginalized by the attitudes of Frenchmen and the policies of the government at a moment when their skills and vigilance were most required.

With the war's end, the German threat dwindled to the point of insignificance. The 11 November 1918 armistice followed by the Versailles agreement scuttled the Kriegsmarine, outlawed the German air force, and shriveled the Kaiser's once redoubtable army into a bite-sized 100,000-man Reichswehr.

But from a secret service viewpoint, the Second Reich, like the Cold War in our own era, had its uses. Germany offered a clear enemy, delineated the frontiers of treason in an uncompromising fashion, and focused French intelligence assets. The question of political loyalty in postwar Europe became more nebulous, less defined. The rise of communist and fascist ideologies offered allegiances which competed with more traditional notions of patriotism. Political instability, apparent diplomatic inconsistency, and economic muddle did little to improve the stature of the Third Republic in its declining years, and offered a formless focus of fealty to the vast majority of the French population, which continued nonetheless to equate loyalty to the Republic with loyalty to France.

In these conditions, it was no surprise that people of both left and right believed France's collapse before the German blitzkrieg in 1940 to have been induced by the regime's "decadence." Therefore, the phenomenon witnessed by Wilhelm Stieber at the end of Louis Napoleon's Second Empire once again reared its head in the politically riven world of interwar France, an atmosphere in which "the impression of betrayal was weak," where those won to totalitarian ideology could convince themselves that "they were acting to liberate their country from the yoke of an execrable prince."[1]

As was the case in Britain, hardly had France won her slim respite from German hostility than a new threat emerged for her secret services—that of communist subversion. In fact, the complications of the Russian Revolution manifested themselves on French soil even before the war's end. As early as 1916, reports began to filter into French intelligence of the "ambiguous attitude of certain Russian representatives in Paris." By the autumn of 1917, several of those representatives had been placed under surveillance. But suspicion focused on Colonel Paul Ignatieff, head of Russian intelligence in France.

The most precise warnings against Ignatieff appear to have reached French intelligence through Colonel Brancaccio of the Italian military mission in France. Brancaccio reported on 27 November 1917 that

Ignatieff and Baron Pietro Wrangel, the Russian naval attaché in Rome, were under suspicion of spying for Germany. His accusations appear to have been based primarily on the revelations of a Polish lieutenant dispatched by Petrograd to Paris in early 1917 to coordinate Russian intelligence on enemy troop movements in the East with information provided by networks run by Ignatieff in Turkey, Switzerland, and Germany. According to the accuser, these networks acquired accurate information on troop movements and on political and strategic viewpoints among the Central Powers. But Ignatieff compromised potentially excellent intelligence by deception and delay.

Ignatieff's claims to have penetrated German counterintelligence in several countries "was more or less German bluff which worked more or less to Ignatieff's advantage." "The [Russian intelligence] bureau was always informed very well and in a timely manner on preparations for enemy offensives [as of the dispatch against Italy of the Fourteenth Army]," the report read. But Ignatieff neutered potentially excellent intelligence by ensuring that it was transmitted too late to be of use. "And if the Entente did not profit sufficiently from this intelligence, it is because it did not always reach the Allies on time, so that the Boches would not be unduly disadvantaged." Ignatieff was also well informed on the "defeatist attitudes" of Lenin and Trotsky, but neglected to inform Kerensky of the danger.

While an investigation revealed the Polish officer to be "corrupt, in debt, and surrounded by doubtful relationships to the point that one can doubt his honor and loyalty," French misgivings persisted and Jules Pam, the Minister of the Interior, ordered a special inquiry. The report, completed on 8 June 1918 and preserved in the French National Archives, was based in part on decrypts of intercepted messages between Ignatieff and Petrograd. While it turned up no hard evidence of Ignatieff's treachery, clearly he kept very bad company. Ignatieff's mother was found to be one of Rasputin's protectors and an active member of the "most ambitiously unhealthy milieux of the Russian court," which was, of course, the pro-German one. General Alexander Ignatieff, who frequently visited Paris to organize the transfer of French war matériel to Russia, had arranged in 1916 for his brother to take over Russian military intelligence in Paris after Paul had been "chased from the *corps de la garde*" for gambling debts and debauchery considered excessive even by the extravagant standards of Czarist Russia.

Ignatieff was basically an opportunist, "without loyalty, looking only to satisfy his need for money by the least recommendable means that wartime Paris has to offer." "All his private relations . . . are suspect," beginning with his mistress, the divorced wife of a German. He traveled frequently to Switzerland, where, both French and Italian intelligence suspected, he regularly passed on documents to German agents. In a book written after the war, Ignatieff admitted his visits to Switzerland, but insisted that it was only to contact spies favorable to the Allies. Both of the·Ignatieff brothers had accommodated themselves well to the fall of the monarchy. The provisional government of Kerensky had sent a Captain Guerbel to investigate Paul Ignatieff, but the government was toppled by the Bolsheviks, who stripped Guerbel of authority. Ignatieff had shifted his loyalties to the cause of the "maximalists" (Bolsheviks) in Russia, and had actively connived to allow revolutionary agents to propagandize among Russian troops in France, an activity which had resulted in the mutinies of those troops in Champagne. [2]

Even before the end of the civil war in Russia, the Soviet government launched an ambitious program of espionage and subversion beyond its borders. France became a prime target for at least two reasons. The first was that in the 1920s Paris was to become the capital of the two-million-strong Czarist diaspora. Paris served as the headquarters of a leading anti-Bolshevik organization, the Russian Combined Services Union (ROVS) under General Aleksandr Kutepov. The young Soviet government, composed of people who had spent most of their lives as hunted conspirators, early on demonstrated a precocious capacity for fabricating conspiracies of "enemies of the people" and for devising ways to thwart them. The fact that these duels were played out on French soil and quickly required the active participation of members of the French Communist Party (PCF) meant that they could not be ignored by French intelligence.

Soviet intelligence, the OGPU, founded a fictitious Monarchist Association of Central Russia, better known as the Trust, staffed by ex-Czarist officers who had sided with the new government. This provided a reassuring link, a point of first contact with the exile community, some of whom could be persuaded to collaborate with Soviet intelligence either because they were disillusioned or demoralized by exile or because they feared for the safety of family left behind in Russia. Through the Trust, Soviet intelligence was able not only to penetrate Kutepov's ROVS at the highest level but also to deceive the secret services of several countries, including France, into providing subsidies and facilitating communications of OGPU agents. And although Kutepov proved to be more than ordinarily inept at organizing internal dissension in the Soviet Union, it is a measure of Stalin's paranoia that he was prepared to run the diplomatic risks of ordering the OGPU to kidnap Kutepov in broad daylight on a Paris street in January 1930, drive him to the Channel coast, and bundle him aboard a Soviet steamer. Unfortunately for the OGPU, Kutepov had been so heavily drugged and mistreated that he died before his ship could reach the Soviet Union for the interrogation which, the OGPU believed, would reveal the true extent of the White conspiracy in Russia.

Kutepov's abduction might actually have improved the efficiency of the ROVS, except that this émigré group displayed a genius for selecting disastrous leadership. Kutepov's successor, General Yevgeni Karlovich Miller, promptly lost the organization's funds to a confidence trickster, and was forced to rent more modest—and thoroughly bugged—premises from an agent of the NKVD (which had absorbed the OGPU in 1934) posing as a businessman.

Miller's ineffectiveness did not save him from being abducted, like his predecessor, in broad daylight off a Paris street in September 1937. Unlike his predecessor, however, Miller survived the voyage home to meet a fate of brutal interrogation and execution. Soon after Miller's disappearance, the ROVS headquarters transferred to Brussels and what remained of their meager efficiency collapsed. But so great was Moscow's suspicion that, when the reports of the NKVD agent who continued to monitor the ROVS headquarters failed to reveal any new plots, the agent was thought to have defected to the Whites. Well into the 1930s, Stalin, whose belief in conspiracies against him had become pathological, continued to blame the failures of his economic policies on the "sabotage" of White Guards in league with a French-led international consortium of plotters working for the overthrow of the Soviet regime and its replacement by a White Russian provisional government.[3]

A second reason why France became a focus of Soviet espionage, like the first, was tightly bound up with the acute insecurity of the Soviet regime. The Kremlin's early hope of exporting the Revolution soon gave way to the task of building "socialism in one country," an experiment which, in Moscow's increasingly twisted view, was under perpetual threat by capitalist encirclement. With Germany defeated, the Austro-Hungarian Empire dissolved into a mosaic of modest states, Britain and the United States withdrawn into isolationism, and the Soviet Union essentially a pariah state, France inherited almost by default leadership of the international conspiracy against the "workers' and peasants' state." France played host to a large population of White émigrés. She supported Poland and Rumania, governments hostile to the Soviet regime, and opposed Soviet-German rapprochement. The Soviet government also believed that the secrets of the French military and of French arms factories held the key to the desperately desired modernization of its own armed forces.

The fact that much Soviet secret service energy in France was expended in spying on White émigrés was probably a good thing, for at least those resources were not directly targeted against French interests. But the activities of nostalgic supporters of the Romanovs did not absorb the complete attentions of Soviet espionage in France.

Efforts to satisfy Moscow's intelligence curiosity were aided by the creation of the French Communist Party, which split from the Socialist SFIO at the Tours Congress of 1920, taking with it the SFIO newspaper L'Humanité. American author David Dallin believed that the early leadership of the PCF, which refused to submit blindly to the orders of the Comintern, and the reluctance of Trotsky, the Comintern's chief for the first five years, to involve local communist parties in Soviet espionage meant that OGPU activity in France was free of PCF participation in the early 1920s.[4] The archives of French military intelligence tell a different story, however.

As early as December 1921, the Deuxième Bureau began to receive reports from Switzerland that Soviet agents had targeted French arms factories for spy networks. Investigations led to Joseph Tommasi, an official in the "Car-aviation Union," who skipped to Moscow one step ahead of the Sûreté in 1923.[5] Espionage and subversion continued to be linked in the armed forces, where intelligence reports indicated cells in several French regiments whose purpose appeared to be to organize protests in 1923 when the French government occupied the

Ruhr in retaliation for Germany's defaulting on her war reparations. "In general, soldiers belonging to the special arms seem most influenced by this propaganda," the Deuxième Bureau lamented on 7 January 1922. *L'Humanité* began a column entitled "Tribune du Soldat," which contained all intelligence sent to it on the subject, "either by soldiers or by their families. The unit commanders have been stripped of practical means to mount effective surveillance," especially as demobilization had removed many veteran NCOs. Throughout the summer of 1922 and into early 1923, military intelligence reported that the communists had stepped up their propaganda campaign among French troops, including those stationed in Germany.[6] A raid on French Communist Party offices in 1923 netted a cache of military documents, presumably purloined by "comrades" in uniform.[7]

The journalist Robert Pelletier was stripped of his editorship at *L'Humanité* when the PCF central committee learned that he had collaborated with Colonel Octave Dumoulin, editor of the left-wing *Armée et démocratie*, to turn over military information to Soviet intelligence. But this sort of righteous indignation on the part of the PCF leadership became a thing of the past once the consolidation of Stalin's power in 1926 promoted the plot of capitalist encirclement into the Imperium of Kremlin ideology. Communist parties abroad were thoroughly Stalinized, and nowhere was the process more successful than in France. Stalin wanted military intelligence. But his neophyte espionage service could only draw upon a motley crew of prewar left-wing refugees who had failed to return to Russia after 1917, few of whom occupied interesting positions in France.

The PCF, its activists, sympathizers, journalists, and trade unionists offered a large pool of potential agents. And even if eventual exposure of PCF-directed espionage activities were to compromise both the party's credibility and the fruits of Soviet diplomacy, so be it! The new PCF leadership, handpicked by Stalin, accepted without a murmur of reservation the notion that the survival of the Soviet Union must become the priority of every communist. This meant total submission to the will of Moscow, to include espionage against one's own country. Jean Cremet, a member of the PCF's central committee, was responsible for coordinating spy activities with OGPU agents operating out of the newly established Soviet embassy.

As Robert Dallin has concluded, "it will probably never be possible to unravel the mesh of contacts, moves, and countermoves involved in the creation of the first Soviet intelligence agencies in France."[8] Much of its success, however, must go to Cremet.

Born in 1892 near Nantes in western France of working-class parents, Cremet began his trade union militancy while still in his teens. He was mobilized in 1914, but his war record remains somewhat mysterious. He returned to trade union militancy in 1917, possibly because a war wound had caused him to be discharged from the army. After the Tours Congress of 1920 split the Socialist Party he sided with the communists and rapidly scaled the party hierarchy. Cremet returned from a trip to Russia in 1925 to become active in the PCF's propaganda campaign against the Rif War, which erupted in the French zone of Morocco in that year, a militancy which earned for him a judicial condemnation for "inciting soldiers to disobedience and plotting against the security of the state." With these *titres de noblesse*, Stalin selected him for the PCF central committee the following year.[9]

Cremet did not create Soviet espionage in French defense establishments, which, as has been seen, had been initiated in 1921 or early 1922.[10] He simply made it more efficient by utilizing his trade union contacts to gather information on French war industries, arsenals, and ports. In this, he was aided by an espionage general staff which included his companion Louise Clarac, Lydia Stahl, a Russian émigré recruited by the Soviets, and three male trade unionists.

On 29 September 1927, the French War Minister received a report which stated that several important French generals were "calling energetically" for the exclusion of communist workers from state arms industries, especially the artillery and aeronautical establishments in the Paris region. The director of the Sûreté Générale reported that workers had been condemned for spying or were under surveillance in the artillery park and the Centre d'Etudes des chars de combat (Tank Study Center), both at Versailles, at the Section Technique d'Artillerie, at the Puteaux arms works, and at the Commission des Poudres de Guerre" (War Powder Commission). The Deuxième Bureau believed the aviation establishments particularly vulnerable, both because the Soviets were especially interested in intelligence on developments in French aviation and because "aviation has a worker who is in general young, without traditions, and among whom extremist elements have a greater influence than in the artillery establishments."[11]

Cremet's main contact with the Soviet embassy was through "Abraham Bernstein," an experienced agent whose real name was Uzdanski-Yelenski and whose wife was a member of the embassy staff. Bernstein both distributed "questionnaires" indicating what specific intelligence was sought by Moscow and received reports provided by Cremet's network. The trouble with Cremet's methods was that they were bound to attract the attention of French counterintelligence, which in the 1920s consisted of about a hundred inspectors who operated out of the Sûreté on Paris' rue des Saussaies and of the Service de Renseignements (SR). This was especially the case as not all French workers who received questionnaires were as convinced as the PCF hierarchy that "protecting the Red Army" or the "defense of workers" required them to flirt with treason. Alerted from several sources, a team led by Louis Ducloux from the Sûreté, which had smashed the spy network of Joseph Tommasi in 1922–23, and Captain Eugène Josset, head of the Russian desk at the SR, fed the communist apparatus false reports until finally, on 9 April 1927, police arrested Bernstein after he had accepted classified reports passed on by communist militants.

The subsequent revelation of a network of almost one hundred spies commanded by the PCF and the Soviet embassy stunned French public opinion; rather than deny the accusations, the PCF brazenly argued that its "questionnaires" were a legitimate form of "defense of class interests" in the face of "war preparations" by "French capitalism," whose goal was the encirclement of the U.S.S.R. Eight people were convicted of espionage in the subsequent trial, including Bernstein and another Soviet agent.

Cremet and Louise Clarac fled to Russia to avoid a five-year jail sentence. In Moscow, Cremet, the exemplary Stalinist in France, apparently displayed insufficient enthusiasm in joining the Stalinist persecution of Trotskyists in the Soviet Union, perhaps because there were none left to persecute. Out of favor, Cremet was gradually stripped of his posts. He continued to work for the French section of Soviet military intelligence until the mid-1930s, when he disappeared on a mission to China.

The most popular of many theories held that Cremet drowned when thrown from a ship off the coast of Macao. French authors Roger Faligot and Rémi Kauffer believe that, aided by French novelist André Malraux, Cremet returned to France, where, under a false identity, he remained active in left-wing and Resistance activities until his death in 1973.

Expelled from the Soviet Union, Louise Clarac returned to France, where she lived for several years in hiding, dying in 1947. Lydia Stahl escaped to the United States, but returned to Paris to avoid charges of passing counterfeit money. In the French capital, she ran a combination literary salon and brothel where Soviet intelligence made contacts with Paris' community of left-wing sympathizers who occupied important research or administrative positions. An arrest of one of her friends in Finland on espionage charges provided the tip which led the Sûreté to Lydia, who in 1934 was given a ten-year prison sentence. In 1940, she was liberated by the Germans, with whom she also appears to have been in contact before her arrest. She subsequently operated in Central Europe for the benefit of the Abwehr, until Hitler's defeat, when she fled with other Nazi refugees to South America.[12]

Imperial subjects residing in France supplied another source of security concern in the decade following the war. World War I had brought an influx of men from the colonies, both to fight at the front and to free French industrial workers for uniformed service. While most of the illiterate workers were repatriated at the war's end, a significant number remained. North and West Africans were left alone by the security services because they were simply too numerous to supervise effectively and because they were little influenced by Marxist ideas. The Indochinese were another matter, however, especially skilled trade unionists and interpreters who remained in France to study and who were joined after the war by students on university scholarships. Influenced by French communists, some of these Indochinese immigrants were, the government complained, regularly implicated in "anti-French activity."

Soon after the war, a Service de Renseignement Politique was created to replace the disbanded wartime Contrôle Général des Troupes Indochinoises and keep watch on these Indochinese. In 1923, this became the Service de Contrôle et d'Assistance des Indigènes en France des Colonies (CAI), attached to the Colonial Ministry, but not appearing on the ministry list. The role of the CAI ostensibly was to provide support groups and aid societies for disoriented Asians in France, so that, according to a 1925 report, they would be kept away from "bad influences" and realize that the Colonial Ministry was "their best friend." But the real goal of the CAI was surveillance. Agents infiltrated into the immigrant communities, reported on Trotskyist, communist, and antifascist activity there, and built up dossiers, especially on the 607 students and 480 navigators residing in France in 1926 and thought to be most vulnerable to communist propaganda. Judging by the number of reports, CAI agents obviously spent a great deal of time attending political meetings and tailing individual Indochinese. But in their own view the interception of mail between immigrants and Indochina paid the greatest intelligence dividends. In December 1920, a Monsieur Josselme, who was in charge of the postal censorship, reported that "each mailbag coming from Indochina brings precious intelligence."

The value of the CAI in maintaining the loyalty of the colonies remains an open question. Certainly, countless hours of police time were invested in surveillance of revolutionary suspects like Ho Chi Minh, who were followed from a café, to the theater, to a restaurant, and then back to their flats, night after night. Reading these voluminous dossiers today, it is difficult to select out anything of substance, like a hint of the troubles which broke out at Yen Bey and in northern Annam in 1930–31. Once the uprisings began, however, the CAI did supply information on which police stations and army posts might become the object of attack. It is more likely that the existence of this surveillance caused resentment which served as an irritant to imperial relations. On 11 June 1938, Galandou Diouf, a deputy for Senegal, complained to the Minister of the Colonies that the CAI "is an organism without great interest, which only centralizes political information of only relative value. The CAI has never been called upon to offer useful intelligence to your ministry on what is really happening in the diverse colonies."[13]

The year 1927 had been fairly calamitous for Soviet espionage, with the smashing of Soviet spy networks in several European countries and in China. These reverses produced two immediate changes in the way Soviet intelligence operated abroad. The first was that, as a result of police raids on Soviet trade delegations and consulates in London and Beijing, Soviet diplomatic outposts were ordered to destroy their intelligence files. The second followed from the French experience—

Soviet intelligence was no longer to call on the services of local parties.

In France, however, this admonition appears to have been little honored. Instead, the decision was taken to "compartmentalize" party and spying activity. Select party faithful were recruited directly by the NKVD for "special" work of spying, transporting currency, or executions, often without the party being informed.[14] In the PCF Politburo, Henri Barbé was assigned to maintain contact with "General Muraille," a former commissar in the Soviet-Polish war of 1920, who expanded the remnants of Cremet's intelligence network until he was denounced and arrested in 1931. After serving a mild sentence of three years, Muraille returned to the U.S.S.R., where he is thought to have perished in the Stalinist purges of the late 1930s. Barbé, summoned to Moscow, failed to convince the Soviets that the employment of French communists in espionage activities was detrimental to the interests of the PCF. He lost his seat on the Politburo after he was denounced by the communist press for "group spirit" and "sectarianism," and resigned from the party in 1934. Meanwhile, the coordination of PCF "special services" fell to another member of the Politburo, Jacques Duclos.

Born in the Pyrenees in 1896, Duclos received only an elementary education before his father's insanity obliged him to be apprenticed as a pastry cook at the age of twelve. During the war, he was wounded at Verdun in 1916 and taken prisoner the following spring in the Nivelle offensive on the Chemin des Dames. In 1919, he settled in Paris and resumed his trade. But Duclos had been profoundly shaken by the experience of the war, in which one of his brothers had died. He joined a veterans association and became a member of the Confédération Générale du Travail (CGT). Active in the PCF section of Paris' tenth arrondissement after the Tours Congress, in 1924 he stood unsuccessfully for parliament. Two years later, Duclos gained seats in the French Chamber of Deputies and in the PCF Politburo. In 1927, prison sentences totaling forty-seven years and 32,000 francs in fines were handed down to Duclos after he published several violently antimilitarist articles. After serving only two months, however, he was furloughed to attend a session of parliament, fled into hiding, and spent the next years in Moscow, Brussels, and Spain. He returned to France in 1931 and, protected by his parliamentary immunity, took a seat on the Politburo. It was around this time that he and André Marty, a fanatical Stalinist who later earned distinction as "the butcher of Albacete" for his purges of Trotskyists in the International Brigades in Spain, became the main contacts for Soviet intelligence in the PCF.

In 1932, Duclos was forced back into hiding when his electoral defeat in May deprived him of the parliamentary immunity required to avoid prosecution in *l'affaire Fantomas*.

The Fantomas (or Phantomas) episode grew out of the "worker-correspondent" movement begun by Lenin in the Soviet Union. Claiming that professional journalists served the interests of capitalism, Lenin invited Soviet citizens to become worker-correspondents—abbreviated to *rabcors* in Russian—by supplying articles on local affairs to party publications. The enthusiastic response of Soviet citizens provided something rather different from the anticipated journalistic harvest. The "articles" more often read like indictments of local officials or inefficiencies prepared by the public prosecutor, who was precisely the person to whom many of these journalistic exercises were forwarded. Stalin depended upon denunciations by what he claimed in 1933 to be three million *rabcors* to maintain his terror machine in the U.S.S.R.

The *rabcors* experiment was imitated by communist parties in several countries, including France. However, it was not until the arrest of Cremet that the *rabcors* movement expanded to become a major source of intelligence on France.

The task of coordinating the reports of the correspondents, mostly young trade unionists in defense-related industries, was given to a committee at *L'Humanité* presided over by Duclos. Reports suitable for propaganda purposes were published in the official PCF newspaper, or in a *bulletin d'information* published by a committee member named Riquier, whose purpose was to denounce the war preparations of French imperialists. Other specialists were mobilized to gather economic intelligence under the auspices of a technical review.

A committee member and Soviet agent named Izaia Bir (or Byr), a Pole who had come to France early in the 1920s, passed on to the Soviet embassy solid intelligence gathered at *L'Humanité* or from one of his agents who regularly visited provincial PCF leaders in touch with local workers. His ability to elude police detection earned him the nickname of "Fantomas," the title of a popular detective novel of the period. In February 1932, Riquier, apparently struck with a case of bad conscience, revealed the workings of the *rabcors* spy network to a Sûreté agent with the improbable name of Charles Faux Pas Bidet. Bir, his chief assistant, and five French communists were convicted as part of the Fantomas network. Duclos fled to Moscow and then to Berlin, where under the name of Lauer he attended two communist conferences. Duclos was rescued by the electoral victory of the left in the November elections when the government, in need of PCF support in parliament, agreed to drop the case against him.

The breakup of the Fantomas network and Duclos' exposure did not slacken the pace of Soviet espionage in France. Traditional defense industry and military targets continued to be the object of numerous reports well into the 1930s. Among several foreigners living in Paris who gathered French defense information for the benefit of Soviet intelligence was Robert Gordon Switz, a wealthy American convert to communism. His arrest at Christmas 1933 led to the arraignment on espionage charges of twenty-nine people, including Lydia Stahl and one of her clients, the ubiquitous Colonel Dumoulin, an expert on French defense problems. After a short prison sentence following his 1927 arrest and a period living in Moscow, Dumoulin apparently had continued to receive a generous subsidy from Soviet intelligence in return for reports found in Switz's possession. Several of those charged, including Switz, escaped prosecution after cooperating with Sûreté inquiries. However, when the remaining suspects were tried in camera in the summer of 1934, they received sentences ranging from five years handed to Dumoulin and ten "unlocated" defendants to three years for others.[15]

In the short run, whatever meager benefits accrued to Stalin through espionage in France were probably more than offset by damage done to the image of the Soviet Union, which saw its diplomacy undermined, its isolation deepened, and its French flagship, the PCF, consigned to a political ghetto. But cognoscenti of espionage had already begun to notice a subtle shift in the attitudes toward illegal Soviet activity in France. The major reason for this was linked to the resurgence of Germany under the Nazi regime after 1933. Cases of Soviet espionage, which had attracted much attention in the decade after the war, were now of diminishing public interest. Even popular books about espionage reflected this shift.

There are several reasons for the popularity of spy literature in the interwar years. Intelligence and espionage were invariably associated with intrigue, mystery, and suspense, escapist themes craved by a public thrown into the midst of the Depression. But beyond this, spy literature found a ready audience in France among those who subscribed to a simplified version of history in which great affairs of state turned on treason, in which an individual altered the course of history through secret means. "Spy fiction needs a success, a danger thwarted, a secret exposed or recovered, an enemy robbed or deceived," an enemy plausible to the public, writes British historian D. Cameron Watt. The public wanted morality tales in which, after a suitable period of suspense, the good reaped their rewards and the treacherous their ruin. In this way, the humble realities of spying, its usually paltry results, were glorified and magnified in the public mind as vast and complex webs of conspiracies spun by mysterious spymasters and their daring agents. It was a game with victory achieved by the side with superior qualities of cerebral courage, bluff, and deceit.

All of these elements were present in the works of Georges Ladoux, who, in the last years before his death, enjoyed considerable success as an author with books on World War I spies Mata Hari and Marthe Richard, published in 1932 and 1933, and *Guerre secrète en Alsace*, published posthumously in 1934. Ladoux's works provide an excellent example of what Westley Wark calls the "faction industry" of spy literature, "deliberately blurring the line between fiction and fact and presenting himself in his texts as a spymaster with a personal knowledge and insight into the threat posed by German spies."[17] Ladoux, considered a rather mediocre counterintelligence officer in real life, presents himself as the vigilant spy chief who manipulated France's enemies. In his accounts of the war, the aging, unintelligent Mata Hari becomes a glamorous vixen playing a daring double game upon which the fate of France might possibly turn. Her arrest by Ladoux is portrayed as one of the greatest French victories of the war.

Opposite the perfidious Mata Hari, Ladoux set the virtuous Marthe Richard, a young war widow who presented herself to Ladoux prepared for any sacrifice to avenge the death of her husband. Ladoux dispatched her to Madrid, where she worked her charms on the German naval attaché, the villainous but stupid Krohn, who made her his mistress and his agent. Over the next months Richard sent messages to Ladoux in invisible ink which revealed a spy network in France, attempts to smuggle arms to dissidents in French Morocco, and U-boat movements. Krohn even sent her on a mission to Argentina to destroy grain stocks and cattle destined for France with chemicals and poisons which he had supplied. But so smitten had Krohn become with his French double agent that he forgave her this "failed" mission.

With the publication of Ladoux's book, Richard overnight became a national heroine. She rushed into print with her own version of these events, *Ma vie d'espionne* (My Life as a Spy) and other books, was awarded the Legion of Honor by a grateful Republic, and launched a political career, the culmination of which was her successful campaign to close the public brothels in France after World War II.

In truth, Ladoux did run a very successful deception operation. But the victims appear to have been the postwar French public rather than wartime German intelligence. Before the outbreak of war, Marthe Betenfeld had married Henri Richer, a wealthy man who indulged his wife's passion for flying and fast automobiles. She was well known in aviation circles when, in 1916, she was recruited by Ladoux. Ladoux's plan was for Madame Richer—thirty-five years old, with gray eyes and an attractive but hard face—to travel to Madrid in the company of Joseph Davrichewy, a Russian pilot who was recovering from an airplane accident. There, the French agents would try to convince the German embassy that Davrichewy should be used to spread pacifist propaganda on the Western Front. In the meantime, having worked their way into the embassy's confidence, they would try to steal the contents of the safe.

From the beginning, the plan was a long shot. The French agents did indeed meet Krohn. But soon afterward they were involved in an automobile accident. The presence in a German embassy vehicle of the naval attaché, a French woman, and a Russian pilot attracted the notice of the Madrid press, and the resulting stories were subsequently picked up by the French press. Their cover blown, Richer and

Davrichewy returned to Paris, the former to await her fame as a result of Ladoux's literary mythmaking.[18]

While Soviet spies were by no means absent from the *La bataille dans l'ombre* (The Battle in the Shadows) series of Jean Bardanne, pseudonym of Georges Bauret, World War I spy adventures and German plots predominated. The *Le poisson chinois* (Chinese Fish) series of Jean Bommart featured Deuxième Bureau captain Georges Sauvin, a male hero with a capacity to foil the plots of German imperialism. Sauvin was modeled at least in part on an "honorable correspondent" of the Deuxième Bureau, the Count of Lubersac, a monarchist whose credo was: "My aim in life is the defeat of Germany." Charles Robert-Dumas' success with the *Ceux du "S.R."* (Those of the Service de Renseignements) series earned for him an assignment in the real thing during the mobilization of 1939. Although André Brouillard made his principal reputation under the pseudonym Pierre Nord after 1945 with books on the Resistance, his first espionage novel, *Double crime sur la ligne Maginot*, appeared in 1936 and was turned into a film the following year.[19]

What was the significance of French spy literature? One interesting thing to note is that, as a genre, it was a generation behind that of the British. By the 1920s and 1930s, Somerset Maugham, Compton Mackenzie, Eric Ambler, and Graham Greene had abandoned the pre-1914 "clash of civilizations" approach of William Le Queux, Erskine Childers, and John Buchan for themes with a pronounced left-wing slant in which Machiavellian vested interests and moral equivocation posed far greater threats to civilization than did a Hun with a monocle. One author has suggested that the moral ambiguity of British spy fiction in the interwar years contributed to the popularity of appeasement.[20] If that is so, one wonders how appeasement became so popular in France without benefit of a supportive spy fiction?

By successfully confounding realism with intrigue, these books helped to glorify and legitimize intelligence agencies in the public mind. Spy novels reflected a conspiratorial theory of history, with the promise that those who positioned themselves on the right side might be able to channel its course. "The fictional glorification of spies enables the real ones to go on playing their sordid games," writes Phillip Knightley.[21] The reputation of the French services was inflated at a time when they were undermanned and starved of funds. Spy fiction allowed intelligence agencies, writers, and readers to play out their fantasies of clandestinity.[22] At least those like André Brouillard would be able to experience those fantasies firsthand in the clandestinity of the World War II Resistance.

The military revival of Germany under Hitler also began to concentrate the minds of the French government in ways which a distant Soviet threat, no matter how distasteful their espionage, could not. Tangible evidence of this shift could be found in French government policy which sought to counterbalance the revival of German militarism by resurrecting the old Franco-Russian alliance of 1894–1917, a diplomatic initiative which resulted in the Franco-Soviet pact of May 1935. It was clearly not in France's diplomatic interest to antagonize the Soviets by a vigorous prosecution of their spies. Nor was it in the political interest of the Radical and Socialist parties to alienate the PCF at a time when they required their parliamentary votes to remain in power, especially following the antiparliamentary riots of February 1934 inspired by the extreme right and the election of the Socialist-dominated Popular Front government of 1936.

These factors contributed to the apparently perverse outcome of the revelation of Duclos' role in the Fantomas network—neither Duclos' career nor his involvement in Soviet spying in France was terminated by the Fantomas affair. Quite the contrary! By 1937, the man generally considered to be the NKVD's impresario in France not only retained his seat in parliament; Duclos was also second-in-command, or more accurately *numéro un bis*, of one of France's major political parties, vice president of the Chamber of Deputies, and became candidate for the presidency of the Fifth Republic in 1969. His survival in the PCF can be explained by the fact that he clearly was Stalin's man in one of the most successfully Stalinized communist parties outside the Soviet Union. But the PCF, too, appeared to have turned over a new leaf, although experienced communist watchers realized that it was merely a tactic rather than the dawn of a new era of reconciliation with the bourgeois order. Its leadership sought to avoid embarrassing their political allies on the left or destabilizing the French government at a moment when Moscow was encouraging a policy of "united fronts" against fascism.

But there was a further factor which accounted for Duclos' re-markable survival, and that was a shift in Soviet espionage priorities. Until 1933, Germany had provided a secure base from which many intelligence operations, including those in France, were run. Hitler ended the tolerant hospitality which Weimar had extended to Soviet espionage services. Some of those services shifted to Paris, like the news agency which employed Arthur Koestler and which continued to function despite the fact that its bulletins found no subscribers.[23] But increasingly their main priority, like that of the Sûreté and the Deuxième Bureau, became spying on Germany.

Stalin, too, had other fish to fry. By the early 1930s, the Soviet dictator's suspicious temperament had flowered into a luxuriant paranoia that would produce his infamous purges. He became obsessed with thwarting imaginary conspiracies of White Russians and Trotskyists against his government. These new tasks were as-signed a high priority in the NKVD, whose work Duclos assisted in France. In 1937, Soviet defector Ignace Reiss was assassinated in Swit-zerland by NKVD agents operating out of Paris. However, Swiss police found the Sûreté decidedly uncooperative when they attempted to extradite the suspects, who were smuggled out of France by Soviet diplomats.

So while the immediate threat for the French intelligence services after 1933 became a resurgent Germany, France's interwar experience with Soviet espionage was to bequeath a legacy that would survive World War II. France had spawned an indigenous communist party whose primary loyalty was to Moscow. And while not all spies acted out of ideological motivation, the fact that the Soviet Union possessed an organization prepared to facilitate its espionage activities, if not furnish vital intelligence outright, would prove a vital factor in its success.

The fact that French governments on too many occasions turned a blind eye to illegal Soviet activities on its soil, whether out of fear of antagonizing Moscow and the PCF or out of fear of divulging state secrets, sent the wrong message to the population and to those responsible for guarding those secrets. *Raison d'état* blurred the lines of loyalty, left Frenchmen unsure of the permissible bounds of behavior where state secrets were concerned, and facilitated the penetration of Soviet moles into positions of greatest importance.

Post-World War II revelations, some of them based on the breaking of Soviet intelligence ciphers (code-named Venona) by the U.S. Army Security Agency from 1948, exposed several prewar Soviet agents in France. Among them was Edouard Pfeiffer, principal secretary to Edouard Daladier, French War Minister from January 1936 to May 1940 and Prime Minister between April 1938 and March 1940. Especially damaging was a nest of Soviet sympathizers revealed in the French Air Ministry under Pierre Cot, Radical Party politician, passionate advocate of a military alliance with the U.S.S.R., and six times Air Minister in the 1930s. That one of the Air Ministry's principal scientists, André Labarthe, was a Soviet agent appears beyond doubt. Whether or not Cot's permanent secretary, Jean Moulin, was also a communist agent continues to be a subject of passionate debate in France, as Moulin was to emerge as the principal hero of the French Resistance in World War II.[24] French historian of the French Communist Party Stéphane Courtois argues that, although Cot and many of his Air Ministry staff in the 1930s were Soviet sympathizers, they were not conscious agents of Moscow. Still, he concedes, they "were under Soviet influence; they could have been manipulated, even without knowing it."[25]

While Moscow undoubtedly obtained much technical and political information from its activity in France in the interwar years, the principal payoff would come in the future. The Soviets appear to have laid a foundation for an extensive spy network in France through the *rabcors* movement, which was particularly strong in the armaments industry and the railways; the communist party; and sympathizers who gradually worked their way into influential state positions. Indeed, French spy specialist Thierry Wolton has suggested that the Air Ministry under Pierre Cot served a function in pre-World War II France similar to that of Cambridge University for Great Britain—as a breeding ground of communists and communist sympathizers destined for influential positions who during and after the war willingly spied and recruited agents for the Soviet Union.

It is very possible that in the early years of the war, as Thierry Wolton speculates, Moscow was much better informed on French industrial production and German dispositions in occupied France than was the Free French intelligence service in London.[26] But this was in the future. In the years which preceded the outbreak of World War II, the attention of French intelligence services became riveted on Nazi Germany.

How did the struggle against Red, and eventually Nazi, spies in the inter-war years contribute to the development of French intelligence? Above all, it continued the trend of the politicization of the services which found it difficult to stake out a position as neutral bureaucracies on the "Anglo-Saxon" model in Frence's divided political culture. Traditions which blurred the frontiers between domestic surveillance and intelligence, the existence of large numbers of communists and communist sympathizers in France whose beliefs made them a threat to the national community, and a political system which accommodated, even perpetuated, this state of affairs, made the services distrustful of their own people and encouraged their alienation from the political system they served. This alienation would be increased by what the intelligence community came to view as the inadequate, even defeatist, response of the political system, and of the French people, to the growing German threat.

SIX

THE GERMAN THREAT

Like most defeats, that suffered by France in 1940 was declared an orphan from birth. So evident was the threat, so obvious the menace which increasingly loomed over France after Hitler's seizure of power in 1933, that it seemed scarcely credible that it could have passed unnoticed by the Deuxième Bureau.

The function of an intelligence service is to protect one's own secrets while penetrating those of the enemy, and possibly of allies as well. It then must see that timely information arrives to guide decision makers.[1] In the immediate aftermath of World War I, however, it appeared that neither mission could be carried out with great effectiveness. The wartime intelligence machine was scaled down, as the defeat of Germany had deprived French military intelligence of its principal adversary. The Service de Renseignements (SR) was assigned responsibility for counterintelligence, or *contre-espionnage* (CE) as the French called it, the handling of agents, spies, telephone taps, and the analysis of foreign newspapers and periodicals. It also contained a Section D, for the interception and deciphering of foreign communications. A Section Matériel de Guerre studied the armaments of foreign powers. Information it collected was passed on to the army's Deuxième Bureau, which also contained a small cryptanalytic section. There it was combined with reports from military attachés or those received through diplomatic channels, and information from the smaller Deuxième Bureau of the navy and air force, to be processed into a daily intelligence summary by the Section des Armées Etrangères.

Hardly was the ink dry on the armistice of 1940 than critics emerged to blast French intelligence for failing to warn of the size and nature of the growing German threat. Among the most bitter of them was General František Moravec, chief of Czech secret services, who in his memoirs condemned the "hear no evil, see no evil" attitude of French intelligence in the face of Czech-supplied evidence of German rearmament. "I also came to the reluctant and astounded conclusion that France . . . was giving us very little worthwhile information . . . because its intelligence service had but little to give," Moravec wrote. "Their desire 'to know' decreased proportionately as the Nazi danger increased," to the point that they even ignored accurate predictions supplied by a Czech agent of the time and place of the 1940 offensive.[2]

One reason why this may have been so was that the French intelligence structure was dysfunctional. A main complaint was that intelligence summaries merely provided a smorgasbord of information rather than a focused analysis of developments, "military and technical details without realizing the grand pattern."[3] Navarre insisted that, as far as this was true, it was because the intelligence services were given inadequate guidance on what exactly the government and high command sought in the way of information, an "intelligence plan."

On the other hand, it was not the role of intelligence to draw their own conclusions or suggest policy directions. When, for instance, Paul Stehlin, who served as air attaché in Berlin in the 1930s, attempted to suggest a direction for French air policy based on his knowledge of developments in the Luftwaffe, he was silenced: "Without rebuking me directly, I was given to understand that no one had asked my opinion; all they wanted was information," he wrote. "I was a young captain, made to observe and report. I was too young to give advice."[4] He lamented the fact that the often uninformed, gossip-laden reports of junior diplomats were preferred to those of well-informed military attachés. He put this down to a diplomatic distaste for soldiers, whom they regarded as social and intellectual inferiors and whose alarmist but accurate reports of German rearmament threatened to ruffle the

harmony of diplomatic receptions.[5] Others claimed that, to curry favor
with their diplomatic superiors, attachés preferred "adopting the ideas
of their ambassadors and turning themselves into the diplomatic counselors of the high command. In Paris, the commanding generals are
receptive to these brilliant dissertations which make a welcome change
from the objective reports of the intelligence service."[6] The Quai
d'Orsay lacked an organization like the SR to coordinate intelligence
information gathered by its diplomats. One result of this, according
to the French commander-in-chief, General Maurice Gamelin, was
that diplomatic reports were superficial and insufficiently attentive to
military questions.[7]

French intelligence officers, however, have rushed to deny that
intelligence failed either because it ignored developments in Germany
or because it was too disorganized to present a coherent picture to
policy makers and strategists. Led by Lieutenant Colonel (later General) Maurice Gauché, who commanded the Deuxième Bureau from
1935, an impressive list of officers credited themselves with producing
"the most perfect work that the Deuxième Bureau could ask for. It is
not humanly possible to come closer to the truth."[8] French intelligence
had chronicled German rearmament, had accurately assessed Hitler's
intentions, and had issued detailed reports on blitzkrieg doctrines which
would be applied with such stunning success against the French in
May–June 1940. In the view of French intelligence veterans, ample
and accurate intelligence was disbelieved, disdained, ignored, or
squandered by France's political and military leaders. If France collapsed, it was not because she had been misinformed or misled by her
intelligence services.[9] On the contrary, the pre-World War II French
intelligence community has sold an image of itself as modern Cassandras whose persistent warnings of looming disaster were received
with ill-humored skepticism bordering on disbelief.[10] This verdict has
received the support of historians, among them Walter Laqueur, who
wrote that "the Deuxième Bureau was second to none" on the eve of
World War II.[11] In his biography of General Maurice Gamelin, English historian Martin Alexander gives an impressive list of French
intelligence accomplishments, beginning with their detection in the
1920s of German steps to evade the arms limitations imposed by the
Versailles Treaty, efforts to produce synthetic oil, the creation of panzer

divisions and operational emphasis on air-tank coordination, and a chronicle of growing German military strength. There was an accumulation of evidence that Hitler was banishing anyone who attempted to exert a moderating influence on his behavior.[12]

Nor were Hitler's intentions ignored: Ample warning was given of the reoccupation of the Rhineland in 1936, the Anschluss (the German takeover of Austria in March 1938), preparations for the invasion of Czechoslovakia in 1938, and the occupation of the rump of that country in March 1939. The invasion of Poland was predicted, and the early signs of the Russo-German pact of August 1939 were detected with a degree of accuracy which forewarned, though alas did not forearm, French politicians and generals.

Contrary to received opinion, while friction among diplomats, attachés, and French intelligence services (caused in part by SR complaints that French embassies were insufficiently security-conscious) certainly existed, its importance must not be exaggerated. Relations between the Quai d'Orsay and military intelligence were good, especially on the embassy level, where attachés regularly briefed ambassadors.[13] Poor intelligence/diplomatic relations, as far as they existed, hardly blinded Paris to the realities of the darkening diplomatic horizon after 1933, even if little action was taken.[14] Certainly, the French ambassador to Berlin, André François-Poncet, and his successor, Robert Couloudre, dispatched long screeds to Paris decrying the German menace. The Quai and the Deuxième Bureau did not cease to communicate essential pieces of intelligence, in part through a permanent liaison officer established to operate between the French general staff and the Quai from 1935. For these reasons, French intelligence officer Henri Navarre conceded that while some divergence of view existed between the diplomats and the Deuxième Bureau, they were not critical. "The overall situation was generally evaluated by them in more or less the same manner."[15]

French military attachés also have been given quite high marks by historians. Whereas before 1914 the primary criterion for the selection of attachés had been the personal fortune each required to hold his own socially in the diplomatic world, in the interwar years the position became more professionally demanding. Candidates were selected on the basis of linguistic ability and experience in foreign military mis-

sions. They were required to spend a training period with the Deuxième
Bureau and produce a study of a foreign army. Not all attachés were
considered top-notch, including General Félix Musse, French attaché
in Poland between 1936 and 1939, and General Henri Didelet in
Berlin, who insisted almost until the opening shots of September 1939
that Germany would not go to war before 1942, when its army and
its economy would be at full strength. He also predicted wrongly that
Germany would move down the Danube rather than against Poland.
Even during the period of "sitzkrieg," Didelet believed that the attack
in the West would not come before Germany's conquests in the East
had been consolidated and its economy had reached peak performance.
Gauché claimed that he had the devil's own time winning Gamelin
away from Didelet's views and persuading him to accept the assessment
of his official intelligence service.[16]

While one may quibble about the accuracy of specific political,
economic, industrial, or scientific intelligence reports supplied by military attachés, they provide, in the view of British historian Martin
Alexander, "a better-informed and more perceptive source about the
policies of foreign powers than did many of the reports of the French
diplomatic corps itself."[17] In general, these officers abroad painted a
fairly accurate picture of Europe's changing military landscape. French
air attachés were well informed on Italian and German air developments, led by the Alsatian Stehlin, whose contacts with the Göring
entourage allowed him not only to take "training flights" over German
defense sites until he was grounded during the Munich crisis of September 1938 but also to purchase the plans for German air rearmament
from a debt-ridden German officer. He also warned Paris of the Anschluss four days before it occurred.[18] Attachés played a leading role
in producing what the Deuxième Bureau regarded as their most successful insights into the development of German armored doctrine and
on the German military buildup in the 1930s, although they also
faithfully reported the views of German officers who advocated a more
plodding infantry support rather than an independent cavalry role for
tanks.[19] Attachés also gave quite adequate warning of the complete
occupation of Czechoslovakia in March 1939, the Nazi-Soviet pact
which was eventually signed in August, and the German staff's conducting war games simulating the invasion of Poland in the spring of
1939.[20]

American historian Steven Ross has modified this picture somewhat, noting that French intelligence made some mistakes in estimating German order of battle in the mid-1930s, paying too little attention to armament and equipment and overestimating the capabilities of German reserve units. Like other intelligence services, the French underestimated the tactical impact of air power, while overestimating its strategic capabilities. On the other hand, their analysis of the German methods in the Polish campaign of September 1939 were excellent.[21] As will be seen, the Service de Renseignements played a significant role in the breaking of the Enigma codes which were to hand the Allies immense intelligence advantages during World War II.

From this survey of the 1930s, it becomes clear that French intelligence in the interwar years had collected enough information to keep French governments adequately informed of events in Germany. And if one adds French successes against Italian codes, then French leaders were also adequately informed about Mussolini's ambitions in the Mediterranean. But was intelligence reaching the policy makers so that it could be factored into decisions? The short answer is that, in the absence of formal records, no one knows for sure.[22] Deuxième Bureau veterans agreed with German intelligence officer Wilhelm Flicke that French political and military leaders "did not make full use" of the excellent intelligence spread before them.[23]

General Moravec became convinced that the only explanation of why the French continued to ignore the excellent intelligence supplied them by the Czechs was that much of it "got lost in transit."[24] In other words, the problem was again one of a dysfunctional bureaucratic structure for transmitting intelligence to the top.

What is certain is that no formal structure existed to give intelligence briefings to ministers on a regular basis, with the exception of a brief period during the Popular Front government of Léon Blum in 1936 when the heads of the Deuxième Bureau and the SR briefed cabinet meetings. Otherwise, Lieutenant Colonel Louis Rivet, head of the SR, complained that he was never asked to give advice to politicians and only rarely to the high command.[25] The two *chefs de cabinet* of Edouard Daladier, who served as both Prime Minister and War Minister from 1938 to the spring of 1940, were notoriously protective of their boss. In any case, the French cabinet usually coordinated policy and did not serve as an important decision-making body in its own right. The Conseil Supérieur de la Défense Nationale was also a staffing and planning body rather than a decision-making one. It prepared reports for the Haut Comité Militaire (HCM) (which after June 1936 became the Comité Permanent de la Défense Nationale—CPDN). It was here that policy decisions were made. But because minutes were infrequently or haphazardly kept, it is impossible to know how far intelligence figured into the decisions of this body.[26] The chief of the Deuxième Bureau was, of course, present at Gamelin's twice-weekly staff meetings.

—

In the absence of official intelligence, some generals, diplomats, and politicians sought private sources of intelligence to supplement or even replace those of the official services. One result was to fragment the intelligence picture. Paul Paillole, who joined the SR in 1936 and remained in French intelligence throughout World War II, complained that ministers were prepared to listen to rumormongers, men who "pretended to know more than anyone else."[27] Stehlin had a low opinion of diplomats who passed on the most frivolous gossip as if it were solid intelligence and of officials who sought out "less pessimistic" intelligence elsewhere if official reports were not to their taste.[28] The same frustrations rumbled through the Deuxième Bureau: "What purpose do we serve?" Paillole's boss, Louis Rivet, railed in frustration at the refusal of French leaders to listen to intelligence reports. "One would think that they only read *Gringoire* [a pro-German newspaper], listen to gossip and live with their heads in the clouds. Each time that Gamelin calls me in—and that's a rare occasion!—it's to talk of a dog run over in the streets. As for the ministers, I never see them! They want to hear only what pleases them and listen only to what corresponds to their wishes."[29]

Fragmentation and consequently frustration were inevitable in part because France had no system capable of analyzing, synthesizing, and distributing intelligence to those who required it. (There is no evidence, however, that other countries, such as Great Britain, were any better organized to integrate intelligence and policy.[30]) Intelligence was squirreled away by Gamelin, or perhaps reached Daladier if it was considered important enough. In other words, there was a demand for intelligence which the Deuxième Bureau was not allowed to satisfy. Therefore, those who fell outside the official intelligence circuit, which included virtually everyone, were forced to gather intelligence where they could find it. The political culture of the Third Republic stimulated this trend—a regime in which rumor was an accepted political currency and in which knowledge, no matter how spurious, conferred status upon those who could claim to possess it.

Canadian historian Robert Young believes that the failure to utilize excellent intelligence was more than just a structural problem. In Young's view, intelligence fitted badly into an army which had a distinct preference for rules, for a "right" and "wrong" way of doing business. Intelligence, especially that which challenged the confident assertions of strategists, tacticians, and policy makers, was like an awkward child who misbehaves at an elegant event.[31] Henri Navarre argued that there was a residual distrust of the secret services dating from the Dreyfus Affair: "For the government and the high command," Navarre wrote, "the Service de Renseignements was a slightly mysterious organization whose necessity was reluctantly acknowledged, but whose initiatives, it was feared, could cause problems."[32]

French generals, presided over by the characterless Maurice Gamelin and his immediate boss, Edouard Daladier, lacked the imagination required to realize that the tank and the airplane had revolutionized warfare. They conceived of battle in the linear terms of World War I trench taking, despite intelligence reports which chronicled the revolution in German tactical and operational theory based on these modern weapons systems. An army which adhered to rules and "lessons" acquired at enormous expense in the trenches of 1914–18 did not so much ignore intelligence as disdain it, as did timid and indecisive political leaders who placed their faith in a policy of Appeasement, a sweeping invitation to Hitler to realize his criminal ambitions.

Young argues that during the interwar years France fell victim to its own sense of self-righteousness: "Did not the French believe that this revealed truth was theirs by right, compensation of divine order for the terrible sufferings of France, France the victim, France the martyr? If such were the case, it may be easier to appreciate why they put such faith in the lessons, the commandments, of the Great War, why they were sometimes tempted into making derisive or patronizing remarks about German military experiments. At the same time, the self-righteousness of a traumatized people may also say something about the difficulties encountered by French intelligence, for their job was to report Olympus from the foothills. What interested them was the work and activity of foreigners, from whom it was at best unclear just how much could be learned. Indeed, perhaps this was the fundamental reason why French intelligence officers often encountered indifference and even disdain from their own colleagues."[33]

This interpretation of the Fall of France assumes that the Third Republic was a regime paralyzed by its own decadence, incapable of devising a logical response to the German menace despite the warnings of its intelligence services. Had a vigorous Republic chosen to resist the remilitarization of the Rhineland in 1936, or intervened to defend her Czech ally in 1938, then the cataclysm of World War II should have died stillborn. With hindsight, the appeal of this interpretation appears irresistible. By refusing to stand up to Hitler, the protagonists of Appeasement, Daladier and Chamberlain, only made him more bold, stripped away the influence of those Germans who urged caution. With each passing month, Hitler's strength increased at a far greater rate than did that of France and Great Britain. The Munich crisis of September 1938 offered the last opportunity for the Allies to confront Hitler with any chance of success.

More recently, the classical view that excellent intelligence fell on the deaf ears of French leaders has been jettisoned for a more subtle interpretation of the interrelationship between intelligence, policy, and military doctrine. The evidence suggests that intelligence reports were read and that they were influential. The problem with French intelligence in the interwar years was not that it failed to give warning of the growing might of Nazi Germany. Rather, it did nothing to shake the faith of French leaders in the correctness of their Appeasement policies or of their military doctrines.

Historians of the 1930s have suggested that in this atmosphere of Appeasement, good intelligence stirred Allied governments to no activity more energetic than lethargy, on the theory that any movement, no matter how slight, would rock an already dangerously unstable boat. Westley Wark has argued that an overblown picture of the efficiency, discipline, and power of the Luftwaffe encouraged by British air intelligence contributed to a disinclination in the Air Ministry, the cabinet, and the British public to do anything which might provoke the Führer.[34] The debilitating effects of a worst-case scenario have also been detected in France. It was not that French politicians ignored intelligence. *Au contraire*, they pondered it to the point of paralysis. Reports of a large and efficient German war machine, which suggested that the costs of confronting it would be catastrophic, provided a comfortable alibi for governments disinclined to action in any case.[35]

To understand the impact of intelligence on policy, one must first comprehend what that policy was. Appeasement was something more than a mere aspiration that Hitler would one day come to his senses, an expression of defeatism. Rather it was a cautious but logical reaction to the German resurgence.

French decision makers did not bury their heads in the sand. They realized perfectly well that a war with Hitler was in the cards. But they preferred that it come later rather than sooner, once Great Britain had been securely bound in as an ally and the French economy was strong enough to support a long war. Then tanks and planes could be produced in quantities which would not dislocate the French economy in the same way that Hitler's rapid rearmament program had forced him to maintain German wage rates at 1933 levels and dangerously overheated his economy. Therefore, French leaders were keen to do nothing which might rush events. The frustrations expressed by French intelligence officers in their postwar writings over what they believed to be the cavalier dismissal of their warnings must be seen in the light of the dramatic failure of Appeasement and the understandable desire of Deuxième Bureau veterans to disassociate themselves from any role in it. What their disavowals fail to acknowledge is that their intelligence reports accommodated themselves perfectly well both to the long-term strategy of Appeasement and to French operational and tactical doctrines.

Intelligence did not lack influence in pre-World War II France. The problem was that intelligence was either interpreted or tailored in ways to fit most snugly with the predispositions of French generals and politicians. Intelligence reports which predicted that Hitler would pick off France's eastern allies encouraged attempts to form an Italian alliance as a land bridge to the East. But as Mussolini slithered toward a rapprochement with Germany after 1935, there was very little France could do for her eastern allies. After all, what are allies for, if not to fight for France? Allies who threaten to draw France into a premature war for the security of some geographical fragment of Eastern Europe were worse than useless—they were a positive danger. So intelligence warnings that Germany would go east confirmed France in the soundness of her Appeasement strategy.[36]

—

Therefore France, and especially Gamelin, had begun psychologically to disengage from its eastern allies even before the Anschluss of March 1938, the timing of which appears to have caught the Deuxième Bureau off guard and convinced the commander-in-chief that any attempts to defend them would be hopeless. Gamelin grew certain that Czechoslovakia was too weak to defend itself. When in September 1938 General Moravec signaled Gamelin that only eight German divisions remained on the half-completed Siegfried Line to oppose fifty-six French divisions, so he could walk into the Rhineland, the regimental bands in the lead, Gamelin could only sigh that he preferred not to initiate "a modernized battle of the Somme."[37] Reports of the Deuxième Bureau of the air force forwarded to Daladier which overestimated the crushing power of the Luftwaffe confirmed the Prime Minister in his disinclination to risk a war for Czechoslovakia.[38] Nor does the Deuxième Bureau appear to have anticipated the final absorption into the Reich of the rump of Czechoslovakia until a few days before Hitler actually marched into Prague on 15 March 1939. Only after the fact did the Deuxième Bureau see the logic in the move which had netted the Germans an enormous arms bonanza and industrial base which would be turned against France in 1940.[39]

While Gamelin had prepared to discount Czech strength because he was disinclined to fight for Prague, he wildly inflated Polish powers of resistance. It is unclear whether this was a result of faulty intelligence, a preference for a Polish over a Soviet alliance, a strategy which sought to tie down German forces in a long campaign in Poland, thus giving France even more breathing space, or a combination of all three. The Poles spoke confidently of their powers of resistance. The deputy chief of staff, General Henri Dentz, with responsibility for intelligence, predicted a Polish resistance of four to six months, when the actual campaign lasted eighteen days. In this atmosphere of wishful thinking, intelligence reports to the contrary, mainly from British and Belgian sources, were, in the words of Martin Alexander, "too inconvenient to be taken seriously,"[40] because they would have discredited France's entire strategy.

Nevertheless, by May 1939, rumors of a Nazi-Soviet pact, and intelligence figures which placed the power of Axis forces at 250 divisions, against 120 Allied divisions in the West and 110 in the East, caused France to flirt once again with the idea of a Soviet alliance to bolster Polish and Rumanian defenses.[41] The inflation of German military numbers was a constant feature of French intelligence, especially after 1938. French intelligence veterans have argued that this was done out of "prudence."[42] But either French intelligence was not as accurate as many of its partisans have claimed or intelligence was being skewed to fit the preconceptions of the consumers. British observers noted that French estimates were generally 20 percent above their figures, which forced the British to push their estimates higher to bring them into line with those of their allies.[43]

French intelligence began to detect the mobilization of German reservists from June 1939, and by 20 August sounded the alarm that Poland was seriously menaced. When September 1939 revealed the naked truth of German power and Polish unpreparedness, the Deuxième Bureau vastly inflated estimates of German troop strength poised to counter a Franco-British invasion in the West—30 to 35 divisions, which it believed could be rapidly reinforced to as much as 60 divisions should the French attack. They also praised the quality of these forces, when the true figure was only 11 divisions backed by some reserves. The Deuxième Bureau also recommended that an economic blockade would be more effective against Germany than an attack. No matter, French intelligence estimates had served their purpose—furnish Gamelin the perfect alibi, so that he could simply stand aside and mutter, "*Quel dommage.*"[44]

French intelligence also closely followed German operational and tactical developments. Yet the limits to the value of even accurate intelligence on German blitzkrieg methods were demonstrated as early as 1935, the year Hitler openly repudiated Versailles and instituted conscription in Germany. Armed with intelligence that Germany had founded its first panzer divisions, French politician Paul Reynaud appeared before parliament on 15 March 1935 to promote Charles de Gaulle's plan for the professionalization and the mechanization of the French army laid out in his 1934 book, Vers l'armée de métier (The Army of the Future).[45] The proposal got nowhere, because it flew in the face of both Republican dogma and prevailing military doctrine. The belief that a professional officer corps imbued with an exaggerated esprit offensif had been responsible for the enormous losses sustained by the French on the Western Front in World War I became an article of faith on the left after 1918. This made left-wing politicians, like Socialist Party leader Léon Blum, predisposed against the conservative political cast of the officer corps in any case, extremely reluctant to adopt an offensive form of military organization which might reproduce the wasteful offensives of World War I. Military leaders like General Maxime Weygand and Marshal Philippe Pétain, who believed matériel no substitute for manpower, were furious with de Gaulle for prodding a hornets' nest by linking the separate issue of modernization with that of professionalization.[46]

Gamelin, who replaced Weygand in 1935, was more innovative. But his power to effect radical changes in the way the French army made war was limited by the political constraints mentioned above, his relatively limited powers to switch military priorities, slender resources, a parsimonious parliament, a complex and inefficient arms procurement system, manpower shortages, and limited sites to train his troops once new weapons like tanks came on-line. Furthermore, Gamelin could not nudge modernization forward by creating a public fuss about French unpreparedness without jeopardizing the British alliance he was keen to create. Guderian's Achtung Panzer! was translated by the Deuxième Bureau and placed in all regimental libraries, and from April 1936 intelligence began to follow the development of German experiments in combined air-tank operations. Unfortunately, until 1938 the Air Ministry was in the hands of Pierre Cot, who was in no haste to modernize the air arm, because to close down factories for retooling would cause unemployment. The French air force remained committed to the creation of a strategic bombing force and disdained close tactical air support.[47]

The Spanish Civil War also supplied a laboratory for the Germans to test many of their methods, and one which the French monitored closely. A Bureau d'Etudes des Pyrénées was created in Toulouse in early 1937 with the mission to study military techniques used in the war.[48] Reports from Spain as well as from observers sent to the Sino-Japanese War, however, concluded that tanks lacked the power to break through a well-organized front backed by artillery and sprinkled with strong points and antitank guns. Studies in 1938 based on intelligence observations supported the French concept of the "methodical battle," a multi-arm, methodical advance by tanks and infantry, backed by massive artillery. The advance of tactical air power was noted, but its importance went unappreciated, in part because the number of planes employed in Spain meant that the operations were still too indecisive to make general conclusions. Nevertheless, the Deuxième Bureau closely followed German army maneuvers and predicted that blitzkrieg concepts were gaining ascendancy in the German army. Deuxième Bureau analyses of the Polish campaign were clear about the deficiencies of Polish mobilization and training, the ability of the Luftwaffe to isolate the battlefield by breaking up communications and to shatter Polish counterattacks, and the rapidity with which panzers, in conjunction with air strikes, reached support positions and disorganized the command structure.[49]

Basically, one can argue that French intelligence reports of tactical and operational developments in Germany did have an impact, especially after 1938, when the combined effects of the Anschluss and Munich forced even the French parliament to recognize that a long-term strategy might be preempted by a German attack. Only then did the French finally get serious about developing tanks and aircraft. Gamelin paid close attention to intelligence summaries of German air and armor coordination in Poland, and these spurred him into intense efforts to form independent tank corps whose mission ultimately was to meet and halt the panzer divisions in an encounter battle on the Belgian plains.[50]

Nevertheless, French intelligence reports were interpreted in ways which supported, rather than challenged, the validity of French doctrine. Methodical battle was operationally and tactically compatible with France's strategic goal of a prolonged war of attrition—parry the initial German offensive, build up Allied strength, and launch a counteroffensive two to three years in the future. Besides, French generals relied on the comfortable fiction that the West would simply not permit the Germans to operate with such devastating effectiveness as she had shown in Poland. The front was too congested, the armies too skilled, "the mouthful too large" for blitzkrieg methods to work.

In sum, the view put forward by intelligence officers that they could do nothing to shake the lethargy of their leaders, that they should, in the view of Paillole, present their views with more force, "upset routines, break through distrust, step over obstacles, and make the truth heard at the summit of the state,"[51] exaggerates the position of prewar intelligence. The truth was that the leaders of the Third Republic in the 1930s were quite adequately informed about the German menace. No one had his head completely in the sand. The purpose of Appeasement, at least in the minds of some, was not to avoid war but to gain time. An absence of knowledge of Hitler's intentions or capabilities was not the problem. Intelligence had no power to alter French policy, which was to solidify the British alliance and prepare for a long war of attrition. France had learned from her 1923 occupation of the Ruhr to collect on Germany's defaulting war reparations payments that unilateral actions were risky. Her goal was to entice Britain out of her postwar isolation and commit her to act in unison with France against German expansionism. It was a costly policy which forced France to stand by as Hitler ran amok. But it was one to which intelligence reports accommodated themselves very nicely.

The French Contribution
to the Enigma Breakthrough

One of the greatest contributions of the French to the ultimate success of Allied signals intelligence in World War II was its role in the breaking of the Enigma codes. Ironically, this success occurred at a moment when French intelligence was deficient in two important areas which would prove vital in cracking the Enigma—cryptanalysis and agents on German soil.

The once redoubtable French code-breaking community slid into irreversible decline in the interwar years. The Sûreté marked time tinkering with invisible ink and practicing on old prewar codes dating from the Caillaux affair, their code-breaking capabilities increasingly suspect. A particularly egregious example of this occurred in 1919, when Givierge was summoned by Haverna, one of the Sûreté's great prewar cryptographers, whose exploits had topped those even of Bazeries, and handed a file of letters intercepted by the police. Haverna complained that they were written in a code which had defeated the best efforts of his cryptanalysts. Upon opening the voluminous dossier, Givierge realized that he had been given a stack of letters written in Yiddish, which "any rag merchant in the Marais [the Jewish quarter]" could have read and which contained nothing more subversive than requests for money sent by an Alsatian Jew to members of his family in America. But on numerous occasions, he was sent wires which they could not translate. "One must not ask of them [the Sûreté] work which was too complicated," Givierge concluded. [52]

French military intelligence was stripped down as most of its prewar cryptographers returned to civilian life or were employed by the Quai. Although allowed a strength of seventeen officers, the cipher section seldom counted more than twelve in the 1920s, and was desperately short of cryptographers and cryptanalysts, who were discouraged by the poor promotion prospects and low prestige of military intelligence. The effects of this deemphasis of code breaking and code security quickly became apparent.

The lack of code security, an old problem which had driven Givierge to distraction during the war, continued after the war. The end of hostilities brought an end to the cryptography classes given at the war college and the artillery school at Versailles. The result was a system which ran from fundamental ignorance of codes in the metropolitan army to "complete anarchy" in the French army in the Levant. For instance, in 1922 a French lieutenant in Beirut was given thirty days' fortress arrest after he asked the Italian liaison officer with the Armée du Levant to help him encode a message. The codes in the French army of the Rhine were so confusing that 30 percent of messages were undecipherable. During the Rif War of 1925, Moroccan resident general Marshal Hubert Lyautey introduced his intelligence officer to a group of visiting Spanish officers as "the one who translates your telegrams for me." The Spanish promptly changed all their codes. Givierge declared that during code exercises for 1927 "more than half of the recipients received untranslatable texts," while officers continued to fill their messages with repetitious phrases like "Do you hear me distinctly?" and "*J'ai l'honneur de vous rendre compte . . .* [I have the honor to inform you . . .]" which made the key easier to discover by eavesdroppers.[53]

Wilhelm Flicke, who served with German communications intelligence through both world wars, discovered that sloppy French communication methods provided a bonanza of useful information for German intelligence. By regularly monitoring French signals during maneuvers in the 1930s, Berlin was handed a very complete picture of French troop organization, tactics employed, weapons committed, march performance, employment of the air force, and important elements of the French air defense system. It was Flicke's opinion that, of all European armies, only Italian radio security was worse. As war approached, the Germans' ability to monitor communications in France and North Africa was improved by the remilitarization of the Rhineland in 1936 and because of growing cooperation with the Italians and Spaniards. French communications security in the colonies ran from abysmal to nonexistent, presumably because the French assumed that the Moroccans or Druse did not eavesdrop on their conversations. But the Germans did. And while this yielded little useful strategic intelligence in the short term, it did sabotage French communications security—for at least two reasons: Flicke argued that communications methods in the colonies offered a poor school for signals troops who might be transferred to Europe. Lapses of French coding security in the colonies was especially damaging because it appears as if the French first tested codes in the colonies or the Middle East before using them in Europe.[54] "The circular traffic employed here," Flicke concluded of French signals, "the frequent transmission of plaintext, the use in France of no less than 78 different types of radio apparatus, the use of signal tables—which were very easy to solve—for brief tactical reports, the tendency to be systematic in the construction of tables of call signs and wavelengths, and many other things, made it certain that in a war between Germany and [France] the intercept service would have the best of success in gathering intelligence."[55] Unfortunately, this proved prophetically true in 1940.

When to the lack of security-consciousness of French military communications is added that of security lapses in French diplomatic missions, then the record of French intelligence in protecting their country's secrets in the 1930s is not good. Much of this was out of their hands, especially where the Quai was concerned. Particularly galling to French intelligence officers was the Quai d'Orsay's resumption of its prewar aloofness in matters of intelligence cooperation. In 1922 the Quai, which throughout the war refused to centralize French cryptanalytic services, ceased to send decoded correspondence to the army, and even insisted that military attachés communicate in special codes that the army could not read because "the war is finished."[56]

The Germans, who had enjoyed good success in breaking European and American diplomatic codes, were allowed even greater access into the mind of the enemy, including the French, with the increase in diplomatic traffic and the increased reliance on the radio to send it, caused by rising European tensions after 1935. The year 1938 appears to have been an especially dismal period, when the cipher security of at least fifteen French embassies and posts abroad was compromised.

But despite these lapses, the Quai treated offers from the Service de Renseignements to provide security officers in foreign posts as lèse-majesté.[57] French embassies enjoyed the dubious distinction of supplying the "bulk of clear texts" intercepted by the Forschungsamt, which became Göring's security and intelligence service. This has led one historian of German intelligence to posit that the ability of the German leadership to read the diplomatic communications of several countries, but especially of France, allowed Hitler "to live more dangerously thanks to the cryptanalytical windows that had steadily opened up during the Weimar era."[58] The plans for the limited offensive which Gamelin carried out in the Saar in September 1939 were betrayed to the Germans by intercepted French signals.[59] The British also appear to have been able to read all French diplomatic ciphers between 1919 and 1935, when they abandoned French ciphers to concentrate on those of Germany.[60]

The decline of cryptology and cryptanalysis in France was especially crippling at a time when both were being altered beyond recognition by the newest postwar innovation—the mechanical cipher or Enigma machine.

Through a combination of rotors and plugboards, Enigma allowed for an infinite number of encoding positions which would revolutionize signals intelligence by 1940. As David Kahn has observed, World War I made cryptanalysis the primary source of intelligence information. At the same time, the volume of traffic and the increasing complexity of the codes had made the old ways of dealing with it obsolete. A large number of messages had to be compared to come up with probable solutions. The idiosyncratic code breaker working alone to devise the brilliant solution became a thing of the past. The question became: How well would the French adapt to the new demands of cryptography?

The French condemned themselves to play an interesting, but altogether secondary, role in this new era. This did not happen out of ignorance. The French were very much aware of the existence of Enigma and, according to Givierge, in 1927, the year after an Enigma machine was adopted by the German navy and the year before the German army followed suit, looked at commercial machines before authorizing their own prototype. But the French Enigma was destined to be stillborn—for several reasons. The first was that French intelligence lacked the technical expertise to develop it. A prototype machine was created by the army ordnance section after both the signals and the artillery technicians declined to do it because they were "overwhelmed with work." But the machine was cumbersome and it was apparent that the designer and the cryptographers "did not share the same conceptions." But Givierge also confessed that when an engineer in the Ministry of Posts and Telecommunications also produced an automatic enciphering system, he "got nowhere." And even if no one strong or energetic enough existed to draw together the technical resources of the French government, why did they not adapt one of the commercial models as did the Germans?

The lack of technical expertise does not appear to have been a problem for the French, although one may well ask if a French military intelligence dominated by conservative soldiers would have reached beyond its milieu to recruit qualified personnel among university professors, as did the Poles and eventually the British. They might have done so had there been a sufficient threat. But the demobilization of the German army after 1919, temporarily at least, had removed any sense of urgency. Therefore, the real problem with adapting Enigma to the French army, in Givierge's view, was less technical than financial and political. A more sophisticated system required a specialized organization in the hands of "well-trained personnel" which France did not possess and was unlikely to acquire unless prepared to reach out beyond the narrow circles of the army and the police. Indeed, when the army did develop an automatic encoding system based on perforated paper, it was dropped because it would require a specialized corps of trained cryptographers.[61]

The second area vital to the Enigma solution and one in which the French were singularly deficient was that of humint. While French counterintelligence complained that the Germans were inundating France with agents by the late 1930s, French intelligence was less successful in infiltrating its main enemy. A 1935 report complained that strict surveillance and draconian penalties meant that "the number of good agents which existed in 1932 is melting away before our eyes [through arrests]" and were not being replaced by the recruitment of new ones. As a result, "we no longer receive any truly important intelligence . . . only fragmentary reports which are often imprecise." It concluded that unless French intelligence got the cooperation of the Berlin embassy both in recruiting agents and in passing back their reports through diplomatic pouch protected from German border police or mail censorship, then French knowledge of German plans would be compromised.[62]

The Germans had every reason to be satisfied with the success of their counterintelligence efforts—almost. During the chaos of the Fall of France in May–June 1940, they seized a trainload of documents which the French command had tried to evacuate to the south. With characteristic thoroughness but without haste, the victors set about establishing an inventory of this intelligence treasure trove, a task which took almost a year and a half. When in early 1942 they began at last to examine their contents, they discovered a list of French agents in Germany, with the sums they had been paid for their information written next to their names. The small amounts of cash doled out proved either that French intelligence were poor paymasters or that the information supplied by their agents was not worth much. But these conclusions were immediately rejected when the Germans spied the large sums of money entered beside the name of one of these agents listed simply as "He."[63]

The role played by the Poles in cracking the German Enigma codes is by now well known. What is less often appreciated is that French intelligence played midwife to that success. Hans-Thilo Schmidt's association with French intelligence began in the summer of 1931, when a letter arrived at SR offices on Paris' Left Bank offering to sell them important documents. The task of contacting this potential spy was assigned to Rudolphe Lemoine, code-named Rex. When Lemoine, a naturalized French citizen of German extraction, met Schmidt on November 1 in a hotel in a small town in eastern Belgium, he discovered a man forty-four years old, a veteran of World War I, who had been trained in chemistry. After the war, Schmidt had opened a soap factory, which failed, forcing him to look for employment. With the help of his brother, one of the Reichswehr's promising young officers, he secured in 1926 a position in the Cipher Bureau (Chiffrierstelle), in the section responsible for compiling and distributing field codes and supervising their destruction when they had expired. But Schmidt remained bitter—he considered his position insufficiently grand for a man of his standing (his mother was a baroness, his father a university professor) and education. His pay was so poor that, to make ends meet, he had been forced to send his family to the country while he remained in the city in a small furnished room. His poverty was matched only by his envy of his brother, who continued his rapid ascent in the army hierarchy. Poverty and envy furnished perfect motives for betrayal. The requirement that Schmidt travel frequently to take codes to the military districts offered the perfect cover for his absences to meet his French contacts.

Rex reported his interview to Captain Gustave Bertrand, founder and head of the SR's D (Deciphering) Section. Bertrand realized that in Schmidt he might have discovered the means to shift his codebreaking program off dead center. As a young private in World War I, Bertrand had been wounded in the Dardenelles campaign of 1915, and subsequently assigned to the cipher section of the French army

in the eastern Mediterranean. The work attracted him, and he remained in the army after the war, slowly climbing to the rank of
captain through assignment to the cipher sections of various staffs. His
service's lack of success against mechanical ciphers served to encourage
Bertrand to experiment with methods less traditionally associated with
cerebral cryptanalysts, like stealing.

When on 8 November 1931 Bertrand returned with Rex to meet
Schmidt at the same hotel in eastern Belgium, the spy turned over
documents which included instructions for use of the Enigma machine
and directions for setting the keys. Bertrand offered Schmidt, assigned
the code name "He" (which French pronunciation eventually transformed to Asché), the princely sum of 10,000 marks, photographed
the documents, and took the train back to Paris. Schmidt, delighted
by his lucrative sideline, agreed to continue as a French agent.

Unfortunately, the documents which Bertrand brought home with
such high hopes did not prove very useful, at least not to French
intelligence. It did no good to hold the directions to the working of a
machine which one did not possess. After showing the documents to
the British, who were equally baffled, Bertrand passed them on to
Polish intelligence. It proved to be an inspired decision. Since 1929,
the Poles had devoted considerable energy to the study of Enigma.
Aided by a team of university mathematicians, Polish intelligence had
been attempting to modify a commercial Enigma into the more complex German military version. Schmidt's manuals, which explained
the key settings, provided the missing information which allowed the
Polish cryptanalyst Marian Rejewski to come up with at least a partial
solution to the wiring of the three rotors. But this did not happen
immediately, basically because the head of Polish intelligence withheld
these documents for some weeks from Rejewski, possibly because he
wanted to see if Rejewski could work out the solution without French
assistance. Only in December 1932, a year after they had been handed
over by Schmidt, was Rejewski given the Enigma manuals, which
allowed him to supply the solution within the month.

But this breakthrough, as important as it was, did not offer a permanent solution to Enigma. The Germans continued to modify their
machines, adding alphabet rings, interchangeable rotors, and new
plugboards which gave Enigma the capacity to produce 10.5 quadril-

lion permutations. The remarkable capacity of the Poles to produce these modified versions of Enigma and to solve their codes has been recounted elsewhere.[64] What is important to note is that, without the assistance of Schmidt's key settings, which he supplied to Bertrand on no fewer than seventeen occasions between October 1932 and August 1938, the Polish achievement might have been consigned to failure. As it was, it came perilously close to collapse in December 1938, when the Germans put two additional rotors into service. Schmidt, transferred from the Cipher Bureau in September 1938, no longer had access to the key settings. The Poles were unable to read German messages. It was clearly only a matter of time before war broke out. The only way out of the impasse was for Polish intelligence to call on the assistance of the British and French.

On 24 July 1939, representatives of British and French intelligence services, including Bertrand, arrived in Warsaw in answer to a summons by Major Gwido Langer, who headed the Polish cryptological section. There they were taken to the cryptological center at Pyry near Warsaw and ushered into Langer's office, where replicas of German Enigma machines constructed by the Poles were displayed. They were also shown the *bomby*, primitive computers used to exhaust the permutations more rapidly. Langer explained that, since the introduction of the additional rotors in December 1938, the Polish ability to read German traffic had come to an end. It was time to call upon the more extensive resources of French and British intelligence. Each of the representatives was given a machine to take home, the British to Bletchley Park, the French to PC Bruno, the code name for their cipher section situated at Gretz a short distance northeast of Paris.

SEVEN

INTELLIGENCE AND
THE FALL OF FRANCE

In theory, Hitler's attack on Poland should have simplified immensely the task of French intelligence. War was no longer a matter of conjecture. The only problem that remained was to predict the time and place of the German attack. Ultimately the inability of French intelligence to do precisely that must count, along with the absence of guidance on the Schlieffen Plan of 1914, as one of its historic failures. Yet even a cursory examination of the Allied situation between the fall of Poland in September 1939 and the German offensive in the West launched on 10 May 1940 reveals the pitfalls and uncertainties faced by the Deuxième Bureau in its attempts to predict the actions of the enemy.

The task of gathering and digesting intelligence, difficult in the best of times, was made more complicated by Gamelin's decision to decentralize his command. The commander-in-chief settled into the gloomy fortress of Vincennes in the eastern suburbs of Paris, while his chief of staff, General André Joseph Doumenc, set up shop at GQG (Grand Quartier Général) at Montry, some fifteen or so miles away. General Alphonse Georges, who commanded the French armies in the north, was dispatched to La Ferté, thirty-five miles east of Paris, but chose to spend much of his time at Bondon, twelve miles from La Ferté. The central command of the French armies, therefore, was actually splintered into four different geographical locations, five if one included the War Ministry on the Left Bank in central Paris. Communications between the various command posts were primitive, and assured in the main by goggled motorcycle dispatch riders who crisscrossed the French countryside with orders, reports, papers, and documents to be signed in their satchels.[1]

Curiously, Gamelin argued that this fragmented command actually made his intelligence services more efficient: All elements concerned with the German army went with Georges to La Ferté while "with the rest, we made up a true Deuxième Bureau of National Defense which I had never been able to organize until then."[2] Unfortunately, many intelligence officers failed to see the gains. The organization, which on a wartime footing was supposed to transform the Deuxième Bureau into a Cinquième Bureau incorporating an administrative section, the SR, and a Section d'Examen to centralize and evaluate intelligence from various sources, fell only slowly into place. Gamelin split the intelligence staff, ordering half to Vincennes with him while the other half remained in the War Ministry close to Prime Minister and War Minister Edouard Daladier. "Yanked between the commander-in-chief and the Minister of National Defense," Paillole complained, "our service does not know to which saint to pray."[3] In October 1939, Daladier ordered the Cinquième Bureau to be attached to the staff of army chief of staff, General L. A. Coulson, whose position both duplicated and in some ways undermined that of Gamelin's chief of staff, General Doumenc.

According to André Beaufre, one of the two officers responsible for coordinating intelligence at Montry, GQG was both upset and disorganized by this new arrangement. He was forced to cope with a daily avalanche of mail, in which routine administrative matters were mixed with urgent and important intelligence. These harassed staff officers sought to determine which information was important enough to bring to the general's attention, a task made more complicated as one of them accompanied Doumenc each time he left his office on a visit, which was frequently. By May 1940, only one intelligence officer remained at the GQG. Beaufre sat next to the teletype, which spewed out information from Belgium, some of it so contradictory and confusing that he nicknamed it the "fiction flood."[4]

The intelligence services now had two separate headquarters, one with Coulson and the other with Georges. A third section was dispatched to North Africa. The situation was even more confused for the German army specialists who were assigned to Georges. Sprinkled over northern France, their locations, rather like the remainder of Georges' headquarters, were determined by the availability of vacant châteaux rather than by any rational plan of command centralization.

Most of the Cinquième Bureau was located in the Château Pereire near Gretz, about twenty-five miles northeast of Paris, and took on the name P[ost] C[commandement] Victor. The cryptographers of the *section du chiffre* were housed in the Château de Vignobles, not far from Victor, called PC Bruno. However, most general staff cryptanalysts stayed behind in Paris " 'to assure the decoding of telegrams requiring rather long study,' which never happened," according to Gustave Bertrand, who commanded the *section du chiffre*.[5]

Much of the intelligence apparatus coagulated around Georges. But it was the distant and isolated Gamelin who retained the ultimate power of decision.[6] Gauché remained near Gamelin at Vincennes, while his deputy, Major Baril, stayed with Georges. Each morning a liaison officer set off from Paris to La Ferté, returning late at night with intelligence reports for Gauché to approve before they could be distributed. Conferences called to sort out disagreements meant that the intelligence commanders lost valuable hours on the road. In periods of crisis, such as during the many alerts which troubled the tranquillity of the Phony War, or during the Norwegian invasion when the Cinquième Bureau was inundated with information, it was simply more difficult to meet and agree on what intelligence was valid and what was to be rejected, or to settle bitter disputes like those over how many tanks the Germans actually had on the Western Front.[7] This system, barely adequate for a static front, was to be put under serious strain by the demands of a war of movement.[8]

And there were other problems. Upon mobilization, the intelligence service was flooded with reservists. Some were extremely useful, like the expert cryptanalysts recruited from among Polish and Spanish refugees. One of these refugees was Marian Rejewski. During his escape from Poland, Rejewski had actually presented himself at the British embassy at Bucharest. But unable to find a British diplomat with time to deal with him, he offered his services to the French, who placed him with fourteen other Polish cryptanalysts at Bruno as "Equipe Z." But for every Rejewski there were dozens of inexperienced reservists who proved more trouble than they were worth, for it was generally reckoned that an intelligence officer needed at least a year to learn his job. Some of the most seasoned men clamored for assignment to combat units, where the work promised to be more glorious and better rewarded.[9] This left intelligence services understaffed and underexperienced, especially as they had to take on extra duties like postal and telephone control which reduced effectiveness. Conflicts, rivalries, and delays resulted and inevitably lowered morale.[10] British general Kenneth Strong noted on a visit to the Cinquième Bureau that he was initially impressed, but soon detected that it was understaffed and demoralized.[11]

The Cinquième Bureau had every reason to feel depressed. Much of the intelligence had dried up with the declaration of hostilities. Agents in Germany had no radios and were forced to communicate, when they could communicate, through mail drops.[12] Hans-Thilo Schmidt, the major French agent in Germany, communicated only infrequently, although his information was accorded prime importance by Rivet.[13] Other sources like POWs which had proved so valuable in the Great War were not available. German domination of the air made air reconnaissance difficult. The Germans had become used to working in secret, which made their plans difficult to penetrate. Hitler kept his own counsel, took decisions with little notice, often gave verbal orders. German radios were liable to fall silent at critical moments, making their units difficult to track. The French set up listening posts in Luxembourg, but the neutral Belgian government refused to allow posts to be established on their territory. Bertrand complained that Luftwaffe traffic was most often intercepted, along with weather reports, and the results were *"faibles."*[14] At PC Bruno, the French, with the help of the Poles and the collaboration of Bletchley Park, made great strides in cryptanalysis. But only on 17 January 1940 did the Poles at Bruno break the first Enigma key of the war. As Allied cryptanalysts gained familiarity with German methods, fully fifty Enigma keys surrendered their secrets. But because of Bruno's inferior resources 83 percent of the honors went to Bletchley.[15] This code breaking might have been of enormous value to the Allies had the Germans not brought in another modification of the indicator system for all army keys on 1 May, which defied the best efforts of the code breakers to crack it for a crucial three weeks.[16]

How important a factor did the fragmentation of the intelligence services become in France's ultimate failure to stop Hitler in 1940? French intelligence veterans have argued that fragmentation was fairly critical; it prevented intelligence from speaking with a common voice and allowed preconceptions, fears, and wishful thinking to substitute for a reasoned study of the facts. This was especially the case in the early autumn of 1939, when the French high command lacked a common view on Hitler's next move or on what the Allies should do about it. Why this was so should come as no surprise. Even as the ruins of Warsaw still smoldered, Hitler and the German high command split over what their next step should be. The Führer was eager to turn his forces West, before the Allies could solidify their defenses, while army chiefs insisted that their forces were badly beat up from the Polish campaign and needed time to rest, retrain, and refit.

Quite naturally, intelligence funneled through the Deuxième Bureau to the high command reflected the enemy's confusion. This made interpretation of intelligence subject to a high degree of wishful thinking, or encouraged commanders to select out of reports intelligence which confirmed their preconceptions. The contentions of Gauché, Rivet, and Paillole to the contrary, one might suspect also that intelligence officers remained true to human nature and slanted intelligence in ways most congenial to command preconceptions. As Martin Alexander has pointed out, Allied commanders were hardly in a state of mind to consider intelligence reports dispassionately; they both feared an early offensive and were alarmed at the prospect of a prolonged stalemate.[17]

Gamelin's reaction to intelligence reports was filtered through a prism of fear—his reactions were based on his reading of Hitler's intentions and French capabilities. An early attack threatened to fall on troops who were far from battle-hardened, whose tanks and planes had yet to come on-line, who were not yet formed into armored divisions and drilled in the intricacies of modern mobile operations.[18] Both Gamelin and Georges, as well as the British command, realized that Hitler's best hope of derailing France's long-war strategy was to preempt it before the Allies' armies were operationally prepared. Consequently, the French generals interpreted intelligence reports which traced the progressive transfer of units from the East to the West, and an order of 9 October in which Hitler instructed the Wehrmacht command to recapture immediately German territory lost to the French in September, as indications of an early offensive. As a consequence, French forces were placed on full alert by commanders who expected an attack on 15 October, when the German command had not even drawn up a plan for an attack in the West. A second alert occurred in mid-November, stimulated by increased German wireless activity, a decoded telegram revealing a meeting of German security officers about achieving "a decision in the West," and rumors that Dutch currency and phrase books were being issued to German troops.[19]

Intelligence to the contrary was not necessarily a comfort. At best, rumors that Hitler might not attack could be the prelude to a treacherous peace offer from Hitler which, like Munich, would simply be a case of *reculer pour mieux sauter* (to step back in order to jump further forward). At worst, they might simply be disinformation designed to lull the Allies into a false sense of security.

Gauché and SR chief Rivet maintained that Hitler would not attack before winter's end. Their certainty was not based on Hitler's intentions, but on their reading of German capabilities. Information, much of it supplied by Asché (Schmidt), which reached the Deuxième Bureau in September and October, suggested that the panzer divisions needed time to refit and were not in a position to attack and that the Luftwaffe was allowing large numbers of pilots and airmen to go on leave.[20] Gamelin listened to these reports, but was not predisposed to believe them, in part because they took no account of Hitler's aggressive intentions, which, Gamelin believed, could not remain long in abeyance.[21] But more important, the French commander-in-chief was keen to implement a preemptive plan of his own. Rumors of an imminent German thrust into Belgium in mid-November allowed Gamelin to override objections in his command and impose a plan to rush French troops into Belgium on the outbreak of hostilities. Therefore, intelligence reports which predicted a quiet winter were at cross-purposes with Gamelin's strategic vision and undermined his ability to achieve it.

Because Gamelin and Georges were disinclined to place great faith in the evaluations of their intelligence chiefs, they sought solace in other intelligence sources which resurfaced with a vengeance. Already a political general par excellence, Gamelin chose to remain in Paris, where "noise"—rumor and false reports, of which there was much in wartime Paris—crowded out good intelligence. Paillole attributed the belief that information obtained through informal sources was superior to official intelligence to "the pride . . . of the military leaders."[22] German "intoxication," political and diplomatic gossip, attaché reports which reached Gamelin and were read by him before they were sent to the Cinquième Bureau were in part responsible for that great plague of the Phony War—frequent alerts. Navarre complained that of the dozen or so alerts which brought French forces to a trembling state of readiness between September 1939 and 10 May 1940, only four or five had been the result of a warning by the SR.[23] The mid-October alert was encouraged by the 9 October Führer directive which reached the French through the Dutch attaché, a link in the friendship which had been established since 1932 between Colonel Hans Oster, deputy of Abwehr chief Admiral Wilhelm Canaris and a fervent anti-Nazi, and the Dutch military attaché in Berlin, Major Sas.

Much has been written on the debilitating effects of the period of *la drôle de guerre* on the combat readiness of the French army. French soldiers endured nine morale-sapping months, constantly on a war footing when there was no fighting, frequently ordered to combat stations during one of the winter's numerous alerts only to find that it was *pour rien*. Sitzkrieg it may have been, but it proved to be a period filled with agitated inactivity. From an intelligence perspective, alerts which are followed by deafening idleness in the enemy trenches incline commanders to dismiss intelligence reports as alarmist and ultimately inaccurate, even though they may have been correct and the enemy simply changed his mind. Such false alerts played an important role in the inability of the French to react to reports of a planned German thrust through the Ardennes.

Nor did the winter of 1939–40 favor a detached assessment of the enemy of the sort that French intelligence might have provided—for several reasons. One was that the period of inactivity had lulled the French into a false sense of security. A common conclusion over the winter was that Hitler hesitated to attack in the West because "the mouthful is too large." While Gauché claimed that the Deuxième Bureau's thorough study of the Polish campaign submitted in October 1939 underlined the "menace" faced by the French army, which was short of antitank and antiaircraft weapons, combat aircraft, and independent tank divisions, this conclusion did not necessarily follow from the evidence presented. Essentially, the report explained how 12 active Polish divisions together with some half-mobilized reserve divisions had been submerged by 70 enemy divisions superior in matériel and able to surge through gaps in the front which the small Polish army was unable to defend. The Luftwaffe, with unchallenged mastery of the skies, was able to pound the Polish high command into paralysis.[24] It was perfectly logical to conclude that such tactics would not work against a Western Front with a much more dense force/space ratio, whose defenses were organized in depth, and which offered no inviting corridors of advance as had Poland.[25]

"The example of Poland did not seem to apply to ourselves with our greater density of troops reinforced by the Maginot Line," Beaufre admitted. "In spite of the study which I had made at Marrakesh of the possibility of armored thrusts, I too fell into this erroneous way of thinking, which shows just how much one's judgment can be affected by one's surroundings."[26] While neither Gamelin nor Georges believed that the Germans would fail to attack, strategically nothing in the Polish experience challenged the wisdom of the basic French strategy, which was to contain the initial German offensive through the Low Countries, stabilize the front, and allow the tide of war gradually to shift against Berlin.[27]

A second consequence of the static front in the West was that it encouraged a flirtation with peripheral operations. The Nazi-Soviet pact and the Soviet invasion of Finland resulted in the most incredible schemes being hatched by the high command for intervention in Finland and attacks on the Baku oil fields, as if it were in the interests of the Allies to add the Soviet Union to a list of enemies which already included Hitler and probably Mussolini.

Stehlin was puce with rage when he returned from an extremely dangerous mission to Hamburg in January 1940, with a detailed report on German air tactics in Poland, only to find that in his absence fighting communists in Finland had replaced Hitler as the major concern.[28] And no sooner had the Finns surrendered than Norway became a focus of attention for Gamelin and Georges, which Paillole believed distracted them from the serious nature of the threat in the West during the spring of 1940.[29] Gamelin admitted that he was preoccupied with Norway because he thought this would delay the start of the German offensive—a conclusion which the small number of German troops actually absorbed by that campaign should have caused to be dismissed out of hand[30]—and that this had taken much valuable time away from preparation for the attack in the West. In early May, on the eve of the attack, he was absorbed in pondering Italian activity in the Mediterranean.[31] So concentration on peripheral conflicts diminished the importance of the primary threat in the minds of the principal commanders.

All of which meant that they failed to focus on the second part of the intelligence task: to determine where the Germans would attack. By concentrating on their own plans, the Allied commanders neglected to think deeply enough about those of the Germans. In their minds, the Dyle Plan—the forward Allied advance into the Low Countries to begin as soon as Germany had violated Belgian neutrality—would buy them the time they needed to defeat Germany at leisure. The logic of this plan, at least in the mind of Gamelin, was impeccable. It would reduce the length of the front by about fifty miles, which, in theory, would provide more troops for the central reserve. It would shift the battlefield away from the industrial areas of northern France and increase the depth of antiaircraft defense. It would bring substantial numbers of Belgian and Dutch divisions into the Allied camp and provide a springboard for eventual offensive operations against Germany. It would appeal to the British by rescuing vast stretches of North Sea coastline from enemy occupation and help to shelter Britain from strategic bombing. The Dyle Plan was motivated by concerns traditional in France since 1918: save French blood, bring in allies against a stronger foe, and avoid the occupation and destruction of French territory.

But despite these advantages, the Dyle Plan also bore great risks.

Several generals, including Georges, opposed it because it pushed French forces too far forward into Belgium, virtually inviting the Germans to cut them off by a thrust through the Ardennes.

While the Deuxième Bureau cannot be blamed for Gamelin's bad judgment, it can hardly claim that it tried to dissuade the commander-in-chief by pointing out some of the plan's weaknesses, notably the poor state of Belgium's defenses, on which it relied for its early success. Paul Paillole remembered that French intelligence was well informed about the Belgian defenses, and Gamelin should have taken note of their reservations.[32] One French author, Michel Garder, is less categorical, asserting that French intelligence possessed "rather vague" information on the actual state of the Belgian defenses which were to delay the German offensive into Belgium and so give Gamelin time to advance his forces into position. Nor was anyone certain of Dutch and Belgian plans to coordinate operations with the French and British.[33] Martin Alexander insists that "the encouraging assessments of Belgian efforts to reinforce their own military security," notably the construction of defensive fortifications such as the multimillion-franc Eben Emael near Liège (which in May 1940 was neutralized by seventy-seven German glider troops in the space of a day), provided a strong argument in favor of the Dyle Plan.[34]

The Dyle Plan had a second unfortunate impact. A defensive strategy such as that chosen by the Allies required sound intelligence. Without a knowledge of where the German blow was likely to fall, then the army on the defensive would not know how to react. The Dyle Plan, however, preempted a flexible response by the Allies and circumscribed their ability to react to the unexpected. Gamelin's mistake was to preordain an offensive plan as part of a defensive strategy, thus creating a need to disregard the intentions of the enemy.

That Gamelin was more intent on putting his plan into effect than in anticipating German moves was forcefully demonstrated by what came to be called the "Mechelen Incident." When a German light plane piloted by Major Erich Hoenmanns made a forced landing in still-neutral Belgium in January 1940 after being lost in the fog, the Belgian police placed Hoenmanns and his passenger, a career officer named Reinberger, in a room while they left to seek instructions. They returned to find Reinberger thrusting pieces of paper into the stove. The

Belgians were able to salvage enough of the charred remains to discover that the staff officer had been trying to destroy a copy of the German plan of attack through the central Belgian plain to the North Sea. On 11 January 1940, Belgian general Raoul François Casimir van Overstraeten conveyed to the British and French attachés the general contents of the documents in a two-page summary without revealing their source, and urged that Gamelin be notified, which he was on the following day. This breach of security convinced Hitler that the Allies would now expect what was in its essential elements a repetition of the Schlieffen Plan. On 24 February 1940, he switched to the risky option of breaking the French lines in the Ardennes and then pushing his armored columns toward the Channel coast, cutting behind the Allied troops advancing into Belgium, a plan which General Erich von Manstein had been elaborating since November 1939. From that moment, the Dyle Plan became a trap.

That Gamelin did not reconsider his strategic options in the light of the Mechelen Incident is all the more surprising in that he could hardly claim in retrospect that the Ardennes plan was the most originally fiendish invention devised by the Teutonic mind since the horned helmet. The Maginot Line Commission and Marshal Pétain had foreseen that avenue of attack during its deliberations in the early 1930s, and recommended that a strategic reserve be stationed near Sedan to cut off such a move. Likewise, the French had war-gamed an Ardennes thrust in 1938, and concluded that, with proper precautions, it could be easily "pinched off."[35] Gamelin, however, appears to have been concerned, even obsessed, with taking the battle into Belgium. As a result, he was insensitive to intelligence reports, many of them coming from Belgium but also from Paillole and the French attaché in Bern, predicting a German attack in the Ardennes. The Belgians complained that their warnings were received with cool disinterest at Gamelin's headquarters. The problem with these charges, as with any failed intelligence, such as Pearl Harbor, is that it is far easier to see the truth in hindsight than from the perspective of intelligence officers forced to deal with a veritable flood of information. "Nevertheless," writes British historian Brian Bond, even with this caveat, "the indictment against Gamelin is damning: not merely was he mistaken about German intentions but he appears to have been unwilling even to consider the possibility of an armored thrust through the Ardennes."[36]

The spectacular success of the German offensive caused contemporaries and historians alike to conclude that the French army must have been "rotten" and incapable of defending itself. Yet a more balanced consideration leads inescapably to the conclusion that, despite its devastating finality, the German victory was potentially a close-run thing. The German success hinged initially on their ability to bring their best troops against the French army's B divisions, stationed in what Gamelin had anticipated would prove a quiet sector. The crack Allied divisions, including the bulk of their tank units, dashed off into Belgium to defend against what amounted to a German feint.

It might be tempting to attribute the Fall of France to the success of German intelligence. Wilhelm Flicke claimed that German intelligence was able to build up a complete picture of the French front through air reconnaissance, espionage, and cryptanalysis. Because of the poor security of French radio communications, including War Ministry cryptograms, "no movement and no dislocation remained concealed from the Germans. The French Air Force was most incautious in its use of radio and the ground stations gave countless clues. The picture was the same as that observed during French maneuvers from 1930 to 1939."[37] Once the breakthrough occurred, German intelligence could assure the panzer divisions racing westward that their vulnerable flank was under no threat of counterattack by French reserves. But as David Kahn has pointed out, German plans were drawn up without benefit of intelligence evaluations, which in any case were limited to locating French units on a map without predicting what the French might do. Hitler "intended to impose his will on other countries," Kahn writes. "For this he needed no intelligence. He concentrated on what he did need: men, guns, tanks, planes, fuel."[38]

From the French viewpoint, intelligence on the German moves, properly gathered and analyzed, might have made the difference, at least snatching a stalemate from the jaws of ignominious defeat. Did they supply intelligence which might have offered potential salvation for French arms? Unfortunately, the answer must be no, although not a resounding no. Paul Paillole claims to have obtained the most promising indication of German intentions when in April he received one of his double agents, a Polish ex-priest named Paul Schlokoff, who told him that he had been ordered by the Abwehr to reconnoiter the roads and bridges between the Ardennes and the mouth of the Somme. "What should I do?" he asked Captain Paillole. Paillole urged Schlokoff to carry out his orders, while he took the information to Gamelin, only to find that the commander-in-chief was in England planning the expedition to Norway. Paillole was then directed to General Georges. Paillole made his case to Georges and Colonel Navereau, Georges' chief of operations. While the three men studied a map, Navereau explained that this contradicted information which predicted an attack farther north. Paillole was thanked for his information, and left.[39] When the final intelligence briefing was given around 5 May, Major Baril, head of the Deuxième Bureau Northeast, would only say that no attack was likely through Switzerland or against the Maginot Line.[40]

Why were preparations for the German attack through the Ardennes not detected? While Gamelin insisted that he always kept an open mind about the prospect of a German offensive through the Ardennes,[41] other factors gradually edged that possibility from consideration. Perhaps the primary one was that French intelligence estimates of the German order of battle did not support the hypothesis of an advance through the Ardennes. On the contrary, the Deuxième Bureau overestimated the number of divisions opposite the Dutch frontier (37 divisions when there were only 29), while it desperately underestimated the number opposite Luxembourg (put at 26 when in reality there were 45). Gauché defended his services, explaining that, in the absence of other intelligence sources such as POW interrogations, the axis of German attack was impossible to predict based merely on a knowledge of the area of German troop concentrations. Perhaps, but intelligence briefings appear to have offered nothing more precise than the miscellany of information contained in the bulletins, vague pronouncements "cloaked in enough imprecision—even contradictions—so that later one can always pretend to have been correct, whatever happens," wrote one observer of 1940. "We will never know the force with which those who believed in an Ardennes offensive put their arguments."[42]

Nor was French intelligence aided as in World War I by air reconnaissance. By 1939, owing to a lack of forward planning and production difficulties, the French air force had well and truly surrendered its superiority to the young Luftwaffe. French air reconnaissance was the most disadvantaged section of an already disadvantaged air force. Although its 14 air groups in September 1939 expanded to 35 at the front by May 1940, many of its pilots had been declared qualified after only a few flights around airfields and without practice in firing or maneuvers with fighters. They were also equipped with a motley of dated aircraft, the most advanced being the Potez 63-11. However, even before the German Bf 109E swept the Potez from the sky above the Western Front in 1940, air reconnaissance over German positions proved a hazardous undertaking. In November 1939, the air force commander-in-chief had retired the vulnerable Bloch 131s from the front and restricted the Potez 63-11s to eleven-kilometer penetrations of enemy territory to conserve his forces for the coming battle. When that great battle came, however, air reconnaissance forces fell in with Gamelin's plans rather than supplying information that might have shown them to be defective.

Although intelligence warnings had placed the French air force on alert on 8 May, air reconnaissance on 9–10 May failed to detect evidence of German offensive preparations anywhere on the front. This was because, during the winter, the Germans had perfected the technique of moving their forces to the starting line in short increments so that an attack could be launched without a series of preliminary movements which would betray it. Once the Dyle Plan went into effect, almost all of France's limited reconnaissance aircraft flew above the First Army slashing into Belgium, leaving the Ninth and Second armies in the Ardennes largely sightless. A veritable slaughter resulted when, on 14 May, General Georges attempted to shift French air resources against the German bridgehead on the Meuse. By 17 May intelligence confirmed that the Germans were heading toward the Channel rather than swinging behind the Maginot Line or toward Paris, and the French air force had virtually ceased to operate as an effective force.[43]

As in the Michael offensives of 1918, the Germans succeeded in blinding French intelligence. "For the Deuxième Bureau to have known the disposition and have an idea of the enemy maneuver would have required an operations order and the adjoining campaign map," Gauché wrote.[44] Agent information, of the sort supplied by Paillole or Paul Thummel, originally a Czech agent passed on to the Allies, who gave a warning through The Hague on 1 May that the German attack was scheduled for 10 May, was lost among many other reports. Many of these were planted by the Germans, and reports predicting attacks elsewhere began to arrive with great frequency from early May.[45] Nor did the humint carry the force of conviction, because agents were considered less reliable than other "objective" forms of intelligence. Navarre believed that no matter how good the intelligence brought in by counterintelligence, the subsection of military intelligence lacked the prestige to have their views given the weight of reasonable doubt.[46]

But the real virtue of the Germans' camouflaging their intentions was that it allowed the French command's preconceptions to remain unchallenged. The most entrenched of these preconceptions was that the Ardennes made a poor corridor of attack. None of the four main possibilities of attack drawn up by Allied intelligence included this option. The British, who were concerned with the Channel coast, and who despite their unfortunate experience in 1914 continued to defer to the French as the experts in matters of German invasion, had no strong opinions on this matter. French operations officers were victims of "mirror imaging"—that is, they would never have attempted such an operation through these wooded hills and so assumed that their enemies would behave as they would.

In the final analysis, if French intelligence proved unable to save France in 1940, it was hardly because they were Cassandras pitted against the *force d'inertie* of the high command.[47] Nor were they howling in a bureaucratic wilderness, cries destined to be silenced by the more authoritative and prestigious opinions of the Troisième Bureau. On the contrary, French intelligence tended to support particular policies and strategies rather than challenge them.[48] This is not to say that they were bad or ineffective. French intelligence was far better than that of the Germans, and, with the exception of cryptanalysis, as good as that of the British in this early stage of the war.

In the final analysis, 1940 offered a repeat of 1914, when Gamelin, like Joffre demoralized by intelligence reports of overwhelming German power, set in motion a strategy anchored in the wishful thinking that a dramatic advance into Belgium and Holland would unhinge the German war plan.

EIGHT

THE BCRA

On the morning of 27 December 1942, Paul Paillole felt like a new man, rested, well received in the homes of high officials of British intelligence, above all with a new suit and complete change of underwear, things virtually unobtainable in wartime France. The nightmare of his almost monthlong journey through southern France, avoiding both French and German police, to find the Spanish *passeur* who guided him through the Pyrenees and put him on the road to Barcelona, was fast receding into distant memory. After what had seemed an almost deliberately prolonged wait at Gibraltar for a space in the belly of a British bomber, Paillole and Colonel Georges Ronin, chief of the SR Air, whom he met in Gibraltar, had arrived in London. Now both men were ushered into the office of the head of the Free French intelligence service, the Bureau Central de Renseignements et d'Action (BCRA).

That this meeting could only take place in 1942, and in conditions of considerable suspicion and mistrust on both sides, was a consequence of the Fall of France in June 1940. The armistice signed between Germany and France permitted the German occupation and administration of northern France, including Paris. However, much of the south was designated as a *zone libre*, or free zone, to be controlled by a French government which set up its "capital" in the spa town of

Vichy. The Vichy government, under the venerable Marshal Philippe Pétain, hero of Verdun, was allowed to maintain an army of 100,000 men, retain its navy and the French colonies, and its intelligence services.

While the vast majority of the French people accepted this solution as a distasteful but unavoidable consequence of defeat, at least temporarily, a small handful of men led by Charles de Gaulle denounced the arrangement as shameful and vowed to fight on from London. This Gaullist or Free French movement, small at first, began to grow as the German attack on the Soviet Union in 1941 pushed a significant number of French communists into active opposition, where they joined other groups and individuals which a combination of German repression, including forced labor, and a desire to join the Allied side had sparked into a growing Resistance.

The rise of a Resistance to the Germans was to create a veritable *crise de conscience* for intelligence officers loyal to Vichy. De Gaulle's Free French movement had established an intelligence service, which after several name changes became the BCRA, both to supply intelligence to the British on developments in France and to coordinate these emerging movements into a coherent Resistance loyal to de Gaulle. As servants of the official government in Vichy, Paillole and Ronin found themselves in a delicate situation. Vichy had declared de Gaulle an outlaw, sentenced him to death in absentia, and denounced the Resistance as a threat to French security. At the same time, the Resistance was organizing against the Germans, the enemies of France, whom Paillole and Ronin also opposed. Thus, for almost two and a half years, Vichy intelligence had faced a moral dilemma which they, like the entire government, increasingly had been unable to resolve: their duty to oppose the Germans, albeit discreetly, against that of fighting the growth of the Resistance and the encroachment of the BCRA in France.

However, in November 1942, the losing battle fought by Vichy intelligence became a defeat when Anglo-American armies invaded French North Africa. In response, the Germans occupied the *zone libre*, disbanded the "Armistice Army," and forbade Vichy to maintain intelligence services. The Vichy Prime Minister, Pierre Laval, declared, "I hope for a German victory," and intensified his campaign against the Resistance in the *zone libre*. Now refugees, Paillole and Ronin had made their way to London, where they now threw themselves at the feet of their Free French rival.

Despite the fact that they had fallen on hard times, this was hardly a meeting of equals, at least in the minds of the visitors. For cognoscenti of intelligence, the events of November 1942 had in no way diminished the status of Ronin and Paillole. In a curious way, exile had actually inflated their prestige. In the world of intelligence, these refugees were aristocracy, *seigneurs* of a dynasty in embarrassed circumstances, perhaps, but lords nonetheless. "To be taken into Paillole's service is considered, by all agents, the supreme consecration," exclaimed the young Lieutenant Roger Warin when he was offered a position in one of Paillole's services in 1941.[1]

Paillole and Ronin looked upon the man who sat before them as Bourbons forced to flee the guillotine might have viewed some Bonapartist parvenu. The parallels were uncomfortably similar had anyone in the room cared to draw them. Like those Bonapartists, the title taken by André Dewavrin, chief of the BCRA, was self-conferred. All of these "Resistance" leaders wore their pseudonyms like an ersatz knighthood. Passy, Dewavrin's pseudonym, had been chosen from a list of Paris metro stations, names to disguise the identity of those "Gaullists of the first hour," to protect their families, potential hostages in France, from reprisals. But even this name choice must have caused the visitors to smile, for it offered yet more evidence of the absence of métier in this so-called intelligence service.

In the first place, it was an idea plagiarized from the Cagoulards— literally "men wearing hoods"—an extreme right-wing group, with links to the Corsican mafia, which had challenged the Third Republic in the 1930s. No wonder critics referred to the BCRA as "an aerie of Cagoulards."[2] In the second place, it was dangerous. One always adopted a pseudonym which began with the same letter of one's true surname, to match the laundry marks on one's clothes. If he intended to poach intellectual property, why had Dewavrin not chosen Dauphine, or Dugommier, or, better yet, Denfert, a name which recalled the heroic resistance of Belfort, a rock which had temporarily parted an earlier flood tide of French defeat in 1870? It was a subtle touch perhaps. But then nuance was a mark of breeding in matters of intelligence—a form, a demeanor, a propriety which separated princes of the blood from mere pretenders.

At first glance, Passy appeared totally out of his depth in the presence of Ronin and Paillole. Tall, with thinning blond hair, his face a bare betrayal of his thirty years, he looked like a subaltern who just stepped off the rugger pitch. His soft voice and the refusal of his blue-gray eyes to fix his interlocutors for more than a second before his gaze resumed its voyage about the room suggested an unease spawned by lack of confidence. But anyone who made that assumption soon realized his mistake. Passy possessed the ordered mind of a mathematician, and political skills which had made him one of the most effective bureaucratic infighters in a Free French camp which was a veritable production line of administrative ambushes. Those who knew him better attributed Passy's air of distraction to a state of dreamy absent-mindedness, which, they insisted, was endemic among alumni of France's elite Ecole Polytechnique, of which Passy was one. But for visitors from a Vichy regime which reverenced experience and especially age, Passy's occupation of such a significant office supplied more evidence, if more were required, that Charles de Gaulle had deliberately selected his disciples with an eye for incongruity.

Passy was the first to admit that, like every other charter member of the Free French, he had quite literally wandered in off the street. The war had caused André Dewavrin to exchange his somber uniform of an officer of engineers and his professorship of fortifications at the French military academy of Saint-Cyr for assignment to the "half brigade" of Chasseurs Alpins which, after a hasty marriage to a "half brigade" of the Foreign Legion, was dispatched on the Narvik expedition of April–May 1940. The collapse of the front at Sedan and the recall of the Narvik expedition had left Captain Dewavrin marooned at Trentham Park near Manchester, where, with the rest of the officers, he debated repatriation to France or enlistment with a newly promoted brigadier named de Gaulle. Passy had no strong political opinions, although he had apparently been moved by one of de Gaulle's appeals, which he heard on 25 June. On the debit side, his wife and children remained in France. He debated until the very last minute before dropping out of the group which entrained for Barry Docks and France.

On 1 July 1940 he traveled to London, located St. Stephen's House,

a gray building which brooded over the Embankment near West-
minster Bridge, and, after a wait which seemed indecently brief, was
admitted into the presence of General de Gaulle. In hardly the time
required to present his résumé, Dewavrin had reemerged from de
Gaulle's office with the task of organizing Free France's Second and
Third bureaus! "Nothing had prepared Passy for this unprecedented
mission," de Gaulle remembered, "but I preferred it that way."[3] Over
the weeks that followed, Dewavrin divested himself of responsibility
for operations, and then even handed off leadership of the Deuxième
Bureau, a superfluous organization in a command without troops, to
concentrate on organizing a Gaullist SR, which, after various name
changes, became in August 1942 the BCRA.

"My ignorance was total," Dewavrin confessed in his account of his
debut as de Gaulle's intelligence chief. He was guided in his first steps
by Sir Claude Dansey, the pugnacious assistant chief of the British
SIS, whose career in espionage stretched back to World War I. But
although Dewavrin affectionately refers to Dansey in his postwar memoirs as "Uncle Claude," relations between the novice Gaullist spymasters and their British hosts were often as laced with suspicion and
distrust as those between Free France and Vichy. Dewavrin and his
associates—three lieutenants in their twenties, who had quite by
chance taken rooms in Dewavrin's bed-and-breakfast on the Cromwell
Road, and three NCOs, all reservists, chosen from "the mass of new
faces" which the fortunes of war had cast upon London—began by
selecting their Resistance pseudonyms from a Paris metro map. And
if in the process they betrayed their amateurism, at least, Passy believed,
for some months they enjoyed the dubious distinction of confusing
enemy services, unaware that any intelligence organization capable of
ignoring such rudimentary organizational rules as respect for the alphabet could, in fact, be real.[4]

On the face of it, intelligence should have been de Gaulle's strong
suit. He was a general without troops, a political leader without a
mandate, for whom military intelligence offered virtually his only
potential capital, "a magnificent currency of exchange," Passy believed, in his dealings with his British hosts, who had desperate need
of it. Unfortunately, the Free French were as bereft of knowledge of
the country from which they were now exiled as were the British,

who, in their haste to depart the Continent at Dunkirk, had neglected to leave behind networks of agents, as the Poles and Czechs, with more foresight, had done. For this reason, British support for de Gaulle was limited to political recognition. In matters of intelligence and special operations, SIS and the newly organized Special Operations Executive (SOE), whose mission was, in Churchill's words, to "set Europe ablaze," found it as difficult as did many of de Gaulle's senior entourage to take the enthusiastic youths in the Deuxième Bureau seriously. They preferred to deal with their ex-colleagues who remained loyal to Vichy, with the Free Poles, or even operate on their own. Even within the Free French organization, Passy's mission was undermined by de Gaulle's *chef de cabinet*, who dispatched people to France to locate sympathizers without even informing the Deuxième Bureau.[5] So, for the moment, Passy was like a banker open for business, but whose vaults as yet remained empty of bullion. When in August 1940 the Deuxième Bureau shifted its two tables, one chair, and two benches to a tiny three-room suite in Free France's new headquarters at 4 Carlton Gardens, the officers had yet to receive their pay, much less any funds to carry out missions. "Go see the English," was de Gaulle's response to Passy's pleas for cash.[6]

Passy's ambition was to create "intelligence networks." Passy's men combed the camps and hospitals of southern England to find soldiers or refugees willing to undertake missions into occupied France. The first insertions were very much of the experimental variety. On 17 July, Jacques Mansion was put ashore in Brittany and managed to return by fishing boat in early September with some information on German dispositions. In late July, the British, worried by air reconnaissance photos which showed intense activity on the Normandy coast near Ouistreham, possibly a prelude to an invasion of England, approached Passy to ask that agents be dropped to investigate. Passy chose two of his closest collaborators, Lieutenants Maurice Duclos, whose nom de guerre was Saint-Jacques, and Beresnikoff, a reserve lieutenant of artillery, who traveled as Corvisart. Saint-Jacques, whose family owned a holiday house in the area, knew the region well. The idea was that both men would spend three days reconnoitering German positions and sending back periodic messages by carrier pigeon, after which Corvisart would return to London while Saint-Jacques would proceed to Paris to establish an intelligence network to cover Normandy. After a crash course in codes, invisible ink, and instruction in the care and feeding of carrier pigeons, on 3 August the Free French officers boarded a patrol boat at Portsmouth for the trip across the Channel.

The beginning of the adventure was a heart-stopper. The two agents sank their small French-made rowboat at the foot of a cliff. However, the early-morning fog of 4 August lifted to reveal that their landing place was crowned by a German sentinel. Saint-Jacques wedged his pigeon cage in a crevice in the rocks, and slowly the two men crawled unperceived past the German to reach Saint-Jacques' holiday house. Unable to retrieve the pigeons, the spies proceeded to reconnoiter the German positions along the coast. But when Corvisart returned to the pickup area at the appointed time three days later, intense fog prevented any signals from being seen. In London, the absence of carrier pigeons and the return of the passengerless patrol boat caused Passy to expect the worst, especially after several other abortive attempts to retrieve Corvisart during the month of August. Apparently abandoned, the two men separated. Corvisart returned to London on 15 January 1941, having made good his escape through Spain. He had been preceded by Saint-Jacques, who, after traveling to Lisbon via Oran, appeared in London on Christmas Day.

One lesson drawn by Passy from these early forays into France was that it was essential to establish an evacuation route through Spain. His choice for this mission fell to Gilbert Renault, a thirty-five-year-old filmmaker who went by the name of Rémy, destined to become one of the most celebrated Free French agents. From the moment in July when Renault presented himself at St. Stephen's House, having left his wife and children in Brittany to hop a fishing boat to England, Passy was struck by his round, strong head, piercing eyes, precise speech, and sympathetic manner. In short, Renault had charisma. He also had contacts in the artistic and diplomatic world in Spain, where he had directed a film about Christopher Columbus. For his part, Rémy remembered having been received by Passy with all the warmth accorded an unwelcome traveling salesman.[7] Dansey was to remark that during his long intelligence career he had never met an agent as skilled as Renault. After the usual crash course in codes and invisible ink, Renault, under the name of Raymond, was put on a plane to Lisbon, but only after Passy had supplied him with a secret French code so that he could correspond independent of the British. By 1 December, Passy was receiving regular messages from Raymond on the French Atlantic harbors, and demands for radios for more rapid translation. Although these beginnings were modest, and failed altogether when agents sent to French North Africa were intercepted, the accumulation of information enabled Passy to draw up lists of people favorable or hostile to Free France grouped by profession and by region, to catalogue German and Vichy police measures, and to organize ways to send mail or evacuate agents through Spain.[8]

If Passy's battles to be treated with something approximating equality by the British lasted as long as the war itself, this was in part because his intelligence service, like the Gaullist movement in general, got off on the wrong foot early on in the relationship. The contentiousness arose from the ill-fated Dakar expedition in the autumn of 1940. That Passy's service was obliged to pay such a heavy price for the failure of Operation Menace was a cruel irony of the Dakar adventure; Passy had warned de Gaulle that opinion in Dakar was "confused" and that even a successful Free French landing could be reversed by Vichy forces operating out of North Africa.[9] The hoped-for spontaneous *ralliement* of Dakar was compromised when a French naval squadron dispatched from Toulon slipped through Gibraltar and reached Dakar ahead of the British fleet in which de Gaulle was a passenger. The presence of the sailors, desperately resentful of the British bombardment of the French fleet at anchor at Mers-el-Kébir, the port of Oran, helped to steel the determination of the Dakar garrison to resist de Gaulle's summons of 23 September 1940 to reenter the war on the side of Free France.

De Gaulle sailed back to London to a welcome which mixed derision with public accusations that Menace had been scuppered by poor security in the Free French camp. Among the many stories which circulated on this subject were those of MI5, British counterintelligence, which reported that de Gaulle had discussed the operation over insecure telephones and had appeared at Simpson's in Piccadilly to announce that he required a tropical kit for his upcoming trip to West Africa. Restaurants and pubs in London and Liverpool did a brisk business in August 1940 for Free French officers hosting *dîners d'adieux* in which the success of "Dakar" was toasted. In some quarters it was even suggested that the Germans had infiltrated an agent close to de Gaulle.[10] While de Gaulle's biographer has concluded that the presence of the naval squadron at Dakar was purely fortuitous, Passy, writing two years after the end of the war, blamed the Dakar debacle on lack of security-consciousness in the Free French camp. This was also the conclusion of British intelligence. Already stunned by what it regarded as questionable operational concepts put forward by the neophyte Deuxième Bureau, the British thus had yet another reason to establish a cautious distance in their working relationship with the Free French.[11] In fact, the Dakar incident cast a long shadow over French intelligence. One result was that de Gaulle was kept in ignorance about every major operation involving France for the rest of the war. Dakar also signaled the beginning of suspicions of penetration of the French services based on poor security which has accompanied them to the present day.

Nor was the memory of Dakar allowed to rest. On the night of 1 January 1941, Passy was informed that the commander-in-chief of the Free French navy, Admiral Emile Muselier, was to be arrested by the British on the personal order of Churchill. The British Prime Minister had been stung to fury by letters brought to him by MI5 allegedly written by the French air attaché in London, General Rozoy, prior to his return to Vichy, which claimed that Muselier had alerted him to the Dakar expedition, conspired to hand over Free France's sole submarine, the *Surcouf*, to Vichy, and had been bribed to sabotage recruitment to the Free French navy. De Gaulle's enemies noted that for once the General did not pitch one of his celebrated temper tantrums at the news of the confinement in Pentonville Prison of a senior member of his staff by the police of a foreign government. This was because Muselier hardly inspired confidence, even among his closest associates. How he rose to admiral's rank remains something of a mystery, given a reputation so somber that in 1940 the French navy preferred to take on the Kriegsmarine single-handedly rather than reactivate the sixty-year-old retired vice admiral. For Passy, Muselier conjured up the image of a buccaneer guiding his brigantine toward some luckless merchantman. Cap invariably pushed back on his head, with tinted mustache, dilated pupils, and glazed eyes, Muselier projected *une impression étrange*, evidence in de Gaulle's mind that the admiral was a "morally unbalanced" drug addict. But in June 1940, when Muselier heaved up in London, de Gaulle was desperately short of flag-rank representatives of any service, and especially from the Vichy-besotted French navy. Passy believed that the French navy remained pro-Vichy precisely because Muselier constituted de Gaulle's nautical alternative to the powerful pro-Vichy Admiral Jean Darlan.[12]

But whatever de Gaulle's reservations about Muselier, given photocopies of the alleged Rozoy letters, he quickly became convinced that they were written in a style unworthy of a French general and graduate of the elite *école de guerre*, of which de Gaulle was also a controversial alumnus. On 8 January 1941, de Gaulle summoned his British liaison officer, General Edward Spears, and informed him that if Muselier was not released, he would break off relations with the British government. By this time, Scotland Yard had been prodded into the recognition that the documents were indeed forgeries. Churchill acknowledged the error, and apologized personally to de Gaulle, who was temporarily mollified with a royal audience. On 10 January a subdued but suspicious Muselier reappeared in his office. Scotland Yard traced the forgeries to Passy's Service de Sécurité, a counterintelligence service created in September 1940 to prevent Vichy infiltration of the Free French. Its head, a Major Meffre, and his assistant, Sergeant Collin, confessed and were given prison terms by the British. De Gaulle struck them from the ranks of the Free French, despite Passy's insistence that this was beyond his powers. Meffre claimed to have been motivated solely by the desire, laudable in itself, to be rid of the pretentious and meddlesome Muselier. But because the two men worked out of an office in Kensington Gardens which had been supplied by the British, de Gaulle and Passy believed that British intelligence, possibly in alliance with Vichy, was behind the Muselier episode. In his memoirs, de Gaulle uncharacteristically resorts to an anglicism to explain the Muselier affair as a dreary *"histoire d'Intelligence,"* surely early evidence of his rapidly developing aversion for all intelligence services, especially his own. This unpleasantness probably helped to ease Passy's service out of its cramped quarters at Carlton Gardens and into a relatively isolated seven-room pavilion at 3 St.

James's Square, well distant, Passy hoped, from the intrigues of Gaullist headquarters. For his part, Passy retained a deep suspicion of British intelligence, which hardly improved relations between the two services.[13]

Passy's suspicion was not without foundation, for the British and Gaullist intelligence bureaucracies reflected competing national interests, a competition which crystallized around the question of the Resistance. British goals were essentially military—to defeat Germany and win the war. Churchill's admonition to his intelligence chiefs to "set Europe ablaze" focused their attentions on the military potential of a European resistance to spy on, sabotage, and eventually rebel against the German occupation. The problem presented by France was that two governments claimed to speak for it. Both SIS and SOE dealt with this by creating separate French sections to deal with each. But this logical administrative arrangement, designed, according to the British, "to give the French every chance of a quite unfettered choice of their own system of government once the war was won," was regarded as a crime by the Gaullists. Worse, it was an error, for the question of who was to be in power "once the war was won" was *the* primary concern of the exiles.[14] So for de Gaulle the Resistance was a military expression insofar as its utility to the Allies gained him political leverage in his dealings with them. But beyond that, the Resistance was to form the basis of his legitimacy, a popular mandate which symbolized the rejection of the armistice, of the occupation, of Vichy. The Resistance was to play a military role, certainly, one which included intelligence gathering. But that role was subordinated to the ultimate political purpose of the achievement of postwar power by Free France.

The question of when the Resistance began to figure in de Gaulle's calculations has been hotly debated by historians, some of whom date its significance in the General's thinking from the December 1941 arrival in London of Jean Moulin, the man who would forge Resistance unity, or from his differences with Roosevelt, who seemed determined to impose any government other than a Gaullist one on France. Many ex-resisters, stung by what they saw as the General's sublime distaste for domestic politics, have wondered if he ever took them seriously at all. But it is clear that de Gaulle was interested early on in the potential of the Resistance, and that the primary function of Passy's intelligence organization was to get it on its feet and direct its loyalty toward the Gaullist cause. The problem for Passy was how to go about this task: "We knew that men of good will, dispersed here and there in France, were ready to engage in violent action against the Germans," Passy wrote of the situation in January 1941. "But we had absolutely no idea how to get in contact with them and, as a consequence, how to organize them. I was afraid that they would become discouraged if they saw no offensive action against the enemy. It was therefore necessary, before one could coordinate sporadic acts, to try to develop a spirit of resistance, which would inevitably favor the birth of more important groups with whom we would have more possibilities to enter into contact by one of our networks or our emissaries."[15]

The fundamental difference between the essentially military goals of the British and Passy's broad political vision of a mass movement provided a basis for yet more conflicts in a security relationship which was already fraught with distrust. The British wanted Frenchmen who could be trained as professional agents and returned to France. Passy countered not only that this would take too long, but would result in the creation of "very small cells, completely isolated." Passy's vision was a much more ambitious one. "We don't want observers, but men able to locate a maximum of informers who, without going out of their way, can tell us precisely what they see, what they know, and what interests us," Passy remembered explaining to Commander Kenneth Cohen of SIS. "Our envoys therefore need only collect the information, organize it, and send it to us as quickly as possible." The advantage of this, in Passy's view, would be "to reestablish communications throughout the country among the groups who could, by their very existence, not fail to snowball, thus favoring the birth of a vast Resistance. This, by its size and strength, would persuade our allies that all of France would little by little reenter the struggle."[16] "The very thought of a circuit snowballing made every officer in Baker Street [SOE headquarters] shudder," writes British historian and former SOE operative M. R. D. Foot. It also gave birth to the complaint that the Free French secret service was more interested in furthering de Gaulle's political agenda than in sabotage and subversion.[17] But because in the summer of 1940 the British were bereft of information on France, and Churchill was demanding results, the SIS agreed to train, supply with codes, and parachute into France a limited number of Free French agents.

The British, who organized SIS for intelligence and SOE for "action," were also distressed by the heresy which had taken hold in the Gaullist services that the two tasks were inseparable.[18] From the British perspective, intelligence collection required discretion, patience, and quiet courage, the ability to persevere through an operation lasting months or even years. Its most effective practitioners were men and women whose very ordinariness allowed them to escape notice. "Action," on the other hand, was a quick, brutal business, organized along military lines, in which casualties were expected. For once, de Gaulle appears to have agreed with the British, at least in 1940, and told Passy to restrict his missions to intelligence gathering.[19] Even some members of the Resistance, like Philippe Thyraud de Vosjoli, became converts to the British view when savage German reprisals for "action" missions made the French population less willing to cooperate with the Resistance and concentrated police efforts on the dismantling of several networks.[20]

Passy argued that action was useless without intelligence, and intelligence ineffective without action.[21] "Every intelligence network *always* possesses a certain number of members capable of military and/ or political action," read a 4 July 1942 BCRA memo to de Gaulle, expounding a philosophy which Jacques Soustelle found alive and well when he succeeded Passy as head of the French secret service in 1944.[22] From the Free French viewpoint, Passy's strategy was logical, even brilliantly so. For all of his distaste for his rivals in the Vichy SR, he shared their dilemma, as well as that of the Poles, of producing intelligence for a command which at this stage of the war was in no position to use it to optimize its action and thereby to increase its political legitimacy. Not content merely to furnish the Allies intelligence which would help *them* win the war and then dispose of the victory as they saw fit, he needed to make an active contribution to the conflict. He needed to show incremental success. In this way, the French people would be offered visions of victory which, no matter how delicate, would offer an alternative to Vichy's melancholy "survive" and "regenerate" strategy. They would be lured back into the war, a process reinforced by the inevitable reprisals by Vichy and their German overseers. And even as this repression reduced the effectiveness of the Resistance as a military and intelligence-gathering organization, as Thyraud de Vosjoli believed, paradoxically it would raise its value as a political movement by discrediting its Vichy rival. In this way, the Gaullists would gain in stature and the Resistance would solidify as a base for and an expression of the Gaullist movement. Therefore, the Resistance networks must prove that they were combatants as well as gatherers of intelligence.

Passy remained faithful to his political vision of the BCRA as impresario of *la France résistante*.[23] Yet many impediments remained before that ambition could be realized. Passy looked for the Resistance organizations to "snowball," but in effect their early progress was sporadic and localized. Unlike the Poles, for whom resistance and insurrection had become part of their national identity, the French had been paralyzed by defeat.[24] The rare Frenchmen who heaved up in London were keen to fight and seldom could be seduced into service with the Deuxième Bureau. Only the German invasion of the Soviet Union in June 1941 began to place the French people on notice that, as de Gaulle had argued since 18 June 1940, the scope of the war was far greater than just another parochial Franco-German conflict. Even when, by late 1942, the Resistance began to assume a vaguely coherent form, much of it was by no means Gaullist. Many early envoys, like Rémy, spent much of their time trying to convince potential resisters that de Gaulle was not a lunatic of the extreme right or a pawn of the left.[25] Of the two largest networks in the *zone occupée*, only Rémy's Confrérie Notre-Dame had been spawned by Free France. Marie-Madeleine Foucarde's larger Alliance was one of several which dealt directly with the British. The left-wing Libération-Nord kept the Gaullists at arm's length. Resistance groups in the *zone libre* eventually organized into Combat, Libération, and Franc-Tireurs et Partisans (FTP). But Henri Frenay, leader of Combat, initially maintained strong links with Vichy, and only began to migrate toward the Gaullists in the summer of 1941 when two of Vichy's top leaders, Admiral Darlan and Prime Minister Laval, became openly collaborationist. And even then, Frenay drove Passy to fury by selling his intelligence to the Americans in Switzerland at excellent rates rather than giving it free to the BCRA. "There are local [Resistance] groups which work directly with the IS [SIS] to which they are completely subordinated," read a BCRA report of 20 August 1942. "For this reason they receive much greater material support than we give."[26]

The Ordre Civil et Militaire (OCM) was composed mainly of ex-soldiers who, though anti-German, listened attentively to Vichy-inspired propaganda which labeled the Gaullists as Jews and clandestine communists. The communist-run FTP, along with groups of antifascist Jews, Poles, or Spaniards with communist loyalties, accepted Gaullist direction with very bad grace, when they accepted it at all.[27] The Red Orchestra, composed of communists planted in Belgium, Holland, and France even before the war began, reported directly to Moscow until its leader, Leopold Trepper, was arrested in November 1942.[28] The Free Poles had wasted little time in organizing two sizable French networks within the large communities of Polish immigrants settled in France, "Nurmi" around Saint-Etienne and Lyon and "Monica" in Lille. And of course there was the Vichy SR, a dependable source of information for the British, which was fiercely anti-Gaullist.

Passy acknowledged divisions within the Resistance, but insisted that they were "more or less artificially maintained, even encouraged, by our allies."[29] Passy was both correct and disingenuous. The different organizational and operational concepts envisaged for the Resistance, as has been seen, were a source of friction between the two allies. Besides, in backing a Gaullist-dominated Resistance, the British were being asked to choose sides in a French civil war, a decision which might well have compromised their basic goal of defeating Germany. And while Passy insists that unification of the Resistance was the raison d'être of the BCRA, the plain fact was that, until the spring of 1942 he and de Gaulle possessed only the most elementary notions of the progress of the Resistance.[30] Besides, the Gaullists, dependent on Churchill's alms, were making war on a shoestring and were unable to communicate with or support Resistance networks to the same degree as were the British and later the Americans. It did no good to play the patriotic card, for at the top many of the leaders were suspicious of the General's ambitions and jealously insulated their commands against Gaullist contamination. Lower down the hierarchy, secrecy meant that Resistance operatives often had no idea for whom they were working. At the Liberation, many courageous men and women discovered to their surprise that they were denied decorations for the mean-spirited reason that the Resistance network in which they had enlisted—when they had even known what that network was—did not figure on the Gaullist-approved list. Passy also declines to acknowledge that his struggles with the British often followed hard upon one of the General's mammoth rows with Churchill.

Passy's principal problem in the early months of the war was that his strategy outdistanced his operational capabilities. For an organization whose business was to gather information, the BCRA remained remarkably uninformed on the progress of the Resistance because he had few agents, no way to send them to France or no means to communicate with them once they arrived. His dearth of agents, he insisted, was a famine deliberately contrived by the British, who intercepted recruits at the London Reception Center, located in the Royal Victoria Patriotic School in Wandsworth. Originally founded to educate the sons of British officers, the school could claim some of its most distinguished alumni among refugees washed onto British shores, men like the writers Maurice Druon and Joseph Kessel, not to mention those who would rise to prominence in the resistance movements of various European nations. Lieutenant Roger Warin, delivered to the Patriotic School in November 1941, described it as a "Tower of Babel" where soldiers, politicians, patriots, refugees, and adventurers deposited by the war onto British shores might spend days slumped on diminutive school benches awaiting interrogation by British intelligence officers,[31] whose job was to unmask German agents and guide choice prospects toward SOE networks. The reception was unfailingly courteous and the food, especially by the standards of occupied Europe, abundant. Nevertheless, some chafed at the interminable interrogations in which the arrival was asked to describe his youth, name his lycée, his professors, the location of the war memorial in his town or village, to describe—yet again!—his escape. When one Frenchman began to show his impatience, his interrogator counseled: "Calm down. Do you realize that in your lot we had two Medical Corps captains? One wasn't a doctor and the other wasn't a captain."[32] The quickest way to be released from the monotony was to volunteer to work for

SOE.[33] In many respects, Passy's complaint was really quibbling over crumbs, but at this stage of the war, crumbs were about all the Gaullists could expect. However, when the Free French asked, as they repeatedly did, to be treated like the Poles and Czechs, who interrogated new arrivals of their nationality, Sir Anthony Eden merely replied that SIS lacked officers with the language skills to interview Eastern Europeans but had plenty who were able to carry out interviews in French.[34]

As in recruitment, Passy strove for independence from the British in operational matters as well. "In fact," Passy wrote, "we had practically no means, while the English had everything." This not only limited Gaullist operational independence; it also made for strained relations between Passy and de Gaulle, who in his imperious manner fumed that his *petit bonhomme* of an intelligence chief was always being "conned by the English of the Intelligence Service."[35] The infant SOE, founded in the same month as de Gaulle's secret service, proved more than willing to use Passy's men for their operations, despite the fact that the first Gaullist agent flown into France on 14 November 1940 refused to jump and had to be returned in disgrace to Carlton Gardens, where he apparently served out the war as a very competent staff officer. Five French agents under Royal Navy direction emerged from a submarine to hijack a fishing boat in the mouth of the Gironde estuary and made useful observations of U-boat traffic before sailing their craft to Falmouth.

In December 1940, Rémy signaled that German bomber pilots were brought to their airfield near Vannes in Brittany in a bus vulnerable to ambush. The British were keen to underwrite an operation which would diminish the number of already scarce German pilots. De Gaulle enthusiastically approved a plan which would demonstrate to the French people the offensive capabilities of the Free French. An officer and four volunteers from the newly constituted Free French paratroop battalion volunteered for the mission, code-named Savanna. There were numerous delays. The RAF argued that while bombing innocent civilians fell within the rules of warfare, Savanna constituted a despicable act of "assassination" of enemy combatants. Finally, on the night of 15 March 1941, five of Passy's men dropped into Brittany only to discover that since the operation's inception in December 1940, the German crews had made independent arrangements to get to work.

So the would-be "assassins" dispersed, three of them to be taken off by submarine a month later. [36]

Operating under British tutelage was hardly Passy's idea of independence, but it was the best deal he could cut for the moment. Besides, the mere participation of his service in these operations signified that in intelligence terms "the Free French had to be accepted as a fact of politico-military life."[37] The British recognized that to operate in France it helped to be French—hence Passy's complaint about the British filtering potential recruits at the Patriotic School. In the long run, it can be argued, failed missions actually paid larger dividends than successful ones. Both Savanna and a subsequent operation, Joséphine B, which targeted an electrical station near Bordeaux, were far less noteworthy for the damage done, which ran from marginal to nonexistent, than for the information which the agents, forced to wander through France in their search for ways to return to London, brought back about life on a German-occupied continent—identity and ration cards, police checks, travel documents, train and taxi service, and so on.

These early operations also revealed that improved training, new ways of getting agents into and out of France, as well as finding ways for them to communicate with London once they arrived, must be devised. In 1941, one of the first French recruits to SOE, Francis Basin, was given a crash course in invisible ink, miniature photography, and lock picking before being sent across England without papers to sketch a map of a military air base. He succeeded so well that he was designated to found a Resistance network, while a job in the Catering Corps was located for the unfortunate base commander. His last exercise required him to appear at an appointed hour at the bar of the Dorchester Hotel. An unknown man approached and, in a loud P. G. Wodehouse accent, exclaimed, "Basin, you're a German! You've been found out and the police are after you." When no one in the crowded bar took the slightest notice, the man leaned over and whispered something in Basin's ear. Every head turned toward them. "You see," explained the man. "Whispers are more dangerous than normal conversations. Take this lesson to heart." He then turned on his heels and departed, presumably leaving Basin to pay the bill. [38]

As the war progressed, instruction gradually assumed a more paramilitary character in training centers located on splendid country estates around the British Isles. Days were spent in running obstacle courses, parachute jumps, self-defense, learning how to set plastic explosives, operate arms from pistols to antitank guns, hijack and sabotage locomotives, and approach specially constructed French-style houses without being spotted. At nightfall, the exhausted recruits returned to their châteaux, where batmen collected their muddy uniforms and shined their boots. One trainee was addressed by a very composed butler of the house who apologized because four recruits would be forced to share only three bathrooms—*à la guerre comme à la guerre!* Still, one could not relax too much. After drinks and a sumptuous dinner in the great hall, an instructor was likely to appear to ask: "How many people were at their table? What were their ranks? Any beards or mustaches?" Then they would be shown a map of the village for a few seconds before being asked to reproduce it from memory.[39]

Placing agents on target and retrieval found the relatively easy solution of light Lysander aircraft. Introduced into the RAF in 1938 as an artillery spotter, the slow, heavy "Lizzy" had seduced few aviators, especially as they proved easy pickings for German fighters. However, from 1941 it discovered its milieu in the clandestine war in France, where the characteristics which had made it a flying coffin on the battlefield were ideal for secret operations. The Lysander's flying range exceeded 1,000 miles when fitted with a supplemental fuel reservoir. Though slow, it could be guided onto a small field along an L-shaped flare path laid out by Resistance "reception committees" under the direction of the celebrated *messages personnels* broadcast by the BBC from June 1941. The Lysander's robust construction enabled it to survive the roughest landings—more than once a posse of Resisters was able to force a bent rudder or flap back into alignment by jumping on it. The Lizzy could discharge and pick up passengers and "mail" and take off in the space of four minutes. While Lysanders continued to be used throughout the war, the problem of their small capacity and relatively short range was compensated for by the introduction of the twin-engine Hudson, capable of transporting a crew of four, twelve passengers, and a ton of baggage over two thousand miles. This required larger reception committees, which were eventually equipped with sophisticated S-phones that allowed a ground controller to guide the pilot down. "Eureka" transmitters, parachuted to agents with precise instructions on their use, also provided a guidance system for landings, and parachute drops and to indicate bombing targets.[40] And while the Hudson proved a useful way to communicate with the maquis, passenger priority on the return flight was often reserved for downed RAF pilots.[41]

Unfortunately for Passy, just as SOE claimed priority on limited Lysander space, so was he dependent on the British for the vital radios that he needed to communicate with his networks. Otherwise information took a minimum of three weeks to travel via Spain, which meant that it was often old news on arrival. Early radios had two characteristics which reduced their suitability for clandestine work— they were cumbersome and they were scarce. The first two radios, sent with agents infiltrated into France through Spain, weighed seventy-two pounds each. They began to broadcast in April 1941, but one quickly went on the blink while the other continued to transmit only because the Germans, who had arrested its operator, took over its maintenance. By the summer of 1941, Passy had two radios in France which transmitted thirty messages daily, inadequate, however, to handle the volume of reports, especially after one of his radios near Rouen was shut down in August. "We took so long to obtain the necessary radios and to get them to their operators that our agents exhausted themselves," Passy complained.[42]

Even this small volume of radio traffic provided yet another excuse for a contretemps with SIS. Messages sent in Morse from agents broadcasting from northern Norway to Spain were received and decoded at the reception center located in the park of a country house in Buckinghamshire, where fifty young women with headsets remained on a permanent twenty-four-hour watch. Decoded, the messages were sent by teleprinter or scrambler telephone to SOE headquarters on Baker Street. To prevent the British from reading his messages, Passy secretly provided BCRA agents with a French code. Thus their messages could not be deciphered at the reception center but had to be dispatched in raw form to London to be delivered by porter to St. James's Square. Despite SIS insistence that this delayed or even denied them vital intelligence, Passy stuck to his guns. By way of retaliation, the British phoned Passy around midnight to announce the arrival of important messages, which Passy and his staff then sat up most of the night deciphering. The next night, "the same comedy was repeated," Passy recorded. Night after night they deciphered messages in their digs at Eaton Place as the blitz raged around them. Passy counterattacked by phoning a high SIS official in the wee hours of the morning to insist that he appear at Eaton Place to receive personally a vital piece of intelligence. The official, snatched from his bed, dutifully arrived to receive some inconsequential anecdote. "This little game lasted three months," Passy remembered. "Finally [the British official], exhausted, abandoned play, and miraculously the telegrams began to arrive at more normal hours." But while he boasted of his victory in his memoirs, in private he realized that he needed the British more than they needed him. [43]

While Passy was generally upbeat, even overly so, about his agents' progress in establishing networks in 1941, especially Raymond and Saint-Jacques, another of his early recruits was having mixed success.

When Captain Pierre Fourcaud appeared at St. Stephen's House on 15 July 1940 asking for an assignment, Passy thought he had stumbled on a prime recruit. Before him stood a man slightly over forty, of medium height, with a full head of black hair and a thin pencil mustache, dressed in the uniform of a Chasseur Alpin which bore decorations from World War I. His arm still in a sling allegedly because of a wound sustained during the collapse of France, Fourcaud began to recount his acts of martial valor, which included his escape from southern France in a boatload of French officers disguised as Poles and Czechs. Despite what Passy thought was a notable lack of modesty, Fourcaud exuded a swashbuckling quality tinged with a hint of sentimentality, a boiling dynamism, a loquacious assurance and easy familiarity characteristic of his traveling salesman's trade which made him infectiously attractive. Fourcaud, using the code name Lucas, was dispatched to the *zone libre* via Lisbon and Madrid with the mission of establishing a Resistance network.

When Fourcaud returned to London in late December, his report astounded Passy. In the first place, his exit from France had been facilitated by a visa delivered by one of Pétain's ministers. In fact, he had spent his autumn working his substantial charms on his old friend

Colonel Georges Groussard, chief of the Marshal's Groupes de Protection, Colonel d'Alès of the Bureau des Menées Anti-nationales
(Bureau of Antinational Activities—BMA), and Commandant Georges
Loustaunau-Lacau of the Légion Française des Combattants, a Vichy
propaganda and spy network. Fourcaud was ebullient about the possibilities for a reconciliation between Pétain and de Gaulle. He brought
a proposal for Free France to finance Loustaunau-Lacau's newspaper
La Spirale to the tune of twenty million francs, and to scatter leaflets
over France from British aircraft advertising the Légion as the only
Resistance group "with no French blood on its hands" (a reference to
Gaullist participation in Dakar).

Fourcaud also announced that Loustaunau-Lacau had drawn up a
plan for the invasion of Sardinia, which he would supply on request.
De Gaulle had a good laugh over the request for money and the leaflets:
"They've got a lot of cheek!" When a furious Passy tried to make
Fourcaud understand the extent of his indiscretion, that he risked
betraying Gaullist sympathizers in France to the BMA or allowing
Vichy to discredit de Gaulle by revealing these contacts with Pétain's
functionaries, the agent was unmoved: "Proof of the good will of Vichy
is that everyone knows me there; they call me 'de Gaulle's represen-
tative,' " he replied. "I was there the entire time and I went wherever
I wanted."[44]

Despite his bizarre behavior, Fourcaud was permitted to return to
France in January 1941. Hardly had they parachuted a radio and
operator for him in March when Fourcaud began to signal that he
wished to bring Groussard to London. After several abortive pickups
by Lysander, due mainly, Passy insisted, to Fourcaud's incompetence,
Groussard simply traveled to Lisbon, where a British plane picked him
up and delivered him to Bristol in June. Groussard and Passy were
not strangers. On the contrary, as commandant of Saint-Cyr in 1939,
Groussard had been Major Dewavrin's commanding officer. Over the
next few days, the two men discussed possibilities for an exchange of
intelligence information on the Germans. Passy gave him two million
francs to build up an intelligence network of officers on "armistice
leave" in cooperation with Rivet's SR. However, Groussard was arrested within days of his return to France. He managed to escape and
flee to Switzerland, but never attempted to reestablish contact with

Passy. In his memoirs, Groussard gave two reasons for keeping his distance from the Gaullists: he had left London with a strong sense that the divisions and intrigues which infected the Free French were as malignant as those which had so disgusted him at Vichy. Second, he sensed that the British—and in particular SIS—were reluctant to throw their full support behind de Gaulle and Passy.[45]

The dissipation of this first contact with Vichy intelligence was followed by another incident, of which, not surprisingly, Fourcaud was the centerpiece. Rather than create an independent Resistance network as instructed, Fourcaud broke contact with London for most of June 1941 as he continued to cultivate anti-German French officers loyal to Vichy as well as political activists. "I have the entire Radical Party behind me," he finally radioed at the end of June, "which is to say more than half of the French. Henceforth I shall designate them by the pseudonym of 'Radish.' " This was among his last messages, for Passy learned at the end of August that Fourcaud had been arrested by the Surveillance du Territoire (ST) after he had barged in on a startled Admiral Jean Joseph de Laborde, commander of the Mediterranean fleet at Toulon, and launched into a confused harangue during which he defended the Gaullist action at Dakar. Fourcaud had waved off those who cautioned that a French navy under Darlan's iron thumb was beyond redemption, insisting that his ribbon of the Légion d'Honneur would guarantee him a fair hearing and a graceful exit. In retrospect, Fourcaud attributed the ensuing disaster to the fact that he appeared just as the remnants of a midday meal of a man who obviously was suffering chronic indigestion problems was being cleared away.[46] Seconds after the mention of Dakar by Fourcaud, the admiral, in a rage, flung his uninvited guest into the street.

Two days later, on 28 August, the Gaullist agent was arrested outside the Gare Saint-Charles, the Marseille railway station, while in the company of young Lieutenant Roger Warin of the BMA. The question of who had denounced Fourcaud was never made clear. Warin blamed Darlan, who had been alerted by Admiral de Laborde. For what it was worth, Fourcaud publicly exonerated Laborde at the admiral's treason trial in 1947, stating instead that Warin and the BMA had been responsible for his arrest. Warin countered that he had been forced to flee France the very next day precisely because the ST returned to arrest him. As for the role of Paillole and the BMA in Fourcaud's detention, the jury probably will be forever out.[47]

In light of the many tragic arrests that led to deportation or death by torture, the detention in August 1941 of an agent considered by most witnesses to be a "mythomaniac" should have been worthy of hardly more than a diminutive footnote in the substantial history of the French secret services. However, this was not to be so. Warin made his way to London, where he presented himself to Passy. On the face of it, Passy might be called mad to employ in a position of immense responsibility someone who had so recently deserted a rival service in circumstances which were certainly suspect. This was especially the case as Passy claimed in retrospect to have detected behind the obvious intelligence reflected in Warin's clear, lively eyes and incisive speech a cold, cynical personality capable, he believed, of cruelty. But few in the trickle of recruits released by the Patriotic School possessed the calm, methodical temperament and common sense required of an agent, or for that matter displayed even a tepid desire to enlist in the secret service. Besides, 1941 had been a tough year for Passy and the BCRA. Agents had been sacrificed through inexperience, incompetence, and, Passy suspected, treason. In November, he had radioed instructions for the return to London of four agents he feared were compromised. A few days later, the men were arrested by the BMA. This was perhaps just a coincidence. But the fear lingered that Vichy had penetrated his organization. An experienced recruit from Paillole's shop might be just the man to organize a counterintelligence service. So that was precisely what Passy did, naming as its director Roger Wybot, alias Warin.[48]

In his memoirs, Wybot claims to have found the atmosphere of Carlton Gardens disturbing: "After the professional rigor of the Bureau des Menées Anti-nationales at Marseille, I had fallen in with amiable amateurs, full of good intentions, who 'pottered about' . . . played at Boy Scout," he wrote. In April 1941, Passy had renamed his Deuxième Bureau the SR, because he was in the business of collecting rather than exploiting intelligence. In July 1941, he created a Section Action to work with SOE. But agents for each, kept strictly separate in England, continued to trip over each other in France.

Relations between the French and British services were periodically poisoned by quarrels between de Gaulle and Churchill, which would result in orders to cease dealings with each other, followed a few days later by a new order rescinding the old one. In October, Passy rationalized his service further by creating a Section Renseignements, and split Action into military and political divisions—escape, archives, and codes and ciphers.[49] But for an organization which was running Resistance networks and planning action missions, St. James's Square had no Paris phone book to verify addresses, no railway timetables to set up itineraries, and no card indexes of agents, so that they were desperately vulnerable to infiltration and deception. None had any direct experience working in the Resistance. In fact, to Wybot, Passy's SR seemed to exist principally to nurture de Gaulle's swollen illusion that the French people lived only for his reappearance on French soil. Passy was disarmingly frank about his ignorance of intelligence work and the defects of his organization. Wybot was the first "real" intelligence officer to enter his SR, which gave him immense prestige. He gave Wybot the green light to reorganize the SR.[50]

In mid-December, Wybot proposed a new organization, the Bureau Central de Renseignements et d'Action (BCRA), divided into intelligence, action, and counterintelligence, to which Passy added a "very important" technical section grouping radio, codes, deciphering, photography, and accounting. An escape section was eventually included to deal with the evacuation of downed Allied pilots.[51] An "M" for "Militaire" was added to the name after the Commissaire à l'Intérieur, former Socialist politician André Diethelm, claimed authority over all "political" intelligence on the very French grounds that soldiers had no business meddling in politics. Although by the summer of 1942 Passy was able to drop the "M" after the Commissariat de l'Intérieur was dislodged from the sphere of active operations, this intrusion touched off another bureaucratic struggle which preoccupied Passy for the first half of the year and contributed to low morale in the BCRAM. And even though the demarcation dispute over "political" intelligence was eventually resolved in Passy's favor, it announced the return of the "Interior" into the intelligence sphere and renewed the prewar fragmentation of the French service. It also suggested the renewal of France's "secret service wars," as Passy confessed to have instructed agents to "intoxicate" the Commissariat de l'Intérieur with false reports.[52] Not without difficulty, Wybot also convinced Passy to lease larger quarters, a modern building near Selfridge's at 10 Duke Street. "The epic of the BCRA began," Wybot announced proudly.

Wybot would not retain good memories of his time there. It should come as no surprise, for his duties as chief of counterintelligence in a service which had experienced a year and a half of unregulated growth was bound to put him at odds with those accustomed to more independent working conditions. Two of his innovations were particularly controversial. The first was the creation of a *fichier*, or card file, which categorized over 100,000 French men and women as hostile, favorable, or "indifferent" to Free France. Passy conceded that it was an unrefined instrument but necessary as a reference point to check the stories of newly arrived recruits and track the relationships of agents in France.[53] However, Wybot's *fichier* was to become a source of friction between the BCRA and some Resistance leaders who saw it as "a means of [Gaullist] political control of the Resistance."[54] It also allowed Paillole to observe that Wybot had created an "internal security service" rather than a counterintelligence section worthy of the name, which encouraged the evolution of the BCRA into a Renseignements Généraux Politique rather than a professional intelligence organization.[55]

Wybot's second innovation was to introduce methods of interrogation for returning agents and potential recruits, who were repeatedly questioned to seek the flaw, the contradiction, the diminutive error which could cause the most expertly crafted tale to unravel. "I was just doing my job," Wybot insisted when he grilled Rémy mercilessly in June 1942 on the grounds that the immense success of his networks appeared too good to be true. "I no longer felt myself capable of hiding my irritation," Free France's most celebrated secret agent wrote of this inquisition by the "cold-eyed" Wybot.[56] De Gaulle personally intervened to short-circuit the investigation of the lawyer André Weil-Curiel, among the first of the Gaullist faithful, after Wybot questioned his prewar friendships with high Nazi officials and his suspicious return to London after his arrest in 1941 by the Gestapo. "Are you trying to land me with another Dreyfus Affair?" the General questioned. Soon the word around 10 Duke Street was that Wybot had contracted a serious case of "spymania." Wybot was particularly proud of his interrogation techniques, which, he insisted, were superior even to those of the Patriotic School. Unfortunately, they soon became the stuff of legend, to the point that lurid stories circulated about torture and even the murder of suspected traitors carried out at Duke Street. And while everyone associated with the BCRA dismissed such stories as ludicrous, the sad truth was that they were given wide credibility in both Washington and London, to the point that the BCRA became a major impediment to de Gaulle's political acceptability among the Allies, reinforcing the view that the Gaullists were little better than a political "gang."[57]

While Passy's service required some serious refinement, one may wonder nonetheless if Wybot's passage through the BCRA did more harm than good. Wybot conceded that his tightening of security measures had not made him popular, because in the process he produced embarrassing evidence of poor practices, especially in the Section Renseignements under air force captain André Manuel. But Wybot's professional criticisms only earned him enmity within the BCRA, especially of Manuel. Manuel conceded that his dislike of Wybot was both personal and professional: Wybot "did not possess a hint of humanity." Manuel also blasted Wybot's Gestapo-inspired interrogation methods.[58] Wybot's *fichier* alarmed important segments of the Resistance and raised the specter of political spying, while his methods of interrogation became the source of stories damaging to the Gaullist movement. One may also doubt the effectiveness of his reforms, as Passy confessed that he enjoyed only intermittent success in getting Lagier and Manuel to apply Wybot's security directives in their services and networks.[59]

The beginning of the end of Wybot's relationship with the BCRA began at around ten o'clock on the night of 3 October 1942, when a car came by his London digs with an urgent summons from Passy. Wybot arrived at secret service headquarters to be confronted by Passy, Manuel, Lagier, and . . . Pierre Fourcaud! Fourcaud, who had escaped his captivity possibly, Wybot believed, with the complicity of his friends at Vichy, began by stating that his long incarceration had given him the leisure to reflect on the circumstances of his capture. This led him to the inescapable conclusion that he had fallen into a trap laid by Wybot, alias Warin. The room was brittle with tension. "Explain yourself!" Passy said drily to Wybot. At two o'clock in the morning, after almost four hours of questions, cross-examination, and theatrical speeches from Fourcaud, the escaped agent suddenly retracted his accusation. The two men shook hands, and the incident appeared to be forgotten. However, Fourcaud's appearance brought out many latent tensions and personality conflicts, to the point that de Gaulle was forced to transfer Wybot's assistant after the officer and André Manuel came to blows in the office. If this was designed to pry Wybot out of his position, it succeeded. Wybot was posted to a fighting unit in Italy, and replaced at the head of counterintelligence by Pierre Fourcaud.[60]

So this was the situation in December 1942 as Passy sat across from Paillole and Ronin to discuss the merger of their services. For the officers of the ex-Vichy SR, this was hardly more than a courtesy call. Although newly exiled, objectively they appeared to hold all the cards. In their eyes, their strength lay with their technical mastery of the intelligence craft. The fact that they had shared intelligence with the Allied services gave them credibility. Though "liberated," French North Africa remained under the control of ex-Vichyites like Paillole and Ronin. Last, their superior knowledge of France guaranteed that the Allies would continue to treat them as partners. The BCRA's long apprenticeship appeared to have brought it no closer to an elusive proficiency, although Passy became testy when Ronin once made a discourteous reference to his "team of amateurs," and delivered an equally pointed commentary on the failures of the Deuxième Bureau in May 1940. But once Paillole, exercising his usual diplomacy, had brought the meeting off the boil, Passy acknowledged that none of his group sought to make a career in the secret services and was happy at the prospect of the arrival of "well-informed technicians."[61]

So the BCRA appeared utterly ripe for a "merger," which could be hardly more than a corporate takeover. It was utterly dependent on the British for its means of operation. It was considered deficient in tradecraft, while its rivalries and methods had served to discredit the Free French in official Allied circles. Paillole had succeeded in excluding the BCRA from French North Africa, which, after Torch and the assassination of Darlan, appeared to offer a secure base for the ex-Vichy, anti-Gaullist conservatives. In effect, it appeared that in the intelligence game, as in the eyes of the Anglo-American Allies, the "Vichy Resistance" was very much in the driver's seat. Roosevelt was in the process of manufacturing a new leader to replace de Gaulle, General Henri Giraud, whose escape from a German POW camp was organized by Rivet's SR. When that happened, the Gaullist "movement" and its BCRA would fade into an interesting but minor footnote in the history of World War II.

NINE

THE WAR OF THE
SECRET SERVICES

The year 1943 would prove critical for France, for it was to determine ultimately who was to represent it in Allied councils and govern it after the war. The Anglo-American buildup in the Mediterranean and in Great Britain, and the inability of German blitzkrieg methods, so effective early in the war, to finish off the Soviet Union, meant that Germany's defeat could only be a matter of time. Nevertheless, the Vichy government, under Marshal Pétain and his Prime Minister, Pierre Laval, continued to follow a collaborationist policy, thereby linking their fate with that of Hitler.

For this reason, three pretenders jockeyed for position as heirs of the French government. The first was the Gaullists, who had staked their claim for French leadership on 18 June 1940 with de Gaulle's celebrated speech to the French people broadcast over the BBC, in which he vowed to fight on. And while from the beginning de Gaulle had received Churchill's support, the General's prickly personality, the turbulent early history of his Free French movement, and his lack of a mandate from the French people made him suspect in the eyes of American President Franklin Roosevelt.

Roosevelt's support was thrown behind a second group of pretenders who collected in Algiers in the wake of Torch—anti-German Vichy refugees who lamented that "the Marshal" had fallen prisoner to his sinister pro-Nazi Prime Minister. Organized behind the leadership of General Henri Giraud, who had been sprung from a German POW camp with the help of Rivet's service and spirited through France to Gibraltar and Algiers, the conservatives hoped that, with American support, they would come to power in France.

A third group of pretenders was the French Resistance. Politically diverse, largely spontaneous, in early 1943 the Resistance "movement" was united only in its opposition to the Germans and, in the south, to Vichy. Its leaders, like medieval barons, were deeply suspicious of both London and Algiers, and reluctant to place themselves under the leadership of either Gaullists or Giraudists.

If de Gaulle ultimately emerged the victor in this three-way struggle, it was in large part due to the success of his secret service. The story of how in 1943 de Gaulle maneuvered Giraud into obscurity and ultimately united the Resistance under his leadership is well chronicled. What the next two chapters will examine is the role, less well known, played by the Gaullist secret service, first in marginalizing its more experienced and professional rival and second in uniting the Resistance behind de Gaulle.

One option which Paillole claimed was considered early on was a merger of Passy's BCRA and Rivet's SR. Paillole and others have viewed Ronin's refusal, apparently on Darlan's orders, to accept Passy's offer to arrange a meeting between the Vichy emissaries and de Gaulle as the missed opportunity of the war for the French secret services, one which could have led to the reconciliation between the two camps.[1] This appears to be wishful thinking, however. Of course, the outcome of such an interview, assuming that de Gaulle would have agreed to it in the first place, can only be a matter of speculation. But it is extremely unlikely, given de Gaulle's distrust of secret services in general, that he would have allowed recent servants of the Marshal to stick their noses under his tent.

That the amalgamation of the two secret services might serve as a vehicle for reconciliation between Gaullists and Giraudists is even more farfetched. In fact, there is much humbug in the assertions of both sides that their willingness to work toward merger broke up on the rocks of their adversary's refusal to see reason. The differences in temperament, recent history, and political support yawned too widely, the bad blood flowed in rivers too broad for a reconciliation to be the work of a few committee meetings. Indeed, Passy confessed that he met Ronin and Paillole only because he wished to dispel his ignorance of the situation in North Africa following Darlan's assassination on Christmas Eve 1942 by a disaffected royalist sailor.[2] But once the Americans, with the complicity of Rivet's service, conjured up General Henri Giraud to supplant Charles de Gaulle as leader of what, since Bastille Day 1942, was now called Fighting France, positions hardened.[3]

One can understand immediately why the officers of Rivet's SR found no difficulty in transferring their allegiance to General Giraud. Tall, elegant, with a superb handlebar mustache, Giraud exuded the heroic presence of a commander of Napoleonic hussars. A veteran of prewar campaigns in Morocco, where he staked out a reputation as one of the French army's coming officers, public rumor whispered in 1940 that Daladier had picked him as Gamelin's replacement as commander-in-chief. The Germans cut short those plans. But Giraud's daring escape from his German prison in April 1942 reaffirmed his reputation for courage. The contrasts between the personalities and views of de Gaulle and Giraud could hardly have been more striking: Whereas a glacial distance usually separated de Gaulle from his subordinates, a gap closed only when he flew into a towering rage, Giraud was the perfect superior—indulgent, affectionate, adored by his men because he listened to their complaints and laughed at their jokes. Both men could be remarkably single-minded. But whereas de Gaulle looked for nuances and did not hesitate to seek political solutions, Giraud's utterances confirmed many in their belief that his athletic abilities had far outstripped those of his intellect. He maintained the classic position that the political arena was no place for any officer worthy of his commission. Above all, this general of the army had no intention of snapping to attention in the presence of a green brigadier. "General Giraud had the charm which de Gaulle lacked," Harold Macmillan, a future Prime Minister, remembered, "but that was all he had."[4] And Rivet's men needed something more substantial than charm if they were to fend off Passy's corporate takeover.

Eventually, of course, a merger of the two French services did occur. But surprisingly perhaps, given the apparent strength of the ex-Vichy

SR, it came about on terms dictated by the BCRA. Of course, the BCRA's trump card was de Gaulle himself. Several witnesses suggest that some sort of arrangement mutually acceptable to the two services might have been negotiated had not de Gaulle personally intervened to make clear that he regarded the ex-Vichy men as tainted patriots.[5] The conclusion, especially by officers of the ex-Vichy services, has been that the end result of a merger in which the BCRA was the dominating element could only be detrimental to the efficiency and stability of the French services. "When I explained to him how I had organized the BCRA," Passy recounted of his 1943 Algiers meeting with Rivet, "I thought he was going to choke, so much did my conception do violence to the classical doctrine. I realized that day that it would be difficult to find common ground in the realm of ideas."[6]

But the BCRA, for all of Passy's modesty about his accomplishments, retained some notable strengths, especially in the battle for influence in the French intelligence community. First was Passy himself, who had succeeded in assembling a service in lean times and despite some rocky moments had established solid relations with SIS and SOE. The intelligence produced by the BCRA might not have been first-class in those early months, or even the first few years. If Wybot is to be believed, when he defected to the Gaullist camp in late 1941, the BCRA seemed to be in the business of stoking de Gaulle's illusion that all available wall space in France was decorated with "Vive de Gaulle!" graffiti, although, he conceded, such statements occasionally were to be read on public urinals.[7] This might have proved to be one instance in which slanted intelligence proved to be good politics, however. Rivet and Passy fundamentally disagreed over the function of the intelligence service. Rivet saw his SR as a strictly "military" intelligence in the service of the general staff, which guaranteed its nonpolitical character. There was a substantial element of hypocrisy in this argument, in that the action of the Vichy SR, and especially of the old BMA, had been very political indeed. Passy countered that, as the BCRA served the chief of state directly, it must have a political function.[8] And while this shocked those like Rivet and Paillole for whom the BCRA was little more than a Renseignements Généraux Politique,[9] who not without reason saw any departure from a strictly "military" intelligence service as a dangerous concept, in terms of the struggle for advantage which now erupted between de Gaulle and Giraud this gave the Gaullist service an incomparable advantage.

And nowhere was that advantage greater than with the Resistance. Passy insisted that a major reason why a quiet accord could never be struck with the ex-Vichy service was that the Resistance would never stand for it. In February 1943, the chief of the BCRA SR, André Manuel, returned from a mission in France, code-named Pallas, to report that Resistance chiefs were "indignant" and had the impression of having been "victims of a hoax" at seeing Giraud, and especially the men of the Vichy SR who had worked against the Resistance, given positions of influence in liberated North Africa. Passy may be accused of biased reporting. But he must be given credit for realizing that de Gaulle could not triumph without the Resistance, and the Resistance could not be mobilized if Rivet, Paillole, and Ronin, all Giraud's men, gained control of the French secret services. It was this realization, Passy confessed, rather than any technical rivalries or doctrinal differences between the services, which made impossible a merger on any basis of equality.[10]

Passy recognized that November 1942 had been a turning point in the history of the Resistance. When, in July 1940, Churchill ordered Hugh Dalton, chief of SOE, to "set Europe ablaze," anti-Nazi patriots all over Europe began to prepare general uprisings against the German occupation. In the case of France, however, it would take nearly a year for the embers of resistance to ignite into flame. In 1940, the French people accepted that the war was over and that the deal between Pétain and Hitler was about the best that could be struck under the circumstances. However, Hitler's June 1941 invasion of the Soviet Union was to have repercussions in France, where an active Communist Party determined to transform France into a front of the "Great Patriotic War," and if possible divert German units from the East. Even before June 1941, French agents in Leopold Trepper's Red Orchestra network, most of them recruited by a German Jewish communist named Henri Robinson, appear to have kept Moscow well informed on developments in French industries, German military dispositions in France, economic cooperation between Germany and Vichy France, as well as snippets of political gossip.[11] Open war was declared on 21 August 1941, when Fredo, later prominent under his

nom de guerre of Colonel Fabien, assassinated Aspirant Moser in the
Barbès metro station. The communist strategy, which aimed to embarrass and ultimately discredit Vichy, worked brilliantly. In response
to an ultimatum from Hitler that a hundred French were to be executed
in retaliation for Moser's death, Vichy Interior Minister Pierre Pucheu
executed six on 28 August, in the hope that Hitler would be satisfied
that Vichy could keep order in France. By taking on this task, however,
he directly associated Vichy with the German repression. The cycle
of assassination and reprisal spiraled upward in the autumn of 1941.
As Pucheu approved lists of hostages for execution, the Vichy argument
that it offered the "Shield of France"—the bulwark which kept France
from sharing the fate of Poland—began to look distinctly threadbare.

It was completely stripped away in the following summer when Pierre
Laval returned as Prime Minister and launched a policy of active
collaboration. After his crackdown on pro-Allied elements in Vichy
in May 1942, in June he announced *la relève*, the policy of sending
French volunteers to work in Germany's factories. Also in that month,
he made a wager for which, ultimately, he would pay with his life:
"*Je souhaite la victoire de l'Allemagne* [I hope for a German victory],"
he thundered in a speech which sent shudders down the spines even
of some faithful Vichyites. In the summer of 1942, Laval obviously
calculated that he faced minimal risks for substantial long-term rewards. With the British confined to their island and the Resistance
not yet a force to be reckoned with, Western Europe was relatively
tranquil. German armies remained on the rampage in Eastern Europe
and North Africa. Whatever latent potential was rumbling to life in
the blast furnaces and military camps of the United States, Laval
believed, would be neutralized once German V weapons came on-
line.[12] As for the rewards, Laval did not cooperate with Hitler because
he admired Nazism. Rather, he was a graduate of the Aristide Briand
school of French diplomacy, which in the interwar years taught that
accommodation with Germany and Italy was France's best option.
With Germany poised to win the war, Laval reasoned, better slide into
the good graces of the Führer by offering French collaboration.

Laval's calculations contained flaws, however, and they were fairly
serious ones. Active collaboration disturbed even some of Vichy's most
devoted supporters, not to mention the mass of the French people

burdened by the deepening rigors of occupation. By August 1942, the tightened application of the "law of hostages" had generated so much business that German officials in France requested extra beer and cigarette rations "to calm the nerves of the executioners" and "prisoners of color" to bury the dead. More, "volunteers" for *la relève* stayed away in droves, so that in September 1942 it was converted into the Service du Travail Obligatoire, the infamous STO. Faced with a summons to forced labor in Germany, many young Frenchmen took to the hills. At a stroke, the opposition, which had hitherto been a mosaic of scattered and largely isolated groups, as yet too insignificant even to have adopted the name of "Resistance" or "resisters," was presented with a recruitment bonanza. The number of clandestine newspapers printed in the *zone libre* had increased to seventy by the autumn of 1942, when the first popular demonstration against STO occurred in Tulle. On 11 November, all across France, citizens responded to the call by the Free French to protest the occupation and the collaboration policy of Vichy.[13] But this lay in the future. In the early autumn of 1941, before Vichy and Hitler had begun to shoot themselves in the foot, Passy had to admit that de Gaulle and *La France libre* were hardly household names in France, that the exile movement had failed to put down roots on the Continent. Then, out of the blue, the means to do so quite literally walked through the door.

Jean Moulin was both a brilliant and ultimately controversial choice to unify opposition to the Germans and Vichy into a movement, in effect to create the Resistance. At first sight, the man who stood in de Gaulle's London office on 25 October 1941 appeared an unlikely candidate for such an intrepid mission. He was small, composed, placid almost to the point of anonymity, and his handsome, well-proportioned face, intelligent brown eyes, and cordial but reserved smile announced a man more accustomed to the elegant salons and sumptuous bureaus of France's *haute administration* rather than a "condottiere" prepared to throw himself into a deadly game of clandestine warfare. Once that might have been so, but the Germans and Vichy had conspired to produce a redoubtable opponent, to draw out what British intelligence officers who first interviewed Moulin in September 1941 recognized as an "exceptional personality."[14] On 17 June 1940, German troops had appeared before the prefecture at Chartres and arrested its occu-

pant. Moulin was tortured for no more worthy goal than to force him
to sign a document claiming that Senegalese troops of the French army
had committed atrocities against French civilians. Released after he
had unsuccessfully attempted suicide by slitting his throat, Moulin
spent the first weeks of the occupation trying to insulate his department
against the exactions of the occupiers. His diligence reaped no
rewards—on 2 November 1940, Vichy fired him on the grounds of
his "attachment to the *ancien régime.*"

Forty years old and unemployed, Moulin, according to his biographer Daniel Cordier, determined to make his way to London. In
1941, this was not easily done. Surveillance and gas rationing had
made it virtually impossible for Breton fishermen to sail to England.
A second, more circuitous route led over the Pyrenees through Spain
to Gibraltar or Lisbon. As surveillance on the Pyrenees tightened,
especially after November 1942, those wishing to take that route had
to put themselves in the hands of a local *passeur* who would guide
them over little-used mountain paths into Spain. Some of these *passeurs* made a habit of collecting their fees twice, first from the refugees
and then from the French police or Germans to whom they betrayed
their charges. Escapees who evaded capture in France, which carried
the penalty of deportation to Germany, seldom avoided lengthy internment in Spain, as the Spanish government, while technically neutral, was sympathetic to the Axis.

Moulin's detractors insist that his delayed departure was only mar-
ginally connected to the difficulties posed by the trip. Rather, they
say, he had little desire to join Free France, and only did so at the
insistence of his mentor and ex-boss, Pierre Cot, who had gone into
exile in the United States after de Gaulle declined his services. It was
Cot who forwarded to Moulin the papers which allowed him to adopt
the identity of Jean Joseph Mercier, professor at the Institut International in New York, so that he could approach the American consul
in Marseille to request a visa to return to his Fifth Avenue residence
via Spain and Portugal. In the meantime, Moulin spent a year in the
zone libre, making contact with embryonic Resistance groups, mainly
through the Cot Air Ministry old-boy network, and in all likelihood
supplying reports to Moscow through Henri Robinson. While Henri
Frenay argued that Moulin's contacts with communists pointed in-

fallibly to the conclusion that he was also a communist, Thierry Wolton suggests that none of this proves incontrovertibly that Moulin was a "conscious agent" of the Bolsheviks.[15]

Finally, on 9 September, his visas in order, Moulin departed France, apparently one step ahead of Paillole's BMA.[16] In Lisbon, Moulin endured another long and frustrating wait of six weeks while he tried to gain passage to London. However, from a Gaullist perspective this proved to be another fortuitous delay, for the administrative formalities and endless interviews insisted upon by the British embassy in Lisbon gave Moulin the leisure to become well informed on the Free French movement, mainly through reading enthusiastic articles in the British press occasioned by the formation on 24 September of the Comité National Français, of which de Gaulle was president. Nonetheless, he maintained an open mind about whether he would offer his services to the British or the "degaullists." For his part, de Gaulle, learning of the arrival in Lisbon of someone who appeared exceptionally well informed on the state of the clandestine opposition, began to prod the British into ending his bureaucratic limbo.[17] On 19 October, a hydroplane took Moulin from Lisbon to Poole, Dorset, and from there he made the inevitable trip to the Patriotic School for four days of interrogations.

The man who stood before de Gaulle, and ultimately Passy, on Saturday, 25 October, possessed what they most wanted after eighteen months of exile—knowledge about growing disaffection in France. In a handwritten report which he had composed in Lisbon, copies of which had been delivered both to SOE and to Passy's SR on the preceding day, Moulin laid out the characteristics of each of the three opposition groups in the zone libre, the milieu in which they recruited, their goals, their potential in terms of propaganda, intelligence collection, sabotage, and military action. Absent from the report was any appreciation of the weaknesses of the Resistance, of which Moulin was only too well aware—its rivalries and divisions, both political and personal, clan loyalties, and lack of means. The silence on these issues was quite intentional; Moulin's purpose was to sell the potential of the Resistance to the British and de Gaulle, not to denigrate it. The strong message of the report, spelled out in the section dealing with the difficulties of communication with England, was that the movements felt isolated, abandoned, and unappreciated by London. The message for Passy was even more subtle, for while Resistance leaders quoted in Moulin's report complained of lack of support from SOE agents, none mentioned ever having set eyes on any of the twenty agents whom Passy had dispatched to France.[18]

Never before had the adage that knowledge was power been more true. To the Free French, Moulin constituted a dangling promise of hitherto elusive political legitimacy. But whether Moulin would place that knowledge in the service of de Gaulle remained an open question. The two men knew of each other, apparently shared a mutual respect, but there was much that potentially divided them. Despite his rebellious, even iconoclastic past, de Gaulle remained a reservoir of conservatism, to the point that republican critics claimed that only his age distinguished him from his archrival and onetime patron, Pétain. On the face of it, his military education, strict Catholic upbringing, even his origins near Lille in the Nord, which he regarded as the "true" France, seemed to offer a defiant antithesis of Moulin. Both men were sons of schoolmasters. But Moulin's father had been a Mason, active in left-wing causes in his native Béziers near the Mediterranean coast. Moulin had remained loyal to his father's beliefs, and carved out a brilliant administrative career backed by the political patronage of his near-contemporary Pierre Cot.

Moulin's close association with Cot offered a likely source of discord, because the former Air Minister, shunned because he was personally blamed for the unreadiness of the French air force in 1940, enjoyed the dubious distinction of being one of only two politicians personally refused admission into the Free French movement by de Gaulle. Snubbed, Cot soon grew tired of living in a modest ten-shilling-a-day bedsit in South Kensington, and, trailing his ostracism, sailed away to the United States to await the outcome of the war. Because Cot's left-wing opinions impelled him to become, consciously or unconsciously, a Soviet spy, some, led by Henri Frenay of Combat, have suggested that, by recruiting Moulin, de Gaulle delivered the Resistance to the communists. Daniel Cordier, Moulin's biographer, disputes this, and insists that despite their divergent backgrounds and beliefs, the *entente* between de Gaulle and Moulin solidified upon a strong sense of service to the state.[19]

Over luncheon, which lasted two hours, Moulin became convinced that de Gaulle was the incarnation of Republican authority. For de Gaulle, Moulin brought two invaluable credentials to Free France: His heroic defiance of the Germans at Chartres in June 1940 made him a "resister of the first hour." Second, Moulin represented a link with republican legitimacy, which helped de Gaulle to counter accusations that he wished to impose an authoritarian government on liberated France.[20] Moulin agreed to carry out three tasks for Free France in the *zone libre*: coordinate the administrative and propaganda activities of the resisters; gain their allegiance to the Comité National Français; unify the paramilitary forces under de Gaulle's command. In the company of Passy, Moulin left for the paratroop training center at Ringway near Manchester, where for five days the two men tested an experimental parachute and discussed plans to unify the Resistance and create intelligence and sabotage networks. The year 1941 drifted away with exasperating tedium as Moulin mastered codes, put the finishing touches on a plan of Resistance organization, and was interviewed by de Gaulle, Passy, and officers of SOE. Again, the delay was not altogether without profit. News of Pearl Harbor focused increased priority on the political importance of Moulin's mission: "Of course, there will be operations, battles, and fights," de Gaulle declared, "but the war is over because the outcome is decided." Free France must put herself in the best position to take advantage of the defeat of Germany. That was Moulin's mission.

Moulin parachuted into Provence in the opening hours of the new year. He immediately began to set up an administrative structure to coordinate propaganda activities and create a plan to administer France after the Liberation. Passy insisted that in these early days of 1942, his purpose was simply to coordinate rather than unify the Resistance. Its unification and eventual subordination to Gaullist direction would begin spontaneously among the *résistants* themselves, he asserted. Because the Resistance groups in the occupied zone of northern France had been largely decimated in late 1941, Moulin concentrated his early efforts on the *zone libre*. But even there Moulin's mission to convince the fragmented Resistance groups to coordinate their activities, operate in a uniform fashion, and eliminate doubtful elements would be difficult enough.[21]

"We were wolves, adventurous ideologues, who didn't want anyone to get their claws on us," remembered Emmanuel d'Astier de la Vignerie, leader of Libération, whose geographical center was Clermont-Ferrand, whom Passy saw as the biggest impediment to unification. But there were others, like the conservative Henri Frenay, leader of Combat, centered in Lyon, who received the idea of London's leadership with a bad grace that bordered on open defiance.

But relations with these independent groups were smooth compared with the difficulties Moulin encountered with the communists. Recent studies based on newly released archives in Moscow show that the goal of the French Communist Party (PCF) was to control the internal Resistance and make it independent of the Free French. It was hoped that these armed Resistance forces under PCF control would provoke a "national insurrection" upon the Liberation that would bring the communists to power. Moulin skillfully thwarted these communist plans, which bolsters the arguments of those who say that Moulin was not working for a communist takeover. [22]

The first step in Moulin's grand plan for the Resistance was the creation in August 1942 of the Armée Secrète. Under General Charles Delestraint, the AS was to coordinate paramilitary action among the three Resistance groups in the *zone libre* in anticipation of an eventual Allied invasion. In February 1943, Delestraint's authority was extended to the northern zone. When the communists refused to integrate their FTP into the AS, Moulin stopped military subsidies from London until they complied. [23] Gradually a parade of visits by *résistants* to London, German military reversals, Laval's intensified collaboration with Germany, the occupation of the southern zone, and the imposition of STO succeeded in breaking down opposition to unity. Moulin set up a wireless and air liaison service under BCRA control. A Comité de Coordination announced the beginnings of political cooperation in the autumn of 1942. In January 1943, a Mouvements Unis de Résistance (MUR), a fusion of Combat, Libération, and FTP, was created, and on 21 February, de Gaulle signed into being a Conseil National de la Résistance (CNR). Moulin's job, as president of the CNR, was to persuade leaders of the Resistance groups, trade unions, and political parties to agree to sit in it. True to their takeover strategy, the communists refused at first to participate, insisting that they wanted an independent "National Front." By again withholding funds, Moulin forced them into the CNR in May 1943. Then he concentrated on bringing in experienced prewar politicians to prevent the communists from turning the CNR into an independent political base to use against London.[24]

The unification of the Resistance was part of a larger Gaullist strategy in which the BCRA played a central role. On 24 January 1943, de Gaulle and Giraud had been brought to Casablanca, where Roosevelt and Churchill were discussing the war's next phase, and made to shake hands before the world press as a symbol of French unity. General Georges Catroux then led a Gaullist delegation to Algiers to discuss transforming this symbolic unity into a unified government. Negotiations stalled, and the Gaullists feared that, unless something was done to get them off dead center, Roosevelt might impose his own solution for the government of France. Moulin returned to London in February 1943 to spend a month closeted with Passy. The priority, they concluded, must be to produce a statement of Resistance support for de Gaulle. After two months of travel and protracted negotiations with Resistance leaders, on 15 May Moulin was able to send to de Gaulle a message from the "parliament" of the Resistance, of which he was "president," to announce its total allegiance to the principles incarnated in Fighting France and a declaration that "the people of France will never accept the subordination of General de Gaulle to General Giraud." Moulin called for "the rapid installation in Algiers of a provisional government under General de Gaulle, who will remain the only head of the French Resistance, whatever the results of negotiations." This declaration had been difficult to secure, because the communists had entered into separate negotiations with an emissary from Giraud, who they believed (correctly) would be easier to manipulate than de Gaulle. Moulin had defeated their motion in the CNR to call for "equality" between Giraud and de Gaulle.[25] This was the declaration which the leader of Fighting France required to establish his legitimacy in the eyes of London and Washington. Two days later, General Giraud invited the Gaullist leader to Algiers.

On 27 May 1943, seventeen men representing Resistance organizations, political parties, and two trade unions gathered in an apartment at 48 rue du Four in Paris for the inaugural meeting of the CNR. The meeting demonstrated the tenuous unity of the Resistance, as well as its lack of security-consciousness—discussion often degenerated into a shouting match as groups accused each other of bad faith, while the communists, ever suspicious of de Gaulle's intentions, repeatedly demanded to know the composition of the government after the Liberation.[26] But the symbolic value was immense, especially when it voted the motion that "France expects that a real government will be formed in North Africa . . . and that it will be headed by General de Gaulle, the soul of the Resistance in its darkest days."

But Moulin sensed that the Germans were closing in. On 7 May, he asked de Gaulle to send a deputy so that he could instruct his "successors." The arrest of a Resistance chief in Marseille who talked to save his skin gave the Germans the means to roll up an important segment of the Resistance leadership. On 9 June, General Delestraint, head of the Armée Secrète, was arrested at the Muette metro station in Paris, the first in a Gestapo line of inquiry which would lead to Moulin.

Moulin moved on to Lyon, but news of his journey traveled with him. The chief of the Lyon branch of Himmler's SS Sicherheitsdienst (SD), Obersturmführer Klaus Barbie, was alerted that an important representative of de Gaulle was to hold a meeting on 21 June 1943. Who tipped off the Germans or how Barbie discovered the place of the meeting was never clearly revealed. But at two-thirty in the afternoon of 21 June 1943, one of the *résistants* who had gathered to meet Moulin looked out from a second-story window of the house of Dr. Dugoujon in the Lyon suburb of Caluire as a large number of men dressed in long leather coats pushed through the garden gate and ran into the house. They barely had time to persuade René Hardy, the only one of them who was armed, not to use his pistol to defend them before the Germans burst into the room. After a preliminary roughing up, the handcuffed occupants were driven to SD headquarters in the Military Medical School of Lyon, but not before Hardy pushed past the Germans and fled into the town. (Hardy was subsequently accused of betraying Moulin, but postwar trials failed to convict him.)

At SD headquarters, they were led into a basement which was already filled with other suspects, and, still handcuffed, were made to face the wall. In ones and twos they were taken upstairs for interrogation. One of those arrested, Henri Aubry, was in the process of being beaten by his interrogators when a large man with a pale complexion walked into the room, threw a stack of mail on the table, and said in French, "Moulin is among them." "Immediately, intense jubilation of Barbie and his acolyte," Aubry recounted. "They came at Lassagne [another resister] and me. We said we didn't know him."

After several more beatings, at eleven o'clock at night the prisoners were thrown into a truck and taken to Fort Montluc. Meanwhile, police sent to Aubry's house discovered a treasure trove of documents relating to the Armée Secrète, which led to more arrests. It took Barbie two days to discover which of his prisoners was Moulin. No method was too brutal for the SS officer—the prisoners were systematically beaten, and lined up before firing squads furnished by the Wehrmacht, only to be reprieved at the last second. On 24 June, Christian Pineau, an arrested member of Libération-Nord, upon whom had devolved the job of prison barber because the Germans had allowed him to retain possession of a mechanical razor, was pulled out of his cell by an SS sergeant to shave a prisoner. "What stupefaction, what horror, when I realized that the man stretched out before me was none other than Moulin. He had lost consciousness, his eyes were sunken as if they had been forced back in his head. There was a terrible bluish wound on his forehead. A faint groan escaped from his swollen lips." The exact date of Moulin's death is not known. The prisoners were transferred to Paris, where the Gestapo attempted to revive Moulin, who had apparently fallen into a coma, for questioning. In the second week of July, he was put on a train for Germany, but was declared dead on arrival at Frankfurt. Only one of those arrested at Caluire survived deportation.[27]

June 1943 was a dreadful month for the BCRA. The SD crowed that the arrest of Moulin and Delestraint had decapitated the Resistance, while three more BCRA networks fell in June, two of them in Lyon. But as far as de Gaulle was concerned, Moulin had accomplished his task—the Resistance had given him a mandate to govern. Never mind that several important Resistance groups remained outside the CNR. It was an endorsement too powerful for the Americans to ignore. Nor had the BCRA in Algiers, under Passy's friend Major Pelabon, another graduate of the Ecole Polytechnique, been idle. On

Sunday, 30 May, a "spontaneous" pro-Gaullist demonstration greeted the head of Fighting France when, without any prior announcement, he appeared to lay a wreath at the Algiers war memorial.[28] On 3 June, a Comité Française de Libération Nationale (CFLN) was created under the dual leadership of Giraud and de Gaulle. On 17 June, the forces loyal to Giraud and those of Fighting France were unified. This had been brought about in part by desertions organized among Giraudist units by Gaullists, and by entire units in Tunisia demanding to be placed under the Cross of Lorraine.[29] Now they could spend the rest of the war fighting the Germans, sometimes on the same side. Finally, on 21 June, the day Moulin was apprehended at Caluire, a de Gaulle–Giraud "dual command" was declared in Algiers. De Gaulle had got his nose well and truly under Giraud's tent.

These developments were most unwelcome to Passy's rivals in Algiers, for whom June 1943 had also proved a dreadful month. The Germans had made over fifty arrests in the destruction of Paillole's Travaux Ruraux networks in Limoges and Clermont-Ferrand. This led them to uncover on 25 June thirty tons of secret service archives left behind after Torch. "What a success for the technicians!" Passy gibed.[30] The Germans also caused significant damage to the Organisation de Résistance de l'Armée (ORA), a Resistance network made up of army veterans whose loyalties were to Rivet's SR. But far worse than these setbacks for Rivet and Paillole had been the arrival of de Gaulle in Algiers on 30 May, which announced the beginning of many political changes, including the "dual command" decree, which, they insisted, was a "revolutionary measure, which had nothing to do with the salvation of the country, and is mortal for the service." Paillole and Rivet submitted their resignations to Giraud, asserting that the SR could serve only "one leader . . . The organization which has just been created is incompatible with the notion of a military SR," which would now be opened to "the influence of partisan politics." Not surprisingly, Giraud refused the resignations. But Rivet and Paillole had put their cards on the table: There could be only one chief and one secret service. From now on the French secret services would fight two wars—one against the Germans and the other against their rivals.[31]

Much to the relief of the Germans, one imagines, the French intelligence officers invested a good portion of their energies in their civil war. Passy complained that Major Pelabon, BCRA station chief in Algiers, was kept under strict surveillance. His three small rooms in a dilapidated building in Algiers were swamped by recruits, many of whom were obviously provocateurs. The Giraudists labeled it a "desertion agency," accusing it of helping to orchestrate blatant Gaullist attempts to entice French soldiers to desert to Gaullist regiments, and worked to have Pelabon expelled. This obviously threatened the viability of a service which insisted that it had a purely military function. Passy claimed that the difficulties created for Pelabon convinced him that a merger of the secret services was a nonstarter.[32]

In September, Giraud reorganized his secret services, all of which were grouped under the command of General Ronin. At the same time, the chief of the American OSS, General Bill Donovan, sent as Roosevelt's personal representative to investigate the intelligence picture in North Africa, recommended that the duality cease in favor of the Giraudists. Both moves backfired. The administrative reorganization of Giraudist services merely served to allow the Gaullists to point out the absurdity of maintaining two separate intelligence organizations, while Donovan's clumsy intervention in internal French matters offered further proof, the Gaullists claimed, that the Giraudists were mere lackeys of Roosevelt. The Gaullist-dominated CFLN intervened on 25 September to strip Giraud of some of his forces and to impose General Cochet of the air force as the head of the combined intelligence services. Ronin resigned in a huff.

While the Gaullists had won a round, the Giraudists still maintained a strong presence at Cochet's headquarters in the Palais Bruce at the entry to the Casbah of Algiers. Rivet presided over the SR, which included Paillole's Securité Militaire, and the technical services. But a section named Services Extérieurs de Renseignements, whose responsibilities remained rather vague, was given to Major Pelabon, who continued to direct the BCRA's Algiers station. For its part, the Giraudists created SR and counterintelligence posts at BCRA headquarters in London. This organization caused desperate problems during the liberation of Corsica in September and in Spain, where much intelligence on occupied France was collected, as intelligence officers of Giraudist and Gaullist services found their ability to communicate with their superiors severely restricted. The recriminations between the two sides burst into open hostility, however, when the Giraudists produced a BCRA order from London instructing its Algiers annex to spy on the Giraudist services. Worse, in November, Paillole learned that the BCRA was trying to convince Cochet that the officers of Paillole's Sécurité Militaire should be excluded from the services because they were "collaborationists and traitors . . . subject to military justice, for complicity of intelligence with the enemy." He fired off a blistering letter to Cochet. But it was too late—on 20 November, Cochet, daunted by the task of the secret service merger, resigned, while Giraud had been maneuvered out of his "dual presidency" role by de Gaulle. Such was Paillole's exasperation, one Gaullist adherent later claimed, that he hatched a plan to have de Gaulle kidnapped from his villa and held hostage on the battleship *Richelieu*, whose sailors still raged against his "treacherous" 1940 attack on Dakar.[33]

On 27 November 1943, Cochet was replaced by Jacques Soustelle. Of all the moves in this undeclared secret service war, this was among the most bizarre. Soustelle appeared an unlikely candidate to preside over, let alone resolve, a bitter feud between military factions if there ever was one. A young academic, a specialist in the early cultures of Central America, Soustelle had never held a rank higher than reserve lieutenant. Nor did he have any experience in intelligence work. His Gaullist credentials were impeccable, however. The war had caught him on a research trip in Mexico, where he rallied to the Gaullist cause. At the time of his appointment, Soustelle was Commissaire à l'Information, but from London he had followed closely the attempts of Passy and Moulin to unify the Resistance. When Giraud protested the appointment of a civilian to head the intelligence services, de Gaulle replied amiably: "If that bothers you, we will dress him up as a general."[34]

Soustelle had two assets that would serve him well. First, he was intelligent, supple, and patient—personal qualities that would put him in good stead to heal this bitter rift. Second, he had reinforced administrative powers as the head of the newly created Direction Générale des Services Spéciaux (DGSS), which superseded the BCRA and under which Passy's, Rivet's, and Paillole's services now fell. At the same time, de Gaulle had created a Comité d'Action en France, which included the Commissioners of War and the Interior, of which Soustelle was secretary, and over which de Gaulle personally presided. In this way, the DGSS answered directly to the chief of state, not to the military command.[35]

Rivet refused to see his SR submerged into what he regarded, not without reason, as a political service, especially after Passy and Soustelle insulted the two Giraudists during a 30 November 1943 meeting to discuss the new organization by demanding that they sign a loyalty oath.[36] Backed by Giraud, Rivet insisted that he would continue to communicate directly with the military command. Attempts to mediate the crisis failed. Rivet's SR and Paillole's SM for the moment remained outside the DGSS.[37] As the Gaullists controlled the CFLN, it appeared that this rearguard action of the "Vichy Resistance" could be easily quelled. However, Rivet found some unlikely allies among those in the Gaullist camp who nurtured no more love for the BCRA than did Rivet—Resistance leaders like Henri Frenay of Combat and Emmanuel d'Astier de la Vignerie of Libération, who resented Passy's cattle drive toward Resistance unity and who communicated these resentments to the Commissariat à l'Intérieur, now led by d'Astier, who sought to break up the BCRA to the profit of the Interior.

D'Astier's oblique support of Rivet was all the more surprising since one of the principal reasons for Rivet's opposition to the Gaullists was the fear that Moulin and d'Astier, whose left-wing political sympathies tilted precariously toward communism, would gain undue influence over French intelligence.[38] Rivet's apprehensions were widely shared. D'Astier topped the bill in a troupe of Resistance leaders and agents who appeared to have been selected for their thespian qualities. Tall, thin, his dark hair rippled above elegant, well-defined features which seemed to testify to his aristocratic lineage, Emmanuel d'Astier sprang from a family which, like the Scottish aristocracy of old, sought to place a son in each political camp. Henri, an outspoken monarchist, was a staunch supporter of Vichy, while François, an air force general, had rallied to de Gaulle. Emmanuel had married a wealthy American woman and espoused right-wing sentiments not uncommon to his class, which included an outspoken anti-Semitism. But he later converted to more radical beliefs, Wybot believed, under the influence of Luba Krassine, daughter of the Soviet ambassador to London, whom he later married.

In 1942, when d'Astier appeared in London to speak for Libération, it became clear that he was an opium addict. The BCRA would not permit his return to France until he had kicked his habit—for fear that, should he be captured, simple drug deprivation would cause him to tell the Germans all he knew.[39] Georges Groussard, who also had been quite taken by Fourcaud, compared the "eagle-profiled" d'Astier with Saint-Just, an aristocratic champion of the French Revolution, an unswerving patriot, and passionate advocate of a cause he believed to be virtuous.[40]

For Passy, however, d'Astier was an unstable fantasist, a "mixture of condottiere and Machiavelli," a "rich man playing at anarchist" cursed with a runaway imagination. His ancien régime charm and mocking smile could turn into "uncontrolled flashes of hateful and violent temper." His positions on issues could shift with equally breathtaking speed. His great strength was that, for reasons which Passy found inexplicable, de Gaulle seemed to like him. In 1942, the General had dispatched d'Astier on a speaking tour of the United States. There he drew ridicule on Free France by giving a press conference with his head covered by a sack to preserve his widely known identity, during which d'Astier's disembodied voice claimed that Libération numbered between thirty and fifty thousand Resistance fighters. While a skeptical Passy had heard these assertions before, by going public d'Astier exposed his delusions to a thorough debunking by a host of foreign affairs and intelligence officials as well as Frenchmen hostile to Free France.[41]

In the midst of this "war of the secret services," d'Astier revived the debate which Passy thought he had won in the summer of 1942. D'Astier maintained that responsibility for "political action" in France should be surrendered to his Interior Commissariat, and found a number of representatives in the Consultative Assembly in Algiers to support his view. Soustelle saw this as merely a communist ploy "to undermine in the spirit of the résistants the authority of the Provisional Government." This produced one of the great ironies of the secret service war: Rivet, who sought to maintain the independence of his service in great part to protect it from communist influence, counted communists led by d'Astier, who now praised Rivet and Paillole in public, among his greatest supporters. This, of course, did not pass unnoticed in the BCRA/DGSS.[42] On 28 December, Rivet's defiance succeeded in winning a personal audience with de Gaulle, who disguised his exasperation with this secret service quarrel long enough to give Rivet's arguments a polite and apparently sympathetic hearing.[43]

But Rivet had succeeded only in producing a temporary tactical stalemate in his war with the Gaullists, for many of the strengths of his SR were fading. Paillole's networks and the ORA led by Generals Aubert Achille Jules Frère and Georges Revers and his TR Jeune under Navarre were badly chewed up by the Abwehr and Gestapo in late 1943. Paillole had even forced them to abandon the landing of agents by submarine on the remote and windswept Cap Camarat near Saint-Tropez after the Germans intercepted one mission in late November. This allowed Soustelle to argue that BCRA/DGSS intelligence on France was now much better than that produced by Rivet's service, which "was very weak . . . Cut off from the complex reality of occupied France . . . they had nothing comparable to the most rudimentary of our networks." Rivet countered bitterly that Soustelle's DGSS was little more than a "Hottentot bazaar," full of pretentious and ambitious men who, eager to evade the dangers of combat, discovered a last-minute enthusiasm for intelligence work, for Gaullism, or for both. Paillole complained that this secret service war went "beyond the bounds of decency," that his mail was opened, and that the Gaullists had placed spies everywhere.[44] But the fact remained that with the approach of D-Day, the Mediterranean theater was fast becoming a secondary front in every struggle but that of the civil war which raged within the French intelligence services. If Passy had chosen to remain in London, it was because Algiers was fast receding into the backwaters of intelligence.

Furthermore, Soustelle had a powerful argument in a debate with men who, each time they received an order, returned with a note signed by Giraud which read: "Colonel Rivet and Major Paillole report to the commander-in-chief and receive orders only from me."[45] Despite Paillole's insistence that only the Germans would profit, the Consultative Assembly gave Soustelle permission in March 1944 to sever Rivet's SR from the accounts of the DGSS. Rivet and Paillole began to discover that their revenues were not keeping pace with their expenditures. To counter this, Giraud insisted that this would lead to the breakup of his secret services, while Paillole attempted to play the American card by having his London chief of station, Major Bonnefous, accredited to Eisenhower's headquarters. And while the agree-

ment to slot a representative of the Service de Sécurité Militaire in
the counterintelligence section of SHAEF headquarters was considered
essential for effective operations in liberated France, predictable difficulties with de Gaulle over questions of sovereignty delayed its implementation until after D-Day.[46] Paillole also sought to strengthen
his networks by infiltrating more agents into France through Spain, a
much longer and more perilous route than via Lysander from Britain.

But in Giraud, Rivet and Paillole had backed the wrong horse. In
the eyes of de Gaulle and his adherents, there was no such thing as
a "Giraudist," merely "Pétainists" in Giraud's clothing. Nor was the
fact that the Giraudists had acquired the dubious assets of Admiral
Muselier and Cot's old associate André Labarthe, after the two had
been cast from the Free French camp, exactly conducive to smooth
relations. Labarthe apparently used his time in Algiers to recruit at
least two men who would become important Soviet spies in the postwar
years.[47] Furthermore, the Giraudists had deepened that distrust by
their open cooperation with the Allies. For Fighting France, heir to
a struggle which began in June 1940, to be recognized as the sole
voice of France, this was an intolerable challenge to de Gaulle's authority. "We are afraid that the Allies can call on someone other than
us," Passy confessed to Paillole. This was why de Gaulle could not
tolerate a separate secret service independent of his will.[48] Even Giraud's most loyal supporters had been soured by his inability to rescue
former Vichy Minister of the Interior Pierre Pucheu from de Gaulle's
firing squad.[49] On 4 April 1944, the post of commander-in-chief occupied by Giraud was abolished by the CFLN, and he was offered
the largely honorific post of Inspector General. On 13 April, Rivet
was promoted to brigadier and retired. Paillole's reputation as France's
master of counterintelligence was such that even the Gaullists recognized the need to continue his services. "I'm counting on you," de
Gaulle told him on 2 May 1944. But Paillole finally resigned in
November 1944, after a further reorganization took counterintelligence
away from the War Ministry and gave it to the Interior.

It was small consolation for Rivet's men, perhaps, but in early 1944
the Abwehr, too, had lost its battle to fend off absorption by Himmler's
SD. Maybe now, at least, the French secret services could get on with
the business of winning the war against Germany.

TEN

THE RESISTANCE

That the Gaullist movement not only succeeded in being recognized by the Allies but obliterated its rivals for the leadership of France in 1943 has entered the historical record as a triumph for the tenacity, not to say the bloody-mindedness, of de Gaulle himself. As the preceding chapter has emphasized, the BCRA played midwife to that triumph. What Paillole and Ronin had missed as they sat smugly before what appeared to be a hopelessly inexperienced Passy in December 1942 was that the world war had transformed the intelligence game beyond recognition. And for no country was this more true than for France. Passy's failings as an administrator and technician of intelligence gathering had been more than compensated for by a vision of the BCRA as a political instrument, rather than a strictly technical service whose role was to inform the commander-in-chief.

Passy's strategy from the beginning was to put the Free French intelligence services in a position to take advantage of the discontent which, given time, was bound to result from German occupation and Vichy collaboration. De Gaulle's success depended ultimately on Passy's and Moulin's ability to create a Resistance out of disparate, spontaneous expressions of rage, despair, or simply quiet patriotism which had begun to ripple through France, and to secure the loyalty of those groups for the Free French. The primary function of the Resistance was to challenge Vichy's authority and underwrite de Gaulle's legitimacy, a purpose essentially accomplished in 1943.

A strong—even primary—component in the legitimacy bestowed by the Resistance on de Gaulle sprang from the moral authority which accrued to those fighting to liberate France. These were the men and women who actively aided the Allied cause by collecting intelligence and participating in military action against the enemy. De Gaulle's enduring row with the British and later the Americans revolved around the issue of sovereignty, about which de Gaulle was especially sensitive. As he represented the legitimate government of France, any Allied operations on French soil required the full consultation and participation of the Free French. The Allies were reluctant to concede this point, and the Americans made preparations to install their own civil administration in France on its liberation. Therefore, de Gaulle and Passy had to prove to the Allies that, without Resistance participation, intelligence gathering and military action in France would be doomed to ineffectiveness. In short, the Resistance must become more than a political platform for Gaullism. It must also become an efficient instrument of intelligence collection and military action during the war, and be prepared to keep order at the end of it. Only in this way would the Free French be accorded credibility in Allied councils of war. The problem for Passy, however, was how to create a useful military, or more specifically paramilitary, force out of a Resistance orchestrated primarily as a political instrument.

The answer to this question has been obscured by the many legends which began to accumulate around the Resistance even before the war's end, legends which afterward became institutionalized in popular and political memory. In countless postwar films and novels, shadowy agents whispered information vital to the war effort, while resisters intrepidly derailed trains, machine-gunned convoys of sinister, Gestapo-stuffed Citroëns, or sent motorcyclists of the *Feldpolizei* and their sidecar passengers careening into ditches along lonely French roads. So powerful was the Resistance mystique, so important did it become to French self-esteem, that only gradually, and not without controversy, have historians been able to assess its size and significance.

In their attempts to reach some sort of objective verdict, historians have not been helped by military leaders of the eminence of Dwight

Eisenhower, who claimed that the French Resistance was worth six divisions during the 1944 invasion of France.[1] The military disasters of the Resistance, like the slaughter at Vercors in July 1944, or the annihilation of the Warsaw uprising, have driven historians toward the conclusion that courageous but lightly armed maquis were no match for disciplined Wehrmacht units in classic combat.[2] But at the time, these pessimistic conclusions could be explained away as aberrations or betrayals depending on one's point of view, uprisings starved of strategic results, deliberately or otherwise, for want of outside assistance. Elsewhere, however, patriots served the cause of the Allies and of national liberation by organizing into maquis units for raids and ambushes or by acting as saboteurs and spies.

If the Resistance *levée en masse* failed to materialize, its image as the eyes and ears of the Allies, as well as creating a "climate of insecurity" behind German lines by sabotage and armed attacks, became accepted even before war's end. SHAEF bulletins in the summer and autumn of 1944 reported thousands of German troops killed in actions with French maquis forces,[3] hence Eisenhower's statement that the Resistance was worth six divisions. After the war, the Resistance became a major industry. Histories like Gilles Perrault's *The Secret of D-Day* or Richard Collier's *Ten Thousand Eyes*, or the memoirs of Resistance leaders Rémy, Henri Frenay, Pierre Nord, and Marie-Madeleine Foucarde, fixed in the historical imagination the vision of a France risen in revolt against her Nazi occupiers.

This Resistance reputation of vitality and efficiency is one which has only grudgingly submitted to close scrutiny. One reason for this is that the view is a perfectly plausible one. On the surface, at least, the Resistance would appear to be a godsend for intelligence and special operations officers. The Allies had Ultra, of course, which contributed a great deal of information about order of battle and, more intermittently, about enemy intentions. But the Resistance furnished an army estimated by Soustelle in 1943 to number 75,000 men and women who held the German occupiers under constant observation, eager to report every movement, every rumor of an impending operation or the appearance of new weapon or defensive work, things which Ultra might not or could not detect.

Although technical intelligence began to replace human intelligence as the primary source of information on the enemy from 1939, according to R. V. Jones, the leader in British scientific intelligence in World War II, humint, including POW interrogations and those produced by SIS, still had the edge between 1939 and 1945. "If we include the tremendous efforts of the Resistance agents in occupied Europe, the balance of [the intelligence] effort may then still have been on the side of gathering intelligence by human observation . . ." Having recounted the valuable work of the French Resistance in piecing together the preparations for the V rocket attacks on London, work which caused them to call down an air strike on a factory staffed by forced laborers in which 500 were killed, Jones enthused, "Can anyone wonder that Langley [head of the escape and evasion section at MI6] and I 'loved our agents'?"[4] Passy claimed that by late 1942 an average Resistance intelligence network was sending 1,000 typed pages of intelligence per month. "Our only strong point was that we were furnishing the Allied general staff with 80 percent of its intelligence on France," Passy believed.[5]

Therefore, even after the revelations of Ultra became public knowledge in 1974, and the results of the Allied bombing campaign closely inspected, the question of Resistance effectiveness has barely been challenged.[6] There may be several excellent reasons for this, a primary one being that a comparison between humint and Ultra would be difficult to quantify. Histories of the French Resistance, even the best ones, seldom rise above the anecdotal, and are much given to accounts of heroic exploits or the tragic decimation of networks. Moreover, to ask questions whose answers might suggest that the courage and sacrifice of so many men and women in the battle against an enemy of such unspeakable immorality had been for naught might be demoralizing or appear disrespectful. The belief that the occupied countries of Europe had played a significant role in their own liberation became a necessary myth, especially in France, where national self-esteem had been dealt a humiliating blow in 1940. Furthermore, high-profile resisters stormed into the postwar era with significant moral and political capital. They drew advantage from the perpetuation of a vision of a divided and prostrate France guided to salvation by the most dynamic and courageous among its people.[7] Finally, the Resistance legend was promoted by those with emotional or bureaucratic capital invested in the wartime Resistance, men like "Wild Bill" Donovan, who successfully marketed the French Resistance to bolster his case with the American government for the need to create a Central Intelligence Agency.

Neither Passy nor Moulin believed that the political mission of the Resistance threatened the effectiveness of intelligence gathering, sabotage, or armed attack. Quite the contrary, Passy recognized early on the value of intelligence and action to gain credibility for his service in British and eventually in American eyes. One of the anticipated dividends of Resistance unity would be to allow the Gaullists to orchestrate their activities and thereby convince the Allies that they required Gaullist cooperation whenever France figured in their campaign plans. De Gaulle was especially keen to avoid a situation in which the Resistance sustained high casualties in military operations beyond their capabilities. He urged Passy to constitute paramilitary groups which could "guide Allied operations thanks to our intelligence on the enemy." But, he insisted, the benefit of these services must ultimately accrue to France; they should not merely smooth Allied operations with no quid pro quo.[8] Moulin was convinced that military action was a "moral question." France must contribute to her own salvation. Military action would offer an outlet for popular frustration and exhibit the incremental success without which the French people would become demoralized. Finally, the Liberation would likely unleash anarchy in France, which could only be controlled by a politically loyal and disciplined paramilitary force.[9]

In theory, at least, Passy controlled the lion's share of humint on France. But that advantage was far from the monopoly that he required to deal with the Allies from a position of strength. In many respects this was a consequence of the Gaullist vision of the Resistance as a mass movement. The British had recommended to Passy that he collect intelligence through professional agents. He had rejected this view, insisting instead that people in place were in a much better position to know what was going on than were itinerant agents cut off from their sources who passed through like traveling salesmen taking orders and making deliveries. Whatever the merits of this view from an intelligence and security perspective (and they were questionable), the result was that the BCRA effectively became a tributary, sometimes even a hostage, to local Resistance groups in intelligence collection and action missions. As the individual Resistance groups produced the product and knew its value to Passy, they exacted a high price for it. Intelligence offered one way in which the internal Resistance in France could influence the external Resistance in London.[10]

And exert influence they did! Probably the most egregious example was that of Henri Frenay of Combat, who sold his intelligence directly to the OSS's Allen Dulles in Switzerland. Passy lamented this "serious loss of weight and of prestige when one realizes the enormous interest which the English attach to intelligence."[11] Frenay usually confined his responses to a business level, arguing that the Americans paid good money for his intelligence, cash he required to run his networks. When the BCRA began to pay the market rate, then it could have exclusive title to the information collected by his resisters. But the plain fact was that, if Passy wanted Frenay's intelligence, he would have to take Frenay's views on the organization of Fighting France into serious consideration. Moulin believed that by doing business directly with Frenay, the Americans sought to split the Resistance and win Combat for the Giraudists.[12] As for action, the Gaullists were increasingly powerless to exert control over the communist-led FTP, who rejected the *attentisme* of London—that is, waiting for D-Day—and pushed for *action immédiate* to create a second front to take pressure off the Soviet Union.

De Gaulle's political rivals also sought to bolster their cause with the Allies by supplying them with intelligence on France. Rivet and Paillole's TR networks in occupied France run by General Henri Navarre, supplemented by the Organisation de la Résistance de l'Armée (ORA), sent information, especially German orders of battle, directly to the Allies through Lisbon and Bern.[13] As has been seen, after Torch the Allied services established very close relationships with Paillole's Direction de la Sécurité Militaire, the successor to the BMA, considered by the Anglo-Americans to be more professional than that of the Gaullists, and even ran double agents jointly with Paillole.[14] Others, like *ci-devant* Vichyite Georges Groussard, maintained Resistance networks independent of Passy because he believed most of the CNR's Resistance leaders were little more than "bandit chiefs."[15] Nor were the Allies content to deal through Gaullist middlemen for their intelligence and sabotage. The British SOE organized their own operations and worked through other groups, the Alliance network being the most celebrated. The Poles had established active and especially effective networks in France very early on, while, from 1942, the American OSS operating out of Algiers parachuted agents into southern France.

Quite naturally, the British, eager to acquire unimpeded access to intelligence that would help them win the war, grew impatient with the Gaullist priority of solidifying the Resistance as a political movement. SIS rightly suspected that, once this occurred, de Gaulle and Passy would use Resistance-supplied intelligence as a currency of political exchange. Some of the earliest conflicts between Passy and the SIS arose over the "nonmilitary" passengers to whom Passy allocated scarce passenger space in clandestine flights from France. While the British sought good agents, Passy wanted men who could extend Gaullist political influence. Passy argued that once a vast political Resistance was in place, the flow of military intelligence would quickly follow. British rejection of this view was only in part attributable to their lack of enthusiasm for de Gaulle.[16] SIS realized that, to be successful, intelligence networks should be small, secretive, tightly organized to insulate them as far as possible against detection and penetration. This was Passy's dilemma: He realized that intelligence networks required tight security. But as he needed to create a mass movement, security could not be his first priority.

The Perils of
Intelligence Gathering

Sloppy security need not have produced devastating consequences had a few precautions been taken, for the quality of the German opposition was far from first-class. The task of combating the Resistance in France fell to two German organizations. Abwehr III, part of the Abwehr which answered to Fremde Heere West (Foreign Armies West) through its chief, Admiral Wilhelm Canaris, was responsible for counterintelligence and security. Its French *Abwehrstellen*—*Ast* for short—was located in the Hotel Lutétia, with outstations at Le Havre, Angers,

Nantes, Bordeaux, Dijon, and Lyon. The *Ast* in Lille was responsible for the Nord and the Pas de Calais and depended on Brussels. The Abwehr and the army shared responsibility for the Geheime Feldpolizei (GFP), or secret field police.

The second service was the Sicherheitsdienst (SD), the Nazi Party security service, whose French headquarters at 82–86 avenue Foch answered to Himmler, chief of the SS and Minister of the Interior. The SD was often referred to as the Gestapo. Technically this is incorrect, as the Gestapo was a branch of the secret political police with its headquarters at 11 rue de Saussaies behind the French Interior Ministry. In fact, the distinction between the SD and the Gestapo was purely academic. Nor must one forget the fifteen separate police organizations run by Vichy, the most redoubtable from a Resistance standpoint being the Milice. Founded in June 1943 under the pro-Nazi Joseph Darnand, the Milice operated only in the southern zone, where by early 1944 it became a fearsome enemy of the Resistance.

This potentially formidable array of repressive power was compromised in practice by bitter rivalry between the Abwehr and the SD/Gestapo, who often refused to cooperate in security operations. That rivalry began at the top. Canaris, a capable U-boat commander in World War I, proved to be a mediocre spymaster, in part because he was strongly anti-Nazi and allowed many unenthusiastic servants of Hitler's Germany to congregate in his service. The result was that, as an intelligence agency, the Abwehr definitely lacked edge—it was unsupervised, often corrupt, and its normal inefficiency was on occasion compounded by deliberate sabotage. The bad news for the French Resistance was that this made the Abwehr vulnerable to a takeover bid by the SD in February 1944, when Canaris lost his job and the staff of the Abwehr was gradually absorbed into the SD. The SD/Gestapo provided the most feared opponents of the Resistance, and they successfully penetrated many of their nets. But this fear stemmed from the barbarity of their methods more than any intrinsic respect for the quality of their police work. The beating death of Jean Moulin by Klaus Barbie's interrogators at Lyon was all too typical of a service which favored brutality over more subtle investigative methods.

The Italian OVRA operated in a half dozen departments close to their frontier until the Italian surrender in 1943. As for the Vichy police, theoretically they were the most formidable because they had local knowledge, although the Germans, too, employed French "mercenaries." But in practice, the commitment of the Vichy police to track down "terrorists," "Judeo-Marxists," and "agents of British Imperialism" might not be all that Laval hoped. Many policemen in the lower echelons were sympathetic to the Resistance, but how they would react depended very much on circumstance. As has been seen, the Surveillance du Territoire spied on French citizens or exploited information received from Paillole's BMA which might lead to the arrest of *résistants* and the destruction of networks.[17]

Given the shaky quality of the visitors, more's the pity the Resistance could not make more of their home-team advantage. Unfortunately, the security-consciousness of most *résistants* ran from minimal to nonexistent, an example which flowed from the top.

On 1 December 1940, Rémy's first report to London seethed with indignation over having been furnished lists of friends or family members of men who had rallied to the Free French in London with the assurance that they were sympathetic to de Gaulle. In fact, several were staunch Pétainists, or worse, so that on several occasions he narrowly avoided arrest.[18]

In January 1943, none other than Passy toured occupied France, thereby courting a human intelligence disaster. For that matter, Rémy also on occasion displayed a reckless disregard for his own safety and consequently for that of his networks. Lower down, resisters too often demonstrated suicidal indiscretion. This was due in part to the nature of Resistance recruitment. The conflict between a tightly organized, discreet intelligence network and the Gaullist concept of the Resistance as a large army, "a national expression,"[19] has already been noted. More, a desire for some sort of military demonstration against the enemy caused the BCRA to pander to the wishes of local networks to mix intelligence and action in the same organization. This virtually guaranteed a more dynamic, and therefore visible, recruit for the Resistance, one keen to carry out attention-grabbing acts and then boast about it afterward. The fact that most resisters were recruited haphazardly by a friend or acquaintance rather than according to any plan of Resistance needs, assuming that one had ever been established, meant that a chain of relationships was created which, once tapped into, might easily be followed link by link.

On the whole young, eager to run risks, the full measure of which they were blithely unaware of, those who enlisted in the Resistance wanted to make a statement. "Actually, our efforts were more a manifestation of resistance against the Germans than really effective action," wrote Philippe Thyraud de Vosjoli, for whom the Resistance became a ticket to a career in postwar intelligence. "We wanted to confuse the enemy and get a measure of revenge. The fear of arrest or torture added spice to our lives, which was necessary when all hope seemed lost. It also was a form of protest against the majority of the population who followed Pétain's example and spent much of their time analyzing who was to blame for the French defeat."[20]

Garrulousness, the endemic affliction of the Resistance, almost proved the undoing of eighteen-year-old Alexandre de Marenches, future chief of the postwar SDECE. In 1942, having succeeded in crossing the Pyrenees and catching a train to Madrid, he engaged in a conversation in English with an elegantly dressed gentleman standing in the corridor, during which he boasted of his escape and stated his intention to join the Free French. "Oh! Really? How interesting!" the man replied. When they reached Madrid and Marenches saw an important retinue waiting on the platform, he was made aware that he had been talking to none other than the German ambassador to Spain! His knees still shaking from his narrow escape, he took a room by chance in the Hotel Florida, which, he quickly discovered, provided the principal lodging for German intelligence officers in Spain.[21] Marenches was more fortunate than many resisters, victims of patrols or crooked *passeurs* in the Pyrenees or picked up in closely watched train stations in France at the end of trips during which they had talked too much.[22] It is hardly surprising, then, that one historian of the Resistance has estimated that 95 percent of *résistants* and agents caught owed their arrests to their own indiscretions.[23]

The vast majority of resisters were enthusiastic recruits pitched into a major war with only a minimal grasp of the tactics required for success and survival. Some, like the increasingly large numbers of young men who took to the hills from 1943 when called up for STO—forced labor in Germany—lived rough, and were increasingly driven into more remote areas by German countermeasures, often resorting to exactions on the local populations to survive. Others were told simply to wait for the general uprising which was to occur on D-Day. They might participate in a parachute drop or a pickup by Lysander or even a local sabotage mission.

But for those called to the clandestine life, existence became more difficult as the grip of the occupation tightened. One of the factors working against them was a system of administrative controls which were intensified by the war. *Résistants* had to construct a false identity that would stand up to a surprise *contrôle* by police or *Feldpolizei* or simply enable them to obtain the ration cards necessary to eat. At first they simply claimed to be from a town whose records had been destroyed by bombardment. But this quickly became inadequate. A lucky or important *résistant* might find a compliant municipal official to furnish the name of someone who had yet to pick up his ration card, in the hope that it was a person whose death had yet to be announced, or who had fled to North Africa, and not someone whose release from prison was imminent. Then the *service faux-papiers* in London or in the Resistance net would produce the identity card, railway pass, tax receipts, membership in a sporting club, all properly stamped, even calling cards, anything needed to bolster the chosen identity.

This in itself could cause unforeseen problems—a prison guard named Mimile, after having arranged a daring prison escape for some resisters, was given a false identity, as was his wife, but under a different name. However, when the ex-guard discovered that his wife was pregnant, he was overcome by a sense of respectability and remarried her under his false identity, which was also passed on to the baby. How the French administration unraveled that one after the war is anyone's guess. Travel by any conveyance more substantial than a bicycle required an *Ausweiss*, or travel pass, which is one reason the bicycle became the favored Resistance mode of transportation. The laundry mark on the resister's clothes had to match the assumed name, and it was helpful to know something of the profession one had assumed, especially if it involved delivering babies. Those who entered most successfully into their assumed identities might discover new vulnerabilities—Henri Noguères confessed to heart palpitations when, quite by chance, he read in the local newspaper the obituary of the man whose identity he had purloined.[24]

But this about stretched the limits of the clandestine imagination, for resisters invariably broadcast their identity in other ways. Smoked glasses, a professorial beard which followed the line of the jaw, and a small briefcase became the accoutrements of a *résistant* Identi-Kit to the point that one newspaper published a "picture" of a resister without face or body but with these three accessories. Even if the Gestapo did not know what a resister looked like, they invariably knew where to find him. To Lyon's boast that it was the "capital of the Resistance," one could append "capital of the Gestapo." Even Resistance leaders acknowledged the folly of assembling so many *résistants* in a city, "where practically you couldn't go ten meters without running into an underground comrade whom you had to pretend not to know . . ." Clandestine rendezvous tended also to be held in a limited and fairly predictable number of places. For instance, the steps of the municipal theater and the Pont Morand at Lyon witnessed so many Resistance encounters that one wonders why Klaus Barbie did not simply set a watch there to arrest anyone who appeared with smoked glasses, a beard, and a briefcase.

And if this "uniform" was not a dead giveaway, resisters often made themselves conspicuous by their behavior. As these meetings often took place in public between men unknown to each other, they usually contrived to call attention to themselves in some way. When Noguères was dispatched to a rendezvous on a railway platform, for example, the prearranged signal for recognition was that he would carry a copy of the *Petit Méridional*. Unexpectedly brisk sales of that newspaper forced him to purchase *L'Eclair* instead. So he paced the platform muttering, "The *Petit Méridional* is sold out. The *Petit Méridional* is sold out." As the person he was meant to meet had missed his train, all he succeeded in doing was to convince most of the passengers that he was stark raving mad. But had an agent of the Gestapo or Milice been present, he might well have been taken in for a *vérification d'identité*, the first leg of a one-way trip to Dachau.[25] Suspicious behavior might also bring on anonymous denunciations, which Passy and Rémy regarded as a real security threat. While many of the anonymous denunciations might have been fabricated by the ST on the basis of telephone taps and the interception of mail, Passy instructed local resistance groups to counter them by sending their own unsigned denunciations of the pro-Allied sentiments of notorious collaborators.[26]

As the war progressed and network after network was decimated by the German or French police, Passy conceded that his Resistance networks must be made more secure and his agents better trained. But this proved very difficult to do. First, because the object of the Resistance was political, leaders were often selected on the basis of their acceptability both to London and to the suspiciously independent Resistance groups, rather than because they demonstrated any particular flair for clandestine warfare. Numerous were the men who were pulled off the street or parachuted into France with little or no preparation to replace some fallen leader or rebuild a decimated network.

In 1942, leadership of the Armée Secrète fell to General Charles Delestraint because he was an "anti-Pétain" soldier who had the backing of Combat's leader, Henri Frenay, whom de Gaulle was eager to mollify. But the sixty-three-year-old general, plucked from quiet retirement at Bourg-en-Bresse in the center of France, displayed little aptitude for clandestine life. "I could never make him understand how a mail drop worked," one Resistance leader complained. "He could not be brought to understand how it was possible to put an envelope with someone's name or a code into a letter box which bore another name."[27] Courageous to a fault, he took no trouble to be discreet, parading about Paris with his erect military bearing and the "tomato" of the Légion d'Honneur prominently displayed in his buttonhole. His solicitous and deferential assistant, another military man, who accompanied him on his missions, could not be broken of the habit of addressing him as *Mon Général* rather than by his Resistance nom de guerre, Monsieur Vidal: "*Après vous, Mon Général.*" "*Je vous en prie, Mon Général.*" "*Bien sûr, Mon Général.*" When in 1943 the unfortunate Delestraint was approached by SD agents pretending to be members of the Resistance, he asked them to drive by to pick up two other *résistants* with whom he was to meet. Quite naturally, they were delighted to oblige.

To be fair to Passy, he had to recruit his resisters where he could find them. Emile Bollaert confessed to his complete surprise when he was approached in his apartment on the rue Vavin in 1943 and asked to become Jean Moulin's replacement on the CNR. Not only did he have a family but he was absolutely ignorant of the Resistance, on which he had to be given a crash course. Noguères was parachuted into France to become the regional chief of the communist FTP, although he was not a communist and knew nothing of the group's structure.[28]

But such were the fortunes of war, which demanded adaptability at short notice. Some inexperienced Resistance leaders did prove quick learners, like Jacques Chaban-Delmas, who two months before D-Day was catapulted by the DGSS, the successors to the BCRA, into the post of *délégué militaire national* with the task of coordinating military action for the invasion. But the sad fact remained that the decimation of Resistance cadres by arrests and by STO sabotaged efforts to create a stable leadership. Rapid growth and the decentralized structure of the Resistance made it difficult to institute practices vital for security in the face of the increased efficiency of the German and Vichy police. In fact, the poor security of BCRA networks, together with more generous American allowances, became one of the OSS's major recruiting pitches to "the de Gaullist-inclined candidates . . . Their security was incredibly bad, which was to a certain extent true, while we functioned on the cellular principle of not mixing people together and thus putting them in jeopardy from one individual being caught and forced to talk."[29]

Passy repeatedly issued orders that "compartmentalization" within and between Resistance groups be respected, and on paper it often was.[30] The larger Resistance groups, like *Mouvements Unis de Résistance* (MUR), had a national director and regional subordinates. They organized into "services" which corresponded to activities, as "maquis," "Secret Army," "medical service," "intelligence," "immediate action," "radio," "false papers," "air operations," and so on, each of which was represented on the national and regional level. In theory, one was expected to belong to only one Resistance group and one service within that group. The communist FTP, taking counsel of the communist party's history of secretiveness and its cell structure, most successfully respected compartmentalization. In practice, however, not only did people belong to more than one Resistance group; the Resistance also reflected French political life in that *cumul des fonctions* (accumulation of jobs) was common. This was especially the case in the various military services, where the tasks overlapped and where coordination across services, regions, and Resistance groups was re-

quired. Regional and even national leaders made frequent visits to
local groups, while efficiency required liaison between groups. This
made for a small world in which systematic sweeps by Gestapo or
police of metro and train stations could have devastating consequences,
especially as in too many cases leaders and agents kept extensive notes
and records of their contacts.[31] "This was the principal cause of the
ravages inflicted upon our networks by the Gestapo," Passy insisted.
The Resistance attempted to attenuate this security risk somewhat by
using women as couriers and liaison agents, because they were not
subject to STO and less likely to be searched than were young men.[32]

Problems with intelligence began with a weak organization at the
top. Separate intelligence and "action mission" sections were created
in BCRA headquarters. But the Resistance networks opposed central
direction. The arrests of Delestraint and Moulin in June 1943 allowed
the base to reassert its authority over the center. The shift of Fighting
France from London to Algiers in the same year split the intelligence
services. Jacques Soustelle, who succeeded Passy as head of the BCRA/
DGSS, was not a member of the Provisional Government, which
refused to define intelligence missions or give him authority to correspond directly to occupied France, although he did it anyway. "My
position each day became more ambiguous," Soustelle complained.
The archives failed to follow the movers from London, which gave
him little to work with.[33] Passy had attempted to resolve the action/
intelligence dilemma by organizing "operational networks" to gather
intelligence from smaller groups. In his view, Rémy's confrérie Notre-
Dame remained by far the strongest intelligence network, while the
communist "Service B," code-named "Fana" for *"Fanatique"* by the
Gaullists, delivered good political intelligence, but "they were deplorable in the military domain," he wrote. "Their reports were very
thin . . . and of a quality which was more than mediocre. One can
affirm, therefore, with proof in hand, that the contribution of the
Communist Party to the French war effort, in the area of intelligence,
was practically negligible."[34] The British did little to help at first, for
they were slow to specify what sort of intelligence they wished to have.
However, Passy boasted that by 1944 he could have a reply to a British
intelligence query on any subject within forty-eight hours.[35]

The best intelligence in the world was worthless if it could not find its way to those who needed it. American intelligence found operations in France an expensive business: 200,000 francs ($4,000 or £1,000) was the standard rate demanded by truck drivers to transport a package of documents to, say, the Pyrenees, where a further 50,000 ($1,000 or £250) francs was required to get it to Spain.[36] The quickest way to speed intelligence was via radio, and it was here that the battle between the Resistance and the Germans raged most fiercely. Passy had to train operators, get them to France, and keep them broadcasting. The Germans had to close them down, thus stanching the flow of information to the Allies. Free France faced many difficulties in running radio nets. One reason was that few of the limited numbers of recruits possessed the special aptitudes required of radio operators. This was probably just as well, because radio technology early in the war was ill-adapted to clandestine living. When Passy dropped into occupied France in January 1943 and saw firsthand the scope of the Resistance movement, he realized that its intelligence potential, especially in the north, could be increased immensely if he could supply more radios.[37]

That resolution depended both on manpower and on equipment. Passy's manpower problem might have been solved had the British allowed him to train radio operators in France. But London would not hear of that. So volunteers had to be combed for potential recruits, who were then trained by the British.[38] Although the first radio contact between London and a field agent had been made in December 1940,[39] everything was limited in the early years of the war—radios, frequencies, and the capacity of the reception center to receive signals. In fact, as late as the first months of 1943, 40 percent of Resistance broadcasts were on frequencies which only the Germans were capable of listening to.[40] The requirement, of course, was to reconcile the need for the rapid transmission of information with security. This was not always easy to achieve. The shortage of "pianists," as radio operators were called, forced Passy to create *centrales* to serve several groups. While this was necessary, it was also risky. The result was that 55 percent of Resistance radio operators were captured.[41]

Most of those captured fell to German radio detection teams, for the ability of the French Resistance to send information by radio was rapidly outstripped by the German capacity to detect the emissions and locate the radio. The type of radio most frequently used in France was a B mark II, capable of transmitting and receiving signals. It weighed thirty pounds and was fitted into a suitcase about two feet long. While it had a wide frequency range, its signal was relatively weak, which required the operator to spread out about seventy feet of eye-catching antenna. Frequencies were changed by replacing fragile crystals. Replacement parts, like batteries, were expensive, when one could find them at all. The result was that the Resistance was desperately short of radios throughout the war.[42]

Given the fact that the Germans had taken fairly elaborate steps to build up agent nets before the war in Czechoslovakia, Poland, and France, they proved remarkably unprepared to deal with the appearance of clandestine stations in countries occupied by the Wehrmacht. The only detection stations available for "radio defense" were those which the police used to apprehend illegal ham operators in Germany.[43] The Germans had only fixed detection stations which had to listen to many frequencies and could take only one directional reading for the radio beam per transmission. For obvious reasons, pianists preferred to broadcast from the *zone libre*, especially after several operators were picked up in the occupied zone in November 1941 and March 1942. In this case, the Germans were reduced to phoning the Vichy *contrôle radio-électrique* at Hauterive in the Allier and ask them for a directional reading on the beam. Hauterive would tell the station to shut down, and then give the Germans a false reading. On 21 September 1942, the Germans began Operation Donar in the *zone libre* in cooperation with the Vichy police, which, Wilhelm Flicke maintained, captured twelve transmitters in three months.[44]

German technical competence also improved in 1942. A "panoramic" receiver placed in a static position, such as the army barracks on the boulevard Suchet in Paris, was able to detect all the radio traffic on a band of 100 kc/s. When a luminous spot appeared on the screen, the operator could check its frequency against the approved list to see if it was a clandestine station. He would then alert the three radiogoniometric centers at Brest, Augsburg, and Nuremberg to tune in to that frequency and send their azimuths, which would cross in a triangle measuring twenty kilometers on each face. By the spring of 1944, this was reduced to a circle with a one-kilometer radius. Then the second German innovation would come into play. The closest SD, Gestapo, or Abwehr station would dispatch mobile RDF (radio direction finding) vans which would move to the edges of the triangle and gradually reduce the field of action until the location of the radio could be pinpointed. The Germans became so practiced that it took only fourteen minutes from the moment the panoramic receiver picked up the transmission until the RDF vars or black Gestapo Citroëns were on the street in front of the pianist's house or apartment. According to Flicke, the Germans were able with these methods to cut an enormous swath through clandestine transmissions: eleven radios complete with transmission plans and crystals taken in Paris in June, thirteen transmitters in July, and forty stations soon after that in the former *zone libre* run by the Deuxième Bureau, each with a number of operators, agents, and codes. [45]

All clandestine transmissions were recorded on magnetic bands, which were handed over to the deciphering service. If they determined that their computer could not break the code, then the order was given to close down the radio immediately. If the code was believed to be breakable, then the order might be given to locate the radio discreetly but allow it to continue to transmit. Passy refused to believe the British when they complained in March 1944 that "every message" the French sent "can be read by the Germans," and accused the British of having used a French code book. So the head of SOE's deciphering section went over to Duke Street, asked the French to encode a message on any subject they chose, and to Passy's astonishment and annoyance broke the code under his very nose. [46] Poor French code security made the British even more reluctant to cooperate too closely with the French. [47] Nevertheless, it is possible that more than one French pianist owed his longevity to poor French codes.

The pianist could adopt several countermeasures, even after German detection vans moved into the *zone libre* prior to Torch. The first was to limit the length of his transmissions by stopping the "conversations" between the pianist and London. Separate and irregular times for sending and receiving messages meant that a pianist would spend less time at his radio. These irregular schedules were established in the first half of 1943, and it was reckoned that they reduced the casualties among pianists. [48] But the number of messages to send and receive, and poor reception sometimes caused by German jamming designed to oblige London to ask for a repetition of all or part of a message, might make that difficult. The pianist could also change frequencies, putting out his call signal on one frequency, getting the acknowledgment of reception on another, and then transmitting his messages on a third. In the midst of his messages, he might also put out a second call signal to make pursuers think there was a second radio.[49] But such radio acrobatics were limited by the skill of the pianist and the patience of the reception center. The Germans also caught on to this technique. When more radios were available, the Resistance pianists might try to saturate an area with radio emissions, forcing the Germans to concentrate their research. In this way, one or two radios might fall, but others would continue to broadcast.

Another option was to change addresses frequently. This, too, had practical limitations. Presumably members of the Resistance responsible for transmitting intelligence had to know where to bring the messages they wanted to send. Police quickly learned to spot suspicious suitcases containing radios. The best option was to have as many as five "music boxes" in different locations, each set to broadcast or receive on a different frequency. The pianist would live in a separate location, where he would encipher and encode his correspondence, and bicycle among his various work stations. This worked better for SOE than for the Resistance, which had few networks rich enough in equipment to make this a universal solution. Also, a pianist stopped by a police *rafle* (sweep) who had in his possession correspondence prepared in the five-letter code groups required for transmission might as well cancel his holiday plans. Lookouts could be placed around radios to spot the ubiquitous RDF vans. But the Germans learned to disguise them as delivery vans. Worse, technical advancements miniaturized detection equipment, so that it could be placed in innocent-looking cars, carried in a suitcase, and by early 1943 worn on a belt with the receiver pressed to the ear of a Gestapo agent walking on a street where a radio had been located.[50] André Heintz, a student at the University of Caen and member of a Resistance network in Normandy, reported that the mere appearance of detector vans in the Calvados, site of the Normandy invasion, caused a shutdown of all radio transmissions to England for a full three weeks.[51]

So the expert detection methods of the Germans could limit the dispatch of intelligence. Paillole admitted that German radio detection was such that his TR officers were reluctant to broadcast intelligence from occupied France to North Africa.[52] It also made the BCRA and the British vulnerable to deception. While the Germans enjoyed nothing of the success in "turning" agents in France as they had in Holland, they did score points. Flicke insisted that 30 percent of the parachute drops to the Resistance were picked up by the Germans as the result of "radio games."[53] In theory, there were ways to guard against this. Each pianist had a "fingerprint," a manner of typing his Morse messages which was distinguishable. If London suspected that the pianist had been given a Gestapo substitute, then the messages could be compared with a magnetic tape to see if the fingerprint matched. But an experienced German wireless operator could imitate a fingerprint, as was proven when half a dozen Germans successfully ran fourteen SOE transmitters in Holland. It was recognized that pianists often operated in desperate conditions, which was more likely than not to alter his fingerprint. Pianists also used local trainees to operate sets, which would change the fingerprint.[54]

Security checks were supposed to guard against an operator being "turned." These might consist of a deliberate spelling or coding mistake specific to each operator. When the Germans discovered this security check, a second one was instituted so the captured operator might give the "bluff check" and keep the "true check" to himself. But in practice, with jamming, bad reception, the strain of sending under adverse conditions, and poor encoding, a pianist often made so many mistakes that the security checks might pass unnoticed, especially in a busy section with a high turnover of its junior staff. The section which actually received the message seldom checked the original enciphered version but merely looked at the translation. If a mistake had been made, there were so many possible reasons for it that virtually no notice was taken. Worse, when the omission of the security check was noticed, too often a message was sent which read: "My dear fellow, you only left us a week ago. On your first messages you go and forget to put your true check." The result was yet more torture for the hapless operator, until he finally gave his true identity, which would produce a message of congratulations from London.[55] It was in this way that the Germans managed to gain control of the SOE Archdeacon net for ten months, pick up fifteen parachute drops, and arrest several agents.[56]

From this brief view of the problems of the Resistance, it might be assumed that the Germans had rendered it impotent. But that was not the conclusion of Gaullist intelligence. "Diverse and reliable sources continue to bring reports of the growth of a national resistance despite the growing number of arrests," de Gaulle's Deuxième Bureau reported on 23 December 1942, "which offers more proof of the insecurity of the occupying authorities."[57] Under normal circumstances, any commander who ascribed such devastating losses to anything other than theoretical shortcomings in his strategic doctrine or the poor performance of his service might be thought to be suffering from advanced dementia. But the ability of the Resistance to replace its losses seemingly at will, especially when placed in the context of a fight waged throughout Europe, did unsettle Wilhelm Flicke. The battle against the Resistance in France, Belgium, Holland, and the Balkans was replicated in the East, where expert Polish operators and Russians with less proficiency but in staggering numbers stretched to the breaking point the German capacity to track them down. "In general, it was a hopeless fight against the agent radios, since for each transmitter which was seized and for every operator who was arrested a new one appeared at a new location, with new characteristics and with a new cryptographic system," Flicke wrote.[58] Had the German services consisted only of the Abwehr, which was a notorious hotbed of anti-Nazi sentiment, defeatist and more easily demoralized, then the morale of German counterintelligence might well have cracked. Unfortunately, the SD and the Milice seemed to feed on the challenge.

The Resistance and Intelligence

So, despite the best efforts of the Germans to stanch it, much intelligence was clearly getting through. There were some fairly spectacular cases of extremely useful intelligence supplied by the Resistance. R. V. Jones was fond of pointing out how the successful British raid in February 1941 to dismantle the German Würzburg station at Bruneval which stood atop a 400-foot cliff on the French coast north of Le Havre would not have been possible without the preliminary re-

connaissance of one of Rémy's agents, Roger Dumont. Dumont discovered that the German soldiers guarding the installation were neither
first-class nor particularly vigilant and that the beach at the foot of the
cliff was not mined and therefore offered an exit for the British raiding
party dropped by air. As the Würzburg stations were vital links in
guiding German bombers to their British targets in 1940–41, in the
opinion of Jones the successful raid gave the British "a first-hand
knowledge of the state of German radar technology," and hence the
keys to counter it.[59]

Humint continued to play an active role in World War II. A message
by Major Philippon on 10 May 1941 that Brest was preparing to receive
a large warship alerted the British to the arrival of the *Bismarck*, which
was intercepted on 28 May.[60] The slaughter of Canadian troops at
Dieppe in the summer of 1942 might have been avoided had an agent
been available to report the guns concealed in the cliffs overlooking
the beach, something which photo reconnaissance failed to detect.[61]
One of the charges leveled by Rivet's service against the BCRA/DGSS
was that they were more interested in political than in military intelligence. Soustelle denied this charge vehemently, claiming that nine-
tenths of the intelligence provided by the BCRA/DGSS was of direct
military value. Certainly, from the beginning Rémy laid plans to gather
military intelligence though Vichy-organized veterans groups, while
Saint-Jacques collected information on German munitions depots.[62]
Nevertheless, Rivet may have had a point. Quite a few of the surviving
reports deal with political events in Vichy and with the state of opinion
in France. And as has been seen, from the beginning de Gaulle, Passy,
and even Rémy saw Free French intelligence as having a supremely
political mission. This sat badly with at least some members of the
intelligence services, who, in an anonymous report dated 22 January
1941, lamented the politicization of the intelligence service which
caused it to distort intelligence to fit the preconceptions of the client,
and the indifference shown by de Gaulle toward intelligence and above
all to proposals of military action.[63]

It is also likely that the secret service furnished political intelligence
because information on the German army in France was hard to come
by. A report of 19 December 1942 of de Gaulle's Deuxième Bureau
admitted that Free France had little hard information on German

troops in France.[64] A report of 1 July 1943 complained that "the contradictions noted in the different information received, the imprecisions of some of these reports, the numerous movements of German troops make it very difficult to establish an exact order of battle of German troops stationed in France." This was in part because the Germans often left behind a *Stamm* (stem) which continued to behave as if it were a full-strength unit, an indication that some of the information was coming through radio intercepts. "If one considers the division garrisons where the presence is certain, one realizes that certain coastal sectors are completely devoid of defense [regiments between the Somme and the Seine, the extremities of Finistère, for example], which seems inconceivable. The number of 22 infantry divisions appears to constitute a minimum *which is certainly false . . .* the real number must be closer to 33 than 22."[65]

"With regard to intelligence gathering," writes American historian of D-Day Stephen Ambrose, "the Resistance was the best possible source on the Atlantic Wall because most of that was built by Frenchmen."[66] But if the Resistance kept the BCRA passably well informed on coastal defenses, it was less precise about the troops manning them. And an order of battle which could be off by eleven infantry divisions does not constitute usable military intelligence, as the report acknowledged. Agent reports of German order of battle reaching British intelligence were often fragmentary, of poor quality, and inconsistent, and only improved as agents began to note the shoulder patch or some other distinguishing unit mark.[67] André Heintz admitted that his methods of tracking German troop movements in the Calvados were unscientific—picking up gossip in the bus queue, checking the unit numbers on the shirt collars of uniforms given to local women to wash, or checking on inscriptions on soldiers' graves, "but you had to wait until one died!" Although civilians were excluded from the coastal zone, he could report the appearance of a new bunker, battery, or minefield by consulting the tax rolls in which farmers reported which of their fields had been taken out of cultivation. However, he lacked the expertise to reply to specific questions like the caliber of a gun in an emplacement, the morale of occupying troops, or how many men would be necessary to invest the place. "It was indeed very difficult to assess for people as inexperienced as most of us were. The only thing it did, in fact, was to make us think that it was not fair to ask us that question unless D-Day was getting near. Other questions were perfectly useless, like finding passwords which were changed every day."[68] The shortcomings of humint need not be fatal to the Allies because they could check the report against Ultra intercepts or photo reconnaissance. But this demonstrates that few in the Resistance were trained to give specific military information.[69]

The contribution made by the Resistance to the intelligence picture before D-Day has also been given high marks. The most spectacular feat was the theft of the plans for the German coastal defenses along the Normandy coast by a *résistant* employed to paint the offices of the Todt Organization in Caen. These plans helped Allied planners to identify the weak points in the defenses.[70] Artillery experts were probably better able to determine the amount of firepower required to reduce specific bunkers.[71] But although much has been made of this celebrated theft, clearly the Resistance was stealing plans of German coastal defenses well before this and continued to do so afterward. In fact, one thing which the rather sparse military intelligence archives preserved at Vincennes do contain are a number of blueprints of blockhouses and topographical sketches of sections of French coastline. Some were probably done on the basis of air reconnaissance photos, but not all—one set of three *documents originaux* of coastal defense maps in the Trouville-Houlgate area just east of the invasion beaches is stamped 13 November 1941. French intelligence was also collecting much Resistance information on German coastal fortifications, much of which was categorized D or C value.[72] But at least these reports could be checked against photo reconnaissance and be added to the large-scale map prepared for the invasion by the intelligence branch of SHAEF, which had found a home in the ladies' corsets department on the second floor of Peter Robinson's shop on Oxford Circus.[73] OSS files stored in the National Archives in Washington contain hand-drawn maps of French airfields, descriptions of coastal defenses, some reports on military trains and German order of battle in Corsica and France, all obviously Resistance-generated.[74]

The problem with D-Day intelligence is that, although the invaders knew everything about the coastline, every house and bunker, intelligence was focused on the problem of getting ashore across a very narrow belt of German defenses. As a consequence, the Allies had only the glimmer of an idea about conditions in the rear areas—what the hedgerows were like or what effects the flooding of low areas behind the invasion beaches might have on operations. In any case, the plan was for Montgomery to seize Caen on D-Day and then break out east toward Paris. Therefore, intelligence on the rear areas was not considered vital.

Probably the most significant contribution of the Resistance was in detecting and defeating the V-1 and V-2 attacks on Europe. The British had received indications of experiments being carried out at Peenemünde on the Baltic coast of Germany as early as 1939. Reports by agents and *résistants* in several countries enabled London to begin to piece together from 1943 that the Germans were experimenting with guided bombs and constructing launch sites along the Atlantic coast. Much of this came through Polish and Alliance networks in France, which gave detailed reports to SOE on experiments at Peenemünde. A French officer and POW working in the RAX works near Wiener-Neustadt sent a very detailed sketch of a V-2 engine, which failed to arrive in London. R. V. Jones believed this a pity, for it would have avoided much speculation about the German engines, which was rife until an experimental V-2 fell into neutral Sweden in June 1944. Pierre Julitte, an officer on de Gaulle's staff, who was sent to France in 1943, captured by the Gestapo, and deported, discovered that he was working in a factory making parts for the V-2 guidance system. He smuggled a report to Paris which brought down an Allied air raid on his own factory.[75]

Donovan believed that the Resistance had saved American and, by extension, Allied lives. Of this, there can be little doubt. However, his own organization concluded on the eve of D-Day that though most humint was supplied by "patriotic Frenchmen," to rely on it was "a false and misleading . . . idea . . . A considerable amount of valuable intelligence is procured by outright purchase from venal people who have always been the traditional purveyors of intelligence." Far more effective, from the American perspective, were a few agents well supplied with cash to buy plans from German officers or bribe French police for tips.[76] Precise agent information proved essential to the success of certain action missions, like the Bruneval raid, and certainly might have made the Dieppe raid less of a bloodbath had it been procured. The precision of the Resistance intelligence on the V weapons proved important in alerting the British to the menace and delaying deployment by pinpointing bombing sites, although this came from several sources, not merely humint. The Resistance also contributed to deception by helping to keep alive the German fear of an attack in the Pas de Calais, even after the Normandy invasion, by continuing to receive radio messages. But the real source of this deception was the phony army created in the southeast of England. Excellent double agents were run by Paillole's Direction de la Sécurité Militaire out of North Africa to deceive the Germans about the time and place of Anvil, the invasion of southern France. But these measures did not keep the Germans from guessing exactly where the Anvil landing would occur in August 1944, even though this knowledge could not save them.[77] And, as will be seen, Resistance-supplied economic intelligence appears to have been good, although it remains an open question how much this was distorted to support Gaullist pressure to limit Allied bombing missions in France.

That said, however, the strategic contribution of the Resistance intelligence to the Allied victory is less evident. It is hard to credit the contention of R. V. Jones that the balance of intelligence in World War II favored humint. The military intelligence supplied by the Resistance appears to have been interesting but hardly critical. More accurate German order-of-battle information could be obtained through Ultra. Resistance intelligence on coastal defenses was certainly helpful so long as the information could be confirmed by photo reconnaissance. Its most useful intelligence appears to have been that associated with the development of the German V weapons. But here again the most valuable reports were those supplied by trained agents or specialists, like Sorbonne professor of physics Yves Roccard, who gave a very accurate appraisal of the German radar beam system, or the French engineer who sent in a detailed report on the Me 163 jet engine, or the French engineer who got a job designing a V-1 site.[78] And while R. V. Jones welcomed intelligence, by his own admission he took it as a professional challenge to figure out the German systems by himself.[79] From the Allied perspective, the real value of humint was that it provided an insurance policy in case the Germans abandoned Ultra for the one-time pad—randomly generated numbers as the basis of a cipher of which only the sender and the receiver have a copy. If the one-time pad is used only once, then the ciphered message is virtually unbreakable.[80] As for Passy, by gradually drawing French recruits toward the BCRA, he forced the Americans to deal with his service and by extension enabled the Free French to acquire radio operators and eventually French members of mixed Jedburgh teams.[81] These consisted of one American, one Frenchman, and a British subject—two of them officers and the third a wireless operator—dropped into Occupied France from June 1944, to provide a command center for local Resistance groups and to coordinate their activities in the interests of Allied strategy.

Intelligence or Sabotage?

One area of Resistance intelligence which did have an impact on policy was economic intelligence. Intelligence began to come in from 1942, detailed from the summer of 1943, to show that Allied bombing frequently targeted factories which were idle or even closed down due to lack of raw materials.[82] Worse, by 1943, complaints from the Resistance, in particular from railwaymen, about the number of French deaths caused by the imprecision of American high-altitude bombing filtered into the BCRA. On 22 September, Georges Boris of the French mission in London visited the American embassy to complain about high-altitude bombing, and received assurances from the Office of War Information that they would call Washington's attention to this.[83] The BCRA reported that the French understood the need for bombing raids. What they could not comprehend was why the USAAF took so little care to avoid civilian casualties, scattering bombs over towns like Annecy, Clermont-Ferrand, or Noisy-le-Sec in perfect weather with no hostile antiaircraft fire. "The British pilots bomb from a low altitude and with precision," a report of 5 June 1944 read. "The population is delighted to applaud the address of the British pilots." Civilian deaths caused by the many stray American bombs were exploited by German and Vichy propaganda. "Now, the Resistance organizations have their roots in these populations and can survive thanks only to their multiple complicities," General Pierre Koenig reported to SHAEF in early June 1944. "The efficiency of their action on D-Day might be diminished."[84]

The BCRA's case against USAAF bombing was supported by economic intelligence, which appears to have been much better than their military intelligence. There are at least three reasons why this was so. First, French intelligence was well placed to provide it through *résistants* working in French firms, factories, and railways. From the middle of 1943, the French Resistance had caught up with that of Belgium in its ability to give systematic reports of rail movements of German troops and war goods.[85] Second, until 1943, when the Germans appeared, at last, to be vulnerable on the battlefield, the British in particular envisaged a war of incalculable length in which victory would be won with the implosion of the German economy. Therefore, through 1943, there was a great demand for economic intelligence which would offer hints of German economic difficulties and guide the Allied bombing campaign. When, on 28 March 1942, the British carried out their first bombing raid in France on the Renault works at Boulogne-Billancourt near Paris, the Resistance was able to provide them with precise accounts of the damage and estimates of how long it would take to get production back to normal.[86]

Finally, bombing provided the incentive for the Gaullists in particular to provide precise economic intelligence, especially once the Americans got into the game. Passy objected that intelligence gathered during the Dieppe raid of August 1942, much of it gleaned no doubt through Source K, a tap placed on the main phone line between Paris and Berlin, demonstrated the German preference for moving reinforcements by road rather than rail. So by bombing rail lines, he argued, the Allies had only succeeded in restricting supplies to the French population.[87] A report by André Manuel on 2 June 1944 complained that the three-month intensive bombing campaign against French railways had damaged only a few hundred of the Société Nationale des Chemins de Fer (SNCF) 8,000 locomotives and a few thousand of their 200,000 freight cars, a minuscule percentage. Rail traffic had not been seriously disrupted. The rail density meant that alternative routes could always be found and, in any case, rail lines could be repaired in two days. "The present methods of bombardment have no effect on military transportation, which always gets through," he wrote. "One can in effect consider a lucky hit on a munitions or troop train or a one- or two-day delay in the arrival of a unit relief as a negligible strategic result." The most useful effect of the bombing campaign, Manuel reported, was that it had slowed down matériel getting to Germany. Its effects could be improved dramatically if Americans would concentrate on choke points, like the twenty-five cranes and the seven or eight repair yards in France, "preferably on a Sunday." Then "the SNCF would be dealt a death blow at little cost."[88]

The French argued that sabotage by the Resistance was superior to bombing, especially high-altitude bombing. Soustelle agreed that the Allied bombing campaign in France, tempting because it was far less lethal than sending planes over Germany, gave the BCRA a real incentive to collect economic intelligence and engage in economic sabotage, to "show [the Allies] the very effective results which could be obtained by our agents."[89] Unfortunately, even BCRA analysis did not always support Soustelle's goal. But at least if locomotives were "vaccinated" discreetly by railway workers, sabotage cost no French lives.[90] In December 1943, the Allies agreed to suspend bombing of rail lines and allow the Resistance to show how effective sabotage could be. The Resistance carried out 220 sabotage missions against the railways in December 1943 alone, and numerous others against electrical pylons and substations in an attempt to stop electric locomotives, a campaign for which Soustelle claimed great results.[91]

The BCRA/DGSS argument that sabotage was more effective than bombing, especially the intense tactical bombing carried out in France during April and May 1944 by the British Second Tactical Air Force and the American Ninth Air Force, betrays a mixture of ignorance and disinformation, perhaps even callousness. Unlike the British and American armies, which had become highly motorized, the German army had remained faithful to its nineteenth-century logistical concepts. Apart from the panzer divisions, most German formations moved short distances on foot with largely horse-drawn transport, and long distances by rail. And even the panzer divisions depended on railways for their logistical support and to move heavy equipment. So the implication of Passy's argument, that by concentrating on rail lines the Allies would do little to diminish the Germans' ability to reinforce the front, was simply inaccurate.

Nor does Passy appear to have appreciated the destructive capacity of tactical bombing. Between 20 and 28 May 1944, Allied bombing destroyed 500 locomotives and caused serious damage to rail lines, repair yards, and bridges. By 6 June, bombing had reduced French rail traffic to 30 percent of its January 1944 level, causing the Germans to wonder if it was even worth attempting to repair the lines. The Germans were barely able to keep their troops in Normandy supplied with the food, fuel, and ammunition required to maintain a static front, let alone maneuver, or even to make a fighting withdrawal.[92]

Why were French intelligence perceptions so far off the mark? It is possible that they simply underestimated the destructive capacity of a modern air force and overestimated the capacities of a Resistance movement. After all, the Free French had no air force to speak of, and so did not carry out the sort of strategic analysis of bombing done in Britain and the United States. They did have a Resistance movement, however, and so they argued for its effectiveness. And to be fair to Passy, the debate over the relative merits of bombing versus sabotage was a lively one at the time and continues to be so among historians.[93]

But Passy's arguments are suspect on political grounds, as he appears to have been quite willing to distort intelligence for the benefit of the Gaullist movement. It is true that the bombing of the French railways hurt the French people, and not simply in terms of those killed by stray bombs. If railway traffic were reduced to a trickle, it was the French who would suffer, as the Germans quite naturally gave priority to supplying their own troops. Vichy propaganda was quick to exploit the destruction and hardship brought upon the French population by Allied bombs. It was in the interest of Passy and de Gaulle to minimize the demands placed by the war on the French population, even if in the short term this aided the Germans. Therefore, Passy argued that in military terms roads were far more important than railways, and that railways could be disabled more effectively by sabotage.

It is hard to imagine that Passy's arguments raised the stock of French analysis in Allied intelligence circles. Nor can one imagine that the French people would have embraced his advocacy of sabotage with enthusiasm, especially as they were the object of German reprisals—indeed, the hostility of the population toward the maquis and SOE operatives furnishes a frequent theme in wartime memoirs. And no wonder! André Heintz reported that when a German troop train was derailed in the Calvados in April 1942, "the Germans immediately shot thirty hostages and threatened to shoot eighty others and deport another thousand. Curfew was brought down to 7:30 in the evening until 6:00 in the morning; all cinemas were closed and no more sports meetings or games allowed; every night—and that lasted for over two years, until the Landing of 1944—French hostages had to spend the night along the railroad that had been blown up and twenty more hostages had to accompany the leave train as far as Belgium and back." But, Heintz admitted, "this did not really stop the acts of sabotage."[94] The German practice of placing an empty freight car or an explosive scoop at the front of a train certainly could reduce the effectiveness of sabotage, however, which obliged the saboteur to use a pull switch which could be fired from cover. As junctions and stations were too dangerous to attack, sabotage was limited to isolated portions of track, causing minor rail damage which could be repaired in a matter of hours. For this reason, the effectiveness of rail sabotage depended upon repetitious disruptions. On D-Day, railwaymen who, with more enthusiasm than prudence, seized upon the news to carry out acts of sabotage were shot on the spot.[95]

A major consequence of sabotage was that it placed the mission of intelligence gathering at risk. BCRA/DGSS directives to the contrary, in practice it was very difficult to separate action and intelligence services in the Resistance networks. As suggested above, this was in part a function of recruitment. Those who had made the decision to join the Resistance were seldom content being assigned to intelligence gathering, a bureaucratic task lacking in romanticism, far less seductive than the prospect of killing Germans or members of the Milice.[96] Résistants engaged in intelligence gathering were denied the elation of contemplating the results of their efforts. They sent their information forward, seldom knowing if it ever reached its destination, or was taken seriously once it did. British air drops organized by SOE favored action services rather than those of intelligence. In 1943, when the intelligence services demanded arms "to protect themselves," Passy concluded that he had to give in; otherwise the intelligence gatherers would simply go off and join action services. "For many months, we only obtained information which lacked precision," Passy complained of his early efforts to collect intelligence.[97] One reason was that intelligence and action were often at cross-purposes. André Heintz remembered that sabotage undermined intelligence because "extensive German reprisals disorganized intelligence networks and made radio transmissions difficult."[98]

M. R. D. Foot has argued that sabotage by SOE and the Resistance had both the direct effect of limiting German resistance in the Normandy campaign and an indirect effect of sapping German morale.[99] How far German morale was undermined before the invasion by French hostility, either active or passive, is difficult to measure. "The French are still apathetic," the Japanese ambassador to Berlin cabled to Tokyo after a visit to the Atlantic Wall in October 1943, "and, while cooperating only reluctantly in the German war effort, are unlikely to do much to hamper German military operations in the event of an Allied landing." British intelligence found this to be "a reasoned and well considered document."[100]

On the eve of the invasion, American intelligence estimated that the French Resistance counted "575,000 men capable of military action."[101] On D-Day, these Resistance elements were to carry out three sabotage plans: *vert* (green) to disorganize the railways; *violet* (purple) for long-distance phone and telex lines; *bleu* (blue) for electricity pylons. Plan Bibendum sought to harass road traffic. According to Henri Noguères, the local Resistance groups poised to carry these out performed much better than Passy had anticipated, in part because they ignored, out of necessity, his strict security directives and recruited saboteurs from whatever maquis groups could furnish them.[102] On the night of 5 June 1944, 950 of 1,050 planned interruptions of railway traffic were carried out by Resistance and SOE teams. Rail traffic was seriously disrupted in the Rhone Valley, around Lille and Tourcoing in the north, and between Paris and Châteauroux.[103] The sabotaging of the rail lines behind the invasion beaches between Avranches and Saint-Lô and Saint-Lô and Cherbourg were considered especially valuable as poor weather limited the ability to bomb.[104] Sabotage, Foot insists, "produced and maintained railway stoppages at an even greater rate than the air forces were able to do." At Saint-Lô and in the Calvados, post office workers cut telecommunication cables,[105] forcing the Germans to use their radios, whose messages could be intercepted.[106] Resistance harassment of the Das Reich SS armored division stationed in the southwest of France delayed the arrival at the front of that important unit by a critical ten days. The constant pinpricks of sabotaged machines which reduced factories to idleness, of trains derailed, gradually undermined German forces in France and reduced their combat effectiveness.[107]

Foot's conclusion that sabotage by SOE and the Resistance was important to the success of the invasion but hardly decisive appears, on the surface, a reasonable one. But was it even important? Certainly, the World War II bombing campaign in France can be considered wasteful when the energy expended is measured against results. The value of the bombing campaign in World War II generally was the subject of considerable controversy at the time, and has continued to be debated by historians. But it is unlikely that, in its absence, sabotage by diverse ill-coordinated and often ill-equipped groups would have been an effective substitute for it, especially bombing of precise targets like bridges and repair centers which was effective and which was beyond the means of most Resistance sabotage teams. Indeed, André Heintz catalogued some of the acts of sabotage carried out for the Normandy invasion, but concluded: "Of course, all this—which implied much risk and required courage—accomplished very little compared to the bombings and the military action in the area."[108] German units struggling to reach Normandy found the hardest going to be the last two hundred miles when they entered the Allied tactical air range, which forced them to suspend daylight movement.[109]

The efficiency of sabotage could have been increased by employing highly skilled teams capable of destroying precise targets of strategic value, as was the case of one SOE team called Armada, which caused havoc far out of proportion to its numbers.[110] As with intelligence, it suggests that action missions could have become a more effective "force multiplier" had they been concentrated in the hands of a few specialists. No one had the capability to do that systematically during the war, least of all the Resistance. The bombing of electrical pylons did not stop rail traffic; there were plenty of steam engines to replace the disabled electric ones. When British economic historian Alan Milward questioned Albert Speer, Reichminister for War Production, on the effects of the French Resistance on German war production, Speer replied, "What French Resistance?" Although Milward cited several instances of successful sabotage, such as the closing of some small wolfram mines in central France, he concluded that the strategic value of Resistance sabotage was negligible.[111]

Tactical Intelligence

Once Allied troops landed in France, many French men and women offered their services as guides or informants on the enemy, suppliers of "combat intelligence," for Allied forces as they moved through France. "All enemy movements were reported in detail. Open warfare and guerrilla attacks deep inside France diverted entire German divisions," William Donovan reported to President Truman. The Resistance guarded the flanks of Allied troops driving up the Rhone Valley and "helped mop up bypassed German units and prevented the demolition of installations vital to the Allies. The battle of France showed as never before the extent of the assistance that an oppressed people, given supplies and leadership, can render to its allies in the course of its liberation."[112]

Donovan claimed that 50 percent of intelligence available to the U.S. Seventh Army during Anvil was provided by OSS humint.[113] Claims for the value of Resistance-supplied tactical intelligence are more plausible, but hardly overpowering. The possibilities of utilizing the Resistance for tactical intelligence only gradually dawned on Allied units. "G-2 thought we were to act as interrogators of French maquisards, translators of reports received from the French SR, which were often not worth translating, and general liaison men to do odd jobs and speak French around the division CP," wrote William Duff, commander of the 45th Infantry Division combat team in Operation Anvil. Many units did not even have combat intelligence teams. In Normandy, so many French men and women came forward to serve as battlefield guides that the OSS set up a special school to train them near Carentan on the Cherbourg peninsula.[114] In the Var, where Anvil took place in August, poor organization had combined with German repression to keep the Resistance weak. While many people came forward to act as guides to the American and French forces, it was very much ad hoc. Most resisters were interested only in liberating their department, and not in accompanying the Allied armies in their drive north. Even American historian Arthur Layton Funk, whose sympathy for the Resistance in Anvil is evident, is forced to conclude that conditions in southeastern France were such that the full potential of Allied-Resistance cooperation could not be realized.[115]

For tactical reconnaissance, the Americans began by using OSS agents, and eventually recruited French people to cross German lines to determine troop strength and pinpoint tanks, heavy weapons, fortifications, or headquarters for artillery fire. Many of these proved very useful. Duff reported that one agent, Marianne, was so well known by GIs of the 45th that she was greeted enthusiastically whenever she appeared. But Duff confessed that many American commanders remained "skeptical of the utility of our operations and of our personal ability . . . The result was that we ran many operations through the French sector."

A second problem with the agents was that their shortcomings were those of the Resistance generally. Some proved extremely resourceful, like the young agent picked up by the Germans as he approached a village in the Vosges in eastern France on a combat intelligence mission for the 45th division. He insisted that he was merely returning home, and to prove it shook the hand of the first Frenchman he encountered and began asking for news about several local people. Fortunately for him, the villager played along and the Germans released the agent to continue his reconnaissance. However, the quality of most agents was uneven, to say the least. "The agents we had proved to be about the best agents in the whole field, or so I am given to understand," Arthur Stratton, charged with recruiting agents for the U.S. Seventh Army in France, wrote to William Donovan in May 1946. But his assessment "was based on two or three superlative men, and a few dozen adequate lesser people . . . The lesser men were, half the time, wholly crooked." This may have been due in part to the fact that the Americans were dependent on the celebrated Free French 2nd Armored Division for their agents, who presumably kept the best for themselves. But many of the agents had no military experience and therefore did not know what to look for. Nor were they given radios until late in the campaign, so that timely intelligence often did not get to the units. Between missions, they were frequently seen wandering about town speaking openly of their work.

Many were simply more trouble than they were worth. To hear

Stratton tell it, he was more like a brothel master than an intelligence director. "Marie . . . was shrewd, not very intelligent, extremely emotional, enjoyed danger, enjoyed the spotlight of being a spy, and enjoyed all the men she could. That was her method of getting information. She was a very hard agent to manage; had no sense of security; disrupted all the household when she was waiting between jobs; and did not bring in first-rate information . . . As a matter of fact, her work for us ruined her, I guess, for life. She stole; she lied; she cheated; and she developed an insatiable appetite for men." A second agent, Ada, "unfortunately got herself pregnant, which involved a great many complications. Another woman, whose name I forget, could not bring herself to jump from the plane. A fourth was so stupid as to be totally useless." He even considered shooting "one failure of an agent . . . He made trouble. He knew too much, and learned more every day . . . I was told that the British and the French—in fact all other spy organizations—did shoot embarrassing people, and thought no more about it . . . Either the spy organization must provide a 'holding area' like a prison, or it must liquidate its embarrassing small mistakes à la Russe."[16]

In sum, German forces fighting in Normandy were significantly weakened by a lack of matériel and reinforcements. Sabotage attacks and harassment by the Resistance and SOE can take some credit for this, although the significance of their contribution is open to serious question. Donovan gave the Resistance, and of course the OSS's part in it, very high marks, as did the French; 87 Jedburgh groups and 19 operation groups composed of two officers and thirteen men with heavy weapons parachuted into France increased immeasurably the combat potential of the Resistance.

In a strategic sense, however, the Resistance can be said to have produced disappointing results, especially when compared with other successful insurgencies like those in the Balkans. In theory, the strength of an insurgency is that a relatively small number of mobile maquisards hidden within the population can tie down or divert a disproportionate number of regular troops. Success for a guerrilla movement is greatest when it can combine and coordinate its actions with a classic military force, thereby confronting the occupying force with a dilemma. Does it spread its forces around the countryside to guard its lines of communication, police the population, and guarantee its political base? Or does it jeopardize or even sacrifice temporarily the security of its rear areas to concentrate against the enemy's main-force units. This strategy worked well for the American Revolutionaries, during the Peninsular campaign of the Napoleonic Wars, and in the Indochina/ Vietnam conflict. Unfortunately, this was not the case in Europe generally and in France in particular during World War II, when a handful of German police backed by Vichy authorities and the ruthless reprisals of the Wehrmacht and SS were enough to keep the population acceptably docile until the very eve of D-Day and beyond.[117]

More, they succeeded in making the majority of the French population very wary of the Resistance. Leaders of Resistance groups tasked with attacking Germans noted that support for their activities among the French population, the sine qua non of a successful guerrilla strategy, ran from apathy to open hostility.[118] And no wonder, as anyone attempting to aid the Resistance—indeed, anyone unlucky enough to be in the general vicinity of a Resistance attack—ran enormous risks. To their credit, the Resistance did not indulge in counterterror, as did the Algerian FLN and the Vietcong, to force the population to assist them.

Eisenhower wrote that Resistance groups had "by their ceaseless harassing activities surrounded the Germans with a terrible atmosphere of danger and hatred which ate into the confidence of the leaders and the courage of the soldiers."[119] Eisenhower's statement was no doubt based on ludicrous OSS reports that Germans were perishing by the thousands in Resistance attacks. The savage reprisals dealt the French populations in Tulle and Oradour-sur-Glane outside of Limoges by the Das Reich Division, reacting to what were little more than pinpricks inflicted by the Resistance, proved beyond doubt the dangerous consequences of even relatively weak Resistance attacks.

British historian Max Hastings has demonstrated that the delayed arrival of the Das Reich Division at the front was self-inflicted, and not the result of successful Resistance ambushes. Hastings' study also makes a mockery of OSS claims that the Resistance had killed 600 soldiers of the Das Reich Division, believing a generous estimate of German deaths from Resistance activity closer to 35 in a division of 15,000 men.[120] Rather than diminishing the German will to resist by creating a "climate of insecurity" behind the lines, in fact it was the Germans who succeeded in creating the "climate of insecurity" for the Resistance. True, Resistance attacks goaded the Germans into the diversion of as many as eight divisions to oppose the Resistance. But these were low-grade divisions whose more rapid arrival in Normandy would have made the Allied invasion more difficult, but hardly impossible.[121] In the end, the Allies achieved victory by outproducing German factories and defeating German armies in the field. Sadly, one is driven toward the conclusion that the contribution of the Resistance to that victory through humint, deception, sabotage, and armed uprising was minimal.

But even if the ultimate effects of Resistance intelligence and action missions weighed little in the war's strategic balance, some historians have fallen back on the ethical defense of the Resistance, agreeing with Jean Moulin that the justification for the Resistance lay ultimately with the "moral question" of associating the French with their own liberation. Thus Max Hastings, whose assessment of the military utility of the Resistance and of SOE is a fairly pessimistic one, can write: "The great contribution of the Resistance—that which justified all that SOE did and made worthwhile the sacrifice of all those who died— was towards the restoration of the soul of France."[122]

But even this argument raises two questions, one factual and the second philosophical. Did the Resistance "associate" the French with their own liberation? In fact, in only five towns was there important combat between Resistance fighters and Germans. In other towns, the Resistance emerged to attack retreating Germans. But 84 percent of French towns "were offered their liberation," writes French historian Philippe Buton, and this may be a low estimate given the tendentious nature of many French wartime memoirs. "One can thus conclude that the 'national insurrection' was a total flop."[123]

No matter that the self-liberation of France was largely myth. "Perhaps in the end one has to see the primary virtue of the Resistance . . . as a contribution to history, to the creation of national pride, and to the renaissance of hope," writes British historian Brian Chapman.[124] Perhaps, but this raises philosophical questions which are impossible to answer. For those who had run those risks, and who had seen many of their companions and countrymen perish, the way that the Resistance had been organized and directed in itself raised moral questions. The Liberation revealed to André Heintz that "five or six groups had been doing exactly the same thing all the time and taking the same risks. It came to us as a great shock and we even thought that it was not fair to have allowed that so many should have taken such great risks . . . It was a costly game."[125] Of course, the counterargument is that several networks had to be assigned the same task to make sure the intelligence continued to flow even if one or two networks were broken up. But one may ask if an enterprise in which around 75,000 French men and women, some of whom were *résistants* while others were mere innocents caught up in savage German reprisals, perished in German concentration camps, and another 20,000 died in France, often after horrible torture, was worth the fairly trifling return in intelligence and "action."[126]

In many respects the question is a pointless one, for the Resistance had been created by spontaneous combustion in France, stoked by Churchill's desire to "set Europe ablaze" and de Gaulle's search for legitimization. What is equally certain is that the political element of the Resistance was converted into a moral imperative. In the view of a French historian of the occupation, "de Gaulle had to convince the French that they had resisted. It was necessary that they disguise the truth from themselves."[127] Otherwise the nation would become demoralized and incapable of assuming the great world role de Gaulle envisaged for it.[128] A bit part in one of the great events of world history was better than no part at all. This was all the more the case because, as Marc Ferro has noted, the growing power of German and Vichy repression more than kept pace with popular disaffection which fed the desire to resist by 1943 or 1944. Consequently, the more the French were psychologically prepared to resist, the less they were able to do so.[129]

The Resistance, therefore, was elevated into a "necessary myth" of which the Gaullists emerged as the major beneficiaries, followed closely by the communists, who redeemed their craven and opportunistic support of the Nazi-Soviet pact of August 1939 through aggressive Resistance and self-proclaimed, if exaggerated, martyrdom as "the party of 75,000 executed." Even though the bill had been a heavy one, for de Gaulle, who saw war as an essential ingredient in the forging of national character,[130] it was a price that he, and apparently France, had been more than willing to pay. "Between ourselves," de Gaulle told a senior member of Free France, André Gillois, "the Resistance, it was just a bluff that came off."[131] The problem for the postwar French intelligence community was that the Resistance "bluff" cut both ways. If it was necessary for French self-esteem to believe that they had played a major role in their own liberation, so they had to believe that action and intelligence-gathering missions of the Resistance had been essential ingredients in the German defeat. This faith, driven by the primacy of the Resistance Myth in postwar France, was a major legacy of the war to the postwar French secret services.

ELEVEN

THE SECRET SERVICES
IN POSTWAR FRANCE

—"That prostitute I put in my pocket."

All Allied intelligence services emerged decisively altered from World War II. But nowhere were the mutations more apparent than in France, where war had bequeathed several legacies to the secret services. The change most obvious was that, on an international level, France was no longer an intelligence power. She had stood on the sidelines of the enormous growth in electronic and scientific intelligence during the war. She lacked the means by herself to compete with the substantial intelligence machine of the Soviet Union and increasingly with those of the surrogate nations of Eastern Europe who did Moscow's bidding. She might have minimized her weaknesses, as did the British to a certain extent, by conserving a caliber of personnel equivalent to the prewar level, developing areas of expertise, and cultivating a close relationship with the CIA. For postwar French intelligence, however, this proved difficult to do with any consistency because poor civil-intelligence relations, made worse by political turmoil, combined to make France's insistence on its global mission difficult for Paris to rationalize and focus its intelligence assets.

The political, bureaucratic, and personality problems that had trailed the services through the war years ripened into something close to complete disarray with the Liberation. Hardly had Paris been liberated, and the DGSS installed in two buildings on the boulevard Suchet recently vacated by the Kriegsmarine, when it was besieged by *résistants* who had discovered "an irresistible vocation for the SR or CE," especially, Paillole noted cynically, when the alternative was incorporation into a fighting unit in Alsace.[1] They swarmed through the offices demanding jobs and decorations, even requisitioning cars at gunpoint, often after having dined—and drunk—at government expense in the service's sumptuous basement restaurant. "Each day lists were passed around, and one simply had to enter one's name to be a candidate for one decoration or another," remembered Thyraud de Vosjoli, who found that "this mixed atmosphere of country fair and revolution was not conducive to serious work." Fortunately, the Indochina section to which he was assigned soon shifted to the Gestapo headquarters on the avenue Foch, vacated by his old adversaries in such haste that they had abandoned many valuable antiques and even their sinister fleet of black Citroën automobiles.[2]

When Roger Wybot appeared in the headquarters of the Surveillance du Territoire on the rue des Saussaies in October 1944, with the mission of transforming it into the Direction du Surveillance du Territoire (DST), he entered into a "din which made me think of the stock market in a moment of madness," where everyone had thrown themselves with enthusiasm into the "hunt for collabos" (collaborators). Hapless victims were dragged in by "agents" who paused briefly to pitch requisitioned jewelry, banknotes, money, even gold bars into a room which quickly took on the appearance of "the cavern of Ali Baba." When Wybot suggested that a detailed inventory of these valuables be made, as they might be used as evidence in court, he was told, "Do you think we have time for these formalities?"[3] Nor were these newly hired agents above cashing in on the great perquisite of Resistance service—the acquisition of several names, which allowed them to draw as many paychecks.[4]

The great postwar challenge of forging a modern intelligence bureaucracy which could serve the national interests faced several impediments, however, not the least of which was the old problem of the fragmentation of the French services. The years of occupation and Resistance, of Vichy and Fighting France, were mere prologue for the turf battles that began in earnest with the Liberation. In November

1944, the DGSS became the DGER (Direction Générale des Etudes et Recherches), with responsibility for foreign intelligence. Like the prewar Deuxième Bureau, the DGER, renamed the SDECE (Service de Documentation Extérieure et de Contre-espionnage) in January 1946, answered to the War Ministry, although various scandals would eventually place it under the direct authority of the Prime Minister. But there the resemblance with its illustrious predecessor ceased. General Rivet had presided over small, exclusively military SR and counterintelligence bureaus. The DGER/SDECE was an elaborate affair which, after swelling to almost 10,000 agents at the Liberation, eventually slimmed down to around 1,500 people, mostly soldiers, in technical, communications, research, and study sections, counterintelligence and others, under a single director. A Service Action, which included the 11ème Choc, a highly trained group of paratroop commandos, eventually settled into a camp at Cercottes near Orléans. And if this were not complicated enough, the Defense Ministry created its own Service de Renseignements Militaires. An early casualty of this reorganization was Paul Paillole, for whom the division of his highly rated counterintelligence section between the DGER and the War Ministry was simply the ultimate insult dealt the old guard of the prewar Deuxième Bureau by the Gaullists. Paillole's delight at returning to liberated Paris was quickly dissipated by the atmosphere of jobbery and revenge which ravaged the secret services like a contagion. So he fled this "monstrous edifice . . . this shapeless magma of the DGER," followed closely in April 1945 by Soustelle, who surrendered the directorship, one imagines with relief, to Passy.[5]

A similar administrative upheaval gripped the Interior Ministry, which presided over three separate intelligence services: the Direction de la Surveillance du Territoire (DST) and the Renseignements Généraux (RG), both of which answered to the Sûreté Nationale, and the Paris Prefecture of Police, which ran its own RG—the RGPP. If this were not complicated enough, the Prime Minister's office eventually added an electronic surveillance bureau. The big winner in the postwar secret service shakeout was undoubtedly the DST—for at least two reasons. The first was that it was able to build on a strong tradition of internal security, which came naturally to a centralized, bureaucratic, and even authoritarian political culture like that of France. But some credit must also accrue to its founder, Roger Wybot, appointed to transform the old ST brigades, which acted only on orders from the army or magistrates, into an active counterespionage service. As has been seen, Wybot's early association with the Vichy services, combined with his cool, not to say condescending efficiency, made him an unpopular addition to Passy's rather freewheeling BCRA and helped to shorten his tenure there. But even making allowance for the boastful overstatement which permeates his memoirs, Wybot brought to the DST two assets in the immediate postwar years. First, an insistence on order and method, a rare quality in the chaos of the Liberation. He established a panoply of sections and services, including desks to specialize in Great Britain, the United States, and the Soviet Union, to collect, centralize, and exploit intelligence, and instruct his agents in interrogation techniques, in the manipulation of double agents, and in codes. Taking inspiration from the Resistance model, Wybot insisted on the strict "compartmentalization" of each service, while the co-ordination of their activities remained in his hands. "The interminable café conversations about life in general" ceased, according to Wybot, and a professional attitude based on rigorous methods and discretion was imposed.[6] Second, he was able to promote and expand the DST on the basis of two missions—the search for collaborators, which converted gently by 1947 into the anticommunist struggle.

This fragmentation brought in its wake the inevitable bureaucratic rivalries and turf battles. While relations between the Sécurité Mili-taire, which keeps files on the political opinions of soldiers and assures the application of security procedures in the armed forces, and the DGER/SDECE were good, the same could not be said of SDECE/DST relations. SDECE resentment of the DST, because it had ab-sorbed some of the army's counterintelligence functions, was mirrored in the Interior Ministry's three separate intelligence services—the DST, RG, and RGPP. The DST's expansion under the relentless Wybot threatened to reduce the RG to a mere subsidiary and increas-ingly caused the DST to muscle in on the sacred Parisian turf of the RGPP and threaten the autonomy vis-à-vis the Sûreté which Paris' Prefect of Police worked to maintain. When the Paris Prefecture of Police refused to supply police support for DST-initiated raids, the DST accused the RGPP of being a hotbed of communist sympathizers.

And as the post-1945 colonial wars more and more disturbed French political life, the Bureau Technique de Liaison et de Coordination (BTLC), yet another independent secret service run by the Colonial Ministry, initiated its own activities among the foreign and colonial populations of Paris.

The rivalries and private agendas of the French services, which eventually became serious enough to shake the foundations of the French state, were envenomed by personal and political rivalries developed during the war, an accretion of new feuds and hatreds added to old ones.[7] Despite his reputation as a loose cannon during the war, Pierre Fourcaud emerged as second-in-command at the SDECE, where his tenure was notable for the feud initiated with his boss, the socialist Henri Ribière, head of Libération-Nord during the war, who succeeded Passy in February 1946. Relations between the two men deteriorated to the point that, despite adjoining offices, they communicated through "aggressive and threatening notes."[8] Thyraud de Vosjoli, who served as Ribière's *chef de cabinet* (private secretary), complained that Fourcaud conspired with SDECE section chiefs to ensure that Ribière saw only low-grade intelligence. When Ribière had a near-fatal automobile accident in 1951, public rumor held that Fourcaud had tampered with the brakes.[9] Rivalries at the top of the DGER/SDECE played out lower down between soldiers and civilians, between alumni of London and Vichy, between those who owed their allegiance to the Gaullists or to the socialists.[10]

Nor were SDECE/DST relations oiled by the feud which Fourcaud continued to prosecute with Wybot, whom despite their wartime reconciliation he continued to hold responsible for his arrest by Vichy in 1941. The rivalry between the DST and the RG to corner the market in the prosecution of collaborators became so intense that RG director Marc Bergé publicly denounced Wybot for stonewalling RG investigations. Wybot retaliated with the nec plus ultra in the Gaullist lexicon of insults, by labeling Bergé an "American agent."[11]

Rather than serving the interests of the French state, the secret services became the Fourth Republic's Achilles' heel. Neither the old Vichy right, unrepentant and well represented in the Christian Democratic MRP, nor the Gaullists were reconciled to the Fourth Republic, while the communists retained their deep suspicion of all bourgeois parties. Rivalries born of fragmentation and politicization joined with an atmosphere boiling with intrigue, rumors of Gaullist coups and communist insurrection, to tempt the services into the political arena.[12] The centrality of the Resistance Myth in the political culture of postwar France, the prominent role played by the BCRA in the organization of the Resistance, and the scramble of the political parties after the Liberation to place their partisans in positions of influence in the secret services meant that they became the source of "affairs" on an almost industrial scale. Politically motivated attacks on the secret services paid off in electoral terms in part because the allegedly sophisticated French voters were in fact deeply suspicious of central authority and avid consumers of conspiracy theories. And their beliefs were given credibility by the numbers of ambitious and unscrupulous men attracted to undercover work in the rapid postwar expansion.

While the Allied services were still getting on with the war, newly sworn French agents flashing their DGER badges as if empowered with police authority arrested or blackmailed collabos and, Thyraud de Vosjoli claimed, even used torture to extract information on the whereabouts of valuables. Illegal currency transactions were commonplace, while two successive heads of his Far East section were dismissed, one for taking bribes for securing business permits and the other for diamond smuggling. "What can I do?" one of Thyraud de Vosjoli's superiors wondered. "Most of the men in this section should be locked up!" Agents supplemented a salary which was pegged to that of the Department of Records and Deeds by reporting intelligence to politicians or supplying birth certificates, police affidavits, and university or medical diplomas counterfeited by DGER/SDECE technicians who had become expert at producing bogus documents during the occupation. "Abandoned to its own corruption," Vosjoli lamented of these early days, "the DGER was dying of scandal."[13]

Wybot joked that the DGER had been involved in so many scandals that his agents referred to it as the Direction Générale des Escroqueries et Rapines (General Directorate of Fraud and Plunder).[14] But Wybot had no reason to feel complacent about the probity of his DST "incorruptibles"[15] after one of his section chiefs, Roger Blément, a bent ex-cop with an exemplary Resistance record, was dismissed for taking bribes to destroy the records of collaborators under threat of indictment. Blément subsequently staked out a brilliant career as one of the "princes" of the Marseille underworld, from which he emerged periodically to give the DST a helping hand, until 1965 when he was gunned down in a gangland shoot-out.[16]

An early victim of the combination of the unsavory reputation of the secret services and the Republican proclivity for spawning scandal was none other than Passy. On 5 May 1946, the ex-head of the SDECE, who had resigned in February 1946, was arrested and confined in the military fortress at Metz. The charges against him were only made clear on 20 May in a long SDECE report to the Prime Minister. In it, Henri Ribière charged that his immediate predecessor had established secret bank accounts in Great Britain and Paris and misappropriated secret service funds. "Where have the BCRA millions gone?" brayed the FTP Resistance journal *France d'abord*. The suicide of Captain André Lahana, responsible for these "accounts," and the arrest of the flamboyant ex-SOE operative Henri Déricourt as he piloted a planeload of pounds sterling and precious metals across the Channel added enough mystery to the affair to give credence to the charge.

In actuality, the truth appears to have been at once simple and complex. Secret accounts were established in Great Britain in the autumn of 1945 after de Gaulle became convinced that war with the Soviet Union was only a matter of time, that France, due to lack of American aid, would be overrun, and that the government must lay money aside for a second exile. It is certainly possible, probable even, that given the amount of money sloshing around for Resistance activities, some of it was diverted to personal use.[17] Other accounts appear to have contained only outdated and worthless scrip. Some "out of budget" funds did go as a loan to the newspaper *France-Soir*. But there was nothing abnormal about the government subsidizing a newspaper with the expected dividend of favorable editorial support, especially as at this stage there was no Gaullist political party and therefore no party publication to counterbalance the political views of the socialist and communist press.

It did not take a brain surgeon to realize that the arrest of Passy was a political shot aimed at de Gaulle. Wilder rumors on the left held that de Gaulle was planning a coup d'état against the Republic, which

Passy's arrest was meant to short-circuit. Wybot's biographer, Philippe Bernert, believed that knowledge of these accounts was exploited by socialists in the Finance Ministry to neutralize de Gaulle.[18] A less hysterical interpretation, however, holds that the "affair" aimed to sabotage a campaign led by the Christian Democratic MRP and supported by de Gaulle to urge Frenchmen to vote *non* in the referendum on the new constitution. It failed. On 6 May 1946, the day after Passy's well-publicized arrest, 53 percent of Frenchmen voted *non*.

The Passy affair also masked other agendas, among them those of the communists. Through most of 1944, the PCF had planned to use its Resistance forces to take power through a "national insurrection." In May 1944, the communists had gained control of the Comité Central des Mouvements de Résistance (Comidac), which controlled the Forces Françaises de l'Intérieur (FFI) and actively tried to create a Resistance movement independent of the government. Frenchmen rushed to join the FFI on the Liberation, so that de Gaulle, fearing a communist coup, dissolved the FFI military staffs and Comidac on 28 August and ordered FFI units to place themselves under the control of the regular French army. Tensions between de Gaulle and the communists mounted in early September as Comidac refused to disband and communist-dominated FFI units declined to join the regular forces at the front. On 15–16 September, however, the communists did an about-face and agreed to submit to regular army discipline. The reasons for this change of heart are complex, but essentially were based on the calculation by the communists that they lacked sufficient support in France, that any uprising would be crushed by Allied troops, and Stalin's view that a civil war in France was against the interests of the U.S.S.R. so long as Germany remained undefeated.[19]

Though their initial strategy had failed, the communists had not given up their ambitions for power. Their new tactic was to infiltrate the state administration, including the army and the secret services. Rebuffed by Soustelle when they had tried to integrate their Resistance intelligence organization, the Service B, into the DGER, the communists sought to discredit the SDECE. Nor were they alone: Georges Bidault, though a Christian Democrat, pressed the Council of Ministers to have the SDECE brought under his Foreign Ministry. Passy had also eliminated around 7,000 ex-*résistants* from the DGER/

SDECE payroll during his tenure, which had won him few friends in the political parties and Resistance organizations which sought to use the secret services as a source of patronage and political control. Finally, some questioned the motives of Fourcaud, who had carried out the initial investigations in Great Britain which called attention to the misplaced "millions," and blew hard on the embers of the affair. The government eventually backed off prosecution, apparently fearing, as President Vincent Auriol noted in his diary, that "Passy would publish part of the BCRA accounts and in this way implicate a number of people. This or that party received millions, what did they do with them? . . . We have to be careful of this sort of revelation, especially as it will be very difficult for those who took money for the purchase of arms, etc., to defend themselves."[20] Released after four months of incarceration, Passy appealed successfully to the Conseil d'Etat, the supreme administrative court, to have his colonel's rank and decorations restored to him. But this incident cured him of any desire to continue in state service, and he resigned from the army to join the private sector.[21]

The Passy affair served as a wake-up call for those who dreamed of re-creating nonpartisan secret services along prewar lines. Clearly, this would be no easier in the postwar world than it had been during the war, and perhaps it would be even more difficult. The charge that Passy's BCRA was an "aerie of Cagoulards" had damaged the credibility of the secret services during the war, both with portions of the Resistance and with the Allies.[22] Now this charge pursued the DGER/SDECE into the peace, for the simple reason that many postwar politicians discovered in the secret services the perfect vehicle through which they could attack the status quo, parade black plots against the Republic before a skeptical but gullible public. Foremost among these were the communists, who denounced the DGER in print as the Direction Générale des Ennemis de la République. Was this charge rooted in reality? If anything, the political antecedents of the BCRA had been more left than right. While BCRA action in drawing together the various Resistance groups into the Conseil National de la Résistance in 1943 had benefited de Gaulle, the left, especially the socialists, had also been big winners.[23] A strong Resistance pedigree remained an important career requirement for both the DGER/SDECE and the

DST until the late 1960s. The DST appears to have retained few veterans of the old ST. Many of Wybot's inner circle had served with him in the Free French forces in Italy. Most of the rest came out of the Resistance.[24]

SDECE recruitment was heterogeneous, combining in the same organization often mutually antagonistic elements. Thyraud de Vosjoli claimed that many of the best wartime members of the BCRA resigned in disgust in the tumultuous postwar months, permitting a return of soldiers, many of them formerly with the Deuxième Bureau.[25] The military occupied around 40 percent of the positions until the 1960s, when de Gaulle raised the proportion of places allocated to soldiers to around 60 percent.

Despite spectacular purges or resignations in 1944 of men like Rivet and Paillole, those who had served the pro-Giraudist Deuxième Bureau reclaimed a prominent presence in the new services, making up about a third of DGER/SDECE personnel. These included Roger Lafont who as Colonel Verneuil headed SDECE's counterintelligence section—Service 23—until his death in 1952; Captain Henri Trautmann, a veteran of the SR Marine, who headed the research division; and Gustave Bertrand in cryptanalysis. The remainder who survived the massive restructuring of 1946–47 were recruited in almost equal portions among survivors of wartime BCRA and from the Resistance networks, especially the socialist Libération-Nord, whose wartime founder, Henry Ribière, directed the SDECE through its early years.[26]

Therefore, it would be impossible to say that, from a recruitment perspective, the French secret services had any specific political orientation, beyond the fact that they were uniformly anticommunist. Ribière's socialist loyalties were matched by those of Wybot, who, although a BCRA veteran, was regarded very much as a client of the socialists. Both men, however, were committed to establishing a professional service, and Ribière caused even more dissension in his party by continuing Passy's elimination from the service of men whose only qualification was that they were ex-résistants.[27] Nevertheless, the SDECE retained a strong Gaullist presence, especially in the Service Action, which grew enormously with the intensification of the war in Indochina. Service Action's politicization was especially apparent among its 7,800-strong reserve contingent, many of whose members supplied the strong-armed *service d'ordre* for the Gaullist Rassemblement du Peuple Français (RPF) during raucous and often violent rallies in the "Red Belt" of communist-dominated suburbs around Paris.[28] What would prove fatal for the Fourth Republic, however, was the strongly procolonialist bias of the French intelligence services.

A further impediment to the constitution of a coherent intelligence organization in France apart from fragmentation and politicization in these early days was the shifting focus of the services. As the Passy affair testified, as early as the autumn of 1945, some on the right, including de Gaulle, began to see war with the Soviet Union as a definite possibility. But planning to prepare the intelligence services to confront the communist threat was fraught with difficulties. For starters, the French Communist Party (PCF) claimed a quarter of the popular vote and until 1947 sat in the government. Their noisy campaign against the intelligence services sought to ensure that the SDECE and DST energies would not be directed against the Homeland of the Revolution, whose interests all good communists must serve. How could the intelligence services defend "national security" if no unanimity existed on where French national interests lay?

Only gradually, as the temperature of the Cold War dropped toward the freezing point, could the secret services reorient their task toward the communist menace. In the war's immediate aftermath, the politically correct task was the hunt for collabos. But this mission in itself caused all sorts of problems for the secret services which had to ferret out the malefactors. Apart from the egregious cases like those who served in the Vichy Milice, worked for the Gestapo, or connived to deport Jews, the line between collaboration and survival—or collaboration and Resistance, for that matter—often proved a fine one which some people had crossed more than once. Was an official who stayed at his desk, a farmer who sold some of his produce on the black market, a businessman who dealt with the Germans, a policeman who arrested a member of the Resistance engaged in illegal activity, or a judge who sentenced him, automatically a collaborator? In theory, the DST was given responsibility for tracking those who collaborated with the Gestapo or Abwehr, while the police and RG hunted down economic or political collaborators. But these divisions, neat on paper, worked out less well in practice. In the confusion of the Liberation, many impeccable Resistance records had been invented, or false accusations of collaboration filed to settle personal scores. Some notorious collaborators, like Joseph Joanovici, who had made a fortune selling scrap iron to the Germans during the war, had established a network of influential political contacts which made them virtually untouchable.

Together with the 10,000 "suspects, spies, Nazis, and collaborators" listed in the "Synthesis of the Organization of German Special Services and Their Operations in France," compiled by Paillole's SSM in Algiers, tons of captured German and Vichy documents had to be examined. Forged documents which implicated in collaboration *résistants* with impeccable records became a minor industry. When Wybot led an unannounced DST raid on the Fresnes Prison, which he had determined was a source of some of these documents, a massacre was only narrowly averted when the prison guards prepared to oppose what they believed was a mass breakout. The two sides held each other at gunpoint until someone rang up the Minister of the Interior to verify credentials.[29]

On the right, the argument of Pierre Laval at his trial for treason that Vichy had been the Shield of France, without which France would have suffered the dreadful fate of Poland, struck a responsive chord, especially among those inclined to blame the Fall of France in 1940 on the rotten governments of the Third Republic. In short, in the fragile political environment of postwar France, the mission was a true hornet's nest, one fraught with dangers for the neophyte secret services because it opened them to the possibilities of corruption, of muddle, and it was bound to add fuel to the fire of interservice rivalry.

The difficulties of organizing a proper counterintelligence service in what Wybot called a *"résistantialiste"* atmosphere were forcefully brought home to the chief of the new DST as early as December 1944. Operating on sound World War II principles, the DST caught an ex-Gestapo agent named Klein, whom they "turned." Hardly had Klein been released in order to trace the whereabouts of other collaborators when he was apprehended by agents working for the Prefecture of Police. According to Wybot, when Klein explained to agents of the Prefecture of Police that he was now working for the DST, they leaked the story to the communist daily *L'Humanité*, which blasted Wybot and the DST for harboring war criminals. The incident brought Wybot to within a whisker of disgrace, and forced him to establish elaborate procedures for running agents in the DST.[30]

In the spring of 1945, American security agents reported that the French were executing willy-nilly any German agents who fell into their hands before they could be interrogated by other Allied services. As a consequence, it was feared that much good intelligence was being lost.[31] Nevertheless, German intelligence documents seized at the war's end did allow the DGER/SDECE to recruit a number of ex-Abwehr and SD "control officers." The purpose was to "recover" former German networks in Eastern Europe and the Near East for use against the Soviets, to guard against the revival of Nazi networks in the West, and to track down collaborators.[32] These activities, common to Soviet and Western agencies, spawned lingering accusations that notorious collaborators had found asylum under the protective umbrella of the secret services.

Although rumors of a Gaullist coup set for May 1946 were followed by those—quite rightly given credence by American intelligence—of an impending communist coup in France, the DST doggedly pursued the hunt for collabos. For instance, in March 1947, Wybot led a raid on a Benedictine monastery in Paris after receiving information that a chain of monasteries had formed an underground railroad to get war criminals out of France and into Spain. The old monk who answered the summons at the gate surveyed the sixty heavily armed DST agents before informing Wybot that he must ask permission of the Father Superior before they could enter. As the Father Superior was celebrating mass, Wybot was invited to stand outside the chapel door until the service was completed. Wybot peered inside the chapel to see the Father Superior raise the host for consecration. After what seemed an interminable period during which various bells rang, he again peered into the chapel to see the chalice being raised. Wybot looked at his watch and waited some time before he realized that he was being duped. His agents flooded into the monastery, only to discover that the suspects had escaped during the interval through an underground passage. Questioned, the Father Superior stood very much on his dignity, insisting that his work was that of God and he had no need to answer the inquiries of agents of the Republic, when suddenly one of Wybot's men appeared with an armload of pornographic literature

collected in the cells of the monks. The confident demeanor of the
Father Superior dissolved, and he offered to reveal all if Wybot would
keep the secret of his monks' bedside reading. But when news of the
raid became public, the DST was denounced for persecuting the
Church, even by those nominally on the left like Albert Camus, who
defended the Church's Resistance record. [33]

The political atmosphere in which the secret services were founded
was to have several consequences. First, it was very difficult for the
services to operate as neutral administrations dedicated to the service
of a nonpartisan view of French interests in such a partisan environment, in which scandal was a potent and profitable political tactic.
Though most of the chiefs attempted to insulate their services against
political interference, it became impossible to hold it at bay completely.
Each time the services seemed on the road to efficiency, a new scandal
would surface to discredit one or more of them. A second problem
was the prominence given to action, a heritage of the London years
when Passy rejected the SIS/Deuxième Bureau view that action and
intelligence gathering must be kept strictly separate and when the
Resistance was locked into an immediate-gratification mode of killing
Germans and Vichy Milice in preference to intelligence gathering. As
will be seen, the involvement of the intelligence services in action
missions would help to discredit them more than once. This was
especially the case in the atmosphere of fragmentation and politicization which would characterize postwar France. The temptation for
a minister or ambitious service chief to court media attention through
some brilliant coup by his personal special service or by a newly created
action branch of a traditional service could prove overwhelming, and
often would end in scandal.

A final challenge to the credibility of the French services was the
specter of communist infiltration. Much has been written on de
Gaulle's flirtation with the communists during and immediately after
the war. Given Free France's weak wartime position, de Gaulle courted
Stalin to bolster his independence vis-à-vis his Anglo-American allies.
The requirement that he not anger Stalin offered one reason why he
had to tread carefully with French communists. A second reason was
that a strong communist presence in the Resistance gave the PCF a
powerful hand to play, especially at the time of the Liberation. As has

been seen, de Gaulle managed to outmaneuver communist plans for a takeover in September 1944. But not before, it was charged, communists well placed in the Resistance, in the Provisional Government in Algiers, and in the Liberation government managed to infiltrate their supporters into influential governmental positions. The PCF leadership especially targeted the army, the police, and the secret services, three institutions which, they believed, formed the most significant impediments to their seizure of power. Communist leader Jacques Duclos demanded that members of the Resistance be integrated into the army as commissioned officers, and some of them were. Special mention was accorded the DGSS, which the communists feared would work with the police to ease their members out of power. Therefore, the secret service was denounced as "a police organ built on the Gestapo model," an "occult power . . . state within the state" with an "uncontrolled" budget. [34]

Quite naturally, the prominent role accorded communists and fellow travelers in the Resistance and in governments in Algiers and Paris on the Liberation opened de Gaulle to charges of giving away the store to them. Henri Frenay argued that Jean Moulin had allowed the communists to dominate the CNR. [35] Peter Wright, a former member of MI5, revealed that his service suspected communist infiltration of de Gaulle's inner circle in the form of André Labarthe, his director for civilian affairs, and Admiral Muselier. This was confirmed in 1964 through VENONA intercepts. VENONA was the code name given to messages sent by the NKGB—the Soviet Security Service—which were intercepted toward the end of World War II. From 1948, the U.S. Army Security Agency began to decrypt these messages which revealed the beginnings of Soviet penetration of the West. VENONA decrypts allowed U.S. and British officials to close in on Burgess and Maclean, and revealed that both Labarthe and Pierre Cot, the Air Minister during part of the 1930s, whom Moulin had served as *chef de cabinet*, had passed on intelligence to the Soviets. [36] The appointment by de Gaulle of Emmanuel d'Astier de la Vignerie, whose sympathies were strongly with the communists, as Commissioner and subsequently Minister of the Interior deeply worried Passy and Soustelle. [37] In the view of many, including the Allies, the entry of communists into the government in Algiers and later in Paris, in which they held four portfolios, flung the doors of government open to communist infiltration in many administrations, including the secret services.[38]

French intelligence began to sense a new coolness on the part of the British and Americans in late 1944, when they discovered that the Bureau Interallié du Contre-espionnage (Inter-Allied Counterintelligence Service), which Paillole had proposed in September 1944 to coordinate Allied activities in Germany, and the British and Americans had at first welcomed, was to be shelved. This estrangement resulted in part from a reorganization of both British and French counterintelligence services which scattered men, like Paillole, who had worked together, and brought in new men unfamiliar with the working relationships of their predecessors. The parochial mission of French intelligence, which busied itself with the hunt for collabos while the British and Americans began to retool for anti-Soviet espionage, offers another explanation. Not only did this mean that the French and Allied intelligence services had different priorities. These missions could also be opposing ones. While, as has been seen, the French did recruit ex-Nazi intelligence officers, they were concerned, at least on paper, that they not be "war criminals."[39] As a consequence, their desire to capture someone like Lyon Gestapo chief Klaus Barbie ran counter to those of American and British intelligence officers eager to turn former enemies and use them against the Soviets.

But the most important reason for the progressive exclusion of the French from Allied intelligence circuits in 1945 stemmed from the fact that the Allies believed they could ill afford to share intelligence with a government which contained communists.[40] And they were correct. By the time the French services began to reorient their activities toward the communists in 1947, the rot of infiltration had spread to the very fabric of the state, or so many—including members of the intelligence services—believed. "France, from August 1944 to May 1947, was a Shangri-la for Soviet intelligence," American researcher David Dallin wrote in 1955.[41] Thyraud de Vosjoli maintained that as long as communist ministers sat in the government, it was "almost impossible" for the SDECE "to carry out any activity . . . As a rule, everyone pretended to be busy, with the aim of being as inefficient as possible." When they were expelled by the government in May 1947, this "instantly cleared the atmosphere."[42]

But almost three years of communist presence in government had taken its toll. Thyraud de Vosjoli decried the fact that Communist Party control of important ministries such as Labor, Air, and Industry allowed them to fill important positions in French industry and government with communists, men like Major André Teulery, an ex-*résistant* named chief of the Air Ministry's security section by communist Minister of Air Charles Tillon. In 1949, Teulery was arrested handing over secret documents to the Yugoslav military attaché.[43] The appointment of the communist professor Frédéric Joliot-Curie as Director of Scientific Research gave the communists a stranglehold on the scientific community, including the French atomic agency and the science section of the DGER. The army had been forced to absorb a number of ex-FFIs, one of whom, Captain René Azéma, was arrested for espionage in 1949. Communist ex-FFIs commissioned into the army at the Liberation were gradually quarantined by the Sécurité Militaire and the SDECE and eventually expelled from the army. The Toulon arsenal was an intelligence sieve where documents from the Scientific Experiments Center in Brest and from the Submarine Research Center found their way into the hands of the Soviets.[44] The secrets of the Ministry of the Interior's services could have been of little mystery to the Soviets, as it transpired that André Blumel, the *chef de cabinet* to Interior Minister Adrien Tixier, was a communist sympathizer.[45]

For an outsider, especially in the light of the Burgess, Maclean, and Philby scandals which rocked the highest levels of British intelligence after the war, these revelations would seem rather trivial. However, even French intelligence specialists argued that they were merely the tip of the iceberg, that far more important spies escaped because it was virtually impossible to bring them to justice. The prominent place held by the Communist Party in the French political system insulated it from prosecution. French politicians instinctively close ranks around comrades or protégés threatened by outside investigation, in part because few have pasts which can endure too searching a scrutiny. So the conditioned reflex of the political and administrative milieus was to show curious police the door. If a member of the French Communist Party or a fellow traveler appeared under threat, the party could orchestrate a press campaign which not only was viciously polemical but could abort justice by publishing fragments of documents so that by the time a case reached court it was thrown out on the grounds that the top-secret information was now in the public domain. Finally, French justice is less independent than its Anglo-Saxon counterparts. Trial judges allow long, rambling speeches which help to obscure an issue, and may be reluctant to pursue a case with strong political overtones because it may jeopardize their promotion to the next judicial level within the Justice Ministry.[46] These are the same problems which Paillole had encountered in the prewar era, and helped to account for the fact that spies like Teulery served only one year of a five-year sentence.

The result was that, in both France and abroad, the French state was thought to be entwined in a web of communist infiltration which stretched to the secret services themselves. When Captain Roger Joint-Daguenet transferred to the SDECE from his signals unit in 1956, he was told during his training that 50,000 communist agents were dormant in France, many of whom were "illegals" who had adopted the identity of someone who had disappeared during the war. Each was supplied with a code that could be activated when needed, "an immense piano with 50,000 keys." His decision to transfer out of the SDECE was motivated in part by his belief that it had been infiltrated by communist moles.[47] "Anti-French feelings ran strongly inside British intelligence," Peter Wright insisted. Nor were these feelings dissipated with de Gaulle's return to power in 1958, both because of the General's notoriously relaxed attitude toward intelligence matters and because of his alleged toleration of communists in high positions.[48] As Ribière's *chef de cabinet* in the 1940s, Thyraud de Vosjoli noted that the SDECE was especially eager that security leaks not jeopardize France's place in NATO, especially as Admiral Rosco Hillenkoeter, former U.S. naval attaché in Paris and now CIA director, made no secret of his disdain for French security.

For Wybot, the Fourth Republic finally began to take the communist menace seriously on 1 December 1947, when it closed Camp de Beauregard.[49] Since its creation on the Liberation at Vaucresson near Paris, as a center from which the Soviets could repatriate their nationals stranded by the war in the West, it had been a constant source of friction, especially as Soviet demands encompassed even those who had acquired French citizenship. When the French failed to comply, the refugees sometimes disappeared behind the gates of Camp de Beauregard. As the camp was under the command of a Soviet colonel, the French liaison officer had been commissioned out of a communist Resistance network, and as François Mitterrand among others in the cabinet agreed with the Quai d'Orsay that any attempt to intervene might jeopardize the return of French deportees from the East, Beauregard was tolerated as a hands-off area for the French.[50]

On 17 November 1947, the DST, led by Wybot in a tank, stormed Camp de Beauregard, ostensibly to recover three kidnapped children. That only a few arms were discovered came as something of a disappointment to Wybot. But his real goal was to wipe out what he believed was a nest of Soviet agents. This was critical, because in 1947 intelligence reports predicting a communist uprising had reached the highest levels of the French government. In fact, the genesis of the raid began in February 1946, when the State Department informed the Quai d'Orsay that information collected by the American embassy in Paris pointed to the likelihood of a communist uprising in France. When Major General Ralph J. Smith, the American military attaché in Paris, met with Passy and Manuel in March 1946, he found the ex-SDECE chief relaxed, almost voluble. Passy "did not display his usual rather self-assured and somewhat austere manner," Smith reported. "He appears not only willing, but eager to express his views." What those views were on the likelihood of a communist insurrection are not clear: "Passy made it very clear that he proposed to remain in France until the last moment prior to a major Communist uprising, at which time he would again become incognito and start reorganizing a *maquis*." But when Manuel said that an uprising was possible but not likely, "Dewavrin [Passy] weakly, and without conviction, indicated agreement with Manuel's views, despite his own previous more alarming predictions."[51]

By the end of 1946, Passy's opinion had hardened, and he appears to have been one of the major sources for the reports dispatched by the U.S. ambassador, Jefferson Caffery, to Washington which predicted a communist uprising. Thorez's visits to Moscow were interpreted as evidence that the Kremlin was putting the finishing touches on the conspiracy. Police in Paris and the provinces, obviously tipped off by informers or by microphones placed in PCF headquarters, reported splits in local communist organizations between revolutionaries and those who displayed more tepid enthusiasm for revolt.[52] The remnants of the International Brigades were being mobilized and armed by parachute drops from Germany, it was believed, while the former Minister of Armaments, the communist Charles Tillon, had ordered the construction of an armored locomotive.[53] Either Monsieur Tillon had concluded that Allied bombing was too inaccurate to hit it or Stalin, who supposedly oversaw planning for the rebellion, was prepared to tolerate a Gallic imitation of his archenemy Trotsky.

By 1947, the SDECE predicted that the rebellion, which would be touched off by a general strike and backed by the International Brigades, was planned for early December. A SDECE note for President Auriol asserted that the members of the International Brigades would move into Yugoslavia, which would serve as a springboard to "liquidate the situation in Greece, and then do the same work in Italy and France."[54] The RG added to the panic by citing increasing militancy in the workplace, and suggested that, when the rebellion occurred, the Gaullists might appeal to the United States for arms, which might then be turned on the Republic. The RG did give to President Auriol the more plausible interpretation that Stalin's discontent with the Marshall Plan was at the origin of the problem, and his goal was to disrupt the French economy to such a degree that the Americans would no longer be willing to invest. But the RG's belief in an uprising to take power persisted, confirmed by U.S. intelligence sources.[55]

Thanks to the research of French historian Philippe Buton in the archives of the Communist International, we now know that the French communists were indeed preparing an insurrection in 1947 and that this was squelched by Stalin. On 22 September 1947, Jacques Duclos gave an impassioned report to the congress of nine communist parties presided over by Malenkov at Szklarska Poreba in Poland. Duclos argued that France was fast falling under the influence of the United States and that something must be done quickly to reverse this trend. Moscow, however, had decided to consolidate its gains in Eastern Europe. For the moment, the Western European parties must bide their time until the next—inevitable—crisis in the capitalist economy would create more favorable circumstances for a takeover. Duclos and the PCF were denounced for their "opportunism." A chastened

Duclos thanked the other communist delegates for showing him the error of his ways. Thus concluded the PCF's attempt to seize power.[56]

The government's concern with communist subversion reinforced and perpetuated into the postwar era the traditional priority accorded counterintelligence in the French intelligence community. Not surprisingly, the DST, and to a lesser extent the RG, emerged as the winners of the new regime. The SDECE was the loser. Distrusted by the Allies, disdained by its own government, confined to a military ghetto, the SDECE was to remain the illegitimate child of the Republic. This was an unfortunate situation, Thyraud de Vosjoli believed, because his service had made good progress. Under Bertrand's direction, the SDECE had made great advances in code breaking. This gave the French "first-rate intelligence on Soviet aims and build-ups . . . Things have changed now, but in the fifties we could easily get a clear picture of their intentions by reading their cables. I do not think that at the time any Western agency had better intelligence on the Soviets." But as French intelligence "was slowly emerging from the confused and chaotic era," it was struck by two important scandals that exacerbated the turf battles and rivalries among the intelligence services, eroded its political support at home, and served to discredit it abroad.[57]

The "Generals affair" had its origins in an obscure fight which on 18 September 1949 broke out on a bus in Paris' Gare de Lyon between an ex-soldier, Thomas Perez, and two Indochinese students just back from the Communist-sponsored World Youth Congress in Budapest. Perez, who disappeared into the Foreign Legion, later claimed that he had been hired by the French colonial intelligence service, the Bureau Technique de Liaison et de Coordination (BTLC), to expose high-level "leaks" in the French government. If Perez's claim is accurate, it worked, for when the two students were interrogated, found in their possession was a copy of a secret report prepared by army chief of staff General Georges Revers and approved by the Comité de Défense Nationale in July outlining the failures of French policy in Indochina and recommending new strategies there. That the Revers report was in communist hands was no secret to French intelligence, as it had been read out over the Vietminh radio in August. After a squabble between the Ministry of Defense and the Ministry of the

Interior over jurisdiction, the DST was handed the case. Investigation recovered seventy-two copies of the report in one of the students' flats. Unfortunately, this proved a mere fraction of the copies of a report which had topped the best-seller list of Paris' large Vietnamese community.

The trail of investigation led to Roger Peyré, a small bald man with furtive eyes who, in Wybot's estimation, "looked like a little accountant."[58] In fact, Peyré was a former member of the pro-fascist Parti Populaire Français, whose prosecution for collaboration after the war had been sabotaged by the intervention of Revers. Peyré had managed to work his way into the esteem of Generals Georges Revers and Charles Emmanuel Mast by convincing them that he had the political contacts to secure for each the posts of commander-in-chief and high commissioner in Indochina. Peyré had collected money from pro-French elements in the Vietnamese community to further the generals' campaigns. At the same time, with Revers' permission, Mast had loaned Peyré a copy of the Revers report to provide discreet evidence to influential members of the Vietnamese community of the two generals' qualifications for the offices they coveted. Instead, Peyré sold it in the Vietnamese community. Peyré and a Vietnamese associate, Van Co, were arrested, but later released. Unaccountably, all of their documents seized in the investigation were returned to them.

According to Thyraud de Vosjoli, the SDECE followed the case with "sad amusement" on the assumption that it had nothing to do with it. The socialist government of Paul Ramadier was content to hush up the affair, and Mast and Revers agreed to resign quietly from the army. But that was to calculate without Pierre Fourcaud. As a protégé of Revers, Fourcaud had visited Indochina in 1949 to help Revers formulate his plan. The deputy director of the SDECE was determined to salvage Revers' career and in the process deliver to the Gaullists and Christian Democrats in the MRP a scandal which would discredit the socialists and thereby spatter his nemesis and boss, Henri Ribière. In the presence of Peyré's lawyer and another SDECE officer, Captain Girardot, who had been detailed by Henri Trautmann, head of the research division, to interview Peyré, Fourcaud offered Peyré money and safe passage to South America in return for a sworn statement that Peyré was a SDECE agent and that Revers had accepted no money from Peyré, and had not leaked the report. Girardot subsequently wrote two reports. The first, supporting the original version of the guilt of Revers, was sent through channels to Ribière and Wybot. A second, supporting the altered version, was handed to Fourcaud.

On the following day, as Peyré set sail for a new life in La Paz, Fourcaud leaked the new version to the press, with the twist that the Prime Minister, Ramadier, had really been behind the leaks and had tried to shift the blame to Revers. The Gaullist press cried scandal while the communists had a field day. In the meantime, under pressure from Fourcaud, Wybot believed, Revers withdrew his resignation. This gave the government no choice but to fire Revers in early December. Tipped off by DST telephone taps on the Paris bureau of *Time* magazine that an article was being prepared damning the hemorrhage of Western secrets through France to the U.S.S.R., the Quai d'Orsay put pressure on Washington to have it suppressed. The request was rejected with indignation, and the *Time* article appeared on 26 December 1949.

An embarrassed Ribière discovered that Fourcaud had opened a can of worms for the SDECE. Peyré had indeed been recruited in 1944, part of a policy to use collaborators to locate other collaborators. One version held that Peyré had been severed from the SDECE payroll in 1947. However, it appears that SDECE patronage of Peyré, possibly ordered by Fourcaud, continued in the form of a gambling casino managed by Peyré to which foreign diplomats and others whom the SDECE wished to court or entrap could be brought. Peyré's SDECE contact, a Colonel Morand, was excluded from the service subsequently by Ribière for "financial irregularities."

As there was an SDECE connection, the DST naturally began to interview Captain Girardot and two other SDECE officers. Fourcaud's arrest followed Girardot's testimony, both to the DST and later before a parliamentary committee of inquiry, about the pressure placed on Peyré by Fourcaud to get him to withdraw his confession. Released on the order of the Prime Minister, however, Fourcaud decided to "declare war" on the DST. He accused Wybot and the DST of destroying documents which would have proved Revers' innocence, a charge given credibility by the fact that inexcusably sloppy work by the DST had resulted in the disappearance of most of Peyré's original testimony. Fourcaud followed this up by producing a list of 97 parliamentary deputies who he claimed had taken bribes from Peyré and other incriminating documents seized at the beginning of the investigation. The parliamentary inquiry sputtered from lack of cooperation from the Justice and Finance ministries, the former because strings had been pulled to abort the charge of collaboration placed against Peyré after the war and the latter because of attempts to conceal the open scandal of the piaster traffic with Indochina. Finally, after several frustrating weeks which implicated another former SDECE colonel but produced only more byzantine intrigue, the committee issued a report calling for a reorganization of the secret services and an end to the piaster traffic.

The Generals affair had at least one beneficial result for the SDECE—Fourcaud was given the sack! But the affair had been terribly damaging, both to the SDECE and the DST. "The scandal of the generals was deeply felt in France," wrote Thyraud de Vosjoli. "It destroyed completely the nation's faith in its army, its police, and its government." Disgusted, Ribière sought to resign, but was persuaded to stay on for another six months. "During those six months we tried to patch up some of the damage caused to the SDECE by the succession of scandals, but our organization had lost all the support it ever had." Because one of the chief beneficiaries of the affair had been the communists, Fourcaud was suspected of having been in contact with them. Though nothing could be proved, "this aura of suspicion poisoned the atmosphere and proved very detrimental to good relations within the military alliance." At the same time, Thyraud de Vosjoli complained that British intelligence, which sought to convince the SDECE to centralize all European intelligence to strengthen the hand of MI6 in dealing with the CIA, had supported Fourcaud's position. "Their interference in French politics had caused hard feelings in our agency, and liaison between the two organizations was at its lowest point since the war."[59]

For its part, Wybot believed that the DST came within a whisker of abolition and that he, denounced for his "totalitarian character" and the "closed, secret" nature of his service, had narrowly escaped early retirement. The new Minister of the Interior, Léon Martinaud-Déplat, a radical who distrusted the DST as a socialist stronghold, made it clear that he wanted "no more scandals." As it was, the DST suffered a debilitating *sauve-qui-peut* as many of its best agents and administrators sought out jobs where tenure was more secure. In the civil service, the DST was tagged as "a place where you hit [career] snags," and recruitment faltered.[60]

In 1954, security leaks and "police wars" again tarnished the reputation of the French services in a spectacular way when top-secret French military reports and the minutes of Comité de Défense Nationale meetings began to find their way into the press. One high-level report was even discovered on the body of a dead Vietminh soldier. Security leaks were especially harmful while the government was in the midst of negotiating a settlement of the Indochinese conflict at Geneva. Meanwhile, French soldiers led by General Henri Navarre and supported by the French right were vocal in their claims that the government's willingness, expressed in February 1954, to negotiate had handed Giap the incentive to invest the lives of his soldiers to overwhelm the French garrison at Dien Bien Phu. The payoff for the Vietminh was to convince the French to leave Indochina. On 2 July 1954, Christian Fouchet, a Gaullist who had just taken up the portfolio of Moroccan and Tunisian Affairs in the new government of Pierre Mendès-France, was visited by Chief Inspector Jean Dides, who ran the 7th Section, a "parallel secret service" for the Paris Prefecture of Police which specialized in the French Communist Party, a service which Wybot dismissed as "a joke."[61] Dides delivered to Fouchet a report on a meeting of the Bureau Politique of the PCF in which a full account of the meeting of the Comité de Défense Nationale of 28 June had been read out. Dides insisted that the document, supplied by an informant inside the PCF, could not be handed over to his superiors because he believed the source of the leak was none other than the new Minister of the Interior, François Mitterrand. Fouchet informed Mendès-France, who had only recently learned of the leaks during the previous government's tenure. The Prime Minister ordered an investigation, but for the moment excluded Mitterrand from it.

Shortly before the 10 September meeting of the Comité de Défense Nationale, in which the initiation of a French atomic program was to be discussed, Mendès-France handed the stalled investigation to Mitterrand. The Interior Minister in turn ordered Wybot to find both the informer of Fouchet and the source of the leaks. Wybot had no trouble tracing Dides, who had repeated his accusations to right-wing deputies, so that Mitterrand's "treason" was openly discussed in Paris. DST agents shadowed Dides, who led them to a communist journalist named André Baranès, who had worked for d'Astier de la Vignerie's Libération and who for four years had been a paid agent of the Prefecture of Police. When they staked out Baranès' apartment building, however, DST agents came to blows with their colleagues from the Prefecture of Police. On 9 September, the day before the CDN meeting, Wybot was ordered to relinquish the case to the Prefecture, which on the next day dropped surveillance of Baranès.

On 18 September, Dides returned to the office of Christian Fouchet with a summary of the CDN meeting of 10 September. Forewarned apparently by a telephone tap, the DST swooped in to arrest Dides. A search of Baranès' apartment revealed other copies without annotations by communist leaders, which made it clear that Baranès was getting them straight from someone in the CDN and not from Communist Party headquarters. Only two people took notes in committee. Those held by Dides and Baranès were reproductions of notes taken by the committee secretary, Jean Mons. Interrogated, Mons denied all knowledge of what happened. Attempts to build a case against Mons, Wybot insisted, simply brought out Mons's powerful friends, Mendès-France and Marshal Alphonse Juin among them, to sabotage it. Suspicion then fell on his two assistants, René Turpin and Roger Labrusse. Labrusse confessed that Turpin recopied Mons's notes, which were given to Baranès and to his boss at Libération, d'Astier. Wybot remained convinced that Mons was guilty as well, but despite active lobbying a court censured him only for negligence. The case against Baranès for the unauthorized possession of secret documents was also dropped because he had acted under orders from Dides. Turpin was given four years in prison, and Labrusse six. Parliamentary immunity shielded d'Astier from prosecution.

What had been the result for the secret services? By giving documents to the right and abandoning surveillance of Baranès to hide the true source of the leaks, Dides and the 7th Section of the Prefecture of Police clearly sought to discredit the government of Mendès-France at a critical time in the Geneva negotiations and smear François Mitterrand. Wybot saw two bad consequences: His belief that Mons was the true culprit deepened his conviction that well-connected spies were virtually immune from prosecution in France, that in France it was not spies who were on trial but those who sought to unmask them. Baranès had been defended by the virulent right-wing lawyer Tixier-Vignacourt, whose real agenda was to attack the regime and in doing so discredit the DST. Wybot also believed that d'Astier was the head of a spy network in France which, had it been exposed, would have rivaled that of Philby in Great Britain or Günther Guillaume, the protégé of Willy Brandt whose unmasking in Germany in 1974 led to the resignation of the German Chancellor.[62] So one of the ironic results for Wybot was that in his attempt to protect the Fourth Republic, he felt more alienated from it. This was to have important consequences in 1958.

A second result was that the leaks once again besmirched the reputation of French security and its espionage services. Thyraud de Vosjoli, who in 1951 had been sent to Washington as SDECE station chief, believed that what had become known in France as the *affaire des fuites* (leaks) might have passed without much comment in the CIA had it not coincided with other events which lowered the stock of the French services. The most blatant was a botched attempt by the SDECE and the DST, before CIA observers, to arrange the defection of a Soviet security agent named Volokitine from the Soviet embassy in Paris. Apparently tipped off, the Soviets spirited Volokitine back to Moscow. According to Thyraud de Vosjoli, to cover their embarrassment, the DST told the Americans that the Soviets had been alerted by none other than their boss, Interior Minister Mitterrand, the very same man responsible for the leaks from the CDN. "After four years of effort to build up confidence between French and American intelligence, I saw the collapse of all my endeavors," Thyraud de Vosjoli anguished. "And who could blame the Americans for being distrustful in the aftermath of their bitter experience with Philby?"[63]

Thyraud de Vosjoli was correct that the CIA was profoundly distrustful of foreign services in general and the French in particular. A series of Soviet defectors in the early 1960s reported that the French services were penetrated. One claimed that in 1952 he had attended a lecture in Moscow by the KGB's deputy chief for disinformation in which he had disparaged French intelligence as "that prostitute I put in my pocket."[64] The most damaging allegations against France came from Major Anatoliy Golitsyn, a KGB agent who defected to the Americans in Helsinki in December 1961. Golitsyn's accusations were given credence in August 1963, when Georges Pâques, a NATO press secretary, was discovered handing over secret documents to the Soviets. Thyraud de Vosjoli believed that Pâques, a frequent visitor to Washington, "had probably passed on to the Russians many valuable pieces of intelligence on U.S. defense plants and on American intentions and potential." He speculated that Pâques had been as valuable to the Soviets as Philby.[65] A KGB officer who defected to the British in September 1963 revealed that his service had ensnared French ambassador to Moscow Maurice Dejean in a "honey trap" with a KGB prostitute in 1958. Dejean was recalled to Paris in 1964 and quietly retired from the diplomatic service.

Whether true or not, these accusations that the French secret services were penetrated by the communists were to have consequences for the efficiency of French intelligence, as they occurred at a period of growing Franco-American tension. In 1964 de Gaulle ordered the SDECE to break off contact with the CIA, an order which stood for three years. Although the CIA lost access to radio traffic picked up by French monitoring stations, the break probably hurt the French, who relied on the CIA for much of their electronic surveillance equipment, more than the Americans. But de Gaulle was apparently more interested in acquiring American nuclear and military secrets than he was in the short-term efficiency of his secret service, which he probably saw as more of a liability than an asset in any case. For his part, Thyraud de Vosjoli departed the SDECE with little regret, insisting that it had been compromised by politics and corrupted by its activities during France's colonial wars, which had absorbed much of its energies since the Liberation.

T W E L V E

I N D O C H I N A

Of the many challenges faced by postwar France, the wars of decolonization in Indochina and subsequently Algeria must count among
the most significant. On one level, both confrontations were what
military theorists call "small wars" or "low-intensity conflicts"—contests in which precise local intelligence often defined the boundaries
between victory and defeat, life and death. At the same time, both
wars acquired an international dimension as they became local battlefields in a global struggle between East and West, an international
contest in which France's future as a great power was at stake. For
French intelligence, these wars would pose challenges beyond the
ordinary ones, difficult enough in themselves, of defining the intentions of the enemy.

The French appeared to be well placed to fight the intelligence war
in Indochina. In occupation of the country since the nineteenth century, the French had assembled a police and intelligence infrastructure
run by men familiar with the country. Likewise, the army and the
Deuxième Bureau could call on commanders with long experience in
Indochina. Before World War II, the Colonial Ministry kept a watchful
eye on the political sympathies of Indochinese in France through the
Service de Contrôle et d'Assistance des Indigènes. By 1946, the prewar
Indochinese population in France of around 2,000 students, seamen,

and domestics had swelled to almost 14,000. In February 1946, the Service de Liaison avec les Originaires des Territoires Français d'Outre-mer, SLOTFOM, was organized to keep tabs on these Indochinese residents. In April 1948, the Colonial Ministry created a Bureau Technique de Liaison et de Coordination (BTLC) to coordinate the flow of intelligence between SDECE, the Deuxième Bureau, the Sécurité Militaire, and the SLOTFOM.[1]

This panoply of intelligence services would deliver excellent intelligence on the Vietminh throughout the Indochina War (1946–54). But excellent intelligence could not in itself be a war winner for the French, especially when fed into a defective governmental and military structure.

One of the great problems for the French was that they were never able to develop a coherent policy for Indochina, one which might have encouraged the emergence of a viable political alternative to the Vietminh. The absence of a coherent policy was the result of indifference and political division in France. One of the heavier legacies of defeat and occupation in World War II was that it served to heighten France's endemic political divisions and institutional instability. Postwar cabinets whose demises and resurrections were announced with embarrassing frequency, a parliament hostage to sectarian ideology or the whims of narrow interests, policies shaped by cowardice or simple inertia, all left the intelligence community rudderless in defining national interests and threats to those interests. Frustrated with France's leadership, stung to fury by the disinterest and even disloyalty displayed by a significant minority of French people during the wars of decolonization, the intelligence community, like large sections of the French army, became increasingly disenchanted and estranged from its political base. It is no surprise that the French secret services were in the thick of the conspiracy against the Fourth Republic which burst into the open in May 1958.

Without a viable policy, the only strategy open to military commanders was that of military victory. However, the prospect of a French defeat of the Vietminh, never very bright, receded over the horizon from 1950 when the victorious Chinese Communists agreed to support their fellow insurgents to the south. Despite excellent intelligence on the growth of Vietminh power, French military commanders never adjusted their expectations and retained their faith in the power of French arms, a faith which led them down the path to Dien Bien Phu.

In retrospect, it is amazing that French intelligence services performed as well as they did in Indochina, given the fact that they began the Indochina War with a considerable handicap. When France fell to Hitler in June 1940, Japan had taken advantage of French vulnerability in the Far East to set up a joint occupation of Indochina with the Vichy French which lasted until 9 March 1945, when, in a surprise attack, Japanese troops overwhelmed the French garrisons there. During the war, the Free French had attempted to set up intelligence networks in Indochina so that de Gaulle could become the essential broker should the Allies decide to invade the French colony. But their efforts had not met with success.[2]

The eclipse of the Giraudists, outmaneuvered by de Gaulle in Algiers, and the liberation of France in the summer of 1944 at least had all Frenchmen in Indochina working on the same side. This helped to improve the intelligence picture in 1945—the Allies became well informed on the numbers of Japanese troops falling back from Burma into Indochina and on the movements of Japanese ships around the coast which allowed American planes to sink fully forty of them in early January 1945.[3] But the leader of Free France never managed to impose a Gaullist intelligence monopoly in Indochina. On the contrary, the Gaullist presence complicated the already byzantine bureaucratic and political rivalries which served to undermine the effectiveness of intelligence gathering in Southeast Asia. Worse, when on 9 March 1945 Japanese forces in Indochina, fearing, in the wake of the fall of the Philippines, that Indochina would be the next Allied target, pounced without warning on the French, arresting, incarcerating, even butchering French soldiers and administrators, intelligence from Indochina dried up overnight.

The 9 March coup also put an end to Gaullist attempts to create a resistance in Indochina. In fact, from the beginning the idea of a resistance, especially a Gaullist resistance, proved a hollow concept, because it was flawed both politically and militarily. It offered an excellent example—alas, not the last—of how a concept shaped in a European milieu was applied in conditions altogether inappropriate for Indochina. In the first place, few in the indigenous population of around 25 million held any deep attachment to continued French governance of Indochina, much less to the Gaullist cause. On the contrary, the only authentic resistance movement in Indochina was organized by the Vietminh with some, very minor, assistance from the American Office of Strategic Services (OSS). So adamant were the French that natives had no role to play in an Indochina resistance that American plans to organize an anti-Japanese guerrilla movement among the hill tribes of northern Indochina collapsed in the face of French opposition. This made nonsense of de Gaulle's vision of a resistance movement as a symbol of Gaullist legitimacy in those colonies. So de Gaulle's resisters had to be recruited among a French population of roughly 30,000 together with 14,500 white soldiers armed with equipment dating from World War I marooned since 1940 in this fragile French enclave in the Far East. What the Free French worked toward was not a resistance movement, but a colonial coup de'état.

Even this population offered stony ground for conversion to the Gaullist cause, for most were staunch Pétainists, either out of conviction or from a sense of self-preservation. Admiral Jean Decoux, governor general of the colony, whose patriotic rigidity was remarkable even by the starched standards of the French navy, reigned from his palace in Saigon in the grand manner of the nineteenth-century admirals who had conquered Indochina. Vichy radio services drew flattering comparisons between Decoux, Marshal Pétain, and Confucius. But beneath his fustian manner, the admiral behaved more like a commander of an unseaworthy ship in a tempest. Unfortunately for de Gaulle, even those most humiliated by the debacle of 1940 and the Japanese occupation were forced to recognize that the French administration of Indochina continued at the sufferance of the Japanese. Overt resistance invited retaliation. Nevertheless, from the promontory from which de Gaulle directed the resurrection of French honor, he judged the "complaisant passivity" of Indochina "unworthy and derisory."[4]

By February 1944, de Gaulle judged the time ripe for Indochina to submit to the authority of his Comité de Libération Nationale. But de Gaulle's choice to lead the resistance, the commander of French forces in Indochina, General Eugène Mordant, proved reluctant to assume the leadership. When on 5 July 1944, François de Langlade, a Malaysian planter, early convert to the Gaullist cause, and chief of the French Indo-China Section of the British Ministry of Economic Warfare in Calcutta, parachuted close to Lang Son with the mission to strengthen Mordant's resolve, the general informed Langlade that "the Indochina army is tired . . . What do you expect it to do?" Mordant's reluctance to serve could not prevent him from being proclaimed "General Delegate to the Action Committee for the Liberation of Indochina" and head of the resistance in August, with the mission to coordinate an uprising against the Japanese which would be a prelude to the intervention of a 15,000-strong French expeditionary force stationed in Ceylon. When Decoux was told that he was now only a front for Mordant, who had the real authority in Indochina, he hit the roof. This touched off a debate over the delimitation of authority between the two men and their entourages which kept the wires warm between Paris and Saigon and required a further parachuted visit by Langlade, one resolved finally by the Japanese on 9 March 1945.

The Japanese followed this activity with interest. When in 1946 the British inventoried the Japanese archives in Singapore, they discovered decrypts of all the French wires. The Japanese also had thoroughly infiltrated the Vietnamese staff of Mordant, a man dropped by de Gaulle into a conspiracy which he lacked the conspiratorial qualities to lead. In fact, the French threw themselves into the organization of the resistance with more enthusiasm than discretion. The South East Asia Command in Ceylon parachuted agents and French officers into Indochina who created a communications network there based on eleven wireless stations. French soldiers openly discussed the possibility of an American landing in Vietnam and trained to assist it. Arms were parachuted to French garrisons in full view of the Japanese. French plans for an uprising were discussed over the wires with General Roger Blaizot in Kandy. Quite naturally, the Japanese preferred to get out in front of events rather than patiently await the rebellion.[5] For its part, rumors of preemptive Japanese action divided, confused, and intoxicated French intelligence, which allowed the Japanese on 9 March to sweep up without difficulty most of the senior administrators and military men in the colony, including Mordant and Decoux. A small force under General Marcel Alessandri made a fighting retreat through northern Tonkin to China. France's links with Indochina were severed.

As so often in his career, de Gaulle proved a terrible tactician but a marvelous strategist. The General attempted to put a good face on the collapse of his resistance and an end to a pretense of French sovereignty in Indochina by insisting in a radio broadcast that the "combat" of isolated French units against Japanese troops had "opened the destiny" of Indochina. In many respects, he was correct. His intelligence organization, however rudimentary, had established a basis for Allied cooperation with the Gaullists in Indochina to provide intelligence and recover pilots.[6]

A further Allied boost for the French in Indochina was provided by the commander of British forces in Saigon, Major General Douglas Gracey, who decided Indochina's immediate destiny by rearming French POWs in September and allowing French forces to return to Saigon from early October 1945. De Gaulle had realized his goal of reclaiming Indochina for France. But he would have to fight for it. For the Japanese surrender in August also "opened the destiny" of the Vietminh, who marched into Hanoi and proclaimed the Democratic Republic of Vietnam on 2 September. Although the French, and later some Americans, accused the OSS of providing the Vietminh with both encouragement and the means to initiate the war, American support for the Vietminh had been minimal. Perception being more important than reality, however, the American involvement in wartime Vietnam left a legacy of bitterness between American and French intelligence services there which persisted beyond Dien Bien Phu to the final French withdrawal from Indochina in 1955.[7] Following fifteen months marred by incidents and mounting tension, the Vietminh commander, Vo Nguyen Giap, quietly surrounded Hanoi with 30,000 troops and at eight o'clock on the evening of 19 December 1946, launched an attack on the French in Hanoi and other garrison towns in Tonkin and Annam.

Given the deteriorating relations between the two sides and unequivocal intelligence warnings, the remarkable thing was that when the uprising began, the Vietminh came within a whisker of repeating the Japanese success of 9 March 1945. Soon after the "Haiphong incident" of 20 November, when French attempts to seize a Chinese junk suspected of smuggling arms to the Vietminh caused a hot skirmish to erupt between the two sides, the Deuxième Bureau had begun to collect information that pointed to an imminent attack.[8] The French high commissioner, Admiral Thierry d'Argenlieu, reported to the Prime Minister that the French commander, General Louis Morlière, failed to act against the obvious military buildup around and within Tonkin's chief city. Worse, when, late in the afternoon of 19 December, Morlière's Deuxième Bureau chief insisted that Giap's attack was only hours—perhaps minutes—away, the general would not order an alert until an intelligence officer dispatched to reconnoiter Hanoi's Vietnamese quarters returned to report alarming military activity there. At eight o'clock in the evening, the Vietminh blew up Hanoi's power station, which plunged the city into darkness and signaled the beginning of the attack. The Vietminh action had been well planned, d'Argenlieu wrote, but "it lacked one element: surprise . . . If this was not realized, it was due to an infinitely precious last-minute piece of intelligence."[9] Forewarned, the French managed to throw Giap out of the city center after a day of very hard fighting. But not before several hundred French and Eurasian civilians had been brutally murdered by the Vietminh. Giap fled to the hills, and the war was on.

From an intelligence perspective, the French appeared adequately organized to carry on the war. Most of the intelligence services fell under the Ministry of Defense, including SDECE, whose two most important roles were surveillance of foreign influence in Indochina and the monitoring of Vietminh radios through the Services Techniques de Recherches, a task supplemented by the Groupement des Contrôles Radio-électriques under the Directeur Général de la Documentation. A Direction des Services Français de Sécurité under the Defense Minister provided the liaison with Vietnamese secret services when these were finally organized after 1950. Its job was to gather political intelligence and ensure the security of French communications. It also specialized in antiterrorism and Chinese activity in Indochina. SDECE furnished a Service d'Etudes Historique (SEH), or 6th Section of the general staff, whose task was "the collection of intelligence in rebel zones" mainly through "operational counterespionage brigades."[10] These organizations were supplemented by the usual panoply of military security organizations coordinated by the Deuxième Bureau.

Hardly two months had passed since the failed Vietminh uprising in Hanoi when d'Argenlieu wrote to the new commander of French forces in Indochina, General Jean Valluy, on 17 February 1947, that intelligence "from various sources" had located the new Vietminh command center in the highlands north of the Tonkin delta. D'Argenlieu insisted in Clausewitzian terms that this formed the rebel "center of gravity" and urged an airborne attack against it within two weeks. Valluy replied two days later that he lacked the troops to carry out the operation and that his intelligence was not sufficiently precise. Even when the operation, baptized Léa, was decided on in principle on 19 May, Valluy insisted that the notion of a Vietminh "capital" was "very theoretical because of the great dispersion of the organs of government and command."[11]

If Valluy was not keen on Léa, the same could not be said of General Raoul Salan. An officer with extensive experience in Indochina and in intelligence, Salan was impressed by his intelligence service, which "gave me very well-thought-out reports," he remembered.[12] With the Vietminh "capital" identified as Bac Kan, Salan believed that he had a chance to make intelligence the servant of strategy by smashing the "head" of the rebellion. Léa had to be postponed while operations were carried out in Cochin China and Annam as a prelude to liberating troops for Léa. In the meantime, extra radio listening posts were established to fix the locations of Vietminh command centers.[13]

At 8:15 in the morning of 7 October 1947, 400 paratroopers came down onto drop zones to the north, south, and east of Bac Kan and moved to the summits of the hills which surrounded it. Two hours later, a second wave of 350 paratroopers dropped out of the sky. By one o'clock in the afternoon, Bac Kan was in French hands. In many respects, the operation was a tremendous success. In the surrounding villages and caves, French troops discovered arms factories and depots. The radio transmitter which broadcast the "Voice of Vietnam" and which probably enabled the French to home in on the Vietminh command post was seized, along with an immense number of high-level documents. A number of hostages were also liberated. Yet the Vietminh government and high command, the real targets of the operation, had melted into the mountains, along with most of their troops, who had not put up a stubborn fight and so had not suffered serious losses. Nevertheless, on 17 November, Salan proclaimed Léa a success, because "the [Vietminh] national redoubt, dislocated and cleaned out, has practically ceased to exist." Léa was followed in early December by Ceinture, which sought to surround and destroy Vietminh troop concentrations near Thai Nguyen. While this time Salan managed to inflict significant losses on his enemy, again the Vietminh chose to live to fight again another day and retreated into the jungle. Valluy proclaimed victory, insisting that the Vietminh had been reduced to "the wandering life of partisans and pirates."[14]

But it was the Vietminh, rather than the French, who learned the lessons of these autumn offensives of 1947. In documents captured by the French, Giap concluded that he must in the future disperse his forces, logistics, and command structures so that they would no longer offer a concentrated target for the French. He must procure more heavy weapons. Deception, camouflage, and better intelligence about French intentions would henceforth become priorities for the Vietminh.[15] All of this would transform the intelligence war against the Vietminh into much more of a challenge.

It was a challenge which gradually exposed several deficiencies in the French intelligence structure in Indochina, a major one being that intelligence was not assigned a high priority in the French army, especially on the unit level. In an army increasingly stretched to the limit to scrape together enough officers to command its fighting units, where a 20 percent officer vacancy rate was common, the appointment of an intelligence officer was often considered an unaffordable luxury, or intelligence was just one of several administrative tasks the intelligence officer was meant to carry out. "A good intelligence officer is worth a whole battalion," one intelligence officer complained. "However, no commander in fact ever deprived himself of a battalion in order to have a competent intelligence officer."[16] And even when an intelligence officer was assigned, the job too often fell to those whose only qualification was their lack of aptitude for command. This was more the pity, because the intelligence officer required very special qualities—curiosity, an open mind, a precise and methodical approach to information, and the firm judgment to allow him to distinguish true from false. Above all, he must "live intellectually with the enemy," understand his mentality, know his possibilities.[17] This was especially difficult in Indochina, where the army had never created a "native affairs" branch as it had in North Africa, so there were few men familiar with local customs and languages, no repository of accumulated experience of Indochina. Furthermore, many Frenchmen long experienced with Indochina were removed after the war because they were considered too pro-Vichy. Therefore, the French became overly dependent on Vietnamese interpreters, men who might be unscrupulous or even Vietminh spies.

The result was too often the predictable one: In their haste to find the needle, the French army many times burned down the haystack. In Englishman Henry Ainley's Legion Battalion, for instance, the intelligence officer ran a *Bande Noire* of Vietnamese thugs and deserters, "grim-faced, cold-eyed killers," who looted and terrorized the countryside and who would bring in Vietminh "suspects" for torture. And while most of the battalion found this distasteful, in the absence of other intelligence sources "the majority regarded the whole matter as a necessary and inevitable evil."[18] If poor intelligence affected the fighting qualities of the French army, it could also encourage retaliatory action against the local population by troops whose inability to distinguish friend from foe put nerves on edge. What began as provocation might easily degenerate into habit. Ainley was shocked to discover that "rape, beating, burning, torturing of entirely harmless peasants and villagers were of common occurrence in the course of punitive patrols and operations by French troops."[19] The result of this undisciplined behavior for battlefield intelligence was nothing short of disastrous, for it merely served to reinforce what French intelligence called the "three khôngs" or "nothings"—See nothing, hear nothing, know nothing— which the Vietminh taught the population was the response of a "good patriot" to French questions.[20]

The insufficiency of French tactical intelligence, and perhaps, too, the excesses of unit intelligence officers, caused Marshal Jean de Lattre de Tassigny to create "counterintelligence brigades" in April 1951 under the command of the SDECE. The next year, the French could claim that the three brigades in the north and one in the south had given good results on the local level, but they admitted that their intelligence summaries "were not done from a sufficiently elevated point of view," that they were "very fragmentary. What is lacking is a general view of the activities of rebel and foreign intelligence services." When Henri Navarre took over command of French forces in May 1953, he expanded them and changed their name to Détachements Opérationnels de Protection (DOP), in part because the Vietminh had identified the organization and so compromised its effectiveness.[21] And while these DOP brigades may have been more professional in their approach to interrogations, some in the service were not above taking advantage of their position, like the two DOP officers hauled before the courts in January 1954 accused of kidnapping a Vietnamese and threatening to kill him if he did not give them 10,000 piasters.[22] The DOPs rapidly acquired a reputation for torture and brutality when they were transferred to Algeria after 1954.

Intelligence officers complained that the troops themselves were not intelligence-conscious and did not realize that they had a responsibility to collect information.[23] But French troops faced enormous disadvantages in intelligence gathering, not the least of which was the fact that they were shifted from area to area and so were constantly fighting in unfamiliar territory, unlike the Vietminh, who invariably had expert local knowledge. The French tried to offset this disadvantage through other means. One was the creation of a Service de Renseignement Opérationel, reconnaissance teams with the mission to penetrate into Vietminh-controlled areas and even into China to a depth of 100 kilometers. In 1952, the French reckoned that their two reconnaissance companies were well worth their 300-million-franc annual cost because they had proved able from time to time to alert posts that were about to be attacked. But they gave little intelligence on "the depth of enemy dispositions," no political or economic intelligence, and the value of their military intelligence was compromised by the fact that, as these units traveled on foot, their information was often stale on arrival.[24]

Air reconnaissance could prove useful, especially in directing set-piece battles when the Vietminh came into the open, as during Giap's all-out offensives against the Tonkin delta in 1951. But in situations of mobile warfare, their effectiveness was limited by bad weather and the heavy jungle cover. After Léa, Vietminh camouflage limited the ability of air reconnaissance to study fixed Vietminh installations. For instance, French planes flying reconnaissance in advance of the ill-fated Groupe Mobile 100 in the Central Highlands in June 1954 reported no enemy activity in the high grass that bordered the An Khe–Mang Yang road just moments before the Vietminh unleashed the massive ambush which wiped out the unit.[25] French reconnaissance capabilities were limited to 350 airplanes, mainly Moranes, Bearcats, and B-26s, or one-eighth of the French air force. The independent, not to say bloody-minded, spirit of air force pilots meant that many preferred to draw up their own reconnaissance plans and overfly areas they knew well, rather than operate on an à la carte basis in response to army demands. On one level, this made sense because the heavy foliage and expert Vietminh camouflage forced the pilots to spend more time over an area to discover any trace of the Vietminh.[26] On the other hand, it did not necessarily serve the immediate needs of army intelligence officers, who might go for months without updated air photos of their sector.[27]

"How often have many of you, commanding a post set up in the rice fields, fallen asleep at night cursing your ignorance of the enemy which surrounds you?" Major F. L. Michel asked officers passing through his intelligence course. Even crack units like the *groupes mobiles*, hard-hitting combined-arms formations, "are obliged to fight blind and exhaust themselves" on operations which "nine times out of ten strike into thin air" because of the "failings of our intelligence services."[28] As a consequence, French patrols tripped out over the paddies and jungles largely blind, often equipped with out-of-date or inaccurate maps, without benefit of air reconnaissance photographs, to wander aimlessly about the countryside. "Our intelligence provided us with a vague image of this enemy," the French postwar self-evaluation noted. "We knew that Vietminh troops had passed the night here or there, or we could deduce that a battalion was to be found within a certain imprecisely defined zone. But all this information was quickly outdated, and the enemy appeared 'a moving cloud of vague and changing contours, either expanding to dissipate itself like a mist, or else condensing into a storm whose violence is quickly over . . . leaving behind it only a blue sky . . . and some ruins.' "

If the Vietminh could catch the French at a disadvantage, however, then units might fall "victims of the most brutal surprises. Every day vehicles were blown up by road mines, patrols either found nothing or fell into ambushes, and when units penetrated into a village, they lacked the information that would have allowed them to screen the people and identify the nonuniformed rebels." Not knowing what was to their front, French forces became hesitant and sluggish in maneuver. They proved quick to adopt a defensive posture, to call in air strikes and artillery, which increasingly forfeited the initiative in combat to the Vietminh.[29] Therefore, poor tactical intelligence had a direct effect on French morale and combat performance and made a significant contribution to the French army's high casualty rates in Indochina.

It was difficult for the French to improve the quality of their intelligence when potential sources were limited or the information collected failed to reach the right people in time. Although the French boasted in 1946 that a network of agents had been created to provide human intelligence, this does not appear to have served the French terribly well. The problem was in part a financial one and, as will be seen, French attempts to solve it caused more problems than it cured. In August 1946, General Valluy complained that no agent network could function without cash, because "to get *worthwhile* intelligence, one has to pay for it, because the life of a clandestine agent is not exactly a leisurely activity in this country. One needs money, lots of money," especially to purchase the loyalty of local chiefs and headmen.[30] The problem with the paid agent was that he was more likely to be a double agent.[31] To be effective the intelligence officers had to operate in a social milieu, to get to know those who circulated freely in Vietminh areas, such as Chinese merchants and Buddhist clergy. They should have won the confidence of the local population, and not have lived isolated on islands of French presence set amidst a population made hostile by Vietminh propaganda and intimidation or by the brutality of French troops themselves. Colonel de Marincourt complained that agent reports, when they arrived at all, were too late to be checked out by air reconnaissance.[32]

But the real problem with human intelligence was that it could not exist in isolation. Valluy recognized this as early as 1947 when he argued that no one would come forward with information so long as the Vietminh was able to "maintain an atmosphere of violence and prolonged insecurity." If the population was assured of protection, then they would willingly offer information.[33] This required a systematic policy of pacification, which the French were never able to achieve.

Few Vietnamese had any incentive to fight for the French. The government of Bao Dai, which began to take form from 1947 to undermine the Vietminh claim that they were the patriotic party, took the position that they were neutrals in the struggle between the French and the insurgents. This compromised the effectiveness of psychological action campaigns upon which the French high command counted heavily to win the war. In early 1946, the French created a Service de Propagande, whose tracts stressed *"l'antivietminhisme . . .* the Vietminh were presented as rebels, outlaws in rebellion against established authority."

After the establishment of the Bao Dai government, joint French-Vietnamese propaganda teams often accompanied by theater groups made up of ex-Vietminh rallied to the French, sought to create a strong core of popular support for the new state by stressing Vietnamese nationalism in conjunction with the creation of a Vietnamese national army. The French psychological action effort was stepped up in 1953 with larger budgets, some of which was provided by the Americans, who also trained several of the French officers at the Special Warfare School at Fort Bragg, North Carolina.[34]

While the French measured the success of their psychological action program by the numbers of Vietminh defectors and the numbers of Montagnards and Catholics who chose to live in the south after the division of Vietnam in 1954, that success is open to question. Apparently, the Vietminh worried about the effects of French propaganda leaflets on civilian morale and required people in their zones to turn them in within three hours or face punishment.[35] In December 1952, a French report claimed that Vietminh leaders in the south attributed the disturbing number of defections from their ranks there to, among other things, the "skillful propaganda and generous attitude of the legal government."[36] But there were limits. Most Vietminh "defectors" were local militia forces who were not keen to be promoted into Vietminh main-force units or who "defected" after being captured or interned. Defections also depended on the tide of military fortunes—defections to the French peaked in the first quarter of 1953 at 10,780 following Giap's devastating setback at Na San in November–December 1952. A year later, as Giap closed in on Dien Bien Phu, however, they had dropped to almost nothing. In fact, the trend had been reversed with a vengeance. So many Vietnamese were deserting French-led units by early 1954 that the Vietminh began to suspect a French plot to inundate their organization with agents.[37] A Vietminh defector claimed in January 1953 that the Vietminh took great pains to see that French propaganda tracts did not reach their soldiers. As for the ordinary peasants, tracts with tables comparing standards of living in French- and Vietminh-controlled areas made no sense to them. Vietminh propaganda, on the other hand, was "well organized and very subtle . . . In the [Vietminh] army propaganda is even more subtle."[38] Legionnaire Adrian Liddell Hart also found this psychological action propaganda cruelly ironic, when after devastating and looting a village, his Legion unit then left behind leaflets which "showed a small chicken, presumably meant to represent the people of Viet-Nam, being swallowed by a large fierce snake which signified the Viet-Minh or Red China. As we were the only people who were preying on chickens at the moment, the propaganda was not particularly apt."[39]

As a viable pacification program would require Vietnamese cooperation, in 1950 the SDECE asked the Bao Dai government to allow the French to guide the creation of a Vietnamese secret service. This was resisted until April 1951, when Bao Dai finally assented. But the subsequent bickering and rivalries among the apprentice Vietnamese spymasters were such that the SDECE sighed that a "French Lawrence" was required to impose some sort of direction. They also began to wonder if they had not created a monster: "The Vietnamese intelligence officer is at once arrogant and ineffective," read a report of November 1951. "Disturbed at seeing his French colleague succeed where he has failed, naturally refusing to admit his own incompetence, he attributes the cause of his lack of success to somber machinations. From that moment, the struggle is on. Under threat of blackmail or bought off, some of our agents go over to the competition, others are 'blown' out of negligence or spite."[40] But in those areas where cooperation was fruitful and a successful pacification program was in place, the results could be excellent: "Informed, for once, by a reliable source," one intelligence officer testified, "I was able in one hour on a certain night to capture all of the political cadres of a rebel village with a handful of men, whereas ordinarily we could not have entered this village with less than a company."[41]

If the French in general were badly or only partially informed about the Vietminh, the rebels, on the contrary, were often very well informed about the French. This was in large part inevitable. Up to 80 percent of French forces were tied down to fixed garrisons and were therefore easier to watch. And the Vietminh watched them very closely. From early in the war, the Vietminh gave a high priority to intelligence, creating a centralized intelligence bureau under the Defense Minister with cells directed by Communist Party members reaching through zones and provinces down to the village level.[42] The Vietminh formed operational intelligence teams, called Trinh Sat, on the Soviet model. Trinh Sat teams were assigned to French units and posts to report on movements, gain plans of defense, collect documents, and prepare attacks. "There is not one Vietminh action, whether it be an ambush or attacks on Dien Bien Phu, that did not involve the use of such intelligence elements, sometimes for as long as several weeks or even months," declared the French postwar study. "All the documents which fell into our hands attested to the wealth of information which the enemy had procured solely through this organization."[43] Indeed, as on the Eastern Front in World War II when the detection of a Soviet operational intelligence team was a sure tip to a German commander of an imminent attack,[44] increased activity of Trinh Sat formations near a post or in an area put French officers on alert that an attack was being prepared. For instance, the discovery, after an action near Son La in the northwestern highlands in July 1952, of the corpse of a platoon leader from the celebrated 426th Trinh Sat Battalion provided an early clue to Giap's autumn offensive into T'ai country which terminated in his reversal before Na San in November–December 1952.[45] The Vietminh also established Dich Van cells in French-led Vietnamese units. These were informers who often were recruited through fear of reprisals against their families and who were instructed to be model soldiers and earn promotion. Their cooperation could be vital in the success of a surprise attack on a French post. Dich Van cells were also created in places frequented by French troops.

One of the consequences for the French of the extensive Vietminh espionage networks was that it was very difficult to keep a secret. Colonel Madre, chief of security of the Défense Nationale des Forces Armées, complained in April 1954 that his soldiers were hopeless at keeping secrets—incorrigibly garrulous in public, especially with prostitutes and dancers, in front of Vietnamese servants in the mess. "Now the Dich Van is 70 percent female," he cautioned.

Units were careless with documents and radio codes, which were distributed too widely and were subject to capture. One unit commander heard about Operation Atlante, an attack on Vietminh strongholds in Annam launched on 20 January 1954, four days before it began from a Chinese returning from Saigon, who said it was common gossip there.[46] The French government and high command had appalling standards of security: Both the Revers Plan of 1949 and the 1953 Navarre Plan virtually became public knowledge from the moment they were drawn up. A trusted interpreter in the office of General René Cogny, commander in Tonkin during the time of Dien Bien Phu, was thought responsible for keeping Giap informed on French intentions during that campaign.[47]

Probably the most damaging indiscretions were caused by sloppy radio security, an old problem for the French army. According to a 1951 Deuxième Bureau report based on information provided by a Vietminh defector, the Vietminh created a small cryptographic bureau late in 1948 with two American radio receivers. Without a cryptanalytic capacity, the rebels began by studying French radio messages in the clear, which, although not terribly useful, at least helped them to establish a French order of battle.

The following year, a larger interception center was set up in the village of La Bang in the highlands near Thai Nguyen which eventually was staffed by ten operators and had two receivers and three other radios. Studies of partially encoded transmissions were begun, "although the procedures were rather basic." In early 1950, the cipher section and listening services were fused into a single section under the Vietminh Deuxième Bureau, and a cryptographic school was created near Binh Yen in the summer to study captured French code books.

Even this modest cryptographic effort paid handsome dividends in

the autumn of 1950 when the French attempted to extract the Cao
Bang garrison down the Route Coloniale 4, a ribbon of road that
twisted through the limestone peaks of upper Tonkin along the frontier
with China. The French plan of action called for a force of 3,500
Foreign Legionnaires and Moroccans under Lieutenant Colonel Marcel Le Page to move up the RC 4 from Lang Son, seize Dong Khe,
a village in Vietminh possession which blocked the escape route, and
so allow the Cao Bang garrison under Colonel Charton to march down
the RC 4 to Lang Son. This rather straightforward plan ran into
problems from the beginning. Le Page failed to seize Dong Khe. With
the RC 4 blocked, both Le Page advancing up the RC 4 from the
southeast and Charton walking down the road from the northwest were
ordered to follow the jungle paths to the west of the town to a rendezvous site in the Coc Xa valley. The result, for the French, was a
disaster. As they slowly hacked their way through the unfamiliar,
jungle-covered mountains, their columns strung out and disoriented
as they climbed and descended abrupt limestone cliffs, Giap moved
in his regular battalions freshly trained in China to attack their flanks
and block their advance. Morale among the French North African
units dissolved. And while the Legionnaires continued to fight bravely,
they were eventually exhausted and overwhelmed. The French lost
almost 6,000 men in the Cao Bang retreat; it was France's greatest
colonial defeat, Bernard Fall insisted, since the loss of Quebec to
General Wolfe in 1759.

Poor French intelligence certainly bore a share of the blame for the
disaster at Cao Bang. But the problem was to divine enemy intentions.
In their after-action report, the Deuxième Bureau of the Tonkin region
confessed that they shared the burden of blame for Cao Bang. Although
they had tracked Vietminh units slipping over the frontier into China
since August 1949, "it was almost impossible to follow them during
their stay beyond the frontier." In a 16 May 1950 report, General
Alessandri, commander of the Tonkin region, confessed that the limited abilities of both air and ground reconnaissance meant that Cao
Bang could face a surprise attack at any time. He speculated that he
should be able to hold off a poorly armed Vietminh attack, but was
less certain of the garrison's ability to fend off one supported by the
Chinese, especially if they brought along their heavy artillery.[48]

While on September 8 the Deuxième Bureau predicted imminent attacks, they were not precise on the objectives or even on the form of the attack. On the contrary, as late as 18 August 1950, the commander-in-chief's Troisième Bureau (Operations) foresaw a Korean-style invasion of Tonkin by Chinese and Vietnamese forces backed by tanks and aircraft, and argued that the frontier posts must be retained as "breakwaters" to protect the Tonkin delta, a perception which further delayed evacuation. When the French commander, General Marcel Carpentier, finally ordered an evacuation, it was to occur before 15 October, because only then were the Vietminh expected to be in strength to oppose it. When the Cao Bang garrison evacuated along the RC 4, the Deuxième Bureau began to realize too late that they had underestimated Vietminh strength by almost a third and their heavy-weapons capacity by almost half. French intelligence, like everyone else, was astonished by the rapidity and maneuverability of Vietminh units coordinated by radio, their generous supply of munitions, their willingness to take casualties, and how their camouflage and ability to dig in nullified the effects of French air power. In short, Carpentier confessed to the French Prime Minister that the complete transformation of the Vietminh "in three or four months" from a ragtag maquis into a modern force had caught him completely by surprise. Finally, the Deuxième Bureau's belief that Giap would continue his advance down the RC 4 to the important garrison of Lang Son contributed to the panicked evacuation of that post at a time when Giap was in no position to take it nor had any intention of doing so.[49]

But if the disaster at Cao Bang exposed glaring French intelligence deficiencies, the battle was a turning point for the Vietminh, not the least from an intelligence perspective. Cao Bang was the first time that the Vietminh employed their still-primitive cryptanalytic and listening services in an "operational" situation. The experiment paid off in spades. According to the Vietminh defector previously cited, two-thirds of Vietminh intelligence came from radio intercepts in that battle. The rebels were able to eavesdrop on French messages announcing the arrival of reinforcements, munitions, liaisons between units, orders from commanders to subordinates—in short, to anticipate French moves as they groped their way through the jungle. Messages broadcast in the clear, "intelligence the French believed without value," could be exploited immediately, those in mixed code and clear with little delay, and even some completely enciphered messages fell to the apprentice Vietminh cryptanalysts. They also carefully built up tables of French frequencies and transmission times, a basic but useful technique. Giap realized that radio intercepts provided fresh intelligence more rapidly than did agents. The cryptographic school was expanded, Chinese cryptographers added to the faculty, and Chinese "technical counselors" attached to the cryptanalytic bureau. French intelligence believed the Russians had also supplied cryptographers.[50]

How useful cryptanalysis and listening proved to be to Giap after 1951 remains a mystery. But if French reports of the continued insecurity of their radio nets are any indication, the Vietminh were offered a potential intelligence gold mine. In early January 1953, General Babet, head of the French Signal Corps in Indochina, carried out a security experiment at the Center for Listening and Radioelectric Security of the General Commanding the Signal Corps. The results put him in a foul temper: "*Utilizing a young operator not broken in in listening,*" he seethed, "[one] could *completely* reidentify the stations of an army network in the south *at the very moment that they were changing their call signs.*"[51] Following Operation Brochet in the autumn of 1953, Babet again complained that "the enemy very quickly obtained a great amount of intelligence, often important, on our order of battle, our movements, *and even our intentions,*" through French radio indiscretions. Entire operation orders were broadcast over the radio and could be intercepted in an "almost complete" form. He did concede that radio security had improved during Operation Mouette in the autumn of 1953, judging by the increased demands by Vietminh intelligence for information on French movements and orders of battle. But it was still far from perfect. Even French commander in Indochina Henri Navarre was moved to complain in November 1953 that there was far too much "chatter," especially among unit commanders. Navarre insisted that one security officer uninformed about an operation "was able *by himself in three hours of listening and without assistance* to reconstruct the march order of the operation," just by paying attention to chatter. And as if the ghost of Givierge hovered over Indochina, Navarre complained that most indiscretions occurred because officers began a sentence in code before they had thought out how to end it, thus supplying the hybrid message which betrayed the code. The *groupes mobiles* were especially guilty of broadcasting in the clear, which obliged the command to dispatch radio security personnel with them on operations. French monitoring of Vietminh radio traffic during Dien Bien Phu also revealed that a number of French messages were being intercepted.[52]

Henri Navarre complained that the Vietminh protected their secrets well, while French security was "a sieve."[53] This was not quite true. When the French did protect their secrets, they could achieve surprise, as during the Lang Son raid, Operation Hirondelle, when two paratroop battalions attacked armaments depots in that city near the Chinese frontier on 17 July 1953. The evacuation of Na San in 1953 was carried out so rapidly that Giap was unable to get sufficient troops there in time to attack the rapidly diminishing perimeter. Even the beginning of Operation Castor, the parachute drop on Dien Bien Phu on 20 November 1953, appears to have caught the Vietminh by surprise.

Nor is it true that the French were uninformed about their enemy. For if the Vietminh learned much from French radio indiscretions, the French learned far more from the poor communications security of the Vietminh. "The study of enemy radio is by far our best source of intelligence," a January 1952 report proclaimed. "After faltering for a long time, this method of research has at last proved itself."

The test had been what the French called the Battle of Tonkin, the series of offensives which Giap, hoping to take advantage of French surprise and confusion after their defeat on the RC 4, had launched against the Tonkin delta in 1951. But if Cao Bang had been an intelligence disaster for the French, it was followed by an intelligence triumph during the Battle of Tonkin. "Certain particularly audacious phases of the Battle of Tonkin could be carried out only thanks to intelligence produced by listening posts," concluded the January 1952 report. Guided by his listening posts who were tracking Vietminh units, intelligence confirmed by air reconnaissance, agent reports, and POW interrogations, de Lattre was able to shift his troops on his interior lines of communications to parry Giap's blows, even to confirm the presence of Chinese units in these offensives.[54]

One of the great paradoxes for the French in Indochina was that the more the quality of their intelligence improved, the less useful it became in improving the chances of victory. The greatest surge in the quantity of French intelligence came from radio intercepts. But if the French were listening to more enemy radio traffic, it was because the Vietminh were acquiring more radios from the Chinese. The radios themselves were but indications of the growing sophistication and capabilities of the Vietminh army. If the surge in Vietminh radio traffic opened opportunities for French intelligence, it also increased the challenges.

By as early as 1952, the French complained that the volume of traffic was outstripping their ability to listen to it because of a shortage of receivers and personnel. Also, the fragmentation of the listening services among the high command, the SDECE, and the high commission diminished its timeliness. These problems had not been resolved by the end of the year, when General Babet again called for listening posts to be centralized under the Signal Corps. His list of complaints might have been lifted from a World War I report: lack of coordination between listening and radiogoniometry, the constant turnover of personnel, shortage of matériel, and lack of mobile listening posts. To deal with the shortage of personnel, the government authorized the hiring of up to 300 civilians to deal with what was expected to be an enormous increase in Vietminh radios supplied by Russia and China and an increase in telephone traffic.[55]

French command of the Vietminh radio nets eventually enabled them to orchestrate deception plans. In general, French intelligence in Indochina was not especially expert in what they referred to as "intoxication," and the Vietminh seldom took the bait.[56] However, they gave themselves high marks for Operation Pelican, a deception plan hatched on 24 September 1953 by the army Deuxième Bureau.

The short-term purpose of Pelican was to prevent the 304th Vietminh Division from rushing to the aid of the 320th Division, which the French planned to attack as part of Operation Mouette. The long-term advantage of Pelican was to make the Vietminh, once they realized they had been deceived, "less aware of real threats." The only real force gathered for Pelican was a naval fleet at Haiphong which was to land French troops near Thanh Hoa, an area populated by Catholics. Operation orders were produced, instructions on what to do after landing, supply manifests, radio call signs, everything an army required for a major surprise offensive, except, of course, soldiers. Senior officers ostentatiously appeared to inspect progress, visits which were faithfully reported by agents and released POWs.

The French were well pleased with the results of Pelican, until they intercepted a radio message from a Vietminh cadre to his high command insisting that these preparations were merely a hoax. So the French stepped up the deception, starting rumors among the ground crews at air bases, bombing the road to Thanh Hoa, printing leaflets instructing troops how to behave toward the Catholic population, and creating another radio net with intense traffic. In the end it worked. The Vietminh held back the 304th as the 320th bore the brunt of the French attack launched on 14 October 1953. On D+3, a regiment of the 304th was sent to Thanh Hoa, where it remained for the rest of Mouette, and no further action was required to keep the 304th in place. The French concluded that, without the ability to monitor Vietminh messages, they would not have been able to intensify the deception when they realized that it was not working.[57]

But the value of French cryptanalysis was limited by the fact that it could not reach into China, where Vietminh forces were being trained and organized by an estimated 15,000 Chinese advisers and technicians. This had been at the origins of the intelligence failure of Cao Bang. In 1952, the French had no complaints about the quantity of intelligence on China produced by spending 100 million francs annually. The quality, however, was suspect: "It is a question of often fragmentary information which one has to carefully evaluate, deception and double agents being common currency in Southeast Asia." The French admitted that careful evaluation was a task which they performed badly, due to lack of time and personnel.[58]

One way in which the French sought to improve their knowledge of what went on in China was through cooperation with the British and the Americans. But cooperation with foreign intelligence services, especially those of their two former allies, could prove an exercise in humiliation for the French. French intelligence appears to have been acutely sensitive to the possibility that these exchanges would reveal shortcomings in their intelligence organization to their allies. "The French 'yellow' with contact in this country, and afraid to 'lose face,' dare not admit to a questioner that they are unqualified to deal with the problems or answer the questions." The French complained that they had been deceived by British intelligence in 1949 when in return for up-to-date information on the Vietminh, they were handed some old maps of Siam. When the French protested, the British replied that, as Siam was a friendly country, to give the French good intelligence about it "would have been an unfriendly act." The British also pointed out that French POW interrogations were very badly done, an observation which, however accurate, could hardly have furthered the cause of intelligence cooperation.[59] The American attitude could mix superiority with disdain: A joint Defense–State Department survey team dispatched to Indochina in July 1950 to assess French military requirements found that the lack of hard intelligence on "the strength and disposition of the Communist-led Vietminh forces" made this difficult to do. "It became increasingly clear that the French did not know this and that what they thought they knew just as likely as not was wrong."[60]

French resentment of American involvement in Indochina ran deeper than professional embarrassment, however. Suspicions that the Americans were trying to displace France in Indochina stretched back to the time of Pearl Harbor and poisoned subsequent Franco-American cooperation both in military assistance and in intelligence cooperation.[61] As early as 1951, de Lattre had banished American air force colonel Edward G. Lansdale from Indochina because he believed that the colorful and controversial counterguerrilla expert would work against French interests. But following these "differences," an accord was struck between Allen Dulles and the SDECE station chief in Washington, Thyraud de Vosjoli, for the exchange of "action missions" and the supply by the CIA of up to 100 radio receivers. Here, and at a subsequent May 1951 Singapore conference between representatives of the French, British, and American intelligence services, they agreed to twice-weekly meetings between the CIA and the SDECE to exchange raw air and naval intelligence and information on China, and to divide the listening duties in China among the French, British, and Americans. Although the SDECE contained Chinese specialists, they were forced to confine their listening to the Vietminh: "Here again we are limited by lack of matériel, money, and personnel."[62]

But these arrangements do not appear to have worked out to the satisfaction of the French, for in the spring of 1953 they complained that their allies were sending in only "syntheses or commentaries" or studies, rather than raw intelligence like Chinese radio decrypts or reports of air reconnaissance missions over southern China. What they did get, especially if it came through the SDECE in Paris, was usually at least a month out of date, which put the commander-in-chief at an enormous disadvantage in the event of a large-scale Chinese intervention in Indochina, which the French obviously thought possible. In December 1953, Navarre allowed the American advisory group in Indochina to import their own combat intelligence detachment to supplement what they considered to be unreliable French intelligence.[63]

By now it will be apparent that intelligence is only as good as the context in which it is applied. The French were in the process of defining their strategic choices in the war, not all of which were to prove intelligence-friendly. But that is not to say that French intelligence and special operations were shouldered out of the process of strategic choice. On the contrary, these services must bear a share of the blame for some of the more disastrous strategic choices made by the French, choices which led them inexorably toward Dien Bien Phu.

THIRTEEN

OPERATION CASTOR
AND THE SINEWS OF WAR

At 10:30 on the morning of 20 November 1953, sixty-five planes appeared over the broad valley of Dien Bien Phu in upper Tonkin just as the last vapors of morning mist burned away. Some 1,827 French paratroops floated out of the sky and, after a six-hour skirmish, chased Dien Bien Phu's Vietminh garrison into the jungle. The opening phase of Operation Castor had achieved complete surprise. The French now occupied a position 220 miles from their center of operations in the Tonkin delta. What did they think they were doing there?

This simple, almost discreet beginning to an operation which was to have such profound consequences for French arms and for French policy in Indochina belied the almost occult nature of the forces which had brought it about. In keeping with the notion that great events must have great causes, the French commander-in-chief, General Henri Navarre, insisted that Castor was carried out as part of a mandate, implied in French treaties with the Associated States, to defend Laos, an obligation which had been sanctioned at the highest levels of the French government. Therefore, he placed a "hedgehog"—a fortified, air-supplied *base aéroterrestre*—astride the strategic gateway to Laos. As the Vietminh commander, Vo Nguyen Giap, could bypass it only with difficulty, he would be forced to renounce his invasion of Laos or attack Dien Bien Phu head-on. An attack, Navarre calculated, would shatter on the French strong point, as had Giap's assault on Na San, another *base aéroterrestre*, in November–December 1952, except this time on an even more devastating scale. This was Navarre's version of events, and he stuck to it to the point that it became the classic interpretation of the strategic purpose of Operation Castor. "Dien Bien Phu reposed on a postulate," writes French historian Philippe Francini in his two-volume history of the Indochina War, "the requirement to defend Laos, and a strategic option, the barrage of a fortified, air-supplied camp."[1]

This interpretation is correct up to a point. Laos did offer a strategic objective of political value for both the Vietminh and the French. But study of the hitherto unexamined documents of the Deuxième Bureau, as well as recently available Chinese sources, suggests that Laos was no more than a secondary consideration for either side. What the communists sought in the autumn of 1953 was to create conditions for a climactic battle which the French must fight at a disadvantage. To achieve this battle, they had to threaten something which the French would venture beyond their base in the Tonkin delta to defend. That thing was a friendly Montagnard "capital" at Lai Chau in the Tonkin highlands.

Lai Chau was the base for a force of T'ai irregulars loyal to the French, which gave it a residual political and military importance in the eyes of the high command. But, on the face of it, this would not be enough in itself to force the French commander, Henri Navarre, to take the risk of flinging 12,000 of his best troops into the Tonkin highlands at the extreme limits of his air range to support what was in essence a marginal maquis. The reason that Navarre was willing to take such risks was that Lai Chau and the T'ais who occupied it controlled the major source of Vietnam's opium. Thus, it is no exaggeration to say that Dien Bien Phu, a remote valley in the Tonkin highlands, became the scene of such carnage because the French fought to maintain control of the opium harvest.

That opium was a commodity valuable enough to draw the war's adversaries into such desperate struggle in 1954 was nothing new. Indeed, opium constituted the war's open secret which has sunk virtually without a trace in histories of the First Indochina War. In some of the most vivid accounts of that war, French journalist Lucien Bodard called opium "the sinew of the war . . . The Viets [Minh] want it. They make enormous profits by selling it in Hanoi, Saigon, Hong Kong, in all the 'capitalist' capitals of Asia . . . But the French go after it with as much energy. To take it keeps the Viets from getting it, from supporting themselves thanks to this robust commerce. On the contrary, [opium] permits the Expeditionary Forces and the Administration to top up their own secret accounts . . . But to take it, to tear it away also from the Meos, the Viets and French are already engaged in a small war."[2] In an extraordinary admission which has passed completely unnoticed, Jean Letourneau, French Minister of the Associated States between 1949 and 1953, admitted not only that opium dictated French strategy in Indochina to significant degrees but also that the French were selling that opium on the open market. "Anyway," he said in an aside to a French parliamentary committee in September 1953, "everyone knows that one of the resources which feeds the Vietminh war budget is opium and that the large operations mounted at certain times in northern Laos or in T'ai country are essentially operations to seize the opium crop to dump it on the international markets."[3]

Even had opium served as a basis for French campaign strategies in the past, this would not explain why in late 1953 both Navarre and Giap were prepared to funnel such a significant portion of their military resources toward such a remote battlefield, virtually to go to the wall at Dien Bien Phu. The sad fact was that by the autumn of 1953, both the Vietminh and French intelligence and special operations shared a dependency—each required opium to finance their war effort. It was this requirement which served as the lure to draw each army out to the remote highlands of northwestern Tonkin. Unfortunately for the French, in their attempt to deny Giap the opium crop, they placed their army in a position in which the consequences of defeat were much more serious for them than for the Vietminh.

How did each side come to take such a risk for opium? For the Vietminh, until late in 1953, opium had been an interesting but hardly vital ingredient in their war effort. In fact, from the beginning of the Indochina War in 1946, the French high command had realized that the fragility of the Vietminh war economy constituted the most vulnerable weakness of the insurgent war effort. As a consequence, much of French strategy sought to dislocate the Vietminh by denying them food and arms. French campaigns to blockade the rice harvests of the Transbassac in Cochin China or of the Tonkin delta met with a good deal of success. Although the Vietminh always managed to smuggle in enough to survive, the margin was a narrow one, and certainly prevented the Vietminh from exporting rice to Thailand for cash, as they had done early in the war.

Indeed, cash became an obsession for both sides. In 1945, when they had occupied Hanoi, the Vietminh temporarily solved this problem by helping themselves to the cash left in French bank vaults. After they were chased into the hills in December 1946, however, the Vietminh faced a financial crisis. In an effort to find hard currency, they forced everyone living in Vietminh areas to exchange the official piasters of the Banque d'Indochine, or BIC piasters, for those of local manufacture, or Ho Chi Minh piasters. The idea was to build up a treasury of hard currency for the purchase of arms and medicines through taxation and confiscation of BIC piasters. These HCM piasters had some value, for in 1948 a scandal broke out in Saigon when it was revealed that the French Sûreté had used the high commissioner's personal plane to fly confiscated HCM piasters to Hong Kong, where they were exchanged for hard currency. When caught, the chief of the Sûreté excused his action with the plea that his budget to pay informers was so ridiculously low that he was forced to smuggle to get money to operate.[4] In the aftermath of this incident, in 1949 the French SDECE flooded the rebel zones with counterfeit HCM piasters, a task which presented few artistic challenges, as the scrip was crudely printed. This turned a devalued currency into a worthless one and caused hyperinflation in Vietminh-held areas. However, the effects on the Vietminh currency were short-lived, because French high commissioner Jean de Lattre de Tassigny called off the operation in late 1950 and because, judging by French intelligence reports, the Vietminh relaxed their regulations to allow other currencies to circulate in their areas.[5]

Nor were these attacks on the HCM piaster likely to be effective so long as the French handed the Vietminh on a platter the means to get hard cash, to multiply their investments, and to purchase arms on the international market. What became known as the "piaster traffic" was a capitalist game so transparent that even the most ideological communist was hard pressed to forgo its temptations, especially when the profits were plowed back into the cause of the revolution. In December 1945, the French government pegged the BIC piaster at 17 French francs, double its free-market value of around 8.50 francs. The idea was to provide a sweetener to entice soldiers and civil servants to Indochina by allowing them to "remit" a portion of their salaries back to France at extremely favorable rates. It also gave a political incentive to the Associated States of Laos, Vietnam, and Cambodia to remain within the French imperial realm. An artificially high piaster served to control wartime inflation by exporting excess currency and making imports cheaper. The governments of the Associated States could also finance their budget deficits through the simple expedient of exporting BIC piasters to Paris, having the French government buy them at exorbitant rates, and transferring the surplus back to Indochina.

But if French soldiers, colonial civil servants, and Associated States could play this game, so could everyone else, including the Vietminh and the communist Chinese. In theory, the remittances were strictly controlled by the Banque d'Indochine and, from 1952, a special Institut d'Emissions des Etats Associés. In practice, neither institution was capable of verifying the origins and validity of the flood of requests for remittances of BIC piasters back to France. The piaster traffic took many forms, including bills of lading by bogus companies for remittance licenses to pay for imaginary goods. In one case, a well-known Paris publishing house created a subsidiary in Saigon, which ordered from its parent company most of its unsalable back stock of books. In Saigon, the books were pulped, while in Paris the publisher replenished its accounts by cashing in its piasters at rates subsidized by the French taxpayer. But the most common dodge began by smuggling gold or dollars into Saigon (or even depositing them in a bank in Bangkok or Hong Kong if one wanted to avoid the negligible risk of being caught). A dollar purchased in Paris for 400 French francs would fetch 50 BIC piasters in Saigon from a Chinese, an Indian, or one of a number of shady networks linked to the Corsican mafia operating out of the Hotel Continental in Saigon. Those 50 piasters remitted to Paris at an exchange rate of 17 francs would translate into 850 French francs—a profit of over 100 percent, minus, of course, the normal 15 percent commission of the middlemen!

The Vietminh and the communist Chinese established the Bank of Communications in Hong Kong, with branches in Saigon, Hanoi, and Haiphong, to carry out their remittances. The Vietminh plowed the profits into U.S. surplus arms purchased in Manila in the late 1940s. Even after the communists gained power in China in 1949 and began substantial aid to the Vietminh, it appears that the Vietnamese were treated in part as cash customers—the Vietminh remained largely faithful to their American weapons supplied from equipment abandoned by Chiang Kai-shek and possibly, too, those captured in Korea in 1950–51.

If the French realized that this system was only aiding the enemy, why did they not change it? The unvarnished answer is that if the Vietminh were profiting from the piaster traffic, so was almost everyone else. In fact, the piaster traffic had become what in modern American political parlance would be called an entitlement program. The governments of the Associated States liked it—Bao Dai and the members of his government financed their lavish lifestyles on the Côte d'Azur, including swarms of high-priced prostitutes, through the piaster traffic. Businessmen, the powerful Banque d'Indochine, and politicians were in the game—the Gaullist party, the RPR, earned an estimated 17 million francs to finance its 1948 electoral campaign by sending a former inspector of finances to Saigon to remit piasters to Paris.[6] Generals whose soldiers were being shot to ribbons by weapons purchased from the benefits of the piaster traffic complained that troop morale would collapse if the piaster was devalued. The old argument that the system was politically necessary, only the lack of enforcement was at fault, was the defense offered by those who subsequently ensured that nothing was done to clamp down on abuses. So the system stumbled forward.

In 1953, however, pressure to end the scandal became overwhelming. One source was the Americans, in particular the CIA, who complained bitterly that the United States had virtually assumed the burden of financing the French war, only to see their efforts undermined by currency and gold smuggling carried out with the merest pretense of discretion by officials of the Banque d'Indochine. By May 1953, the CIA noted that while it had shut down gold smuggling to Bangkok and Singapore, Air France planes continued to shuttle between Paris and Saigon with gold shipments of the Banque d'Indochine, which were subsequently transferred to Macao for sale to the Vietminh. These were turned over to the communist Chinese, who purchased arms for the Vietminh through Moscow. According to the CIA, French bankers were clearing a 50 percent profit on the deal, which put roughly 500 tons of arms in the hands of the Vietminh each month.[7]

The second factor which forced a change was the bombshell which detonated in Paris with the publication in 1953 of *Le Trafic des piastres*. The author, a disgruntled ex-employee of the Banque d'Indochine named Jacques Despuech, published his book despite bribes, lawsuits, and finally threats on his life and that of his wife. Even after his book appeared, his detractors mounted a sophisticated campaign to discredit him, while the Banque d'Indochine attempted to buy up and destroy as many copies as possible.[8] But Despuech had blasted his whistle so loudly in a study which detailed how many in France and elsewhere profited from a system which sent French soldiers to their graves by the thousands, that the shrill pierced even the hushed indifference of the French parliament. The parliamentary committee of inquiry established in the wake of the uproar over Despuech's book was never able to gauge the extent of the traffic, in part because of a government gag order which forbade officials in the Ministry of Finance to testify. Nor, in the absence of Vietminh cooperation, were they able to assess its value to the enemy, beyond the fact that it was substantial. But the tumult was enough to force the French government in May 1953 to devalue the piaster from 17 to 10 French francs, thereby killing the piaster traffic.[9]

The end of the piaster traffic and what appears to be a CIA-led crackdown on gold smuggling left the Vietminh essentially with only two other sources of income to sustain their insurrection beyond whatever aid the Chinese communists or the Soviets cared to bestow on them gratis: the limited taxation they dared impose in areas which they could control, and opium. But the Vietminh discovered in 1953 that they had fierce competition for control of the opium market, competition which came from none other than the French secret services and special operations.

To unravel the opium connection, one can begin by cutting through all the rhetoric and mutual accusations which churned the French army and government following Dien Bien Phu, a debate which has completely distracted historians from the true intent of Operation Castor. French intelligence reports make that answer immediately clear: the French had come to Dien Bien Phu to support the resistance which they had created among the Montagnard hill tribes of upper Tonkin. "Our presence [in northwestern Indochina] manifests itself by the action of our maquis," wrote Lieutenant Colonel Eugène Guibaud of Navarre's Deuxième Bureau on 8 November 1953. "The very existence of [the maquis] *resides essentially* in our establishment of a strategic position in the territory, in this case Lai Chau. It is therefore certain that our withdrawal from this locality without a compensatory occupation of an equivalent point—from a psychological angle—in the same territory will mean the rapid collapse of the French presence in all of northwestern Indochina."[10]

The resistance to which Guibaud referred was that of the semiautonomous T'ai Federation, whose president, Deo Van Long, had established his capital at Lai Chau in upper Tonkin under French patronage in 1946. Part of a traditional "divide and rule" policy followed by French colonial administrators, this T'ai Federation assumed military importance in the eyes of the French in late 1950, following the disastrous collapse of a string of French posts along the Route Coloniale 4. The loss of 6,000 men and the strategic barrier along the Chinese frontier in the space of a few days left the Vietminh camped on the fringes of the populous Tonkin delta. The Tonkin delta, a triangle of flat, fertile rice land whose base opens to the east along the Gulf of Tonkin with an apex formed at the point where the Red River flows like an artery out of the Tonkin highlands and China beyond, became France's northern bastion. It formed the center of her economic and military power enfolding both Hanoi and its port city, Haiphong, and which, from October 1950 until the war's bitter conclusion in 1954, Vietminh forces appeared capable of overwhelming.

To soldiers besieged in Hanoi, men trained in conventional notions of European warfare, Lai Chau appeared an island of French influence in a Vietminh sea, a citadel which, in their haste to overrun northern Tonkin and reach the delta, the Vietminh had incautiously neglected. A second, more recent experience which these French officers had brought to their traditional military education had been that of the French Resistance in World War II. The military value of the French

Resistance in creating a "climate of insecurity" in the German rear areas had achieved the status of dogma among these men. In this respect, French officers merely shared the psychological heritage of their countrymen, among whom the Resistance had become a "necessary myth," an unguent for French self-esteem, the antidote to charges of complacency, dissension, even cowardice, leveled against the French nation and its army following the stunning defeat of May–June 1940.

The French did not suddenly discover what they chose to call the maquis in late 1950. In fact, these plans had been brewing in the fertile minds of officers of the French intelligence service, the SDECE, earlier. They had even managed, briefly, to court the complicity of the CIA, a cooperation which faltered after only a few months. The French forged ahead with plans to create a maquis, their efforts animated by the French army's most dynamic advocate of unconventional warfare, Major, later Colonel, Roger Trinquier. The original idea of a Service Action appears to have been merely to kidnap prominent Vietminh leaders. But with the collapse of the RC 4, the idea, under Trinquier's energetic promotion, blossomed into the creation of a full-blown underground in Vietminh-controlled areas. The missions assigned to this maquis—establish escape routes, participate in special sabotage missions, sometimes in collaboration with regular troops, gather intelligence—took inspiration from experience in another war on another continent. There is no evidence that the French command ever questioned whether these missions were adapted to Indochinese realities. Indeed, there is no evidence that the high command ever evaluated the usefulness of maquis operations in the World War II European theater before French commander Jean de Lattre de Tassigny presided over the birth of the Groupement de Commandos Mixtes Aéroportés (GCMA) in December 1951.[11]

Despite a dearth of officers familiar with Montagnard languages and customs, this command registered early success in creating resistance groups among T'ai and Meo tribesmen in Tonkin and Laos. The technique employed by Trinquier was to fly over Montagnard villages in a light plane in the hope of eliciting some sort of hospitable response, as, for instance, the waving of a tricolored French flag. When this happened, he would land and convince the village headman and a group of his followers to fly to the GCMA training camp established at Cap Saint-Jacques, near Saigon. There they were trained in counterinsurgency tactics, given arms, radios, and cash, and reinserted into the mountains, often accompanied in the early months by Nationalist Chinese officers driven into Indochina by the Chinese communist victory of 1949. GCMA action appeared to pay dividends as early as June 1952, when the 148th Vietminh Regiment at Lao Kay on the Red River was so hard pressed by French-led Meo Hundreds—so called because each section was meant to contain one hundred men—that they were obliged to call for Chinese help. When the Chinese 302nd Division crossed the Vietnamese border in June 1952, some units were badly mauled by ambushes, mines, and French air strikes called in by the guerrillas. But the success proved fleeting—by August, the Chinese had succeeded in driving the resistance into jungle caves, where they were eventually annihilated and their leaders assassinated, sometimes by their own followers, who might well have been infiltrated by the Vietminh. It was a rerun of the disaster which befell the French Resistance when many of its members congregated on the Vercors plateau in southeastern France in the summer of 1944. Had their commitment to the maquis been based on reason rather than theology, then the French might have been driven toward the inescapable conclusion that massing resistance groups for set-piece battles against regular forces was a recipe for collective suicide.

Unfortunately, neither the GCMA nor the French high command accepted the conclusion that stared them in the face, even after a similar fate met the T'ai resistance in the autumn during Giap's Black River campaign. As the Vietminh drove in from the northeast on the isolated French posts between the Red and Black rivers, including Dien Bien Phu, in October, French commander Raoul Salan ordered his troops to fall back toward a hastily constructed *base aéroterrestre* at Na San. It was a footrace won by the French—when Giap attacked Na San in late November and early December, he was bloodily repulsed. But this victory for the *base aéroterrestre* concept was bought at the price of the dispersal or destruction of the maquis, which had been ordered to delay the pursuit by Vietminh units. French cadres with the guerrillas were hunted down and killed or captured. Two commando leaders escaped by floating down the Red River. Na San had two consequences. First, it convinced the French of the inviolability of the air-supplied base of the type they were to create at Dien Bien Phu. Second, despite the disasters which met the maquis, or perhaps because of them, the French threw themselves into the task of rebuilding the Montagnard resistance shattered in 1952.

Why the French decided to invest so many of their limited resources into resurrecting the maquis appears irrational given the meager military results of the enterprise. A French intelligence report of late 1952 pointed out that the modest successes of the resistance were more than outweighed by its weaknesses, which included poor training, poor security, inadequate radios, and a lack of aggression. They could be armed and supplied only with great difficulty, especially with enough food for them or their families, without which the Hundreds would simply break up and go home to plant. Early Montagnard successes depended upon surprise. But once alerted to the guerrilla threat, the Vietminh moved effectively to crush it. The value of the maquis as an intelligence organization was also called into question: "As 98 percent are illiterate, they are incapable of giving precise intelligence," the report complained. Moreover, they were more concerned with gathering intelligence directly related to their specific mission than with supplying information which might help construct a general picture of the enemy—ironically, an echo of a major weakness of French Resistance-supplied intelligence in World War II. Not only did many of the Montagnard guerrilla leaders fail to serve the goals of French strategy—if, that is, the French command ever bothered to integrate the maquis into any sort of unified strategic plan—they actually undermined them by behaving more like bandit chiefs. Backed by French arms, cash, and authority, they alienated many Montagnards, creating a disgruntled population ripe for Vietminh exploitation. All of this confirmed observations expressed in the spring of 1952 that the French lacked a "dynamic ideology or a xenophobia" on the Vietminh model to motivate the maquis.[12]

This report is the first hint of a realization in the French camp of the dangers of following the mirage of the Montagnard maquis. It suggested that the traditional *politique des races* which French colonial administrators used to "divide and rule" their subjects was of limited military utility. To be historically anti-Vietnamese offered insufficient motivation to the Montagnard peoples to take up arms against the Vietminh for the benefit of the French. Moreover, the suggestion that these maquis actually threatened to produce more support for the Vietminh than for the French proved disastrously prophetic at Dien Bien Phu. Last, it suggested that for the French high command to base strategic decisions on such a fragile reed as the maquis would be dangerous, even foolhardy.

But several factors beyond adherence to a World War II Resistance Myth conspired to draw the French back into the guerrilla business. One was that even the pessimistic report of the spring of 1952 argued that the maquis had succeeded in fostering a climate of insecurity behind Vietminh lines by keeping contact with the local population, laying ambushes, and assassinating Vietminh cadres. In fact, the maquis was in part a response to the recognition of the increasing ineffectiveness of traditional French elite forces in the conditions of Indochina. From early in the war, the French had begun to launch commando operations against Vietminh command centers or supply depots. However, while often spectacular, these operations enjoyed diminishing success as inadequate intelligence, Vietminh dispersion, the difficulty of extracting airborne troops dropped into Vietminh-controlled areas, lack of secrecy, and increasingly bloody Vietminh reprisals against populations loyal to the French or against soft French targets like the convalescent center at Cap Saint-Jacques compromised their effectiveness.[13]

As early as 1950 the French concluded that these commando operations produced only minor inconvenience to the Vietminh while devouring a disproportionate share of French resources and diverting too many of the French army's best elements to operations of dubious value. Clearly a new tactic had to be found.[14] For the French, the military payoff for their small maquis investment came in the form of the disproportionate number of troops which the Vietminh had deployed to contain the resistance threat. So the spectacular disasters of the resistance in 1952 in a perverse way confirmed its usefulness in the minds of French special operations.

But these tactical arguments were mustered to distract from the real—though unspoken—factor which powered French strategy in late 1953: opium. According to Trinquier, the opportunity for a comeback in the highlands was handed to the French when the Vietminh seized the opium crop from the Montagnards in 1952, sold it on the market in Bangkok, and used the money to buy arms from the Chinese. The GCMA capitalized on Montagnard rage to purchase the 1953 crop. This was to have at least three consequences. First, it aborted Giap's 1953 offensive into Laos, which ran out of steam not, as has often been suggested, because Vietminh forces outdistanced their logistics. Rather, according to Edward G. Lansdale, who was sent to Vietnam in 1953 as a CIA observer, it was because Trinquier and the Deuxième Bureau had beaten Giap to the opium crop, which had been the objective of his campaign in the first place, and killed his incentive to continue.[15] Second, according to Trinquier, the commercial relationship restored the ties between the French GCMA and the Montagnards. Last, when the secret service sold the opium on the Saigon black market, the windfall furnished them with the resources to finance the maquis.[16] Trinquier was perhaps correct to argue that the resurrection of the maquis was linked to control of the Montagnard opium crop. But what he neglected to confess was that by 1952 the SDECE, the Deuxième Bureau, and the GCMA had become as addicted to that drug as the most emaciated habitué of a Cholon opium den.

Before World War II, the French colonial administration held a monopoly on the importation, refinement, and sale of opium, an extremely profitable state enterprise which had financed many administrative expenses and capital improvement projects. This source of revenue had been threatened during the Japanese occupation, which severed Indochina from its principal source of raw opium in China. To keep its revenues flowing, the French reversed their previous policy and encouraged the planting of the opium poppy in the high ridges of Laos and upper Tonkin occupied by Meo and T'ai tribesmen by forcing them to pay their taxes in opium. Hardly had the Japanese surrendered, however, when the French colonial administration bowed to international pressure to pull out of the opium trade altogether in 1948. But here the problems began, for French intelligence and the French army moved in to fill the vacuum. The reason for this was simple—opium provided an excellent source of revenue for these money-starved services and political leverage with certain groups. In what became known as Operation X, Trinquier's GCMA planes collected opium from Montagnard tribesmen and flew it to their training camp at Cap Saint-Jacques, where it was transferred to SDECE trucks and taken to Saigon to be refined in one of the two boiling plants directed by Binh Xuyen gangsters who ran the Saigon underworld. Opium was the product which guaranteed the loyalty of the Binh Xuyen, who, working with Captain Antoine Savani's Deuxième Bureau, kept the Vietminh contagion under control in Saigon. The Binh Xuyen sold the refined opium through Chinese and Corsican mafia networks, many of which were also involved in the piaster traffic, sharing the profits with Trinquier and Savani. This meant that some of the drugs turned up in Europe and the United States.[17]

The resurgence of the maquis from early 1953 was also related to the fact that both General Raoul Salan and his successor as commander-in-chief in Indochina, Henri Navarre, accepted their military value as an article of faith. Both also signed on to a strategy which sought to deny the valuable opium crop to the Vietminh.[18] It is impossible to believe that Salan did not know of Operation X and personally approve of it. Indeed, it was said that he himself freed the funds which allowed the Deuxième Bureau and the GCMA to purchase the opium crop in 1953.[19] But his attachment to the maquis was as much emotional as professional. "This population [the Montagnards] deserves our nurturance and protection," Salan wrote in his memoirs. "It loves us, it places its confidence in us. We do not have the right to abandon it."[20] The maquis also formed an essential operational component of the *base aéroterrestre* concept applied at Dien Bien Phu, as well as of France's political strategy in the highlands.[21] Salan caused substantial resources to be devoted to training Montagnard guerrillas at the GCMA's counterinsurgency training camp at Cap Saint-Jacques. He silenced the opposition of paratroop leaders of a more traditional stamp, like Brigadier General Jean Gilles, who objected to the diversion of scarce special operations resources to resistance forces, and he was especially keen to construct maquis networks around his *base aéroterrestre* at Na San. Because of Salan's support, by the summer of 1953 French intelligence could boast that Montagnard guerrillas had been "organized in record time" to collect elements of French garrisons dispersed by Giap's April 1953 thrust into Laos and to "harass the rebels on their axis of attack."[22]

Salan's departure in the spring of 1953 hardly caused the GCMA to miss a beat, for his successor, Henri Navarre, saw a strong maquis as his "artillery" which guaranteed French strategic mobility beyond the Tonkin delta by preparing the ground for the regular troops. He maintained Salan's faith in the resistance, with the difference that he sought to increase its effectiveness by using it as partisans to operate in conjunction with main-force units.[23] By early 1954, the maquis counted 15,000 men, according to French estimates. It was allotted 300 to 400 hours of scarce B-26 bomber support per month and a monthly budget of over six million piasters. And plans were in the works to more than double its strength. Ironically, this came at a time when the maquis was demonstrating its ineffectiveness in resounding terms. As in 1952, promising beginnings merely proved a prelude to disappointment.

Trinquier's GCMA had succeeded in creating three maquis—a Meo group in Laos, a T'ai maquis under Deo Van Long in northwestern Tonkin around Lai Chau—"the most loyal" according to Trinquier —and a Meo maquis in north-central Tonkin east of the Red River. On 3 October 1953, partisans backed by French paratroops and with air support mounted a spectacular raid on Lao Kay, the purpose of which was to divert Vietminh attention so that maquis could be created in other areas.[24] Even when Navarre ordered the evacuation of Na San between 4 and 8 August 1953 to regain six battalions for use elsewhere, he sought to retain a foothold in the region by creating three underground groups of around 1,000 men each. The maquis formed an integral part of the Na San evacuation plan by seizing Son La to distract Giap, and by blocking the Route Provinciale 41 to delay the arrival of the Vietminh 312th Division by ambushes and mines and forcing the Vietminh to deploy to deal with the guerrillas until the garrison could be airlifted to safety. But while French special operations officers trumpeted the Na San withdrawal as a success for the maquis, the slow reaction of the Vietminh was due to several factors, which included successful French efforts to protect the secrecy of the operation and Vietminh problems with their radio communications and logistics.[25]

The expansion of the maquis had several important consequences for the French war effort in Indochina. The first was that the more

the Vietminh main-force units outmanned, outgunned, outmaneuvered, and forced the French back to the tenuous security of the Tonkin
delta, the more French military leaders clutched at the hope that the
maquis offered a way to redress the deteriorating military situation and
furnish them strategic mobility. In early 1954, at the very moment
when Giap's legions were closing in for the kill at Dien Bien Phu, the
Comité d'Orientation de l'Action composed of high-ranking representatives of the army general staff and the SDECE laid plans to "create
an immense guerrilla zone, in the interior of which our maquis organization will be invulnerable to Vietminh attacks and which will
constitute in their rear a true second front."[26] Plans were made to open
three new camps to train both French and Montagnards in guerrilla
warfare and to increase the maquis to 40,000 men.[27]

The problem for the French was that their strategy had fallen hostage
to the need to support the Montagnards, out of a misplaced faith in
the military effectiveness of the highland maquis, joined with what
many saw as a moral obligation and political requirement to support
the Montagnards.[28] And then there was the tremendous stake which
the Deuxième Bureau and the GCMA had in controlling the opium
crop. The French intelligence community depended on opium to keep
the Binh Xuyen in line and for much of their cash flow. Loss of the
opium would swell the treasury, and consequently the arms depots,
of the Vietminh. Such was the French attachment to protecting the
opium that, as will be seen, all the enemy had to do was to threaten
it for the French dangerously to extend themselves. All of these motives
coalesced at Dien Bien Phu.

One of the great ironies of Operation Castor, which was launched
to rescue the maquis, was that there were no maquis organizations
near Dien Bien Phu,[29] nor did French-led partisans ever play an
effective part in the battle. The reason for this was linked to poor
political decisions on the part of the French and to the excesses of
Trinquier's opium policy. Dien Bien Phu nominally fell into the
geographical area of the semiautonomous T'ai Federation created by
the French in 1946 with its capital at Lai Chau. To lead the Federation,
Saigon had chosen the French-educated Deo Van Long, who previously had served them in minor administrative posts, including during
World War II that of collecting the opium crop from Meo tribesmen

in northwestern Tonkin. This choice proved disastrous. Deo Van Long was a White T'ai, a minority group of 25,000 rice-planting valley dwellers in a federation which included 100,000 Black T'ai and 50,000 highland Meo. This might not have been a fatal disqualification had not Deo Van Long proved to be a leader of great brutality.

Around 1950, French journalist Lucien Bodard flew over the heavily forested highlands and suddenly descended into a deep canyon on the Black River, at the bottom of which sat Lai Chau. Bodard's impression of having stumbled upon a "happy valley, undiscovered, away from everything," was quickly dispelled as he was rowed across furious rapids and led up a rocky outcropping, past heavily guarded prisoners in rags, to an agglomeration of concrete blockhouses which constituted Deo Van Long's "palace." There, Bodard discovered "the Middle Ages with machine guns," the heart of a regime which sustained itself on force, capital punishment, and the marriage of the leader's numerous off-spring with local T'ai notables. According to Bodard, Van Long was "a man of about sixty years of age, smooth and fat. His face is a mask, his voice is slow, colorless. He never becomes animated, but remains hunched up, swathed in a military garb which is not French, but Nationalist Chinese." Despite Van Long's boasts that he had been a pupil at Paris' Lycée Vincent Auriol, Bodard believed his education owed more to his father, a chief of Black Flags, the Chinese pirates who had terrorized Tonkin at the turn of the century. Van Long had gained his office by garroting the previous occupant, a man named Deo, forcing his daughter to marry him, and adopting the name of her father, a fait accompli recognized by the French. His substantial maquis, trained by Trinquier and armed both by the French and with weapons purchased in China and stored in the palace cellars along with his treasury of gold and silver bars, was seldom used against the Vietminh. Rather, it served to force the Meo to sell their opium at reduced prices and to quell opposition among the Black T'ai provoked by his heavy-handed administration of their territory. Unfortunately for the French, the Black T'ai were the very group which occupied the region of Dien Bien Phu. Neither the Meo nor the Black T'ai had any reason to support Deo Van Long and the French. In fact, these groups were counted by Giap among his most enthusiastic guides and porters during the siege.[30]

It is clear that the French had a significant strategic, operational, emotional, and, with the opium, financial investment in the maquis. But how did this lead to Dien Bien Phu? The truth was that the French army in Tonkin realized that the war had inexorably tilted against them by the autumn of 1953. Despite significant American aid and attempts to Vietnamize the war by raising a friendly Vietnamese army, Vietminh forces, backed by communist China, were gaining strength as the French grew steadily war-weary. As the Americans later discovered, Vietnamese recruits to the incumbent forces lacked the stomach to fight, as increasingly did the North Africans and Senegalese upon whom the French continued to rely in Indochina. Deprived of French conscripts because of hostility or indifference to the war in France, the French effort fell more and more on the shoulders of elite paratroop and Foreign Legion formations. Giap controlled the strategic pace of the war, electing to fight the French only on conditions favorable to the Vietminh. For their part, the French had to be strong everywhere, and alternated between exhausting and unprofitable strikes into the highlands to maintain their "strategic mobility" and scattering their troops in isolated garrisons where they could be overwhelmed virtually at will by Vietminh attacks.

This was the situation which Henri Navarre inherited when he took command in the spring of 1953. How did the new French commander plan to deal with it? What became known as the Navarre Plan was drawn up in the early summer of 1953. In fact, American sources suggest that Navarre really had no plan, but adopted one thrust upon him by the U.S. Pacific commander, General John W. "Iron Mike" O'Daniel, a hard-nosed, cigar-chomping general who insisted on addressing his French counterpart as "Navarrie." O'Daniel's job—contrary to French suspicions that the Americans wanted to kick them out and supplant them—was to keep French forces in the Indochina fight for as long as possible. The Navarre/O'Daniel Plan called for a reorganization of French forces, to get them out of their static positions and, with the aid of additional troops drawn from Europe, create a *corps de bataille* capable of inflicting severe damage on Giap's regular divisions in open warfare. As this reorganization would take fully a year, the goal was to avoid a major battle against Vietminh strength in Tonkin during the *cap dangereux* of the winter of 1953–54.

The problem, as with so many military plans, was that it neglected to calculate the intentions of the enemy. This was not entirely surprising; until the autumn of 1953, the enemy, too, remained undecided on its strategy. That this was so was due in part to divisions between the Chinese, who from 1950 had assumed a leading role in the war's strategic planning, and Giap, who had his own ideas about the campaign of 1953–54. Giap believed that the time had come to launch the third phase of the revolution in the north as envisaged in the theories of Mao: a general offensive which, when combined with a popular insurrection, would overwhelm the French colonialists. On 22 August 1953, the Vietnamese politburo accepted Giap's plan to launch an offensive against the Tonkin delta with the aim of liberating Hanoi and Haiphong.

This decision had been taken without consulting the Vietminh's powerful ally, however. Once this news became known in Beijing, the Chinese wired their disagreement to their Vietnamese counterparts. In the Chinese estimation, the Vietminh were not yet strong enough to take on the French in the delta. The Chinese military mission argued that the Vietminh must seek to draw the French into the open, away from their area of strength, and fight them at their disadvantage—as in 1950 on the RC 4. How were they to entice Navarre to come out of the delta? Launch an offensive against Lai Chau, whose loss would "limit the human and financial resources of the enemy and separate enemy troops, leaving the enemy in a disadvantageous position." In September, the Vietnamese again met to discuss the strategy for 1953–54 and, with Ho Chi Minh backing the Chinese proposal, the vote went against Giap. In October and early November 1953, Giap and his Chinese advisers drew up operational plans which called for the seizure of Lai Chau, which would then become a base of operations for a Vietminh invasion of upper and central Laos. A second thrust against southern Laos would be launched from the Central Highlands of Annam. The Vietnamese politburo approved the plan on 3 November, and in the middle of the month five Vietminh regiments moved toward Lai Chau.[31]

If French intelligence remained unaware of the strategic debates going on within the enemy high command, its intelligence reports did divulge its shift in priorities. In mid-September 1953, the Deuxième

Bureau reported that Giap was massing his main divisions around the Tonkin delta. But although they were able to track Vietminh divisions through radio intercepts, they had no way of knowing whether Giap intended to launch an attack against the delta or turn his troops toward Laos.[32] Writing twenty-five years after the event, Navarre claimed to be more worried about the first possibility. Giap had already launched a full-fledged offensive against the delta in 1951, only to be bloodily repulsed by de Lattre. But the situation was different three years later. The French army was battle-weary, while the Vietminh army was large, well trained, and equipped with heavy artillery. A Vietminh attack against the delta, using a combination of infiltration and classic attack formations, would bring the full force of Giap's troops to bear on the French and could be launched without warning. The goal of the attack, Navarre believed, would be to cut off Hanoi from its harbor city, Haiphong, and overwhelm one or both of them. "It is very probable that we would have been submerged," he argued.[33] Navarre's response was to carry out a series of spoiling operations and peripheral raids like Operation Mouette, launched on 15 October against the 320th Division south of the delta. This kept Giap off balance and delayed the expected offensive against the delta.

Had Giap had his way, Navarre's plan would have been appropriate, even masterful. However, by the time the French commander applied it, the Vietminh had set their sights on Lai Chau. Wiser than the Vietminh, the Chinese had discovered Navarre's Achilles' heel—the French commitment to Deo Van Long's maquis and to their opium strategy.

French intelligence documents for the first time give a clear view of how Operation Castor developed and the fundamental assumptions and strategic priorities of the French high command. One of the dubious advantages which accrued to the French from the increasing sophistication of Vietminh forces was that they were able to gain much better intelligence on the enemy through radio intercepts. In November 1953, the Deuxième Bureau of the army general staff announced the movement of the Vietminh 351st Division and the "probable movement" of the 316th Division in early November toward the Tonkin highlands, and predicted "the imminence of a rebel action against our maquis in T'ai country. *As a consequence*, the Franco-

Vietnamese command launched on 20 November an airborne offen-
sive on Dien Bien Phu."[34] Colonel Guibaud of Navarre's Deuxième
Bureau summed up the feelings of his commander, that to abandon
T'ai maquis to their fate would offer a "gratuitous success" to the
Vietminh and undermine all confidence in French promises.[35] As Lai
Chau, set in a canyon, was considered too difficult to defend, the
French settled on Dien Bien Phu, the broadest valley in the Tonkin
highlands, as the spot for a *base aéroterrestre* to which they could
transfer the new capital of the T'ai maquis.

By deciding to accept battle at Dien Bien Phu, Navarre ran a risk,
but one which he probably believed he could not refuse. A veteran of
the French Resistance and of French intelligence, he subscribed
wholeheartedly to the maquis myth. But more important, as the
Chinese realized, Navarre was likely to follow traditional French campaign patterns which held that the opium harvest must be denied the
enemy. This strategy had assumed an even greater importance in the
autumn of 1953 with the demise of the gold and piaster traffic. Navarre
calculated that he could simply not stand by and allow the Vietminh
to replenish their war chests with Montagnard opium. Therefore, from
a strategic perspective, the French occupation of Dien Bien Phu was
neither the foolish nor the shortsighted decision that has often been
portrayed.

From an intelligence perspective, however, Navarre's decision to
occupy Dien Bien Phu appeared ominously reminiscent of 1914 and
1940. How can intelligence effectively serve a country and a command
which display an innate genius for choosing policies and strategies
beyond their means? As was the case with Joffre and Gamelin, it was
not up to the Deuxième Bureau to talk Navarre out of a particular
course of action. They simply presented the evidence. It is up to leaders
to know the limits of intelligence, and the capabilities of their own
forces. In other words, net assessment is not a job for intelligence
alone. Like Joffre and Gamelin, Navarre appears to have become
unhinged by the increasing power of his adversary, to the point that
he abandoned his own "Navarre Plan." He concluded that a defensive
posture was a strategy for defeat in the long term, and adopted a course
of action anchored in the wishful thinking that a dramatic initiative
would somehow unhinge the plans of his Vietminh adversaries.

FOURTEEN

DIEN BIEN PHU:
THE INTELLIGENCE DIMENSION

Dien Bien Phu must count as one of history's most studied battles. Indeed, so investigated has been the decision by the French
commander-in-chief in Indochina, General Henri Navarre, in November 1953 to occupy a remote valley in upper Tonkin, a decision
which led inexorably to a battle whose outcome terminated nearly a
century of French rule in Indochina, that nothing appears left to be
said about it.

As has been seen, however, Navarre's justification for his occupation
of Dien Bien Phu—that his "hedgehog" would force the Vietminh
commander, Vo Nguyen Giap, to renounce his invasion of Laos or
attack Dien Bien Phu head-on—has concealed the true intention of
French strategy, which was to protect the maquis and deny the opium
crop to the Vietminh. And while both constituted perfectly valid reasons for Operation Castor, the mistake made by Navarre was to place
his forces in a position where they had more to lose from a bad outcome
than did the Vietminh. In other words, while the loss of the opium
and the destruction of the maquis in upper Tonkin, even the eventual
occupation of much of Laos, might have been unfortunate, it would
not have proved fatal for Navarre. On the contrary, it would have
allowed him to husband his resources in the Tonkin delta and force
the Vietminh eventually to attack his strength there. On the other

hand, in trying to protect these two assets, Navarre not only lost them but also sacrificed much of the cream of the French expeditionary force, a situation which drove the French to the peace table in Geneva in the summer of 1954 hat in hand.

Responsibility for the decision to go to Dien Bien Phu has been obscured by postwar polemics over the battle and by the absence of archives. The first point made much of during the postbattle autopsy was that the French high command was divided over the purpose of Dien Bien Phu, when they were not skeptical of the entire operation. This was the line of defense pursued by Navarre's principal subordinate, the commander of the Tonkin theater, General René Cogny. Cogny insisted that he never shared Navarre's concept of Dien Bien Phu as a breakwater against a main-force Vietminh invasion of Laos. Rather, it was meant to be a *point d'amarrage*, or anchor point, for mobile operations to support French-led Montagnard irregular forces in the Tonkin highlands. Military historians especially have focused on this debate over the strategic purpose of Dien Bien Phu. But the general conclusion has been that the French high command did not speak with a common voice in Indochina. Dien Bien Phu symbolized the inadequacies on several levels: a failure to coordinate policy and strategy, of matching means to ends. It offered a striking example of the command's inability to achieve a unified strategic view of the war, to undertake operations in harmony with the French army's tactical and operational capabilities. The course of the battle revealed grave professional shortcomings in the army, as well as a serious decline of morale in a heterogeneous expeditionary force.

It would seem reasonable to suppose that, had French intelligence been on its toes, had it been able to assess Vietminh intentions and capabilities, then Navarre might well have been able to avoid the trap that the Chinese set for him in upper Tonkin. Good intelligence could have resolved some of the disputes within the French high command and supplied information that might have guided Navarre toward a more rational strategic choice in the late autumn of 1953. Why did this not happen? Navarre's answer was categorical: because French intelligence failed him badly. The French commander-in-chief complained that because of the lack of security-consciousness among French forces his moves were an open book for Giap. Meanwhile, his intelligence was utterly unable to discern Giap's intentions.

Navarre complained that all he got from his Deuxième Bureau were radio intercepts of "intermediate echelons" of Vietminh forces and information on the volume of Chinese supplies sent over the border into Tonkin. So while he knew where Giap's units were, he could not predict what the Vietminh commander intended to do with them. Nor could he know what support the Chinese were prepared to lend to the insurgents, both critical factors, he claimed, in his defeat at Dien Bien Phu.[1]

In a perverse way, it was only appropriate that none other than Giap himself supported Navarre's version of events, for it is now clear that both men were driven into a battle by the Chinese, who emerged as its principal beneficiaries. Giap boasted that he had laid a careful trap, undetected by French intelligence, into which Navarre obligingly stumbled. The massing of Vietminh forces as if he were preparing a major offensive against the Tonkin delta was merely a *ruse de guerre*; he intended to move into upper Tonkin all along. By sending only a few battalions against French-led Montagnard forces in upper Tonkin, he convinced the French that the occupation of Dien Bien Phu carried few risks for them. Once they had been drawn out into the highlands at the extreme limit of their air support, he could move in to finish them off. This military strategy was coordinated with the political goal of delivering a resounding victory to strengthen the Vietminh bargaining position at peace talks which in October 1953 Ho Chi Minh had decided to initiate.[2] Contemporary historians have tended to agree that Dien Bien Phu was essentially an intelligence failure. "The one fundamental calculation which underlaid Navarre's decision, the one reason which to Navarre justified the operation," writes American historian Lieutenant General Philip B. Davidson, who served as General Westmoreland's intelligence chief in Vietnam, "*was the estimate by his intelligence staff that the operation carried little or no risk*."[3]

But how accurate is this view of Dien Bien Phu? Must intelligence share the burden of blame for the disastrous decision and might strong intelligence warnings have averted disaster? One of the themes of this book has been that intelligence can only be judged by the context in which it operates. Certainly, in light of the mutual recriminations and the attempts to evade responsibility for the defeat which occurred after the battle, the French command appeared to be hopelessly confused and riven over the strategic purpose and operational concepts applied at Dien Bien Phu. But a closer look at the documents suggests that, on the contrary, there was a remarkable unity of vision over what Dien Bien Phu was meant to do, and that subsequent arguments by the main protagonists of the defeat have obscured that reality. In fact, the French command had a purpose, and believed they possessed the capacity to succeed, and this despite, not in the absence of, accurate assessments of Vietminh capabilities delivered to the high command by the Deuxième Bureau. Furthermore, Chinese military documents reveal that at Dien Bien Phu the French came within an ace of success. Had it not been for active Chinese intervention in strategic planning, logistical support, tactical direction, and, finally, boosting faltering Vietminh resolve, it would have been Navarre, not Giap, who emerged as the victor. It appears that Dien Bien Phu was indeed a trap, one set by the Chinese both for Giap and for Navarre. But if the Deuxième Bureau failed to discover the full scope of Chinese-imposed strategy until well into the battle, they did supply more than adequate information for Navarre to have made a more intelligent strategic choice and for the French command to have turned in a better tactical performance.

The first claim, that Navarre and Cogny were divided over the purpose of Dien Bien Phu as a hedgehog to stop a major attack, as at Na San, or, as Cogny claimed, an anchor point to support mobile operations, can be dismissed by a study of French army doctrine and the strategic situation of Dien Bien Phu. This poses the problem of Dien Bien Phu in the artificial terms of an operational dilemma. The beauty of the *base aéroterrestre* concept, in French eyes, was that it could perform both functions: "have enough personnel to permit extensive patrolling and to permit counterattack and the carrying of the fight beyond the defensive complex," as the French postwar study of their performance noted. "When the enemy commits major forces, our mobile elements fall back on the entrenched camp. If need be, these are reinforced by land, air, river, and maritime routes . . . The enemy is then forced to undertake veritable siege operations, which are long, costly, and difficult, and which require large forces vulnerable to air attack . . ." Interestingly, even in the aftermath of defeat, the French refused to concede that Dien Bien Phu invalidated the concept of the *base aéroterrestre*. This offered "a solution well suited to the problem of reestablishing our power and our influence in regions which are remote from our bases"—the only way which they could maintain strategic mobility in Indochina.[4]

Clearly, the French saw the *base aéroterrestre both* as an anchoring point *and* as a hedgehog. The fall of Dien Bien Phu was something beyond the norm, an exceptional case brought on by exceptional circumstances. Navarre insisted that while there were plenty of people around to say "I told you so" after his camp had been overrun, at the time only the head of the air force expressed reservations about supporting a camp at the limit of air range.[5] And while historians have chipped away at Navarre's assertion of quasi-unanimity in the French command, the main debates appear to have been about *how* the camp was to be defended rather than *if* it could be defended. And this despite the fact that in late November, French intelligence began to track the shift of Giap's divisions from the delta toward the highlands, a sure indication that the Vietminh would mount a major effort to seize it. True, at this stage, Navarre did not know that the Chinese were prepared to sustain a major Vietminh operation at Dien Bien Phu. But as he insisted that Laos was the objective of Giap's thrust, he must have known that the enemy effort might be considerable.

Despite this intelligence, Navarre and Cogny made a series of operational judgments which ultimately proved fatal to the garrison. These errors were moored in the dual role of the *base aéroterrestre*, which, when combined with the French goal of protecting the maquis and the opium crop, contributed to the demise of the camp in at least three important ways.

First, the anchor-point portion of the concept called for the appointment of an officer of light armor, Colonel Christian de Castries, as the camp commander, whereas events proved that an engineering officer expert in siege warfare would have been a happier choice. Second, the use of the garrison in mobile operations in the critical first weeks contributed to the neglect of the defensive positions which so weakened the French. Why should French soldiers already exhausted from patrols and reconnaissance missions worry overmuch about the strength of their bunkers or the depth of their trenches when it was they who held the operational initiative? The third weakness of the *base aéroterrestre* concept was that it was based on a belief in the

the military effectiveness of the Montagnard resistance which it was meant to support.

As has been noted, one of the goals of Castor was to transfer the T'ai capital from Lai Chau to Dien Bien Phu, which would become a new, more defensible base for partisan activity in the highlands. But when Deo Van Long's maquis attempted to depart Lai Chau for Dien Bien Phu in early December 1953, they were ambushed by soldiers of the 316th Division. American USIA representative Howard Simpson, present at Dien Bien Phu in December 1953, remembered the arrival of the remnants of Deo Van Long's T'ai maquis as "a scene from an old World War II film—until you realized the wounded were stained with real blood . . . The T'ai had come shuffling through the dust in a long column, arms slung, leading small, heavily laden mountain ponies. Their gaunt faces were blank with exhaustion. Some were carrying their wounded on makeshift bamboo litters, others supported a limping comrade. The slow-moving cavalcade exuded an aura of defeat. The members of the Dien Bien Phu garrison watching the column's arrival were grim-faced and thoughtful. One sensed a certain resentment on their part, as if the partisans had brought with them some unwanted, threatening virus." A battered jeep containing one of Van Long's lieutenants, a stocky man dressed in khaki, a .45 holstered on his hip, slid to a halt before Simpson's group: "The T'ai officer began to shout and curse, berating the French officers, his voice rising as he stamped back and forth, gesticulating . . . As I was politely but firmly hustled from the scene, I heard him repeat the word *trahison*—betrayal."[6]

The decision in December to continue with Operation Castor, given the state of the T'ai maquis which it was meant to support, was questionable, to say the least. The sad truth for Navarre was that Dien Bien Phu would never serve as an anchor point for anything, much less a friendly maquis operating in Giap's rear. The French postwar study complained that the maquis was never able to harass seriously Vietminh supply lines to Dien Bien Phu. Despite the monthly investment by 1954 of 1,500 flight-hours of C-47s, 300 flight-hours of reconnaissance aircraft, numerous B-26 missions, and airdrops of close to 300 tons of supplies and ammunition, "at no time did the Vietminh high command seem to be disturbed by the operations of our regular units," the French concluded disconsolately.[7] Roger Trinquier, the driving force behind the maquis experiment, acknowledged the failure of his partisans, but he was not short of excuses—the high command never supported them and, second, his Meos from Laos got their marching orders to attack the Vietminh rear only when the battle was virtually lost.[8] The truth lay elsewhere, however. The problem was that the high command not only supported the maquis, it mortgaged its strategy to them at Dien Bien Phu. Trinquier rather undermines his second accusation with the admission that the Meos would not move until paid in silver bars, the only currency which they recognized.[9] In any case, Trinquier's Meos from Laos had no local knowledge and no local support,[10] which must form an essential element of any successful guerrilla operation. The maquis served the French as a political symbol and a source of opium income, not as even a quasi-effective military force.

So if, as the French believed, the fall of Dien Bien Phu was an exceptional case brought on by exceptional circumstances, this leaves intact the "stab in the back" thesis—Navarre's accusations that events in Paris reduced his essentially sound strategy to rubble. Navarre claimed that his decision to drop on Dien Bien Phu was perfectly logical given the situation in November 1953, one which conformed to his plan of drawing Vietminh troops away from the Tonkin delta and avoiding a major battle. Cabinet "leaks" which eventually evolved into a full-blown political scandal in the *affaire des fuites* revealed that the French were overstretched in upper Tonkin. This was merely an inconvenient indiscretion, however, compared to the blunder which followed Ho Chi Minh's announcement in November that the Vietminh were willing to negotiate an end to the war. On 18 February 1954, the government foolishly agreed to meet with the Vietminh in Geneva, a decision that, according to Navarre, "overnight upset all my calculations." This gave the insurgents and the communist Chinese the incentive to commit a disproportionate number of forces to overwhelm the garrison at Dien Bien Phu and collect the political payoff.[11]

Chinese sources now show Navarre to have been correct, at least partially. To fully understand communist strategy, Dien Bien Phu must be placed in the context of major diplomatic initiatives which followed the end of the Korean War in July 1953. As part of a calculated "peace offensive," in late September, Moscow proposed a five-power conference to include China whose goal was to reduce international tensions. Beijing supported the Soviet initiative, publicly stating that the Indochina situation should be resolved by a meeting of the big powers. Chinese pressure was at the origins of Ho Chi Minh's stated willingness in November 1953 to negotiate an end to the war with France. In late January 1954, a four-power conference in Berlin agreed to meet in Geneva to discuss the restoration of peace in Korea and Indochina. The strategy which China forced on Giap sought to put the communists in the best possible negotiating position—if the French tried to defend their maquis in Tonkin and Laos, then they would be overextended and would open themselves to defeat. If they hunkered down in the Tonkin delta, then the communists would carry a very favorable "war map" to Geneva. In short, the Chinese had designed a "win-win" situation, at least for them.[12] In retrospect, even the French army's official study of the Indochina War blamed the Deuxième Bureau for failing to sniff out this carefully crafted ruse, one which conformed to Giap's strategy of enticing the French, and later the Americans, into the outlying regions where they could be isolated and overwhelmed by a superior force.[13]

While it is true that French intelligence did not supply Navarre with a blueprint of the communist master plan, to shift the blame for the defeat onto the shoulders of the Deuxième Bureau—or French politicians, for that matter—is unfair. Granted, the French response to the communist challenge was fragmented and inadequate. But French intelligence did give the French commander-in-chief a picture of the enemy which should have allowed him to make more judicious decisions, had he kept an open mind. French intelligence documents suggest that Giap was keeping his options open until well into November. On 23 September, French intelligence reported that Vietminh divisions concentrated around the delta were in a defensive position but had begun to infiltrate some regiments through the so-called de Lattre Line of blockhouses placed around the delta. "We retain the hypothesis that the campaign can begin by infiltrations in the delta," it concluded. On 22 October, it reported that Vietminh intelligence officers from the 312th and 308th divisions had been reconnoitering attack sites on the northern fringes of the delta, while elements of the

312th were training for urban warfare, which "would seem to indicate that the 312th is preparing to attack urban centers." But French maquis attacks against Lao Kay on the Red River near the Chinese frontier had caused some Vietminh troops to be diverted there. On 13 November it noted, in a report based at least in part on a defector's information, that two divisions and part of another were prepared to intervene in the delta, possibly by 1 December, while a regiment of the 325th Division stationed near Vinh in Annam had been ordered toward the delta on 6 November. But the shift of Vietminh divisions toward the northwest in late November was immediately detected by the Deuxième Bureau, who also drew the proper conclusions from it. "The [Vietminh] high command has manifestly changed its plan," it declared on 7 December. "Rather than aim at the delta, the principal Vietminh effort seems to be directed toward the northwest."[14] At this point, French intelligence attributed the change in plan, not to Chinese influence, as we now know to be the case, but to the success of the Navarre/O'Daniel Plan. The French raid on the Vietminh supply base at Lang Son in July, Mouette, and the attack on Lao Kay in October had produced "indecisiveness" in the Vietminh high command. Giap renounced his idea of attacking the delta and decided to deal with the easier target of the maquis in upper Tonkin.

Navarre complained that virtually his only intelligence on the enemy came from radio intercepts. But these gave him an enormous amount of information and allowed him to monitor the reactions of his enemy to his every move. On 28 November 1953, barely a week after the surprise French occupation, French intelligence reported that the paratroop drop on Dien Bien Phu initially had puzzled the Vietminh because its purpose was not readily apparent. At first they believed that it was a deep raid like that launched against the Vietminh supply base at Lang Son in the summer of 1953. But Giap quickly reached the correct conclusion that the purpose of Operation Castor was to support French-led Montagnard guerrillas in upper Tonkin. On the day after the landing, according to the report, he began to order troops toward Dien Bien Phu in the belief that the French might be forced to withdraw or defend their base. French intelligence believed him especially eager to deal with the guerrillas before they could disrupt his "supply lines."[15]

Historians have echoed Navarre's cri de coeur in awarding low marks to French intelligence for gravely underestimating Vietminh ability to bring so many troops, so much artillery, and so many antiaircraft guns to besiege the French camp successfully.[16] But even a cursory scan of the intelligence documents reveals that these provided the French commander with enormously useful information, enough to serve as the basis for a sound decision to stand and fight or cut and run. When the French seized Dien Bien Phu to derail Giap's offensive against the maquis, Navarre took the risk that his *base aéroterrestre* could take the best that Giap could throw at it. In making that calculation, he held in his hand intercepts which enabled him to trace the movement of Giap's divisions as they disengaged from the delta and threaded their way through the mountains toward Dien Bien Phu in November and December 1953, divisions that included the 351st heavy artillery division and the 367th antiaircraft regiment.[17] Navarre's insistence that he was unaware of the potential of Chinese assistance also rings hollow. Six weeks before Castor was launched, the Deuxième Bureau had reported an enormous increase in Chinese aid, which *"has now lost its character of the improvised supply of heterogeneous surplus, and once again underlines the effort of rationalization undertaken by the Vietminh."*[18] And in any case, the possibility should always have been in the forefront of his calculations. Ultimately, Chinese intervention proved to be the decisive factor, in the tactical as well as the strategic phase of the campaign.

After the decision was made to accept battle, French intelligence gave the high command more than adequate warning of Giap's every move. Radio intercepts of 22 December revealed Vietminh observers posted on the heights above the valley openly discussing ways of attacking the French position. Even at this early date, they divulged that their priority would be to neutralize Dien Bien Phu's airstrip, the key to the campaign.[19] Navarre was aware that Giap had contemplated a January assault on Dien Bien Phu, but had been deterred by Chinese advice, by the fact that his artillery was not yet in place, and by an unexpectedly swift French buildup. Requests for supplies, deliveries of vast quantities of munitions throughout the battle, the arrival of artillery and reinforcements around Dien Bien Phu in the winter of 1953–54 allowed the French to draw up an accurate enemy order of battle, revealing his logistical and military capabilities. Even the code names which the Vietminh established for their own units and for the French positions did not baffle French intelligence, including the identity of the man referred to as Mr. Ngoc or Hong Linh, who was none other than Giap himself.

Radio intercepts alerted the French in early January that the Vietminh had located the bunkering station for the airstrip and the munitions depot, and that enemy unit intelligence officers had been called in to discuss attack plans around a carefully constructed model of the French position. These open discussions revealed to de Castries and Cogny that Giap, at Chinese insistence, would attack the valley strong point by strong point, rather than attempt a "human wave" assault designed to swallow the entire position.[20] The Vietminh broadcast the results of POW interrogations over the radio, and the hours when French guard details changed, so that raids and sabotage missions could be planned for those times. Even when the French systematically ambushed Vietminh intelligence and raiding parties which crept into their positions at night, it never occurred to the Vietminh that their radios were being read like a book. "It is possible that spies have denounced Vietminh activities in the area of Fu Tuu [Béatrice?]," concluded a radio intercept of 11 March. At seven o'clock on the night of 13 March 1954, the Vietminh radio broadcast an appeal to their soldiers to "win the battle of Dien Bien Phu." Attack assignments and times were sent out. The Vietminh artillery barrage which slammed into Béatrice announcing the beginning of the battle came as no surprise to the French, who knew the precise time and the main axis of the Vietminh advance.[21]

If the Chinese are to be believed, it is clear that without their substantial assistance Giap probably could not have won at Dien Bien Phu. And this despite the fact that the French were shoehorned into poorly conceived and constructed defensive positions, lacked air support, were completely dominated by Vietminh artillery, and only a quarter or so of their forces, namely paras and Legionnaires, put up serious resistance. Chinese advisers trained Vietminh troops in tactical methods perfected in Korea, which included sniping and engineering techniques. At Chinese insistence, the Vietminh converted some infantry units to two new artillery divisions. When Vietminh morale began to falter due to high casualties caused by frontal assaults, the Chinese organized a new tactic which spun webs of trenches around French positions, which, isolated, would fall to attackers who charged from close quarters. These changes were recorded by French radio intercepts and air reconnaissance photographs. It is not clear that the French caught wind of a slackening of Vietminh resolve as the monsoons approached, a resolve stiffened by Chinese insistence that Dien Bien Phu must be taken before a cease-fire was declared. To make sure that Giap persisted, they trained and equipped two Vietminh battalions with 75 mm recoilless guns and Katyusha multitube rocket launchers for the final assault. On 7 May, the garrison surrendered, de Castries, still wearing his red spahi cap, taken as he sat in his bunker.[22]

It is obvious that the French had more than adequate intelligence on the Vietminh, and still it did not save them. Why? Because Navarre failed to make logical decisions on the basis of his intelligence information. He continued to believe, as did the vast majority of French officers, that despite the Vietminh buildup, Dien Bien Phu would remain inviolate. The charge that the Deuxième Bureau did not warn Navarre that he was headed for disaster is unconvincing. That was simply not the role of military intelligence, whose function was to provide information on which the commander-in-chief could base his decisions. And if French intelligence did nothing to challenge the firm belief that Dien Bien Phu would shatter Giap's attacks as had Na San in 1952, what would have been the result if it had? Would such a challenge, assuming that there had been any intelligence officer bold, clearsighted, or foolhardy enough to have made it, have fundamentally altered Navarre's decision? The answer must be no.

That said, however, the Deuxième Bureau was not above placing its evidence in terms emphatic enough so that only the most obtuse commander could ignore it. On 24 January 1954, Cogny's Deuxième Bureau produced a report detailing the increase in Vietminh strength between Na San and Dien Bien Phu and concluding ominously that Giap "will increasingly throw his best elements into what he intends to be a battle of destruction."[23] In early February, the Deuxième Bureau was more precise, noting that while at Na San, Giap had mustered 30,000 troops, he had almost doubled that number at Dien

Bien Phu, whose garrison barely outnumbered that at Na San. "Along with this progress in the campaign plans," the report concluded, "we have noticed a corresponding progress in the Vietminh force structure."[24] But the increase in Vietminh strength and capabilities was no secret. In fact, the Deuxième Bureau was merely stating the obvious. After all, the recognition of growing Vietminh power and a corresponding decline in French strength formed the entire rationale for the Navarre Plan of 1953. Navarre confessed that his multiethnic French expeditionary force resembled "the Roman legions in the last stages of decadence."[25] The T'ai maquis, the raison d'être of Castor, had been destroyed as an effective force in December. Despite all of these factors, Navarre decided to accept battle in any case.

The reason for the marked improvement in Vietminh capabilities, the February 1954 report pointed out, was related directly to an increase in Chinese aid, especially heavy artillery and antiaircraft guns, to which the Deuxième Bureau had called attention when Castor was barely a twinkle in Navarre's eye. Nor can French intelligence be accused of failure to place the campaign in its political context. It reported that, in moving his regular divisions toward the northwest from November 1953, Giap hoped "to improve the 'war map' by the conquest of vast territories and reinforce the international position of the Vietminh government."[26] When it became obvious that Navarre had decided to make a stand at Dien Bien Phu, the Vietminh, with strong Chinese encouragement, direction, and support, acquired the political will to turn in a logistical, operational, and tactical performance the scale of which the French had yet to witness. That is not to say that French intelligence thought their enemies incapable of it. Merely that they did not suspect that the Vietminh possessed the will to push their desire for victory to the very brink of military collapse. It was not Giap's military capabilities they had misjudged, but the lengths to which he was prepared to go for victory. But they caught a glimmer of it on 27 December, when Navarre's Deuxième Bureau made the connection between the increased Chinese interest in providing aid and Ho Chi Minh's willingness to negotiate, which he announced in November. Then "everything is seen in a new light," they reported.[27]

Of course, the French had made the political calculation that it would be disastrous to abandon the maquis and forfeit the opium crop.

But by making this decision, they ignored initially the political calculations of the enemy. One criticism which can be directed at French
intelligence in Indochina, especially given the fairly sophisticated international calculations of the communists, was that its focus was too
narrowly military. This stemmed in part from administrative arrangements which fragmented French intelligence services in Indochina
while creating an artificial separation between "political" and "military" intelligence. In 1949, a Direction Générale de la Documentation
(DGD) had been created to circulate information among the various
intelligence organizations in Indochina and to centralize intelligence
for the benefit of the high commissioner. When de Lattre became
high commissioner and commander-in-chief in 1951, he insisted that
"the DGD could not, in his opinion, impose a sufficient coordination
because it did not have the necessary authority." As de Lattre was both
political and military chief in Indochina, he demanded that intelligence be coordinated in his person and dissolved the DGD. When he
departed his position after barely a year, de Lattre left behind no
institutional structure to coordinate political and military intelligence.
The result of the abolition of the DGD, according to an April 1952
report, had been "dispersion, intelligence work carried out in an isolated environment, without orientation, without coordination and synthesis of political and military intelligence at the highest echelon."
This situation persisted down to the grand finale of the battle itself—
as late as 12 November 1953, Colonel Cann called for a reorganization
of French intelligence, complaining that the Deuxième Bureau was
concentrating on purely military subjects.[28]

But if French intelligence cannot be saddled with the blame for the
defeat at Dien Bien Phu, neither can it be exonerated entirely. Probably
the most damning charge which can be leveled against French intelligence is that important segments of that community had linked
French strategy, and ultimately the fate of French Indochina, to opium. The GCMA worked hard to resurrect the maquis after its virtual
destruction in 1952, no doubt calculating that if they did not retain
control of the opium, then the Vietminh would use it to buy arms.
Opium and the maquis were intertwined, assets which the intelligence
officers were determined to defend. Even those unaware of the opium
connection—and it is difficult to believe that Navarre counted among

them—could be persuaded that the maquis were politically important, and succeed in deluding themselves that it also had value as a military force. As Giap closed in on Dien Bien Phu, Navarre elected to make a stand rather than cut his losses and flee back to the relative sanctuary of the Tonkin delta.

Would Navarre have made a different decision with different intelligence? Certainly one may argue that the more sober assessments of the increase in Vietminh capabilities came too late. However, the issue ultimately was not about whether intelligence reached the *décideur*—the person making the decision—after the deadline for a pullout. Navarre would have taken this decision in any case, based on his desire to protect the maquis and the opium crop and to shield Laos, and because of his belief that a *base aéroterrestre* could defend itself. Intelligence cannot be influential as an objective factor in the decision-making process when it is applied in a flawed strategic context. French military intelligence, and the French high command generally, took little interest in the political calculations on which Giap based his military campaign. So Navarre chose to fight a battle in which, ultimately, he had far more to lose from defeat, and far less to gain from victory, than did his opponent.

In retrospect, it was not Navarre but Giap and Ho Chi Minh who could more plausibly claim to have been "stabbed in the back." At Geneva, Vietminh and Chinese interests were shown to diverge. In 1949, China had come to the support of the Vietminh largely because it had wanted to eliminate Tonkin as a possible base for a Nationalist Chinese resurgence. Now that Dien Bien Phu had achieved that goal, China needed time to put its domestic house in order and end its diplomatic isolation with openings to the Western powers. Therefore, the Chinese Premier, Zhou Enlai, agreed to the partition of Vietnam, thus undercutting the Vietminh desire for unity under their rule. When the Soviets backed the Chinese view, Ho had no choice but to accept a cease-fire based on the "temporary" partition of Vietnam.[29] Thus, Dien Bien Phu proved a trap for the Vietminh as much as it had been for Navarre.

Indochina: A Final Encore

Though Dien Bien Phu offered a spectacular finale for France's rule in Indochina, incredible as it may seem, French intelligence still retained the energy for an encore. The primary reason for this was that, although France agreed in Geneva to end Vietnam's imperial status, she still hoped to maintain French influence in the south. Throughout the war, the Vietminh had registered fewer successes in South Vietnam than they had in Tonkin—for several reasons. But a significant factor was that in Cochin China the French had shared power with a mosaic of quasi-independent and well-armed religious sects—the Cao Dai and the Hoa Hao—as well as the Saigon underworld controlled by the Binh Xuyen. While these groups did not necessarily support French interests, they made it difficult for the Vietminh to establish firm roots in the areas they controlled.

In the political vacuum which developed in the south following the French defeat in 1954, these groups emerged as major power brokers. The Emperor Bao Dai remained in gilded exile on the French Riviera, copulating with high-class prostitutes and wasting enormous sums at the tables in Monte Carlo. His benediction, as well as that of the United States government, eventually was bestowed on Ngo Dinh Diem, a fiercely anti-French Catholic nationalist, who became President of the Republic of Vietnam in July 1954. But though Diem reigned in Saigon, he did not govern. Despite the defeats, the deceptions, the agony of struggling to defend a land at the far frontier of the French imperium, France hoped to reserve a tutorial role in her former colony.

Though defeated, 80,000 French troops remained in Indochina as permitted under the Geneva Agreement. Diem's Gallophobia hardly pleased them. To the French secret services fell the task of enforcing French interests, a charge which they assumed with the self-interested conviction of a service some of whose members had developed a cozy business relationship with the Binh Xuyen through the opium and gold trade, which stretched via the Corsican underworld to Marseille.

On the face of it, the French services appeared to be in a commanding position to conjure up more mischief than the new Diem regime, virtually under siege in Saigon, could hope to quell. Diem's army chief of staff, General Nguyen Van Hinh, was in their pay and made no secret of his presidential ambitions. The sects remained jealously vigilant over the autonomy which they had carved out under the French. As the French secret services would discover to their peril, however, once the Americans dispatched Colonel Edward Lansdale to shore up the Diem regime, they were playing out of their league. Lansdale was one of the most controversial characters to amble through the pages of American intelligence history. Born in Detroit in 1908, a graduate of UCLA who had pursued an advertising career until World War II had drawn him into the OSS, Lansdale had accepted a regular commission in the air force after the war. But special operations remained his passion. Lansdale made a memorable impression on those who met him—he served as the inspiration both for Colonel Edwin B. Hillandale, the mad but charismatic "Ugly American" in the Lederer and Burdick novel,[30] and for British novelist Graham Greene's "Quiet American," Alden Pyle.[31] Lansdale arrived in Saigon in the early summer of 1954 from the Philippines, where he had played midwife to President Ramon Magsaysay's successful campaign against the communist insurgency. At the head of a small team whose job it was to make life difficult for the new Hanoi government, he set about fabricating documents discrediting the communists and sending sabotage squads to destroy oil and coal stocks in the north. These were directed by Major Lucien Conein, a short, muscular Frenchman raised in the unlikely surroundings of Kansas City, who had enlisted in the U.S. army in World War II. Assigned to the OSS, Conein had worked in occupied France and, in 1945, as part of a Franco-Vietnamese commando group charged with attacking Japanese garrisons in Vietnam and liberating French POWs. "Black Luigi" would continue to serve as Lansdale's right-hand man in Vietnam. But as French distaste for the Diem regime hardened into outright hostility, Lansdale set about making life difficult for his opposites in the French secret service.

In early 1955, the French relinquished their control over the South Vietnamese army (ARVN) after Lansdale had foiled a coup by pro-French General Nguyen Van Hinh. Meanwhile, Lansdale, supplied with substantial funds through the American embassy, set out to buy the neutrality or cooperation of several of the militias and maquis of the religious sects. However, according to Lansdale, French intelligence tried to counter the growing American influence in March 1955 by organizing a United Front of disaffected religious leaders and Binh Xuyen. Lansdale reasoned that as gangster cash held the United Front together, then the elimination of the Binh Xuyen would cause it to collapse. A special Military Security Service, composed of up to 300 reliable Vietnamese police, tracked down and eliminated Binh Xuyen "action committees" in Saigon and Cholon which had been so effective for French intelligence in neutralizing Vietminh cadres there. Meanwhile, the ARVN commander of Saigon, under Lansdale's direction, drew up plans to assault Binh Xuyen strongholds in his city.

In the fighting which broke out between the ARVN and Binh Xuyen on 28 April 1955, the two intelligence services, one French and the other American, coached from opposite sidelines. In his memoirs, Lansdale suggests that he merely awaited the outcome in his bungalow. But even his brief account reveals that he was actively consulted by the Vietnamese government. On the French side, Captain Antoine Savani of the Deuxième Bureau is alleged to have installed himself in Binh Xuyen headquarters near the Y Bridge in Cholon while Deuxième Bureau officers worked to coordinate intelligence and operations for Binh Xuyen units. When a United States Information Service representative in Saigon, Howard R. Simpson, was brought to Binh Xuyen headquarters during a lull in the fighting in the hope of persuading the American embassy to withdraw their support for Diem, he was amazed "when a French captain emerged from the radio room. His shirtsleeves were rolled up and he held a clipboard full of papers . . . Seeing me, he stopped dead in his tracks, turned, and disappeared behind the door." But the coming and going of French dispatch riders left Simpson in no doubt that "the French are running the goddamn show."[32] Offers of rewards for the capture of Lansdale, who, it was promised, would have his entrails cut open and stuffed with mud, were broadcast on Binh Xuyen radios.

After several days of destructive fighting in the streets of Cholon, by 3 May the Binh Xuyen had been driven into the swamps south of town. Lansdale complained that French "soreheads," presumably from the Deuxième Bureau, began to carry out a terror campaign against

Americans in Saigon, to which he responded with a counterterror campaign of his own aimed at French intelligence officers.[33] On 11 May 1955, French Premier Edgar Faure agreed to withdraw all French forces from Indochina. It was not a moment too early. Like the army, French intelligence already faced a new challenge in Algeria.

FIFTEEN

THE ALGERIAN WAR

If the French had decided to disengage from Indochina, it was largely because all of France's military and intelligence resources were required to deal with an insurgency that had erupted in another French possession—Algeria. The plastic explosives which rocked Algiers and other Algerian cities on 1 November 1954, explosions which announced the beginning of the Algerian insurrection, caught the French government completely by surprise. Interior Minister François Mitterrand summoned Roger Wybot and demanded to know why the DST had produced no warning. It was a fair question. Algeria, after all, was considered an integral part of metropolitan France and had a complete panoply of police services whose job it was to keep a finger on the pulse of the population. The director insisted that since January 1954 police in Algeria and France had reported the discovery of arms stocks, propaganda tracts calling for an independent Algeria, and plans for a general uprising against French rule in North Africa. A long report laid on the desk of Mitterrand's predecessor in March had merely gathered dust, while authorities in France and Algeria had resisted the implementation of plans for Operation Sirocco, which aimed to destroy potential insurgent networks, calling them provocative and alarmist.[1]

Wybot's exculpation may be dismissed as special pleading, but it probably wasn't. For in truth, it required willful blindness in the

French administration to ignore the fact that Algeria simmered with latent revolt. The humiliation of 1940 followed by the successful Allied invasion and occupation of North Africa in 1942 had encouraged a thousand expressions of native discontent while World War II was still in progress, from anti-French graffiti on public urinals (reported by police as a particularly accurate barometer of public opinion) to widespread evasion of conscription notices, rumors of a general strike, and even arms traffic.[2] Nationalist opposition spilled into the open at Sétif on 8 May 1945. But while French intelligence in North Africa had sniffed trouble, its scope took them completely by surprise.

The attack which erupted in Sétif, a grid of bleached habitation scratched out of the desiccated uplands of the Constantinois in eastern Algeria, during wreath-laying ceremonies to celebrate the German surrender, resulted in the deaths of 102 Europeans. French repression was both general and specific. The general contribution was supplied by the French army, which, with the help of armed Italian POWs, quelled it in traditional fashion with indiscriminate force and generalized terror. The number of Algerian Muslims who perished in the retribution which followed Sétif has been the subject of some dispute, but it was no fewer than 3,000.[3] On 11 May 1954, 15,000 members of the Babor and Oued Marsa tribes gathered on the beach of Les Falaise east of Bougie. Their backs to the sea, they formally requested an *aman*, or pardon, from General Henry Martin, thus punctuating the end of the "rebellion" in the time-honored fashion of North Africa. Rebellion, repression, *aman*—the imperial trinity complete, General Martin urged the ex-insurgents to "return to the path of worthiness, work, and peace."[4] For the army, the incident was closed. But not quite, for the Deuxième Bureau identified and apprehended the principal troublemakers through a network of informers in the Muslim population who traveled under code names like Philinte or Denis and native affairs officers who lived among and administered the indigenous populations.[5] Although how many were true political activists and how many had been denounced by native "agents" for private reasons is a matter of open conjecture.

It may be generous to give French intelligence and the French police the benefit of the doubt on this score. The criticism leveled at French repression of nationalist movements in their colonies generally was that it tended to fall on "the usual suspects"—high-profile moderate nationalists whose public criticisms of French policies caused them to have voluminous police dossiers. Violent revolutionaries and clandestine conspirators escaped arrest or capture by fleeing underground or into exile. For instance, the political moderate who urged Paris to integrate Muslims into the full rights of French citizenship, Ferhat Abbas, and 4,500 of his followers were arrested in police sweeps although he had nothing to do with Sétif. This French reaction was identical to the one which had followed nationalist agitation in Vietnam in 1930–31. The arbitrary and indiscriminate nature of French repression in both Indochina and Algeria actually worked to the benefit of the revolutionaries both by alienating the population and by eliminating or discrediting moderates like Ferhat Abbas. Even in 1954, normally lucid and reform-minded Prime Minister Pierre Mendès-France proved reluctant to negotiate with Abbas in part because French intelligence reports labeled Abbas as "the archetypal extremist."[6]

Unfortunately, the French learned no lessons from Sétif. Nor, in truth, could they, as French policy there fell hostage to the one million *pieds noirs,* Algerians of European extraction, who ruled Algeria for their own benefit. The fragmented National Assembly of the Fourth Republic awarded the twenty *pied noir* deputies political leverage far out of proportion to their numbers. Therefore, the *pieds noirs* continued to sabotage reforms demanded by moderate Muslim leaders and to stuff ballot boxes with scandalous impunity. Not surprisingly, in this atmosphere of disenfranchisement and intimidation, anti-French incidents began to multiply from January 1954 when three French soldiers were assassinated and four civilians wounded on Algiers' rue d'Isly. Nor was the tense atmosphere dissipated by news from Indochina, where the capitulation of Dien Bien Phu in May stripped away yet another layer of *baraka* from an army whose military reputation in the eyes of Algerians was already threadbare.[7]

The tragic fact for Algeria and for France was that virtually every enemy of accurate intelligence available to French authorities was present in Algeria and Paris in the summer and autumn of 1954, the most prominent of which was wishful thinking. When in April 1954 the Service des Liaisons Nord-Africaines reported that a revolutionary element no longer content to await the pleasure of Paris for reform had split from the Mouvement pour le Triomphe des Libertés Démocratiques (MTLA), senior administrators breathed a sigh of relief. This report offered proof, if more were needed, that the Algerian nationalist movement was hopelessly riven and incapable of action.[8] Over the summer reports began to filter gradually into prefectures and subprefectures in the Constantinois in eastern Algeria, into Algiers itself, and finally even into Oran in the west, traditionally the least restive area of Algeria, of arms stocks, bomb factories, and even groups of armed men circulating in remote regions like the Aurès Mountains, which separate the Constantinois from the Sahara. But they could be dismissed as alarmist by administrators who refused to pass them up the chain of authority. After all, the Aurès were rather like Corsica, a half-policed aerie of bandits and highwaymen. With the army in Indochina, and great slabs of Algeria with as few as nine policemen per 100,000 inhabitants, it was only natural for criminal activity to increase. Wishful thinking, even racism, stoked the eternal wars between the RG, the Prefecture of Police, and the army, predisposed to disbelieve any report which might suggest a hint of competence on the part of their bureaucratic rivals. They clung to the comfortable fiction that Algerians were incapable of organizing revolution on a national level—even well into the war, many insisted that Cairo had supplied the brains and the organization for the rebellion, which was beyond the competence of mere Algerian Muslims.[9]

The Armée d'Afrique's Affaires Indigènes and the Deuxième Bureau, which traditionally kept an eye on native populations, had been gutted by World War II and Indochina, and its networks of informers in place in 1945 allowed to languish. Few old hands, fluent in Arabic or Kabyle with close contacts with the native population, remained to raise the alarm. The cold indifference of the Muslim population toward the French, and pressure from the FLN, which had even extended to the prostitution trade—a traditional intelligence window on the mood of the Muslim population—left the government dependent on the fragmentary and uncoordinated reports of civil administrators of "mixed communes," French-appointed caids in Muslim areas whose information was seldom reliable, and the gendarmerie. "Progressively, the civil and military administration was cut off from the reality of the *bled* [the Algerian hinterland]," writes French historian Jean-

Charles Jauffret, "confident in the apparent calm which reigned in Algeria."[10] Even those who received the reports tended to dismiss intelligence as unimportant—let the Muslims rise if they dare, and we shall smash them as always.

By October 1954, however, the reports flowing into the office of Governor General Roger Léonard had become too numerous to ignore. Worse, they suggested a national pattern of activity, a conspiracy for concerted action. Still, Léonard was in an awkward position. Like his subordinates, he knew full well that it was bad form to be alarmist in prefectural circles, that careers seldom advanced on the back of bad tidings—which, according to Wybot, was why Léonard dismissed DST warnings as "alarmist."[11] And of no time was this more true than in the autumn of 1954, when the very conditions which made insurrection most likely in Algeria made Paris least receptive to the warning signs. Both Tunisia and Morocco were in nationalist turmoil. Prime Minister Mendès-France, inclined to cede independence to these two protectorates, hardly needed to stretch his wafer-thin credibility still further to deal with Algeria. Nor were *pied noir* notables, traditionally suspicious of mainland meddling in their affairs, eager to promote alarmist reports which suggested that they were not in absolute control of their country, and thus jeopardize the generous metropolitan subsidies which injected badly needed capital into their backward economy. A few military units were shipped into eastern Algeria in August 1954. But these were conscripts, inexperienced in insurgency warfare and depressed beyond measure at being plucked from posh garrisons on the Côte d'Azur and deposited in the scorched Algerian uplands. Léonard had already been warned that army reinforcements in any quantity could not be expected before Easter 1955. Better just close one's eyes and hope for the best.

Administrative complacency cannot be the absolute answer to French unpreparedness—the Algerian revolutionaries can take some credit, for they had learned more from Sétif than had their French opponents. Formed into the Organisation Spéciale (OS), which on 10 October 1954 became the Front de Libération Nationale (FLN), the insurgents had concluded that the war would be a protracted one. Sétif had proven that a spectacular rebellion only called down an equally spectacular repression from the French. The beginning of the insurgency would be announced by the bombing campaign of 1 November 1954. Their theory of victory may be described as modified Mao, or Mao manqué. Unlike the Vietminh, the FLN never believed that they would ever be powerful enough to achieve Mao's "Third Phase" of revolutionary warfare when the insurgent forces would overwhelm the colonialist army. The likelihood that the Armée de Libération Nationale could produce a Dien Bien Phu on Algerian soil was discounted from the beginning. The military portion of their strategy called for a combination of terrorist and guerrilla actions against soft targets like settler farms, isolated police stations, and Muslims inclined to cooperate with the French. This would create a climate of insecurity in Algeria and provoke the French to retaliate against a Muslim population in which they could not distinguish friend from foe, thereby driving the Muslims into the arms of the FLN. Military commands, the *wilayas*, would gradually build up their forces to take on mainline French units in open combat. Unlike the Vietminh's, the FLN's goal was not to clear and secure territory, but to inflict increasing casualties on the French and erode their will to continue.

The political portion of FLN strategy sought to isolate the French both diplomatically and from the Algerian Muslims. Diplomatic missions in Arab capitals and the United Nations would promote the FLN as the "legitimate" representative of Muslim Algerians. Meanwhile, inside Algeria six-man cells would organize shadow governments to collect intelligence and funds, distribute propaganda and justice. The endgame would be a revolutionary uprising which would deliver a political and psychological defeat to a weary France, demonstrate the futility of a French strategy based on military superiority alone, and convince France to abandon Algeria.

Although François Mitterrand is alleged to have censured his subordinates following the bombings of 1 November 1954 over their failure to alert him, apparently the rebellion did not catch the Interior Minister and future President of the Fifth Republic completely off guard. French historian Yves Courrière argues that of all French politicians Mitterrand was most acutely aware of the potential for insurrection in Algeria. However, his instincts were political rather than based on intelligence sources—when Mitterrand explained to Mendès-France that he "smelled something in Algeria," the Prime Minister asked for hard

evidence rather than a reading on the Interior Minister's "snout meter."
Mitterrand traveled to Algeria, but was constrained by the requirement
to show no disrespect to *pied noir* notables, on whose support the
government's fragile majority depended, by asking searching questions
which might suggest that the Muslim proletariat was not completely
in hand. Radical division of opinion among administrators confused
the intelligence picture still further. The report composed by the RG
in Algeria on 23 October predicting some sort of trouble before Christmas was forwarded to Mitterrand by Léonard, but a subordinate official
who considered it unduly alarmist consigned it to the archives. The
RG report did prod Léonard into belated action. The governor general
journeyed to Constantine on 29 October for a conference about the
deteriorating situation there. But the meeting was gutted of results by
sharp differences between soldiers and administrators and conflicting
reports over the scope of the threat. Only on 31 October, barely twelve
hours before the insurrection, were steps taken in the Defense Ministry
to liberate credits to buy essential military supplies, like mules, and
transfer extra soldiers to Algeria. For all practical purposes, the revolutionaries had achieved surprise.[12]

The Algerian rebellion was certainly not guaranteed success at the
outset. If the 1 November bombings had caught the French unprepared, the revolutionaries were even more at a disadvantage. Few in
number, poorly armed, with little support in a population whose most
politically aware elements clamored for integration into the full rights
of French citizenship, the insurgents had only one slim asset in these
early days—the support, largely rhetorical, of Cairo. Their goal in this
first winter of rebellion was merely to survive. In this, their best allies
were their adversaries. In the short run, they were aided by the absence
of force available to the French and the timid patrol methods of those
who were in Algeria. As the French began to recognize the seriousness
of the threat, their policy sought to isolate the FLN from the Muslim
population. But as French leaders were held hostage in parliament,
and in Algeria, by a *pied noir* population dead set against all reform
which would have given the Muslim population a stake in the continued French presence in Algeria, the margins of political maneuver
were close to zero.

"*L'Algérie, c'est la France,*" Mendès-France thundered before the

Chamber of Deputies on 12 November 1954. "And who among you
. . . would hesitate to employ every means to preserve France?"[13] Put
that way, those who suggested any sort of accommodation with the
rebellion were immediately branded as traitors. This was especially the
case after August 1955, when in the aftermath of the Philippeville
massacres the brutal slaughter by the FLN of unarmed *pieds noirs*
down to babes in arms caused a sickened and angry Governor General
Jacques Soustelle, who had arrived with intentions of pursuing genuine
reform for the Muslims, to rule out all compromise until the rebellion
was crushed. This was a significant gain for the FLN, for the French
had committed themselves to a policy of military victory stripped of
any political dimension, patent nonsense in any counterinsurgency
campaign which demanded political reform as the basis of winning
the allegiance—the "hearts and minds"—of the population. The
FLN's goal was to present themselves as the only alternative to a
French/*pied noir* condominium in Algeria. They sought to abolish the
middle ground, to force Muslims to take sides. The fact that Paris was
in the pocket of the *pieds noirs*, the arrest and harassment of moderate
Algerians who might have supported a reformist French policy, the
torture and indiscriminate reprisals carried out by the French in reaction to FLN outrages like the Philippeville massacres, all worked to
the FLN's advantage. All the rebels had to do was intimidate or assassinate any holdouts, and victory would come to them in the fullness
of time.

The generally accepted wisdom is that the French understood that
poor intelligence had been a great weakness in Indochina, and sought
to rectify that deficiency in Algeria. The sad truth was that intelligence
within a political vacuum could be no more effective over the long
run than could military operations severed from any coherent political
strategy. Worse, as will be seen, much intelligence activity actually
served to weaken France's argument—directed particularly at allies
and the United Nations—that she was dealing with a civil war, an
internal French matter of no concern to the outside world. This was
no mere diplomatic subterfuge. It was an ethnocentric vision which
shaped and guided French policy and one to which the French intelligence community subscribed wholeheartedly: Algerians were incapable of organizing rebellion on their own. Only outside assistance

kept the FLN and its military wing, the Armée de Libération Nationale (ALN), in business. A top priority of French strategy against the FLN became to isolate the battlefield, to sever the FLN/ALN from their outside sources of support. But in striking at those sources, the French sped up the internationalization of the conflict, thus undermining their own arguments that it was merely an internal French affair.

Outside support for the insurgents came principally from three sources. The Arab states, the Egyptian regime of Gamal Abdel Nasser first among them, gave the FLN a political refuge and a certain amount of rhetorical support. From 1956, when France freed them from protectorate status, Tunisia provided the principal base for the ALN, while Morocco offered a secondary insurgent platform. A second source of support for the insurgency came from the large numbers of Algerian workers in France whom the FLN milked for funds. The international arms trade which supplied the FLN was a third focus of support.

Arab diplomats offered a viable intelligence target, as a source of information on the FLN, but especially because diplomatic recognition of the Algerian insurgents held out the prospect of respectability and support for the FLN. Thyraud de Vosjoli, the SDECE representative in Washington, claimed there was no shortage of Arab diplomats eager to barter for information on FLN activities. So French diplomats could keep their hands clean; the SDECE distributed funds to representatives of some of the smaller nations at the UN—which became a significant battleground in the FLN war for international support—in exchange for voting the French position. While this may have retarded the formation of an anti-French majority on the Algerian question in the General Assembly, it could not keep it indefinitely at bay. The United States, which had backed France in Indochina to the point of paying 50 percent of the war costs by 1953, turned a deaf ear to arguments put forward by French psychological action officers like Roger Trinquier, who insisted that the FLN was simply another tentacle on the octopus of international communism. By the autumn of 1956, Thyraud de Vosjoli discovered that "the State Department and American intelligence categorically refused to help the French."[14] Following the February 1958 French bombardment of Sakiet, an ALN base in Tunisia, both Washington and London dropped any pretense of Allied solidarity and offered to broker a settlement between Paris and the FLN.

In Paris, SDECE attention focused on the Egyptian embassy, whose military attaché was active in coordinating FLN affairs in France. Responsibility for its surveillance was given to Service 7, known in SDECE headquarters as the "burglars," or *cinéma et publicité* (films and advertising), which had been created in 1954 as Service 25 2/4 under ex-Breton resister Marcel Le Roy especially to spy on Paris embassies and open diplomatic pouches. Most of the information supplied by Service 7, however, had proven to be of limited interest. But with the Algerian War raging, it set to work bugging the Egyptian embassy and bribing its concierge to supply copies of embassy correspondence. When nothing concerning FLN activity was discovered in this way, Le Roy and another Service 7 agent entered the embassy at night to crack the safe. Surprised by the approach of a guard, they dodged into the basement and burrowed behind stacks of papers stored there. Daylight came before they could flee, so they were condemned to remain in their hiding place for an entire day.

Toward late morning, a member of the embassy staff came into the basement to throw some more papers onto the stack. To his surprise, Le Roy discovered that the staff member had hurled lists of payments made to FLN operatives in France only a few feet from his hiding place. When night fell, the two agents made their escape. The following day they reappeared at the embassy disguised as workmen sent to clear out the papers in the basement. Not only were they allowed to cart away the papers which only hours before had provided a hiding place, but before they left, an official asked them to clear out the archive room as well.

This operation proved a bitter success for French intelligence. The SDECE turned over the papers to the DST, who called in the Egyptian military attaché. During the course of his interrogation, the DST agent showed him the pilfered documents as proof of his support of the FLN. The existence of Service 7 and the identity of its chief must have been no great secret to the Arabs, for a few days later three North African thugs knocked at the door of Le Roy's apartment. When his wife opened the door, she was given a beating of such severity that she never recovered, and in fact she died two years later as a result. Service 7's tendency to play fast and loose with legality would also lead to the arrest of Le Roy and the dissolution of the service following the Ben Barka scandal some years later.[15]

Nor were Arab political leaders immune from attack. In January 1956, Service Action hired two Paris gangsters to assassinate Allal El Fassi, leader of the Moroccan Nationalist Party, Istiqlâl, at the Hotel Dersa at Tétouan in the Spanish zone of Morocco. The two men got drunk on the plane and dropped a sack of grenades which they were carrying. This obliged them to get down on all fours to retrieve the grenades, which had rolled under the seats of the other passengers. In Tétouan, they made a mess of placing the charge, so that it harmed no one. Alerted, the Spanish police picked them up, forcing the SDECE to insist that they were wanted for a serious crime in Paris to secure their extradition. The Tétouan fiasco illustrates, first, how French intelligence operations carried out on foreign soil made other states, in this case Spain, less sympathetic with Paris' position that the Algerian problem was one of internal French concerns. Second, it betrayed a naive streak in the SDECE, which obviously believed that hiring criminals offered an efficient method of striking at terrorist targets. In this instance, they were repaid, quite literally, in their own currency. Although the criminals had been advanced a substantial sum of money for "expenses" as well as some sophisticated radio equipment (which they subsequently sold), for an operation which they had completely botched, the underworld demanded full payment nonetheless. When Service Action refused to pay, the gangsters threatened to murder the second-in-command.[16]

If, as will be seen, the DST increasingly ceded primacy of place in Algeria to military intelligence,[17] it still had a significant role to play in the battle to limit FLN influence among the hundreds of thousands of Algerian Muslims in France. From January 1957, the FLN began to deepen their influence in France's community of Algerian students, workers, and shopkeepers. In his memoirs, Wybot boasts of the great success the DST registered against the FLN. While all intelligence services played a role, "only the DST launched the operations which led to the complete disorganization of the leadership of the rebellion in France, and struck deeply at FLN morale in Algeria." His methods, Wybot insisted, were those of the Resistance—introduce double agents into networks devoted to terrorism or to collecting funds, assist their advancement by allowing the success of their operations, many of which were bogus, while aborting those of their rivals. "Some of our agents arrived at the highest echelons of the FLN leadership," Wybot boasted, even though this activity absorbed 70 percent of DST manpower. Wybot did concede that on occasion the FLN successfully circumvented DST action against money collection in France by utilizing "objective allies"—that is, left-wing French sympathizers whom the left-leaning governments of the Fourth Republic were reluctant to prosecute—as *porteurs de valises*.[18]

British historian of the Algerian War Alistair Horne contests Wybot's version of DST achievement, however. The FLN enjoyed remarkable success until the end of the war in imposing its authority on the Algerian community in France and in collecting substantial funds from them. "Objective allies" certainly played a significant role in this FLN triumph. One of the most important networks operated for three years under the direction of Marxist professor Jean Jeanson, and specialized in hiding terrorists, spiriting French deserters out of the country, and above all in smuggling an estimated ten billion francs from France to Switzerland for the FLN. Horne attributes the extraordinary longevity of the Jeanson network less to government protection than to the "extraordinary incompetence" of the DST. When the DST finally did move in on the Jeanson network in 1960, Jeanson escaped and continued to give press conferences under the very noses of the police and publish ringing indictments of French policy in Algeria.[19]

The principal reason why it was important to dry up monetary support for the FLN was that the money collected was invested in arms to fight French forces in Algeria, a third way in which intelligence sought to isolate the battlefield. The importance of blocking the arms shipments became obvious in February 1955, when a Jordanian royal yacht loaded with arms beached off the coast of Morocco and the weapons were carried into the mountains. At the beginning of the war, the SDECE realized that they knew little about the arms trade, and had to establish a list of known arms depots and dealers. Arms shipments could be traced by keeping a close watch on catalogues of armaments inventories and then keeping close tabs on shipping cables, sources which could be supplemented by reading FLN radio codes, tapping phone lines at Egyptian embassies in Switzerland and Germany, or through Israeli sources. The SDECE also used deception—it established a company in Madrid to sell arms to the FLN. It then alerted French maritime and air services of the destinations, so that the arms could be repossessed, and presumably sold again. The SDECE's war against the arms trade was to have a profound influence on French policy.

On 14 October 1956, a decommissioned British minesweeper, the *Athos*, flying the Sudanese flag, was intercepted by the French navy. On board were enough weapons to equip 3,000 men, weapons which had been loaded at Alexandria. Whether the interception of the *Athos* came about as a result of a tip by the Israeli secret service, the Mossad, or, as French journalists Roger Faligot and Pascal Krop insist, was a purely SDECE-inspired bust,[20] the impact on French policy was significant. The French were already enraged by Nasser's political support for the FLN and by the asylum which he had extended them. Indeed, this allegedly had resulted in an unsuccessful 1954 SDECE assassination attempt against the Egyptian leader.[21] The seizure of the *Athos* and firm evidence of Cairo's support for the FLN tipped the French government into its decision to unleash the Suez operation, which began on 5 November 1956 and ended ignominiously in withdrawal forty hours later. It also appears to have occasioned at least one more unsuccessful attempt on Nasser's life.[22]

Having succeeded in slowing the flow of arms to the FLN in 1956 and 1957 while the French army gained the upper hand in Algeria, the SDECE began to operate ruthlessly against the arms trade. In truth, French intelligence had ample provocation—in December 1957, the Cairo conference brought promises of increased money for arms from Arab and Eastern bloc countries. A Yugoslav ship, the *Slovenija*, carrying 148 tons of arms, many of Czech origin, was intercepted by the French navy off Oran in January 1958. But after de Gaulle came to power in May 1958, he was reluctant to allow his services to intercept ships from communist countries, whose cargoes were usually listed as destined for North Vietnam.[23] The FLN, their pockets fairly bulging with money, also began to attract merchants of death, some of whom were former SS or Sicherheitsdienst operating out of Egypt, Germany, and Switzerland. Some SDECE actions fell into the category of *la bonne guerre*, like supplying instantaneously fusing grenades from SDECE-run arms factories in Spain or Switzerland or substituting cargoes of cheese for arms. In all, six ships were boarded on the high seas and their cargoes seized between 1956 and 1961.

But as early as September 1956, the SDECE was sponsoring assassinations of arms suppliers and their FLN contacts in Germany and Switzerland under the auspices of Operation Homo (for "homicide"). German arms dealer Otto Schluter canceled his contracts with the FLN after his mother was vaporized by a car bomb. In March 1957, the Swiss Attorney General committed suicide after it was revealed that he had handed over to the French names of FLN arms suppliers and transcripts of telephone taps on the Egyptian embassy in Bern. An FLN representative was gunned down in the streets of Bonn in November 1957. Another German arms dealer, Hans Paulman, was captured when his plane with its cargo of arms, which he had attempted to fly into North Africa from Italy, was forced down in Oran.[24]

Much SDECE attention focused on the German Georg Puchert, a man whom the Algerian War had transformed from a petty smuggler of whiskey and cigarettes who operated out of Tangier into one of the FLN's major arms suppliers in Morocco. A Service Action team was sent to Tangier to sink Puchert's boats, only to discover on their arrival that they had neglected to bring explosives, so that a naval mine had to be dispatched to Tangier on board an Air France plane. Although Puchert lost several of his speedy boats, he failed to be dissuaded. Service 7 even infiltrated one of its agents into Puchert's organization to track his shipments. The agent displayed his lack of professional commitment, however, when he fell madly in love with Puchert's daughter, failed to keep the SDECE informed, and even tried to warn the smuggler when he learned that the SDECE planned to assassinate him. Enraged to discover that his daughter's lover was an SDECE agent, Puchert threw him out of the house. In September 1958, one of Puchert's explosives experts was found dead in a Geneva hotel, a poisoned dart embedded in his neck. In that same month, the freighter *Atlas*, whose hold was filled with Norwegian dynamite destined for the FLN, blew up in Hamburg harbor. The fact that the Service Action had employed an easily traceable French naval mine caused the enraged burgermeister to deny French ships entry into his port. Six months later, a bomb containing ball bearings placed under the seat of Puchert's Mercedes in Frankfurt exploded and killed him.[25] These assassinations were blamed on a shadowy and probably fictitious organization called the Main Rouge—the Red Hand.[26] But the only hand which most chose to see behind these assassinations was that of the SDECE's Service Action.

On balance, one can argue that the SDECE campaign against the arms dealers was counterproductive. It is certainly true that by the end of 1958, if not before, the French army in Algeria had taken the measure of the ALN, which had to abandon its Maoist-inspired goal of equaling and then besting the French army in the field, as had Giap. The interruption of the arms trade played some part in enabling the French to outgun the ALN, but probably a far less important part than had barrier interdiction along the Tunisian and Moroccan borders. The SDECE could do little to interrupt the flow of arms to the ALN in Tunisia, where it maintained a substantial force as an important political symbol of the FLN's determination to continue the struggle. But by the end of 1958, the FLN had shifted its goal from military to political victory. Its *katibas* (companies) broke up into small terrorist squads whose purpose was to commit outrages that would keep the struggle going within Algeria, while the FLN isolated France politically at the UN and gradually convinced Paris that it must cut its losses in Algeria. The SDECE contributed to the success of FLN strategy in at least two ways: First, by exporting the struggle, extending the battlefield to other nations, Service Action operations succeeded in making even France's allies eager to end the war. As a result, they began to pressure France to come to terms with the FLN.

Second, SDECE operations abroad helped to neutralize potential French propaganda victories in the face of FLN terrorist outrages. It served to deepen de Gaulle's professed distrust of his intelligence services which employed "methods not worthy of gentlemen."[27] According to the anti-Gaullist Thyraud de Vosjoli, however, though de Gaulle may have disapproved of Service Action methods, he was not above using them. "Assassination is part of the daily routine of the men in the Service Action of the SDECE," Thyraud de Vosjoli insisted. "They dutifully carry out their orders and are proud of their skill, confident that it is equal to that of the Gestapo or the KGB." Such was the depth of their vengeance, Thyraud de Vosjoli insisted, that in October 1962, after the Algerian War was over, they even assassinated Italian oil magnate Enrico Mattei, whose plane crashed after he had signed a deal with the FLN to exploit Saharan oil.[28] Intelligence officials dismiss Thyraud de Vosjoli's accusations as the ranting of a disaffected agent.[29] Yet it is quite clear that French intelligence officials were prepared to go to extraordinary lengths to pursue their own aims, as the Ben Bella episode was to prove.

Ahmed Ben Bella was a well-decorated veteran of the French army in World War II, revolted enough by Sétif and *pied noir* electoral frauds to join the nationalist Organisation Spéciale. In 1949, he was arrested by the French after he led a botched bank raid to secure funds for the OS. His prison escape came about by methods so banal that it is hard to imagine that French jailers failed to detect it—Ben Bella sawed through the bars of his cell with a file smuggled into prison in a loaf of bread! In 1954, Ben Bella numbered among the *neuf historiques*—nine founders—of the FLN. Charged with gathering financial support and arranging arms deals for the FLN in Cairo, Tunis, and Rabat, Ben Bella had been singled out by French intelligence as their prime target. This was a sort of decapitation strategy dominated by the ethnocentric—not to say racist—assumption that if the FLN stimulus outside of Algeria could be removed, then the rebellion within Algeria would collapse for lack of any solid base of internal support. French assassination teams led by the *pied noir* André Achiary, a sometime SDECE agent with a checkered past and strong ties with organized crime, had failed to kill Ben Bella. An Achiary assassin had crept into Ben Bella's hotel room in Cairo in mid-December, fired a shot at the Algerian, and missed! A bomb which exploded in front of Ben Bella's Cairo office in early 1956 left the Algerian unscathed, as did a *pied noir* assassin who tracked him down in Tripoli but who was himself killed for his trouble.

In October 1956 at the moment the French were contemplating the Suez operation, Ben Bella was in the Spanish Sahara preparing for the reception of the *Athos* and its cargo of arms. Ben Bella's movements were tracked by Colonel Jean Gardes, who headed the Deuxième Bureau at Rabat. Howard Simpson, a United States Information Service representative who had met Gardes when he had headed the French Army Information Service in Saigon, described him as "a whirlwind of energy and ideas," one of a clutch of young French officers eager to integrate the ideas of Mao into the service of counterinsurgency warfare.[30] Although it has been suggested that Israeli intelligence was instrumental in helping the French keep track of Ben Bella, Colonel Henri Jacquin insists that his movements were well known because his meetings with Mohammed V were well publicized by the FLN as evidence of the Sultan's support for the rebellion. What the FLN was especially proud to announce was that Ben Bella had been issued an invitation to fly from Rabat to Tunis for a "summit" between Arab and FLN leaders on board the Sultan's private plane.[31]

On 22 October 1956, Gardes phoned Colonel Ducournau, a tough paratroop officer serving as military adviser to the governor general of Algeria, Robert Lacoste, to announce a change of plans. Ben Bella and four other FLN members would not be traveling aboard the Sultan's private plane but would be on an Air Atlas DC-3. Algiers realized that they had a golden opportunity to hijack Ben Bella as he flew past Algeria. When the Air Atlas plane made an intermediate stop at Palma de Mallorca, Oran radioed the pilot, who, like the rest of the crew, was a French national, and relayed orders from the French Defense Ministry to fly directly to Algiers. The pilot, an air force reservist, obeyed after orders were broadcast in the clear to shoot down his plane if he tried to return to Morocco. The air hostess distracted the Algerians with idle chatter and cards and pulled down the blinds so that the passengers would fail to notice that the plane was circling to approximate the Tunis arrival time. Only when they saw the French troops and tanks drawn up on the tarmac did the Algerians realize that they had landed at the Maison Blanche airport in Algiers.

The capture of Ben Bella, who languished for the remainder of the war in French prisons, was a brilliant intelligence coup, a tactical masterpiece which spawned a strategic disaster. Although the army, the intelligence services, and the *pied noir* community were transported by the news, the government was deeply embarrassed by the international outcry over the violation of international law, which included resignations of French diplomats and anti-French riots in Morocco that claimed the lives of forty-nine French civilians there. Government officials scurried to declare failure an orphan, and to this day it is unclear who, if anyone, in a position of political responsibility approved the operation.[32] The French Prime Minister, Guy Mollet, a socialist, considered releasing the Algerians, but feared that the *pieds noirs* would explode with rage. Therefore, he elected to digest the fait accompli presented him by his intelligence services.

The most serious consequence of Ben Bella's arrest was that it scuttled attempts by Tunisian President Habib Bourguiba and Mohammed V of Morocco to broker a settlement between the French and the FLN. Bourguiba, who had festooned Tunis for his Arab summit, was enraged by the French action and resolved to support the ALN on his territory. For his part, the Sultan took the removal of passengers, whom he considered his guests, from a plane of his nation as a personal insult. Hard-liners in the FLN, though outwardly incensed, were secretly delighted that the French had eliminated the most powerful opponent of the unbending stance taken at the Soumman Conference in the summer of 1956, that the FLN would fight until all French were driven from Algerian soil—no partition, no dual citizenship, no "Third Force" government, no compromise. Had Ben Bella been left at liberty, he would no doubt have accentuated the divisions in the FLN leadership and softened their uncompromising positions, thereby offering an alternative to protracted war. It was the old story of French repression falling hardest on moderates, eliminating the middle ground, and stiffening the resolve of their opponents to fight on. Once again, the secret services had proved to be a loose cannon, an organization out of control, of dubious moral value, whose actions served no general strategic plan.

The conclusion is inescapable that the combined efforts of the secret services to combat the external threat posed by FLN leaders abroad and arms dealers undermined, rather than advanced, long-term French interests. On one level, one must not be too hard on the secret services. France, after all, had no policy in Algeria beyond military victory. Therefore, the tactics of the secret services simply mirrored the operational approach to the Algerian problem followed by the French army. On a policy level, assassinations, bombings, and hijacking simply produced a harvest of bad publicity and served to eliminate any spirit of compromise in moderate Arab leaders who had no interest in prolonging the conflict. But operationally, too, these secret service actions were counterproductive, for they neglected to consider war as an interactive process. The FLN's access to arms actually increased as a result of these actions, for it turned to larger corporations not so easily intimidated by SDECE assassins, or to communist bloc countries. Arms could be off-loaded without difficulty in Libya and shipped to the ALN bases in Tunisia, whose numbers were swelling as the result of French repression within Algeria. A smaller but significant traffic filtered through Morocco.

But by 1958, the FLN's ability to acquire arms was to have little impact on the war. In September 1957, the French completed the Morice Line, which ran the length of the Tunisian frontier from the Mediterranean to the Sahara's Grand Erg of trackless dunes. Bloodily repulsed each time they tried to go around, under, or through the Morice Line, the 10,000 ALN troops in Tunisia were effectively severed from the battlefield by April 1958. Similar fortifications kept smaller FLN forces in Morocco at bay, while naval patrols along the coast of Algeria stopped infiltrations of arms and troops. The FLN could and did import heavier weapons. But they could never match the French in the competition of firepower. Furthermore, in 1959, the French commander in Algeria, General Maurice Challe, perfected a series of mobile operations which left the *katibas* reeling.

The FLN realized that attempts to mass even limited numbers of troops against the French was suicidal. Forced to reassess their strategy, they elected to abandon their regional command structures inside Algeria, the *wilayas*, to their own fates, maintain their army in Tunisia as a symbol of continued resistance, and seek the political victory which SDECE actions had made more, not less, possible.

SIXTEEN

THE WAR WITHIN ALGERIA

If French intelligence played a role of dubious value in the external war against the FLN, it did prove indispensable in the battle against the FLN within Algeria. As Sir Robert Thompson, the man who guided the British to victory in the insurgency war in Malaya between 1948 and 1960, recognized, unless priority is given to intelligence gathering in an insurgency war, then the government forfeits all hope of victory.[1] On the other hand, the lesson of Algeria, as at Dien Bien Phu, is that good intelligence cannot in itself supply the margin of victory in an insurgency war. This lesson was not immediately apparent to the French, however, whose tactical, as opposed to strategic or operational, intelligence in Indochina had generally been of poor quality. The fact that the French knew little of their adversary in the early days of the rebellion, and that they lacked planes for air reconnaissance, condemned their early tactics of *ratissage* (combing an area) and *bouclage* (sealing a sector and then "beating" the ground in the direction of the blocking force) to disappointment, and allowed the rebellion to survive its first winter. Throughout 1955, French officials merely posted new eruptions on the "syphilis chart," the map used to track new outbreaks of insurgent activity.

In fact, it appears that the French army did not get serious about organizing their intelligence services until the spring of 1956, when

Governor General Robert Lacoste began to exploit the special powers granted him by the French National Assembly. In part, the lag can be explained by the slow disengagement of French forces from Indochina and by the fact that it took some time for the French government to admit that Algerian operations were anything more than a "maintenance of order." Only after a successful raid against an FLN hideout in the south in the autumn of 1955, almost a year after the outbreak of the rebellion, netted a rich harvest of FLN documents did the Deuxième Bureau begin to build up a clear picture of the enemy.[2] Indeed, like the French Resistance in World War II, the FLN lacked security-consciousness—it generated enormous amounts of paper, often explaining in detail a plan or an operation, or demanding a citation or decoration for a particular individual, which supplied the French with a great deal of information throughout the war.

Still, the absence of any urgency given to the intelligence dimension of the war is somewhat surprising given the fact that the resident minister in Algeria in 1955 was none other than Jacques Soustelle, former head of the BCRA/DGSS. But intelligence had seldom been given a high priority on the unit level in the French army. Ambitious officers shunned intelligence work, which usually devolved, along with a multiplicity of other duties, upon a relatively junior officer. The army discovered that it had to train 600 intelligence officers and create a panoply of structures to centralize and analyze intelligence and integrate it into operations. It also needed dramatically to expand the Section Administrative Spécialisée (SAS) and Section Administrative Urbaine (SAU), direct heirs of the old Arab Bureau, made up of officers who spoke the indigenous language and could live among the native populations.[3]

Worse, the French army in the colonies proved to be its own worst enemy when it came to efficient intelligence gathering. Students of the Algerian War have explained French military practices there, such as "collective responsibility"—an indiscriminate retaliation against the Muslim population in response to sabotage or ambushes—and torture of FLN suspects as spontaneous ad hoc responses by French units powerless to distinguish friend from foe, unable to identify precise culprits or targets. But French units did not resort to these dubious practices because they lacked intelligence. Rather, they lacked intelligence because they resorted to these practices. Algeria was not the exception but rather the place where the French army revived, refined, and institutionalized habits developed over years, habits which could only erode hopes of French victory.

Collective responsibility received quasi-official benediction in Algeria when the indiscriminate reprisals of French paratroops and *pieds noirs*, enraged by the atrocious massacres of seventy-one Europeans by the FLN at Philippeville on 20 August 1955, caused the deaths of at least 1,273 "insurgents."[4] But these habits had returned with French troops from Indochina. "Unfortunately brutality and bestiality were not exclusively reserved for official suspects," wrote the Englishman Henry Ainley, who served in Indochina with the Foreign Legion in the early 1950s. "Rape, beating, burning, torturing of entirely harmless peasants and villagers were of common occurrence in the course of punitive patrols and operations by French troops, throughout the length and breadth of Indochina; the same measures evidently being applied to *bona fide* Vietminh as well. Nor were these measures exclusively applied by the men; officers and NCOs assumed an active and frequently dominating role."[5]

The devastating impact of these practices on the collection of tactical intelligence was a lesson which went unlearned. Englishman Simon Murray, serving with the Legion in the Aurès Mountains in 1961, noted that the population fled at the mere sight of their patrols, leaving the Legionnaires to wring the necks of the chickens, kill the livestock, and burn the villages. "The order to burn the huts came in each case from a captain of the Deuxième Bureau who was with us and presumably knew that these were the dwellings either of the fellagha themselves or sympathizers . . ." Murray wrote. "Just before noon we came across some *mechtas*, and this time the men had not had time to flee. Under questioning by the officer of the Deuxième they refused to admit that they had any dealing with the fell and in fact they had very little to say at all. This all changed when they were put inside one of the huts and it was set ablaze. They started to scream blue murder and when we let them out we couldn't stop them talking.

"One of them was finally elected as spokesman and he said he could lead us to a cache that was filled with arms, and so off we set. We followed him over hills and plains and valleys for about fifteen miles, at the end of which time he said he couldn't find it. We had all stopped and were lying about waiting for the order to move on while the Arab explained his problems to the Deuxième captain. I was sitting just above the Arab who was jabbering away to the officer and waving his arms around in desperation. They were below me on the side of a small valley with a dried-out stream bed at the bottom.

"Suddenly the officer grabbed a sub-machine-gun off a Legionnaire standing near him and as the Arab started to scream in protest he kicked him in the side and sent him rolling down the hill. The machine-gun came quickly to the officer's shoulder and he squirted bullets into the writhing body of the Arab as he rolled down into the dried bed of the stream. When he reached the bottom he was as dead as the stones around him. We left him. We had a long walk back and in between us and our lorries was a mountain barrier 5,000 feet high. Nobody mourned the Arab—it was too hot and we were too tired."[6]

This sort of behavior may have satisfied the thirst for vengeance. But as a quasi-official policy, which it effectively became in the wake of the Philippeville massacres, it served to lock French and Algerians into an upward spiral of violence and retaliation which worked to the FLN's advantage. It was but a short step from Philippeville to a generalized policy of collective responsibility to include indiscriminate bombing of villages in rebel-controlled areas and to "resettlement" (regroupement) of populations in French camps, all of which were military and public relations disasters for France. They were also intelligence disasters, for a wedge of suspicion, hatred, and fear was driven between the French and the very people upon whom they should have relied for intelligence. It also pushed back hopes for political compromise, to the delight of FLN hard-liners. It served FLN needs in courting world opinion, for in the wake of Philippeville the UN General Assembly agreed for the first time to discuss the Algerian problem. The French delegation stormed out in protest over UN interference in what it insisted was a French domestic dispute. But Jacques Soustelle noted with lucidity that the General Assembly vote was "worth more than a convoy of arms."[7] All the more reason that early on he should have concentrated his intelligence assets on the war within Algeria.

The Battle of Algiers

But even the struggle for tactical intelligence would prove disastrous for the French, for a group of officers stormed in to fill the intelligence vacuum in Algeria with more enthusiasm than professionalism. In the process, they imported a hard-hitting "para" culture into a field of endeavor which favored patience and a more cerebral approach. If a trained intelligence officer like the one who accompanied Murray's Legion patrol was behaving with callous brutality late in the war, he was merely following a pattern that had been established early on. The issue that came to exemplify most clearly a flawed vision of intelligence collection, which took hold in the French army, was that of torture. Torture became a public issue during the Battle of Algiers when Jacques Massu's crack 10th Parachute Division was called in to deal with the crisis caused by a wave of FLN bombing in Algeria's first city in January 1957. The general excuse has been that torture was an ad hoc solution forced on the paratroops by exceptional circumstances. Unfortunately, this was not so. Torture, like the indiscriminate, gratuitous brutality often inflicted on the Algerians, had been practiced in Indochina. Massu admitted this but claimed that torture had been used only by a few Vietnamese interpreters, who employed "ancient methods practiced among them, such as suspension by the wrists, perhaps followed by forced swallowing of water."[8]

Massu was probably correct in his charge that most of the torture carried out in Indochina was the work of Vietnamese. But French intelligence officers were hardly innocent witnesses to a few deplorable excesses of Oriental behavior, as Massu implies. Torture had been widespread enough in 1949 for the left-wing Catholic journal *Témoignage chrétien* to write that "it is permitted, recognized, and no one complains." This produced a brief outcry in Christian Democratic circles, which was drowned in the French reversals of 1950 on the RC 4.[9]

In what was most probably a fairly typical pattern of intelligence gathering in French garrisons, Henry Ainley reported that his battalion intelligence officer in Indochina directed a *Bande Noire* made up of a few French NCOs and "Viet deserters, local thugs and fugitives from justice . . . Torture and brutality were routine matters in the questioning of suspects, and frequently I was obliged to be an unwilling and disgusted witness, powerless to intervene," he wrote. Although their job was to collect intelligence on the Vietminh, they "did very well on the side," shaking down the local population. "The *Bande Noire* in various forms and under various appellations was an intrinsic and vital part of the different units forming the French expeditionary force," Ainley insisted.[10]

In fact, the *Bande Noire* to which Ainley refers appears to have been composed of detachments of the Operational Counterintelligence Brigades, each commanded by an SDECE officer, formed in Indochina in April 1951. In 1953 when he became commander-in-chief in Indochina, Henri Navarre expanded and camouflaged them under the name Détachements Opérationels de Protection (DOP).[11] It was possibly members of an intelligence organization of this ilk which Foreign Legion sergeant Henryk Szarek encountered in 1951 on the Paul Doumer Bridge, a mile-and-a-half-long span over the Red River at the entrance to Hanoi: "At nightfall no vehicle is supposed to cross the bridge. I stopped the jeep at the entrance of the bridge coming from downtown. I saw that there was some kind of a sack on the back seat. There were four men in the jeep and they were a little impatient. One of them was a captain, but since I was in charge of the guard I asked them for a special pass they had to show me. After inspecting the pass and counting the number of people, I asked them, 'What's in the sack?' 'None of your business,' was the reply. I then told them, 'Do not stop on the bridge. My men have orders to shoot at any vehicle that stops on any part of the bridge.' 'No, we won't stop.' I let the jeep go by. Soon I heard a couple of shots. The jeep had stopped about two-thirds of the way across the bridge, and then kept on going. I called the opposite side of the bridge to tell them to stop the jeep, but it was too late. The guard was on the phone to me when the jeep sped by."

At dawn, the guard led Sergeant Szarek to the spot where the jeep had stopped. "I looked down and saw not only one sack but quite a few sacks containing skeletons, chains, and some lead weights to keep the sacks down on the bottom. After reporting to my commanding officer, we went back onto the bridge with the Duty Officer. That day the river was lower than normal and we could see many skeletons. The DO said: 'Yes, I now know why. The men in the jeep were from intelligence. They were dumping bodies of certain individuals who were no longer of value to them after interrogation. They were Viet-minh who did not want to cooperate under questioning.' I was really angry. Even an enemy shouldn't be treated like that after interrogation . . . but there was nothing I could do to change things."[12]

In Algeria, the DOPs were integrated into the Dispositif de Protection Urbaine (DPU), created by Robert Lacoste and directed by Colonel Roger Trinquier. Despite his forceful advocacy of the failed Indochina maquis and his role as a prime catalyst in the disaster of Dien Bien Phu, Trinquier had emerged as France's greatest theorist of counterinsurgency warfare. Intelligence officer Henri Jacquin complained that Trinquier, and other high-profile advocates of counterinsurgency theory like Yves Godard, now inflicted their "often contradictory and fraudulent theories" on intelligence.[13] The DOP divided the Algiers casbah into sectors, subsectors, blocks, and even buildings, each with a Muslim *responsable*. As Alistair Horne notes, the sort of accountability which this produced did lead to arrest of suspects. But it also often forced the block wardens to choose between assassination by the FLN and lying to the French.[14]

While death at FLN hands hardly offered an alluring prospect, Muslims regarded a tête-à-tête with a French DOP squad as an alternative of almost equal unattractiveness. To be fair to French soldiers, both the DST and the RG in Algiers resorted to the beating of suspects to gain information.[15] The difference now came down to the fact that, while the police selected their victims on the basis of probable cause, the military net was thrown so wide that many innocent young males stood a fair chance of spending an evening with a DOP squad. The French technique was to pick up suspects in the dead of night and then try to break them before the curfew lifted at dawn so other suspects might be caught in their beds. This task fell to the DOP detachments, who, after trying gentle persuasion or the technique of presenting the suspect with a hooded "informer," were "obliged to have recourse to violence," the most infamous being electric-shock torture—the *gégéne*. Massu defended his unit's use of torture in 1957 as necessary to "obtain urgent operational intelligence, upon which depended the lives of innocent human beings, deliberately sacrificed by the FLN to gain its objectives." Torture, he insisted, won the Battle of Algiers for the French.[16]

Even if one accepts Massu's debatable assessment of the value of torture, it is equally certain that it helped to lose them the war. The practice of using the military—especially an elite military unit called in from the exterior like Massu's 10th Paratroop Division—for an internal security operation violated Sir Robert Thompson's first rule of intelligence collection: Intelligence is best collected by a static police unit with established contacts in the population.[17] The French practice of rounding up "suspects" willy-nilly and turning them over to the DOPs to find un bon—that is, a legitimate FLN runner or money collector—was utterly counterproductive. In the first place, the use of the cell system meant that, where it was properly respected, a real terrorist should know only two others. The use of aliases made it difficult to trace the FLN organizational structure to its top levels through interrogation. A much better picture of enemy organization and the identities of many FLN adherents could be discerned through the study of captured documents. The random nature of the French selection of suspects meant that an estimated 40 percent of the male population of the casbah was detained at one time or another. Almost 4,000 people in French custody "disappeared." In other words, there was hardly a Muslim family in Algiers which did not have a family member tortured, unaccounted for, or, at the very least, detained by the French. In this way, the French army in Algiers created a climate of hostility, fear, and antagonism, a policy which reaped the dubious dividend of creating more terrorists than it snagged in the long run. It stimulated bitterness against the French in the Muslim population, which was targeted by the French simply because they were Muslims. It often produced inaccurate intelligence, because suspects said any-thing simply to put an end to the pain. Finally, torture became a serious moral issue in France, where it served to undermine support for the war there. And because the debate over torture was carried out in full view of the world press, France's international reputation suf-fered. For these reasons, Massu's claim that his forces won the Battle of Algiers is open to dispute. For while his intelligence methods had served to hand the FLN a military defeat in a narrow sense, they allowed the FLN to claim a moral and political victory in the Battle of Algiers.

The War in the Bled

The concentration of French military resources in Algiers and along the Morice Line in 1957 and early 1958 had succeeded in isolating the battlefield and allowed the French to inflict significant casualties on the ALN, who threw themselves with desperate abandon at the Morice Line in an attempt to aid the hard-pressed *wilayas*. One of the unintended consequences of French operational superiority was to throw the balance of power within the FLN to the "exterior" leadership in Tunis. These men realized that, even though the ALN had suffered serious military defeats within Algeria, they had made significant progress in advancing their cause in world opinion—in the United Nations, in Paris, and among Algerian Muslims. Therefore, they decided to shift the goal of their struggle from that of military victory against the French army—clearly an impossible task—to that of gaining a political victory. Militarily all they needed to do was to keep the struggle going through terrorist attacks by small suicide teams, while their diplomats worked to pressure the French to realize that *Algérie française* was not worth the costs of continued conflict. However, as the FLN shifted to a political strategy, the French continued to pursue a military victory, to employ their increasing operational superiority in an effort to eliminate the ALN altogether. That task, in which operational intelligence would play a significant role, fell to General Maurice Challe, who took command of French forces in Algeria in the closing weeks of 1958.

On the face of it, Challe made an unlikely candidate to lead a French army on the offensive, his most salient disqualification being that he was an air force general. But he had strengths, the most obvious being a mastery of the requirements of mobile warfare. His exemplary Resistance record, for which he had received the British DSO and Churchill's personal commendation, his contacts in both the Republican camp, which he had served as Prime Minister Guy Mollet's military representative to Anthony Eden during the Suez campaign, and among the Gaullists made him politically correct. Round-faced, pipe-smoking, of jolly and relaxed disposition, Challe was popular with subordinates and superiors alike.

The French commander's first priority when he took command in December 1958 was to locate the fellagha in the countryside. In Challe's case, the problem was not so much to build an intelligence organization as to focus the intelligence resources which the French had been steadily accumulating since the war's beginning. In 1957, a Centre de Coordination Inter-armées (CCI) had been created under Colonel L. Simoneau to oversee all intelligence gathering in Algeria. Divided into "Operational Intelligence," counterintelligence, "Technical," and "Action" services, the CCI utilized 400 officers, sometimes inserted within regular units such as the 157th Infantry at Constantine or the 61st at Oran, whose mission was to provide tactical intelligence. Unfortunately, the CCI had not escaped the general condemnation for the excessive measures used against Muslim "suspects" and their European sympathizers during the Battle of Algiers.[18]

As in Indochina, electronic surveillance offered the French significant intelligence advantages, although the primitive nature of the FLN limited these somewhat. The FLN first began to use radios in 1956, run by Egyptian-trained operators. FLN ciphers posed few mysteries for SDECE code breakers, and intercepted messages had proven useful in predicting ALN attacks on the Morice Line in 1957 and early 1958. By 1960, thirty FLN radios were operating in the interior. Pinpointed by airborne direction finding expanded by Challe, these radios gave away the positions of some command posts and allowed the French to attack them. A few radios were preserved nevertheless to gather information on the state of the maquis, their morale, movements, and matériel situation. For instance, radio intercepts enabled the French to track the disaffection of the commander of wilaya 4, Si Salah, and guide his defection. No political advantage was gained from the Si Salah episode. After meeting with Si Salah, de Gaulle ignored his approach in favor of another appeal to the Algerian Provisional Government (GPRA) in Tunis. The General's biographer gives no satisfactory explanation for this conduct. It is possible, however, that de Gaulle bought into intelligence reports that the GPRA was badly split and on the verge of collapse, and wished to use the Si Salah episode to pressure them into a compromise peace.[19]

In March 1960, an FLN code book captured in *wilaya* 5—the Oranie in western Algeria—allowed the French to track its commander, "Colonel Lofti," and kill him in an ambush. They then substituted a false "Lofti" who called for arms, money, and reinforcements, all of which fell into French hands, until the Algerians finally detected the ruse. As usual, however, eavesdropping worked both ways, and listening posts established in Morocco and Tunisia by Egyptians and East Germans, and possibly on Soviet trawlers offshore, allowed the FLN to listen in on police and possibly army radios, which too often broadcast in the clear. However, because this was done only in late 1960, and because the FLN lacked the communications to enable them to act on the tactical intelligence which this provided, it was probably of limited significance. However, by monitoring police radios, the FLN could contact journalists as soon as one of their number was arrested and launch a press campaign for the person's release.[20]

Air reconnaissance accorded the French advantages in tactical intelligence they had lacked in Indochina. In 1954, there were only twenty aircraft in Algeria, a paucity of air resources which crippled the ability of the French to track down the mobile *katibas*. French air power expanded dramatically in the first six months of 1956, which gave the French the ability, when combined with direction finding and *commandos de chasse*, to locate the *katibas*. This intelligence information was centralized by Jacquin's Bureau d'Etudes et des Liaisons (BEL). When the *katiba* had been spotted, then Challe's second innovation, a "general reserve" of paratroops, Legionnaires, and other elite forces, was ferried in. The combination of a general reserve and the helicopter, which began to appear in ever increasing numbers and varieties from 1955, was to give the French a new strategic mobility. These troops established a perimeter sometimes as large as ten miles in diameter, which was gradually contracted to corner the rebel units. When this was done, air and artillery strikes would be called in, after which the general reserve forces would move in to finish the job. So at last intelligence was slotted into an operational framework in which it could prove to be a great benefit.

The French also appear to have had more success in raising indigenous forces than they had in Indochina—for several reasons. In Algeria, the French reversed the Vietnamization programs of Indochina which had sought to build up a regular Vietnamese National

Army. Desertions among regular Algerian *tirailleur* units caused the French to reduce that once proud force and to limit its employment. Instead, as the war progressed, the French came increasingly to rely on Algerian irregulars, called *harkis*. The first *harkis* began as a tentative experiment in eastern Algeria in the opening months of the war, part of an embryonic pacification program involving the SAS. The presence of a French officer schooled in the native languages and customs formed an essential ingredient in the program's success, and rested on a long tradition in Algeria of native *goums* and police organized by Arab Bureau officers. The *harkis* acted as local village militias, designed to protect and give intelligence, rather than as shock troops. Their numbers rose rapidly from 1957 until they incorporated 60,000 men, which allowed the French to claim with some justification that more Algerians fought for them than for the FLN.

The *harkis* were an important experiment which allowed the French to prevent and even roll back FLN infiltration in certain areas. The fact that from late 1958 the ALN was on the defensive within Algeria reduced the temptation to join the insurgency, unlike Indochina, where from October 1950 the Vietminh were increasingly in the ascendancy. Also, FLN attempts to infiltrate the *harkis* were stymied by the fact that the local, even family, nature of these groups meant that an alert SAS officer could detect an outsider by his dialect, accent, or customs. But though a success, the *harkis* could not be a war winner for the French. There were never enough of them to cover the entire country. And because the SAS program was under the jurisdiction of the Ministry of the Interior, a coordination of strategy with main-force units was too often neglected. A sweep by a general reserve of paras or Legionnaires which treated all Muslims as potential enemies could wipe out in a matter of minutes several months—even years—of patient political work by an SAS officer.

Nor did the French fully trust their *harkis*. They proved reluctant to furnish the *harkis* the arms they required. Problems also occurred when the French tried to transform the *harkis* into something other than local militias. Not surprisingly, these experiments were usually the work of the Service Action forces which had been active in Indochina, with the same sort of mixed results. Some of these forces slipped the leash altogether and managed to become virtual private forces operating for their own accounts, smaller but not unlike the Cao Dai or Binh Xuyen in Vietnam. One such group was led by "General" Bellounis, whose self-styled Armée Nationale Populaire Algérienne was at first supported by the French as an alternative to the FLN in *wilaya* 6 north of the Sahara. But Bellounis was liquidated by Trinquier in 1958 when his actions were deemed no longer to be in French interests.[21] Utterly ignorant of the complex social and linguistic culture of North Africa, French Service Action officers, unlike the more knowledgeable SAS, opened their units to FLN infiltration.

The most notorious example of FLN infiltration occurred during the secret Oiseau Bleu operation of 1956, when an elite *harka* known as Force K, run by elements of the 11ème Choc, turned out to be controlled by the FLN. Paratroops had to be called in to hunt it down, killing 130 of them. However, 600 escaped to the *wilayas*. Wybot condemned the army's handling of Bellounis and other double agents as amateurish, which often led to their discovery and assassination.[22]

On the positive side for the French, the *harkis* provided the nucleus of the *commandos de chasse* developed by Challe to stalk the *katibas* in the mountains. And although the French claimed great success for them, the chart of achievement was not always in the ascendant. The *commandos de chasse* came about after the attempts of purely French commandos of the 11ème Choc enjoyed little success in 1954–56. They were inspired by the legend of the GCMA in Indochina, of whom several were veterans, to "cut lines of communications" and to create "a constant insecurity" by ambushing *wilaya* headquarters. They then tried to play the old French game of exploiting ethnic divisions, in this case those between Arab and Berber, with the creation of Force K in the Kabylia, "General" Bellounis and "Kobus,"[23] which enjoyed as much success as pitting Meo against Vietnamese in Indochina. The ratio of contacts to operations attributable to the *commandos de chasse*, as opposed to radio detection, air reconnaissance, or humint, is not recorded.

What seems to have happened increasingly with the *commandos de chasse* is that they slotted too easily into the French counterterror operations in the countryside, operations of dubious political value. They also played a part in the deception, or *bleuite*, techniques developed during the Battle of Algiers by Captain Christian Léger, head

of the Groupement de Renseignement et d'Exploitation, another organization linked to Trinquier's DPU.

A Moroccan-born *pied noir*, Léger had dark features that could allow
him to pass for a North African. Experienced in clandestine operations
in France, a veteran of Trinquier's GCMA in Indochina who is alleged
to have participated in the assassinations of arms dealers during a tour
at SDECE headquarters between 1955 and March 1957,[24] practiced
in both Arabic and Kabyle, Léger became a natural coordinator for a
plan to infiltrate FLN ranks. Alerted by an intelligence officer or a
DOP squad that they had a "suspect," Léger would arrive: "Each time,
my technique was the same," Léger remembered. "We would talk and
I would turn him. You know, at the time, it wasn't difficult. You just
had to tell them that it was a civil war, French against French . . .
between a Mohammed and a Dupont. There was never any problem.
Except a few, the purists, who absolutely insisted on an independent
Algeria."[25]

However, a fairly straightforward plan to infiltrate double agents into
the FLN took an original twist when, during one interrogation, Léger
left the room to answer the phone. With the door ajar, he noticed
that the suspect, a young woman, began to examine forged documents
left on the desk which appeared to prove that a well-known FLN leader
was in touch with French intelligence. When Léger released the
woman, she remained in contact for about a week, and then redefected
to *wilaya* 3, where she told of the documents she had seen. This
triggered the natural tensions which lurked barely beneath the surface
of the *wilaya* commands, groups not generally distinguished by their
conviviality, which tended to kill suspects out of hand, often after
torture revealed the names of other suspects, real or imagined.

Why these officers believed that French torture of FLN suspects
gave good intelligence, while FLN torture of suspected infiltrators in
their ranks spread distrust and disinformation, remains one of the least
logical features of the intelligence war on the French side. But when
Léger realized the success of his exercise in *wilaya* 3, he began to
introduce more double agents into the FLN supplied with false information. Dressed in the *bleus du travail*, the workingman's blue-
dyed coveralls common in France, the captured guerrilla was returned
to the casbah or the *bled* as a double agent. If he remained faithful to

Léger, then he could help the French ferret out his former comrades. It was largely through intelligence provided by double agents, and by good police work, rather than by information gained by DOP torture, that the FLN terrorist Yacef and his bomb squad, which had terrorized French Algiers during much of 1957, were tracked down. If the double agent redefected to the FLN, he would produce panic in the *wilayas*, where he would be tortured to get the names of other suspects. Léger fed this panic by spreading false documents which seemed to compromise leaders or suggested widespread infiltration.

Henri Jacquin, commander of the Deuxième Bureau in Algiers, who in 1959 became head of the Bureau d'Etudes et des Liaisons (BEL), into which Léger's team was integrated, trumpeted Léger's success as a perfect use of intelligence to exploit the enemy's main weaknesses—"his natural absence of objectivity, his brutality, his cruelty." He claimed that almost 5,000 executions in the *wilayas* between 1958 and 1960 were the result of the *bleuite*. An ever increasing number of defections occurred because some *wilayas* were systematically executing all FLN ex-POWs who had "escaped" from the French. But one must be careful not to overstate the success of the *bleuite*. By 1960, the FLN was under substantial pressure within Algeria from all directions—the Challe offensives, the Morice Line, the *harkis*, which denied them friendly villages and forced them into caves in the mountains. The numbers of ALN POWs increased from 1960 as members of the *katibas* began to lose faith in the ultimate victory. Certainly, if the FLN executed 5,000 of their own as a result of the *bleuite*, then it was a success cheaply bought. But French intelligence had been notorious for overstating the "climate of insecurity" created by its special operations in Indochina. Also, the *bleuite* actually appears to have compromised intelligence gathering in the *wilayas*, where legitimate double agents introduced by the Centre de Coordination Inter-armées (CCI) fell victim to FLN suspicion.[26]

Nor was the *bleuite* an unqualified success for the French. Suspicion and fear were not confined to the insurgents. The FLN appears to have worked successful deceptions of its own which played on the natural French mistrust of Muslims.

In 1958, the FLN managed to convince the French that the *harka* of Belhadj Djillali, alias "Kobus" or "Pistol," was in fact disloyal. The

French withdrew their support from him, he was assassinated by one of his lieutenants, and several of his followers who defected to the FLN were executed by the revolutionaries. This was one more debacle to add to that of Force K and Bellounis which caused the French to be cautious in their support for the *harkis*.[27] It also provoked complaints from Roger Wybot, perhaps motivated by jealousy but worthy of consideration nonetheless, that Trinquier and Léger had plunged into an intelligence war in which they were out of their depth.[28] The *commandos de chasse*, originally conceived as a tool to provide tactical intelligence, were redirected by the *bleuite* into a sort of counter- or rather extraterrorist unit, perhaps an indication that they were not locating many *katibas* (or that there were a diminishing number of *katibas* to locate). By posing as ALN *katibas*, the *commandos de chasse* would request aid from a village, and then mete out savage reprisals if the village actually provided it. The purpose of this ruse was obviously to dry up support for the FLN by making the population distrustful of everyone.[29] The political benefits the French reaped from this technique were, to say the least, questionable.

So if no counterinsurgency operation can hope to be successful without intelligence, French intelligence can certainly be said to have made a contribution to the decline in the ALN's operational effectiveness. In the absence of documents, it is difficult to know what proportion of success in tracking down *katibas* and cells to attribute to electronic surveillance, air reconnaissance, *commandos de chasse*, torture, careful police work, or a combination of all of these. *Bleuite* introduced confusion into the *wilayas*. Together with other operational innovations, such as the Morice Line, which essentially sealed off the battlefield, they left the ALN within Algeria suspended by a thread. But counterintelligence and counterinsurgency methods could not be decisive so long as they served a policy that was utterly defective. On the contrary, they actually contributed to the French defeat, for they served to root hatred of the French firmly in the Muslim population.

But it is perhaps the *bleuite* which offers the most appropriate metaphor for the dilemma of both sides in this war of deception and distrust fostered by French intelligence. The FLN in the interior was reduced to hunted bands of desperate men, clinging to survival in mountain caves, afraid to act for fear of French countermeasures, deeply fearful of betrayal. This sense of suspicion pursued the FLN in victory after 1962, when a splintered and beleaguered resistance movement offered a weak base for Algerian national unity. But, as has been suggested, the French were not spared the effects of their own tactics. Muslim cooperation must comprise an essential ingredient of any French victory. But the French army never trusted the people it sought to master, and of no group was this more true than of French intelligence.

French intelligence was infected by their own *bleuite*, a paranoia which increasingly came to focus on their own government and ultimately on their own people. The French secret services, mired in their war against the enemy, severed themselves from their political base, lost sight of the purpose of a war which they pursued with such determination. In the end, the French services became the mirror image of the enemy they despised—factious, brutal, distrustful, and ultimately disloyal.

Intelligence and the Fall of the Fourth Republic

To a degree, it appears unfair to blame intelligence for an application of methods which failed to serve the ends of policy, when, as in Indochina, the French government seemed incapable of defining a firm policy. But here again, French intelligence must shoulder its share of the blame for limiting the government's political options. Like the rest of the army, French intelligence was firmly committed to *Algérie française*. For all their talk of reforms to ensure equality for the Muslim population in Algeria, ultimately they supported the interests of the one million *pieds noirs*. The response of the French intelligence community to the eruption of *pied noir* discontent in May 1958 put this beyond doubt.

The insurrection which was to topple the Fourth Republic began on 13 May 1958 with ceremonies before the Algiers *monument aux morts* for three French POWs executed a few days earlier by the FLN. Although the fact that a popular explosion was being actively plotted by several antigovernment groups was the worst-kept secret in France, the government was remarkably unprepared to defend itself. It required only a brief harangue by *pied noir* political activist Pierre Lagaillarde for the *mèche* of rebellion to ignite. Standing before the war memorial, which provided a natural podium at the top of a long flight of steps, Lagaillarde, arrayed in a paratroop uniform and flanked by a dramatic personal bodyguard of four fully armed *harkis*, invited the 20,000 frenzied *pieds noirs* at his feet to rebel. The mob lurched toward the building which housed the Gouvernement-Général, symbol of the despised Fourth Republic, brushed aside a cordon of French riot police who fired a halfhearted volley of tear-gas canisters in retreat, and sacked the building. To demonstrate, to France and the world, their break with the present, they conjured up a powerful image of France's Revolutionary past by forming a Committee of Public Safety. If Lagaillarde cast himself as Robespierre, Massu and Trinquier, who instantly became members, would fumble through roles as Danton and Marat. But the Algiers Committee of Public Safety would prove a pale shadow of the original version of 1793.

When Wybot learned that the Algiers antenna of the DST had also formed a Committee of Public Safety, he ordered it disbanded. But this was not because he opposed the rebellion. On the contrary, his house on Paris' rue d'Ankara had become a nest of secret service intrigue against the Republic. Members of several branches of the police, including the Renseignements Généraux and paras from the SDECE's Service Action, who had collected to plot and plan, sprawled over his house and garden. Every hour the DST chief in Algiers phoned with news of the latest developments supplied by Colonel Yves Godard, another Service Action officer who had joined the rebellion and who had seized control of the Algiers Sûreté.

On the evening of 17–18 May, Wybot received word that a Major Vitasse of the 60th Airborne Company and a personal emissary of Massu, had arrived in Paris from Algiers and wished to speak to him. Vitasse suggested a meeting at a café on the Place Trocadéro. Wybot had no doubt that the paratroop major wanted to discuss Operation Resurrection, the plan hatched by the rebellious soldiers in Algiers led by Massu and Trinquier to invade France and overthrow the government. Nevertheless, because "confidence did not reign at first" and because he feared a trap by rival police, he appeared at the meeting with a substantial bodyguard. As Vitasse had taken identical precautions, the café quickly filled with heavily armed French secret service agents and paras dressed in civilian clothes who eyed each other warily as their chiefs strolled up and down the avenue Georges-Mandel locked in conversation. Displaying the para preference for dramatic entrances, Vitasse requested that the DST secure the Champs de Mars as a landing zone so that the Algiers rebels could parachute in and, with DST complicity, seize the Interior Ministry and other strategic locations in Paris. "My job is to overthrow my boss, Jules Moch," Wybot remembered of those days in May as he canvassed the complicities of top police officials and the SDECE's Service Action for a coup d'état.

His task was a delicate, but not especially difficult one. Like sections of the French army, the secret services had become deeply politicized by the war against the FLN. The Fourth Republic counted few sympathizers among men who viewed all politicians as weak, potentially or actively corrupt, a pusillanimous category of humanity whose predisposition was to cut and run in Algeria, but who were too timorous even to take counsel of their own instincts. Gaullist influence had been assiduously cultivated among the 150 officers and 450 NCOs and soldiers of the SDECE's Service Action by Jacques Foccart. Foccart had also turned the Amicale Action, which grouped the SA's 7,800 reservists into a Gaullist front. Many of these reservists were also active in the RPF's Service d'Action Civique (SAC), which provided both a "security service" for RPF rallies and gangs of toughs to disrupt communist meetings in Paris' Red Belt of suburbs. An unofficial council composed of ex-BCRA and RPF activists led by Foccart regularly met with Action director Colonel Roussillat at his headquarters at Cercottes "to keep them abreast, grosso modo, of what the service was up to."[30] On May 24, elements of the 11ème Choc based in Calvi, with the complicity of pro-Gaullist officials, spearheaded the occupation by paratroops of Corsica, an action in which Foccart played an active coordinating role through military, secret service, and old Resistance contacts. Amicale Action reservists, "thinking they were serving the cause of Algérie française," began to gather at Cercottes, prepared to seize targets designated by Gaullist plotters. One of those targets was SDECE director General Paul Grossin, who, when he caught wind of it, surrounded the SDECE's headquarters on Paris' boulevard Mortier with members of the 11ème Choc loyal to him.[31]

Meanwhile, Moch, declaring that "I won't be Kerensky," continued to hold meetings with his security chiefs "in an atmosphere of growing panic." Wybot was even asked by his boss to provide radios and secret codes so that a Republican commando could infiltrate Corsica. "With Jules Moch, we spent hours putting the final touches on a secret code which, in a Corsica gone over to the revolution, would obviously never be put in service," Wybot wrote. "But that is the sort of game an ago- nizing Republic played right to the end."[32] On the other hand, Moch does not appear to have been completely oblivious to the fact that ele- ments of the Service Action were organizing a pronunciamento.[33]

On 27 May, just hours before Operation Resurrection was to break upon the French capital, de Gaulle announced that he had "begun the regular process necessary to the establishment of a Republican government." The next day, Prime Minister Pierre Pflimlin resigned. On the morning of 29 May, the President of the Republic, René Coty, made public the fact that he had invited Charles de Gaulle to form a government. Twenty-four hours later, the General appeared before the National Assembly to demand full powers to rule by decree for six months, an enforced four months' "holiday" for the deputies, and authority to submit a new constitution. His requests were voted 329 to 224. The Fourth Republic had chosen suicide over assassination by a troika of *pieds noirs*, the army, and its security services.

Disengagement from Algeria
and the War Against the OAS

Given his ill-disguised contempt for *des affaires de basse police*, as de Gaulle is alleged to have categorized intelligence work, it is surprising that French intelligence services should have been high on his list of concerns once back in power. One answer to this is that, contrary to his legend, de Gaulle was very interested in police matters, and with good reason. During World War II, it was the BCRA which had fashioned a political base for the General from the disparate elements of the Resistance. The BCRA had extended its influence over wartime Action missions in France to the point that the Allies had to recognize de Gaulle as a force which had to be taken seriously. The BCRA/ Resistance presence had been the mainstay of the RPF during de

Gaulle's years in the political desert of Colombey-les-Deux-Eglises. Without police and secret service connivance, de Gaulle neither could have returned to power nor, once in power, could he have long survived. According to François Mitterrand, de Gaulle's apparent contempt for his *basse police* was only feigned. The General very much expected them to keep him informed.[34]

De Gaulle appears to have recognized the need to exert as firm a grip over his intelligence services as that which he began to apply to the armed forces. In December 1958, Wybot was put on notice that his fifteen-year tenure as head of the DST had run its course. He was replaced by Gabriel Eriau, former high commissioner of and then ambassador to Morocco. Wybot took the news of his disgrace no better than had his distant predecessor Fouché—he claimed to the end that he had been "sacrificed to the somber mythology" of DST intrigue.[35] More likely, de Gaulle was increasingly aware that he needed to replace some of the more *Algérie française* service directors with others able to distinguish between Gaullism and what the General had come to regard as a failed policy of imperial overstretch. This was especially the case as the FLN commitment to unconditional independence for Algeria made it unlikely that France would be able to wring any face-saving concessions from its intransigent enemy. That prospect would present the Fifth Republic and its President with the greatest threat to its stability—the Organisation Armée Secrète (OAS).

The OAS began life as a gesture of defiance and despair as it began to dawn on die-hard partisans of *Algérie française* that de Gaulle was wavering on what they believed to be his commitment to victory over the FLN. In June 1960, the General publicly offered to open peace talks with an enemy which many of his champions regarded as little better than criminals. Utterances of *"Algérie algérienne"* coming out of the Elysée caused Salan to issue a public caution to the President, who in turn forbade the former French commander-in-chief in Algeria to return there. By February 1961, conspirators were laying the groundwork for an organization to defend French Algeria, an organization which took wings in the wake of the failed April 1961 putsch in Algiers by disaffected French soldiers and *pieds noirs*.[36] Active among the conspirators was a trio of colonels with extensive experience in intelligence, psychological action, and counterinsurgency warfare—

Antoine Argoud, Jean Gardes, Yves Godard. All offered excellent examples of the corrosive effects, both morally and politically, of an excess of intelligence work during a particularly dirty war. Argoud, a graduate of the elite Ecole Polytechnique, was the youngest colonel in the French army and thought to be its most intellectual. He approached the study of counterinsurgency warfare as if it were a metaphysical experience, but practiced it with a ruthlessness during the Battle of Algiers remarkable even by the standards of the 10th Paratroop Division. While head of the Deuxième Bureau in Morocco, Jean Gardes had triggered the Ben Bella kidnapping, after which he returned to Algeria as head of the Cinquième Bureau, which specialized in psychological action. Godard was a veteran of the maquis of the Haute-Savoie in 1944, ex-commander of the 11ème Choc in Indochina, who unsuccessfully had tried to fight his way to Dien Bien Phu with a Laotian maquis in 1954. During the Battle of Algiers, Gardes had served as chief of staff in Massu's 10th Paratroop Division. Throughout the bloody months of 1957, he had become expert on the FLN infrastructure, an expertise which he now harnessed to the cause of rebellion, creating the organizational structure for the OAS based on a hybrid of the FLN and Trinquier's Dispositifs de Protection Urbaine (DPU).

What the OAS hoped to accomplish, beyond the creation of absolute chaos in Algeria and Paris, is unclear. But for men steeped in the theories of *la guerre révolutionnaire*, the evocation of the maquis in their early propaganda tracts had a decidedly Maoist ring about it.[37] Bombings of property began in March 1961, the prelude to the failed putsch of 21–22 April. OAS outrages soon escalated to assassinations of prominent government officials in Algiers, random murders of Muslims, and bank raids. But appeals from officials in Algiers to Interior Minister Roger Frey and even to de Gaulle himself to dispatch reliable police and intelligence teams to Algeria fell on deaf ears in the summer of 1961.

That what was in effect a very small group of active conspirators could achieve results out of all proportion to their numbers appears strange at first. As Wybot's dismissal would appear to suggest, de Gaulle was keen to gain control of his intelligence services. And although Paul Grossin was retained at the SDECE, Jacques Foccart increasingly appears to have taken control of the struggle against the OAS.

The problem was that the French secret services appear to have

been struck by a disarray so remarkable that they were utterly unprepared to confront a threat to French disengagement from Algeria and
to the stability of the Fifth Republic, which the blind could see must
come. This was especially important as the OAS counted some remarkable strengths. First, open support for the April 1961 putsch by
several high-ranking generals including Salan, Challe, André Zeller,
and Edmond Jouhaud offered a thumping endorsement of its ideals.
They were joined by two prominent political figures: Georges Bidault,
the man who had taken over as head of the Conseil National de la
Résistance on the death of Jean Moulin in 1943, and who after the
war had founded the Christian Democratic Party (the MRP), and served
several times as Foreign Minister in the Fourth Republic. The second
was former intelligence chief and governor general of Algeria, Jacques
Soustelle. Next, an especially determined band of killers trained in
the hard war in the *bled* against the FLN supplied its shock troops,
men able to operate with effectiveness because they enjoyed the sympathies of the *pied noir* population of Algiers. And last, the ability of
the new Gaullist government to track them down was compromised
by the complicity with the OAS among police, DST, RG, and Action
officers. In fact, it is not unfair to say that French intelligence was
deeply involved in the war against the OAS—on both sides!

It is difficult to know how far inaction by Paris was due to lack of
concern, to a concentration of the security services in the war against
the FLN and the arms dealers, or to an absence of reliable elements
in the secret service willing to take on the OAS. The SDECE, deployed
principally against the FLN arms networks, proved to be very much
a marginal player in the battle against the OAS, its role limited to
telephone taps of suspected OAS sympathizers, on the pretext that the
OAS was an "internal" problem.[38] But it is difficult to escape the
conclusion that the SDECE kept to the sidelines of this battle largely
because it was riddled with OAS sympathizers, from its *pied noir*
director, Paul Grossin, through the large numbers of men in the Action
branch who had taken on the war against the FLN as a personal
crusade.[39] Even Foccart recognized that the faithful Gaullist legions
so painstakingly cultivated for almost a decade were betraying a reluctance to make war on their former colleagues—in fact, Foccart
scathingly dismissed the Service Action as "an OAS rabble."[40]

Into the autumn of 1961, OAS Delta Force teams led by Roger

Degueldre exacted an increasingly bloody toll of police casualties. This was in part retaliation for some police successes against the OAS— the apprehension in September of an OAS courier with a briefcase full of documents on the Paris–Algiers flight enabled police to sweep up a number of senior army officers in France with OAS sympathies, while in October a renegade police inspector under torture directed his colleagues to the lair of a Delta Force commando in Algiers. But by November 1961, the OAS appeared to be operating at will in Algiers. OAS assassins had created a considerable stir in France when they had struck down the mayor of Evian, where talks between the French government and FLN representatives were being held. De Gaulle had also narrowly escaped an assassination attempt at Pont-sur-Seine.[41]

One security force which did square off against the OAS was the Sécurité Militaire (SM). Normally a sort of military RG which builds up voluminous dossiers on French soldiers, the SM had caught the Action disease. Under its ex-Free French director, air force general Charles Feuvrier, it created a Division des Missions et Recherches to identify and retire officers believed loyal to the OAS and to unmask pilots acting as OAS couriers. But that is not all it did. It infiltrated one of its members into OAS ranks, an ex-parachutist who was subsequently assassinated. It hired a gangster, Jean Augé, whom it sent to Algeria to assassinate two SDECE officers who had gone over to the rebels.[42] When six prominent cafés frequented by OAS sympathizers in Algiers were ripped apart by explosions in November 1961, the culprit was identified as a pro-Gaullist political group, the Mouvement pour la Communauté (MPC), under a former radio producer named Lucien Bitterlin. Bitterlin had been given the explosives by none other than the Sécurité Militaire. With official blessings, Bitterlin formed a group to combat Delta Force, which French intelligence called the *spéciaux* but which the press, with more imagination, dubbed the *barbouzes* (spooks).

Whether the *barbouzes* were amateurs, innocent victims of their own idealism, or sinister elements entirely worthy of the fate which they courted is not entirely clear. A 1982 parliamentary committee dismissed the legend that they had been recruited among the Gaullist Service d'Action Civique, after hearing testimony that the SAC was too *Algérie française* to be considered entirely reliable.[43] Alistair Horne classified the *barbouzes* as a motley of Jewish *pieds noirs*, four Vietnamese experts in torture, and other odds and ends recruited mainly in Algiers karate clubs and weight rooms and from the ranks of nightclub bouncers.[44] Thyraud de Vosjoli believed the criminal elements were dredged up, in the wake of Action refusal to act against the OAS, by two of Foccart's friends—Dominique Pontchardier, a naval officer with special operations experience in Indochina and a sadistic streak, who wrote espionage fiction in his spare time; and Pierre Lemarchand, a defense attorney whose clientele were drawn principally from *le milieu*, the French underworld. Pontchardier provided the Vietnamese, while many of the rest were recruited among Lemarchand's clients of pimps and petty gangsters.[45] Lucien Bitterlin admitted that the 200 or so men recruited for this duty came from disparate backgrounds, but insisted that they were patriots.[46] For Jacques Harstrich, a member of an eighty-man DST/RG Bureau de Liaison (BDL) created to operate against the OAS, "these men were adventurers . . . dropouts," with whom the BDL refused to work.

The BDL collected intelligence based on RG files, telephone taps, informers, and surveillance and passed it to a team of 200 inspectors from the Police Judiciaire known as Force C.[47] It is not clear how much intelligence was provided by the *barbouzes*, although Alistair Horne credits them with guiding Force C toward many of the 600 arrests of OAS suspects, of whom 69 were active assassins.[48] If the principal role of the *barbouzes* was to discourage the *pied noir* population from supporting the OAS by creating the impression of a vast parallel network of Gaullist agents,[49] Thyraud de Vosjoli insisted that goal was soon drowned in an orgy of gratuitous cruelty and sadism.[50] The *barbouzes* certainly distracted Delta Force commandos, who launched spectacular attacks on the various villas which housed the *barbouzes* in December 1961–January 1962. On 29 January 1962, eighteen of the *barbouzes* clustered around a crate which contained a printing press sent from Paris to enable them to print propaganda. As one of them pried it open, a terrific explosion destroyed the three-story building they were in, killing everyone inside.[51] A few days later, a contingent of 25 *barbouzes* were besieged for forty-eight hours in their seedy hotel by Degueldre and his Delta Force. The police did not intervene. The few wounded *barbouzes* who attempted to flee were set upon and their car set alight by *pied noir* onlookers, who danced gleefully around the pyre. So ended the *barbouzes* experiment. Only later did OAS activists conclude that they had wasted their energies attacking a visible target, allowing Force C and the Sécurité Militaire to work at leisure.[52]

Meanwhile, arrests considerably thinned the ranks of the OAS in Algiers and France, and forced others, like activist Captain Pierre Sergent, into a clandestinity so profound that their ability to work mischief bottomed out. But it was also difficult to be effective when the OAS possessed no coherent strategic plan. Sergent organized a few desultory attacks on French communists based on the specious logic that they had provided the true support for the FLN. Another OAS member, André Canal, a businessman and friend of Salan known as "Le Monocle" because of a black monocle worn over an eye injured in an automobile accident, arrived from Algiers with orders from Salan to step up the bombing campaign. This he succeeded in doing in January 1962 in the face of what Alistair Horne categorizes as the "extraordinary lethargy" of the security services.[53] Perhaps the lethargy arose from the fact that the targets of the bombs were mainly left-wing critics of the Algerian War, like Jean-Paul Sartre. But the bombing campaigns had also succeeded in turning French public opinion definitely against the partisans of Algérie française, lubricating de Gaulle's task of disengagement.

Between March and May 1962, the BDL and Force C police gradually decapitated the OAS in Algiers and Paris, using double agents and other tips. Generals Salan and Jouhaud, who had gone into hiding after the failed April 1961 putsch, were arrested, as was Roger Degueldre.[54] "Le Monocle" was apprehended in May, and on 17 June the OAS declared a truce. But OAS diehards, led by Lieutenant Colonel Jean-Marie Bastien-Thiry, set another ambush for de Gaulle at Le Petit-Clamart near Paris on 22 August 1962. De Gaulle, who displayed little concern for his own safety, was outraged that the assassins had attacked him while in the company of his wife, and made Bastien-Thiry's apprehension a personal affair. The authors of the Petit-Clamart ambush were captured in a café in Montmartre on 5 September after a tip by a police informer. All were condemned to death. But of these only Bastien-Thiry was executed.

The OAS was now well and truly on the run. It is alleged that some of its members with BCRA, SDECE, or Action pasts were quietly folded into the networks which Foccart was spinning in the French colonies of sub-Saharan Africa, a prerequisite for the "neocolonialism" de Gaulle planned to practice there. Colonel Argoud, the brilliant maverick who had been rescued by his SDECE friends in the wake of the April 1961 Algiers putsch, had spent two years in meandering exile, alerted by friends in the Interior Ministry or the SDECE so that he could stay one step ahead of those who would kill or kidnap him. In February 1963, on the orders of the Minister of the Interior, Roger Frey, Argoud was kidnapped from the lobby of his Munich hotel by what he insisted were three gangsters. He might be forgiven his error, for at this stage of the battle against the OAS it had become virtually impossible to distinguish at sight officers of the Sécurité Militaire from hit men from le milieu.[55] A few hours later, Argoud was "found" in the back of a van in Paris. Protests poured in from the West German government. The Italians proved more cooperative. They harassed Georges Bidault, who had succeeded Salan as head of the OAS, and renamed it, with more than a touch of nostalgia, the Comité National de la Résistance, until he struck out for South America. The OAS had been shattered. A long, destructive war for France and for her intelligence service came, mercifully, to an end.

In retrospect, France's wars of decolonization in Indochina and Algeria demonstrated how the performance of the French services was shaped by a unique culture of French intelligence. Once again, France had mobilized her intelligence services to support a policy beyond her means. In these conditions, the military character of French intelligence, normally an asset in wartime, became a liability against Vietminh and FLN opponents armed with a sophisticated comprehension of the political dimension of strategies of national liberation. By contrast, French intelligence, keeping faith with French strategy generally, pursued operational solutions which were not only barren of political content but actually counterproductive, because they undermined support for the wars both in France and among the indigenous populations. Finally, the "Action" heritage of the French Resistance was accentuated in the conditions of imperial conflict. French policy appeared barren of result as special operations became a panacea to extricate French policy from inextricable strategic problems. The Indochina "maquis," the bleuite, and the commandos de chasse offered straws to be grasped by leaders desperate for success, to the point that operations came to substitute for strategy and policy.

SEVENTEEN

INTELLIGENCE IN DE GAULLE'S REPUBLIC

—"De vulgaire et de subalterne"

Observers of French intelligence have viewed de Gaulle's ascension to power as the turning point for the secret services. According to Socialist Party deputy Jean-Michel Bellorgey, who led a 1982 parliamentary investigation into secret service activity, intelligence agents driven by Cold War phobias and obsessed with the "enemy within" "took liberties . . . with legality and Republican tradition." For Bellorgey's parliamentary committee, the cold facts were that, during twenty-three years of conservative rule between 1958 and the left-wing electoral victory of 1981, French intelligence agencies accumulated a record of "failures, scandals, and doubtful operations," shielded from accountability by the inflexible law of *"secret-défense."*[1]

Something had certainly changed for French intelligence with the advent of the Fifth Republic. For starters, Wybot was given the sack on 15 December 1958. While the disgraced DST director blasted Gaullian ingratitude, in his more lucid moments he conceded that the General's policy swerve which placed Algeria on the path to independence required men in key positions less committed than Wybot to *Algérie française.*[2]

But the reassuring notion shared by Gaullist and opposition politicians alike that those changes occurred because at a stroke the services had been emancipated from Republican notions of propriety, was on closer examination to prove a politically driven myth. French intelligence services did not mutate virtually overnight into collections of rogue operatives whose mischief was limited only by their imagination, political fanaticism, or personal interests. It takes a selective memory indeed to forget the "failures, scandals, and doubtful operations" of intelligence services in the Fourth Republic. After all, had not the intelligence chiefs, Wybot among them, contributed their own trifle of treachery during the assassination of the Fourth Republic in 1958?

On the face of it, the secret services should have come into their own after 1958. The strong presidential system of government established a consistency of policy which freed French political life from the tyranny of ministerial instability. In theory, this allowed strong and stable links to be established between the politicians and the intelligence community, whose natural conservatism should have accorded well with the views of those in power. But this did not happen. In fact, one can argue that politicians in the Fourth Republic, like Vincent Auriol, relied more on the regular services than did their successors in the Fifth Republic. Why?

Pierre Marion, who took over as SDECE chief in 1981, complained that more than two decades of conservative rule had witnessed the "marginalization" of French intelligence services. The reason for this, he believed, began at the top.[3] One explanation is that the Presidents of the Fifth Republic—de Gaulle (1958–69), Pompidou (1969–74), Giscard d'Estaing (1974–81), and Mitterrand (1981–95)—arrived in office skeptical of the value of intelligence. As early as 1962, de Gaulle compared the SDECE to a popular puppet theater, derisively titling it *"le Guignol."*[4] The General's disdainful February 1966 categorization of the Ben Barka affair as representing all that was *"de vulgaire et de subalterne"* seemed neatly to sum up his attitudes toward intelligence.[5] "The situation under the next two Presidents did not improve," complained Marion, echoing an opinion generally shared by observers of French intelligence. "What use is your thingamajig?" de Gaulle's successor as President, Georges Pompidou, is reported to have asked of SDECE chief General Paul Grossin, insisting that bankers, of which he was one, were better informed than France's intelligence chiefs.[6] Alexandre de Marenches claimed that a year into his presidency, Pompidou contemplated shutting down the SDECE altogether and rebuilding from scratch. And no wonder, as Marenches claims to have taken over an organization more like the mafia than a state agency: "Some agents were running drugs and guns; others were engaged in kidnapping, murder, and the settling of the most bloody scores." For a bribe, criminals could have their police records destroyed. SDECE-produced counterfeit pesetas financed groups intent on destabilizing the Algerian regime. But the SDECE's main product was political scandal generated to discredit powerful politicians, up to and including the President of the Republic.[7] This distrust of the secret services survived the Fifth Republic's lurch to the left in 1981. President François Mitterrand, whose platform promised the abolition of the SDECE, has categorized his secret services as "a costly farce," whose sole purpose is to serve as a vehicle for American influence.[8]

But these attitudes did not come out of thin air. In fact, it is not obvious that de Gaulle initially held deep prejudices against his intelligence services. As has been seen, the BCRA had been virtually the only weapon which he had possessed during much of World War II. Through Passy, de Gaulle manipulated his intelligence service adroitly to organize and dominate the Resistance, the basis for Free France's legitimacy in the eyes of French men and women and allies alike. In 1958, he also appears to have contemplated an important role for the intelligence services in the Fifth Republic. Unfortunately, if his new ministers, inexperienced in government service, had even the most elementary concept of the role of intelligence in a modern state, it was not immediately apparent. When de Gaulle questioned his new cabinet on what sort of intelligence they would find useful, the lengthy silence was eventually broken by Foreign Minister Maurice Couve de Murville, who, choosing an appropriately Gallic culinary metaphor, asked that intelligence be served up à la carte. With a grunt of displeasure, de Gaulle adjourned the meeting, smothering the Conseil Supérieur du Renseignement in its cradle.[9]

Certainly, distrust of the secret services accompanied Pompidou to the Elysée as part of his baggage. And, as will be seen, with good reason! Marion argued that the same could be said for Valéry Giscard d'Estaing, under whose presidency the SDECE was permitted to slide into gentle decomposition under its chief, an affable aristocrat named Alexandre de Marenches. Marion charged that, to Giscard's great annoyance, Marenches preferred to jet around the world hatching plots with foreign services, thus leaving his service leaderless on Paris' bureaucratic fields of battle.[10] Of course, Marion's observations are hardly free of bias. Giscard did take an active interest in certain intelligence operations, especially in Africa, while the SDECE budget increased dramatically during his presidency.[11] Although, as has been suggested, Mitterrand's attitude toward intelligence runs from ambivalent to mistrustful, he among all Presidents put intelligence to best use. The DST's intelligence coup—the intelligence bonanza on Soviet spying in the United States and Europe supplied by a KGB agent which became known as the Farewell dossier—was utilized by Mitterrand to demonstrate to allies and French people alike that, though he had communists in his government, he had no intention of going soft on the Soviets. One consequence has been that the DST in particular has been given far more prominence under Mitterrand.[12]

In the absence of archives, it is difficult to assess the extent of the decline of secret service prestige in the Fifth Republic. The rhetorical commitment of the right wing to the secret services appears to remain strong, especially during annual debates over the intelligence budget, which, like that of defense in earlier days, has supplied a symbolic battleground over which left and right skirmish. But the allegations of the intelligence chiefs seem to ring true for at least two reasons, one systemic, the other more prosaic and historically induced. The creation of the Fifth Republic saw a changed relationship between politicians and civil servants. Under the Fourth Republic, ministries were fragile multiparty coalitions which came and went with dizzying frequency. Politicians composed a vulnerable class, under constant threat from political enemies, eager for any scrap of information which might guarantee their survival in a turbulent parliamentary world. In this situation where ministers were forced to devote most of their time to parliamentary business and their energies to ensuring their political survival, the permanent civil servants supplied the institutional memory, and above all the information, upon which a minister relied. No one party dominated parliament, which gave civil servants independence and autonomy. In any disagreement with a minister, the permanent secretary simply had to hunker down secure in the knowledge that in a matter of weeks, if not hours, he would have a new boss, possibly a complete neophyte, who would be dependent almost completely on him for information. In a regime of this composition, chiefs of the DST, the RG, and even the SDECE could be real powers in the state, with a virtual intelligence monopoly.

This was to change radically under de Gaulle's Republic, although these changes did not occur overnight. In 1958, and for practical purposes for the next two decades, the Gaullist party became what political scientists call a "hegemonic party." The increased powers of the executive and the absence of coalition governments lent greater stability to the regime. Freed from the need to spend most of their days in parliament trying to ensure their political survival, ministers could devote more attention to ministerial business, become more informed, and assume greater control, all of which devalued the quasi-monopoly on information once held by senior civil servants. The result was to subordinate the bureaucracy to the political sector to a degree unknown before 1958. The role of the bureaucracy was to serve the interests of the ruling party.[13] And of no bureaucratic sector was this more true than of the secret services.

The second development which occurred in the Fifth Republic was that the political priorities of the President, especially de Gaulle, diminished the central role of the secret services. Not only that, but increasingly de Gaulle and Pompidou especially came to see the secret services as liabilities rather than assets. It is axiomatic that intelligence is more valuable to the side on the defensive. From 1963, however, de Gaulle seized the initiative in diplomatic affairs. His goal was to project France into the imperium of world powers, a program which required that he loosen the grip of the United States—and eventually the U.S.S.R.—on Europe, which would in turn reassert its independence behind French leadership. Intelligence was not to guide this policy. Quite the contrary, de Gaulle recruited his storm troopers in the Quai d'Orsay, not out of his secret services.

But together with these institutional and policy shifts which contributed to the "marginalization" decried by Marion, government/secret service relations were shaped by more direct differences. Increasingly, Presidents of the Fifth Republic, led by de Gaulle, came to distrust their secret services, regarding them as liabilities rather than assets. Although the Presidents arrived at this conclusion by different routes, their basic response has been the same—to create ad hoc intelligence organizations, temporary structures which they control, duplicating and bypassing the work of the regular services. This pattern is reproduced on the ministerial level. The result has been that, while Marion is correct to argue that the intelligence services have been "marginalized," in a generic sense intelligence has remained a central player in the political history of France for nearly forty years.

For de Gaulle, the problem was that his services did not adapt rapidly enough to his policy shifts. The first crisis came over his abandonment of *Algérie française*, which had firm secret service support, and the subsequent war against the OAS. As has been seen, he had to resort in part to parallel networks, the *barbouzes*, to do work which his regular services were loath to undertake. The same thing occurred after 1963, when his services did not shuffle quickly enough into line behind the radical new Gaullist direction in foreign policy. As a consequence, de Gaulle made it plain that he intended to carry out his foreign policy with his diplomats, not his "irresponsible secret services," who were ordered to sever all relations with the CIA, upon whom they depended for much of their foreign intelligence.[14]

It is ironic, perhaps, that the SDECE has been credited in some circles for the intelligence coup which provoked the very event that allowed de Gaulle's dramatic and revolutionary foreign policy initiative. Ordinarily, Cuba might be considered of fairly peripheral interest to the SDECE. However, this changed when Cuban diplomats began transporting FLN correspondence in their diplomatic pouches and even creating FLN training camps in Cuba, an experiment whose utility was somewhat compromised, according to the SDECE station chief in Washington, Philippe Thyraud de Vosjoli, by the atrocious French spoken by Cuban instructors and Algerian guerrillas. Though SDECE interest in Cuba again waned with the end of the Algerian War in 1962 and the fight against the OAS, Thyraud de Vosjoli maintained his network there, one of the few, he insisted, which survived Castro's crackdown after the March 1961 Bay of Pigs fiasco. By the summer of 1962, Cuban refugee circles in Miami were alive with rumors of Soviet missiles on the island, a state of affairs encouraged if not created by *Our Man in Havana*, a film about a vacuum cleaner salesman who photographed his product and passed off the pictures as those of missiles. Thyraud de Vosjoli claims to have flown to Havana in July and brought back the first reliable agent information about the missiles.[15]

Undoubtedly, Thyraud de Vosjoli's claims for the SDECE are exaggerated. While he probably maintained an agent network there, one possibly financed by the CIA,[16] and while his agents might actually have seen missiles, they were SAMs rather than MRBMs and IRBMs, which arrived only on 8 September. The SDECE station chief fell victim to "agent intoxication," a condition which occurs in intelligence services when agents verify the very intelligence they are asked to check. Thus, when asked if they have spotted any missiles, agents will invariably produce reports of missiles! While the CIA had detected the construction of suspicious sites in August, it was the huge Soviet armada moving toward Cuba in early September which confirmed what was until then only wild agent speculation that the Soviets intended to install intermediate-range missiles in Cuba.[17]

Khrushchev's retreat over the Cuban missile crisis convinced de Gaulle that the U.S.S.R. was no longer a threat to Western Europe. Therefore, he risked little in jeopardizing Franco-American relations to break off in a new foreign policy direction. A nuclear *force de dissuasion* would eliminate any residual Soviet threat to Western Europe.[18] De Gaulle's initiatives came at an awkward time for the French services, for across the Atlantic a secret interrogation was taking place which would sow the seeds of suspicion between de Gaulle and his agents, as well as discredit the SDECE in the eyes of many. On 15 December 1961, a thirty-five-year-old KGB agent named Anatoliy Mikhailovich Golitsyn defected to the American CIA station chief in Helsinki. During the weeks of debriefing by the CIA, Golitsyn charged that Soviet moles had infiltrated NATO headquarters in Paris, important French ministries, and even de Gaulle's intimate entourage. Finally, a spy ring which carried the KGB code name Sapphire had infiltrated the confines of the SDECE. So dire did these warnings seem that in the spring of 1961 the head of CIA counterintelligence, John Jesus Angleton, recommended that CIA director John McCone ask President Kennedy personally to warn de Gaulle. Kennedy duly dispatched a letter to the French President by diplomatic pouch, warning of the Soviet penetrations and expressing full confidence in the reliability of the defector's information. The letter, delivered personally to the Elysée by the CIA station chief in Paris, was read in glacial silence by de Gaulle. Though he expressed disbelief, after uttering various oaths about the spy business the French President promised the CIA representative an investigation.

Kennedy's personal warning was to have unfortunate consequences for the SDECE. Although delivered in a spirit of naive good faith, the American President's letter was interpreted by de Gaulle as a clumsy attempt by the CIA, in league with sympathetic elements in the SDECE, to discredit the Fifth Republic and undermine de Gaulle's credibility at the very moment that he had begun to lead French policy in a direction which the Americans opposed, and he ordered SDECE–CIA contact virtually to cease.[19] This was only one small nail in the coffin of Franco-American relations, which were on the downward slide in any case. But they simply confirmed de Gaulle's distrust of his services.

The investigation promised by de Gaulle also threw the SDECE into turmoil. The Prime Minister's office dispatched General Jean-Louis du Temple de Rougement to debrief Golitsyn, assigned the code name Martel by the French. Impressed, Rougement suggested to de Gaulle that Martel should undergo intensive interrogation by the French. A combined SDECE–DST debriefing team began to shuttle back and forth across the Atlantic with batches of secret documents and dossiers of suspects, many among de Gaulle's and the SDECE's most trusted officials, to be examined by the defector, as Angleton looked on.

As the French investigation achieved an almost frenetic pace, CIA observers began to wonder why no arrests had been made. The obvious answer is that Martel's information was vague and imprecise, spun out and embroidered to enhance his own credibility. But Angleton, who his biographer believes had traversed by this point the narrow border-land which separates professionally cultivated suspicion from profound paranoia, suspected treasonably induced foot-dragging in the allied service. In October 1962, the new SDECE chief, General Paul Jacquier, appeared in Washington for a courtesy call. Instead, he was barbecued by a posse of CIA officials led by Angleton who demanded that he de-mole his service. Predictably in periods of high paranoia and suspicion, senior SDECE officers reciprocated with suspicions that Martel's allegations were a CIA conspiracy to destabilize their service.

This changed somewhat in August 1963, when Martel's claim that there was a spy in NATO headquarters led to a deputy press secretary, Georges Pâques, who was caught red-handed passing NATO documents to his contact in the Soviet embassy. Pâques had apparently been recruited in Algiers in 1944 by André Labarthe.[20] While the capture of a spy normally leaves counterintelligence in a self-congratulatory frame of mind, in this case the mood was less festive. Pâques's arrest appeared to lend credibility to Martel's other allegations, the investigation of which had been utterly stalled for over a year. Worse, Pâques could not have been the source of the paper flow between Paris and Moscow in the late 1950s when Martel had seen the purloined documents—for the simple reason that he had not taken up his NATO post until 1962. At the request of the DST, in November 1963 Prime Minister Pompidou intervened to order an investigation of Colonel Léonard Hounau, General Jacquier's assistant, and an ex-SDECE official, François Saar Demichel, a Resistance hero who had retired from the SDECE in 1949 to direct a profitable import-export business with Eastern Europe. The investigation was entrusted to Colonel Georges de Lannurien. When Lannurien again interrogated Martel in late November 1963, the Soviet defector insisted that at least a dozen SDECE officers were in the pay of the KGB. When this was reported to Pompidou, he ordered Hounau dismissed. Unfortunately for Lannurien, his name was included among the dozen, and he resigned in disgust in 1964.

Another casualty of Martel's accusations was the SDECE station chief in Washington since 1951, Thyraud de Vosjoli. In 1962, when Martel's accusations broke, the SDECE was in the midst of the battle against the OAS. As lists of new suspects poured almost daily from Thyraud de Vosjoli's telex into SDECE headquarters, confusion in Paris ripened into perplexity, and eventually suspicion. Might not Thyraud de Vosjoli's accusations be part of a plot to discredit de Gaulle's Algerian policy by demonstrating that it was formulated by Soviet moles? Had he been recruited by the CIA? To test his loyalty, Thyraud de Vosjoli was instructed by Lannurien to set up a network to gather defense-related intelligence in the United States. But the effect of this request was to confirm Thyraud de Vosjoli's growing conviction that moles abounded around de Gaulle and that he was distrusted by Jacquier and Lannurien. This belief and his distaste for spying on the United States made him a willing accomplice when Angleton, with higher approval, decided in the summer of 1963 to burgle the French embassy in Washington. The objectives of Angleton's embassy expedition were the code books which would allow him to read French diplomatic telexes to find out what, if anything, the French were doing about Golitsyn's Sapphire allegations. Although Thyraud de Vosjoli denied all association with Angleton's burglary, when he was recalled to Paris on 16 September 1963 he claims to have feared that he would be murdered by KGB agents in the SDECE. He sent off a screed of protest to Jacquier in which he announced his resignation. Angleton threw a party for his French friend in a Georgetown restaurant, after which Thyraud de Vosjoli packed his Volkswagen camper and, mistress in tow, fled in secret to Mexico.[21]

In the last few years, students of intelligence have begun to conclude that mole hunts actually do more damage to intelligence services than the actual moles themselves. British historian Phillip Knightley has argued that the impact of spies and moles has been seriously overrated. For instance, while the value to Soviet bomb makers of spies like Klaus Fuchs and the Rosenbergs was negligible, the revelation of these spy rings allowed the CIA to blame their own poor estimates of Soviet nuclear capabilities on internal treason and demand a bigger budget. Even the failure to create a resistance in Albania after the fall of that country to communism, regarded as one of the greatest covert operation failures of post-World War II Western intelligence agencies, could not be attributed to Philby's betrayal, as is often alleged, but rather to CIA–SIS incompetence, lapses in communications security, and the vigilance of the Albanian security police.[22] Georges Pâques certainly believed that the value of the NATO documents, including the plans for NATO's defense of Western Europe, which he delivered to the Soviets was such that it influenced Soviet policy—his handlers obligingly produced a personal letter from Khrushchev attesting to this, although naturally they could not allow Pâques to retain a copy for his files.[23] American historian John Lewis Gaddis has also questioned the impact of spies and moles. Information they supplied was often filtered or disbelieved, the most notorious case being Stalin's dismissal in the summer of 1941 of warnings of Hitler's imminent attack on the Soviet Union. It is unlikely that moles like Philby or Alger Hiss had the power to impact policy formulation in large government organizations. On a lower level, moles might compromise covert operations, most of which offer scant promise of success in any case. At the time of writing, this appears to have been the greatest impact of the Aldrich Ames case on the CIA. Technical intelligence can provide shortcuts, but its value depends on context.[24]

Where moles and fear of moles do exercise a profound influence is on the psychology of intelligence organizations. An "obligatory paranoia" is built into all intelligence organizations. It is a necessary requirement of the job. But it sometimes takes only a slight jolt to transform a free-floating suspicion which prevails in intelligence organizations into what is known as "sick think," a feeling that no one can be trusted, even within one's own organization. This can destroy the morale, efficiency, and value of an intelligence organization, as the Sapphire episode illustrates.[25] The Martel allegations produced false trails similar to that which tied MI5 in knots during the "Fifth Man" search of the 1980s. So debilitating was that episode for British intelligence that the British came to suspect a deliberate destabilization campaign fostered by the KGB. But as British historian of the KGB Christopher Andrew has noted, the equally paranoid Soviets, upset that their spying activities had become a source of media speculation in Britain, believed the Fifth Man mole hunt to be part of a sinister plot by British intelligence to discredit the KGB.[26] The unfortunate effect of Sapphire, however, was that, unlike the Fifth Man, this episode stimulated distrust between two allied services.

Though no moles as important as Burgess, Maclean, Philby, Blunt, or John Cairncross were discovered in France, Andrew believes that Soviet penetration there, especially of the SDECE, was "as least as successful" as in Britain.[27] This was certainly the conclusion of the CIA, where Sapphire reawakened old suspicions of the French services which dated at least from the 1954 *affaire des fuites*. It was widely believed, in America as well as in France, that the leader of Sapphire was none other than Jacques Foccart, the diminutive protégé of the

General who had organized Gaullist party "security services" in the 1950s and who coordinated intelligence services from an office in the Elysée Palace.[28] Both Foccart and Lannurien subsequently went to court to clear their names. De Gaulle's increasingly anti-American policy, which obliged the SDECE to spy *à tous azimuts* (in all directions)—that is, against friend as well as foe—simply confirmed for CIA observers the pro-Soviet sentiments of his entourage.

If the investigation touched off by the Martel accusations induced more turmoil within the SDECE than the Fifth Man mole hunt did in the British services in the 1980s, it was because the French were particularly vulnerable to accusations of Soviet penetration. A psychosis of penetration hovered over the SDECE from the day it inherited the intelligence mission from the BCRA/DGSS, a state of mind rooted in the fear, the certainty almost, that French communists had taken advantage of their positions in the National Council of the Resistance, in the Provisional Government in Algiers, and in the early ministries of the Fourth Republic to infiltrate sympathizers into the secret services. It is alleged that had Admiral Muselier succeeded in replacing de Gaulle as head of the Free French in September 1941, he would have appointed at least three men with direct links to Soviet intelligence to the equivalent of ministerial rank.[29] Pâques, a Free French official who had been recruited in Algiers in 1944 and channeled into high-profile civil service assignments in ministerial cabinets and NATO, seemed to underline that vulnerability. It also appears that Algiers was the venue for the recruitment of Maurice Dejean, who eventually was appointed French ambassador to the Soviet Union by de Gaulle. It is highly probable that Cot's protégé in the French Air Ministry in the 1930s, André Labarthe, used his extensive contacts in the scientific and technical community for the benefit of Soviet intelligence.[30] According to Peter Wright, a senior official in MI5, the low esteem in which French intelligence was held by the British services in the post–World War II period stemmed in part from alleged Soviet penetration of the Free French movement through two of its ministers and Resistance chief Jean Moulin.[31] When Angleton took advantage of a 1963 visit to Washington by DST chief Daniel Doustin to reveal that he suspected that the SDECE's deputy director, Colonel Houneau, had been recruited by the Soviets during his time as French military attaché in Prague,[32] he was probably only confirming Doustin's general mistrust of the SDECE in any case.

In these conditions, it took little for the paranoid tendency to get the upper hand in the SDECE. Colonel Roger Joint-Daguenet, a communications officer who served in the SDECE in the 1950s and 1960s, rejected a promotion to the directorship of SDECE security because this would require him to go after moles in his service. As these suspects inevitably had political connections, and because, he claimed, French politicians would not support a thorough shakeout of the SDECE, he preferred to abandon intelligence work altogether. "I didn't have shoulders large enough to pursue the investigations," he confessed.[33] Alexander de Marenches, SDECE chief under Pompidou and Giscard, adopted the very original defense that Soviet penetration of his service was a compliment to the quality of the SDECE's intelligence product. Although secret microphones had been discovered at SDECE installations, and each year personnel had been dismissed for security reasons, "I hope nonetheless that [the penetration] is not at an important level," he said.[34] Accusations of Soviet penetration of the SDECE have even outlived the Cold War. Oddly enough, even in the left-wing coalition government of François Mitterrand which came to power in 1981, a government which included communist ministers, Interior Minister Gaston Deferre refused to allow his DST to cooperate with Pierre Marion's SDECE because he believed it "a nest of Soviet spies."[35]

The Sapphire affair had a happy outcome for at least one of its dramatis personae—Thyraud de Vosjoli made a fortune by successfully suing Leon Uris, whose 1967 book *Topaz* and the subsequent 1969 film directed by Alfred Hitchcock were based on his experiences. French intelligence specialist Pierre Péan has concluded that "in his novel, Leon Uris was not far from the truth" and that an important Soviet network made up of former attachés and diplomats who had been recruited during postings in Eastern Europe did in fact exist in Paris. He also speculates that the publication of *Topaz* might have been timed by the CIA to destabilize Franco-Soviet détente in 1966.[36] But even if this were so, one can legitimately ask: What difference did it make? For de Gaulle's attempt to end the Soviet status quo in Eastern Europe was a nonstarter in any case, as the 1968 invasion of Czechoslovakia demonstrated in resounding terms.

If the Sapphire episode brought home to de Gaulle that intelligence services were a source of vulnerability rather than of power in the state, the disappearance in broad daylight of Mehdi Ben Barka from the busy boulevard Saint-Germain-des-Prés in the heart of Paris' Left Bank on 29 October 1965 struck at the very foundation of his regime. Ben Barka was a prominent leader both of the Moroccan opposition and of the Nonaligned Movement living in exile in Geneva, and his disappearance could not long remain unnoticed. An investigation quickly revealed that Ben Barka had been detained by two policemen, Roger Voitot and Louis Souchon, attached to the Renseignements Généraux of the Paris Prefecture (RGPP). He had been driven to a house in the Paris suburb of Fontenay-le-Vicomte which belonged to a notorious gangster, Georges Boucheseiche. There, he had been tortured in the presence of General Mohammed Oufkir, Morocco's Minister of the Interior, who apparently was trying to extract the combination of a safe where information on the Nonaligned Movement was kept. Ben Barka, or his body, was then spirited through Orly airport on the night of 30 October with the complicity of the Air France station manager, Antoine Lopez, who had previously managed Air France's operations in Rabat.

On 4 November, de Gaulle personally dispatched a high official from the Quai d'Orsay to meet with King Hassan II to demand the extradition of Oufkir, who up until only a few hours before had been entertained lavishly in official receptions given by his French counterpart, Roger Frey. Hassan II shrugged off all knowledge of the affair, and categorically refused to surrender his Interior Minister, in retrospect a mistake, as Oufkir perished in 1972 while leading an unsuccessful coup against the King. Livid, the French President went on a rant against the ungrateful "little king" who had dared insult him in his own country. He sent a personal letter to Ben Barka's mother promising that "justice will be carried out with the greatest rigor and the greatest speed." By 11 November, Lopez, Souchon and Voitot, and a Moroccan "spy" named El Mahi had been arrested. By the end of the month, a journalist named Philippe Bernier, who had been used to draw Ben Barka to the rendezvous on the pretext that he was to meet a filmmaker, had joined the four in prison.[37]

More was at stake than the General's exaggerated sense of personal dignity. The Ben Barka episode coincided with the beginning of his campaign for a second presidential term. Surprisingly, only one of de Gaulle's four political opponents—François Mitterrand—made an allusion during the campaign to "the unhealthy activities of certain members of the political police who carry out the government's dirty work." And although Mitterrand hinted that the kidnapping had been ordered by Minister of the Interior Roger Frey, even he absolved de Gaulle of any responsibility. De Gaulle sailed back into office on 19 December 1965 with 54.6 percent of the vote.

As the investigation which he had promised Ben Barka's mother progressed into the early months of 1966, embellished with press speculation, rumor, and conspiracy theories, it increasingly appeared that Mitterrand had missed an opportunity to make an issue of the role of the secret services in the state. When assigned to take Ben Barka into custody, Souchon had formally protested to his superiors but was told to proceed nevertheless. Both RGPP agents were cleared of conspiracy but were given six years each for participating in a criminal act.

Lopez, who received eight years in prison, had been in the pay of Marcel Le Roy, whose Service 7 in the SDECE specialized in opening diplomatic pouches, briefcases, and luggage (access to which was obligingly provided by Lopez), searching hotel rooms, and other illegal activities. Le Roy was imprisoned for "nondenunciation of a crime." He was released after 117 days when he began a hunger strike. The trial of the suspects, which began in the summer of 1966 and lasted over a year, eventually cleared Le Roy, "because one had to whitewash the special services."[38] Despite his acquittal, the SDECE refused to reinstate him. Boucheseiche fled to Morocco, where Oufkir housed him in a luxurious villa in Rabat. But he disappeared in August 1982 following Oufkir's unsuccessful coup attempt. Georges Fignon, a character with criminal ties who was believed to have arranged the fatal rendezvous, died by gunshot. Though his death was classified by the police as suicide, the bullet which killed him had been fired from some distance away, causing speculation that the SDECE had used the underworld to silence him. In fact, the investigation revealed a complex and sordid relationship between the Service Action and the underworld. Many, even among de Gaulle's own supporters, began to demand that he make a clean breast of it. Cornered at a 21 February press conference, de Gaulle suggested that his "inexperience" had allowed the Ben Barka affair to get out of hand, a statement which produced an outbreak of mirth in the audience, not all of it cynical. He denounced the kidnapping as a Moroccan affair, "perpetrated with the complicity of agents or members of the French secret service and the participation of criminals recruited here." He castigated the press attention lavished on "a vulgar affair involving subordinates." It was a "mediocre" drama unworthy of France, of "limited" importance, the product of a grotesque fascination with "the mysterious *barbouzes*" and James Bond.[39]

As usual, intelligence was forced to shoulder the blame for bad policy decisions. While de Gaulle biographer Jean Lacouture agrees that the Ben Barka affair was "vulgar," he doubts whether only subalterns were involved. Nor, judging by de Gaulle's reaction to the affair, is it likely that the General believed it of trifling importance. According to one of his close military colleagues, "the Ben Barka affair was for [de Gaulle] as terrible a spotlight on the vulnerability of the system as the putsch of April 1961."[40] It was an attempt to discredit his regime, his NATO policy, and above all his desire to pry the underdeveloped nations away from the two blocs and toward a Gallocentric Third World order. According to this scenario, the kidnapping and probable assassination of a pivotal figure in the Nonaligned Movement like Ben Barka on French soil was a deliberate attempt to sabotage that policy. No one appears to have asked the basic question: What difference did Ben Barka's kidnapping make on the success or failure of de Gaulle's policies? If those policies were realistic, if they had more than a shadow of a chance of success, then Ben Barka was hardly a blip on the screen. If they had no chance of success, then Ben Barka was a nasty episode, certainly, but hardly a critical one.

But from the Gaullian perspective, the French state was under assault by secret forces. Who was to blame? The CIA certainly, believed de Gaulle. The Agency, he was sure, had conspired with Oufkir to embarrass his opening to the Third World and punish him for distancing France from NATO.[41] Suspicion also fell upon Israel. The intelligence relationship between France and Israel predated the foundation of the Jewish state, a bond cemented by the anti-British attitudes of the intelligence services of the two countries. In the immediate postwar years, de Gaulle's services had facilitated Zionist arms-buying sprees in France, allowed the Haganah to establish training camps on French estates, and above all assisted Jewish refugees in their flight to Palestine through Marseille. Early on, Mossad, the Israeli intelligence service, had established close links with the DST, while the Israeli Defense Force from 1949 became successful clients of French and Italian services for military intelligence. This relationship continued into the Algerian War, when Israeli intelligence on the FLN and on Egypt was exchanged for arms and the release of Jews from Morocco and Tunisia. France became a major arms supplier for Israel, and had provided the expertise which allowed Israel to build its nuclear program. It has even been alleged that a tip from Mossad aborted an OAS attempt on de Gaulle's life.[42]

Mossad's role in Ben Barka's kidnapping was probably only a minor one. Mossad had close links with the Moroccan services. According to one account, Oufkir may have used threats against Jews in Morocco to gain Mossad cooperation in luring Ben Barka from Geneva to Paris. De Gaulle did not spare Mossad, and ordered cessation of relations between French and Israeli services in the wake of Ben Barka.[43] Still, this was merely the prelude to the significant breakdown in relations which followed the Six-Day War of 1967. Furious that Israel's preemptive strike in that war had jeopardized his opening to the Arab world, de Gaulle retaliated by suspending sales of Mirages to Israel, followed in 1968 by a complete arms embargo. This brought on a wave of Israeli spying on France which netted the blueprints for Mirage IIIs, and the dramatic theft on Christmas Eve 1969 of patrol boats ordered from France but not delivered.[44] Some elements in the French intelligence services went so far as to blame the events of May 1968, when widespread disorder in France caused de Gaulle's regime to totter, on the Mossad in retaliation for the General's pro-Arab policies. For their part, Mossad accused the French of turning a blind eye to the presence of Arab terrorists in France.[45]

Nor were the French services, the Trojan horse through which old Vichyites or OAS sympathizers hostile to his regime could conspire to discredit him, spared the General's attentions. The RGPP, for which Souchon and Voitot had worked, and which reported to the Prefect of Paris, was fused with the Sûreté Nationale to give the Interior Minister better control over it. The SDECE was taken from the Prime

Minister's office, the hapless Georges Pompidou absorbing the General's ire in front of his entire cabinet for slack supervision, and placed under the Defense Ministry, where he assumed it would be given a dose of military discipline. Jacquier, regarded as loyal but unqualified for intelligence work, was sacked, his place taken by General Eugène Guibaud, unfairly blamed for poor intelligence at Dien Bien Phu.[46] Le Roy's Service 7 was abolished, many of its members seeking employment in the clandestine arms trade, according to Le Roy.[47] De Gaulle disbanded the 11ème Choc, put the Service Action "to sleep," and, according to French writer on intelligence Philippe Bernert, barred the SDECE from internal surveillance operations. So distrustful was de Gaulle of his intelligence services that, when important documents were put before him, he immediately suspected them to be forgeries.[48]

These administrative rearrangements did little to resolve the problems of the French services. On the contrary, as John Lewis Gaddis has noted, "in this field, as in most others, what particular individuals do to, within, and apart from bureaucracies is generally more important than the structure of the bureaucracies themselves."[49] But several factors converged to shape the development of the intelligence services. The first was that, as the Gaullist party settled into its hegemonic position, it became easier to identify national interests with those of the party in power. Intelligence professionals, like other functionaries, were expected to abandon any residual commitment to a politically neutral concept of state service and to support the Gaullists. The intelligence services failed to follow this general bureaucratic development in lockstep, however, for the simple reason that, since the days of the OAS, de Gaulle was never confident that his intelligence services would support his policies. This attitude resulted in two contradictory developments within the French intelligence community. First, intelligence was increasingly pressed into the service of domestic surveillance. Second, de Gaulle tolerated the creation of parallel intelligence networks, with informal links to the regular services, to carry out policies he preferred not to entrust to his regular services. Each practice proved to be dismal legacies to the secret services of the Fifth Republic.

EIGHTEEN

TERRORISTS, PARALLEL
NETWORKS, AND MONSIEUR
PASQUA'S LUNCHEONS

On paper at least, the labor within French intelligence services seems to be logically divided. The SDECE, which in 1981 became the Direction Générale de la Sécurité Extérieure (DGSE), like the CIA or MI6, aimed to gather intelligence on foreign threats to France, while the DST, like the FBI or MI5, is responsible for internal security. However, France has been spared neither the muddle over the frontier between external threat and counterintelligence nor the confusion of competing intelligence services which afflict other nations. The result has been that the SDECE/DGSE and the DST, in waging the espionage battle against the enemies of France, are not always on the same side.

But the French secret services have a third dimension which attracts little attention outside the hexagon but which is a source of significant controversy within France—a panoply of services "unprecedented in a democracy"[1] which focus on the collection of domestic intelligence, the most prominent of which is the Renseignements Généraux (RG). The official mission of the 3,800 employees of the RG is defined as the "research and transmission to the government of necessary information in the political, social, and economic domains." To this end, it prepares reports, conducts briefings, and carries out secret polls for the Minister of the Interior or prefects on popular views on issues or the electoral prospects of individual candidates. It also initiates individual investigations in response to requests by the police, the judiciary, or other sectors of the administration. To this end, it keeps an enormous file of hundreds of thousands of dossiers on individual French men and women built up through surveillance, infiltration of political groups and trade unions, opening mail, tapping telephones, or even simply soliciting opinions. RG files are supplemented by those of the Renseignements Généraux de la Préfecture de Paris (RGPP), whose 700 employees answer to the Prefect of Paris. A third service, the Sécurité Militaire (since 1981 called the Direction de la Protection de la Sécurité de la Défense—DPSD), also plays a role in domestic surveillance. Heir of Vichy's Bureau des Menées Anti-nationales, the DPSD employs 1,660 people, almost as many people as the DST, in an agency "without ideological nuance" to keep a watchful eye over military bases and defense establishments and for subversives in the ranks.[2] In response to intelligence failures in the Gulf War, in April 1992, a Direction du Renseignement Militaire (DRM) was created.

The predictable objection that such an elaborate network of domestic surveillance constitutes a permanent threat to the individual liberties of Frenchmen is countered by the insistence that the RG, RGPP, and SM/DPSD compose a necessary, benign, and neutral tool to protect the state against spies, terrorists, and criminals. While few would question the need to protect society from the three aforementioned categories, the major criticisms are that these services overstep their mandate. Nor can they be accused of benign neutrality. In the 1960s, these intelligence organizations were indentured to Gaullist service, and in the process acquired a right-wing ideological focus which Giscard d'Estaing was unable to broaden by more diverse recruitment. Even the most "objective" intelligence product supplied by these agencies has been a source of conflict. A statistical and polling service (OCSS) was created within the RG in 1964 to conduct opinion polls and prepare surveys or reports to serve as the basis for government electoral programs or predict the outcome of elections. While the quality of its product has been criticized,[3] OCSS public opinion surveys are widely used in government circles, not least by President Mitterrand, who has relied heavily on them to prepare his public broadcasts on contemporary issues.[4] The major complaint about this area of RG activity is that its research is initiated and pressed into the service of the party in power.[5]

RG agent Jacques Harstrich has charged that the partisan character of the RG's role goes beyond its polls and reports. As an RG department chief in the communist-dominated Red Belt of Paris suburbs, Harstrich was expected to maintain a claque of paid "supporters," some of whom most probably were members of an undercover Gaullist organization, the Service d'Action Civique, to turn up at majority political rallies where a public appearance by a minister or even the President of the Republic would otherwise produce an embarrassingly modest, even a hostile, turnout.[6] The RG's mental image of the French population is shaped by a nineteenth-century vision of national purity untainted by notions of democratic pluralism. For instance, during the legislative elections of June 1988, all Jewish residents of Paris' 1st Electoral District received an invitation from a small Jewish organization to a reception for a local Gaullist candidate. It transpired that the guest list was supplied by the 6th Section of the RGPP, which is tasked with the surveillance of foreigners in Paris! The RGPP maintains a classification system which assigns ethnic, cultural, or religious groups to the 6th Section, even those established in France for centuries, according to Vichy-like criteria for "foreignness."[7]

The persistence of such a classification system in a nation whose struggle to define the frontiers of Frenchness is perpetual and highly polemical can hardly bring comfort to groups which might find themselves locked out of the national community. But if the system defines and tags groups, it also catalogues private lives. The invitation to abuse is obvious, especially in a political culture which relies on relationships heavily oiled by personal favors, in which the frontier between private and public interests has become increasingly blurred. The charge is that RG dossiers can contain hearsay, malicious or vindictive information, without benefit of evaluation, the sorts of denunciations which allegedly shocked even the German occupiers of France in World War II by their sheer volume. So long as these remain buried in the RG archives, the damage may be minimal. For high-profile public figures or journalists, especially those of the opposition persuasion, RG files thick with allegations of indiscretions can lie like time bombs waiting to explode. But ordinary citizens, too, may discover that their dossiers have been visited by employers or potential employers. Even one of France's main police unions has blasted the *"véritable pillage"* of RG files for the benefit of private employers.[8]

Portions of these personal files may be composed of telephone taps, a particularly controversial source of domestic intelligence collection. Those who defend telephone taps insist that they have played the critical role in the breakup of various terrorist networks, especially in the 1980s,[9] and in criminal investigations. But more to the point, domestic spying is so embedded in French political culture that politicians, police, and even judges rarely saw a telephone tap they did not like. While phone taps, like opening mail, have always been a bow in the quiver of French secret services, phone tapping in France took off in 1962 during the Gaullist campaign against the OAS with the creation of the Groupement Interministériel de Contrôle (GIC).

The historical context in which phone tapping was expanded is important. The OAS posed a serious terrorist threat for France and one which needed to be eradicated by any means, including phone taps. However, the problem for de Gaulle was that the sense of betrayal expressed by the OAS found a wide audience, even among those in high administrative positions, who were not necessarily prepared to participate in the OAS conspiracies. Therefore, the phone-tapping net had to be spread widely, because opponents of Gaullist disengagement in Algeria automatically fell under suspicion. The scattershot approach of the early days has made phone tapping an activity as difficult to regulate as was the distillation of bathtub gin during Prohibition. The advance in cellular phone communications has produced the novel justification that since eavesdropping is now available to virtually anyone with the necessary equipment, there is little reason for the secret services to show scruples over using it.

In theory, telephone taps, which fall into one of two categories—administrative or judicial—are subject to strict controls. An administrative tap, requested by the Ministry of Defense, the Ministry of the Interior, or the Prefecture of Police, is approved by the Prime Minister's office and forwarded to the GIC's computerized phone-tapping center in the Caserne de Latour-Maubourg, on the avenue de Tourville on Paris' Left Bank, or in one of a number of smaller provincial centers. Phone conversations are taped, a transcript of the conversations is typed, and dispatched for analysis by motorcycle courier to the ministry or service which requested it. The original tape remains with the GIC.

The problems associated with administrative taps are not difficult to imagine. The most frequent accusation is that administrative taps are used for spying on political opponents, journalists, trade unions, even colleagues or other administrations. When the Gaullist Charles Pasqua inherited the Interior Ministry from the socialist Pierre Joxe in 1986, he discovered that his voluminous RG dossier contained transcripts of his private telephone conversations. Reporters who witnessed Pasqua's subsequent show of indignation as he denounced his predecessor who had turned the RG into a "political police force," must have thought it a bid for an Oscar nomination: "I could care less about knowing with whom Monsieur Joxe had lunch," Pasqua declared. "But apparently, he was very interested in my lunches, and in the lunches of the other members of the opposition. We prefer to use public servants in the Criminal Investigation Department for repressing bandits and gangsters."[10] If sighs of resignation were to be heard in the living rooms of France, it could come as no surprise. The politicians who out of power complain loudest about the infringement on individual liberty by the intelligence services of the police are the first to defend domestic surveillance as a requirement of state security once the files and phone taps fall under their management. Still, those who accept domestic surveillance as a noxious if incurable fact of political life in France are able to console themselves with small acts of vengeance on the system. One senator who, knowing that his phone was tapped, ended each conversation with an invective—"*merde au préfet!*"—encountered the prefect at an official reception one day and was asked, "Why do you dislike me so?" A journalist sent his greetings to "the honorable correspondents of the Interior Ministry" each time he picked up his phone. Others have resorted to installing scramblers or jamming devices on their phones, or simply finding an alternate means of communication.[11] The satirical left-wing weekly *Canard enchaîné*, the taps on whose telephones were discovered in a celebrated 1973 incident, has sought its revenge by seeking out spies and whistleblowers in the ministries: "Since the [Fifth Republic] came to power," the editor explained, "we have lived in a society which is more and more secretive. So in the milieus of judges, of tax collectors, of the police, of customs, there are people who are disgusted. We have informants in each of these milieus."[12]

While the abuse of administrative taps by officials has caught public attention, cognoscenti of French domestic intelligence insist that it is the judicial tap which is most subject to abuse.[13] Authorized to carry out a tap by an examining magistrate for whom a case is incomplete without a bulging *dossier d'écoutes* (tap record), the police frequently turn to one of several private firms, enterprises usually run by ex-policemen. It is charged that the authorization of phone taps by examining magistrates has become such an automatic reflex that one judge discovered to his dismay that he had consented to a tap on a member of his own family.

If the number of phone taps in France is a subject of great debate, this is not entirely due to politicians who decry, then deny, the existence of domestic spying. For there also exists a third category of tap more difficult to enumerate—the *sauvage* or unauthorized tap. For instance, an administrative tap can easily become *sauvage* when an official demands a *blanc*, or transcript for which no copy is filed. Judicial taps might also slither into the unauthorized category, especially as they are frequently carried out by private agencies. Phone-tapping agencies might install a tap as a "favor" for ex-colleagues without going through judicial formalities. To these must be added the unauthorized activities of the Elysée Palace, which under both de Gaulle and Mitterrand stands accused of establishing in-house telephone devices to monitor the phones of enemies and of their own staffs.[14] The assumption by any foreign embassy in Paris that its phones are secure from eavesdroppers is a foolish, possibly even dangerous, one to make. Estimates of as many as 72,000 judicial and 30,000 administrative taps are dismissed as wildly exaggerated and beyond the technical capabilities of the listening services. Still, they appear to have become so commonplace that unionized telephone repairmen, who once might have ripped out a tap in the routine course of repairs, now hardly bat an eye.[15]

As will be seen, when properly targeted, as, for example, against a foreign embassy suspected of aiding terrorists, phone tapping can provide useful intelligence. However, as a general rule, the return France has received for its enormous investment in domestic spying is an open question. Transcripts of taps are not admissible as evidence in court. The knowledge that one is likely to be recorded induces caution in politicians, journalists, lawyers, or criminals, who avoid using their phones, speak in code, or devise other evasive techniques: one closely monitored criminal was discovered after the fact to have coordinated his operations from the phone at the neighborhood bakery.[16] Close links between hunters and game in France mean that the latter can be tipped off that their phone and probably their mail are being monitored, as one lawyer who specialized in defending terrorist suspects noted.[17] From the admittedly anecdotal evidence available, it appears that unsuspecting foreigners, especially diplomats apparently unaware that France has been intercepting their dispatches and listening in on their phones for years, are more likely to give away useful information over the phone than are Frenchmen less naive about the capacities of their secret services.

Even in the best of circumstances, the volume of information and the number of the different services involved make coordination, digestion, and the timely use of intelligence acquired in this way a difficult task.[18] But French police do not work in the best of circumstances and the inevitable fragmentation of investigative and intelligence services is complicated by jealousy and rivalry among them. Daniel Burdan, who served in the DST's antiterrorist division, insisted that "the retention of information becomes a sport among the police services," to the point that they are reduced to spying on each other.[19] Jacques Harstrich confessed that May '68 caught the RG completely by surprise because they had utterly ignored the left-wing groups based in universities which touched it off. The names of those who emerged as leaders, such as Alain Geismar and Daniel Cohn-Bendit, were nowhere to be found in the RG's voluminous file of personal dossiers. This changed radically when Interior Minister Raymond Marcellin and his RG chief, Jacques Lenoir, focused substantial resources on the "antileftist struggle," infiltrating left-wing groups and establishing enormous files based on phone taps, mail interception, and informers in schools and universities.[20] The value of such an elaborate apparatus of state surveillance in a period when small cells of left-wing militants, not to mention the general student population, had long ceased to pose a threat to the stability of the Fifth Republic never appears to have been assessed.[21]

Like counterintelligence in general, domestic spying can institutionalize a dangerous mind-set in that portion of the secret services responsible for it. As métiers go, counterintelligence should require a hazardous-to-your-health warning. The search for spies and revolutionaries can, if perpetual and left unevaluated, result in a dangerous psychological disequilibrium, an eternal mole hunt in which the state treats its own citizens as potential subversives. Such was the case of the FBI during the McCarthy era, when anonymous denunciations, which carry with them an automatic presumption of guilt, created a climate of intolerance. France's secret services achieved this psychological condition in the first two decades of the Fifth Republic. De Gaulle's distrust of his own supporters who sympathized with the OAS was easily shifted to the communist left and, in May '68, to the student movement. When services which already "bathe in an atmosphere of spying"[22] fall under a Minister of the Interior obsessed by the threat of the *ennemi intérieur*, the potential for abuse spirals.

Historically, this has proved especially true when the secret services decide to become more "operational," on the theory that they should be able to act on intelligence they generate. Of course, the SDECE operated Service 7 to intercept diplomatic pouches and suitcases and break into the hotel rooms of foreigners. However, in the wake of the May 1968 disturbances, Pompidou's Interior Minister, Raymond Marcellin, possibly influenced by DST and RG reports which associated the disturbances with foreign subversion,[23] decided to take a more muscular approach. The SUBAC group created by Marcellin in the DST to investigate "revolutionaries"[24] received unwelcome public attention in December 1973 when its agents were surprised planting microphones in the editorial offices of *Le Canard enchaîné*. The plumbers were tracking the source of a leak to the newspaper on an investigation linking an important Gaullist deputy with a drug deal. As often happens in scandals involving the secret services, debate raged over whether it was a rogue operation or had been ordered by Marcellin himself, possibly with the cooperation of the CIA.[25]

Under Marcellin, the RG exceeded its acquisition and filing role to acquire a Brigade Opérationnelle Centrale (BOC), whose mission, according to its chief, Jacques Harstrich, was to "destroy" left-wing movements in France. The BOC began to burglarize, introduce agents provocateurs to transform left-wing demonstrations into riots, intercept mail, place taps on telephones, and concoct compromising photos to blackmail political opponents. Marcellin justified this sort of action with the accusation that the people targeted served foreign intelligence services or, like the Maoists supported by Jean-Paul Sartre, they had the potential to evolve into terrorist groups.[26] The official word was that Giscard d'Estaing gradually transformed the BOC into a "research" division after he became President in 1974. But the RG has continued to be a center of scandal. In 1979 it was charged that the BOC had slipped the addresses of two Basque exiles in France to Spanish police, who had them assassinated.[27] According to Jean-Marc Dufourg of the RG's "manipulation section," the communication of identities to Spanish police of Basque militants in France who were subsequently assassinated continued into the Mitterrand presidency, with the blessing of the Elysée. And this despite secret understandings between the French secret services and the ETA of no interference in return for abstaining from terrorist acts in France.[28]

The widely publicized assassination of the Protestant pastor Doucé in July 1990 opened a can of worms in France with the revelation that the RG was implicated in a range of illegal activities including wiretaps, intercepting mail sent to the Communist Party, break-ins of left-wing organizations like SOS Racisme, and, in the Doucé case, the blackmail of pedophiles. This raised calls in parliament for outright abolition of a service whose more serious activities merely duplicate those of journalists and professional pollsters and whose more imaginative ones represent a permanent threat to democracy. It appears, however, that the socialists are content to make the RG more accountable to the police hierarchy, which they decreed in 1992, perhaps eventually merge it with the DST, and clean up its image.[29] "Twenty years ago, I was asked to do illegal things," an RG inspector confessed in 1993. "I diverted mail, conducted stakeouts in front of houses, and planted microphones in offices. Nowadays, only the services involved with terrorism use these methods . . . to my knowledge, anyway. We simply came to the realization that in the matter of political analysis, too many risks were being taken for too few results."[30]

One may doubt the sincerity of these claims. In July 1994, the leadership of the Socialist Party cried foul when Le Canard enchaîné revealed that an RG officer had eavesdropped on a closed-door meeting of the Socialist Party executive. In this way, the Interior Ministry, run by the conservative Charles Pasqua, was able to learn of the resignation of Michel Rocard as party leader at the same moment as the socialist leadership. In its defense, the police inspectorate pointed out that presence at political meetings was part of the RG's mandate, which socialists had defended, when they had been in power, against charges that the RG was harassing Gaullist politicians. Pasqua insisted that these RG reports were no longer useful and ordered that the service stop reporting on political parties. The left-wing *Libération* produced a cartoon of an official comforting a tearful RG officer with the reminder that he was still allowed to spy on trade unionists, journalists, and judges. "Only on the day when the right or the left proposes a law to disband the RG can one take this shrieking seriously," *Le Monde* concluded in an editorial.[31]

The methods of those involved in counterterrorism are of more than academic interest in France, which in the 1980s was struck by a plague of terrorist attacks. The fight against terrorism in France encountered several obstacles from the perspective of the secret services, not the least of which was the sheer numbers of groups, actual or potential, who might engage in terrorism.

During the 1986 parliamentary elections, the right insisted that "France was paying for four or five years of indifference, irresponsibility, and laxity in the face of the problem of international terrorism."[32] The explanation favored by the right has been that France's tradition of asylum, or more specifically her lax immigration laws, has allowed a number of communities with terrorist potential, especially Arab but also Armenian, to settle there. This is not entirely without foundation, especially when external terrorists are able to seek support within communities established in France. But governments of both the right and the left have struck deals of noninterference with political groups which have terrorist potential in return for abstention from attacks on French soil. Such a strategy hardly serves to make France popular with nations that are the object of attacks by terrorists, who then slip back into their French sanctuary. The accusations by the Israelis following the 1972 Lod airport massacre that Paris had become a terrorist crossroads, in keeping with the pro-Arab slant of French policy from 1967, led to friction with the Mossad, which sought to settle accounts with its Arab enemies on French soil. American sources claimed that France and Italy struck agreements with Libya and the PLO in the 1970s for free use of their territory in return for immunity from attack. Without denying these charges, the French government responded with Gaullian indignation: France reserved the right to determine her own policies.[33]

Nor does the collection on French soil of terrorists under a banner of truce exempt France from terrorist problems in the long run. Police can deal with this, as has been seen in the case of the Basques, by leaking information to their natural predators so that France can become the scene of what is known as "a settling of accounts." Truces are also subject to breakdown, as in the summer of 1983 when bomb attacks on Turkish Airways at Orly and other targets in Paris announced that the understanding reached in the late 1970s with the Armenian group ASALA (Armenian Secret Army for the Liberation of Armenia) had lapsed. The books on the ASALA were quickly closed by the DST, because most of them were French residents or citizens with RG files. This was a considerable feather in the cap of these two services and helped to rehabilitate them in the eyes of the socialist government.[34]

The essential cause of the terrorist problem, however, was directly linked to French policies in Lebanon and in the Iran-Iraq War. French intervention in Lebanon opened her to terrorist attacks by radical Arab factions which had always denounced Paris' "pro-Zionist policies." More important, however, Lebanon became entwined in the minds of Iran's leaders with Paris' support for Iraq. A direct link between Lebanon and Iran was supplied when a five-person commando led by the Lebanese Anis Naccache was imprisoned in 1980 after a botched attempt to assassinate the Shah of Iran's last Prime Minister, Chapour Bakhtiar, in the Paris suburb of Neuilly. To liberate these "resisters" and change French policy, Iran organized the taking of French hostages in Lebanon.

Pierre Marion insisted that it was difficult to organize a secret service response to the terrorist threat essentially for two reasons: because French policy in the Middle East was mortgaged to the arms trade and because the response of the secret service community was plagued by the old problems of fragmentation and lack of trust. According to Marion, no consistent counterterrorist policy, especially toward the

Islamic world, could be devised in a state whose Arab policy had fallen hostage to the latest arms deal. "The influence of pro-Iraqi, pro-Libyan, pro-Palestinian lobbies dictates the orientation of external action and blends its effects with the military-industrial complex to increase arms sales," Marion charged.[35]

The sale of French arms to Iraq, which began in 1974, had assumed substantial proportions by 1982, when Baghdad began to insist that unless Paris delivered Super-Etendard fighter-bombers armed with the redoubtable French Exorcet missile, they stood to lose the war. As France did not have enough in stock, in October 1983 five bombers belonging to the French navy were flown by French pilots in the temporary employment of the Dassault arms firm to Baghdad, where they were turned over to the Iraqis. The consequences were not long in coming. At 6:20 on the morning of 23 October 1983, just minutes after a truck loaded with explosives crashed into the U.S. Marine barracks in Beirut killing 241 U.S. troops and wounding 105, a second vehicle barreled toward a nine-story building on Beirut's seashore named the Drakkar, headquarters of the French forces in Beirut. Fifty-eight French paratroops died and fifteen were wounded as the Drakkar pancaked to the ground.

As in the United States, arms, terrorism, and hostage taking became irrevocably intertwined in the Lebanese situation. When the French Director of Industrial Affairs, General René-Pierre Audran, the man responsible for controlling French arms exports, was assassinated as he left for work on 25 January 1985 by members of the French terrorist group Action Directe, the Elysée Palace was furious because, soon after it took office, it had amnestied two leaders of that organization against a promise to cease terrorism, a promise which Action Directe failed to respect.[36] But after a few false starts, French intelligence eventually linked Audran's assassination to a series of Iranian-sponsored bomb blasts which in December 1984 had resulted in the expulsion from France of six Iranian diplomats.

Audran seems to have been the victim of confused French policy at the top. While the Quai d'Orsay continued to back a pro-Iraq policy, Defense Minister Charles Hernu had begun secret arms negotiations with Iran through Audran. According to one theory, Audran's assassination was ordered by Rafsanjani when Mitterrand intervened to prevent the filling of the orders which Audran had taken in Teheran.[37]

Mitterrand's prohibition was short-lived, however, for on 28 February 1986 the *Presse de la Manche* revealed that at least three freighters filled with munitions had cleared Cherbourg harbor with manifests listing Brazil, Thailand, and Portugal as their unlikely destinations. In fact, the three freighters docked at the Iranian port of Bandar Abbas. Marion complained that the influence of the arms dealers reached into the military hierarchy and the SDECE/DGSE itself, which made it difficult to restrict and control arms policy.[38] By December 1987, the fact that France was selling arms to Teheran had been reported in both the American and the British press.[39]

The second obstacle was the fragmented nature of the response of the French government and its secret services to the terrorist threat. Marion fumed that the SDECE/DGSE was completely cut out of the antiterrorist struggle by the DST and the Elysée Palace. But, by his own admission, his service appears to have been badly placed to take a lead in the counterterrorist campaign. An "antiterrorism and anti-subversion" unit existed in the early 1970s which cooperated closely with Mossad on Arab terrorists and their links with Corsican nationalists and built up a substantial dossier on the Basque ETA.[40] When Marion took over the SDECE in 1981, he found only one officer assigned to counterterrorism. The SDECE had done no systematic research and analysis of terrorist groups and had no plans to infiltrate them.[41] The former colonial officers who manned the SDECE's Arab desk "worked at a very colonial cadence" and made no secret of their pro-Arab sentiments. Relations with Mossad, which had excellent intelligence on Arab groups, had been severed. Marion established close contacts with Mossad, the CIA, and the services of Morocco and Tunisia and beefed up his Beirut station, which, he claimed, gave the SDECE, renamed the DGSE in 1982, a better picture of Arab terrorism.

Marion inherited a service which traditionally had reveled in its poor relations with the left, not to mention with the DST. Nor did the DGSE act to retrieve its reputation in the eyes of the Elysée Palace. In the wake of the Drakkar bombing, the DGSE had produced reports blaming it on the KGB. When information collected by West German intelligence through contacts with the Turkish service pointed the finger of guilt at Teheran, the Action section of the DGSE was directed by Mitterrand to prepare an act of revenge. On 7 November 1983, a French jeep full of explosives was parked against the wall of the Iranian embassy in Beirut. However, the detonators failed to work. The Iranians had no trouble tracing the jeep and the explosives to the French. Following a formal protest to the French ambassador in Teheran by the Iranian Minister of Foreign Affairs, the French trade mission there was closed down. The French President, already badly disposed toward the DGSE, fumed against the "incompetence" of his intelligence service. Nor was the reputation of the DGSE salvaged on 17 November when an air raid carried out by eight Super-Etendard fighter-bombers launched from the French carrier *Clemenceau* on a Shiite barracks in the Bekaa Valley apparently produced a shorter than anticipated casualty list. In the recriminations which followed, it was unclear if DGSE intelligence was faulty or if, tipped off in advance, the Shiites and their Iranian advisers had partially evacuated the premises.[42] DGSE efforts to locate French hostages in Lebanon and launch a commando raid to rescue them in 1985 came to nothing, either because, as DGSE sources insisted, they were called off in the wake of the *Rainbow Warrior* scandal of that summer or, as the Quai d'Orsay maintained, Lebanon simply comprised a Sahara of secrets for the DGSE.[43]

The DST's record in the antiterrorist campaign, though far from perfect, appears to have been more credible. One reason why Marion found the SDECE/DGSE so poorly prepared to deal with terrorism may be that Giscard d'Estaing had assigned the DST priority in this mission during his presidency. By some accounts, counterterrorism was a mission accepted with less than resounding enthusiasm by the DST, which saw its central purpose as that of protecting France against penetration by Eastern bloc services. Nor was enthusiasm kindled in 1975 after two unarmed DST agents were shot dead when they surprised the terrorist Carlos in a Left Bank hotel room.[44] A recent book claims that the DST masked their incompetence by creating a myth, with the help of compliant journalists, of Carlos as a glamorous international terrorist, when in fact he was a desperate little man who had few international contacts and whose marksmanship left much to be desired.[45] It is quite possible that this antiterrorist mission overwhelmed the DST's 2,000 agents: "Thus, they are expected to know

the communists, the leftists, the terrorists, the Basques, Occitan, Breton separatists, the movements of the extreme right," wrote Jacques
Harstrich, who complained that his RG was stripped of his informers,
whose "manipulation" was given to the DST. "As they are professional
encyclopedias, they commit errors of interpretation and their informers
begin to have doubts about the quality of their handlers."[46] Gendarme
captain Paul Barril agreed that the twenty-five agents which the DST
assigned to counterterrorism were "completely overwhelmed." But
when in 1981 fifty new posts were created to deal with counterterrorism, according to Barril the DST simply used the windfall to scatter
the new positions through the various services rather than concentrate
them in the counterterrorism division. Still, Barril rated DST work in
this field better than that of the SDECE/DGSE.[47]

The DST appears to have occupied a more central role in the
counterterrorism struggle under the socialists than did the DGSE—
for at least two reasons. The first was that the Farewell dossier—and
the quick roundup of the Armenian terrorists of ASALA after the Orly
bombing redounded to the credit of the DST in Mitterrand's eyes.
The second was that the socialist victory of 1981 found the police, of
which the DST and the RG are part, in a filthy mood, some sections
virtually on the verge of revolt. Mitterrand and his Interior Minister,
the mayor of Marseille, Gaston Deferre, launched a "charm offensive"
toward the police, which included improved career advantages and a
highly publicized "tour of the Paris police stations" in January 1984
by Mitterrand. Once the Prefect of Police and top police slots were in
safe hands, the socialists appear to have felt more confidence in the
DST.[48] This did little to dilute the bad blood between the DST and
the DGSE. Quite the contrary! During the Greenpeace fiasco of 1985,
the DST cooperated with the New Zealand police by handing over
information on DGSE operatives involved in that operation.[49]

In the counterterrorist battle, however, Mitterrand was not content
to rely entirely on the DST. Rather, he obeyed an ancient tradition
in intelligence gathering to create his own secret service, in this case
an antiterrorist cell in the Elysée. Although Pierre Marion denounced
this as the most egregious example of the President's "surprising conceptual and operational incapacity" in questions of intelligence,[50] in
fact Mitterrand was merely acting in a long tradition of French political

leaders who preferred back-channel intelligence, even action, to the official product. To understand that tradition, and how it played out in the crisis of terrorism in the 1980s, one must return to the Fifth Republic's early days and its impresario of parallel secret services, Jacques Foccart.

Parallel Services

In 1958, Thyraud de Vosjoli was escorted into a small side office near the entrance of the Elysée Palace where he discovered a small, bald man who could almost have passed for a cleric, except that he addressed Thyraud de Vosjoli with all the courtesy a senior NCO reserves for a raw recruit. Foccart periodically interrupted his questions about how the CIA organized hit squads, or made contact with the American mafia—"The services of a few thugs could be useful at times"—silently to pick up the receiver attached to an impressive switchboard which sat next to his desk, and take notes. "I had the unpleasant feeling that he was purely and simply listening to conversations not meant for him," Thyraud de Vosjoli concluded.[51]

Thyraud de Vosjoli certainly cannot be taken as an impartial observer. But the shadowy and ill-defined role which Foccart played in the Fifth Republic suggests that he made it his business to listen to conversations not meant for him. The extent of Foccart's powers are almost as mysterious as the question of how he came to acquire them in the first place. A native of Guadeloupe, Foccart had been mobilized in 1939, but had managed to evade capture during the Fall of France. By the war's end, he had emerged as the leader of an important Resistance network in the Basse Normandie whose task had been to delay the arrival of German reinforcements behind the Allied beachhead. According to his biographer Pierre Péan, Foccart's version of his Resistance record in itself constitutes an impressive display of deception. Foccart offered his arrest by the Germans in the summer of 1943 and his subsequent escape into the Resistance as proof of his patriotic bona fides. In fact, Foccart's choice of the Resistance was rather forced upon him after he had jumped bail on a fraud complaint filed by the Todt Organization, charged with construction of the German Atlantic fortifications among other things, for which he worked. No matter, his association with the Resistance, with U.S. army tactical reconnaissance, which awarded Foccart the Medal of Freedom, and above all his contacts with the rising stars of Gaullism like Jacques Chaban-Delmas, cleansed any past misdemeanors (the state paid off Foccart's bail debt) and swept Foccart into Gaullism's inner circle.

Foccart had two strengths required by these upstart Gaullists, who began to assemble their faithful into a political party, the RPF—he was well connected in the SDECE and in the French colonies, especially Africa. Foccart managed to combine these two competencies into what his critics allege was in its day nothing short of a subversion of the French state. While the view of Foccart presented by the left as a cross between Fouché and Himmler is overdrawn, the analogies are not completely fanciful. The controversy swirls around the Service d'Action Civique (SAC). The official line insisted that SAC was merely a high-minded association of Gaullist faithful which traced its origins to the electoral campaign of 1947–48, when the newly founded RPF required a *service d'ordre*, or storm troopers, to fight what became known as the battle of the (Paris) suburbs. With a membership drawn from the nearly 8,000 "reservists"[52]—and possibly an occasional active member—of the SDECE's Service Action and its elite combat unit, the 11ème Choc, the *service d'ordre*'s task was to maintain the upper hand during political rallies in the face of communist militants whose specialty was to silence Gaullist orators by hurling lug nuts from the floor, and to protect Gaullist politicians or groups putting up Gaullist political posters.[53] During electoral campaigns, SAC operatives could provoke "grave incidents" without implicating the Gaullist party politicians. "It was a very useful sacrificial lamb," a 1981 parliamentary investigation of SAC activities recorded.[54]

But the same inquiry insisted that Foccart's ambitions for the organization were not limited to guaranteeing Gaullist politicians their First Amendment rights. Rather, as the "spiritual father" of SAC, he sought to infiltrate the state administration with men utterly loyal to de Gaulle and prepared to act in Gaullist interests. Operating through Masonic and Resistance contacts, Foccart found willing recruits among the police and the secret services, milieus which traditionally believed democracy incompatible with order and secrecy.

By all accounts, Foccart was remarkably successful. The action school, established at Cercottes near Orléans in 1950, became a place of pilgrimage for SAC members in the 1950s where the embers of "the Resistance spirit" were fanned to flame among muscular Gaullists led by Foccart who gathered to parachute, blast, and karate-chop their way to spiritual renewal. When the RPF disbanded in 1954, the faithful in the *service d'ordre* stayed in touch, and helped Foccart to play midwife to de Gaulle's return to power in 1958.[55] In December of the following year, SAC was officially organized.

Under the Fifth Republic, SAC became a sort of Gaullist praetorian guard, "a refuge of Gaullist purity" which reflected the General's distrust of all political parties, including his own. Its self-proclaimed mission was "to support the action of General de Gaulle."[56] The way SAC did this was to become a new Gaullist "Resistance"—a back-channel intelligence, action, and police service for de Gaulle, a band of men under Foccart's orchestration upon whom de Gaulle could count when so many in the regular French services and even RPR officials had been contaminated by *Algérie française* and OAS senti-ments. The commission concluded that the files of the RG and the RGPP were virtually open books for SAC in the 1960s and 1970s, which allowed SAC to keep their own intelligence networks and file system up to scratch. Local SAC militants were not above using theft, false police identifications, or contacts in the DST, RG, or private security services to collect documents relating to political, university, and union affairs.[57] The allegations are that service directors in the SDECE received instructions from Foccart through SAC contacts to spy on or disrupt unions and student groups. Likewise, information reached him directly without passing through the hands of the SDECE chief. The parliamentary committee concluded that SAC had attracted a number of men with criminal records,[58] and had financed itself in mysterious ways, including through SDECE funds and the drug traffic. Under de Gaulle, SAC became so powerful that when he resigned in 1969, other members of the RPF led by Pompidou and Charles Pasqua wanted to carry out a serious purge of SAC membership, if not elim-inate it altogether, because they believed SAC was a threat to the party's control of the Gaullist movement.[59]

SAC and the secret services provided a vehicle through which Foccart developed his second area of expertise—his relations with France's African colonies. To hear his many enemies tell it, when Foccart was not at Cercottes, he could be seen in Dakar, Abidjan, or Libreville engaged in assiduous courtship of French diplomats, civil servants, and African leaders seen as comers. Through the SDECE, SAC, and Safiex, his import-export business, Foccart made important contacts with French companies with African interests. When de Gaulle returned to power in 1958, Foccart became the agent through which the General sought to coordinate and apply his African policies. "It is no accident," the 1982 parliamentary committee concluded, "if viewed from a foreign perspective [especially that of the United States], the actions of the SDECE and SAC beyond our frontiers are intimately linked."[60]

At the heart of that policy lay de Gaulle's decision to shed France's sub-Saharan colonies. For the French President, however, decolonization was meant to be merely a tactical readjustment, not a strategic retreat. From a Gaullist perspective, Africa offered an area where France could demonstrate that she still had cultural, political, and economic clout, which in turn could be bartered for influence in Europe, with the United States or the Soviet Union. Foccart was assigned the task of orchestrating an arrangement whereby French interests could maintain the upper hand in her former colonies, for whom she had done virtually nothing to prepare for independence. It was an assignment ideally suited to Foccart's clandestine methods, for the primitiveness of the place, the diminutive size of its educated elite, the utter dependence upon French economic and financial advisers to manage its economy, French soldiers and gendarmes to defend and police it, technicians to maintain its infrastructure, and French companies to supply its needs, left few levers of control which Paris did not manipulate.

Presiding over the weekly meetings to coordinate African policy, Foccart translated the Gaullist vision into practice. Paris scuttled the old colonial divisions of French West Africa and French Equatorial Africa favored by African states because Foccart felt that a jumble of financially strapped African countries would be more easily controlled than two large blocs.[61] And controlled they are, as Paris has nailed them to the cross of the franc zone, floated loans on easy terms to cover national debts, and given generous aid. But the cost in political independence and economic development has been high. The predominance of French firms turned the capitals of the Ivory Coast, Gabon, and Senegal virtually into company towns, where costs of living soared because, until 1994, French interests blocked devaluations which would lower the value of their assets, where national economies have fallen hostage to the export of overpriced, hence uncompetitive, commodities like coffee and cocoa, and where the mass of the population has borne the burden of depressed incomes and stagnating economies.[62]

Although such a relationship has been denounced as neocolonialist, in the Cold War context this arrangement kept a great patch of Africa in the camp of the "Free World." Unfortunately, even this modest gain was tarnished by what American diplomat and African expert Francis Terry McNamara has called a "paranoid brutality" perpetrated by "a picturesque gang of mercenaries and Gaullist political action thugs."[63] The SDECE formed an Africa section of around 150 agents led by Colonel Maurice Robert, who established his headquarters, called Bison Base, in the Invalides. There, "driven by a compulsive phobia of 'reds,' which they saw everywhere," they dedicated themselves to maintaining French control of their former colonies.[64] When one African leader, Sékou Touré of Guinea, requested the option of a "free" association with de Gaulle's French community, de Gaulle, who feared that the Guinea example would prove contagious,[65] took it as a personal affront. According to the version one reads, either Sékou Touré cleverly invented French plots to bolster his political position or Foccart and the SDECE had been given the green light to destabilize the country with bribes, floods of counterfeit currency, commando raids, and insurrections.[66] The fact that none of these conspiracies against Touré succeeded does little to settle the argument.

But if covert operations failed to rattle Sékou Touré's control in Guinea, they had more success elsewhere. Apparently de Gaulle, so eager to exert France's independence against the two power blocs, was loath to allow his former African colonies to follow his example. The SDECE's Africa section made certain that loyal opposition, not to mention disloyal ones, found no future in the ex-colonies. If Sékou Touré survived to die in his bed, such was not the fate of Felix Moumié, who fled to Accra after the rebellion which he headed in Cameroon in 1958–60 was brutally crushed by French troops. An Action reservist posing as a journalist convinced Moumié to travel to Switzerland for medical treatment, where the African died in agony after the SDECE agent put poison in his drink.[67]

In 1964, French troops, spearheaded by Robert's Action service, intervened in Gabon to reinstate the unpopular regime of Léon M'ba, temporarily embarrassed by a military coup. Gabon became a test case as well as a stronghold from which, according to his accusers, Foccart and the *clan des Gabonnais*, armed with undated requests for intervention signed in advance by the presidents of Gabon, Cameroon, the Ivory Coast, and Chad, applied the "Gabonese cocktail" in greater or lesser strength in other former colonies. SDECE agents covered Africa, doubled by Foccart's parallel networks of informal contacts in police forces, administrations, and businesses. But their influence was especially potent in oil-rich Gabon, where the Elf group led by Foccart's friend Pierre Guillaumat was eager to suborn the government to exclude foreign oil companies who were offering much better terms to Gabon. The country's oil resources were siphoned off to imperceptible national benefit, while financial scandals, brutalities, and land seizures were perpetrated to the benefit of a small claque of Foccart supporters. So pervasive was the network said to have become that Gabon acquired the unflattering nickname of "Foccartland."[68]

Not content merely to guarantee the "stability" of France's friends in Africa, Foccart also sought to play an active political role in countries outside the community of former French colonies. The motives for stirring the troubled waters of the former Belgian Congo, and later Nigeria, sprang in part from a situation of Foccart's own making. Having broken up the old French colonial blocs to create small countries easier to control, he had left them vulnerable to larger, potentially more powerful neighbors.

De Gaulle gave Foccart and General Grossin the task of supporting the 1960 rebellion of Moïse Tshombé in mineral-rich Katanga. Foccart's team of business interests swarmed into Katanga offering contracts to exploit mineral rights. In January 1961, none other than Roger Trinquier was pulled from retirement at Nice and sent to act as Tshombé's military adviser, at the head of a clutch of ex-Legion paras and members of the 11éme Choc. Although Trinquier vanished once France withdrew its official support for his mission, Katanga launched the mercenary presence in Africa which would add petroleum to the fires touched off by the turmoil of African independence. Afterward, the links between the SDECE, Foccart, and the mercenaries become more difficult to pin down. They were very much in the condottiere mold, an ad hoc group which shattered like a ball of mercury, only to re-form. Although they were by no means all French, one of the most celebrated was a former French sailor and policeman named Bob Denard, who earned his spurs unsuccessfully defending Tshombé against the invasion of UN troops who swarmed into Katanga in December 1961, driving Denard into headlong flight to Angola.

Denard claimed that he always received approval from the Elysée and the SDECE before he undertook a contract. Though this was impossible to prove, before his long career was completed Denard was able to construct a curriculum vitae which destined him either for glory or for incarceration. Presumably the suspended sentence handed down by the French judge in Denard's 1993 trial on the charge of "criminal association" for his participation in a 1977 coup in Benin was meant to preserve just that balance. The machinery of judicial leniency was no doubt greased by the testimony of former SDECE chief General Jeannou Lacaze, who told the court that he could not imagine Denard operating without official approval, and that of Jacques Foccart, who insisted that Denard's only ambition was to act in French interests.[69] In 1967, France again pressed Denard into the service of those very interests.

Ever since it had been carved out of what France saw as her natural sphere of influence in West Africa in the nineteenth century, Nigeria had been looked upon with suspicion by Paris. In the postcolonial world, Dahomey, Niger, Cameroon, and the Ivory Coast felt threatened by the presence of a large Nigeria. Nor was de Gaulle well disposed toward that country after Nigeria broke off diplomatic relations in 1960 over the General's insistence on exploding his atomic weapons at Reggane in the Sahara. The French President seized on the rebellion which broke out in Nigeria's eastern province of Biafra in 1967 as an opportunity to fragment the former British colony. From Abidjan in the Ivory Coast, one of Foccart's associates, in touch with the Biafra

Historical Research Center in Paris, whose "historical" research was apparently limited to collecting the names of mercenaries and weapons merchants, supervised the supply of both fighters and arms to Denard and the rebellion. The key to success was diplomatic recognition for the rebellion. Once again, however, in Biafra intelligence and action resources proved to be committed to failed policy.

Neither Washington nor London favored the breakup of Nigeria and little appreciated de Gaulle's not very covert support for the rebellion. The Soviet Union, eager to recapture its fading influence in Africa, backed the Nigerian central government.[70] Of the West African countries, only the Ivory Coast, out of its President's loyalty to de Gaulle, and Gabon, reluctantly and out of fear of Foccart and the SDECE, recognized Biafra. They were joined by Zambia and Tanzania, the latter apparently influenced by the Chinese, who had a large development mission there. By July 1968, French "humanitarian" aid, stimulated by de Gaulle's survival of the tumult of May '68 and the press coverage of starving Biafrans, became more overt. Between September 1968 and March 1969, planes from Libreville in Gabon flew 70,000 tons of arms and munitions and another 1,200 tons of food and medicines to airstrips within the ever diminishing frontiers of the secessionist province. Planes bearing markings of the French Red Cross flew combinations of all cargoes.

But Paris was approaching the limits of its ability to impose French policy in Africa. Trouble which broke out in Chad in 1968, requiring French intervention, put it at full stretch militarily. It became increasingly apparent that French intervention could only retard Biafra's defeat, not ensure victory for the secessionists. Furthermore, French policy had contributed to its isolation in Africa, not the least because it was supported by the secret services of Rhodesia, South Africa, and Portugal, countries which had vested interests in undermining the power of black African states, and whom France aided through secret sanction busting. Other African nations, France's ex-colonies among them, were acutely aware of the bad precedent which a successful Biafran secession might set. At home, too, de Gaulle was in trouble. The Minister of Foreign affairs was forced to concede in January 1969 that, once again, the world seemed incapable of appreciating "the profound worth of General de Gaulle's policy." In May 1969, de Gaulle resigned when his referendum on decentralization was rejected by the French. Foccart was fired by the interim President, Alain Poher, and France pulled the plug on Biafra.[71]

What de Gaulle's successors were to discover was that Foccart's creations, like all irregular intelligence and covert action structures, rather resembled nuclear waste in one very important respect—they created a disposal problem, foremost among which was Foccart himself. Even while he was de Gaulle's Prime Minister, Pompidou had become concerned about the close relationship which SAC had struck with the police and secret services, as well as a thug element attracted by SAC's Wild West behavior. Nor was he alone in his fear that SAC, whose members saw themselves as above and beyond the influence of the party, might resent the mantle of the movement falling on the shoulders of a "technician" like Pompidou.

Pompidou's problems with SAC, the secret services, and indirectly with Foccart began with an investigation into the October 1968 discovery in a rubbish dump in a Paris suburb of the body of Stefan Marcovic, a former bodyguard of French actor Alain Delon. Rumor rife in government circles was soon spilled to the press that the police investigation had tied Pompidou and his wife into a fast-moving crowd of socialites and gangsters. Even de Gaulle at first refused to dismiss out of hand sordid rumors of photographs of Madame Pompidou engaging in sexual orgies, an attitude on the part of the General which resulted in an unbridgeable breach between the two men.[72]

Testifying before the 1981 parliamentary committee convened to study the activities of SAC, Foccart denied the committee president's contention that the Marcovic affair had prompted Pompidou's decision to purge SAC. But as Foccart denied much else, including his association with SAC or that he had ever created any networks in Africa, the committee refused to believe him, as does his biographer Pierre Péan. Pompidou appears to have been eager to keep SAC from getting involved in the elections, especially when his political opponent, Poher, raised "the scandal of the parallel networks . . . and organization of clandestine armies" as an election issue. After Pompidou won the June election, he resisted Foccart's reinstatement. And when he finally yielded to pressure from African heads of state in the French Community to reappoint Foccart general secretary of the community, he excluded him from any dealings with the secret services.

Under orders from Pompidou, newly appointed SDECE chief

Alexandre de Marenches carried out a purge in the SDECE which hit hardest at those believed involved in the Marcovic affair.[73] The debris of his networks in Africa proved tougher to root out, however. Marenches discovered that the situation of the secret services in the former French colonies was "confused" by a profusion of sometimes overlapping official and unofficial networks. Nevertheless, he denounced as "unpleasant" a situation in which a company like Elf run by Foccart's friend Pierre Guillaumat but owned by the French government could finance a service run by former SDECE employees which could virtually shut out his official agents.[74] Elf virtually carried out its own foreign policy in Africa, one which sought to extend its influence in areas like the Angolan dependency of Cabinda. And while Marenches claimed that he took tough action against the Foccart networks in Africa, Foccart's biographer believes that the SDECE basically left de Gaulle's old *éminence grise* alone to stir his own African cauldron.[75]

The prolongation of Foccart's political life also gained time for mercenaries like Bob Denard, who remained on the payroll in Gabon, which he used as a launching pad to involvement in Africa's civil and colonial wars, or coup d'états. His career came to an end when French intervention forced him to abandon the Comoro Islands, where he and his mercenaries had behaved with a murderous impunity which even Paris could not continue to ignore.

Foccart was dismissed a second time by Giscard d'Estaing in 1975. However, upon his nomination as Prime Minister in 1975, former SAC president Jacques Chirac recalled Foccart as his adviser on African affairs. SAC did not long survive the victory of the left in 1981. After a former chief of SAC in Marseille, police inspector Jacques Massié, was murdered with his entire family in July 1981, communist deputies in the National Assembly demanded an investigation of SAC. After listening to six months of testimony, the parliamentary committee concluded in December 1981 in a voluminous report that the actions of the SDECE, SAC, and the unofficial networks in Africa "are intimately linked." The committee denounced SAC as a dangerous organization which had served as a parallel police, infiltrated the public administrations to influence decisions, and carried out acts of violence, and deemed its continued existence "incompatible with the laws of the Republic." The government agreed and ordered SAC disbanded in July 1982.[76] However, it appears that the terrorist crisis of the 1980s intervened to give Foccart's African networks a new lease on life.

Mitterrand and
the Elysée Cell

If the history of parallel secret services has not proved particularly distinguished in France, the practice of creating such networks there is firmly established. Its appeal rests on the mistrust of many French leaders for official intelligence. And while this mistrust had usually evolved over time, Mitterrand came to it quite naturally.

As a man of the left, Mitterrand hardly required instruction in the statistical section's perfidy during the Dreyfus Affair. But he received hands-on experience during the 1954 *affaire des fuites*, when he was cited as the source of the leaks concerning French policy in Indochina which Navarre and his supporters claimed had brought about the fall of Dien Bien Phu. And although Wybot at the DST cleared Mitterrand of suspicion by finding the true source, the future French President was left with a profound distrust, not to say paranoia, toward all intelligence organizations, which he believed capable of any "treason."[77] Nor was his sense of discomfort in any way lessened by the fact that by 1981, when he assumed the presidency, those very services had been under conservative management for twenty-three years. Mitterrand was well aware that they could prove the source of scandals through which the opposition might seek to tarnish his presidency.

Mitterrand is given high marks as the one President who actually used an intelligence coup to political advantage—namely, during the Farewell affair. In the late 1970s, a disgruntled KGB agent who once had been stationed in Paris contacted the DST to offer his services. What followed was a bonanza of information on Soviet industrial spying, the Soviet space program, and lists of KGB agents, among other things. By admitting Reagan into this secret during the Ottawa Conference of 1981, Mitterrand established his credibility with a conservative U.S. administration deeply suspicious of a French regime which counted communist ministers in its government. The Farewell dossier also helped Mitterrand establish his credibility with the Soviets.

In 1983, when the Soviet ambassador to France arrived at the Quai d'Orsay formally to protest the expulsion of forty-seven Soviet diplomats from Paris after the French discovered that the Soviets had intercepted all diplomatic messages between their Moscow embassy and the Quai since 1976, the Foreign Minister simply spread out on his desk a lengthy KGB document taken from the Farewell dossier detailing Soviet spying in France.[78]

One of the paradoxes of the Mitterrand presidency is that, although the socialist President had employed intelligence to greatest effect in policy, he arrived in office determined to keep his secret services at arm's length. Distrustful of the political biases of men who would have considered Richard Nixon a crypto-communist, who complained that the socialist government was in itself a threat to national security, Mitterrand remained deeply suspicious of "manipulations." When the Farewell affair was leaked to the press in 1985, a furious Mitterrand fired the DST head, Yves Bonnet. Mitterrand apparently came to the conclusion that Farewell had been a CIA plant to test him: "I have no proof," he told journalists in 1989, "but if this was the case [that I was manipulated], we must have looked stupid, Chesson [the Minister of Foreign Affairs] and I, in front of Reagan and Haig at Ottawa when we revealed the affair to them."[79]

No surprise, then, that the new President, who doubted his services, who found their chiefs mediocre and the product suspect, anodyne, or merely misinformed, also sought to operate outside the official system. Pierre Marion, who complained that he was not admitted into Mitterrand's inner council, conceded that the SDECE/DGSE was so penetrated by what he saw as Foccart's influence that he was hard pressed to have his orders obeyed. The situation was absolutely out of control in Africa, where the Minister of Cooperation was running arms into Chad through a private firm. Worse, Foccart's networks, which dominated Togo, Cameroon, and Gabon, were conspiring with Eastern bloc services to discredit the SDECE, while channeling funds from Gabon and Iraq into Gaullist party coffers. Marion complained that his attempts to change this were sabotaged by Mitterrand's son, whom the President named as his special adviser on African affairs.[80]

Apparently Mitterrand, too, became upset in October 1981 after "our uncontrollable special agents in Africa," with what he believed to be CIA collusion, tried to trick him into intervening in Chad by reporting a false alert of a coup.[81] Therefore, he took a page out of de Gaulle's book and placed his own "Foccart" in charge. François de Grossouvre, along with African specialist Guy Penne, set out to re-structure, revivify, and re-create parallel networks in Africa, through Masonic contacts and even calling for help from loyal servants of the *ancien régime* like Alexandre de Marenches and Pierre Dabezies, ex-colonel of the 11ème Choc, who in 1982 was made ambassador to Gabon.[82] The same reflex was apparent in France, according to Marion, who was appalled that Grossouvre continued to send men fired from intelligence "for political reasons" with the recommendation that he create parallel networks with them, "and little by little to empty the SDECE of its substance." He concluded that the Elysée Palace under Mitterrand was more interested in creating parallel networks than in the streamlining and coordination of the official services.[83]

When Mitterrand turned to the Groupement d'Intervention de la Gendarmerie Nationale (GIGN) to lead his counterterrorist campaign, he did so out of distrust of the regular services and doubts about their competence. Furthermore, as has been seen, it was by no means an original reaction. Marion saw this as an eccentric decision, and from a professional perspective he was correct. Part of the Gendarmerie Nationale, which under the complicated French administrative structure is a police formation which answers to the Ministry of Defense, the GIGN was created in 1974 principally as an action team of around ninety officers and NCOs to deal with hostage situations. As such, it had achieved a nodding acquaintance with the Islamic world when, together with an SDECE action team, it led the recapture of the mosque at Mecca seized by Muslim fundamentalists in 1979.[84] The GIGN, under its dynamic chief, thirty-eight-year-old Christian Prou-teau, had attracted Mitterrand's attention by demonstrating through staged "ambushes" and "bombings" the inadequacies of the President's security staff. A sobered Mitterrand appointed Prouteau as his chief of security.

In the aftermath of an August 1982 bombing of a well-known kosher restaurant in the traditional Jewish quarter's rue des Rosiers, Mitterrand was especially eager to refute charges that the socialists were soft on terrorism. It was entirely in keeping with the President's character, however, that he apparently feared that the professionalism of his secret services would be corrupted by their desire to embarrass his government.[85] Therefore, the French President assigned to Prouteau "the mission of coordination, intelligence, and action against terrorism." To establish their credibility with intelligence and police communities stunned by Mitterrand's promotion of Prouteau, whom they regarded as little more than a "cowboy," the elite gendarmes of the "Elysée cell" arrested three Irish nationals in their apartment in the Paris suburb of Vincennes. A presidential communiqué announced that an important gang of IRA terrorists wanted by Scotland Yard, complete with arms and explosives, was now behind bars. However, the following summer a gendarme from the Vincennes brigade, in judicial trouble of his own, charged that irregularities had been committed during the Vincennes raid. Investigating magistrates established that the Elysée cell had planted the evidence in the apartment of the "terrorists," who were freed.

Like Foccart's mercenaries, Prouteau presented Mitterrand with a disposal problem. But rather than absorb a lesson about the dangers of a parallel service out to feather its own nest, Mitterrand instead believed that the *affaire des Irlandais* was a DST manipulation to discredit his Elysée cell, and stood by his man.[86] After the usual maneuvers, denials, prevarications, and trials, Paul Barril, who led the raid, was eventually dismissed, and reconverted into the private security business. Prouteau was finally charged in 1987. But Mitterrand courted substantial unpopularity in police and secret service circles when, rather than throw Prouteau to the wolves, he instead promoted him to prefect in charge of security for the 1992 Winter Olympics. So far, under Mitterrand's protection, Prouteau has proved to be untouchable.[87]

But this is to leap ahead. Prouteau's Elysée cell furnished the guts of Mitterrand's counterterrorist effort, especially from 1985, when the terrorist campaign against France reached crisis proportions. In the first half of 1985, eight Frenchmen were seized by pro-Iranian groups in Beirut. On March 10, 1985, pictures of the body of one of them, Michel Seraut, were sent to the Associated Press by the terrorist group Islamic Jihad, with a note which explained that the unfortunate Seraut had been executed in reprisal for the murder of one of two Iraqi dissidents rounded up by the DST on 19 February and, drugged and handcuffed, placed unceremoniously aboard a flight to Baghdad. This proved typical of the confused French approach to the terrorist crisis.

Once the Quai d'Orsay realized that the Ministry of the Interior had expelled the dissidents, it moved heaven and earth to retrieve them. But Saddam Hussein, who had benefited so greatly from French arms largesse, refused to return the favor. The best the French could do was to exact a promise from the Iraqi dictator not to execute them, against a threat of the suspension of arms shipments. British intercepts of a 6 February radio message from the Iranian embassy in Damascus and the Ministry of Foreign Affairs in Teheran suggested that Seraut had died well before the extradition of the two Iraqis and a false communiqué by Amnesty International that one of them had been executed. Seraut's widow, Mary Seraut, refused to be mollified. Tearful and bitter, she appeared on television to place responsibility for the execution of her husband squarely on the shoulders of Interior Minister Pierre Joxe and the DST.[88]

A second factor which encouraged the resort to parallel services was the March 1986 parliamentary victory of the right. For the first time since its inception, the Fifth Republic had a split government—that is, the Prime Minister was not of the same persuasion as the President. The socialist Mitterrand and the Gaullist Prime Minister, Jacques Chirac, both eager to reap the political benefits, became locked in competition for the release of French hostages in Lebanon. To complicate matters, in September 1986, Paris was rocked by a wave of bombings which culminated on the afternoon of 17 September when a bomb placed in a trash can exploded on the rue de Rennes, crowded with rush-hour traffic, killing six and wounding fifty.

France now had both a resurgence of terrorism and a hostage problem. The secret service response, according to Daniel Burdan, who worked in the DST's antiterrorist division, was "an implacable struggle" among the DST, the DGSE, and the Elysée cell, each of which "jealously keeps its information to itself, manipulates the other services, and practices 'disinformation.' "[89]

Mitterrand, feeling cut off by the conservative government from access to DST intelligence,[90] had given the Elysée cell a huge computer linked to those at the SDECE/DGSE and the Centre d'Exploitation du Renseignement Militaire (CERM), assigned a Middle Eastern expert from the Gendarmerie Nationale, and allowed Prouteau a free hand to pursue his antiterrorist campaign with presidential backing. But despite boasts by Interior Minister Charles Pasqua that he would "terrorize the terrorists," Chirac decided that the solution to the crisis of terrorism lay with diplomacy rather than repression. The key would be to win the support of Syria, whose power in Lebanon was on the increase. Journalists close to Mitterrand have alleged that visits to Damascus in late September 1986 by government and DST officials resulted in an agreement whereby the Syrians would supply intelligence to the DST on Lebanese terrorists, in return for arms, economic aid, and the abstention of France from U.S. and British condemnations of Syrian-sponsored terrorism. When the deal was revealed by *Le Monde* on 29 October, the government denied it, but insisted on the right "to get its intelligence where it thinks it can find it." In any case, terrorist attacks on France ceased.[91] But part of the price was a moral compromise in which, in the interest of good relations, Paris was required to look the other way when Syrian-sponsored terrorist groups attacked U.S. and Israeli diplomats.[92]

France does appear to have received some return on its Syrian investment, for in November 1986 three French hostages held by Syrian-controlled groups were released. But to credit the Syrian initiative for the cessation of terrorist attacks in Paris appears to be going too far. Initially, the French services had linked the September bomb blasts with Arab terrorists held in French jails, despite the insistence of Mossad and the Palestinians that they were linked to Iranian interests still upset with French arms sales to Iraq. The DST got a break in February 1987 when a Tunisian living in Tours spontaneously came forward with an offer of information on an Iranian-sponsored terrorist cell in France in return for a million francs and a new life in the United States. A meeting was arranged between the Tunisian and the leader of the network in a room alive with DST microphones. The result was a wave of arrests of a number of men linked by their studies at Qom, the hotbed of Khomeinian agitation in Iran. The young Tunisian and his family, with CIA assistance, flew to a new beginning in North America.

In its eagerness to retrieve the hostages and so reap the benefit of electoral success, the government offered itself as hostage to the intermediaries and even to the very terrorists with whom they dealt.[93] Given the political stakes, competition between left and right to secure the release of the hostages was an intense, no-holds-barred affair. In January 1987, the French newspaper *Le Matin* published accusations, based on documents supplied by socialist sources, probably with Elysée approval, that just days before the March 1986 elections which brought him to power, Chirac had sabotaged a hostage release by promising Teheran a better deal when he came to power. This raised a fierce, if inconclusive, polemic, whose result, especially after Iranian Prime Minister Rafsanjani said it was so, was to slow the normalization of French-Iranian relations which Chirac had begun on assuming office. The breakup of the Iranian terrorist cell brought these negotiations to the verge of breakdown, for DST investigations revealed the contact for the terrorist cell to be none other than the spokesman and interpreter for the Iranian embassy in Paris, Wahid Gordji. But when on 3 June the DST appeared at his house to take him in for interrogation, Gordji had disappeared, apparently tipped off by a French diplomat upset by the sabotage of French-Iranian relations.[94]

Phone taps on the Iranian embassy revealed that Gordji had sought refuge there rather than flee the country. French police surrounded the embassy and demanded that Gordji come out. Teheran recipro-cated with a blockade of the French embassy, and seized a French diplomat whom it accused of espionage. Both countries were now locked in a "war of the embassies." Only when they had brought things to a crisis did the government realize that it had no firm proof tying Gordji to the terrorist cell, just the accusations of one of the arrested terrorists and some phone taps and radio intercepts. The situation was further complicated because Mitterrand, cut out by Chirac, had dis-patched men from Prouteau's Elysée cell to Damascus and Beirut to gather information. Pasqua had also sent a former SDECE agent, Jean-Charles Marchiani, and a Lebanese businessman to try to find a way to liberate the hostages. The result was a cacophony of intelligence from several, often contradictory, sources and confused initiatives as the DST and the Elysée cell each sought ways to end the embassy standoff.

Despite the severing of diplomatic relations between the two coun-tries, the crisis gradually resolved itself in the autumn of 1987. The first indication of a resolution occurred when two of the five French hostages were released on 27 November, a success claimed by Mar-chiani, who nonetheless had kept in close touch with the Elysée cell and the DST. The following day at the Karachi airport in Pakistan, Gordji was exchanged for the French diplomat "spy" taken by Teheran.

The terrorist and hostage crises became the subject of bitter recrimination during the presidential debates of 28 April 1988. After a general exchange of charges of cowardice and incompetence, each candidate for the presidency became more specific. Chirac broadsided Mitterrand for the amnesty of Action Directe terrorists in 1981 who were subsequently involved in murders. A scorched Mitterrand fired back at Chirac for the release of Gordji despite "crushing" proof of guilt. On 5 May, three days before the vote, Chirac sought to snatch victory by two electoral coups with secret service connections. One was the successful assault by elements of the 11ème Choc and the GIGN on a cave in New Caledonia to liberate twenty-two policemen held hostage by natives demanding independence. The second was the release of the three remaining French hostages in Lebanon. The price? The U.S. and British press insisted that France had agreed to limited arms shipments to Iran. There was also the accusation that Chirac had revived Foccart's contacts to funnel a large ransom payment to the kidnappers. Nor was there agreement on whether the final release had been delayed by the Syrians, miffed at being circumvented by the diverse French emissaries, or was related to internal Iranian politics. In any case, it failed to save Chirac, whose opponent captured 54 percent of the vote.[95]

Rather than rationalize and modernize the relationship between French intelligence services and the state, the Fifth Republic has accentuated some of the worst features of French intelligence culture: the intermixing of domestic or counter-intelligence with foreign intelligence continues because the frontiers between internal and external enemies have not been easy to define. French leaders continue to distrust regular intelligence services, which causes them to resort to parallel services. This accentuates the old problem of the fragmentation of intelligence and a preference for intelligence which tells leaders what they want to hear. The temptation of services to resort to an "operational" approach to validate their service or when confronted with an apparently insoluble intelligence problem remains strong. Finally, rather than being seen as a neutral bureaucracy in the service of the state, intelligence is politicized because it continues to be used as a weapon in quarrels between politicians. All these elements were present in the *Rainbow Warrior* affair.

NINETEEN

L'AFFAIRE RAINBOW WARRIOR

If ever a botched intelligence operation pointed up in stark terms the dysfunctional relationship between an intelligence organization and its political masters, it was *l'affaire Rainbow Warrior*. Indeed, the sinking of the *Rainbow Warrior*, a ship which belonged to the environmentalist group Greenpeace, in Auckland harbor on the night of 10 July 1985 can safely be said to be a prototype case through which relations between the state and the intelligence services in France can be analyzed. Ultimate responsibility was assigned to Defense Minister Charles Hernu and DGSE chief Admiral Pierre Lacoste, who took the blame and resigned. However, observers have suggested that such an operation could never have been carried out without the expressed consent of the Elysée Palace, which appears to have supplied the funds for the operation. One great irony of the *affaire* is that a government of socialists who evinced such concern for rogue operations carried out by the intelligence services should themselves stand accused of using the DGSE, not to inform policy, but to make it. In the process, they not only supplied a thumping illustration of the counterproductive use of covert action but called into question the nature of state-intelligence relations in France.

One may never know the full truth of the *Rainbow Warrior* affair. But some officials appear to have tumbled with their old nemesis in the DGSE into what British spy novelist John le Carré has called "the oldest trap in the trade," the belief that the real world's imperfections can be redressed by the secret world."

The first ingredient in an ultimately poisonous union of government and intelligence was a *Weltanschauung*, or vision of the world and France's place in it, which bordered on hysteria. From Paris' viewpoint, the real world's imperfections stem from the jealousy occasioned by France's desire to claim great power status through possession of the bomb. Indeed, so potent was this bomb-induced jealousy that it appeared able to draw the world's most unnatural allies together into the Mother of Unnatural Alliances.

According to Roger Faligot and Pascal Krop, French experts on the SDECE/DGSE, this mind-set gave birth to a bizarre conspiracy theory spun out in the minds of the DGSE and the gendarmes of the Moruroa atoll, where French nuclear testing was conducted. Soldiers there saw France's nuclear independence under threat from a coordinated and implausibly diverse conspiracy of jealous "Anglo-Saxons," long-haired environmentalists, island nationalist groups financed by communists, and the Soviets, whose submarines lurked in the azure waters off the atoll. French nuclear explosions had drawn acerbic condemnation from South Pacific nations, fed by charges laid out in a 6 November 1981 issue of *Libération* of sloppy safety practices which had resulted in widespread nuclear contamination and had so weakened the atoll's underlying crater that a devastating nuclear accident was possible. More, these issues had become intermingled with increasingly vocal independence movements in Tahiti and New Caledonia, which argued that Paris' refusal to make even minimal concessions to regional autonomy was the direct result of fear for the security of its nuclear program. Foreign threat and domestic subversion coalesced in the form of a growing French ecology movement which increasingly questioned the government's commitment to nuclear power plants in France and whose leader, Brice Lalonde, captured almost 4 percent of the popular vote in the first round of the 1981 presidential elections. Lalonde, whom socialist leaders increasingly had to accommodate, was no stranger to the DGSE as a veteran of the sea battles off Moruroa in the 1970s.[2]

The sinking of the *Rainbow Warrior* was not an instant inspiration, but the fruit of a long-term contingency plan which stretched back to the 1970s when the SDECE contemplated sinking the ships of ecologists protesting French explosions in the Pacific. These had never been put into practice. Instead, the SDECE/DGSE had confined its retribution to malicious, if nonlethal, acts of sabotage.[3] As the 1985 tests approached, however, naval authorities, in particular Admiral Henri Fages, head of the Direction du Centre d'Expérimentations Nucléaires, which organized the test operations on Moruroa, feared a Greenpeace effort to block vital testing of the warhead for the M4 submarine-borne missile, that for the medium-range Hadès, and finally of a tactical neutron bomb. The question became what to do about it. At this point, however, the defects in intelligence-state relations, their lack of maturity, kicked in.

On the intelligence side, a combination of military dominance of the DGSE and an intelligence organization with a strong action culture combined to sabotage a rational analysis of the situation. Military control of the DGSE meant that, rather than being an independent organization capable of analyzing the situation in a detached way, intelligence became one of the players with a vested interest in the outcome. The DGSE fell into the trap of confusing tactics with strategy, means with ends. A "worst case" analysis on the strategic level combined with a "best case" on the operational level to make for an operation whose major ingredient was wishful thinking.[4]

The second problem was one of political leadership. Ultimately, it falls to the political leadership to ensure that a clear frontier between politics and intelligence is maintained. The political leader should act as a brake on operations which are likely to be counterproductive. This did not happen. Credit for pushing the plan forward is usually assigned to Defense Minister Charles Hernu. Jovial, immensely popular with the French electorate, and a close friend of Mitterrand, the sixty-two-year-old mayor of the Lyon suburb of Villeurbranne owed his post as Defense Minister to the fact that he was one of the few qualified military experts in the socialist camp. Indeed, it was he who in the 1970s had won Socialist Party support for the Gaullist-inspired *force de frappe*, thus giving the left much credibility with the French electorate. The principal charge against Hernu was that this son of a gendarme was eager to the point of desperation to ingratiate himself with the military, to prove that the left which came to power in 1981 was as committed to a strong defense as were the conservatives. But in his desire to be congenial to the military, he allowed himself virtually to be taken over by them and began to share their obsession with Greenpeace. Some have claimed that Hernu was fed a steady diet of selective information by the DGSE, which alleged that Greenpeace had been infiltrated by the communists, that the Soviets had allied with independence activists in the South Pacific to "pull strings" to stop French nuclear testing, and that British Petroleum was financing Greenpeace operations to stir up trouble for the French nuclear industry.[5]

Troubles in the French possession of New Caledonia and the July 1984 election in New Zealand of outspoken antinuclear Prime Minister David Lange fueled the tension in the Pacific. For French intelligence and military officers, the problem was the old one of French weakness and apparent lack of alternatives. The world seemed to be opposed to French nuclear testing. Greenpeace was simply the agent of this web of intrigue, both international and domestic, which no amount of diplomatic or military pressure could resolve. Why one of the world's major navies should tremble at the prospect of attack by an unarmed boatload of ecologists is unclear. The most obvious option was to form a naval cordon around the atoll which would keep the ecologists at bay. But the size of the 417-ton *Rainbow Warrior* and the negative publicity which would inevitably ensue from attempts to ram and round up ecologists apparently ruled out this possibility.[6] Better to nip the ecologist operation in the bud.

Both Hernu and DGSE head Admiral Pierre Lacoste subsequently denied that they had given the order to sink the *Rainbow Warrior*. This is quite possible in a technical sense, but irrelevant. In the first place, as the responsible leaders, it was up to them to maintain political control of intelligence operatives. Clearly, they did not do this, but instead allowed the boundaries between intelligence and policy to become blurred. Second, it is probable that they allowed this to happen quite intentionally, a process which political scientists call "plausible denial."

Plausible denial occurs when politicians find it difficult formally to order an operation which contradicts ethical values or policy. Never-theless, they can hint that such an operation would be desirable, rather like Henry II wishing ill of his nemesis Thomas à Becket within the hearing of his devoted knights. If the operation succeeds, then the intelligence service has the undying gratitude of the politician. If it fails, the politician can deny all responsibility.[7] The link in the French action might have been a line in Admiral Fages's report to Hernu which suggested that the DGSE should "anticipate Greenpeace actions." According to one source, when Hernu passed on Fages's report to Lacoste, the word "anticipate" had been underlined twice. In any case, a large degree of local control appears to have devolved to the man on the spot—Admiral Fages—to the point that he may have set in motion the events which led to the bombing. So, while Hernu and Lacoste may never have ordered the operation in a formal sense, and may never have been informed of the exact plan of its execution, it is highly improbable that they were unaware that some sort of action was to be taken against Greenpeace, and that they had tacitly approved that action in principle.[8]

Opinion is divided over Mitterrand's role in the operation,[9] as is the attitude of the Service Action. A second brake on lunatic schemes should be an intelligence organization's sense of professionalism—indeed, of its own survival. For instance, in the Iran-Contra episode during the Reagan administration, the CIA refused to become involved because they judged that the operation could not be kept secret and because it took them over the line into the controversial realm of policy making. Therefore, the Reagan administration was forced to carry out their operation with members of the NSC staff and private business contacts.[10] Likewise, the risk of exposure in any operation to sink the *Rainbow Warrior* was extremely high for the DGSE. It should have been obvious to anyone who gave the matter more than five seconds' thought that whatever advantage may have accrued to them by ingratiating themselves with Hernu would be more than offset by the subsequent scandal and damage of public trust. Some sources suggest that the plan appeared so amateurish that the Service Action had to be prodded virtually at gunpoint to execute it. Nice thought! But if true, it proved an insufficiently powerful motive to abort the operation. The real problem was that the intelligence culture in France which constantly blurred the lines between politics and intelligence, which saw no contradiction in using intelligence for partisan ends, and a low level of professionalism in the DGSE conspired to corrupt any system of control. In fact, others insist that the *Rainbow Warrior* operation was embraced with enthusiasm by the DGSE as a way to retrieve Action's tarnished reputation in the wake of the embarrassing episode of November 1983 when the Iranians discovered a French jeep loaded with explosives against the wall of their Beirut embassy.[11]

The DGSE succeeded in transforming a badly conceived plan into a disastrously mismanaged operation. Agents arrived in New Zealand by various conspicuous routes to join Lieutenant Christine-Huguette Cabon, who had infiltrated the Greenpeace organization in New Zealand. Cabon, apparently a commando-trained parachutist with experience in covert operations in the Middle East, managed to disguise herself as a fervent ecologist to secure a position of trust within the Greenpeace headquarters in Auckland. From there she dutifully reported the various plans, many quite harebrained, for sabotaging French nuclear testing, schemes which included launching an invasion of Tahitian outrigger canoes or landing prominent politicians directly on the atoll. Among those who arrived by yacht were DGSE frogmen from the Aspretto base in Corsica.

On the night of 10 July, two frogmen swam through the ink-black water to fix two mines to the hull of the *Rainbow Warrior*, set the timers, regained the surface, and jettisoned their equipment, to be collected by the Surface Protection Team. A half hour later when two agents, Major Alain Mafart and Captain Dominique Prieur, traveling with Swiss passports as Alain and Sophie Turenge, appeared to collect the gear, they were spotted by suspicious night watchmen, who noted the license number of their rental car. When, near midnight, the first mine exploded, the twelve people on board scrambled out of the ship as they were meant to do, so that no loss of life would occur when the second mine exploded. Unfortunately, this precaution collapsed when a photographer working for the organization returned to the ship to collect his equipment. He died in the explosion of the second mine.

So clumsy was the operation, so indiscreet the agents, so obvious the trail of evidence linking the explosion to the French secret service, that even one DGSE operative was moved to remark that the agents might as well have left a beret, a baguette, and a bottle of Beaujolais at the scene of the crime.[12] Indeed, the operation was so ill conceived, so amateurish, that New Zealand police, hardly more than a country constabulary but able to break the case in an eyelash, suspected at first it must be a frame-up.[13] The "Turenges" were detained when they returned their rental car. Their Swiss passports were obvious forgeries, and they were charged with murder and arson.

For someone who had worked with intelligence since her commissioning in 1976, Dominique Prieur proved to lack the most elementary notions of security. Unlike the heroines in spy novels, Sophie Turenges failed to swallow the pages of her notebook upon which several Paris phone numbers were written. Contacted by the New Zealand police, the DST was only too delighted to verify that the numbers belonged to the French Defense Ministry.[14] On the harbor shore, the frogmen abandoned their oxygen bottles with French markings and the zodiac, which was traced to a French purchaser.

Those who, in their naiveté, believed it impossible to make a more thorough mess of an operation were proven wrong by the attempt at a cover-up. The French press got wind of the affair and doggedly pursued it, despite a DGSE disinformation campaign, leaked through selected journalists, claiming that the Greenpeace photographer killed in the operation was a KGB agent, that the Rainbow Warrior carried "equipment capable of analyzing the effects and parameters of a neutron bomb,"[15] and that the whole affair was a plot by the Anglo-Saxon services to discredit France—an accusation which produced heated press debate over whether French Foreign Minister Roland Dumas owed a formal apology for this remark to British Foreign Secretary Sir Geoffrey Howe.[16] The only result of this clumsy attempt to trigger nationalist support by conjuring up the time-honored Anglo-Saxon bogey appears to have been to short-circuit an initiative to request the good offices of MI6 to settle the affair amicably between the two countries.[17]

Several explanations have been advanced to explain the government's subsequent prevarication, the most flattering of which was that Paris sought to gain time so that the other agents could make good their escape. If so, the agents took their time leaving the country, at least two of them dawdling until the end of July. Mitterrand's instincts were to ignore the affair in the hopes that it would simply fade away during the sacrosanct August holiday. It is also possible that Prime

Minister Laurent Fabius was initially misled by Hernu into believing the DGSE was not responsible. In any case, Fabius seemed unable to decide what action to take.[18] For whatever reason, the government's foot dragging reflected badly on its credibility.

By the end of August, when an independent investigation entrusted by President Mitterrand to the jurist Bernard Tricot exonerated the DGSE from responsibility for the attack, the public sensed that it was being governed by failed comedians. "Tricot [sweater] Washes Whiter!" newspaper headlines screamed, refusing to be fobbed off by government insistence that only a reorganization imposing more "discretion" on the DGSE was required—the usual list of reforms trotted out in bad times to include better recruitment, job rotation, and superior career prospects.[19] When Tricot's daughter committed suicide a few days later, observers speculated that it was out of shame over her father's credulous report.[20] On 17 September the prestigious newspaper Le Monde published an explosive article which demolished the Tricot report. It denounced as "stupid and criminal" the DGSE action which had considerably damaged France's position in the Pacific and blasted the government cover-up.

Mitterrand's calculation that the hair-trigger nationalism of the French would cause them to rally round this attack on the secret services having failed, he needed a scapegoat. By refusing to reveal the truth of the affair even to the Prime Minister, Lacoste selected himself to be sacrificed by socialists already uncomfortable with the attitude of defiant independence adopted by the DGSE chief. But the sacking of Lacoste was insufficient propitiation for what, after all, had become a "crime of state." Reluctantly, on 19 September, Mitterrand ordered Fabius to accept the resignation of Charles Hernu. But a chorus of journalists and politicians continued to insist that this was no rogue operation concocted on the authority of a coterie of admirals, but stretched to the Elysée itself, which had authorized and financed the operation. Attempts by Hernu's successor at the Defense Ministry, Paul Quilès, to discover the truth slammed into a wall of service silence.

It is probably no accident that the English language has purloined "déjà vu" and "plus ça change" from the French without amendment. The procrastination and denial which had marked the socialists' handling of the *Rainbow Warrior* affair so resembled that of an earlier set of French politicians with regard to Dreyfus that the comparisons were almost eerie. Mitterrand had based his initial strategy, which was to smother the affair, on Hernu's stoutly patriotic insistence that the secret services furnished the cornerstone of French defense. While this had failed initially to quiet the press, by late September, when Hernu was dismissed, the Defense Minister had become a hero to many. By insisting that he would get to the bottom of the *Rainbow Warrior* episode, Fabius began to understand that, though the least involved, he had cast himself as a villain in the mind of a French public whose Machiavellian attitude was that France had a right to sink the *Rainbow Warrior*. The DGSE's sin was to get caught.[21] As with Dreyfus, what had begun as a blunder of French intelligence spun quickly into a question of the honor of the DGSE and, by extension, the armed forces. Fabius realized that politically the *Rainbow Warrior* episode was barren, and so dropped it. But the damage had been done, for a small crack of suspicion and distrust opened between Mitterrand and his heir apparent which gradually widened into a chasm.[22]

The new DGSE head was chosen to inspire confidence in the French public that the situation was under control. General René Imbot, Legionnaire and former army chief of staff, exuded an air of command on 27 September as he appeared on television to denounce the "veritable evil operation" to destabilize the French secret services. Imbot insisted that he had "cut off some rotten limbs"—by which he meant the arrest of four DGSE officers who were accused of leaking information to the press to embarrass the government—and "bolted the door" on the archives. *L'affaire Rainbow Warrior* was at an end.[23] Imbot's message might have been scripted by a distant predecessor, General Galliffet, who in 1899 had announced, *"L'affaire est close!"* Galliffet, of course, had been referring to Dreyfus.[24]

In the meantime, the prospect of a public trial of DGSE agents on murder charges was a profound blow to French prestige in an area of the world where its nuclear policy was much criticized. Fabius urged New Zealand to release the French agents, who could be guilty of no crimes because they had acted under orders—the most vigorous defense of *raison d'état* since Nuremberg, believed *The Times* of London.[25] The two agents pleaded guilty to involuntary manslaughter to spare the French government and the DGSE a long and revelatory murder trial. On 22 November, they were sentenced to ten years in prison. When France retaliated with extremely dilatory customs checks of New Zealand goods to pressure Wellington for an early release, the Labour Prime Minister, David Lange, dug in his heels. However, when in 1986 the government of the Gaullist Prime Minister, Jacques Chirac, looked as if it might make good on its threat to have the EEC raise the tariff on New Zealand butter, Lange was forced to take notice. Former Canadian Prime Minister Pierre Trudeau brokered an agreement whereby France would pay the family of the dead photographer 2.3 million francs, reimburse Greenpeace for the loss of its boat, and offer New Zealand a formal apology. In return, the captured French agents were released to French custody in July 1986.

According to the terms of the agreement, Mafart and Prieur were to remain until July 1989 on the atoll of Hao, a French base 500 nautical miles east of Tahiti. Chirac failed to abide by the agreement. Mafart was evacuated to France in December 1987 with gastroenteritis. When Dominique Prieur proved to be annoyingly disease-resistant, Chirac transported her husband to Hao with orders to impregnate his wife. Though not exactly a solution in the best traditions of Mata Hari, it worked—in May 1988, the happy mother-to-be was returned to France. Like New Zealand, a United Nations tribunal was less moved by tummy troubles and birth announcements among DGSE agents than was Chirac. It denounced France's "bad faith" and ordered Paris to pay New Zealand $2 million in compensation.[26]

The *Rainbow Warrior* episode and the government's reaction to it revealed, if more revelation was required, the paradoxical relationship between the Fifth Republic and its intelligence services—governments do not trust their intelligence services, but at the same time they appear powerless or unwilling to reform them. Once again, as in the cases of Ben Barka and Marcovic, the secret services had been the means by which the government had been discredited. The opposition brayed loudly that the socialists were incapable of controlling the secret services.[27] Nor were they entirely wrong. The DGSE fumed that the DST cooperated with the New Zealand police and leaked information to the press, possibly part of a move by Interior Minister Pierre Joxe to diminish political rival Charles Hernu.[28] In private, Mitterrand drew parallels with Ben Barka, and denounced the *Rainbow Warrior* episode as "an idiotic affair of the secret services, full of bandits and pathetic people," pushed to it by admirals.[29] When Fabius and the new Defense Minister, Paul Quilès, had asked to see the case files, they were told that these had mysteriously vanished. The French Prime Minister had publicly acknowledged that the issue at stake in the *Rainbow Warrior* affair was essentially one of "the control of the intelligence services in a democracy."[30]

That control has been difficult for French governments to achieve, despite what one would imagine to be the strong incentive of repeated scandals. Governments, both left and right, have generally agreed with François Mitterrand's observation of Marenches, that secret service chiefs are more dangerous within the corridors of power than confined to their lair on the boulevard Mortier.[31] Parliamentary demands in the wake of the *Rainbow Warrior* that the secret services be brought under strict control proved to be, as in the past, so much posturing. Neither side glimpsed political benefit in doing battle with the DGSE, especially as it would invariably mean conflict with the powerful military lobby. Fabius quietly abandoned the parliamentary committee of inquiry he had pledged to form.[32] In the process, he swept off the table two proposals for secret service reform, both of which take their inspiration from the American example—parliamentary control and the creation of a National Security Council.[33]

In any case, the benefits of applying an American model in France are uncertain, in part because the advantages for Washington are not altogether obvious. Students of the CIA have noted that the safeguards applied in the United States are more honored in the breach among politicians who are reluctant to shoulder "co-responsibility" for actions whose outcome is unknown but who can earn thousands of political frequent-flier miles by posturing amidst the wreckage of failed operations.[34] In the wake of the *Rainbow Warrior* fiasco, opponents of parliamentary control of the secret services, like former SDECE chief Alexandre de Marenches, argued that it was ill adapted to French political culture. Unlike the United States, France does not have bipartisan agreement on defense and foreign policy to serve as a basis for DGSE orientation.[35] Marenches argued that the presence of communists on parliamentary committees raises the possibility of deliberate treason, a threat far more serious than the garrulous indiscretions of congressmen or their aides at Washington cocktail parties. Given the important role played by intelligence-induced political scandals in modern French history, it can come as no surprise that French deputies have concluded that binding their political futures to the next operation of the DGSE's Service Action would be like playing Russian roulette with all the chambers loaded. The powerful chairman of the Senate Defense and Foreign Affairs Committee, Jean Lecanuet, denounced public oversight of the secret services through parliament as "non-sense . . . Parliamentary control is dangerous." His colleagues appear to have taken his advice to heart, to the point that intelligence chiefs never appear before parliamentary committees, while, as in the United States, budgets for French intelligence organizations are kept secret even from otherwise powerful finance committees. Basically, French politicians have concluded that the secret services bring them no votes when things go right and only headaches when there is a _bavure_, a mistake.[36]

But even some opponents of parliamentary control see great gains for French secret service efficiency in the establishment of a National Security Council. In the view of CIA veteran Ray Cline, the creation of the National Security Council in 1948 reflected "a national commitment to establish a procedure for orderly deliberation and decision on military and diplomatic policy . . . A critical element in this structure was that both the CIA and the Joint Chiefs of Staff reported directly to the NSC on foreign situations, trends, threats, and opportunities. Thus an objective intelligence data base was available to the President along with technical evaluation of military risks and requirements."[37] Whatever else they disagree on, and it is much, both Marenches and Marion have endorsed the creation of an NSC. Marenches argues that such a body would stop the fragmentation of intelligence and its filtration through the Defense and Interior Ministries before it reaches the "decider" at the Elysée. It would also help to avoid "affairs," or at least insulate higher authority from their political impact.[38] Pierre Marion agrees, pointing out that the current French system leaves the Prime Minister completely out of the intelligence loop, as the _Rainbow Warrior_ affair demonstrated. An NSC in which the secret services were represented by a Director of Intelligence would also give them an independence of assessment which they dare not assume when under the direct authority of a minister. [39]

Of course, the purpose of the NSC in its original conception was not so much to inform American foreign policy as to give the intelligence and military constituencies a voice in the formulation of that policy. [40] Rather than lead to genuine reform, the result for the DGSE of the *Rainbow Warrior* episode was exactly as CIA director Stansfield Turner would have predicted—even an intelligence service which boasts an excellent record can be practically "obliterated by a very small number of harebrained enterprises." Worse, the tendency is to overreact by becoming too cautious and conservative to the point that even beneficial operations are curtailed. [41] Imbot's televised speech, delivered in full uniform, served notice to the DGSE that he intended to defend it, but in return it must "go back to its shell." "We were obliged to do it," one socialist politician confessed. "One had to turn the screws and he did it. After that, the DGSE plunged back into mediocrity. That's what we wanted . . ."[42] For Marion, it was merely one more nail in the marginalization of the DGSE to the benefit of the DST, although he admitted that the soldiers of the DGSE had only themselves to blame. [43]

For France, it was a rather depressing conclusion, one more missed opportunity for reform, for the maturation of state-intelligence relations which could have led to an effective system of political controls on the DGSE and greater integrity in the organization. It was yet another indication that France would continue to pay the price for a lack of real interest in intelligence issues in parliament, the media, and the public, and for the blurring of boundaries between intelligence, policy, and personal ambition in the political culture.

TWENTY

CONCLUSION

Although the fascination with spies is decades, perhaps centuries, old, serious attempts to trace the fingerprint of espionage and intelligence on the course of history has been a fairly recent phenomenon. Given a history of war, invasion, and empire, one might logically conclude that, of all countries, intelligence should play a critical, central role for France. But one message of this account might be that, while that relationship has been central, it has seldom been critical. Why? One possible explanation is that French intelligence has simply not been very good, or—to make the accusation even more sweeping—that intelligence seldom matters in any case. This has not been the conclusion of this study. Rather, the intelligence failures in France are related both to limitations of intelligence in general and specifically to the context of what might be called intelligence-state relations in France.

Thus, where ideally intelligence might have supplied an important "force multiplier" to inform policy and strategy at significant moments in French history, it has seldom functioned efficiently in that capacity. But this is not to say that the role of the French secret services over the past century can safely be ignored. Intelligence estimates have, at various times, influenced policy formulation or strategic decisions, although often in ways so oblique and subtle that its actual role has been opened to misinterpretation, even to charges of total failure, as at Dien Bien Phu. Second, the secret services have operated in ways which have influenced the political process more directly.

One result has been that French intelligence organizations founded to "reduce uncertainty" have often increased it. In other words, ⟨intelligence becomes part of the problem, not the solution. And while this is hardly unique to France, the consequences have been heavily felt there—for at least four reasons: First, the political culture in which French intelligence operates, one churned and even driven by scandals whose origins lurk deep in secret service conspiracies. Second, the military domination of foreign intelligence, which departs from the "norm" of an independent civilian organization standing outside of policy. In other words, intelligence has been captured by one of the players within the process. Third is the strong action culture in the French intelligence community. This legacy of the French Resistance has been given special prominence in France because action or special operations are seen as a tactical solution to intractable strategic problems caused by failed policy or national weakness. The problems occur when action solutions impinge on domestic politics, which causes the intelligence organization to be perceived as dangerous and makes it distrusted.

This brings up the fourth and final problem of French intelligence—the role of domestic intelligence or counterintelligence. Theorists of intelligence who take Anglo-Saxon models as the norm, tend to include counterintelligence in the category of police work or even repression, rather than that of intelligence. This does not make sense in the French case, where the line between internal and external enemies has not always been easy to draw, and where taking a position on a foreign issue can place one in a very delicate position domestically. Indeed, because of France's divided political culture, and a vision of nationhood as a cultural and linguistic communion in constant danger of subversion or overthrow by groups whose national origins, religious beliefs, or political allegiances cause them to be insufficiently integrated into the national community, it is hardly surprising that French leaders have on occasion shown a marked inability to distinguish between the two. Nor must one forget that zealous pursuit of political or personal advantage requiring the assistance of domestic intelligence or counterintelligence has been accorded a central position in French political culture.

If intelligence is the "pursuit of secret advantage,"[1] over both external and internal enemies—or even friends, for that matter—one may legitimately ask: What advantage has accrued to France from the quest for intelligence? A hypothetical French intelligence professional whose career has spanned the lifetime of this book might be tempted to agree with an equally hypothetical British colleague who is alleged to have admitted only two lapses in his long career—the failure to forewarn of either World War I or World War II. The most egregious failures assigned French intelligence include the strategic surprises of the Schlieffen Plan of 1914 and the 1940s Ardennes breakthrough, and the failure to predict Giap's ability to overwhelm Dien Bien Phu in 1954. In other words, as critics chided the CIA for its inability to predict the collapse of the Soviet Union or Saddam Hussein's invasion of Kuwait,[2] so the French services, while perhaps useful tactically or operationally, stand accused of strategic failures monumental enough to have changed the course of French history.

The classic defense of French intelligence advanced by some of its ex-practitioners, such as Paul Paillole or even Henri Navarre, has been that intelligence was perfectly adequate but French politicians and generals did not bother to heed it. This study does not disagree with this view. Intelligence in France was hardly an unrelieved series of disastrous predictions and ignominious failures. Far from it. But simply to plead "we were right, but not listened to," defines the problem of intelligence generally, and French intelligence in particular, in terms too simplistic to make sense out of a complex relationship. Rather, as students of intelligence are only beginning to understand, the relationships among information, policy, and strategy are seldom as clear-cut as both critics and apologists would suggest.

Ideally, intelligence stands outside of policy, a source of information untainted by prejudice or preconception, a corrective which, if heeded, can inform and guide policy and strategy. From this perspective, the Deuxième Bureau and French military attachés before both world wars provided perfectly adequate documentation of the growing power of German arms, their combat doctrines, and their capabilities. The problem is that intelligence interacts with its environment in ways such that it seldom operates as a neutral, objective force, but one which is softened and shaped by government structure, bureaucratic or political pressures, or ethnocentric views of the world beyond one's borders.

Ultimately, the most important factor is what the decision maker wants to do in any case, a decision more likely to be informed by a strong dose of wishful thinking than solid intelligence. In other words, "what is the concept," what do French policy makers expect of their intelligence organizations? This places intelligence officers in a difficult—not to say impossible—dilemma. They can "go with the flow," supply intelligence which does not challenge the leader's perceptions, in the hope of preserving at least some shreds of influence. The risk in this course of action is that they become irrelevant, and ultimately are excluded from the very councils in which they hope to preserve their influence.[3] This is hardly a problem unique to France. Canadian historian Westley Wark noted that British intelligence in the interwar years was far more likely to reflect existing perceptions and interests than to criticize them. Nor does intelligence evaluation remain static, especially in crisis situations when it may reflect different viewpoints or even shift positions. Furthermore, visions of a "worst-case scenario" painted by intelligence analysts can induce fatalism in politicians and soldiers. The question becomes not why intelligence fails to act as a corrective, but how it ever succeeds at all.[4] Given these underlying conditions, American scholar Richard Betts has argued that intelligence failure is not the exception, but inevitable.[5] When the factors which lead to selectivity, distortion, or simply dismissing intelligence are appended to the equation, then the performance of the French secret services over the last half century becomes less a question of "Did they get it right?" than one of how the secret services have behaved within the French political and military contexts. And while one of the themes of this book has been that these problems are common to all intelligence communities, in France they have been made particularly acute because the environment in which the secret services operate has reflected the idiosyncratic, at times even irrational, priorities and visions of French policy makers and strategists, as well as the fundamental problems caused by French weakness.

French intelligence has had to adapt to an idiosyncratic, even a hostile political environment in order to survive, while in their view preserving the integrity of their product. So far as one can tell, a basic strategy followed by the Deuxième Bureau before both world wars, one bequeathed to the postwar SDECE/DGSE, has been a sort of smorgasbord approach—spread the intelligence before the decision makers in all of its infinite variety and allow them to draw their own conclusions and select those elements which reinforce their own pre-dispositions and preferences. In the case of France's major enemy, Germany, the weight of the evidence inevitably amounted to a "worst case" assessment. Before 1914, this intelligence-supplied vision of growing German power caused politicians to cling more firmly than ever to their Russian alliance and impelled Joffre to risk all on an offensive strategy as the only way to overcome apparently hopeless odds. Likewise, in the interwar years, the "worst case" assessment encouraged the policy of appeasement and convinced Gamelin to attempt to seize a battle line in Belgium as far forward as possible.

In both wars, therefore, the question of where exactly the Germans would attack was not provided by French intelligence. Shards of the answer can be found by historians digging through the debris of Deux-ième Bureau reports. But giving opinions, especially strong opinions, to politicians and generals was not their style. And what if it had been? Would Joffre or Gamelin have changed their plans? Before 1914, French intelligence supplied enough indications that the Germans might attempt a wide sweep through Belgium to convince at least some officers, including the French commander-in-chief in 1911, General Michel, that he should provide a defense against it. Joffre, however, had other priorities. Likewise, the French committee led by Marshal Pétain which designed the Maginot Line in the interwar years, and those who led the French war games in 1938, all thought an Ardennes thrust a threat serious enough to devise ways to counter it. As Gamelin insisted on applying a strategy which was opposed by all of his major subordinate commanders, one can only conclude that it is unlikely that, even had his Deuxième Bureau chief spoken with certainty of a German thrust into the Ardennes, Gamelin would have abandoned his Dyle/Breda Plan, any more than Joffre would have jettisoned Plan XVII.

It is no exaggeration to say that French intelligence at the time of Dien Bien Phu had never been better, in its ability both to track enemy movements and to assess Vietminh potential in logistics, armaments, and manpower. If Navarre opted for Castor in 1953 in the teeth of intelligence-compiled evidence which should have induced caution, it was because his desire to protect his highland maquis and their opium crop was more powerful than the fears that he might be sticking his head into a noose. So if intelligence available to Navarre should have induced caution, he calculated that his strategy would negate that of Giap, thus making the enemy's plans and his own intelligence on enemy intentions and capabilities irrelevant. This can, in the right circumstances, offer a commander a perfectly legitimate reason for ignoring or overruling his own intelligence. The fundamental require-ment of success, of course, is that one's strategy is firmly grounded in a realistic appraisal of one's own capabilities, and not in wishful think-ing. When Giap's offensive began, the French knew the objective and time of virtually every attack. But even intelligence of such precision could not rescue bad judgment. In all three instances, intelligence fell like drops of water on a stone, persistent, but powerless to make even a slight indentation.

It is also true that leaders are apt to influence intelligence more than intelligence influences leaders. This is especially the case in areas where a leader feels particularly knowledgeable, when he has com-mitted to a line of action, or where significant national or personal interests may be at stake. Any intelligence adviser or agency which persists in producing intelligence which runs counter to a leader's policies or visions condemns itself to marginalization or utter oblivion.[6] Therefore, if the policy is flawed or even irrational, the intelligence process will likely mirror, even reinforce, its defects.[7]

This was especially the case under de Gaulle. Intelligence played no role in shaping the General's geopolitical vision either of guaran-teeing for France a great power role in World War II or of shattering the status quo of the two power blocs after 1963. A strong personality, master of diplomatic surprise, of creative, innovative diplomacy, de Gaulle embarked on a strategic offensive, much as had Joffre and Gamelin. The General was more interested in translating a diplomatic vision into reality than in reacting to the moves of other powers, and as such he had scant use for intelligence. As far as he found a role at all for his secret services, both official and unofficial, it was a tactical one—to organize the Resistance into a political base for Fighting France, to create the nucleus of a political party in the 1950s, to fight against the OAS, and to solidify French control over her former African colonies. Intelligence was pressed into the service of the Gaullist vision even if this meant spying à tous azimuts—"in all directions"—or subsidizing Quebec separatism with secret service funds.[8] It is possible that de Gaulle's inability to achieve many of his policy goals encouraged French intelligence organizations to take extreme, even foolhardy, measures in pursuit of success. This can lead to failure, and cause intelligence services to court low esteem, even derision.

Such has been the case in France. The low esteem in which French intelligence, especially foreign intelligence, has been held has helped to diminish its influence, because leaders believed it inefficient, politicized, or both. And the strength of this belief has turned it into a self-fulfilling prophecy. While on paper the various intelligence agencies may appear to have defined the frontiers of their tasks quite clearly, in practice there is much rivalry between them, a rivalry which can on occasion spill over into hostility. In theory, at least, competitive intelligence organizations need not be a bad thing in themselves, for they can produce a system known as "multiple advocacy." Multiple advocacy should eliminate "groupthink" and offer a leader multiple channels of information, rather than allow his advisers to present a limited range of options or even a unanimous recommendation cooked up in advance.[9]

If, however, multiple advocacy is likely to fall short of its theoretical promise in any political context, it is a model which is especially ill adapted to France. Since the Dreyfus Affair, there can be few French politicians unaware that, as the British historian of intelligence Phillip Knightley reminds one, all intelligence organizations are essentially bureaucracies interested in perpetuating and extending their own power, with elaborate defense mechanisms for explaining away failure.[10] In practice, the struggle for influence can mean that few are willing to put forward intelligence uncongenial to a leader's views, especially a leader uncomfortable with debate among his advisers.[11] The bottom line for an intelligence advocate is not veritas, but survival, influence, and a disproportionate share of resources, all of which can undermine the coherence of the intelligence picture presented to the decision maker.[12]

Students of multiple advocacy have noted that, to be effective, it must be part of a controlled system, with an executive presiding over an orderly presentation of views and options.[13] Traditional distrust of intelligence services, the fragmentation of political power in the multiparty system with a weak executive, which characterized the Third and Fourth Republics, the rivalries between President and Prime Minister in the Fifth Republic, made especially acute by the "cohabitation" of the socialist Mitterrand with conservative Prime Ministers in the 1980s and 1990s, has done much to ensure the failure of multiple advocacy in France.

French leaders fear that their position will be diminished, even sabotaged, by intelligence functionaries, and so can keep them at arm's length or, better, favor tame intelligence organizations, especially ones created to support a leader's policies rather than challenge them. Political favoritism, rivalry and distrust among intelligence organizations, the military control of foreign intelligence, the priority accorded domestic spying, has meant that competence, information, and analytical resources are unevenly distributed among the various intelligence services, which has created an unlevel playing field on which the game of intelligence advocacy is played. This has placed some services—notably the DST—in a far stronger position to advocate than their rivals. Last, the secretive nature of French decision making caused by fear of scandal, by fears that rivals in the cutthroat world of French politics might seize political advantage from a leak, or by resistance to parliamentary control of intelligence has meant that decisions are often taken by a restricted circle of people on the basis of a limited spectrum of intelligence evaluation. One wonders, for instance, if the lunatic order to sink the *Rainbow Warrior* would have been given had a properly functioning system of multiple advocacy been in place, one which required the discreet consultation of opinion outside a narrow circle in the DGSE, the Defense Ministry, and possibly military advisers in the Elysée Palace. In other words, because the French intelligence system is both fragmented and enclosed with narrow orbits of different services or parts of services, it leads to the same sort of "groupthink" which multiple advocacy is meant to avoid.

Overall, French political leaders have seldom been impressed by the intelligence product. This is in part because traditionally the French services are better at collecting raw data than at producing a finished product. Once again, while this phenomenon constitutes almost a universal law of intelligence, it is true nonetheless that French foreign espionage traditionally has placed a low premium on analysis. Vincent Cannistraro, until recently chief of operations and analysis for the CIA's Center for Counter Terrorism, has argued that the DGSE's "principal handicap resides in a limited capacity for analysis and the provision of operational synthesis" to French leaders, a charge leveled also at the SGDN.[14] The explanation for the diminished analytical capacities of French intelligence lay in part with the military nature of the SDECE/DGSE. While it is certainly true that since Bazeries some of France's most remarkable intelligence officers have been drawn from the ranks of the military, as even Cannistraro concedes, generally speaking the hierarchical values of loyalty and obedience sit uneasily with an intelligence culture which requires independence of mind and the pursuit of "truth."[15] Therefore, the absence of strong analyses which may run counter to policy or strategy becomes a bureaucratic defense mechanism particularly congenial to a military culture, which rewards "team players" and condemns officers who demonstrate too much independence of spirit as argumentative or maverick, or—worse by far—consigns them to that circle of the damned reserved for "les intellectuels."

This clash of cultures, one military, the other in theory closer to something resembling an academic environment, plays out on a bureaucratic level in France. Intelligence in the French army is not a distinct branch of service, so that the organizational independence which is a prime component of intelligence effectiveness is in part compromised by the career structure. Officers who have thrown themselves into intelligence work, such as Paillole or Rivet, often arrive by accident and remain, so far as regulations allow, out of a liking for the work and a strong sense of duty. Such was the experience of Roger Joint-Daguenet, a communications officer co-opted by the SDECE during the Fourth and Fifth Republics, who discovered that he was neither fish nor fowl—intelligence work offered no career pattern, yet when he returned to his arm for the command time required for promotion, he was regarded as an outsider and given the least attractive assignments. The result has been organizational turbulence and demoralization which can hardly benefit the quality of analysis. Joint-

Daguenet agreed with Marion that while SDECE recruited some excellent personnel and technicians, their effectiveness was compromised by lack of means and by poor middle management—the desk officers or *analysts de zone* chosen because they were ill, because they needed to be in Paris, or for any reason other than a demonstrable skill as analysts. Either they would send out intelligence requests, "*notes d'orientation* . . . which were completely crazy[Once [while serving in India\ I received a note asking me to count the number of blades on the propellers of Soviet fishing boats. Obviously this interested someone very much. But I never found out the answer]" Or they would water down or refuse to pass on a report which would be badly received higher up.[16]

One irony is that, while official France is a closed, even a secretive society, it has a weak culture of intelligence. Intelligence professionals decry their inability to be taken seriously by national leaders, which some have come to see as a Gallic character flaw, an element of "our national failings: the absence of an intelligence culture, a consequence of a lack of seriousness in the French spirit which prefers the immediate to the long-term, the brilliant spectacle to the quiet contemplation of the monk in his cell," writes General Jean Pichot-Duclos, head of the Institute for Economic Intelligence Studies and Strategy. ["There is also the Gallic spirit, quick to cultivate differences, to throw up barriers, to break into factions.]"[17]

While the explanation which interprets the absence of an intelligence culture in France as an inevitable consequence of a national character flaw has a certain superficial attraction, in the final analysis it is a lame excuse for poor civil-intelligence relations there. All politicians operate on the basis of short-term calculations. Few in any country like to waste time contemplating events beyond the next critical parliamentary vote or local election. As noted before, how to have one's intelligence factored into a political process which invariably neglects long-range considerations and makes decisions on an ad hoc basis is a problem for *all* intelligence organizations, not just those of France. However, the problem is made more acute in France for historical reasons—French decision makers simply place little faith in their intelligence organizations because they distrust them. As a consequence, intelligence organizations feel powerless because they cannot make their influence felt. Therefore, civil-intelligence relations in France have become locked in a vicious circle, in which intelligence organizations are frustrated and bitter because their product is largely neglected by leaders who do so because they distrust the motives or abilities of those who supply the information.

For instance, Pichot-Duclos' image of the intelligence professional as a monk lost in quasi-monastic contemplation should be enough to make most French politicians choke on their morning croissant. All intelligence agencies have their own prejudices and agendas, see the world and their role in it refracted through their own peculiar lens. In France, the struggle between objectivity and mirage has been especially acute because of the country's precarious military position during much of the century and France's divided political culture. The result has been the politicization of the intelligence services which began in earnest in the interwar years when they defined themselves as anticommunist and anti-Nazi, and often decried the timid, slothful, or self-interested response of governments in the face of imminent national peril so voluminously chronicled by the Deuxième Bureau and military attachés.

That politicization was given a new twist during World War II, when the intelligence services in the Vichy and Free French camps were pressed into the service of radically different visions of French interests. The French services in the postwar world found it difficult to recover completely their political objectivity, as political parties sought to place their surrogates in the intelligence services. The process of politicization was furthered in the Fifth Republic, when the services were expected to support the interests of the hegemonic power. As American intelligence specialist Michael Handel has noted, while ideally intelligence work should be objective and autonomous, in fact it is closely bound up with policy to the point that it is difficult to know where intelligence stops and policy begins.[18] In France, intelligence ceased to be an objective, neutral bureaucracy, but rather became one whose mission was to support conservative governments. But this transition came at a price, even for the Gaullists, who until 1981 were the prime beneficiaries of the process. In effect outsiders who inherited the state apparatus, they proved deeply distrustful of their regular intelligence services. In opposition, the Gaullists, like the left, had been targets of intelligence-inspired coups—de Gaulle with the *affaire Passy* and Mitterrand with the *affaire des fuites*. Nor did these fears diminish once the men came to power. On the contrary, parties in power became especially vulnerable to scandals of murky secret service inspiration—the Ben Barka affair for de Gaulle and the Marcovic episode for Pompidou have been mentioned. In September 1979, the SDECE was tainted by the part they played in an episode of political corruption, when a regiment of French paratroops working for the SDECE's action service smuggled an opposition politician into Bangui, the signal for an uprising in the Central African Empire to overthrow Emperor Bokassa. Bokassa had become an embarrassment for the French for several reasons, not the least being that he allegedly had threatened to reveal the names of politicians upon whom he had showered gifts of diamonds. High on that list was President Giscard d'Estaing. The "popular uprising" was a great success, marred only slightly from a covert-action perspective by the paratroops' insistence on a victory parade down Bangui's main street. Nor did the French President have occasion to be completely satisfied with the SDECE after leaks from Bokassa's archives, seized and transported by them to Paris, revealed the very information that the "uprising" had been contrived in part to keep hidden.[19]

The left, which seized power in 1981, came by their distrust of the secret services quite naturally. Since the Dreyfus Affair, many on the left especially have placed little faith in the objectivity, not to mention the sense of fair play, of intelligence services dominated by military men who owe their careers, and hence their primary loyalty, to the armed forces. One obvious step toward making intelligence more palatable to political leaders, especially on the left, would have been a thorough reform of the SDECE, to include removing it from military control. This should have caused few problems as the SDECE's information gathering had long since broken the bounds of strictly military intelligence, which comprises probably no more than a fifth of its intelligence product,[20] and as roughly half of SDECE employees are civilians. In 1981, Mitterrand named a civilian, Pierre Marion, to head the SDECE, and the following year changed the name to the DGSE.

However, tentative steps by Mitterrand to slip policemen into senior roles at the DGSE and the SGDN from 1989 were reversed with the right-wing electoral victory of 1993, which presided over, in the opinion of *Le Monde*, "the recovery by the military of two of the Republic's most senior bodies dealing with security and intelligence matters, at the highest levels of state."[21] So long as military control of the DGSE remains a political issue, its influence over policy must remain muted. But Mitterrand's distrust has not been reserved for the DGSE. Even intelligence coups which have redounded to his credit, like the DST-produced Farewell dossier, have been perceived by him as vehicles to realize the malicious intentions of his enemies in and through his intelligence services.

Because French political leaders so often distrust official intelligence organizations, they prefer to keep them inefficient, thus perpetuating the vicious circle which has done so much damage to civil-intelligence relations. At the same time, at least since Joseph Caillaux, if not before, they require intelligence if for no other reason than to spy on their political rivals and advance their own interests. One way out of this dilemma has been to create new parallel services acting outside normal channels, special ad hoc formations of men whose agent status depends utterly on their loyalty to the minister or President. The Elysée cell under Christian Prouteau is but the latest example of this practice, which would include the anti-OAS *barbouze*, SAC, and the mesh of networks, agents, and mercenaries in Africa which, tradition has it, have answered to Jacques Foccart. The defense of these arrangements with Paris is that they have provided stability for a large part of Africa, have kept the ex-colonies free of Soviet and Eastern European interference during the Cold War, and shored up French economic, political, and cultural interests. Against these benefits, these countries must balance the costs of a particularly stringent version of neocolonialism in which national sovereignty is severely circumscribed by a France which aggressively demands it for herself. Nor has France hesitated to employ several of these countries as bases for some of Paris' least commendable interventions in the internal affairs of other African nations. Indeed, some observers traced the leaks during the Bokassa diamond episode to dissident elements in the SDECE who were upset at being employed as "intelligence mercenaries" in the private interests of Monsieur Foccart and friends, rather than those of France.[22] Mitterrand appears to have interfered little in these arrangements, although there is some evidence, now that the Cold War is over, that the United States is no longer willing to tolerate what one Clinton official called "France's . . . exorbitant and anachronistic . . . privileges in black Africa."[23]

A further legacy of France's Resistance past, of her post-1945 colonial wars, and the tendency to resort to parallel services has been to give French intelligence an operational dimension through a marriage with action and special operations. Once again, a problem which affects all intelligence organizations becomes an especially corrosive one in France. As with the intelligence services of several countries, this marriage began in World War II when intelligence gathering and sabotage missions behind enemy lines became a high priority for Allied intelligence and special operations. In the French case, however, one result has been that some of the shortcomings of the Resistance as an intelligence organization were perpetuated in the postwar era. During World War II, action distorted and even undermined intelligence, for the requirements of the immediate operation took priority over the dull, thankless, and, to those unable to see the results of the labors, apparently fruitless task of intelligence collection.

But it was in the excitement and drama of action in France's shadow war against the Nazi occupier that reputations were made. The ex-resisters, cradled in the necessary myth that the maquis had made a significant contribution to the German defeat, transferred their taste for action into the postwar services. There it was fed by Jacques Foccart in his search for corps of muscular Gaullist faithful and a *service d'ordre* to protect the General's political rallies from communist disruption. The SDECE's Service Action and the 11ème Choc were actively courted—some insist infiltrated—by the Gaullists, as insurance against any future need to suborn the Fourth Republic or defend the Fifth. Covert action helped to shape Foccart's interventionist approach to African affairs and bequeath to that continent an unhappy legacy of mercenaries ready to stir the bubbling cauldrons of African instability. The benefits of such activity proved marginal—either they failed, as in Guinea and Biafra, or gave French policy a cynical and thuggish patina which tarnished any political and economic advantages which accrued to France through these methods. The image of prominent ex-directors of the SDECE testifying to Bob Denard's fundamental patriotism, at his recent trial for murder and extortion during his long and bloody mercenary career, hardly reflected great credit on the "civilizing mission" of France in Africa.

Many of these mercenaries were graduates of the "low-intensity conflicts" fought by France in Indochina and Algeria, wars in which clandestine operations were pressed into the rescue of a weak policy and confused strategy. Soldiers like Roger Trinquier, eager to apply maquis methods, were paired with sympathetic commanders like Salan and Navarre in unions which, at Dien Bien Phu at least, were politically and militarily disastrous. To this already lethal and romantic mixture of the Resistance heritage, the political benefits of courting support among action volunteers, and the prolonged wartime atmosphere were added a number of unstable, criminal, or merely "cowboy" elements normally drawn by exotic or exciting images of the secret services. The preference for action has been encouraged by the military character of the SDECE/DGSE. This has had an especially noxious effect because, as Pierre Marion discovered when he became SDECE chief in 1981, the Service Action is a commando formation rather than one prepared for "a light and clandestine intervention."[24] One result has been that politicians desperate for a quick fix, a rapid or spectacular exit from a political problem, especially when a policy appears to have encountered stiff opposition, may opt for an action solution in totally inappropriate circumstances. The New Zealand fiasco of 1985 offers a striking example of how intelligence and special operations can court disaster when they are fed into an irrational political process.

Given the lack of parliamentary or institutional restraint beyond that imposed by the lingering memory of the last secret service-induced *affaire*, intelligence agencies too often fall back on the principle that the requirement to defend French interests justifies almost any means.[25] While this attitude is by no means limited to France, its consequences are more evident there. Apologists for excesses of intelligence agencies operating abroad will invariably insist that license is a necessary attribute for those operating in an anarchic political system. Only the prevalence of this Machiavellian acceptance of *raison d'état* can account for French tolerance of Chirac's disgraceful settlement of the *Rainbow Warrior* episode. One consequence of this attitude is that it too often extends to a tolerance of domestic spying as well.

There are several reasons why the French have come to accept domestic spying as an unavoidable fact of life. Generally speaking, domestic spying becomes acute when governments fear that threats abroad can translate into unrest and subversion at home.[26] This has reinforced in France the persistent belief that great affairs of state can turn on treason, and has combined with popular tolerance of an invasive state bureaucracy to open the door to abuses. France is caught in the contradiction of two conflicting images of itself. On one hand, since the French Revolution, France has prided itself on being a destination for Europe's politically oppressed. At the same time, the invasion of foreign refugees and immigrants feeds the persistent French fear that the cultural and linguistic homogeneity by which they define their national character, as well as their very security, is under threat. Indeed, it is quite clear that at least from Clemenceau's first ministry (1906–9) if not before, the French state has commingled notions of internal surveillance of foreigners, colonial subjects, ethnic, national, or religious minorities resident in France, and external intelligence to the point that the two tasks have become in effect indistinguishable. So long as surveillance of "foreigners" in France, supplemented by intelligence on them gleaned from abroad, was carried out, then France could be protected from outside influence and could enjoy real political freedom at home.[27] It is hardly surprising that secret services charged with standing watch over French security, especially the DST and the RG, may violate many of the principles they claim to uphold. Perhaps it is only natural for men who work in secret to mirror-image, to see conspiracies as the source of their problems and seek to remedy them through clandestine and conspiratorial means. The tendency might be given full rein when a conspiratorially minded Interior Minister takes charge.

For Interior Minister Raymond Marcellin, for instance, to whom the DST answered, the outbreak of the May '68 troubles in France had nothing to do with deep-seated social or economic causes. He linked them directly to revolutionary groups of Trotskyists, Maoists, and other left-wing extremists—an implausible conspiracy of "Germans and Jews"—of which the French services remained ignorant.[28]

Likewise, Marcellin remained convinced that, of all Western countries, France was the most deeply penetrated by Soviet espionage, a penetration which even Mitterrand's expulsion of forty-seven diplomats in April 1983 did little to diminish.[29] When the world is viewed in such a way, automatically to make fellow citizens suspect and to regard political adversaries as potential subversives, then abuses like the bugging of the *Canard enchaîné* office become not only possible; they are in danger of becoming the norm, especially when internal autonomist groups of Bretons, Basques, or Corsicans, or—far worse—a growing Muslim population threaten the homogeneity, and consequently the security, of the national culture.

Certainly, Soviet and Eastern bloc services have been very active in France. France's advanced armaments and technological industries, and, until the mid-1960s, a significant NATO presence, supplied the East with useful targets. Paris was swamped with foreign agents who, under diplomatic cover, could easily recruit people in need of money, who were ideologically sympathetic to the Soviet Union, or those of Russian extraction vulnerable to emotional appeals in the name of Mother Russia. To this, one can add the presence of a large indigenous Communist Party, some of whose members were assigned espionage duties.

How did the DST rise to the challenge of foreign espionage? Since Wybot, the DST has seen itself as the elite service of the police, from which its agents are recruited, as in the SDECE/DGSE, by co-option. Like any secret service, the DST is prepared to accept credit for its successes and shift blame for failures onto external causes—lack of security-consciousness among the French, lax courts, or government officials who fear that revelation of an espionage network will hurt French prestige or that the expulsion of a foreign diplomat will damage foreign relations.[30] The DST is generally considered the most professional of France's secret services. According to Pierre Marion, not an unbiased source certainly, the DST director was suspected by Mitterrand to be "unreliable and probably ill disposed toward the new government" in 1981. But while socialist suspicion was extended with commendable lack of bias to all the secret services, the DST alone was able to settle into a cozy relationship with the socialists by producing the Farewell dossier and by smashing several terrorist networks.[31]

Farewell was an intelligence coup which fell into the lap of the DST. Other espionage affairs, however, had to be ferreted out. And with these, the DST faced substantial obstacles in the waning years of the Cold War. With fewer than 2,000 agents, the DST found it difficult to keep pace with the sheer volume of spies or potential spies. Critics of the DST say it is too compartmentalized, which leads to duplication and lack of focus, and "drowns itself in personnel inquiries" and fiches.[32] The task of keeping up with Eastern bloc spies was complicated further by the assumption of counterterrorist or political spying missions. The potential for espionage and internal subversion has remained the excuse for maintaining some of the least attractive aspects of counterintelligence in France. All of this appeared to act as a Cold War alibi for men like Marcellin who were convinced that democracy—open, generous, trusting—had disarmed itself before its Soviet adversary. "That's why the intermittent efforts of democracies to practice Christian virtues bring about derisive results," insisted Marcellin, "from which spring their momentary paralysis in the face of triumphant and joyously ironic adversaries." In Marcellin's view, the problem was not to justify telephone taps, secret microphones, and the opening of letters. Rather, it was to find ways to make these practices more efficient.[33] It comes as no surprise, then, that the DST has hardly been scandal-free. The *Canard enchaîné* episode is the most celebrated only because of the sensational manner in which it was revealed. The DST also stands accused of "provocation," such as setting off bombs which were subsequently attributed to Breton nationalists. But during the 1980s, the DST has certainly become more efficient at counterterrorism, both by its own efforts and through increased cooperation with the police and intelligence agencies of other nations.

The Future of the French Secret Services?

This prompts one to ask: What roles might the French services adopt in the future? It is not an easy question to answer. Certainly, there is no lack of intelligence missions—counterterrorism, the traffic of arms and drugs, the proliferation of nuclear and ballistic technologies, and the circumvention of embargoes prominent among them. The essential problem for the French government will be to prioritize its intelligence missions to tailor them to the capabilities and resources of its secret services. France lacks the intelligence assets to be strong in all areas. But it need not be. Counterintelligence should pose fewest problems, for it is an area in which the strengths of French intelligence services have traditionally been located. It is also there where the two most obvious threats lie—terrorism and industrial/scientific espionage. The realignment of foreign intelligence priorities will be less easy, for it will require the French political leadership to confront the contradictions of an attitude which combines disdain for the intelligence community with a Gaullist-inspired insistence on France's status as a great power.

How can France be a power which insists on a position of independent, almost Olympian, conduct in world affairs, including an independent nuclear force, without intelligence to inform policies and target missiles? The short answer is that it cannot. So it needs to focus its intelligence assets on those areas of the world of most interest to it—in particular Europe, especially Germany, whose reunification and future policies are once again of vital importance to France, and also North Africa. Elsewhere, it will need to cooperate closely with other intelligence services, most notably with the CIA.

The role which French intelligence will inevitably continue to assume with least adjustment is that of counterintelligence, especially counterterrorism. Persistent incidents of terrorism by Corsican and Basque nationalists, and fears that political and religious disputes in the Middle East and North Africa will play out among France's significant Islamic population, caused the government to form an interministerial committee to coordinate the antiterrorist campaign in September 1993.[34] The aggravation of the situation in Algeria potentially has serious repercussions for France, especially if it produces a wave of refugees prepared to carry on their civil war between Islamic fundamentalists and pro-Western Algerians on French soil.[35] The deteriorating situation in Algeria, in which French nationals have been assassinated, has placed French politicians in a dilemma. Interior Minister Charles Pasqua has favored tough measures against fundamentalists in France. Over the long term, this will require the development of networks in the Islamic community, possibly within Algeria itself, to deliver humint. However, this tactic courts two dangers, both of which France has encountered before.

The first is that, as in the past, France itself could become the victim of a campaign of Islamic terrorism, requiring the government to reverse course, to ignore or dismantle its counterterrorist strategy, and instead seek to appease the fundamentalists in some way. Former Iranian President Bani-Sadr recently claimed France was doing just that when it refused in 1993 to extradite two Iranian terrorists to Switzerland to stand trial for the murder of an Iranian dissident, and instead extradited them to Teheran. Bani-Sadr suggested that the French strategy was to convince Iran to stop financing fundamentalist terrorism in Algeria, an interpretation adopted by other sources.[36]

The second danger is that French swoops on fundamentalist "bases" in France have netted only relatively moderate elements who are opposed to assassination and merely seek to open a dialogue with the Algerian government. One interpretation is that Pasqua was only trying to send a signal to militant Algerians that their activity must remain within acceptable limits and to assure the French people that its government is on the qui vive.[37] The danger, of course, is that the relatively moderate religious elements will be either discredited or shoved into the ranks of the extremists, as happened in Indochina and Algeria in the colonial days.[38]

A second area on which French intelligence resources should be concentrated is the field of industrial and scientific espionage. Claude Silberzahn, named to head the DGSE in 1989, declared that he intended to do just that: "Espionage today is essentially economic, scientific, technological, and financial," he insisted. Indeed, given the large role played by the French state in industrial planning and scientific and technological development, the government's ownership of major sectors of the economy, not to mention the importance of major industries, like that of armaments, to the health of the French economy, industrial and scientific intelligence is a good investment for France. To this end, the DST has proposed to absorb the RG so that it can more effectively concentrate on protection against industrial espionage.[39]

Unfortunately for France, intelligence activity in this area has not won France many friends abroad, especially in the United States, upset by revelations that the French have launched a campaign of intensive industrial espionage against her ally. In an interview soon after taking office, Silberzahn explained that the viability of France's defense industry was a high priority for French intelligence, for without it France could have "no independent national defense."[40] When in April 1993, the Knight-Ridder news agency released a document allegedly prepared by the DGSE which prioritized systems developed by various U.S. aerospace firms as the object of espionage, the result was a virtual boycott in June 1993 of the celebrated Paris Air Show by the Pentagon and several of the American firms on the list.[41]

Although the French insisted that the documents were produced by a "malicious individual" eager to discredit the DGSE,[42] the news should have come as no shock to the CIA or the FBI. Thyraud de Vosjoli, after all, claims that he fled the SDECE outraged at being asked to spy on America. House Intelligence Committee chairman Dan Glickman of Kansas insisted that the United States had been "at the top of the [French] list" since de Gaulle.[43] In a September 1991 *Exposé* program aired on ABC television, Pierre Marion boasted that he had organized a twenty-man industrial espionage unit in the SDECE in 1981. The results had been impressive, and included plans of aircraft and marketing strategies which allowed France to close deals with India on the purchase of jets. In 1989, Jacques Isnard, who specializes in defense and intelligence matters for *Le Monde*, wrote that much information came through former Soviet agents who passed on to the French the fruits of Soviet industrial espionage in the West.[44] Both the DST and the DGSE solicited information from "correspondents" working for subsidiaries of foreign firms in France.[45]

When, in 1990, the French press insisted that the CIA had become so upset with French spying that virtually all exchange of "information on sensitive issues" had ceased, the DGSE dismissed them as "old stories" cleared up "a long time ago."[46] Old stories perhaps, but cleared up they certainly were not. The *Sunday Times* quoted a CIA official in 1993 who insisted that a cache of *"secret défense"* documents given to the CIA was "incredible stuff. They had got our position on the GATT negotiations in advance of talks, material on the President's private life, future weapon buys, everything they might want to gain political and economic advantage over us."[47] Business and government circles have expressed concern that poor protection of U.S. industrial and technological secrets accounts in some measure for the loss of U.S. competitive edge and the CIA has begun to reorder its priorities to a more economic, trade, and technology focus, although this falls short of industrial espionage.[48]

While French intelligence has been the object of significant anger, one may ask if it is really deserved. Certainly, some of the SDECE/ DGSE's past employees like Pierre Marion or Marcel Le Roy have proved the very souls of indiscretion, putting forward extravagant public claims of espionage successes against the United States. In the wake of these indiscretions, anecdotal evidence which allegedly pointed to a concerted French effort to discover American technological and scientific secrets began to build up. The French consul in Houston was allegedly discovered by the FBI rifling the trash cans of his neighbors in search of industrial secrets. Alerted, U.S. officials and businessmen have become more aware of searches of hotel rooms or briefcases when in France, and possibly less open with teams of French experts visiting the United States.

But when viewed in context, industrial spying by official French agencies is likely to be fairly small potatoes. In the first place, spying among corporate competitors appears to dwarf anything done on the state level. According to a 1987 study, espionage cost U.S. businesses $50 billion a year.[49] Furthermore, it is virtually risk-free. Trade secrets are easy to access through computer break-ins or the monitoring of faxes. The advantages for companies can be immense. As the KGB realized before its fortunate demise, industrial and technological spying can offer a shortcut which can save substantial sums in research and development. But companies which are the targets of spying report that product development is the most likely area to attract attention, while basic research draws little curiosity. Nor is the image of government spooks poking through wastebaskets an accurate one. When outsiders are involved in cases of industrial espionage, they are usually former employees.[50] The most skillful companies do their spying the old-fashioned way—they simply hire away a competitor's key personnel, as demonstrated by the Lopez affair between Volkswagen and General Motors.

Nor, if the DGSE is engaged in industrial espionage, do they appear to have been universally effective—for instance, intelligence, however precise, proved powerless to prevent the award of a huge Saudi Arabian contract to Boeing in 1994 at the expense of Airbus. Indeed, the complaint of French industrialists, in particular arms manufacturers, is that the DGSE supplies them with no intelligence on the proposals submitted to foreign customers in Asia and the Near and Middle East by their U.S. rivals so that the French can better counter them. The DGSE defends itself by arguing that it is being made a scapegoat by industrialists desperate for alibis to excuse their own competitive shortcomings. Many impediments exist to the implementation of an adequate system of economic espionage in France, critics maintain. The *énarques*—graduates of the elite Ecole Nationale d'Administration, who hold most of the important government and industrial posts in France—communicate only among themselves and regard intelligence as beneath their consideration. Companies do not define their intelligence needs, refuse to recognize that useful information carries a price tag, and have no mechanism for handling secret intelligence when they receive it, often mingling it with open research, or ignoring it in favor of a decision-making process which places a premium on corporate intuition. French banks, notoriously conservative, hesitate to take risks even when they are supplied with good financial intelligence.[51] Worse, businessmen lack the discretion to handle confidential information. One theory holds that the 1993 leaks of documents which alleged a concerted program of French industrial spying in the United States was the work of disgruntled French arms manufacturers eager to spite the DGSE for what they claim is a deliberate and discriminatory policy of withholding intelligence vital for the success of business deals.[52]

While the DGSE and the DST are no doubt guilty of siphoning off U.S. trade secrets, one suspects that they are the focus of such resentment simply because they are French. Though spying on allies is an unattractive business, intelligence experts have concluded that allied industrial spying on the United States has soared since the end of the Cold War, but that the French are far from the worst offenders. On the contrary, France trails at least a dozen countries, including Japan, Italy, Taiwan, and Germany. Among "enemies," China possibly tops the charts.[53] And it would be naive to believe that the CIA refuses to direct tidbits of industrial espionage back to Washington. French intelligence simply does not have the resources for widespread spying in the United States. The companies most vulnerable to French industrial espionage are those with subsidiaries in France. "It is hard to get information on weapons development," a CIA expert in industrial espionage said, noting that in the Gulf War even the most advanced French conventional weapons were comparatively out-of-date. "Besides, weapons espionage [against allies] is going beyond the bounds of the game. It is easier to go for more high-tech things, like computers. Industrial espionage is not central to French defense. It is not large."[54] Silberzahn, like Robert Gates of the CIA, has recognized that, with the internationalization of corporations, corporate and national interests may not go hand in hand.[55] As has proved to be the case with the SDECE/DGSE in Africa, intelligence agencies fueled by patriotism are reluctant to become industrial mercenaries pressed into the service of private interests, even when those are nationalized industries.[56] And if French businessmen are anything like their American counterparts, they may be reluctant to accept espionage help from secret services unschooled in business methods or needs, or who may request favors in return, such as cover for an agent and even a say in corporate decisions. Indeed, in the absence of official cooperation, industries are increasingly turning to private intelligence agencies. But, as in the public sector, the problem of French industry appears less in the acquisition of "real time" intelligence and more in its integration into a strategic decision-making process on the corporate level.[57]

In addition to counterterrorism and economic, industrial, and scientific espionage, France must also refine its priorities in the field of foreign intelligence. While the CIA, for instance, has to provide a global intelligence stretch, the DGSE cannot hope to do so. For this reason, the Gulf War was for the French government a wake-up call. The conflict exposed in all its nakedness the absurdity of France's ambitions to play the role of a great power with complete "freedom of assessment, decision making, and action for its benefit alone,"[58] and the fact that its intelligence services are unable to support this attitude. Again, it must be stressed that the problem was not uniquely a French one—no intelligence service did well in predicting Saddam Hussein's incursion into Kuwait, including the CIA and Mossad. After all, intelligence, especially military intelligence, focuses on capabilities and priorities, not intentions. But what was a universal problem was once again accentuated by the old problem of French weakness—France's insistence on playing a role beyond its capabilities.

The Gulf War broke over a military intelligence structure which was fragmented, undermanned, and undervalued. At the beginning of the crisis in August 1990, Major Philippe Debas warned that, if fighting came, the French army would pay the price of a policy which favored the purchase of tanks and frigates over satellites. "The President of the Republic will continue counting Russian rockets through American eyes," Debas predicted, noting that the Spot satellite system used by the French was far less precise than the U.S. version.[59] This proved prophetic—President Mitterrand had to be briefed about the Iraqi buildup in the Persian Gulf by American admiral Philip Dur, who traveled to the Elysée armed with satellite photographs. Mitterrand expressed enormous admiration for the precision of the American photographs. However, the briefing ended badly with the French President apparently feeling "humiliated" when Dur refused his request to leave the photographs behind so that they could be studied by French experts.[60] This constituted a poetic justice of sorts for a French President who had denounced "this sort of intellectual submission to the Americans" of his own intelligence services.[61] The French realized that their tributary position had considerably limited their capacity for independent decision making. "It was the United States that provided us with the bulk of the information necessary for conducting the conflict when and as it wished," Joxe confessed.[62] Joxe acknowledged the paradox of a country which maintained a force and constructed weapons systems for the projection of power but which, when the moment came, could only aim in the dark. With only 150 personnel, the Centre d'Exploitation du Renseignement Militaire (CERM) was too small to advise the high command.

One consequence of this lack of intelligence on the French side was that it brought out deep Gallic suspicions of its American ally. French intelligence claimed subsequently that they had suspected that Saddam Hussein's desperate financial situation and the proliferation of arms in the Middle East would require the Iraqi President to take offensive action once his war with Iran had been brought to a conclusion, but what that would be they had no ability to predict. Given the quality of U.S. satellite surveillance, however, the Americans *must* have been aware of Saddam's intention to invade Kuwait. For this reason, the French were deeply skeptical of the U.S. explanation of a "disagreeable surprise" at the Iraqi move, and suspected from the beginning that they were being set up by the Americans, who, with almost Bismarck-ian deviousness, were trying to draw them into a preplanned conflict.[63] This may help to explain the shifts between conciliation of Saddam and alignment with the Allies which characterized Mitterrand's policy practically up to the launching of Desert Storm in January 1991.

The absence of intelligence in theater also tied French forces in the Gulf closely to the apron strings of U.S. intelligence. "Without Allied intelligence, we were almost blind," Defense Minister Pierre Joxe confessed, citing weaknesses in all areas, including that of interpre-tation and integration of intelligence into the general plan of opera-tions. Some battlefield intelligence could be supplied by French air surveillance, a radio intercept service which worked in close contact with a CERM spy ship which carried a full complement of Arabic translators. But the French admitted that it was no more than a modest contribution to the Allied intelligence "pool."[64] Special operations support was provided for the Division Daguet in the form of commando teams, which travel under the unfortunate acronym of CRAP. Some 120 CRAP commandos, paratroops trained in various intelligence and special operations specialties, including photography, engineering, communications, foreign weapons systems, etc., were sent to the Gulf virtually at the last minute. Their task was to provide intelligence and take out specific enemy positions in advance of the French forces, a task in which two commandos died during the advance.[65]

Furthermore, it is clear from the Gulf War that the military staff structure lacked the personnel to digest the intelligence it received, much less deal with an influx of new intelligence. No combat intel-ligence arm exists in the French forces as in those of the United States, an omission which particularly hurt the Division Daguet. James J. Cooke, a U.S. army reservist assigned to intelligence duties with the French in Desert Storm, noted that the French were so limited in staff personnel to deal with intelligence that they would have been utterly lost had the Americans not supplied them. "All in all, the IPB [Intelligence Preparation of the Battlefield] system works well if you have the trained personnel . . . to analyze the information and con-tinually produce and interpret the overlays," Cooke writes. "Therein rested a French problem, for they had only a small number of support personnel to meet their needs, and these were taxed to the limit." He

494   THE FRENCH SECRET SERVICES

also noted that their POW interrogation methods were rendered almost useless by strict guidelines, a reaction to the torture of the Algerian War, Cooke believed.[66] One of the post-Desert Storm reforms proposed by Joxe has been to reorient the Interbranch Intelligence and Language School (EIREL) in Strasbourg away from its traditional curriculum of Czech and Russian to "four or five rare languages."[67] Never mind the "rare languages"! French officers better begin by learning the languages spoken by their most likely allies, starting with English. "The messages from the XVII Airborne Corps were in English, and the ability of the French personnel to comprehend important material was thus limited," Cooke records. "The critical nature of many messages did not leave room for an error of interpretation—a mistake in translation could potentially be fatal."[68]

Some of these French failures must be placed in context, for American intelligence, too, was forced to acknowledge that the Gulf War exposed some systemic weakness: no clear notion of what sort of intelligence could be provided; lack of "real time" intelligence; no standard methods of battle-damage assessment or methodology for analysis among the different services; poor radio communication among the services; lack of cooperation between the CIA and the Pentagon.[69] Still, the DGSE acknowledges that it owes Saddam Hussein its undying gratitude, for he accomplished what the *Rainbow Warrior* affair failed to do: forced the French government to recognize that it had neglected intelligence for over a century and prodded the French leadership into an apparently serious attempt at secret service reform. It is unlikely that French politicians wanted to go so far as to create an American-style NSC when in April 1989 the French cabinet discussed the need to reorganize and modernize the French secret services. The result was the creation of a Comité Inter-ministériel de Renseignement (Interministerial Intelligence Committee—CIR), which incorporated the ministries most interested in intelligence and the directors of the DST and the DGSE. In November 1993, Defense Minister François Léotard announced plans to press ahead with a French version of an NSC.[70] But doubts remain over the sincerity of French reform attempts, illustrating once again that it is difficult to transpose an intelligence model from one political culture, in this case the United States, to another. The conclusion that French politicians are actually happy with the fragmentation of the secret services is virtually inescapable, and it is easy to see why. Given the politicization of the services, it is much safer to keep them inefficient, weak, and dependent on crumbs of political patronage than to form a powerful state intelligence apparatus. After all, the same is true in the United States, where the creation of the NSC did not prevent the fragmentation of the intelligence services between the Defense Intelligence Agency and the CIA.

French investigative journalist Thierry Wolton remains skeptical of the ability of "those running the country to use these organizations as sources of reliable information and no longer as a lever in their political backstabbing." In other words, the history of French intelligence since Caillaux indicates that even reliable intelligence—especially reliable intelligence!—fed into a flawed and vindictive political process must lead invariably to scandal and abuse. It was clear in the late 1980s that the CIR was no NSC, and unlikely to become one so long as French politicians maintained their "archaic" attitudes toward intelligence agencies,[71] and the turf disputes between the DST and the DGSE continue to adjourn the restructuring of the French secret services.[72] The political and intelligence cultures in France appear to be a long way from seriously tackling the issues of accountability, executive leadership, efficiency, and ethics, especially in the area of covert operations and parallel services, which must serve as the basis of serious reform.[73]

As has been noted, attempts to bring senior civilian leadership with DST experience into the DGSE from 1989 foundered on the right-wing electoral victory of 1993. For this reason, it seems likely that the left will continue to distrust the DGSE, while the right will defend the army's right to impose its mediocrity on it. Claude Silberzahn, named to head the DGSE in 1989, recognized that serious intelligence reform faced an uphill struggle in France, where the absence of "a real intelligence culture" makes "it very difficult to integrate [intelligence] and its personnel into the decision-making process."[74] Silberzahn's priorities were to improve recruitment, to restructure the DGSE so that it could be in a better position to inform policy, and then to redirect its interests away from the old Cold War focus. Because of French weakness, the intelligence structure has to be flexible, prepared to shift priorities, and work in harmony with leaders.

Silberzahn's appointment to the DGSE was in itself a radical departure from past tradition—both he and a number of senior subordinates whom he has appointed come from the DGSE's rival, the DST, which at least held out the promise of better interservice relations. Silberzahn sought to raise the quality of DGSE personnel and lift its pay and career structure up to DST standards.[75] As in the DST, "walk-ins" are traditionally suspect in the DGSE. But this service, between 30 and 40 percent of whose 3,500 personnel are military, appears to be in less of a position to quibble—in the early 1990s, the DGSE and its Service Action actually began a "target" advertising campaign for mathematicians, computer scientists, communications specialists, and other technicians. Successful applicants realize that the "company" to which they have applied is a DGSE front. Silberzahn, the sixth director since Mitterrand came to power in 1981, promised to set up "a homogeneous structure" which would "create stronger company loyalty and put an end to the rivalry between the military and civilians."[76]

But better pay is unlikely to improve the morale and efficiency of the DGSE. Respect and influence, the need to have their product taken seriously and factored into the decision-making process, is the real goal of intelligence services. The inability to achieve any real influence ultimately condemned Silberzahn's reforms to failure. Like many French intelligence experts, Silberzahn sought to establish a central clearinghouse for intelligence as a means to inform government policy, similar to the function performed by the CIA. To overcome skepticism of the value and even distrust of DGSE intelligence in government circles, he had to improve the product. This required better cooperation within the organization between those who gather, analyze, and disseminate intelligence. The problem came down to the DGSE's corporate culture, which Silberzahn defined as one of "command" infused with military values and priorities. The DGSE had to become more like a research institute made up of specialists, technicians, and experts focused on the problems of the post-Cold War era rather than a military unit.

In June 1992, France pulled her fragmented military intelligence organizations into a single Military Intelligence Directorate (DRM). The DRM groups various Deuxième Bureaux of the three services, the CERM, which runs its own communication spy ship and planes in liaison with the Air Command for Surveillance, Information, and Communication (CASSIC), the DPSD (formerly the Sécurité Militaire), the Délégation Général de l'Armement, which oversees arms shipments abroad, and the communications sections of the DGSE. The 13th Paratroop Special Operations Regiment, technically part of the First Army, and the 1st Paratroop Hussars at Tarbes specialize in deep penetration operations, and have been used in Afghanistan and Cambodia. (Their last-minute commitment in the Gulf War limited their usefulness there.) For covert action, the DGSE can call on the 11ème Choc, revived after the *Rainbow Warrior* affair, and its naval section transferred from Aspretto to Quelern in Brittany, often transported by the Combined Air Group 56 in Evreux in western France. Most airborne regiments also maintain CRAP teams for deep reconnaissance.[77]

Under Silberzahn, the DGSE budget increased significantly to recruit more civilian personnel and improve France's technical capabilities. An Hélios satellite surveillance system appeared in 1994, and an Osiris radar detection satellite is scheduled for the next century, as is the Syracuse telecommunications system to supply secure communications. An electronic warfare brigade was organized in 1993, helicopter-mounted Horizon radar with a 150-mile range ordered for tactical reconnaissance, and an updated Sarigue electromagnetic system mounted on DC-8s to collect intelligence further afield.[78] Nevertheless, the French are likely to remain dependent on the United States for intelligence should they wish to engage in large-scale operations beyond the Mediterranean or in the Near East.

On the surface at least, this would suggest a revolution in French attitudes toward intelligence. Critics, however, argue that the reforms are cosmetic. After all, what is the point in investing heavily in a technical upgrade for a flawed intelligence system? Nor will such investment pay off so long as France has not defined its intelligence priorities. Complaints continue to be heard that the DGSE is still short on humint, and outclassed by the British in technical means, especially as London cooperates closely with Washington. Obviously, France will need to consult more closely with Washington in intelligence matters to make the best use of its scarce resources. But this will take a revolution in French policy toward cooperation with the United

States within the NATO structure. While the DRM with its significantly increased budget has been advertised as a new commitment to military intelligence, critics argue that it has only supplied another layer of bureaucracy which further marginalizes military intelligence, which competes with rather than rationalizes the intelligence-gathering mission with the DGSE. More, it offers another path through which the dead hand of military authority asserts its control over the French intelligence community, especially as the government persists in the appointment of active soldiers or men with military backgrounds to top positions in the DRM and the DGSE.[79]

Silberzahn argued that the DRM eliminated overlapping tasks in the DGSE and allowed it to place purely military intelligence in a broader context and refocus the DGSE's mission. When the new director took office in 1989, he discovered that the DGSE's intelligence product, half political analysis and the other half divided between military and economic information, was best in those areas where France had declining interests, notably Africa, "respectable" in Europe, and "significantly worse in Asia and sometimes outright mediocre in the Americas." Silberzahn's complaint was that the DGSE's intelligence was mainly tactical, uninformed, or lacking "broad-ranging ideas . . . and a very clear and intelligent vision of policies," past, future, or recommended. Nor was the sort of information it gathered very useful—political information, which makes up half its product, often duplicates that supplied by the Quai d'Orsay or the press, although DGSE reports are less inclined to exaggeration than are those of journalists and more in depth.

Have the Silberzahn reforms significantly altered the character of the DGSE and the quality of its product? Anyone with a historical perspective on the French secret services must remain skeptical. Attempts to give the services a "new look," tried before, all foundered on the poor image of agents as "toughs" and "shady characters" or "amateurs." The real high fliers of the French civil service, the graduates of the Ecole Nationale d'Administration, the celebrated énarques, have expressed scant interest in a career in which the senior positions to which they would aspire in other ministries or in industry are reserved for soldiers and cops.[80] Only three graduates of the elite Ecole Polytechnique and two énarques were to be found in the DGSE in

1993. In 1990, DGSE employees complained personally to the director of the "bitterness . . . despair . . . [and] exasperation" over crushing bureaucracy, poor efficiency, and low pay.[81] By 1993, however, Silberzahn could claim that pay raises which brought DGSE employees to a level with those of the DST and a better image had produced such a flood of recruits that the selection machinery had been completely overwhelmed.[82]

The massive investment in electronic gadgetry may assuage French pride bruised by dependence on the Americans. But it really amounts to tinkering with a faulty machine. The problem for the SDECE/DGSE has seldom been lack of intelligence. Rather it has been the generally poor quality of analysis and the unwillingness of the political structure to integrate intelligence into the decision-making process. Whether progress made will be reversed following the return of the DGSE to military control by the right in 1993, and Silberzahn's subsequent resignation, remains to be seen. Defense Minister François Léotard, complaining that French intelligence services are half the size of those of Germany and number only one-third of the British establishment, produced a massive budget increase for the DGSE, DRM, and DPSD along the lines of 25 to 30 percent in 1994.[83] The preliminary report of the Marceau Long Commission on defense reorganization has understood that the "ability to assess an international situation . . . starts with the possession of a whole panoply of intelligence and of what is called 'aids' to informing the command. The Americans have understood that and have made a spectacular effort in the sphere of C3I [Communications, Command, Control, and Intelligence] technology."[84]

If, as is sometimes alleged, ignorance of the past condemns America to repeat its mistakes, the French are so aware of their history that they fall prisoner to it. This would suggest that the prospects for major intelligence reform in France are limited. If, as Le Monde's intelligence and defense expert Jacques Isnard believes, intelligence has now become a "crisis management" tool,[85] it can be effective in that role only if the government is prepared to use it as such. France still possesses no structure to integrate intelligence into decision making beyond the willingness of the President to consult with his service chiefs on an ad hoc basis. There is little evidence that French leaders have abandoned their preference for parallel networks or information collected through informal means over that supplied by official services. Nor did they take much trouble to offer the collectors of intelligence guidance on issues important to the government. This has become especially critical as the single enemy has imploded. Secret services must be guided in their tasks by government. Within the services, analysts must tell collectors what they are collecting and guide technicians on how to utilize their equipment to best effect. Likewise, analysts must be sufficiently talented to cover the wide range of issues which will now fall to services to examine, and of sufficiently different backgrounds to look at problems from different angles, a cross-check on conclusions. One way around limited staffs is to draw on outside expertise in think tanks and universities,[86] a process in its infancy in France, where the DGSE has isolated itself by the very military nature of its recruitment. This is a tall order for a relatively small service held in low esteem both within the military and on the outside, because it is military.

Although Silberzahn's four-year tenure brought about significant budget and staff increases, efforts to change the DGSE's corporate culture, to distance it from the defense establishment, were bound to meet resistance. All intelligence organizations, to be successful, must readapt habits acquired during a lifetime of Cold War service. The clandestine habits which segregated operators and analysts within the same organization, the reports whose conclusions were shaped and prodded to fit a Cold War outlook, are legacies which all Western services must work to shed. In France, these legacies are further complicated by the predominance of a strong action culture inherited from the Resistance and by the military character of the DGSE, which reasserted itself with a vengeance in 1993. To hand the agency for foreign intelligence over to soldiers is automatically to reduce its significance; unlike the U.S. army or even the British army, the French army occupies a marginal and contested place in the political culture. No other world power—neither the United States, Great Britain, Russia nor Israel—has placed its major foreign intelligence agency in the hands of the military. Finally, it is unlikely that DGSE effectiveness can improve so long as Paris clings to attitudes of Gaullist independence which strain the capacities of its intelligence services. Like the British, the French lack the technical capacity for a global intelligence reach. While the British have compensated for their weaknesses by close cooperation with the United States, political considerations mean that the DGSE can do this only on an intermittent basis. However, as the breakup of the Soviet Union creates a more fragmented, less polarized world more congenial to the Gaullist vision, perhaps the French will be able to improve cooperation with other services.

With the end of the Cold War, all major intelligence agencies face significant challenges of change and adaptation. These trials promise to be particularly acute for the French services, especially the DGSE, because it limps toward the twenty-first century burdened by the baggage of the twentieth. The road from Colonel Schwartzkoppen's wastebasket has been too uneven, too cratered for one to predict that France will learn to coexist in relative serenity with its secret services.

APPENDIX

ENCRYPTION/DECRYPTION

There is no single process that will reliably produce a decoded text from its encoded version. Decryption is very much an art and not a science. While successful code breakers may follow a general pattern of analysis to decrypt a message, the success of their efforts is more the result of intuition, insight, perseverance, trial and error, and good luck than the general process they pursue.

Theoretically, the means available to encrypt a message are limited only by the imagination of the person designing the encryption system. The more complex the decrypting system, the more secure it is. Practically, however, real-world limitations usually require simplicity and a minimum portability of decryption systems. This is particularly true for military cryptography, which must be suitable for field use and able to provide a timely information flow. All encryption systems reflect a compromise between facility and security.

Encoding. There are two general processes whereby an unencoded message (plaintext) is encrypted. The first, transposition, is simply the systematic rearranging of the plaintext letters. The world "cryptanalysis" might be rearranged to become "atanpyylrciss." The other method, substitution, involves a systematic substitution of one or more letters, numbers, or symbols for plaintext letters and numbers.

In this case, "cryptanalysis" might become "1 23 45 5 12 2 30 2 15 45 8 18 8" or "mnxjqsgsexoao." This last example was encoded using monoalphabetic substitution and the following substitution alphabet.

plaintext alphabet: abcde fghij klmno pqrst uvwxy z
cipher alphabet: simpl ctyab defgh jknoq ruvwx z

When two or more cipher alphabets are used in a systematic way, then the process is called polyalphabetic substitution. In this case, any plaintext letter would be represented by more than one cipher symbol.

Serious students of cryptography distinguish codes from ciphers. "A code consists of thousands of words, phrases, letters, and syllables with the *codewords* or *codenumbers* (or, more generally, the *codegroups*) that replace these plaintext elements. A portion of code might look like this:

Codenumber	Plaintext
3964	emplacing
1563	employ
7260	en-
8808	enable
3043	enabled
0012	enabled to"[1]

This latter system, while virtually unbreakable, is very unwieldy, as it requires a very large encode-and-decode book to handle all of the possible word and phrase forms. This system would generally not be used in an environment requiring timeliness and ease of use. In military field use, it would also be susceptible to capture by the enemy.

Decryption. The easiest, and preferable, way to decrypt a message is to use the same process that the intended recipient uses to decode the message. While this is generally impossible for an unintended recipient, it is not always so. Code systems can be compromised in numerous ways: espionage, capture of encoding systems, or poor security practices such as allowing an unintended recipient to compare the plaintext and enciphered version of the same message. This latter insecurity allows the encoding system to be derived from a comparison of the two versions. Once obtained, this knowledge would allow the cryptanalyst easily to decode other messages in the same encoding system. Similarly, a successfully decrypted message allows cryptanalysts to decode other messages in the same system and key.

When these easier solutions are not available, the cryptanalyst must derive the plaintext from an analysis of the encrypted message or messages. To do this, he must have a detailed understanding of the letter frequencies and associations of the plaintext language.[2] The letters in every language have certain frequencies of occurrence and association with other letters. For example, a "frequency table of 200 letters of normal English is

Occurrences:	16	3	6	8	21	4	3	12	13	1	1	7	6
Letters:	A	B	C	D	E	F	G	H	I	J	K	L	M
Percentage:	8	1.5	3	4	13	2	1.5	6	6.5	.5	.5	3.5	3

Occurrences:	14	16	4	.5	13	12	18	6	2	3	1	4	.5
Letters:	N	O	P	Q	R	S	T	U	V	W	X	Y	Z
Percentage:	7	8	2	.25	6.5	6	9	3	1	1.5	.5	2	.25"[3]

However, common variations among these normal percentages do not permit the cryptanalyst simply to substitute plaintext letters for cipher letters based only upon letter frequencies. While it is very probable that individual letters will not exhibit their average frequencies in any specific case, it is also very unlikely that their frequency of occurrence in any specific text will substantially deviate from the expected averages. "Thus e, t, a, o, n, i, r, s, and h will normally be found in the high-frequency group; d, l, u, c, and m in the medium-frequency group; p, f, v, w, g, b, and v in the lows, and j, k, q, x, and z in the rare group."[4]

Just as every letter has a predictable frequency of occurrence in a given language, it also has a predictable frequency of association with other letters in the alphabet. For instance, not only is e a letter of the highest frequency, it also has the highest association with every other letter in the alphabet. The vowel digraph io is fairly frequent while the vowel digraphs *oi, ia, ai, oa,* and *ao* are fairly rare. Eighty percent of the time, *n* is preceded by a vowel. The digraph *he* is very common but *eh* is rare. *H* precedes vowels ten times more frequently than it follows them. *R* more often associates with vowels while *s* more often associates with the consonants.

Letter association frequencies, in conjunction with letter frequencies, allow the cryptanalyst to make good educated guesses as to what many of the more frequently appearing letters represent. As certain groups of letters become apparent, other letters are suggested by what would produce meaningful text. For instance, *?ith* suggests that the letter preceding the *i* is probably a *w.*

"Because it is difficult to remember an incoherent string of 26 letters that constitutes the set of cipher equivalents, cipher alphabets are often based on a single word that is easy to memorize. Various derivations are possible, but the simplest is just to write out the keyword, omitting repeated letters, then to follow it with the remaining letters of the alphabet. Thus the cipher alphabet springing from the keyword CHIMPANZEE would be:

```
plaintext:    a b c d e f g h i j k l m n o p q r s t u v w x y z
ciphertext:   c h i m p a n z e b d f g j k l o q r s t u v w x y"⁵
```

Because this is a common means of creating an easily memorized cipher, the cryptanalyst will also fill in the ciphertext letters, below their plaintext equivalents, as he makes his educated guesses. If a pattern develops in the ciphertext alphabet, it will lead to determinations of additional letter equivalences.

Additionally, certain words and letters can be determined on the basis of knowledge of common salutations, forms of address, routine formatting, knowledge of events causing the message to be sent, etc.

The cryptanalyst's job can be made more complicated by use of polyalphabetic substitution, null characters, and other devices intended to destroy the basic letter and letter association frequencies. Additional techniques, beyond the scope of this appendix, have been developed to assist the cryptanalyst, but in the final analysis, a more or less informed set of trial-and-error guesses is required until the message is broken. In *The Codebreakers*, David Kahn quotes from Parker Hitt's *Manual for the Solution of Military Ciphers*: "Success in dealing with unknown ciphers is measured by these four things in the order named: perseverance, careful methods of analysis, intuition, luck."[6]

BIBLIOGRAPHY

NEWSPAPERS

Le Canard enchaîné
L'Evénement du Jeudi
L'Express
FBIS—Western Europe
Le Figaro
Libération
Le Monde
Le Point
Le Quotidien de Paris
The New York Times
Sunday Times

BOOKS

Abtey, Jacques, and Dr. Fritz Unterberg Gibhardt, *2ème Bureau contre Abwehr*, La Table Ronde (Paris, 1967).

Adamthwaite, Anthony P., *France and the Coming of the Second World War*, Frank Cass (London, 1977).

Ainley, Henry, *In Order to Die: With the Foreign Legion in Indochina*, Burke (London, 1955).

Albertini, Luidi, *The Origins of the War of 1914*, Vol. II: *The Crisis of July 1914: From the Sarajevo Outrage to the Austro-Hungarian General Mo-*

bilization, Oxford University Press (London, New York, and Toronto, 1953).

Alexander, Martin, *The Republic in Danger: General Maurice Gamelin and the Politics of French Defence, 1933–1940*, Cambridge University Press (Cambridge, Eng., 1992).

Amouroux, Henri, *La Grande Histoire des français sous l'occupation, 1939–1945*, 6 vols., Fayard (Paris, 1977–83).

Andrew, Christopher, *Her Majesty's Secret Service: The Making of the British Intelligence Community*, Viking (New York, 1985).

—— and David Dilks, eds., *The Missing Dimension: Governments and Intelligence Communities in the Twentieth Century*, University of Illinois Press (Urbana, 1984).

—— and Oleg Gordievsky, *KGB: The Inside Story*, HarperCollins (New York, 1990).

Andrews, William C., and Stanley Hoffman, eds., *The Fifth Republic at Twenty*, SUNY Press (Albany, N.Y., 1981).

Arendt, Hannah, *The Origins of Totalitarianism*, World Publishing (New York, 1972).

Argoud, Antoine, *La Décadence, l'imposture et la tragédie*, Fayard (Paris, 1974).

Les Armées françaises dans la Grande Guerre, Service Historique, Imprimerie nationale (Paris, 1922–).

Armengaud, General Jean-Louis, *Le Renseignement aérien, sauvegarde des armées*, Librarie aéronautique (Paris, 1934).

Arnold, Eric A., Jr., *Fouché, Napoleon and the General Police*, University Press of America (Washington, D.C., 1979).

Aubert, Jacques, Michel Eude, Claude Goyard, et al., eds., *L'Etat et sa police en France (1789–1914)* (Geneva, 1979).

Auriol, Vincent, *Journal du septennat, 1947–1954*, Vol. I: *1947*, Armand Colin (Paris, 1970).

Bar-Joseph, Uri, *Out of Control: Intelligence Intervention in Politics in the USA, Britain and Israel*, Ph.D. dissertation, Stanford University, 1990.

Barnet, Frank R., R. Hugh Tovar, and Richard H. Shultz, eds., *Special Operations in U.S. Strategy*, National Defense University Press (Washington, D.C., 1984).

Barril, Paul, *Missions très spéciales*, Presses de la Cité (Paris, 1984).

Barthelemy, Chef de bataillon, *L'Officier de renseignement outre-mer*, Centre d'information et de spécialisation pour outre-mer, DOC 9593, SHAT (Vincennes, 1958).

Beaufre, André, *1940: The Fall of France*, Knopf (New York, 1968).

Bennett, Ralph, *Ultra in the West: The Normandy Campaign of 1944–45*, Scribners (New York, 1979).

————, *Ultra and Mediterranean Strategy: The Never-Before-Told Story of How Ultra First Proved Itself in Battle, Turning Defeat into Victory*, Morrow (New York, 1989).

Bernert, Philippe, *Roger Wybot et la bataille pour la DST*, Presses de la Cité (Paris, 1975).

————, *S.D.E.C.E. Service 7*, Presses de la Cité (Paris, 1980).

Bertrand, Gustave, *Enigma ou la plus grande énigme de la guerre, 1939–1945*, Plon (Paris, 1973).

Beschloss, Michael R., *The Crisis Years: Kennedy and Khrushchev 1960–1963*, Edward Burlingame Books (New York, 1991).

Bézy, Jean, *Le SR Air*, Editions France-Empire (Paris, 1979).

Bitterlin, Lucien, *Nous étions tous des terroristes: L'Histoire des "barbouzes" contre l'O.A.S. en Algérie*, Editions du témoignage chrétien (Paris, 1983).

Black, Ian, and Benny Morris, *Israel's Secret Wars: A History of Israel's Intelligence Services*, Grove Weidenfeld (New York, 1991).

Bloch, Gilbert, *Enigma avant Ultra, 1930–1940*, author's publication (September 1988).

Bodard, Lucien, *La Guerre d'Indochine*, Vol. I: *L'Enlisement*. Gallimard (Paris, 1963).

Bodinier, Gilbert, *Indochine 1947: Règlement politique ou solution militaire, textes et documents*, SHAT (Vincennes, 1989).

Bond, Brian, *France and Belgium, 1939–1940*, Associated University Presses (Cranbury, N.J., 1979).

Booth, Ken, *Strategy and Ethnocentrism*, Holmes & Meier (New York, 1979).

Borchers, Major, *Abwehr contre Résistance*, Amiot-Dumont (Paris, 1949).

Brédin, Denis, *The Affair: The Case of Alfred Dreyfus*, George Braziller (New York, 1986).

Brook-Sheperd, Gordon, *The Storm Birds: Soviet Postwar Defectors*, Henry Holt (New York, 1989).

Buchheit, Gert, *Secrets des services secrets: Missions, méthodes, expériences*, Arthaud (Paris, 1974).

Burdan, Daniel, *DST: Neuf ans à la division antiterroriste*, Laffont (Paris, 1990).

Buton, Philippe, *Les Lendemains qui déchantent: Le Parti communiste français à la Libération*, Presses de la Fondation Nationale des Sciences Politiques (Paris, 1994).

Calmitt, Arthur, *L' "O.C.M.," Organisation Civile et Militaire: Histoire d'un mouvement de Résistance de 1940 a 1946*, Presses Universitaires de France (Paris, 1961).

Calvi, Fabrizio, *OSS. La Guerre secrète en France: Les Services spéciaux* américains, la Résistance et la Gestapo, 1942–1945, Hachette (Paris, 1990).

———— and Olivier Schmidt, Intelligences secrètes: Annales de l'espionnage, Hachette (Paris, 1988).

Carré, Captain Claude, Les Attachés militaires français, 1920–1945: Role et influence, Mémoire de maîtrise, Paris I Sorbonne, 1975–76.

Carrias, Eugène, Les Renseignements de contact, Charles-Lavauzelle (Paris, 1937).

————, La Pensée militaire française, Presses Universitaires de France (Paris, 1948).

Castellan, Georges, Le Réarmement clandestin du Reich, 1930–1935, vu par le 2ème bureau de l'état-major français, Plon (Paris, 1954).

Cave Brown, Anthony, Bodyguard of Lies, Bantam (New York, 1975).

Chairoff, Patrice, Dossier B . . . comme barbouzes: Une France parallèle, celle des basses-oeuvres du pouvoir en France, Alain Moreau (Paris, 1975).

Christienne, Charles, and Pierre Lissarrague, A History of French Military Aviation, Smithsonian Institution Press (Washington, D.C., 1986).

Churchill, Winston, The World Crisis, 1911–1914 (London, 1923).

Clausewitz, Carl von, On War, Princeton University Press (Princeton, N.J., 1984).

Codevilla, Angelo, Informing Statecraft: Intelligence for a New Century, Free Press (New York, 1992).

Collier, Richard, Ten Thousand Eyes, Dutton (New York, 1958).

Cooke, James J., 100 Miles from Baghdad: With the French in Desert Storm, Praeger (Westport, Conn., 1993).

Cordier, Danier, Jean Moulin: L'Inconnu du Panthéon, Vol. III: De Gaulle capital de la Résistance, J. C. Lattès (Paris, 1993).

Courrière, Yves, Les Fils de la toussaint, Fayard (Paris, 1968).

Croizat, V. J., Lessons from the Indochina War, Rand Corporation (Santa Monica, Calif., May 1967).

Cruttwell, C. R. M. F., A History of the Great War, 1914–1918, Paladin (London, 1982).

Dallin, David, Soviet Espionage, Yale University Press (New Haven, Conn., 1955).

Danielsson, Bengt, and Marie-Thérèse Danielsson, Poisoned Reign: French Nuclear Colonialism in the Pacific, Penguin (London, 1986).

Daudet, E., La Police politique: Chronique des temps de la Restauration d'après les rapports des agents secrets et les papiers du cabinet noir, 1815–1820 (Paris, 1912).

Daudet, Léon, L'Avant-guerre: Etudes et documents sur l'espionnage juif-allemand en France depuis l'affaire Dreyfus, Nouvelle Librairie nationale (Paris, 1925).

————, *Magistrats et policiers*, Grasset (Paris, 1935).

Davidson, Philip B., *Vietnam at War: The History, 1946–1975*, Presidio Press (Novato, Calif., 1988).

Deacon, Richard, *The French Secret Service*, Grafton Books (London, 1990).

de Gaulle, Charles, *The Complete War Memoirs of Charles de Gaulle*, Simon & Schuster (New York, 1964).

Delarue, Jacques, *OAS contre de Gaulle*, Fayard (Paris, 1981).

Derogy, Jacques, and Jean-Marie Pontaut, *Enquête sur trois secrets d'Etat*, Laffont (Paris, 1986).

Desplanches, Hervé, *Les Français face à l'Afrique Orientale Italienne, 1938–1940: L'Action subversive en Pays Abyssin*, Maîtrise d'histoire contemporaine, Université de Provence, 1991.

Despuech, Jacques, *Le Trafic des piastres*, La Table Ronde (Paris, 1974).

Diamant, Commissaire, *Les Réseaux secrets de la police*, Editions la Découverte (Paris, 1993).

Dion, J., *Historique du SLOTFOM*, Archives nationales, Section Outre-Mer, Répertoire numérique.

Dolent, Jean, and Thomas Daquin, *La Sécurité militaire*, Editions du Cerf (Paris, 1981).

Dostoievsky, Fyodor, *Summer Impressions*, John Calder (London, 1955).

Droz, Humbert, *L'Oeil de Moscou à Paris*, Juillard-Archives (Paris 1964).

Du Camp, Maxime, *Souvenirs d'un demi-siècle: Au temps de Louis-Philippe et de Napoléon III, 1830–1870*, Hachette (Paris, 1949).

Ducloux, Louis, *From Blackmail to Treason: Political Crime and Corruption in France, 1920–1940*, André Deutsch (London, 1958).

Dufourg, Jean-Marc, *Section manipulation: De l'antiterrorisme à l'affaire Doucé*, Michel Lafon (Paris, 1991).

Dyson, John, *Sink the Rainbow Warrior! An Enquiry into the "Greenpeace Affair,"* Victor Gollancz (London, 1986).

Elmer, Alexander, *L'Agent secret de Napoléon, Charles-Louis Schulmeister*, Payot (Paris, 1932).

Elting, John, *Swords Around the Throne: Napoleon's Grande Armée*, Free Press (New York, 1988).

L'Espionnage et le contre-espionnage: Pendant la Guerre Mondiale, d'après les archives militaires du Reich, Payot (Paris, 1934).

Faligot, Roger, and Pascal Krop, *La Picine: Les Services secrets français, 1944–1984*, Seuil (Paris, 1984).

————, *La Picine: The French Secret Services Since 1944*, Basil Blackwell (Oxford, 1989).

Faligot, Roger, and Rémi Kauffer, *Les Résistants: De la guerre de l'ombre aux allées du pouvoir, 1944–1989*, Fayard (Paris, 1990).

————, *Histoire mondiale du renseignement*, Vol. I: *1870–1939*, Laffont (Paris, 1993).

Favier, Pierre, and Michel Martin-Roland, *La Décennie Mitterrand*, Vol. I: *Les Ruptures, 1981–1984*, Seuil (Paris, 1990); Vol. II: *Les Epreuves*, Seuil (Paris, 1991).

Ferro, Marc, *Pétain*, Fayard (Paris, 1987).

Flicke, Wilhelm F., *War Secrets in the Ether*, 2 vols., Aegean Park Press (Laguna Hills, Calif., 1977).

Foot, M. R. D., *SOE in France*, Her Majesty's Stationery Office (London, 1966).

————, *Resistance*, Granada (London, 1978).

Fourcade, Marie-Madeleine, *L'Arche de Noé: Réseau "Alliance" 1940–1945*, Plon (Paris, 1989).

Fournier, Nicolas, and Edmond Legrand, *E . . . comme espionnage*, Alain Moreau (Paris, 1978).

Francini, Philippe, *Les Guerres d'Indochine*, 2 vols., Pygmalion (Paris, 1988).

Frenay, Henri, *La Nuit finira: Mémoire de Résistance 1940–1945*, Laffont (Paris, 1973).

Funk, Arthur Layton, *Hidden Ally: The French Resistance, Special Operations, and the Landings in Southern France, 1944*, Greenwood Press (New York, 1992).

Furse, Colonel George Armand, *Information in War: Its Acquisition and Transmission*, William Clowes & Sons (London, 1895).

Galtier-Boissière, Jean, *Mysteries of the French Secret Police*, Stanley Paul (Plymouth, Eng., 1938).

Gamelin, General Maurice, *Servir*, 3 vols., Plon (Paris, 1946–47).

Garder, Michel, *La Guerre secrète des services spéciaux français, 1935–1945*, Plon (Paris, 1967).

Gauché, General, *Le Deuxième bureau au travail (1935–1940)*, Amiot-Dumont (Paris, 1953).

Gerdan, Eric, *Dossier A . . . comme armes*, Alain Moreau (Paris, 1975).

Giap, Vo Nguyen, *People's Army, People's War*, Foreign Languages Publishing House (Hanoi, 1961).

————, *Dien Bien Phu*, Foreign Languages Publishing House (Hanoi, 1964).

Gillois, André, *Histoire secrète des français à Londres de 1940 à 1944*, Hachette (Paris, 1973).

Giraud, Henri-Christian, *De Gaulle et les communistes*, Vol. I: *L'Alliance: Juin 1941–mai 1943*, Albin Michel (Paris, 1988); Vol. II: *Le Piège: Mai 1943–janvier 1946*, Albin Michel (Paris, 1989).

Givierge, Marcel, *Au service du chiffre: 18 ans de souvenirs, 1907–1925*, Bibliothèque nationale, NAF (Amiens, 1930).

Granatstein, J. L., and David Stafford, *Spy Wars: Espionage and Canada from Gouzenko to Glasnost*, Key Porter Books (Toronto, 1990).

Gras, Yves, *Histoire de la guerre d'Indochine*, Plon (Paris, 1978).

Groussard, Georges A., *Service secret, 1940–1945*, La Table Ronde (Paris, 1964).

———. *Chemins secrets*, Bader-Dufour (Paris, 1948).

Guillaume, Gilbert, *Mes Missions face à l'Abwehr*, 3 vols., Plon (Paris, 1973).

Guisnel, Jean, and Bernard Violet, *Services secrets: Le Pouvoir et les services de renseignements sous François Mitterrand*, Editions la Découverte (Paris, 1988).

Gunsburg, Jeffrey, *Divided and Conquered: The French High Command and the Defeat of the West, 1940*, Greenwood Press (Westport, Conn., 1979).

Hamon, Alain, and Jean-Charles Marchand, *P . . . comme police*, Alain Moreau (Paris, 1983).

Handel, Michael, *Masters of War: Sun Tzu, Clausewitz and Jomini*, Frank Cass (London, 1989).

———, ed., *War, Strategy, and Intelligence*, Frank Cass (London, 1989).

———, ed., *Leaders and Intelligence*, Frank Cass (London, 1989).

Harstrich, Jacques, and Fabrizio Calvi, *R.G.: 20 ans de police politique*, Calmann-Lévy (Paris, 1991).

Hastings, Max, *Das Reich: The March of the 2nd SS Panzer Division Through France*, Holt, Rinehart and Winston (New York, 1981).

Hawes, Stephen, and Ralph White, *Resistance in Europe: 1935–45*, Pelican (London, 1976).

Hinsley, F. H., *British Intelligence in the Second World War*, 5 vols., Cambridge University Press (New York, 1979–90).

Hitchcock, Lieutenant Colonel Walter T., ed., *The Intelligence Revolution: A Historical Perspective*, Office of Air Force History (Washington, D.C., 1991).

Homberg, Octave Marie Joseph Kerim, *Les Coulisses de l'histoire: Souvenirs 1898–1928*, Fayard (Paris, 1938).

Horne, Alistair, *The Price of Glory: Verdun 1916*, St. Martin's Press (New York, 1963).

———, *A Savage War of Peace: Algeria 1954–1962*, Macmillan (London, 1977).

Howard, Michael, *British Intelligence in the Second World War*, Vol. V: *Strategic Deception*, Cambridge University Press (New York, 1990).

Howe, Russell Warren, *Mata Hari: The True Story*, Dodd, Mead (New York, 1986).

Jacquin, Henri, *La Guerre secrète en Algérie*, Olivier Orban (Paris, 1977).

———, *Guerre secrète en Indochine*, Olivier Orban (Paris, 1979).

Janowitz, M., *The Military in the Political Development of New Nations: An*

Essay in Comparative Analysis, University of Chicago Press (Chicago, 1964).

Jauffret, Jean-Charles, *La Guerre d'Algérie par les documents*, Vol. I: *L'Avertissement, 1943–1946*, SHAT (Vincennes, 1990).

Joes, Anthony James, *Modern Guerrilla Insurgency*, Praeger (Westport, Conn., 1992).

Jomini, Baron de, *The Art of War*, Greenwood Press (Westport, Conn., 1977).

Jones, R. V., *Most Secret War: British Scientific Intelligence, 1939–1945*, Cornet (London, 1978).

———, *Reflections on Intelligence*, Heineman (London, 1989).

Kahn, David, *The Codebreakers: The Story of Secret Writing*, Macmillan (New York, 1967).

———, *Hitler's Spies*, Macmillan (New York, 1978).

———, *Seizing the Enigma: The Race to Break the German U-Boat Codes, 1939–1943*, Houghton Mifflin (Boston, 1991).

Karnow, Stanley, *Vietnam: A History*, Penguin (London, 1984).

Kauffer, Réne, *Service B*, Fayard (Paris, 1985).

———, *O.A.S.: Histoire d'une organisation secrète*, Fayard (Paris, 1986).

Kegan, John, *The Second World War*, Penguin (London, 1989).

Kennedy, Paul, ed., *Grand Strategies in War and Peace*, Yale University Press (New Haven, Conn., 1991).

Kennett, Lee, *The First Air War, 1914–1918*, Free Press (New York, 1991).

King, Michael, *Death of the Rainbow Warrior*, Penguin (Harmondsworth, 1986).

Knight, Frida, *The French Resistance*, Lawrence and Wishart (London, 1975).

Knightley, Phillip, *The Second Oldest Profession: Spies and Spying in the Twentieth Century*, Norton (New York, 1987).

Lacouture, Jean, *De Gaulle: Le Rebelle, 1890–1944*, Seuil (Paris, 1984).

———, *De Gaulle: Le Politique, 1944–1959*, Seuil (Paris, 1985).

———, *De Gaulle: Le Souverain, 1959–1970*, Seuil (Paris, 1986).

———, *De Gaulle: The Ruler, 1945–1970*, Norton (New York, 1992).

Ladoux, Georges, *Les Chasseurs d'espions: Comment j'ai fait arrêter Mata-Hari*, Editions du masque (Paris, 1932).

———, *Marthe Richard: Espionne au service de la France: Août 1914–octobre 1917*, Editions du masque (Paris, 1932).

———, *Mes Souvenirs*, Les Editions de France (Paris, 1937).

Lambry, Emile, *Les Mystères du cabinet noir sous l'Empire et la Poste sous la Commune*, E. Dentu (Paris, 1871).

Lansdale, Edward Geary, *In the Midst of Wars: An American's Mission to Southeast Asia*, Harper & Row (New York, 1972).

Laqueur, Walter, *A World of Secrets: The Uses and Limits of Intelligence*, Basic Books (New York, 1988).

Le Clère, Marcel, *La Police*, Presses Universitaires de France (Paris, 1972).

Lederer, William J., and Eugene Burdick, *The Ugly American*, Norton (New York, 1958).

Liang, Hsi-Hue, *The Rise of Modern Police and the European State System from Metternich to the Second World War*, Cambridge University Press (Cambridge, Eng., 1992).

Liddell Hart, Adrian, *Strange Company*, Weidenfeld and Nicolson (London, 1953).

Liddell Hart, B. H., *History of the First World War*, Pan Books (London, 1970).

Lilienfeld, Jean-Marie, *La Résistance et la répression Allemande dans le Calvados*, DES d'Histoire, University of Caen, June 1966.

Lorain, Pierre, *Armement clandestin: France 1941–1944*, Author's copyright, 1972.

McCoy, Alfred W., *The Politics of Heroin in Southeast Asia*, Harper & Row (New York, 1972).

Madelin, Louis, *Fouché*, Plon (Paris, 1903).

Mangold, Tom, *Cold Warrior. James Jesus Angleton: The CIA's Master Spy Hunter*, Simon & Schuster (New York, 1991).

Marcellin, Raymond, *La Guerre politique*, Plon (Paris, 1985).

Marenches, Count de, and David A. Andelman, *The Fourth World War: Diplomacy and Espionage in the Age of Terrorism*, Morrow (New York, 1992).

Maricourt, Colonel de, *Les Opérations aériennes en Indochine: Conférence faite au CEAA en mai 1952*, manuscrit conservé au SHAT.

Marion, Pierre; *Le Pouvoir sans visage*, Calmann-Lévy (Paris, 1990).

———, *La Mission impossible: A la tête des services secrets*, Calmann-Lévy (Paris, 1991).

Marrus, Michel, *Les Juifs en France à l'époque de l'Affaire Dreyfus*, Calmann-Lévy (Paris, 1972).

Massu, Jacques, *La Vrai Bataille d'Alger*, Plon (Paris, 1971).

May, Ernest, ed., *Knowing One's Enemies: Intelligence Assessment Before the Two World Wars*, Princeton University Press (Princeton, N.J., 1984).

Melman, Yossi, *Every Spy a Prince: The Complete History of Israel's Intelligence Community*, Houghton Mifflin (Boston, 1990).

Michel, Chef de bataillon F. L., *Cours de renseignement*, Section de documentation militaire d'outre-mer, Doc. 8428, SHAT (Vincennes, 1955).

Michel, Henri, *Jean Moulin l'unificateur*, Hachette (Paris, 1964).

———, *Bibliographie critique de la Résistance*, Institut pédagogique nationale (Paris, 1964).

Millar, George, *The Bruneval Raid: Flashpoint of the Radar War*, Bodley Head (London, 1947).

Millet, Allan R., and Williamson Murray, eds., *Calculations: Net Assessment and the Coming of World War II*, Free Press (New York, 1992).

Minart, Colonel Jacques, *P.C. Vincennes: Secteur 4*, Berger-Levrault (Paris, 1945).

Mitchell, Allan, *The German Influence in France After 1870: The Formation of the French Republic*, University of North Carolina Press (Chapel Hill, 1979).

———— *Victors and Vanquished: The German Influence on Army and Church in France After 1870*, University of North Carolina Press (Chapel Hill, 1984).

Mitterrand, François, *Le Coup d'état permanent*, Plon (Paris, 1965).

Moravec, General František, *Master of Spies: The Memoirs of General František Moravec*, Doubleday (Garden City, N.Y., 1975).

Moréas, Georges, *Un Flic de l'intérieur*, Edition 1 (Paris, 1985).

————, *Ecoutes et espionnage*, Stock (Paris, 1990).

Morin, Henri, *Service secret: A l'écoute devant Verdun*, G. Durasse (Paris, 1959).

Mulle, Raymond, and Eric Deroo, *Services spéciaux: Armes, Techniques, Missions. GCMA—Indochine 1950/54*, Editions Crépin-Leblond (Paris, 1992).

Murray, Simon, *Legionnaire: My Five Years in the French Foreign Legion*, Times Books (New York, 1978).

Navarre, Henri, *Le Service de renseignements, 1871–1944*, Plon (Paris, 1978).

————, *Agonie de l'Indochine, 1953–1954*, Plon (Paris, 1956).

————, *Le Temps des vérités*, Plon (Paris, 1979).

Neilson, Keith, and B. J. C. McKercher, *Go Spy the Land: Military Intelligence in History*, Praeger (Westport, Conn., 1992).

Nicholai, Walter, *German Secret Service*, Stanley Paul (London, 1924).

Noguères, Henri, *Histoire de la Résistance en France*, 5 vols., Laffont (Paris, 1967–81).

————, *La Vie quotidienne des résistants de l'Armistice à la Libération*, Hachette (Paris, 1984).

Nord, Pierre (pseudonym of Colonel Brouillard), *Mes Camarades sont morts*, 3 vols., Librairie des Champs-Elysées (Paris, 1947–49).

————, *L'Intoxication: Arme absolue de la guerre subversive*, Fayard (Paris, 1971).

Ockrent, Christine, and Alexandre de Marenches, *Dans le secret des princes*, Stock (Paris, 1986).

Paillole, Paul, *Services spéciaux (1935–1945)*, Laffont (Paris, 1975).

————, *Notre espion chez Hitler*, Laffont (Paris, 1985).

Paléologue, Maurice, *Journal de l'affaire Dreyfus, 1894–1899*, Plon (Paris, 1958).

Paquet, Charles, *Etude sur le fonctionnement interne d'un 2ème bureau en campagne*, Berger-Levrault (Paris, 1923).

———, *La Défaite militaire de l'Allemagne en 1918*, Berger-Levrault (Paris, 1925).

———, *Dans l'attente de la ruée: Verdun (janvier–fevrier 1916)*, Berger-Levrault (Paris, 1928).

Passy, *Souvenirs: 10 Duke Street, Londres (le BCRA)*, Raoul Solar (Monte Carlo, 1947).

———, *Missions secrètes en France: Souvenirs du BCRA. Novembre 1942–juin 1943*, Plon (Paris, 1951).

Paxton, Robert O., *Vichy France: Old Guard and New Order*, Barrie & Jenkins (London, 1972).

Payne, Howard C., *The Police State of Louis-Napoleon Bonaparte, 1851–1860*, University of Washington Press (Seattle, 1966).

Péan, Pierre, *Secret d'état: La France du secret. Les secrets de la France*, Fayard (Paris, 1986).

———, *La Menace*, Fayard (Paris, 1987).

———, *L'Homme de l'ombre: Eléments d'enquête autour de Jacques Foccart, l'homme le plus mystérieux et le plus puissant de la Ve République*, Fayard (Paris, 1990).

———, *Les Deux Bombes*, Fayard (Paris 1992).

———, *Le Mystérieux Docteur Martin, 1895–1969*, Fayard (Paris, 1993).

Pedroncini, Guy, ed., *Histoire militaire de la France*, Vol. III: *De 1871 à 1940*, Presses Universitaires de France (Paris, 1992).

Perrault, Gilles, *The Red Orchestra*, Simon & Schuster (New York, 1967).

———, *The Secret of D-Day*, Little, Brown (Boston and Toronto, 1965).

Pilleul, Gilbert, ed., *Le Général de Gaulle et l'Indochine*, Plon (Paris, 1982).

Planchais, Jean, *Une Histoire politique de l'armée*, Vol. II: *1940–1962: De de Gaulle à de Gaulle*, Seuil (Paris, 1967).

Poincaré, Raymond, *Au service de la France: Neuf années de souvenirs*, Vol. I, Plon (Paris, 1926).

Pontaut, Jean-Marie, *Les Secrets des écoutes téléphoniques*, Presses de la Cité (Paris, 1978).

Porch, Douglas, *The March to the Marne: The French Army 1871–1914*, Cambridge University Press (Cambridge, Eng., 1981).

"Rapport de la commission d'enquête sur les activités du Service d'Action Civique," *Assemblée Nationale. Seconde session ordinaire de 1981–1982*, No. 955, 2 vols., Alain Moreau (Paris, 1982).

Records of the Foreign Office, 1782–1939, Her Majesty's Stationery Office (London, 1969).

Rémy (pseudonym of Gilbert Renault-Roulier), *Mémoires d'un agent secret de la France Libre*, 3 vols., Editions France-Empire (Paris, 1983–84).

Richard, Marte, *Ma Vie d'espionne au service de la France*, Editions de la France (Paris, 1938).

Rivière, P.-Louis, *Un Centre de guerre secrète: Madrid 1914–1918*, Payot (Paris, 1936).

Robrieux, Philippe, *Histoire intérieure du Parti communiste*, 4 vols., Fayard (Paris, 1980–84).

Rochet, Jean, *5 ans à la tête de la DST, 1967–1972: La Mission impossible*, Plon (Paris, 1985).

Ruffin, Raymond, *Résistance P.T.T.*, Presses de la Cité (Paris, 1983).

Savant, Jean, *Les Espions de Napoléon*, Hachette (Paris, 1957).

Schecter, Jerrold L., and Peter S. Deriabin, *The Spy Who Saved the World: How a Soviet Colonel Changed the Course of the Cold War*, Scribners (New York, 1992).

Select Committee on Intelligence, *Activities of "Friendly" [KCIA] Foreign Intelligence Services in the United States: A Case Study*, 95th Congress, 2nd sess., U.S. Government Printing Office (Washington, D.C., 1978).

Simpson, Howard R., *Tiger in the Barbed Wire: An American in Vietnam, 1952–1991*, Brassey's (U.S.), (Washington, D.C., and New York, 1992).

Smith, R. Harris, *OSS: The Secret History of America's First Central Intelligence Agency*, University of California Press (Berkeley, Los Angeles, London, 1972).

Soustelle, Jacques, *Envers et contre tout*, Vol. I: *De Londres à Alger, 1940–1942*, Laffont (Paris, 1947); Vol. II: *D'Alger à Paris, 1942–1944*, Laffont (Paris, 1950).

Spears, General E. L., *Liaison, 1914*, Doubleday, Doran & Co. (Garden City, N.Y., 1931).

Spector, Ronald, *Eagle Against the Sun: The American War Against Japan*, Free Press (New York, 1985).

———, *Advice and Support: The Early Years of the United States Army in Vietnam, 1941–1960*, Free Press (New York, 1985).

Stead, Phillip John, *The Police of Paris*, Staples Press (London, 1957).

———, *Second Bureau*, Evans Brothers (London, 1959).

Stieber, Wilhelm, *Espion de Bismarck*, Pygmalion (Paris, 1985).

Stinglhamber, Colonel B. E. M. Gustave, and Paul Dresse, *Léopold II au travail*, Editions du Sablon (Brussels and Paris, 1944).

Strong, Major General Sir Kenneth, *Intelligence at the Top: The Recollections of an Intelligence Officer*, Cassels (London, 1968).

Suleiman, Ezra N., *Politics, Power and Bureaucracy in France: The Administrative Elite*, Princeton University Press (Princeton, N.J., 1974).

Szulc, Tad, *The Secret Alliance: The Extraordinary Story of the Rescue of the Jews Since World War II*, Farrar, Straus & Giroux (New York, 1991).

Thiebault, Paul, *The Memoirs of Baron Thiebault*, Macmillan (New York, 1896).

Thomas, Bernard, *Les Provocations policières*, Fayard (Paris, 1972).

Thompson, Robert, *Defeating Communist Insurgency: Experiences from Malaya and Vietnam*, Macmillan (London, 1966).

Thyraud de Vosjoli, Philippe, *Lamia*, Little, Brown (Boston and Toronto, 1970).

———, *Le Comité*, Editions de l'homme (Montreal and Brussels, 1975).

Trepper, Leopold, *Le Grand Jeu*, Albin Michel (Paris, 1975).

———, *The Great Game: Memoirs of the Spy Hitler Couldn't Silence*, McGraw-Hill (New York, 1977).

Trinquier, Roger, *The Indochina Underground*, Foreign Technology Division, Air Force Systems Command (1984).

Turner, Stansfield, *Secrecy and Democracy: The CIA in Transition*, Houghton Mifflin (Boston, 1985).

Vaillé, Eugène, *Le Cabinet noir*, Presses Universitaires de France (Paris, 1950).

Verines, Colonel Guy, *Mes Souvenirs du réseau Saint-Jacques*, Charles-Lavauzelle (Paris, 1990).

Verity, Hugh, *We Landed by Moonlight: Secret RAF Landings in France, 1940–1944*, Allan (London, 1978).

Villelume, Paul de, *Journal d'une défaite*, Fayard (Paris, 1976).

War Department, *Civil Affairs Information Guide Survey of French Underground Movement*, Washington, D.C., 25 May 1944.

Wark, Westley, ed., *Spy Fiction, Spy Films and Real Intelligence*, Frank Cass (London, 1991).

Wheelwright, Julie, *The Fatal Lover: Mata Hari and the Myth of Women in Espionage*, Collins & Brown (London, 1992).

Wiart, E. Carton de, *Léopold II: Souvenirs des dernières années, 1901–1909* (Brussels, 1944).

Williams, Philip M., *Wars, Plots and Scandals in Post-War France*, Cambridge University Press (Cambridge, Eng., 1970).

Wolton, Thierry, *Le KGB en France*, Grasset (Paris, 1986).

Woytak, Richard A., *On the Border of War and Peace: Polish Intelligence and Diplomacy, 1937–1939, and the Origins of the Ultra Secret*, Columbia University Press (New York, 1979).

Wright, Peter, *Spy Catcher*, Dell (New York, 1988).

ARTICLES, CHAPTERS, AND REPORTS

Alexander, Martin, "Did the Deuxième Bureau Work? The Role of Intelligence in French Defence Policy and Strategy, 1919–39," *Intelligence and National Security*, VI, No. 2 (April 1991), 293–333.

———, "In Lieu of Alliance: The French General Staff's Secret Cooperation with Neutral Belgium, 1936–1940," *Journal of Strategic Studies*, XIV, No. 4 (December 1991), 313–27.

Amery, Julian, "Of Resistance," *Nineteenth Century Magazine*, March 1949, 138–49.

Andrew, Christopher, "Déchiffrement et diplomatie: Le Cabinet noir du Quai d'Orsay sous la Troisième République," *Relations internationales*, No. 5 (1976), 37–64.

Anon., "Le Réseau F2," *Revue historique de l'armée*, I, No. 4 (December 1952), 81–116.

Armengaud, General Jean-Louis, "La Reconnaissance de l'ennemi par l'armée de l'air et la manoeuvre stratégique des armées de terre," *Revue militaire française*, No. 154 (April–June 1934), 43–81.

Austin, Roger, "Surveillance Under the Vichy Regime: The Service du Contrôle Technique, 1939–1945," *Intelligence and National Security*, I, No. 1 (January 1986), 123–37.

Betts, Mitch, "CIA Steps Up Foreign Technology Watch," *Computerworld*, XXVI, No. 16 (20 April, 1992), 121.

Betts, Richard, "Analysis, War and Decision: Why Intelligence Failures Are Inevitable," *World Politics*, XXXI, No. 1 (1978), 961–88.

Bissy, J. de Lannoy de, "Les Photographies aériennes et leur étude au point de vue militaire," *Revue militaire française*, XII (April–June 1924), 257–77.

"Blame the U.S.: Another French Plot," *U.S. News & World Report*, L (May 15, 1961), 84 ff.

Borrus, Amy, "Should the CIA Start Spying for Corporate America?" *Business Week*, No. 3235 (14 October 1991), 96–100.

Boumaza, Bechir, "Torture in Paris: An Excerpt from 'La Gangrène,' " *Harper's*, CCXX (March 1960), 87 ff.

Brady, Thomas F., "Paris Rumors on CIA—Despite U.S. Denials, Speculation Persists Agency Aided Algiers Revolt: Reprinted from *The New York Times*, May 2, 1961," *Congressional Record*, CVII (2 May 1961), 7023–4.

Bréguet, Claude, "La Reconnaissance aérienne et la bataille de la Marne," *Revue historique des armées*, No. 166 (March 1987), 92–100.

Buffotot, Patrice, "La Perception du réarmement allemand par les organismes de renseignement français de 1936 à 1939," *Revue historique des armées*, III (1979), 173–84.

Cartier, François, "Souvenirs du Général Cartier," *Revue des transmissions*, No. 85 (July–August 1959), 23–51.

Chapman, J. W. M., "No Final Solution: A Survey of the Cryptanalytical Capabilities of German Military Agencies, 1926–35," *Intelligence and National Security*, I, No. 1 (January 1986), 13–47.

Cluseau, Captain D., "L'Arrestation par les Allemands du personnel du 2ème bureau français," *Revue d'histoire de la Deuxième guerre mondiale*, No. 29 (1958), 32–48.

Cobban, Alfred, "The Great Mystification of Méhée de la Touche," *Bulletin of the London University Institute of Historical Research*, XLI (May 1968), 100–6.

Dainville, Colonel A. de, "Une Résistance militaire 1940–1944: La naissance de l'O.R.A. Ses problèmes et son activité en 1944," *Revue historique des armées*, No. 3 (1974), 11–36.

d'Esneval, Captain, "Fonctionnement d'un 2ème bureau: Le 2ème bureau de la 4e armée au cours de la période 18 au 22 août 1914," *Revue militaire française*, No. 185 (November 1936), 214–58.

Farson, Stuart, "Schools of Thought: National Perceptions of Intelligence," *Conflict Quarterly*, Spring 1989, 52–104.

Ferris, John, "Whitehall's Black Chamber: British Cryptology and the Government Code and Cypher School, 1919–1929," *Intelligence and National Security*, II, No. 1 (1987), 54–91.

——, "The British Army and Signals Intelligence in the Field During the First World War," *Intelligence and National Security*, III, No. 4 (October 1988), 23–48.

——, "Ralph Bennett and the Study of Ultra," *Intelligence and National Security*, VI, No. 2 (1991), 473–86.

French, David, "Sir John French's Secret Service on the Western Front, 1914–15," *Journal of Strategic Studies*, December 1984, 423–40.

Gardner, Michael, "Searching for Safe Procedures," *Security Management*, XXXII, No. 9 (September 1989), 179–82.

George, Alexander, "The Case for Multiple Advocacy in the Making of Foreign Policy," *American Political Science Review*, LXVI, No. 3 (September 1972), 751–90.

Givierge, Marcel, "Questions de chiffre," *Revue militaire française*, No. 36, 1 June 1924, 398–417; July–September 1924, 59–78.

Green, William C., "The Historic Russian Drive for a Warm Water Port: Anatomy of a Geopolitical Myth," *Naval War College Review*, Spring 1993, 80–102.

Handel, Michael, "Technological Surprise in War," *Intelligence and National Security*, II, No. 1 (January 1987), 1–53.

Heintz, André, "Preparing for 'D' Day—the French Resistance in Caen and Calvados," unpublished paper.

Hess, John L., "CIA, Satire and Scandal: Why 'Le Canard' Endorses Domestic Intelligence," *Politicks & Other Human Interests*, 14 March 1978, 27 ff.

Howe, Quincy, "At Random: The CIA in France," *Atlas*, XXII (March 1976), 5 ff.

"Intelligence Successes and Failures in Operations Desert Shield/Storm," Report of the Oversight and Investigations Subcommittee of the Committee on Armed Services, House of Representatives, August 16, 1993, U.S. Government Printing Office (Washington, D.C., 1993), 1–29.

Isnard, Jacques, "Quand l'armée se renseigne sur l'adversaire intérieur," *Le Monde*, No. 8945 (17 October 1973), 16.

Johnson, William, "Information Espionage: An Old Problem with a New Face," *Computerworld*, XXIII, No. 43 (23 October 1989), 85.

"Lo, the Poor Spy: Financial Aspirations of French Spies," *Newsweek*, LXVI (27 September 1965), 50–1.

Mariel, Pierre, "Les Postes d'écoute et la bataille de Verdun," *Geographia*, No. 106 (1960), 39–43.

May, Ernest R., "Intelligence: Backing into the Future," *Foreign Affairs*, LXXI, No. 3 (Summer 1992), 63–72.

Mitchell, Allan, "The Xenophobic Style: French Counterespionage and the Emergence of the Dreyfus Affair," *Journal of Modern History*, 3 September 1980, 414–25.

Morgan, Ted, "When the Maquis Stood and Fought," *Military History Quarterly*, II, No. 2 (Winter 1990), 104–11.

Naftali, Timothy J., "The DSM and the Politics of Allied Counterespionage," unpublished paper.

Painvin, Georges Jean, "Conférences de M. Georges Jean Painvin," *Bulletin de l'Association des réservistes du chiffre*, VII (May 1961), 5–47.

Paquet, Commandant, "Le 2e bureau en campagne," *Revue militaire française*, No. 22 (1923), 83–102; No. 23 (1924), 181–201.

Pichot-Duclos, General Jean, "L'Evolution actuelle des services de renseignement français," *Bulletin de AASSDN*, II, No. 158 (1993), 12–15; II, No. 159, 6–9.

———, "Vers une culture de renseignement," *Défense nationale*, May 1992, 73–85.

Porch, Douglas, "French Intelligence and the Fall of France, 1939–40," *Intelligence and National Security*, IV, No. 1 (January 1989), 28–58.

Powers, Thomas, "The Truth About the CIA," *The New York Review of Books*, XI, No. 9 (13 May 1993), 49–55.

Resis, Albert, "Russiaphobia and the Testament of Peter the Great, 1812–1980," *Slavic Review* Winter 1985, 681–93.

Ribadeau Dumas, General, "Essai d'historique du chiffre de l'armée de terre," *Bulletin de l'Association des réservistes du chiffre*, nouvelle série, No. 2 (1974), 25–61.

Ruat, Colonel, "Les Services spéciaux français dans les conflits d'outre-mer, 1945–1962," *Bulletin de l'AASSDN*, IV, No. 152 (1991), 28–35.

"Rumor or Fact: Did the CIA Interfere in Algeria?" *Newsweek*, LVII (15 May 1961), 50–1.

Rusbridger, James, "Between Bluff, Deceit and Treachery: The Story of Henri Déricourt and an SOE Disaster in France," *Encounter*, May 1986, 5–23.

Santa, Jean Della, "Cassandre, ou le renseignement jamais cru," *Revue militaire suisse*, No. 3 (March 1972), 117–30.

Scuro, Daniel P., "The Dangers of Openness," *Security Management*, XXXIV, No. 9 (September 1990), 93–5.

Steadman, Michael J., "Industrial Espionage: What You Don't Know Can Hurt You," *Business and Society Review*, No. 76 (Winter 1991), 25–32.

Trumpener, Ulrich, "War Premeditated? German Intelligence Operations in July 1914," *Central European History*, IX, No. 1 (March 1976), 58–85.

Viasse, Maurice, "L'Evolution de la fonction d'attaché militaire en France au XXe siècle," *Relations internationales*, No. 32 (1982), 507–24.

Wark, Westley K., "British Intelligence on the German Air Force and Aircraft Industry, 1933–1939," *Historical Journal*, XXV, No. 3 (1982), 627–48.

———, "Introduction: The Study of Espionage: Past, Present, Future?" *Intelligence and National Security*, VIII, No. 3 (July 1993), 1–13.

Werth, Alexander, "The CIA in Algeria," *The Nation*, CXCII (20 May 1961), 433–5.

Young, Robert J., "French Military Intelligence and the Franco-Italian Alliance, 1933–1939," *Historical Journal*, XXVIII, No. 1 (March 1985), 143–68.

Zhai, Qiang, "Transplanting the Chinese Model: Chinese Military Advisers and the First Vietnam War, 1950–54," *Journal of Military History*, No. 57 (October 1993), 689–714.

NOTES

1. THE BIRTH OF THE MODERN FRENCH SECRET SERVICES

1. Eugène Vaillé, *Le Cabinet noir*, Presses Universitaires de France (Paris, 1950), 2.

2. Vaillé, *Le Cabinet noir*, 51–74, 200–1, 226.

3. Vaillé, *Le Cabinet noir*, 304–5.

4. Louis Madelin, *Fouché*, Plon (Paris, 1903), I, 467–8.

5. Vaillé, *Le Cabinet noir*, 307–8, 321.

6. Phillip John Stead, *The Police of Paris*, Staples Press (London, 1957), 78.

7. Quoted in Eric A. Arnold, Jr., *Fouché, Napoleon and the General Police*, University Press of America (Washington, D.C., 1979), 78, and notes 28, 29 on p. 85.

8. Carl von Clausewitz, *On War*, ed. and trans. Sir Michael Howard and Peter Paret, Princeton University Press (Princeton, N.J., 1984), 117, 199, 202–3.

9. Clausewitz, *On War*, 198–9, 454, 545.

10. Baron de Jomini, *The Art of War*, trans. Captain G. H. Mendell and Lieutenant W. P. Craighill, Greenwood Press (Westport, Conn., 1977), 209–10, 270–1, 273–4. Discussed in Michael Handel, *Masters of War: Sun Tzu, Clausewitz and Jomini*, Frank Cass (London, 1992), Ch. 11.

11. See Paul Thiebault, *The Memoirs of Baron Thiebault*, Macmillan (New York, 1896).

12. Jay Luvaas, "Napoleon's Use of Intelligence: The Jena Campaign

of 1805," in Michael Handel, ed., *Leaders and Intelligence*, Frank Cass (London, 1989), 40–54.

13. Arnold, *Fouché*, 170–1.

14. Alfred Cobban, "The Great Mystification of Méhée de la Touche," *Bulletin of the London University Institute of Historical Research*, XLI (May 1968), 100–6.

15. On Schulmeister, see Jean Savant, *Les Espions de Napoléon*, Paris (Hachette, 1957), and Alexander Elmer, *L'Agent secret de Napoléon, Charles-Louis Schulmeister*, Payot (Paris, 1932).

16. Arnold, *Fouché*, 88–96. Savary did this out of personal spite and also because he believed that Fetny was a double agent in Austrian service. Nevertheless, his information was considered as valuable as that supplied by Schulmeister before Austerlitz.

17. John Elting, *Swords Around the Throne: Napoleon's Grande Armée*, Free Press (New York, 1988), 118 and passim.

18. See Albert Resis, "Russiaphobia and the Testament of Peter the Great, 1812–1980," *Slavic Review*, Winter 1985, 681–93; L. R. Lewitter, "The Apocryphal Testament of Peter the Great," *Polish Review*, Summer 1966, 37; William C. Green, "The Historic Russian Drive for a Warm Water Port: Anatomy of a Geopolitical Myth," *Naval War College Review*, Spring 1993, pp 83–4, 91–2.

19. Vaillé, *Le Cabinet noir*, 349–51.

20. Vaillé, *Le Cabinet noir*, Part 2, Ch. 12. See also E. Daudet, *La Police politique, chronique des temps de la Restauration d'après les rapports des agents secrets et les papiers du cabinet noir, 1815–1820* (Paris, 1912).

21. Hsi-Hue Liang, *The Rise of Modern Police and the European State System from Metternich to the Second World War*, Cambridge University Press (Cambridge, Eng., 1992), 52.

22. This argument is made in the context of the military by M. Janowitz, *The Military in the Political Development of New Nations: An Essay in Comparative Analysis*, University of Chicago Press (Chicago, 1964), 65.

23. Marcel Le Clère, *La Police*, Presses Universitaires de France (Paris, 1972), 28.

24. Howard C. Payne, *The Police State of Louis-Napoleon Bonaparte, 1851–1860*, University of Washington Press (Seattle, 1966), 258–60.

25. Jacques Aubert, Michel Eude, Claude Goyard, et al., eds., *L'Etat et sa police en France (1789–1914)* (Geneva, 1979), 102, 105.

26. Vaillé, *Le Cabinet noir*, 394–5.

27. Maxime Du Camp, *Souvenirs d'un demi-siècle: Au temps de Louis-Philippe et de Napoléon III, 1830–1870*, Hachette (Paris, 1949), 168–70.

28. Emile Lambry, *Les Mystères du cabinet noir sous l'Empire et la Poste sous la Commune*, E. Dentu (Paris, 1871), 25, 39.

29. Du Camp, *Souvenirs*, 169.

30. Christopher Andrew, "Déchiffrement et diplomatie: Le Cabinet noir du Quai d'Orsay sous la Troisième République," *Relations internationales*, No. 5 (1976), 40.

31. Liang, *The Rise of Modern Police*, 45–6, 89, 109.

32. Dennis E. Showalter, "Intelligence on the Eve of Transformation: Methodology, Organization, and Application," in Lieutenant Colonel Walter T. Hitchcock, ed., *The Intelligence Revolution: A Historical Perspective*, Proceedings of the Thirteenth Military History Symposium, U.S. Air Force Academy, Colorado Springs, Colorado, October 12–14, 1988, Office of Air Force History (Washington, D.C., 1991), 18.

33. Henri Navarre, *Le Service de renseignements, 1871–1944*, Plon (Paris, 1978), 15. Also "Le Service des renseignements secrets," Bibliothèque nationale, NAF 20642.

34. Her Majesty's Stationery Office, *The Records of the Foreign Office, 1782–1939* (London, 1969), 47.

35. Otto Pflanze, *Bismarck and the Development of Germany: The Period of Unification, 1815–1871*, Princeton University Press (Princeton, N.J., 1963), 449.

36. Wilhelm J. C. E. Stieber, *Espion de Bismarck*, Pygmalion (Paris, 1985), 132–67.

37. Colonel George Armand Furse, *Information in War: Its Acquisition and Transmission*, William Clowes & Sons (London, 1895), 36, 55, 60–2.

38. Allan Mitchell, "The Xenophobic Style: French Counterespionage and the Emergence of the Dreyfus Affair," *Journal of Modern History*, 3 September 1980, 418.

39. Liang, *The Rise of Modern Police*, 96, 98–102, 112–29, 147–50, 156–7, 177–81.

40. Liang, *The Rise of Modern Police*, 140–7.

41. Colonel B. E. M. Gustave Stinglhamber and Paul Dresse, *Leopold II au travail*, Editions du Sablon (Brussels and Paris, 1944), 51.

42. Andrew, "Déchiffrement," 42.

43. E. Carton de Wiart, *Leopold II: Souvenirs des dernières années, 1901–1909* (Brussels, 1944), 196.

44. For instance, ex-Deuxième Bureau officer and historian of early military intelligence Henri Navarre writes that Schnaebelé worked for the Statistical Section, when he depended on the Sûreté. *Le Service de renseignements*, 16.

45. Michel Marrus, *Les Juifs en France à l'époque de l'Affaire Dreyfus*, Calmann-Lévy (Paris, 1972), 219.

46. Jean-Denis Bredin, *The Affair: The Case of Alfred Dreyfus*, George Braziller (New York, 1986), 46.

47. 3 October 1888. Cited in Liang, *The Rise of Modern Police*, 94–5.

48. Bredin, *The Affair*, 51.

49. Mitchell, "The Xenophobic Style," 424–5.

50. General Louis Ribadeau Dumas, "Essai d'historique du chiffre de l'armée de terre," *Bulletin de l'Association des réservistes du chiffre*, nouvelle série, No. 2 (1974), 27–32.

51. Showalter, "Intelligence on the Eve of Transformation," 19.

52. For a more thorough explanation of how these systems worked, see the classic work by David Kahn, *The Codebreakers: The Story of Secret Writing*, Macmillan (New York, 1967), 230–44.

53. Andrew, "Déchiffrement," 43–4. Translations of Italian diplomatic telegrams date from 1887, those of Great Britain from 1891, German communications from 1899, although these certainly were broken earlier. Turkish correspondence dates from 1898 and Spanish from 1906. Andrew concludes that this list is not complete. For instance, no evidence exists of translations of Russian or Austrian telegrams, although some Russian police codes were read at least by 1905.

54. Andrew, "Déchiffrement," 45.

55. Kahn, *Codebreakers*, 245–6.

56. Kahn, *Codebreakers*, 250.

57. Hannah Arendt, *The Origins of Totalitarianism*, World Publishing (New York, 1972), 101.

58. Douglas Porch, *The March to the Marne: The French Army 1871–1914*, Cambridge University Press (Cambridge, Eng., 1981), 66.

59. In a book recently published in France, author Jean Doise argues that the Statistical Section refused to admit their mistaken accusation of Dreyfus, not because of anti-Semitism or a belief in the infallibility of their codes, but because they needed to protect Esterhazy, through whom they were passing information to deceive the Germans about the development of the 75 mm artillery piece. Few historians of the period give much credence to this theory, however. Jean Doise, *Histoire militaire de l'Affaire Dreyfus ou un secret bien gardé*, Seuil (Paris, 1994).

2. SUCCESS AND SCANDAL, 1900–14

1. John Ferris, "Before 'Room 40': The British Empire and Signals Intelligence, 1898–1914," *Journal of Strategic Studies*, XII, No. 4 (December 1989), 432, 446. The British could intercept diplomatic messages passing through India, however.

2. Christopher Andrew, *Théophile Delcassé and the Making of the Entente Cordiale: A Reappraisal of French Foreign Policy, 1898–1905* (London,

1968), 98–100. Erroneous decrypts also led Delcassé to believe in 1901 that England and Italy had signed a nonexistent naval treaty. Ibid., 188–9.

3. *Les Carnets de Georges Louis* (Paris 1926), II, 18–19. Quoted in Christopher Andrew, "Déchiffrements et diplomatie," *Relations internationales*, No. 5 (1976), 55.

4. Denis Showalter, "Intelligence on the Eve of Transformation," in Lt. Col. Walter T. Hitchcock, ed., *The Intelligence Revolution: A Historical Perspective*, Proceedings of the Thirteenth Military History Symposium, U.S. Air Force Academy, Colorado Springs, Colorado, October 12–14, 1988, Office of Air Force History (Washington, D.C., 1991), 21–2.

5. Ferris, "Before 'Room 40,' " 447–8.

6. Henri Navarre, *Le Service de renseignements*, Plon (Paris, 1978), 16–17. See also Christopher Andrew, "France and the German Menace," in Ernest R. May, ed., *Knowing One's Enemies: Intelligence Assessment Before the Two World Wars*, Princeton University Press (Princeton, N.J., 1984), 135–6.

7. *Journal officiel. Documents parlementaires, Chambre* (1913), No. 3318. Quoted in Andrew, "France and the German Menace," 133–4.

8. This was true not only for intelligence but even for important policy questions. For instance, not until June 1909 were the soldiers told of the secret treaty between Italy and France of November 1902. This proved a rather serious oversight, as it had profound implications for French mobilization plans. "As a result," wrote French commander-in-chief Joseph Joffre, ". . . we continued to maintain on the Alps a substantial and unnecessary army." Joseph Joffre, *Mémoires*, Plon (Paris, 1932), I, 104. For its part, the War Ministry kept the Quai d'Orsay in the dark about Franco-British staff talks begun in the wake of the Tangier crisis of 1905.

9. Octave Homberg, *Les Coulisses de l'histoire: Souvenirs 1898–1928*, Fayard (Paris, 1938), 38–9.

10. Homberg, *Les Coulisses*, 43.

11. Andrew, *Delcassé*, 300–1.

12. Archives nationales, F7 14605, Haverna, "Note sur l'organisation et le fonctionnement du service cryptographique de la Sûreté générale," 7 September 1917, 2–4.

13. Marcel Givierge, *Au service du chiffre: 18 ans de souvenirs, 1907–1925*, Vol. I, Bibliothèque nationale, NAF 17, 353, 40.

14. Archives nationales, F7 12829, 27 December 1909.

15. Givierge, *Au service du chiffre*, 37, 41, 45.

16. Haverna, "Note," 2–4.

17. Showalter, "Intelligence on the Eve of Transformation," 18.

18. Maurice Paléologue, *Un Grand Tournant de la politique mondiale, 1904–1906*, Plon (Paris, 1934), 64–5.

19. Jean-Baptiste Duroselle, *La France et les français, 1914–1920*, Editions Richelieu (Paris, 1972), 45.

20. Showalter, "Intelligence on the Eve of Transformation," 19; Gerhard Ritter, *The Schlieffen Plan: Critique of a Myth*, Greenwood Press (Westport, Conn., 1978), 42–4.

21. Navarre, *Le Service de renseignements*, 18.

22. Jan Karl Tanenbaum, "French Estimates of German Plans," in May, *Knowing One's Enemies*, 158–60. Andrew, "France and the German Menace," ibid., 137. Indeed, it appears that the French were not above planting bogus intelligence themselves, as when, for instance, in 1909 the Deuxième Bureau gave the British a document which claimed to be a plan for a German invasion of Great Britain, probably to encourage the British to be more forthcoming in the Anglo-French staff talks.

23. Andrew, "Déchiffrement," 53–4.

24. Haverna, "Note," 6–8, 12. Givierge, *Au service du chiffre*, 41.

25. Haverna, "Note," 12.

26. Andrew, "France and the German Menace," 144–45.

27. Andrew, "Déchiffrement," 56.

3. THE FAILED MIRACLE

1. Charles Christienne and Pierre Lissarrague, *A History of French Military Aviation*, Smithsonian Institution Press (Washington, D.C., 1986), 42–5, 50–3, 77–9.

2. General E. L. Spears, *Liaison, 1914*, Doubleday, Doran & Co. (Garden City, N.Y., 1931), 71. Indeed, Spears complained that, at this stage of the war, the Germans posed far fewer dangers than French troops, who were firing at everything, including British officers.

3. Marcel Givierge, *Etude historique de la section du chiffre*, Vol. I: *1896–1916*, Bibliothèque nationale, NAF 24353, 34, 37–8, 45.

4. Service Historique de l'Armée de Terre (SHAT), 16N 918, "T.S.F. allemande," 31 July 1914.

5. François Cartier, "Souvenirs du Général Cartier," *Revue des transmissions*, No. 85 (July–August 1959), 27.

6. Michael Handel, ed., *War, Strategy, and Intelligence*, Frank Cass (London, 1989), 239.

7. "Note sur des renseignements récent relatifs à la mobilisation et à la concentration allemandes," 8 March 1904. SHAT, 7N 1756. "Note," 23 January 1908, SHAT 7N 670. Quoted in Jan Karl Tanenbaum, "French Estimates of German Plans," in Ernest R. May, ed., *Knowing One's Enemies*, Princeton University Press (Princeton, N.J., 1984), 154, 156.

8. "Les Chemins de fer allemands à la fin de 1909" and "Note sur les

chemins de fer allemands à la fin de 1910," SHAT 7N 672. Cited in Tanenbaum, "French Estimates of German Plans," 158–9.

9. SHAT, 7N 1111, 6 July 1912. Tanenbaum points out, however, that Pellé rarely ventured an opinion on German strategy. "French Estimates of German Plans," 160.

10. Winston Churchill relates that when he attended a meeting of the Committee of Imperial Defense during the 1911 Agadir crisis, "overwhelming detailed evidence was adduced to show that the Germans had made every military preparation for marching through Belgium . . . The great military camps in close proximity to the frontier, the enormous depots, the reticulation of railways, the endless sidings, revealed with the utmost clearness and beyond all doubt their design." *The World Crisis, 1911–1914* (London, 1923), 57. This knowledge makes the British decision to accept Plan XVII without question, and to join their small army to the French left wing, thereby placing them in the direct path of the German juggernaut, appear all the more negligent.

11. Henri Navarre, *Le Service de renseignements*, Plon (Paris, 1978), 18.

12. Tanenbaum, "French Estimates of German Plans," 161.

13. "Commentaires," 1911, SHAT, 7N 1112, dossier 1907–1914, p. 3. Quoted in Tanenbaum, "French Estimates of German Plans," 162.

14. Beyond these technical objections lurked a political agenda. In 1910, French socialist leader Jean Jaurès had published *L'Armée nouvelle*, a blueprint for a root-and-branch reform of the French army along Swiss lines. The Jaurès plan, which he placed before parliament in an unsuccessful but widely followed debate, called for a very small number of regular officers, trained in universities rather than in inbred and narcissistic military colleges, to lead a citizen militia. As these citizen soldiers and their largely civilian cadres would be incapable of offensive maneuver, they could only adopt a defensive strategy. A defensive-minded citizen militia, Jaurès reasoned, would in itself lessen the risks of war by removing the temptation to strike the first blow. While many left-wing politicians were not prepared to go as far as Jaurès, *L'Armée nouvelle* did articulate a distrust of military leaders accentuated by the Dreyfus Affair. It also began a process which, in the popular mind, associated defensive warfare with a broad-based citizen army composed mainly of reservists. The implications of intelligence that Germans would integrate active and reserve divisions was simply too unsettling. If the French followed suit, the poor quality of French reserves would require the high command to adopt a defensive strategy. Jaurès would at least get some satisfaction. For a discussion of reserve issues, see Douglas Porch, *The March to the Marne: The French Army, 1871–1914*, Cambridge University Press (Cambridge,

Eng., 1981), Ch. 10. Tanenbaum, "French Estimates of German Plans," 162–3.

15. Tanenbaum, "French Estimates of German Plans," 158–62.

16. Christopher Andrew, "France and the German Menace," in May, *Knowing One's Enemies*, 145.

17. General Louis Ribadeau Dumas, "Essai d'historique du chiffre de l'armée de terre," *Bulletin de l'Association des réservistes du chiffre*, nouvelle série, No. 2 (1974), 34.

18. Raymond Poincaré, *Au service de la France: Neuf années de souvenirs*, Vol. I, Plon (Paris, 1926), 224–5. Joseph Joffre, *Mémoires*, Plon (Paris, 1932), I, 49–54.

19. One former French intelligence officer charged that the arrogance of French military theorists, the heirs of Napoleon who disdained German strategists as mere Teutonic upstarts, meant that French soldiers were little concerned about the plans of their primary enemy in any case. Eugène Carrias, *La Pensée militaire française*, Presses Universitaires de France (Paris, 1948), 289. Yet, in the aftermath of the Prusso-German victory over France in 1870–71, Germany served as the model for French military reforms, and books by German theorists continued to be translated, widely read, and hotly debated in France. Therefore, this explanation for the ignorance of German military theory would appear to drop short of the mark. See Allen Mitchell, *The German Influence in France After 1870: The Formation of the French Republic*, University of North Carolina Press (Chapel Hill, 1979); and *Victors and Vanquished: The German Influence on Army and Church in France after 1870*, University of North Carolina Press (Chapel Hill, 1984).

20. Joffre, *Mémoires*, I, 192–201.

21. This was precisely the conclusion which Joffre drew on 21 August 1914, when he responded to news that the mass of the German forces were wheeling through Belgium by ordering an offensive into Lorraine. Joffre, *Mémoires*, I, 283.

22. Andrew, "France and the German Menace," 146–9.

23. Holger H. Herwig, "Imperial Germany," in May, *Knowing One's Enemies*, 94.

24. See Porch, *The March to the Marne*, Ch. 11, for the author's argument about how the weaknesses and doctrinal confusion of the French army contributed to the popularity of the offensive. At the height of the 1911 Agadir crisis, Joffre informed French Prime Minister Joseph Caillaux that French arms could not be assured of the 70 percent chance of victory which Napoleon believed the critical precondition for accepting battle. France's military position actually deteriorated in the two years before the war. In 1912 and 1913, Germany passed laws which increased the size of its standing army, which sharpened the enemy's edge in virtually every category of arms and

manpower, at the very moment when massive French intervention in Morocco absorbed funds badly needed for army modernization. During the 1913 debates over the three-year-service law, the French government argued that the growing strength of the German army made an extra year's service necessary. In a stormy parliamentary session on 14 July 1914, Senator Charles Humbert laid bare the enormous deficiencies of the French army compared to that of Germany, especially in the area of heavy artillery, in which the French were almost totally deficient.

Certainly, France hoped to offset the German advantages through Russian and British assistance. But even at its optimal level, French strategists calculated that they would be forced to bear the brunt of the German offensives for the opening weeks, a critical time when France's ability to survive would be tested to the limit. "First and foremost," General de Laguiche, the military attaché to Russia, wrote in 1913, "we must count on ourselves." And that was not an alluring prospect as the realization that war must be fought sooner rather than later began to take hold in the French high command. Joffre admitted in his memoirs that optimistic reports and pronouncements at odds with reality had flowed from the War Ministry in the three years before the outbreak of the war. But this had been done "for reasons of morale, especially to avoid discouragement . . . our inferiority could escape no one . . ." Indeed, British colonel E. L. Spears, sent as a liaison officer with French intelligence in 1914, discovered a lack of faith in the training and discipline of French troops, especially of the reserves, in the French high command, which convinced them, in keeping with common military wisdom, that the offensive was the tactic of choice with poorly trained troops.

25. SHAT 7N 1771, "Concentration des armées allemandes," n.d. (probably 1913). Quoted in Tanenbaum, "French Estimates of German Plans," 166–7.

26. Indeed, Joffre charged that the warnings of the Fifth Army commander, who anchored the French left wing, General Lanrezac, that he was to be attacked was based upon "divination" rather than firm intelligence. *Mémoires*, I, 267–8 note. The dispute between the two men was especially bitter because Joffre subsequently relieved his subordinate of his command.

27. Tanenbaum, "French Estimates of German Plans," 170–1. For his part, Joffre complained of contradictory intelligence summaries, citing a 9 October 1913 study of the German army which stated that "reserve forces are employed in the same manner as active troops" but then went on to say that poor leadership, inadequate artillery, and a separate organizational structure meant that German reserves could not possibly be integrated into active formations initially and would be retained behind the lines until needed. *Mémoires*, I, 249–50.

28. Luigi Albertini, *The Origins of the War of 1914*, Vol. II: *The Crisis*

of July 1914: From the Sarajevo Outrage to the Austro-Hungarian General Mobilization, Oxford University Press (London, New York, and Toronto, 1953), 600.

29. Joffre, *Mémoires*, I, 117–18, 212, 215. Joffre includes the dispatch of the French ambassador in Berlin on 21 July claiming that the Germans had begun preparation for mobilizing, when it is clear that they had done nothing of the sort.

30. The Deuxième Bureau complained that these agents' reports were subject to "the inevitable delays, which vary between twelve and twenty-four hours." SHAT, 16N 918, "Note à Monsieur le Général Chef d'Etat-Major Général de l'Armée." n.d. (obviously July 1914).

31. Ulrich Trumpener, "War Premeditated? German Intelligence Operations in July 1914," *Central European History*, IX, No. 1 (March 1976), 75–9. Joffre, *Mémoires*, I, 217, 221–2.

32. Albertini, *The Origins of the War of 1914*, II, 614, 628–9.

33. Trumpener, "War Premeditated?," 69, 74.

34. SHAT, 16N 918, 1 August.

35. Joffre, *Mémoires*, I, 213. Only on 6 August was Joffre satisfied that he had enough forces mobilized to deal with a surprise *"attaque brusquée"* (p. 242).

36. Trumpener, "War Premeditated?," 68–9.

37. Spears, *Liaison*, 26.

38. SHAT, 16N 918. These reports are in the *bulletin de renseignements* for 7 and 8 August 1914, although Joffre reports receiving them on the previous days.

39. Joffre, *Mémoires*, I, 244, 256–7. Although the last Liège fortress did not surrender until 20 August, the way was clear for the passage of the German First Army by the 14th. Far more damaging to the Germans ultimately was the destruction of railway tunnels and bridges by the Belgians, which diminished their ability to supply and reinforce their right wing. This author found no evidence that this significant information was picked up by French intelligence. Joffre continued to be distracted by reports of German troop movements east of Metz.

40. Joffre, *Mémoires*, I, 250.

41. Joffre, *Mémoires*, I, 91–3. The German army could utilize a greater percentage of its reservists on mobilization in part because German reservists were staffed with a higher percentage of professional officers and NCOs than were those of France. For a discussion of the French reserves, see Porch, *The March to the Marne*.

42. Joffre, *Mémoires*, I, 251.

43. For a discussion of the shortcomings of the French high command, see Porch, *The March to the Marne*, 171 passim.

44. SHAT, 16N 918, 14 August 1914.

45. Joffre, *Mémoires*, I, 261, 263, 266. Joffre also appears to have been distracted by "fantasist" intelligence reports out of Italy and Switzerland announcing the arrival of Austrian troops on the French front (p. 265).

46. Joffre, *Mémoires*, I, 266.

47. SHAT, 9N 918, "Note au sujet des formations de réserve et de Landwehr," 16 August 1914.

48. SHAT, 16N 918, 15 August 1914.

49. Joffre, *Mémoires*, I, 270–1, 273.

50. SHAT, 16N 918, "Note au sujet des formations de réserve et de Landwehr," 25 August 1914. Not only were French army commanders informing headquarters of this clever piece of German deception but on 24 August the Deuxième Bureau reported that the British had detected the ruse.

51. *Les Armées françaises dans la Grande Guerre*, Tome 1, Vol. II, Imprimérie nationale (Paris, 1925), 20–1. Spears, *Liaison*, 84–5, reported that on 17 August a downed German pilot revealed to the Deuxième Bureau of the French Fifth Army that reserve corps were following closely on the heels of active units marching through Belgium.

52. C. R. M. F. Cruttwell, *A History of the Great War: 1914–1918*, Paladin (London, 1982), 19.

53. B. H. Liddell Hart, *History of the First World War*, Pan Books (London, 1970), 54.

54. Joffre complained on 14 August that his pilots' reports gave "almost no precision" on enemy movements. *Mémoires*, 265.

55. "Aircraft Work at the Front," *Flight*, 9 October 1914, p. 1017. Quoted in Lee Kennett, *The First Air War, 1914–1918*, Free Press (New York, 1991), 32.

56. Christienne and Lissarrague, *A History of French Military Aviation*, 80.

57. Joffre, *Mémoires*, I, 277–8.

58. Claude Breguet, "La Reconnaissance aérienne et la bataille de la Marne," *Revue historique des armées*, No. 166 (March 1987), 92–100. Joffre appears unable to have made up his mind about Kluck's objectives. On 1 September, Joffre had concluded from various intelligence sources that Kluck would not attack Paris, a decision which he reversed on the next day. He was still undecided until late on 3 September. *Mémoires*, 365, 369, 378.

59. Wilhelm F. Flicke, *War Secrets in the Ether*, Vol. I, Aegean Park Press (Laguna Hills, Calif., 1977), 22.

60. Joffre, *Mémoires*, 352–3.

61. SHAT, 16N 918, 27 August 1914. Joffre interpreted the division to mean that the German advance would probably slow down, as the Second Army was given the task of besieging Maubeuge. *Mémoires*, 325.

62. Flicke, *War Secrets*, 23–4.

63. Cartier, "Souvenirs," No. 87 (November–December 1959), 15–9.

64. Marcel Givierge, *Au service du chiffre*, Vol. I, Bibliothèque nationale, NAF 17,573, 142. Joffre confirmed that news from various intelligence
sources that the Germans were exhausted, although "we ignored to what
degree this weakening was to our advantage," at least gave hope for a successful
outcome on the Marne. *Mémoires*, 399.

65. SHAT, 16N 918.

66. Flicke, *War Secrets*, 31–2.

67. David Kahn, *The Codebreakers: The Story of Secret Writing*, Macmillan (New York, 1967), 301–3.

68. Marcel Givierge, "Questions de Chiffre," *Revue militaire française*,
No. 36 (1 June 1924), 402–8. Kahn, *Codebreakers*, 299–304.

69. Cartier, "Souvenirs," 38.

70. Givierge, *Au service du chiffre*, Vol. I, NAF 17,573, 152–54.

4. THE TRENCH DEADLOCK

1. Colonel Charles Paquet, *Etude sur le fonctionnement interne d'un
2e bureau en campagne*, Berger-Levrault (Paris, 1923), xv.

2. Paquet, *Etude*, 7. On the issue of integrating intelligence into operational plans, see Michael Handel, ed., *Intelligence and Military Operations*, Frank Cass (London, 1990), 5–6, 25.

3. Paquet, *Etude*, xvi.

4. David Kahn, *The Codebreakers: The Story of Secret Writing*, Macmillan (New York, 1967), 299, 313.

5. Marcel Givierge, "Questions de chiffre," *Revue militaire française*,
Tome 13e (July–September 1924), 72.

6. Marcel Givierge, *Au service du chiffre*, Vol. I, Bibliothèque nationale,
NAF 17,573, 155.

7. Kahn, *Codebreakers*, 305–6. By November 1915, Paris was organized
into a Bureau du Chiffre for encoding and decoding messages; a Radio Bureau
for listening services and liaison with Russia; a Cryptologic Service for studying
codes; a Translation Bureau; a Radiogoniometry Service, which centralized
its findings with the Belgians and the British; and an Administrative Section.
Givierge, *Au service du chiffre*, Vol. I, NAF 24,353, 418.

8. Paquet, *Etude*, 50.

9. Kahn, *Codebreakers*, 313.

10. Givierge, *Au service du chiffre*, Vol. II, NAF 17,574, 439; Vol. III,
688–94.

11. "Vth Army Staff, 2e bureau, 16/1/17: "Instructions on the Intelligence Service in the Divisions," Nolan Papers, U.S. Army War College,
Carlisle Barracks.

12. Ibid.

13. Givierge, *Au service du chiffre*, Vol. I, NAF 24,353, 118, 142, 182,

197, 208, 251–2, 254; Vol. II, NAF 17,575, 425; Vol. III, 694. For instance, Givierge noted in May 1918 that American listening posts intercepted 5,980 calls to 1,750 for French posts: Vol. III, 696; Vol. II, NAF 17,574, 506. Many of these issues are also discussed in General Louis Ribadeau Dumas, "Essai d'historique du chiffre de l'armée de terre," *Bulletin de l'Association des réservistes du chiffre*, nouvelle série, No. 2 (1974), 37–61. Similar disruption appears to have been caused in the spring of 1917 when Philippe Pétain replaced Robert Nivelle as commander-in-chief, which was one reason why American intelligence officers, who were visiting the French army during this changeover, opted to model U.S. intelligence practices on those of the British army. "I got the distinct impression that French intelligence was suffering some kind of a shock, that the rest of the French army had suffered in the great failure of the Nivelle offensive, which is only natural as they would be involved in the failure," remembered General Denis Nolan, who was part of that mission. "General Nolan's notes on Secret Service: Dictated 25 January 1932," 9/5, Papers of Colonel Denis E. Nolan, G-2 of GHQAEF, U.S. Army War College, Carlisle Barracks.

14. Paquet, *Etude*, 52; Givierge, *Au service du chiffre*, Vol. I, NAF 24,353, 320–21; NAF 17,573, 247–48. "Questions de chiffre," *Revue militaire française*, No. 36 (1 June 1924), 411–2.

15. Givierge, *Au service du chiffre*, Vol. II, NAF 17,574, 464.

16. Givierge, *Au service du chiffre*, Vol. I, NAF 17573, 258. See also Henri Morin, *Service secret: A l'écoute devant Verdun*, G. Durasse (Paris, 1959). Wilhelm Flicke, *War Secrets in the Ether*, Vol. I, Aegean Park Press (Laguna Hills, Calif., 1977), 28. By 1918, the Germans had 292 of these devices in operation. David Kahn, *Hitler's Spies: German Military Intelligence in World War II*, Macmillan (New York, 1978), 35.

17. Paquet, *Etude*, 59; Givierge, *Au service du chiffre*, Vol. II, NAF, 17,574, 466. For German exploitation of lapses in French communications security, see Flicke, *War Secrets*.

18. Givierge, "Questions de chiffre," Tome 13e (July–September 1924), 63; *Au service du chiffre*, Vol. II, NAF 17,574, 535–6, 541–2.

19. Kahn, *Codebreakers*, 308.

20. Flicke, *War Secrets*, 35–6.

21. Givierge, *Au service du chiffre*, Vol. II, NAF 17,574, 543, 564. Walter Nicholai, chief of the German espionage service during World War I, agreed that the Germans were able, through a variety of sources, to establish an accurate French order of battle at the front. However, they were less adept at locating reserve divisions. Nor did this information give them much insight into the intentions of the Allied commanders. Walter Nicholai, *German Secret Service*, Stanley Paul (London, 1924), 196.

22. Givierge, "Questions de chiffre," No. 36 (June 1924), 413.

23. Givierge, "Questions de Chiffre," No. 36 (June 1924), 412–14. *Au service du chiffre*, Vol. II, NAF 17,574, 454, 461, 464, 551–2, 564–5. Kahn, *Codebreakers*, 314–15.

24. Givierge, *Au service du chiffre*, Vol. II, NAF 17,574, 551–2.

25. Commandant Paquet, "Le 2e bureau en campagne," *Revue militaire française*, No. 22 (1923), 97, 87.

26. 2e bureau, VIth French army & "Memorandum report of visit to HQs, Ist French army" by Major Kerr T. Riggs, 25 January to 7 February 1918. Nolan Papers, U.S. Army War College, Carlisle Barracks. American officers noted complaints by General Pétain in 1917 that the form and even the scale of these maps varied from army to army.

27. Lieutenant Colonel Arthur L. Conger, 18 July 1918, Nolan Papers, U.S. Army War College, Carlisle Barracks.

28. Paquet, *Etude*, 7, 40, 43.

29. Paquet, "Le 2e bureau en campagne," 102.

30. Captain James R. Sloane, 20 February 1918. See also Nolan's unpublished memoirs, Ch. 3, p. 17. It is possible that the French may have bugged POW cells as did the British, but there is no evidence of this in the records. I thank John Ferris for this information. For French handling of POWs on the Somme in 1916, see Paquet, "Le 2e bureau en campagne," 180–91, 200.

31. Papers of Major General Ralph H. Van Deman, p. 57, U.S. Army War College, Carlisle Barracks.

32. David French, "Sir John French's Secret Service on the Western Front, 1914–15," *Journal of Strategic Studies*, December 1984, 428–9.

33. General Nolan's notes on Secret Service, 9/2, U.S. Army War College, Carlisle Barracks.

34. Nicholai, *German Secret Service*, 155–9. Christopher Andrew, *Her Majesty's Secret Service: The Making of the British Intelligence Community*, Viking (New York, 1986), 139–65.

35. See, for instance, Commandant Georges Ladoux, *Guerre secrète en Alsace*, Editions du masque (Paris, 1934). For a contemporary account, see Pascal Krop, *Les Secrets de l'espionnage français de 1870 à nos jours*, J. C. Lattès (Paris, 1993), Chs. 1–4.

36. Nolan thought agent intelligence of even less value to the Americans, but confessed that there were no agents left by the time the Americans arrived in 1917. His only option, he believed, was to hire them away from the British and French by paying higher fees, which he claimed he was loath to do.

37. "General Nolan's Notes on the Secret Service," 9/2, 7/21; Captain James Sloane; Papers of Ralph H. Van Deman, 31, 57, U.S. Army War College, Carlisle Barracks.

38. Paquet, "Le 2e bureau en campagne," No. 22, 87; No. 23, 191–6.

39. Paquet, *Etude*, 71. On founding of the SR Artillery, 25.

40. "Memorandum report of visit to HQs, 1st French Army," Nolan Papers, Army War College, Carlisle Barracks.

41. This was largely because observation planes seldom flew "deep" missions but remained close to their own lines, engaged in combat only to defend themselves, and by the winter of 1917–18 were regularly assigned fighter escorts. Charles Christienne and Pierre Lissarrague, *A History of French Military Aviation*, Smithsonian Institution Press (Washington, D.C., 1986), 130.

42. Out of 16,458 pilots and 2,000 observers who served during the war, 5,553 men died in combat or accidents. Christienne and Lissarrague, *A History of French Military Aviation*, 130.

43. J. de Lannoy de Bissy, "Les Photographies aériennes et leur étude au point de vue militaire," *Revue militaire française*, Tome 12 (April–June 1924), 257–77; Christienne and Lissarrague, *A History of French Military Aviation*, 69–75, 80, 90–1; Lee Kennett, *The First Air War, 1914–1918*, Free Press (New York, 1991), Ch. 2; *Revue Icare*, Nos. 85 and 88; Krop, *Les Secrets*, 141–44.

44. Bissy, "Les Photographies aériennes," 269–73; Christienne and Lissarrague, *A History of French Military Aviation*, 95–6, 106–7, 125.

45. Givierge, *Au service du chiffre*, Vol. II, NAF 17,574, 385, 411. He claims that he was never given English or Japanese wires.

46. François Cartier, "Souvenirs du Général Cartier," *Revue des transmissions*, No. 85 (July–August 1959), 49–51.

47. Givierge, *Au service du chiffre*, Vol. III, NAF 17,575, 762–3.

48. Kahn, *Hitler's Spies*, 36.

49. Russell Warren Howe, *Mata Hari: The True Story*, Dodd, Mead (New York, 1986), 139–44. Howe concludes that Kalle deliberately fabricated an exchange with Berlin in an old code which he knew was read by the French, to convince the French to arrest her. French intercepts show that Kalle broadcast that H-21 only pretended to work for France. "She has furnished very complete reports on subjects which I have transmitted to you by letter or telephone," Kalle wired. Service Historique de l'Armée de Terre (SHAT), 5N 83. While Givierge does not mention Kalle's use of broken codes, he did record that Kalle was forever sending messages which suggested that he had highly placed agents in France, reporting wild rumors such as that the French had formed special units at the front to finish off their own wounded because there was a shortage of ambulances and medicines, or suggesting projects like importing livestock infected with anthrax into England and France. (Givierge, *Au service du chiffre*, Vol. III, NAF 17,575, 763–5).

50. For a description of Mata Hari's final moments, see Julie Wheel-

wright, *The Fatal Lover: Mata Hari and the Myth of Women in Espionage*, Collins & Brown (London, 1992), 98–9.

51. Nicholai, *German Secret Service*, 183.

52. Kahn, *Hitler's Spies*, 32–7.

53. "General Nolan's notes on the Secret Service," 9/2, Nolan Papers, Army War College, Carlisle Barracks.

54. AN, F7 14607, 8 June 1918.

55. Alistair Horne, *The Price of Glory: Verdun 1916*, St. Martin's Press (New York, 1963), 53.

56. These claims are repeated in a recent work, Krop, *Les secrets*, 149–57.

57. Colonel Charles Paquet, *Dans l'attente de la ruée: Verdun (janvier–février 1916)*, Berger-Levrault (Paris, 1928), x.

58. SHAT, 16N 1073, "Attaque de Verdun," 29 February 1916. See also daily assessments for 9, 10, 11, 13, 15, 21, 22, and 25 February. Eugène Carrias, *Les Renseignements de contact*, Charles-Lavauzelle (Paris, 1937), 57–69. Alistair Horne, *The Price of Glory: Verdun 1916*, Penguin (London, 1962), 53–4, 62–5.

59. Paquet, *Dans l'attente de la ruée*, 92; Horne, *The Price of Glory*, 63–4.

60. Paquet, *Dans l'attente de la ruée*, 18.

61. SHAT, 16N 1073, "Attaque de Verdun."

62. Paquet, *Dans l'attente de la ruée*, 92.

63. Givierge, *Au service du chiffre*, Vol. II, NAF 17,574, 370–7. Givierge complained that GHQ was soon stripped of code breakers, who, because they were counted as "detached" rather than transferred, could not be replaced. The result was that "the morale of my (overworked) officers declined." A second consequence, a particular hobbyhorse of Givierge, was increased insecurity in army staffs who lacked the most elementary notions of secrecy, who placed code breakers amidst the controlled pandemonium of central offices, or who recruited men who had demonstrated no particular competence or skill at that delicate task other than that of being unfit for other duties. His depression may have also been connected to the staff turnovers which accompanied Joffre's departure as commander-in-chief in December 1916.

64. Givierge, *Au service du chiffre*, Vol. III, NAF 17,575, 691.

65. SHAT, 16N 945, 4 March 1917.

66. SHAT, 7N 757, 18 September 1915.

67. SHAT 7N 757, 16 April 1916.

68. SHAT, 7N 758, 29 March 1917.

69. Paquet, "La 2e bureau en campagne," No. 23, 197–200.

70. SHAT, 7N 758, n.d. but certainly 1916.

71. SHAT, 16N 1172, 28 August 1917.

72. SHAT, 16N 1617.

73. Givierge, *Au service du chiffre*, Vol. II, NAF 17,574, 547. "Questions du chiffre," Tome 13 (July–September), 1924, 69–70, 73.

74. *Les Armées françaises dans la Grande Guerre* (AFGG), Tome 6, Vol. I (1931), 235–6.

75. AFGG, Tome 6, Vol. I, annexe 435, and Vol. II, 4, 25–6.

76. Marcel Guitard, "Conférences de Marcel Guitard," *Bulletin de l'Association des réservistes du chiffre*, VII (May 1961), 49. Quoted in Kahn, *Codebreakers*, 341. General Cox, in charge of establishing the German order of battle for GHQ, reported on 21 April 1918 that he "has lost the German Army!" John Ferris, "The British Army and Signals Intelligence in the Field During the First World War," *Intelligence and National Security*, III, No. 4 (October 1988), 40.

77. AFGG, Tome 6, Vol. II, 76–77.

78. For a more complete explanation of this complicated system, see Kahn, *Codebreakers*, 339–47.

79. AFGG, Tome 6, Vol. II, 264–5. Also François Cartier, "Souvenirs du Général Cartier," *Revue des transmissions*, No. 87 (November–December 1959), 19–20. Cartier notes that the most puzzling aspect of this message is that no other listening post had picked it up.

80. AFGG, Tome 6, Vol. II, 428–33, 486; Bissy, "Les Photographies aériennes," 273–4.

81. SHAT, 16N 1617. "Offensive allemande du 15 juillet 1918."

82. Flicke, *War Secrets*, I, 37.

83. "Nolan's notes on the Secret Service," 9/2.

84. General Ribadeau Dumas writes that "camouflage . . . is an anachronism" in the context of French World War I radio security, "for it was not until 1939–45 and above all subsequently that a clear distinction was established between code breaking and the very limited security procedures applied in small units." "Essai d'historique du chiffre," 49.

85. For instance, in the autumn of 1918, German intelligence appears to have had more luck establishing the French and American orders of battle than that of the British, whose techniques of signals deception improved dramatically in the late summer of 1918. John Ferris, "The British Army and Signals Intelligence," 41–2, 45.

86. Kahn, *Codebreakers*, 348–50.

5. TRACKING THE RED MENACE

1. Wilhelm Stieber, *Espion de Bismarck*, Pygmalion (Paris, 1985), 132–67.

2. Archives nationales, F7 14607.

3. Christopher Andrew and Oleg Gordievsky, *KGB: The Inside Story*, HarperCollins (New York, 1990), 122, 150–3, 163–4.

4. David Dallin, *Soviet Espionage*, Yale University Press (New Haven, 1955), 25–7.

5. Roger Faligot and Rémi Kauffer, *Histoire mondiale du renseignement*, Vol. I: *1870–1939*, Laffont (Paris, 1993), 195.

6. Service Historique de l'Armée de Terre (SHAT), 7N 2570. See especially 22 December 1921, 7 January 1922, 5 April 1922, 23 and 30 May 1922, 16 January 1923.

7. Faligot and Kauffer, *Histoire mondiale*, 376.

8. Dallin, *Soviet Espionage*, 30.

9. Philippe Robrieux, *Histoire intérieure du Parti communiste*, Vol. IV, Fayard (Paris, 1984), 151–2.

10. SHAT, 7N 2570. Reports of communist plans for espionage in French arms industries date from 22 December 1921. The Deuxième Bureau lamented the dissolution of the wartime Service de Garde et de Protection des Etablissements Travaillant pour la Défense Nationale (SGPE) on 24 April 1919.

11. SHAT, 7N 2579, 29 September 1927.

12. Dallin, *Soviet Espionage*, 32–9; Robrieux, *Histoire intérieure*, IV, 151–2; Faligot and Kauffer, *Histoire mondiale*, 195–8, 210–13.

13. J. Dion, *Historique du SLOTFOM*, unpublished manuscript, Archives Nationales Section Outre Mer. See also SLOTFOM I 4 for quotations cited. Série III 128 for reports on Yen Bey and Annam in 1930–31. Many surveillance reports are to be found in IX 11 and 12, XIII 2 and 3, on anti-French activity among colonial subjects in France.

14. Stéphane Courtois, "Jean Moulin et les communistes," *L'Histoire*, No. 166 (May 1993), 9.

15. Dallin, *Soviet Espionage*, 60–7. Faligot and Kauffer, *Histoire mondiale*, 207–10. A 19 November 1934 letter from the Minister of the Interior to the War Minister, presumably in response to a request for more police protection for defense industries, stated that ministerial-level meetings had been held on several occasions since 1925 to discuss the problem of communist cells in defense plants. SHAT, 7N 2570.

16. D. Cameron Watt, "Afterthoughts and Alternative Historico-Literary Theories," in Westley K. Wark, *Spy Fiction, Spy Films and Real Intelligence*, Frank Cass (London, 1991), 214. See also David Stafford, *The Silent Game: The Real World of Imaginary Spies* (Toronto, 1988); Michael Denning, *Cover Stories: Narrative and Ideology in the British Spy Thriller* (London, 1987).

17. Wark, *Spy Fiction*, 1.

18. Pascal Krop, *Les Secrets de l'espionnage français de 1870 à nos jours*, J. C. Lattès (Paris, 1993), 244–9.

19. Faligot and Kauffer, *Histoire mondiale*, 384–91.

20. Eric Homberger, "English Spy Thrillers in the Age of Appeasement," in Wark, *Spy Fiction*, 92–116.

21. Phillip Knightley, "Spy Lies," *Saturday Night* (September 1988), 72.

22. Wark, *Spy Fiction*, 2–3, 8.

23. Arthur Koestler, *The Invisible Writing*, Macmillan (New York, 1954), 303.

24. Andrew and Gordievsky, *KGB: The Inside Story*, 215, 445–7.

25. Courtois, "Jean Moulin et les communistes," 10.

26. Thierry Wolton, *Le Grand Recrutement*, Grasset (Paris, 1993), 284–5. Wolton also supplies examples of the sort of information communist informers were passing on to Moscow in 1941 (pp. 220–5).

6. THE GERMAN THREAT

1. See Elisabeth du Réau, "L'Information du 'décideur' et l'élaboration de la décision diplomatique française dans les dernières années de la IIIe République," *Relations internationales*, No. 32 (1982), 525–41.

2. General František Moravec, *Master of Spies: The Memoirs of General František Moravec*, Doubleday (Garden City, N.Y., 1975), 41–2, 103, 175.

3. Martin Alexander, "Did the Deuxième Bureau Work? The Role of Intelligence in French Defence Policy and Strategy, 1919–39," *Intelligence and National Security*, VI, No. 2 (April 1991), 326.

4. Paul Stehlin, *Témoignage pour l'histoire*, Laffont (Paris, 1964), 56.

5. Stehlin, *Témoignage*, 120, 156, 162.

6. Michel Garder, *La Guerre secrète des services spéciaux français, 1935–1945*, Plon (Paris, 1967), 148.

7. Réau, "L'information," 530.

8. General Maurice Gauché, *Le Deuxième Bureau au travail (1935–1940)*, Dumont (Paris, 1953), 101.

9. Even before Hitler's arrival in power, the French had detected German plans to strengthen the Reichswehr and lay the basis for the massive rearmament of the late 1930s. (See Georges Castellan, *Le Réarmement clandestin du reich, 1930–1935, vu par le 2ème bureau de l'état-major français*, Paris [Plon, 1954], 541–3, 548–52.) The evolution of German tactical doctrine, and especially the tandem of independent tank divisions and close air support, probably made the Deuxième Bureau more knowledgeable about German doctrine than were many German generals. (Stehlin, *Témoignage*, 55–6, 58. Robert J. Young, "French Military Intelligence and the Franco-Italian Al-

liance, 1933–1939," *Historical Journal*, 28/1 [March 1985], 288–9.) French intelligence even had Guderian's *Achtung Panzer!* translated and distributed to garrison libraries. (Garder, *La Guerre secrète*, 31.) The stunning success of blitzkrieg methods employed in Poland in September 1939 was the object of detailed reports of French intelligence. (André Beaufre, *1940: The Fall of France*, New York [Knopf, 1968], 146. Jeffrey Gunsburg, *Divided and Conquered: The French High Command and the Defeat of the West, 1940*, Greenwood Press [Westport, Conn., 1979], 93.) Therefore, the French command certainly could not claim to have been surprised by the shape and ferocity of blitzkrieg warfare. Also, as will be seen, the series of German moves beginning with the reoccupation of the Rhineland in 1936 also failed to catch French intelligence off its guard.

10. Lieutenant Colonel Jean Della Santa, "Cassandre, ou le renseignement jamais cru," *Revue militaire suisse*, No. 3 (March 1972), 117–30. "I believe that I already told you, my goal is to offer once again proof of the efficiency of the French *service de renseignements* and in this way to demonstrate the incompetence of the Allied governments." (Letter from Paul Paillole to David Kahn, 26 March 1984.)

11. Walter Laqueur, *A World of Secrets: The Uses and Limits of Intelligence*, Basic Books (New York, 1985), 11. See also Robert J. Young, "French Military Intelligence and Nazi Germany, 1938–1939," in Ernest J. May, ed., *Knowing One's Enemies: Intelligence Assessment Before the Two World Wars*, Princeton University Press (Princeton, N.J., 1980), 187.

12. Martin S. Alexander, *The Republic in Danger: General Maurice Gamelin and the Politics of French Defence, 1933–1940*, Cambridge University Press (Cambridge, Eng., 1992), 35, 43–4, 46–7, 49, 50–1, 76, 159. See also Young, "French Military Intelligence and Nazi Germany," 280, 287.

13. Robert J. Young, "French Military Intelligence and Nazi Germany, 1938–1939," in May, *Knowing One's Enemies*, 283.

14. Journal de Marche (Cabinet Gamelin), 18 and 21 September 1939. SHAT Fonds Gamelin, 1K 224, Carton 9, quoted in Alexander, "Did the Deuxième Bureau Work?," 324.

15. Henri Navarre, *Le Service de renseignements, 1871–1944*, Plon (Paris, 1978), 77. See also Alexander, *The Republic in Danger*, 46–7.

16. Maurice Viasse, "L'Evolution de la fonction d'attaché militaire en France au XXe siècle," *Relations internationales*, No. 32 (1982), 511–12, 522. Gauché, *Le Deuxième Bureau au travail*, 96, 180–81.

17. Alexander, "Did the Deuxième Bureau Work?," 323.

18. Jean Bézy, *Le SR Air*, France-Empire (Paris, 1979), 19–21; Stehlin, *Témoignage*, 77, 96–98.

19. Patrice Buffotot, "La Perception du réarmement allemand par les

organismes de renseignement français de 1936 à 1939," *Revue historique des armées*, No. 3 (1979), 177. The Deuxième Bureau, "in the final analysis, did not believe in tank battles," Buffotot concludes, although they did point out that the Germans did (p. 179).

20. Stehlin, *Témoignage*, 136–8, 148, 153–4.

21. Steven Ross, "French Net Assessment," in Williamson Murray and Alan Millet, eds., *Calculations: Net Assessment and the Coming of World War II*, Free Press (New York, 1992), 168–9, 171.

22. Anthony P. Adamthwaite, "French Military Intelligence and the Coming War, 1935–1939," in Christopher Andrew and Jeremy Noakes, eds., *Intelligence and International Relations, 1900–1945*, Exeter University Publications (Exeter, 1987), 202.

23. Wilhelm F. Flicke, *War Secrets in the Ether*, Vol. I, Aegean Park Press (Laguna Hills, Calif., 1977), 115.

24. Moravec, *Master of Spies*, 102.

25. Navarre, *Le Service de renseignements*, 41.

26. See Alexander, "Did the Deuxième Bureau Work?," 300–7, for a discussion of French government structure.

27. Paul Paillole, *Services spéciaux (1935–1945)*, Laffont (Paris, 1975), 78.

28. Stehlin, *Témoignage*, 78.

29. Paul Paillole, *Notre espion chez Hitler*, Laffont (Paris, 1985), 105–6.

30. F. H. Hinsley, *British Intelligence in the Second World War*, Cambridge University Press (New York, 1979), I, 98–9.

31. Young, "French Military Intelligence and Nazi Germany," 296–9.

32. Navarre, *Le Service de renseignements*, 46.

33. Young, "French Military Intelligence and Nazi Germany," 308–9.

34. Westley Wark, "British Intelligence on the German Air Force and Aircraft Industry, 1933–1939," *Historical Journal*, XXV, No. 3 (1982), 646–7.

35. Ross, "French Net Assessment," 168.

36. Alexander, *The Republic in Danger*, 50–1, 282.

37. Moravec, *Master of Spies*, 136–7. Maurice Gamelin, *Servir*, Vol. II, Plon (Paris, 1946), 345. Nicole Jordan, "Maurice Gamelin, Italy and the Eastern Alliances," *Journal of Strategic Studies*, XIV, No. 4 (December 1991), 436–7. Jordan says that the Anschluss caught the Deuxième Bureau by surprise, which is disputed by Ross, "French Net Assessment," 164.

38. Robert Young, "Le Haut Commandement français au moment de Munich," *Revue d'histoire moderne et contemporaine*, Tome 24 (janvier–mars 1977), 128.

39. Young, "French Military Intelligence and Nazi Germany," 285.

40. Alexander, *The Republic in Danger*, 289.

41. Anthony Adamthwaite, *France and the Coming of the Second World War*, Frank Cass (London, 1977), 311. Williamson Murray, *The Change in the European Balance of Power, 1938–1939: The Path to Ruin*, Princeton University Press (Princeton, N.J., 1984), 301.

42. Navarre, *Le Service de renseignements*, 82. Canadian historian Robert Young has defended it as necessary: "Whereas the historian may judge these estimates wildly inflated, particularly with respect to the mobilization schedules," Young writes, one must understand that "for the French general staff it was, potentially, a question of national survival." Young, "French Military Intelligence and Nazi Germany," 293.

43. Major General Sir Kenneth Strong, *Intelligence at the Top: The Recollections of an Intelligence Officer*, Cassels (London, 1968), 58. French historian Patrice Buffotot notes that while before 1938 the tendency of French intelligence was to underestimate German capabilities, after 1938 it systematically overestimated them. Buffotot, "La Perception du réarmement allemand," 176. Hinsley, *British Intelligence*, 112, 115.

44. Alexander, *The Republic in Danger*, 284–5, 287, 289, 311, 319, 321; Jordan, "Maurice Gamelin, Italy and the Eastern Alliances," 437–8; Buffotot, "La Perception du réarmement allemand," 181.

45. Alexander, *The Republic in Danger*, 40.

46. Philip Bankwitz, *Maxime Weygand and Civil-Military Relations in Modern France*, Harvard University Press (Cambridge, Mass., 1967), 153.

47. Alexander, *The Republic in Danger*, 159–61.

48. Roger Faligot and Rémi Kauffer, *Histoire mondiale du renseignement*, Vol. I: *1870–1939*, Laffont (Paris, 1993), 304.

49. Ross, "French Net Assessment," 169–73.

50. Alexander, *The Republic in Danger*, 315, 343–6.

51. Paillole, *Notre espion*, 151.

52. Marcel Givierge, *Au service du chiffre*, Bibliothèque nationale, Vol. III, 17,575 NAF, 899, 979.

53. Givierge, *Au service du chiffre*, Vol. III, 17,575 NAF, 930, 947, 937, 943, 927, 961.

54. J. W. M. Chapman, "No Final Solution: A Survey of the Cryptanalytical Capabilities of German Military Agencies, 1926–35," *Intelligence and National Security*, I, No. 1 (January 1986), 34.

55. Flicke, *War Secrets*, 93, 95, 97, 99, 100, 102.

56. Givierge, *Au service du chiffre*, Vol. III, 17,575 NAF, 973–4.

57. Henri Navarre, *Le Temps des vérités*, Plon (Paris, 1979), 47–8; Alexander, "Did the Deuxième Bureau Work?," 324. Gustave Bertrand complained that the Italians had a specialized safe-cracking team, "P-Squadra," which managed to steal the codes of all embassies in Rome with the exception

of those of Japan and the U.S.S.R. Gustave Bertrand, *Enigma ou la plus grande énigme de la guerre, 1939–1945*, Plon (Paris, 1973), 17.

58. Chapman, "No Final Solution," 35. Unfortunately, no examples of intercepted intelligence playing a role in Hitler's decisions are offered. German intelligence also noted that the French were often slower to put new codes in place than were other nations, and were more likely to send nonurgent cipher cables *en clair* because of limited encoding and deciphering capabilities in embassies and missions (pp. 34–5, 39).

59. Paillole, *Notre espion*, 169.

60. Alistair Denniston Papers, Churchill College, Vol. 1/4, 7. Quoted in John Ferris, "Whitehall's Black Chamber: British Cryptology and Government Code and Cipher School, 1919–29," *Intelligence and National Security*, II, No. 1 (January 1987), 72–3.

61. Givierge, *Au service du chiffre*, Vol. III, 17,575 NAF, 930–31.

62. Service Historique de l'Armée de Terre (SHAT), 7N 2570, 9 February 1935.

63. Flicke, *War Secrets*, 113. Flicke, writing in 1945, avoided using Schmidt's complete name to protect the family.

64. See David Kahn, *Seizing the Enigma: The Race to Break the German U-Boat Codes, 1939–1943*, Houghton Mifflin (Boston, 1991), chs. 4 and 5.

7. INTELLIGENCE AND THE FALL OF FRANCE

1. Brian Bond, *France and Belgium, 1939–1940*, Associated University Presses (Cranbury, N.J., 1979), 100–1.

2. Maurice Gamelin, *Servir*, Vol. I, Plon (Paris, 1946), 71. Italics in original.

3. Paul Paillole, *Services spéciaux (1935–1945)*, Laffont (Paris, 1975), 163.

4. André Beaufre, *1940: The Fall of France*, Knopf (New York, 1968), 165.

5. Gustave Bertrand, *Enigma ou la plus grand énigme de la guerre, 1939–1945*, Plon (Paris, 1973), 70.

6. Disagreements between the two men over the French war plan caused the command structure to be altered again in January 1940. Gamelin claimed that his reshuffle had actually increased Georges' authority, but the result was the exact opposite. Gamelin, *Servir*, I, 61–2. Jeffrey Gunsburg, *Divided and Conquered: The French High Command and the Defeat of the West, 1940*, Greenwood Press, (Westport, Conn., 1979), 129–33.

7. General Maurice Gauché, *Le Deuxième Bureau au travail (1935–1940)*, Dumont (Paris, 1953), 201–2. Michel Garder, *La Guerre secrète des services spéciaux français, 1935–1945*, Plon (Paris, 1967), 155.

8. As was British intelligence. See F. H. Hinsley, *British Intelligence in the Second World War*, Cambridge University Press (New York, 1979), I, 147.

9. Garder, *La Guerre secrète*, 155.

10. Paillole, *Services spéciaux*, 164.

11. Major General Sir Kenneth Strong, *Intelligence at the Top: The Recollections of an Intelligence Officer*, Cassels (London, 1968), 57.

12. Garder, *Guerre secrète*, 149–50.

13. Paul Paillole, *Notre espion chez Hitler*, Laffont (Paris, 1985), 169.

14. Gauché, *Le Deuxième Bureau au travail*, 162. Bertrand, *Enigma*, 75.

15. This may have been in part because Bletchley and Bruno divided the labor, with Bletchley working on exploitation of the codes and Bruno doing the research. But some of the Poles were especially critical of the organization of Bruno. See Gilbert Bloch, *Enigma avant Ultra 1930–1940*, chez l'auteur, September 1988, E. 8.

16. Hinsley, *British Intelligence*, Vol. III, Part 2, 952–53. See also Jan Stengers, "Enigma, the French, the Poles and the British, 1931–1940," in Christopher Andrew and David Dilks, eds., *The Missing Dimension: Governments and Intelligence Communities in the Twentieth Century*, University of Illinois Press (Urbana, 1984), 135.

17. Martin S. Alexander, *The Republic in Danger: General Maurice Gamelin and the Politics of French Defence, 1933–1940*, Cambridge University Press (Cambridge, Eng., 1992), 327.

18. Journal de Marche (Cabinet Gamelin), 14 October 1939. SHAT, Fonds Gamelin, 1K 224, Carton 9, quoted in Alexander, *The Republic in Danger*, 333.

19. Colonel Jacques Minart, *P.C. Vincennes. Secteur 4*, Berger-Levrault (Paris, 1945), II, 6–7; Alexander, *The Republic in Danger*, 332, 335.

20. Paillole, *Notre espion*, 170–1; Gauché, *Le Deuxième Bureau au travail*, 183–6, 191–3; Alexander, *The Republic in Danger*, 334–5.

21. Minart, *P.C. Vincennes*, II, 7.

22. Paillole, *Service spéciaux*, 183.

23. Henri Navarre, *Le Service de renseignements, 1871–1944*, Plon (Paris, 1978), 100.

24. Gauché, *Le Deuxième Bureau au travail*, 165–77.

25. Gunsburg, *Divided and Conquered*, 93–4.

26. Beaufre, *1940*, 146.

27. For French strategy, see Douglas Porch, "Arms and Alliances: French Grand Strategy and Policy in 1914 and 1940," in Paul Kennedy, ed., *Grand Strategies in War and Peace*, Yale University Press (New Haven, Conn.,

1991), Ch. 8. For a contemporary view, see Paul de Villelume, *Journal d'une défaite*, Fayard (Paris, 1976), 251.

28. Paul Stehlin, *Témoignage pour l'histoire*, Laffont (Paris, 1964), 208–10.

29. Paillole, *Services spéciaux*, 188.

30. Gauché, *Le Deuxième Bureau au travail*, 214.

31. Gamelin, *Servir*, III, 205, 308.

32. Interview with author 8 August 1991.

33. Garder, *La Guerre secrète*, 192.

34. Martin Alexander, "Did the Deuxième Bureau Work? The Role of Intelligence in French Defence Policy and Strategy, 1919–39," *Intelligence and National Security*, VI, No. 2 (April 1991), 321.

35. Guy Pedroncini, ed., *Histoire militaire de la France*, Vol. III: *De 1871 à 1940*, Presses Universitaires de France (Paris, 1992), 369.

36. Bond, *France and Belgium, 1939–1940*, 63–7, 78–81.

37. Wilhelm F. Flicke, *War Secrets in the Ether*, Vol. II, Aegean Park Press (Laguna Hills, Calif., 1977), 133.

38. David Kahn, *Hitler's Spies*, Macmillan (New York, 1978), 423, 528–9.

39. Paillole, *Services spéciaux*, 185–6, and interview with author. See also Garder, *Guerre secrète*, 152–3.

40. Gauché, *Le Deuxième Bureau au travail*, 213.

41. Gamelin, *Servir*, I, 401–3.

42. Lieutenant Colonel Jean Della Santa, "Cassandre, ou le renseignement jamais cru," *Revue militaire suisse*, No. 3 (March 1972), 126–7, quoting Jacques Nobécourt.

43. Charles Christienne and Pierre Lissarrague, *A History of French Military Aviation*, Smithsonian Institution Press (Washington, D.C., 1986), 332–3, 338, 345–6, 358.

44. Gauché, *Le Deuxième Bureau au travail*, 118, 215, 222–3.

45. Gauché, *Le Deuxième Bureau au travail*, 210–12. Santa, "Cassandre," 117–30.

46. Paillole, *Notre espion*, 180.

47. Santa, "Cassandre," 126–8.

48. Alexander, "Did the Deuxième Bureau Work?," 321.

8. THE BCRA

1. Philippe Bernert, *Roger Wybot et la bataille pour la DST*, Presses de la Cité (Paris, 1975), 24.

2. The idea of adopting metro names was apparently suggested by Lieutenant Maurice Duclos, one of Passy's early collaborators, who had been

associated with the Cagoulards. Early members of the Deuxième Bureau denied that the Cagoule had inspired the choice. See Daniel Cordier, *Jean Moulin: L'Inconnu du Panthéon*, Vol. III: *De Gaulle capital de la Résistance*, J. C. Lattès (Paris, 1993), 654 and notes.

3. Charles de Gaulle, *Mémoires de guerre*, Vol. I: *L'appel* (Paris, 1954), 129.

4. Colonel Passy, *Souvenirs*, Vol. I: *2e bureau Londres*, Raoul Solar (Monte Carlo, 1947), 65, 56.

5. Cordier, *Moulin*, 655.

6. Cordier, *Moulin*, 656.

7. Rémy, *Mémoires d'un agent secret de la France Libre*, Editions France-Empire (Paris, 1983), 52–3.

8. Passy, *2e bureau Londres*, 63–74. Rémy's early activities are described in Rémy, *Mémoires d'un agent secret de la France Libre*, Vol I. 63–74 Henri Noguères, *Histoire de la Résistance en France*, Vol. I: *Juin 1940. Juin 1941*, Laffont (Paris, 1967), 118–20.

9. Jean Lacouture, *De Gaulle*, Vol. I: *Le Rebelle, 1890–1944*, Seuil (Paris, 1984), 430.

10. M. R. D. Foot, *SOE in France*, Her Majesty's Stationery Office (London, 1966), 151.

11. Lacouture, *De Gaulle: Le Rebelle*, 434, 437–8, writes that the squadron had been dispatched to Douala in Cameroon, which had just declared for the Free French, met the British-led fleet by chance, and sought refuge in Dakar. For the British reaction to the lack of security-consciousness in the Free French camp, see Christopher Andrew, *Her Majesty's Secret Service: The Making of the British Intelligence Community*, Viking (New York, 1985), 464. Passy, *2e bureau Londres*, 94.

12. Passy, *2e bureau Londres*, 83.

13. For his part, Muselier was convinced that de Gaulle was behind the affair, which began a deterioration in the relations between the two men which eventually led to the admiral's resignation from the French National Committee in March 1942. Lacouture, *De Gaulle: Le Rebelle*, 489–92; Passy, *2e bureau Londres*, 127–33.

14. Foot, *SOE*, xxi.

15. Passy, *2e bureau Londres*, 142–3.

16. Passy, *2e bureau Londres*, 60.

17. Foot, *SOE*, 152, 232.

18. Foot, *SOE*, 152.

19. Cordier, *Moulin*, 666.

20. Philippe Thyraud de Vosjoli, *Lamia*, Little, Brown (Toronto and Boston, 1970), 19.

21. Archives nationales, Fla 3727, 19 July 1943.

22. AN, Fla 3727. To separate action and intelligence was "an abstraction, a fiction," Soustelle was told. Jacques Soustelle, *Envers et contre tout*, Vol. I: *De Londres à Alger, 1940–1942*, Laffont (Paris, 1947), 319.

23. Passy, *10 Duke Street, Londres (le BCRA)*, Raoul Solar (Monte Carlo, 1947), 13.

24. Marc Ferro, *Pétain*, Fayard (Paris, 1987), 712.

25. Cordier, *Moulin*, 670–8.

26. AN, Fla 3727.

27. Ferro, *Pétain*, 333–5.

28. Leopold Trepper, *Le Grand Jeu*, Albin Michel (Paris, 1975).

29. Passy, *10 Duke Street*, 12.

30. Lacouture, *De Gaulle: Le Rebelle*, 569.

31. Bernert, *Roger Wybot*, 52.

32. André Gillois, *Histoire secrète des français à Londres de 1940 à 1944*, Hachette (Paris, 1973), 112.

33. Gillois, *Histoire secrète*, 125.

34. AN, Fla 3727, contains numerous letters on the subject. See also Passy, *2e bureau Londres*, 171.

35. Passy, *2e bureau Londres*, 145–6.

36. The volunteers returned with much useful information on life in France, which was put to good use by other agents. Cordier, *Moulin*, 719–22; Foot, *SOE*, 152–4.

37. Foot, *SOE*, 152.

38. Gillois, *Histoire secrète*, 122–3.

39. Gillois, *Histoire secrète*, 123–5.

40. Pierre Lorain, *Armement clandestin: France 1941–1944*, author's copyright, 1972, 86–95. For an exciting personal account of a Lysander pilot, see Hugh Verity, *We Landed by Moonlight: Secret RAF Landings in France, 1940–1944*, Allan (London, 1978).

41. This was not bad in itself, as pilots could be a burdensome encumbrance to Resistance groups. Passy, *2e bureau Londres*, 181.

42. Passy, *2e bureau Londres*, 185.

43. "The British secret services are *administrative* services who would envisage a rupture with the French secret services with regret perhaps but certainly not with despair," Passy wrote on 18 March 1942. He also noted that in radios and codes, and perhaps also in the reception of messages, as in the area of agent recruitment, the Poles and Czechs were given an independence by the British denied to him. AN, Fla 3727, "BCRAM mémorandum pour M. le chef de l'Etat-Major Particulier du Général de Gaulle," 18 March 1942. Passy, *2e bureau Londres*, 172–3, 182–4.

44. Passy, *2e bureau Londres*, 123–7.

45. Georges A. Groussard, *Service secret, 1940–1945*, La Table Ronde (Paris, 1964), 203–4.

46. Bernert, *Roger Wybot*, 27.

47. Bernert, *Roger Wybot*, 25–30. Noguères, *Histoire de la Résistance*, ii, 96–8, says that Paillole denied any role, while, according to Passy, Paillole insisted that he arrested the garrulous Gaullist agent to protect his contacts; *2e bureau Londres*, 203–4. In his book, Paillole says that Fourcaud's arrest followed on naturally from that of Groussard on 15 July; Paul Paillole, *Services spéciaux (1935–1945)*, Laffont (Paris, 1975), 323.

48. Passy, *2e bureau Londres*, 224; *10 Duke Street*, 20–1.

49. Passy, *2e bureau Londres*, 222–23.

50. Passy, *2e bureau Londres*, 226; Bernert, *Roger Wybot*, 57.

51. Passy, *10 Duke Street*, 30–5.

52. Passy insisted that the creation of a rival service had resulted in low morale and that the distinction between political and military intelligence was one which members of the Resistance were incapable of making. "The only distinction they respect is that of intelligence [political and military]." AN, Fla, "BCRAM mémorandum," 18 March 1942. The reorganization required the BCRA to create a "Section Non-militaire" for political intelligence. Passy, *10 Duke Street*, 86–95, 233–7. See Soustelle, *De Londres à Alger*, 314–20, for a discussion of this issue.

53. Passy, *10 Duke Street*, 22–3.

54. Bernert, *Roger Wybot*, 67–9.

55. Paillole, *Services spéciaux*, 433 note, and interview with author. The Renseignements Généraux is a section of the French police which amasses personal files on French citizens to be used as the basis of investigations.

56. Rémy, *Mémoires d'un agent secret de la France Libre*, Vol. II, Editions France-Empire (Paris, 1984), 27.

57. Lacouture, *De Gaulle: Le Rebelle*, 524, 538. Wybot traced the origins of these stories to the attempt of a double agent to jump out a third-floor window on Duke Street when he was unmasked. Bernert, *Roger Wybot*, 62–3.

58. Gillois, *Histoire secrète*, 130.

59. Passy, *10 Duke Street*, 24.

60. Fourcaud remained as chief of counterintelligence barely a month before being replaced by Pierre Bloch, former socialist deputy and future Gaullist minister. Bernert, *Roger Wybot*, 76–9. Passy wrote that he regretted Wybot's departure, but he was ordered by de Gaulle to get rid of him. Fourcaud quickly showed himself "incompetent" in Wybot's old job. Passy, *10 Duke Street*, 253.

61. Passy, *Missions secrètes en France. Souvenirs du BCRA. Novembre 1942–juin 1943*, Plon (Paris, 1951), 295.

9. THE WAR OF THE SECRET SERVICES

1. Paul Paillole, *Services spéciaux (1935–1945)*, Laffont (Paris, 1975), 433; Jean Bézy, *Le SR Air*, Editions France-Empire (Paris, 1979), 104–5 and note.

2. Passy, *Missions secrètes en France. Souvenirs du BCRA. Novembre 1942–juin 1943*, Plon (Paris, 1951), 295.

3. Giraud's escape from his prison at Königstein to the *zone libre* in the summer of 1942 had been organized by Rivet's service. As soon as de Gaulle learned that Giraud was in France, he ordered the BCRA to contact him. Henri Frenay, leader of the Resistance network Combat, also appealed to Giraud "not to ignore the attractive force of the symbol of de Gaulle." These were rejected by Giraud. Jacques Soustelle, *Envers et contre tout*, Vol. I: *De Londres à Alger, 1940–1942*, Laffont (Paris, 1947), 433–43.

4. Jean Lacouture, *De Gaulle, Vol. I: Le Rebelle, 1890–1944*, Seuil (Paris, 1984), 652–53.

5. According to Wybot, Paillole and Passy were mutually agreeable to his taking over a combined counterintelligence section as the first step toward merger, but this was vetoed by de Gaulle. Philippe Bernert, *Roger Wybot et la bataille pour la DST*, Presse de la Cité (Paris, 1975), 82–4. Thyraud de Vosjoli blamed Giraud for opposing any merger plan which threatened to take intelligence beyond a purely military function. *Lamia*, Little, Brown (Toronto and Boston, 1970), 72. Jean Lacouture makes clear that de Gaulle saw his battle with Giraud simply as a continuation of the "moral" debate he had carried on with Vichy since 18 June 1940. *De Gaulle: Le rebelle*, 651.

6. Passy, *Missions secrètes*, 296.

7. Bernert, *Roger Wybot*, 55–6.

8. Passy, *Missions secrètes*, 296–8.

9. Paillole interview with author.

10. Passy, *Missions secrètes*, 11–14.

11. Thierry Wolton, *Le Grand Recrutment*, Grasset (Paris, 1993), 222–5.

12. Marc Ferro, *Pétain*, Fayard (Paris, 1987), 402.

13. Ferro, *Pétain*, 407, 469–72.

14. Daniel Cordier, *Jean Moulin: L'Inconnu du Panthéon*, Vol. III: *De Gaulle capital de la Résistance*, J. C. Lattès (Paris, 1993), 791.

15. Wolton, *Le Grand Recrutement*, 267, 269–70, 275–7, 282–3.

16. Cordier attributes Moulin's escape to lack of cooperation between the BMA and the Surveillance du Territoire, which had been following his activities for some time, knew he was an ex-prefect, but had been confused

by his pseudonym of Mercier, which they never connected with Moulin. *Jean Moulin*, 849–50.

17. The Gaullists subsequently charged that Moulin's stay in Lisbon was intentionally prolonged by SOE, who hoped to recruit him, and that he was allowed out of London only after de Gaulle had sent a strongly worded letter to Anthony Eden. The British replied that this was never their intention, but that the weather was exceptionally bad in September, thus restricting the number of flights available. De Gaulle's letter to Eden, of which there is no archival record, could not have been the reason for Moulin's release from Lisbon, for he was already bound for London at the time de Gaulle claimed to have sent it. Cordier, *Jean Moulin*, 473–4.

18. Cordier, *Jean Moulin*, 789–801.

19. Cordier, *Jean Moulin*, 815. For charges that Moulin was a communist, see Henri Frenay, *La Nuit finira*, Laffont (Paris, 1973), and *L'Enigme Jean Moulin*, Laffont (Paris, 1977); Henri-Christian Giraud, *De Gaulle et les communistes*, 2 vols., Albin Michel (Paris, 1988–89), and Wolton, *Le Grand Recrutement*.

20. Lacouture, *De Gaulle: Le Rebelle*, 581.

21. Passy, *10 Duke Street*, 118–33.

22. Philippe Buton, *Les Lendemains qui déchantent: Le Parti communiste français à la Libération*, Presses de la Fondation Nationale des Sciences Politiques (Paris, 1994), 19–20.

23. Buton, *Les Lendemains*, 22–3.

24. Buton, *Les Lendemains*, 24–5.

25. Buton, *Les Lendemains*, 25–6, 29.

26. Passy, *Missions secrètes*, 240–42.

27. Lacouture, *De Gaulle: Le Rebelle*, 580–91, 704–22; Henri Noguères, *Histoire de la Résistance en France*, Vol. III, Laffont (Paris, 1972), 439–78, 499–500. Moulin's body was returned to Paris and buried in the cemetery of Père-Lachaise. On 20 December 1964, his remains were transferred to the Panthéon. General Delestraint, transported to Dachau, was shot by SS guards on 19 April 1945, just days before the arrival of American troops.

28. Philippe Thyraud de Vosjoli, *Lamia*, Little, Brown (Boston and Toronto, 1970), 69.

29. Lacouture, *De Gaulle: Le Rebelle*, 686–88.

30. Passy, *Missions secrètes*, 299.

31. Michel Garder, *La Guerre secrète des services spéciaux français, 1935–1945*, Plon (Paris, 1967), 365–71.

32. Passy, *Missions secrètes*, 287–88, 297–300.

33. Lacouture, *De Gaulle: Le Rebelle*, 694.

34. Lacouture, *De Gaulle: Le Rebelle*, 696.

35. Jacques Soustelle, *Envers et contre tout*, Vol. II: *D'Alger à Paris, 1942–1944*, Laffont (Paris, 1950), 292–93.

36. Paillole, *Services spéciaux*, 535.

37. In his memoirs, Wybot writes that both Passy and Paillole agreed to have Wybot nominated as head of a unified counterintelligence section, but that this was vetoed by de Gaulle because Wybot "has already resigned once and that's enough!" Bernert, *Roger Wybot*, 83–4.

38. Interview with Paillole.

39. Bernert, *Roger Wybot*, 69.

40. Georges Groussard, *Service secret, 1940–1945*, La Table Ronde (Paris, 1964), 142.

41. Passy, *Missions secrètes*, 83–5.

42. Soustelle, *D'Alger à Paris*, 304, 324–25; Garder, *La Guerre secrète*, 403.

43. Garder, *La Guerre secrète*, 396. Paillole and Lacouture give less placid accounts of this interview; *Services spéciaux*, 535–6; *De Gaulle: Le Rebelle*, 695.

44. Paillole, *Services spéciaux*, 540–41; Soustelle, *D'Alger à Paris*, 284–86; Lacouture, *De Gaulle: Le Rebelle*, 695.

45. Soustelle, *D'Alger à Paris*, 327.

46. F. H. Hinsley and C. A. G. Simkins, *British Intelligence in the Second World War*, Vol. IV: *Security and Counter-espionage*, Cambridge University Press (New York, 1990), 264 and note.

47. Wolton, *Le Grand Recrutement*, 235, 238.

48. Paillole, *Services spéciaux*, 528.

49. Pucheu had been Vichy Minister of the Interior from July 1941 to April 1942. The principal charge against him was that he had ordered the execution of forty-seven communist hostages at Châteaubriant in October 1941. In February 1943, Pucheu had written to Giraud and asked to come to North Africa to fight the Germans. Giraud agreed to "welcome him and give him a place in a combat unit," under an assumed name. However, his lack of discretion caused him to be interned in Morocco, and arrested in August on orders of the Comité Français de Libération Nationale. In France, the Conseil Nationale de la Résistance voted for his death on 3 September, and on 2 October the CFLN created a military tribunal competent to hear his case. Communist deputies in the Consultative Assembly demanded the death sentence. His trial opened on 9 March 1944. The principal witness against him was the communist deputy for Saint-Denis, Fernand Grenier, who had escaped from Châteaubriant, who denounced him in vigorous terms. Although Pucheu's direct complicity in the execution of the hostages was never proven, on 11 March 1944 the military tribunal condemned him to death with a recommendation of clemency. Despite Giraud's appeals for

clemency, de Gaulle merely insisted that "we will find the evidence at the Liberation." On 20 March, Pucheu was executed in the courtyard of the prison of Hussein-Dey in Algiers, denouncing Giraud and insisting till the end that he was the victim of a "political assassination." Giraud's statements "declining all responsibility" for Pucheu's execution were badly received by his supporters, for whom the political refrain became: "A passport signed Giraud will lead you directly to the stake." Lacouture, *De Gaulle: Le Rebelle*, 754–56; Paillole, *Services spéciaux*, 531–34.

10. THE RESISTANCE

1. Julian Amery, "Of Resistance," *Nineteenth Century Magazine*, March 1949, 138–49.

2. John Keegan, *The Second World War*, Penguin (London, 1989), Ch. 26.

3. SHAEF G-3: "Summary of SAS/Special Force and Etat-major of the FFI operations under SHAEF control," Arthur S. Nevins Papers, U.S. Military History Institute, Army War College, Carlisle Barracks.

4. R. V. Jones, *Reflections on Intelligence*, Heineman (London, 1989), 98, 43–44.

5. Passy, *10 Duke Street, Londres (le BCRA)*, Raoul Solar (Monte Carlo, 1947), 295, 275. Colonel, and future Lieutenant General, William W. Quinn, G-2 in General Alexander Patch's Seventh Army, tasked with the invasion of southern France in 1944, agreed with Passy on the value of humint. "I was absolutely astounded at what OSS was doing there in North Africa. I was astounded that they had 28 agent chains in the southern part of France in which we were particularly interested. These agents were reporting every day. They all had radios. They were all French and they were reporting on the German dispositions, fortifications, aircraft, logistics, order of battle, command posts—everything that we wanted to know." Quinn insisted that the Seventh Army lost only 140 men on the beaches, "and it was because we knew the underwater obstacles, we knew *everything* about that beach and where every German was, and we clobbered them!" U.S. Army Military History Institute, Senior Officer Oral History Program, Project 81-E, Interview of Lieutenant General William W. Quinn, Army War College, Carlisle Barracks.

6. Rather, academics have often outdone themselves in discovering new ways to approach Resistance studies. In the process, the question of the efficiency or utility of the Resistance has become mired in debates over whether the Resistance included only those who actively participated in a network or everyone who quietly withdrew their allegiance from the Vichy government. See Marc Ferro, *Pétain*, Fayard (Paris, 1987), 712. With such nebulous frontiers, as Jean Moulin anticipated, the Resistance has been dis-

cussed primarily as a moral obligation or ethical statement. Thus, the editor of one study of the Resistance resolved opposing comparisons of the relative merits of bombing versus sabotage by resistance groups in occupied France by concluding that "in broader and more obviously moral terms" the advantage went to the Resistance. Stephen Hawes and Ralph White, *Resistance in Europe: 1935–45*, Pelican (London, 1976), 223–4.

7. See, for instance, Roger Faligot and Rémi Kauffer, *Les Résistants: De la guerre de l'ombre aux allées du pouvoir, 1944–1989*, Fayard (Paris, 1989).

8. Daniel Cordier, *Jean Moulin: L'Inconnu du Panthéon*, Vol. III: *De Gaulle capital de la Résistance*, J. C. Lattès (Paris, 1993), 839.

9. Cordier, *Jean Moulin*, 825–7.

10. Jean Lacouture, *De Gaulle, Vol. I: Le Rebelle, 1890–1944*, Seuil (Paris, 1984), 571. One author has suggested that de Gaulle and Passy intentionally allowed the Resistance to remain leaderless for several months after the arrest of Moulin in 1943 because they feared that the CNR, with a strong communist representation, would actually become a rival to London Gaullists. Henri-Christian Giraud, *De Gaulle et les communistes*, Albin Michel (Paris, 1988), II, 50–1.

11. Passy, *Missions secrètes en France. Souvenirs du BCRA. Novembre 1942–juin 1943*, Plon (Paris, 1951), 212.

12. Jacques Soustelle, *Envers et contre tout*, Vol. II: *D'Alger à Paris, 1942–1944*, Laffont (Paris, 1950), 165–66. Soustelle argued that whatever the immediate value to Combat "the Swiss affair" was a serious error in the context of the internal politics of the Resistance, for it helped Frenay's bitter rival d'Astier to solidify his hold over the Commissariat à l'Intérieur and further divide French intelligence. "Therefore, one can see one of the long-range causes of the misfortunes and disillusions of the following years," Soustelle believed.

13. Interview with Paillole.

14. Timothy J. Naftali, "The DSM and the Politics of Allied Counterespionage," unpublished paper, 12–13. Also Michael Howard, *British Intelligence in the Second World War*, Vol. V: *Strategic Deception*, Cambridge University Press (New York, 1990), 85.

15. "We were even in agreement on the Resistance" was Groussard's judgment after a postwar conversation with de Gaulle. "For if I judged it harshly, he was no less severe, because, he told me, 'I was looking for leaders. I only found bandit chiefs.' " André Gillois, *Histoire secrète des français à Londres de 1940 à 1944*, Hachette (Paris, 1973), 67.

16. Passy, *10 Duke Street*, 164–69.

17. M. R. D. Foot, *SOE in France*, Her Majesty's Stationery Office (London, 1966), 116–19; Howard, *Strategic Deception*, 47–51. Henri Noguères, *La Vie quotidienne des résistants de l'Armistice à la Libération*, Ha-

chette (Paris, 1984), 97–105. See also Henri Noguères, *Histoire de la Résistance en France*, Vol. II, Laffont (Paris, 1969), Annexe VIII, 698–700, for Paillole's insistence that the BMA had no police functions and if some officers turned over information on Resistance networks to the ST, it was the result of a few "errors" or "mistakes" and not part of BMA policy.

18. Cordier, *Jean Moulin*, 679.
19. Passy, *10 Duke Street*, 167.
20. Philippe Thyraud de Vosjoli, *Lamia*, Little, Brown (Toronto and Boston, 1970), 16.
21. Christine Ockrent and Alexandre de Marenches, *Dans le secret des princes*, Editions Stock (Paris, 1986), 19–20.
22. Noguères, *Vie quotidienne*, 56.
23. Gillois, *Histoire secrète*, 122.
24. Noguères, *Vie quotidienne*, 54–5, 50.
25. Noguères, *Vie quotidienne*, 53, 44.
26. Passy, *10 Duke Street*, 51. It is unclear why Passy thought this tactic would work. Denunciations of notorious collaborators would probably be dismissed out of hand and therefore not overload the system. Nor would it discourage denunciations, most of which probably came from very average French men and women who felt threatened by any abnormal activity.
27. Noguères, *Histoire de la Résistance*, II, 614–16; *La Vie quotidienne*, 16.
28. Noguères, *La Vie quotidienne*, 16–19.
29. National Archives, Entry 97, box 32, folder 578, report n.d.
30. Passy, *10 Duke Street*, 105–6.
31. Noguères, *La Vie quotidienne*, 23–30, 33–40.
32. Passy, *10 Duke Street*, 296; *Missions secrètes*, 94.
33. Soustelle, *D'Alger à Paris*, 257, 271.
34. Other authors have disputed this, claiming that the communists had extensive contacts in France and Switzerland, and were especially good at providing intelligence on German rail movements in France. But even these concede that relations between the BCRA and Service B were fraught with distrust, and hampered by poor communications and German repression. See Roger Faligot and Rémi Kauffer, *Service B*, Fayard (Paris, 1985), 114.
35. Passy, *10 Duke Street*, 297–306; *Missions secrètes*, 100; Soustelle, *D'Alger à Paris*, 286, 306–8.
36. National Archives, Entry 97, box 32, folder 578.
37. Passy, *Missions secrètes*, 90–1.
38. Passy confessed that, even though the British schools were excellent, his agents were not given adequate instruction. This was because, Passy believed, the British training centers lacked the "moral climate in which we

would have liked to bathe our agents." The waiting lists for a place in a school were too long. Those who had been brought out of France often had to be returned before the completion of their course, lest an overly long absence cause suspicious local officials to ask questions on their return. The French were allowed to set up their own radio training school at Ealing, a basic training which was then completed in a British school.

39. Cordier, *Jean Moulin*, 686.

40. Passy, *10 Duke Street*, 183.

41. Passy, *10 Duke Street*, 177–81, 289.

42. Americans discovered that radio batteries, when they could be found, cost 20,000 francs ($400) in France. National Archives, Entry 97, box 32, folder 578. See Entry 97, box 42, folders 724–5, for "urgent" requests by the BCRA for radio equipment in 1943 and 1944.

43. Wilhelm F. Flicke, *War Secrets in the Ether*, Aegean Park Press (Laguna Hills, Calif., 1977), II, 170.

44. Flicke, *War Secrets*, 235.

45. Flicke, *War Secrets*, 236.

46. Foot, *SOE*, 105, 241.

47. Public Record Office, CAB 122-1347 for a 17 February 1944 meeting of the Joint Intelligence Committee in which Sir Stewart Menzies complained that codes used by the French armed forces and the French National Committee "are dangerously insecure." There follows a long correspondence which includes French denials and finally a 27 September recommendation from the Joint Chiefs of Staff to drop the matter, as it was "not . . . worth antagonizing the French" over the issue.

48. Foot, *SOE*, 106.

49. Gilles Perrault, *The Red Orchestra*, Simon & Schuster (New York, 1967), 67–70.

50. Pierre Lorain, *Armement clandestin: France 1941–1944*, Author's copyright, 1972, 24–31. Flicke, *War Secrets*, II, 172. Fieseler-Storch planes with RDF equipment might also be used for radio detection, especially in Eastern Europe.

51. André Heintz, "Preparing for 'D' Day—the French Resistance in Caen and Calvados," unpublished paper in the possession of the author.

52. Paul Paillole, *Services spéciaux (1935–1945)*, Laffont (Paris, 1975), 393–4.

53. Flicke, *War Secrets*, 245.

54. Foot, *SOE*, 109.

55. Foot, *SOE*, 107–9, 329–30.

56. Noguères, *La Vie quotidienne*, 42–3.

57. Service Historique de l'Armée de Terre (SHAT), 4P 16.

58. Flicke, *War Secrets*, 169–71. Flicke says that the Russians trained 30,000 radio operators to work behind German lines.

59. R. V. Jones, *Most Secret War: British Scientific Intelligence, 1939–1945*, Cornet (London, 1978), 316–17. Also George Millar, *The Bruneval Raid: Flashpoint of the Radar War*, Bodley Head (London, 1974).

60. Noguères, *La Vie quotidienne*, 202.

61. F. H. Hinsley, *British Intelligence in the Second World War*, Cambridge University Press (New York, 1981), II, 699–700.

62. Cordier, *Jean Moulin*, 679–80, 685.

63. Cordier, *Jean Moulin*, 682–3, 704–5.

64. SHAT, 4P 16.

65. SHAT, 5P 34.

66. Stephen Ambrose, *D-Day, June 6, 1944*, Simon & Schuster (New York, 1994), 100.

67. Hinsley, *British Intelligence*, III, Part 2, 20.

68. Heintz, "Preparing for 'D' Day."

69. This would explain in part Soustelle's criticism that the Resistance group ORA was "too imbued with its technical superiority because it was run by professional soldiers [and] wanted to act like lone horsemen." Soustelle complained that the ORA preferred to give its intelligence to Rivet's SR. Soustelle, *D'Alger à Paris*, 304. American intelligence reported that the soldiers within the Resistance group Ordre Civil et Militaire (OCM) had limited its effectiveness, "partly by the conspicuousness of its members, partly by the fact that it has no mass following, and partly by the professional soldiers' skepticism toward military unorthodoxy." War Department pamphlet, *Civil Affairs Information Guide Survey of French Underground Movement*, 25 May 1944, 21.

70. Richard Collier, *Ten Thousand Eyes*, Dutton (New York, 1958).

71. Letter to author from M. R. D. Foot.

72. SHAT, 7P 135.

73. Letter to author from M. R. D. Foot.

74. National Archives, Entry 97, box 19, folders 330–1, 337, 339–40.

75. Hinsley emphasizes the role of Polish networks based on the Polish community in Lille: *British Intelligence in the Second World War*, Vol. III, Part 1, 349, 376–7, 420, 439–40. Jones, *Reflections*, 43–4, 126, 221–23; Jones, *Most Secret War*.

76. National Archives, Entry 97, box 32, folder 578.

77. Howard, *Strategic Deception*, 159.

78. Jones, *Most Secret War*, 335–8, 460–2; Hinsley, *British Intelligence*, III, Part 1, 349.

79. Jones, *Most Secret War*, 305.

80. M. R. D. Foot, *Resistance*, Granada (London, 1978), 309.

81. Letter of 10 January 1944 from Henry Hyde to Colonel Galvin saying that Passy's pressure on French recruits had created a shortage of radio operators available to the OSS. National Archives, Entry 97, box 32, folder 568. See also folder 578, cited above.

82. Archives nationales, Fla 3727.

83. AN, Fla 3727, 22 September 1943.

84. AN, Fla 3727, Manuel report of 2 June 1944. Also "Des Bombardements de l'aviation anglo-américaine et les réactions de la population française," 5 June 1944. And bombing reports for individual cities.

85. Hinsley, *British Intelligence*, III, Part 2, 28. SHAT, 4P 16, report of 19 December 1942, does demonstrate that rail movements were under surveillance.

86. SHAT, 4P 16, 19 December 1942. Hinsley, *British Intelligence*, II, 167.

87. Passy, *Missions secrètes*, 108–9.

88. AN, Fla 3727.

89. Soustelle, *D'Alger à Paris*, 310.

90. For instance, the French reported in June 1944 that only about 70 per month were being hit by bombs, and of these only about 35 were seriously damaged, which had cost the lives of 78 French railwaymen and wounded another 378. At the same time, around 40 locomotives were "vaccinated" (Resistance argot for sabotaged) each month. As roughly 20 percent of locomotives were normally in for repair at any one time, the effects of sabotage and bombing were negligible. AN, Fla 3727, "Des Bombardements de l'aviation anglo-américaine." The Americans reported that the FTP had claimed 357 locomotives put out of action in the "North zone" alone between 1 April and 1 September 1943. War Department pamphlet, *Civil Affairs Information Guide*, 39.

91. Soustelle, *D'Alger à Paris*, 311–20.

92. Keegan, *The Second World War*, 406.

93. See especially the chapters by Alan Milward and M. R. D. Foot in Hawes and White, *Resistance in Europe*.

94. Heintz, "Preparing for 'D' Day," 5.

95. Author's interview with Michel Briens, who in June 1944 was an SNCF employee at Caen. He saw two railwaymen who had sabotaged a locomotive shot out of hand by the Germans.

96. Noguères, *La Vie quotidienne*, 201.

97. Passy, *10 Duke Street*, 172.

98. Heintz, "Preparing for 'D' Day," 5.

99. Foot, *SOE*, 438, 440.

100. Hinsley, *British Intelligence*, III, Part 2, 775.

101. War Department pamphlet, *Civil Affairs Information Guide*, 8.

102. Noguères, *La Vie quotidienne*, 37–8.

103. Foot, *SOE*, 389.

104. Hinsley, *British Intelligence*, III, Part 2, note 107, 114–15 and note.

105. Raymond Ruffin, *Résistance P.T.T.*, Presses de la Cité (Paris, 1983), 100, 107, 202.

106. Foot, *SOE*, 440.

107. Foot, *SOE*, 440–41, 438.

108. Heintz, "Preparing for 'D' Day," 19.

109. Max Hastings, *Das Reich: The March of the 2nd SS Panzer Division Through France*, Holt, Rinehart and Winston (New York, 1981), 210–2.

110. Foot, *SOE*, 437.

111. Alan Milward, "The Economic and Strategic Effectiveness of Resistance," in Hawes and White, *Resistance in Europe*, 193, 197. See also Foot, *Resistance*, 313. Hastings drew the same conclusions for SAS operations in occupied France: *Das Reich*, 209.

112. Memorandum for the President, 4 May 1945, Donovan Papers, Box 80 A, Army War College, Carlisle Barracks. Also *Résumé de l'historique de l'état-major des FFI*, Box 120 B, file 97.

113. "Specific Achievements," 31 August 1945, Box 80 A, Donovan Papers, Army War College, Carlisle Barracks.

114. Heintz, "Preparing for 'D' Day," 19.

115. Arthur Layton Funk, *Hidden Ally: The French Resistance, Special Operations, and the Landings in Southern France, 1944*, Greenwood Press (New York, 1992), 65–9, 120–1, 259.

116. "Combat Intelligence," lecture at Fort Benning, May 1946, by William Duff, and letters from Arthur Stratton 26 May and 1 June 1946, Donovan Papers, U.S. Army Military History Institute, Army War College, Carlisle Barracks.

117. Brian Chapman, "The German Counter-Resistance," in Hawes and White, *Resistance in Europe*.

118. "It is regrettable to have to insist on the surfeit of difficulties which were imposed on us by the attitude of the civilian population in the Orne, and even more in the Calvados," read the official report of Plan Tortue, the Resistance plan to attack German troops behind the lines in Normandy. "Everywhere, we came up against the inertia and the feeling that we threatened the interests of the Norman peasants. Apart from a few exceptional people who sacrificed everything, we were given little aid. Even after the invasion, the peasants preferred to sell their butter to the retreating Germans rather than to our men, who were considered suspect. Outside of the traitors who denounced patriots and revealed our caches to the Germans or the Milice, the major part of the population was hostile and capable of any cowardly act

to preserve their goods." Pierre Péan, *L'Homme de l'ombre: Eléments d'enquête autour de Jacques Foccart, l'homme le plus mystérieux et le plus puissant de la Ve République*, Fayard (Paris, 1990), 131–2.

119. Report of the Supreme Commander to the Combined Chiefs of Staff on the Operations in Europe (Washington, D.C., 1946), 53. Quoted in Funk, *Hidden Ally*, 20.

120. SHAEF G-3: "Summary of SAS/Special Force and EM des FFI Operations under SHAEF Control," July 1944, Arthur S. Nevins Papers, U.S. Army Military History Institute, Army War College, Carlisle Barracks, quotes the figure of 600. Hastings, *Das Reich*, 217.

121. Hastings, *Das Reich*, 217.

122. Hastings, *Das Reich*, 219.

123. Philippe Buton, *Les Lendemains qui déchantent: Le Parti communiste français à la Libération*, Presses de la Fondation Nationale des Sciences Politiques (Paris, 1994), 105–6.

124. Chapman, "The German Counter-Resistance," 185, 224.

125. Heintz, "Preparing for 'D' Day," 17–18.

126. Foot, *SOE*, 424.

127. Gillois, *Histoire secrète*, 101.

128. Lacouture, *De Gaulle: Le Rebelle*, 340.

129. Ferro, *Pétain*, 528.

130. Lacouture, *De Gaulle: Le Rebelle*, 527.

131. Gillois, *Histoire secrète*, 164.

11. THE SECRET SERVICES IN POSTWAR FRANCE

1. Paul Paillole, *Services spéciaux (1935–1945)*, Laffont (Paris, 1975), 563.

2. Philippe Thyraud de Vosjoli, *Lamia*, Little, Brown (Boston and Toronto, 1970), 117–8, 125–6.

3. Philippe Bernert, *Roger Wybot et la bataille pour la DST*, Presses de la Cité (Paris, 1975), 96.

4. Philippe Bernert, *S.D.E.C.E. Service 7*, Presses de la Cité (Paris, 1980), 36.

5. Paillole, *Services spéciaux*, 564–5.

6. Bernert, *Roger Wybot*, 108.

7. Philip M. Williams, *Wars, Plots and Scandals in Post-War France*, Cambridge University Press (Cambridge, Eng., 1970), 38.

8. Bernert, *Roger Wybot*, 231.

9. Thyraud de Vosjoli, *Lamia*, 157, 143; Bernert, *Roger Wybot*, 228.

10. Bernert, *S.D.E.C.E. Service 7*, 38–40.

11. Roger Faligot and Rémi Kauffer, *Les Résistants: De la guerre de

l'ombre aux allées du pouvoir, 1944–1989, Fayard (Paris, 1989), 120–3.

12. Williams, *Wars, Plots and Scandals,* 50.

13. Thyraud de Vosjoli, *Lamia,* 125, 130, 159–60.

14. Bernert, *Roger Wybot,* 105. Roger Faligot and Pascal Krop enumerate some of these scandals in *La Piscine: Les services secrets français, 1944–1984,* Seuil (Paris, 1985), 32–6.

15. Faligot and Kauffer, *Les Résistants,* 116.

16. Bernert, *Roger Wybot,* 111–13. Also Faligot and Kauffer, *Les Résistants,* 134–5.

17. These fears of a second Fall of France, this time to Soviet arms backed by a French Communist Party fifth column, were communicated to Passy's successor, Henri Ribière. Ribière launched Operation Arc-en-ciel (Rainbow), which sought to put an underground network in place in peacetime and prepare to transfer the government and secret services to North Africa. Arc-en-ciel was discontinued in 1958. Faligot and Krop, *La Piscine,* 88–90.

18. Bernert, *S.D.E.C.E. Service 7,* 40.

19. Philippe Buton, *Les Lendemains qui déchantent: Le Parti communiste français à la Libération,* Presses de la Fondation Nationale des Sciences Politiques (Paris, 1994), 108–31.

20. Vincent Auriol, *Journal du septennant, 1947–1954,* Vol. I: *1947,* Armand Colin (Paris, 1970), 254–4.

21. Jean Lacouture, *De Gaulle,* Vol. II: *Le Politique, 1944–1959,* Seuil (Paris, 1985), 263; Faligot and Krop, *La Piscine,* 38–41; Faligot and Kauffer, *Les Résistants,* 122, 155–8; Thyraud de Vosjoli, *Lamia,* 143–53.

22. Daniel Cordier, *Jean Moulin: L'Inconnu du Panthéon,* Vol. III: *De Gaulle capital de la Résistance,* J. C. Lattès (Paris, 1993), 717–18.

23. Lacouture, *De Gaulle: Le Politique,* 210.

24. Faligot and Kauffer, *Les Résistants,* 116–17.

25. Thyraud de Vosjoli, *Lamia,* 134.

26. Faligot and Krop, *La Piscine,* 184. The figures supplied by Faligot and Krop, based on a 1960 budget report, are slightly confusing, as they add up to more than 100 percent.

27. Faligot and Krop, *La Piscine,* 59.

28. Pierre Péan, *L'Homme de l'ombre: Eléments d'enquête autour de Jacques Foccart, l'homme le plus mystérieux et le plus puissant de la Ve République,* Fayard (Paris, 1990), 217–18.

29. Bernert, *Roger Wybot,* 124–7.

30. Bernert, *Roger Wybot,* 107–9.

31. National Archives, RG 226, box 22, folder 165, 12 February 1945.

32. *Le Monde,* 31 March 1983, p. 8.

33. Bernert, *Roger Wybot,* 135–40.

34. Philippe Robrieux, *Histoire intérieure du Parti communiste,* Vol. II,

Fayard (Paris, 1981), 52–4, 73; Buton, *Les Lendemains*, 133–53, 164, 200–5.

35. Passy, *Missions secrètes en France. Souvenirs du BCRA. Novembre 1942–juin 1943*, Plon (Paris, 1951), 413–15. As stated above, Jean Lacouture argues that Passy saw to it that the socialists dominated the Comité Nationale de la Résistance; *De Gaulle: Le Politique*, 210.

36. Peter Wright, *Spycatcher*, Dell (New York, 1987), 301–2; Stéphane Courtois, "Jean Moulin et les Communistes," *L'Histoire*, No. 166 (May 1993), 10.

37. Jacques Soustelle, *Envers et contre tout*, Vol. II: *D'Alger à Paris, 1942–1944*, Laffont (Paris, 1950), 304.

38. French journalist Thierry Wolton estimates that around 20 communists managed to make a career in the SDECE. *Le KGB en France*, Grasset (Paris, 1986), 31.

39. *Le Monde*, 31 March 1983, p. 8.

40. Memorandum, Norman Holmes Person to James R. Murphy (Chief of X-2), June 8, 1945, Record Group 226, Entry 109, Box 26, National Archives, Washington, D.C.; cited in Timothy J. Naftali, "The DSM and the Politics of Allied Counter-espionage," unpublished paper, 22.

41. David Dallin, *Soviet Espionage*, Yale University Press (New Haven, Conn., 1955), 307.

42. Thyraud de Vosjoli, *Lamia*, 154.

43. Dallin, *Soviet Espionage*, 317–18.

44. Thyraud de Vosjoli, *Lamia*, 129; Dallin, *Soviet Espionage*, 308, 317–19.

45. Dallin, *Soviet Espionage*, 308.

46. Wolton, *Le KGB en France*, 131–2.

47. Joint-Daguenet interview.

48. Wright, *Spycatcher*, 302–3.

49. Bernert, *Roger Wybot*, 168–73.

50. Auriol, *Journal*, I, 587.

51. National Archives, XL47861, 28 March 1946.

52. Auriol, *Journal*, I, 339, 358, 367, 480.

53. Robrieux, *Histoire intérieure*, II, 181–4.

54. Auriol, *Journal*, I, 616.

55. Auriol, *Journal*, I, 155–6, 480–1, 485–6, 521–2, 606–7, 612, 616, 622, 629–30, 632, 639, 649.

56. Buton, *Les Lendemains*, 298–314.

57. Thyraud de Vosjoli, *Lamia*, 209, 186, 162–3.

58. Bernert, *Roger Wybot*, 207.

59. Thyraud de Vosjoli, *Lamia*, 208–11. For a detailed discussion of

the Generals affair, see Williams, *Wars, Plots and Scandals*, 38–48; Bernert, *Roger Wybot*, 181–275; Faligot and Krop, *La Piscine*, 126–31.

60. Bernert, *Roger Wybot*, 272–5.

61. Bernert, *Roger Wybot*, 284.

62. Bernert, *Roger Wybot*, 410, 415, 417, 421–2, 428, 430, 440.

63. Thyraud de Vosjoli, *Lamia*, 240. He also complained that security in the French embassy in Washington was so lax that even the State Department broke its normal reserve to complain, especially as, to show their disapproval of McCarthyism, many French diplomats in Washington were expressing pro-Soviet opinions. The French services raised skepticism in the CIA by their "puerile" insistence that members of the French Communist Party were never used for espionage. There were also tensions over Indochina (pp. 241–3, 217–22).

64. Jerrold L. Schecter and Peter S. Deriabin, *The Spy Who Saved the World: How a Soviet Colonel Changed the Course of the Cold War*, Scribners (New York, 1992), 237.

65. Thyraud de Vosjoli, *Lamia*, 245.

12. INDOCHINA

1. This reorganization did not meet with the approval of everyone. A 1951 report complained: "Since 1948, the BTLC has annexed the SLOTFOM. In principle, nothing has changed. But in fact since 1949 the SLOTFOM has been disorganized and now works under more and more difficult conditions. It has been stripped of most of its resources. The Service de Renseignement Général, created . . . to replace the BTLC, has no more resources . . . It is therefore certain that with the abolition of the SLOTFOM a very serious void will open in our relations with members of the Associated States [Indochina] living in France. Our already fragmentary intelligence . . . will plunge to absolute zero." J. Dion, *Historique du SLOTFOM*, Archives nationales, Section Outre-Mer, Répertoire numérique 8.

2. The Free French military mission in China established an SR d'Extrême-Orient (SREO) under Major Tutenges to gain intelligence on Japanese installations suitable for Allied bombardment and to establish contacts in the French garrisons in Indochina. De Gaulle insisted that all intelligence gathered in Indochina must be communicated to the Allies "in the measure and only in the form compatible with the interests of France in the Far East," to establish beyond doubt that in Indochina the Allies "absolutely need our help." Christophe Babinet, "L'Action du général de Gaulle en Indochine à partir de la Chine," in Gilbert Pilleul, ed., *Le Général de Gaulle et l'Indochine, 1940–1946*, Plon (Paris, 1982), 42.

Tutenges' efforts to establish contacts with French garrisons in Tonkin had disappointing results. For instance, when SREO agent Lieutenant Pierre Boule, future author of *The Bridge on the River Kwai*, floated into Tonkin down the Black River in July 1942, he was arrested and imprisoned by the Sûreté. In the main, therefore, Tutenges was obliged to work through networks controlled by the Chinese Central Investigation and Statistics Bureau, an organization of agents, opium dealers, and assassins under the secretive and sinister General Tai Li. This arrangement did produce some useful intelligence, some of it provided by the Bureau de Statistique Militaire in Hanoi, such as a plan of Japanese defenses at Cam Ranh Bay. But in a conscientious inversion of the Christian spirit, Tai Li received far more than he gave. Besides, it could only be a matter of time before this "Chinese Himmler," as he was described in one American report, turned his pathological hatred of foreigners against the Gaullists. In 1943, he established cordial relations with naval commander Robert Meynier, who arrived in Chungking to head a Giraudist mission. American intelligence in China also found Meynier a more congenial working partner than the prickly Gaullists or the untrustworthy Tai Li. He also had good contacts among the Vietnamese through his Vietnamese wife, and in the Indochina garrison, men humiliated by Vichy neutrality but as yet unwilling to throw in with the Gaullists. Meynier regularly furnished the Americans with information on political developments, Japanese troop movements, and bombing targets to supplement their own extensive "GBT" network. Ronald Spector, *Eagle Against the Sun: The American War Against Japan*, Free Press (New York, 1985), 469–70. Also Ronald Spector, *Advice and Support: The Early Years of the United States Army in Vietnam, 1941–1960*, Free Press (New York, 1985), 21–35. Meynier was removed by de Gaulle in January 1944. Henri Jacquin, *Guerre secrète en Indochine*, Olivier Orban (Paris, 1979), insists that the GBT network, named for three businessmen refugees in China, was more interested in commercial than military intelligence (p. 117). While this may have been true early in the war, as the network's original purpose was to look after Allied business property in Indochina, its activities had an increasingly military orientation.

3. William H. Wainwright, "Faits et événements essentiels," Pilleul, *De Gaulle et l'Indochine*, 62.

4. A few men in Indochina were willing to run the risk of resistance, among them a Captain Philippe Milon, stung by the treacherous September 1940 Japanese attack on his garrison of Lang Son which had inflicted 800 casualties on the French. In March 1943, he slipped away from his artillery battery there and made his way to Algiers, where he received instructions, radio codes with which to contact the military mission in Chungking, and orders to return to Indochina. As the would-be resisters would discover to their cost, it was very difficult, if not quite impossible, to organize a clandestine

movement in a country where a large percentage of the population appeared to be in the pay of Tai Li, the French Sûreté directed by the veteran Commissaire Louis Arnoux, or the remarkable Japanese network whose primary agents were trained in Tokyo's Nakano Gakko military spy academy. Some no doubt worked simultaneously for all three.

5. Pilleul, *De Gaulle et l'Indochine*, 152-3. Gaullists and ex-Vichyites bitterly contested the role of the resistance in precipitating the Japanese coup of 9 March 1945. General Jean Lecomte insisted that the archives of the Japanese naval commander in Indochina revealed that he took the decision to act against the French in September 1944, a view shared by Decoux's principal adviser, General Gautier (p. 225). Others argue that the Japanese decision was taken in Tokyo on 20 February 1945 and was based solely on the strategic rationale that Indochina would follow the Philippines as the next American objective in the Pacific (p. 221). There is really no contradiction here. An Allied invasion would be assisted by the French population in Indochina, so that French sovereignty in Indochina had to be terminated. See Philippe Francini, *Les Guerres d'Indochine*, Pygmalion (Paris, 1988), I, 183.

6. One of the great historical myths of the French in Indochina is that the Americans did not lift a finger to help French forces in March 1945. In fact, the U.S. Fourteenth Air Force flew numerous missions and parachuted mixed Franco-American commando teams in support of Alessandri's retreating column. It was the first open commitment by the United States to aid the French in Indochina. Decisions by Washington in the summer of 1945 to support French resistance groups and clandestine operations in Indochina served as a de facto recognition of a French claim on the area. And if subsequent joint Franco-American commando teams failed to harass the Japanese in Indochina, it was because the real resistance in Indochina, the Vietminh, were extremely anti-French. Spector, *Advice and Support*, 40-1, 47-50.

7. Spector, *Advice and Support*, 42. Spector argues that the Vietminh-OSS cooperation in the summer of 1945 was "limited and almost accidental." Only 5 percent of Vietminh small arms in March 1946 had been provided by the United States, and some of these had been given them by French intelligence agents. Most Vietminh arms had been collected from the Japanese. "That Washington, more than three months before V-J Day, had virtually capitulated to French demands for the return of all of Indochina, that American material aid to the Viet Minh had been inconsequential, and that the very existence of the Viet Minh was largely a response to French exploitation and oppression were rarely acknowledged by the men who would lead France to Dien Bien Phu," concludes Spector (pp. 72-3).

8. Gilbert Bodinier, *1945-1946: Le Retour de la France en Indochine*,

textes et documents, Service Historique de l'Armée de Terre (SHAT) (Vincennes, 1987), 332–33, 336–37, 343.

9. Gilbert Bodinier, *Indochine 1947: Règlement politique ou solution militaire, textes et documents,* SHAT (Vincennes, 1989), 1 January 1947. One reason that General Morlière failed to act against the obvious Vietminh preparations was that he had strict orders not to place upon France the onus of initiating hostilities. On the other hand, he seems to have shared the belief of some French that the war preparations were the work of a handful of extremists who would be controlled by Ho Chi Minh, and was reluctant to go on alert on the 19th. And d'Argenlieu to the contrary, the attack had some notable organizational failures, possibly because it was carried out by only a faction of the Vietminh. Yves Gras, *Histoire de la guerre d'Indochine,* Plon (Paris, 1978), 151–4.

10. SHAT, 10H 266, "SDECE en Indochine," n.d.

11. Bodinier, *Indochine 1947,* 289–90, 328.

12. Raoul Salan, *Mémoires: Fin d'un empire,* Vol. II: *Le Viêt-Minh mon adversaire,* Presses de la Cité (Paris, 1971), 99.

13. Bodinier, *Indochine 1947,* 294, 296, 306.

14. Gras, *Histoire de la guerre d'Indochine,* 207.

15. Bodinier, *Indochine 1947,* 325, 327, 361–2, 393, 417.

16. SHAT, 10H 375, 3e régiment étranger d'infanterie, 1st semester 1951. V. J. Croizat, *Lessons from the Indochina War,* Rand Corporation (Santa Monica, Calif., May 1967), 57.

17. Chef de bataillon Barthelemy, "L'Officier de renseignement outre-mer," Centre d'information et de spécialisation pour outre-mer (SHAT, 1958), Doc. 9593, 3, 19. SHAT, 10H 273, "Procès-verbal de réunion d'information et de coordination du renseignements," 1954.

18. Henry Ainley, *In Order to Die: With the Foreign Legion in Indochina,* Burke (London, 1955), 37.

19. Ainley, *In Order to Die,* 30.

20. Chef de bataillon F. L. Michel, *Cours de renseignement,* Section de documentation militaire de l'outre-mer (SHAT, 1955), Doc. 8428, introduction.

21. SHAT, 10H 266, "Coût et rendement des organismes de recherche du renseignement," n.d. but around 1952. Also report on Brigade de CE Opérationnel. A brigade was commanded by an SDECE officer and included two SDECE NCOs, two inspectors from the Army Service de Sécurité, two from the Vietnamese Sûreté, three interpreters, and a support staff of eleven. See also Colonel Ruat, "Les Services spéciaux français dans les conflits d'outre-mer, 1945–1962," *Bulletin de l'Amicale des anciens membres des services spéciaux de la défense nationale et réseaux F.F.C. correspondants,* IV, No. 152 (1991), 37.

22. SHAT, 10H 266, 15 January 1954.

23. Barthelemy, "L'Officier de renseignement," 18.

24. SHAT, 10H 266, "Coût et rendement."

25. Bernard Fall, "La Fin du groupe mobile 100: Une unité motor-isée dans la guerre de jungle." WWR, II.60, 606. SHAT, Indochine géné-ralités.

26. Colonel de Maricourt, "Les Opérations aériennes en Indochine. Conférence faite au CEAA en mai 1952." SHAT, 21–6.

27. Croizat, *Lessons*, 57.

28. Michel, *Cours de renseignement*, 4.

29. Croizat, *Lessons*, 56–7, 94–5, 150–1, 220. "It was practically im-possible to find out the strength of the Vietminh forces, their dispositions, and their movements by local means alone," the commander of a *groupe mobile* noted. "The little intelligence that was available was most often un-reliable and, above all, was usually too late to be useful" (p. 149).

30. Bodinier, *1945–1946*, 280.

31. SHAT, 10H 273, "Procès-verbal de réunion d'information et de coordination du renseignement," 1954.

32. Marincourt, "Les Opérations aériennes," 30.

33. Bodinier, *Indochine 1947*, 191.

34. "Historique de l'action psychologique en Indochine de 1945 au 20 juillet 1954," SHAT; carton has no number.

35. SHAT, "Historique."

36. SHAT, 10H 271, 18 December 1952.

37. SHAT, "Historique," annexe, ralliements VM: 1,415 first semester 1951; 3,228 first semester 1952. 10H 271, 23 February 1954. The Vietminh command insisted that defectors be sent to do agricultural work rather than be incorporated into military units.

38. SHAT, 10H 612, 13 January 1953.

39. Adrian Liddell Hart, *Strange Company*, Weidenfeld and Nicolson (London, 1953), 138–40.

40. SHAT, 10H 266, 28 July 1952.

41. Croizat, *Lessons*, 58.

42. Bodinier, *Indochine 1947*, 123.

43. Croizat, *Lessons*, 59–60. Each Vietminh infantry division had a Trinh Sat company of three platoons, each regiment contained a reduced three-squad Trinh Sat platoon, and each battalion had a detachment.

44. David Glantz, "Soviet Operational Intelligence. A Case Study," in *The Intelligence Revolution*, Office of Air Force History (Washington, D.C., 1991), 161.

45. Jacquin, *Guerre secrète en Indochine*, 213–14. Unfortunately, it did not provide conclusive proof, because the Deuxième Bureau believed that it

might be part of a deception campaign to distract attention away from the Tonkin delta. Gras, *Histoire de la guerre d'Indochine*, 474.

46. SHAT, 10H 266, 6 April 1954.

47. Jacquin, *Guerre secrète en Indochine*, 232, 236.

48. SHAT, 10H 1142, 16 May 1950.

49. SHAT, 10H 1142. Especially report of 18 August 1950: "Les événements en zone frontière du Nord-est d'après les ordres V.M. interceptés," and 13 October 1950: "Quelques idées sur les combats." American observers in Indochina also blamed the Cao Bang disaster in part on poor French intelligence. But they also appear to have believed a conventional invasion of Tonkin possible. See Spector, *Advice and Support*, 125–6.

50. SHAT, 10H 1869, Deuxième Bureau report of 21 April 1951.

51. SHAT, 10H 1869, 4 January 1953.

52. SHAT, 10H 1874, 3 November and 24 November 1953. Navarre also pointed out that French attempts at radio deception were clumsy and unconvincing, that units continued to commit the "heresy" of changing call signs without changing frequencies, and that far too much information, including cryptographic documents and complete lists of call signs, were distributed to lower-echelon units which did not require them and where they were more likely to be lost or captured. The practice of changing call signs and frequencies once a month was introduced in 1951. By 1954, this was to occur every week. 18 March 1954. 10H 266, 6 April 1954. 10H 1160 for Dien Bien Phu.

53. Henri Navarre, *Le Temps des vérités*, Plon (Paris, 1979), 257–9.

54. SHAT, 10H 1869, 2 January 1952.

55. SHAT, 10H 1869 17 October, 9 December, 17 December 1952.

56. Jacquin, *Guerre secrète en Indochine*, 209.

57. SHAT, "Historique." "Etude du bureau de la guerre psychologique sur les opérations de déception." Also 10H 614.

58. SHAT, 10H 266, "Coût et rendement." Roger Faligot and Pascal Krop, *La Piscine: The French Secret Service Since 1944*, Basil Blackwell. (Oxford, 1989), 85, also notes the poor quality of agent intelligence from China.

59. SHAT, 10H 266, 29 May 1951. Among the shortcomings listed were the lack of security, the confusion of raw intelligence with syntheses because of poor delineation between "research" and analysis, and the poor quality of French interrogations of Vietminh POWs.

60. John F. Melby, "Vietnam—1950," *Diplomatic History*, VI (Winter 1982), 99; quoted in Spector, *Advice and Support*, 111–12.

61. See Spector, *Advice and Support*, Ch. 6.

62. SHAT, 10H 266, 5 September 1951.

63. SHAT, 10H 612, 27 March, 3 April, 11 May 1953. "It is no longer

possible to make a distinction between Vietminh and Communist Chinese. Various sources indicating the training of Vietminh pilots in China are numerous enough for the study of air activity in southern China to be a constant preoccupation of the [French] command." The 11 May report further complained that the reports drawn up by the Direction Générale de la Documentation "were not done by a specialist in aviation or intelligence, and certain affirmations of the superiority of Russian over American matériel must be reviewed in the light of the Korean War experience. [Since the beginning of hostilities, 522 MIG 15s have been shot down in dogfights against 50 Sabres.]" Also Spector, *Advice and Support*, 180.

13. OPERATION CASTOR AND THE SINEWS OF WAR

1. Philippe Francini, *Les Guerres d'Indochine*, Pygmalion (Paris, 1988), II, 97.

2. Lucien Bodard, *La Guerre d'Indochine*, Vol. I: *L'Enlisement*, Gallimard (Paris, 1963), 355.

3. *Assemblée Nationale, Deuxième Législature, session de 1954, annexe au procès-verbal de la séance du 17 juin 1954. Rapport fait au nom de la commission chargée d'enquêter sur le trafic des piastres indochinoises.* Cited in Jacques Despuech, *Le Trafic des piastres*, La Table Ronde (Paris, 1974), 217.

4. Despuech, *Le Trafic des piastres*, 241–2.

5. Service Historique de l'Armée de Terre (SHAT), 10H 273, "note verbal, 23 mai 1952."

6. Known as the "Diethelm affair." Despuech, *Le Trafic des piastres*, 243–4.

7. SHAT, 10H 273, 19 May 1953.

8. The latter piece of information was confirmed to the author by a former CIA agent.

9. Despuech, *Le Trafic des piastres*, from which much of the above information is taken. The 1974 version contains transcripts of the Mondon Committee, which investigated the traffic in 1953.

10. SHAT, 10H 1161.

11. Two years later the name was altered to Groupe d'Intervention Mixte (GMI). Trinquier recounts that there was opposition to the GCMA and a reluctance to serve in it because it was considered a career risk. But this originated more from competition between traditional "paras" and "action" officers for scarce air support resources than from any fundamental analysis of the value of the resistance. Roger Trinquier, *The Indochina Underground*, Foreign Technology Division, Air Force Systems Command (1984), 46.

12. SHAT, 10H 338, "Activité du GCMA, 1 janvier–31 mars 1952"

and "4ème trimestre 1952." Subsequent evaluations were even more damning. A 1 October 1953 report noted that "sabotage" was a European concept which was nullified in Indochina by the dispersion and flexibility of the Vietminh. And how could one establish escape routes along the rare jungle trails, all of which were controlled by the Vietminh? The maquis, it concluded, was little more than a collection of "static village militia." Trinquier, *The Indochina Underground*, 151. See also 16 November 1954 for the mission of resistance. "Rapport du Lt.-col. Trinquier . . . sur l'action menée en Indochine par la groupement mixte d'intervention: 9 juin 1955."

13. V. J. Croizat, *Lessons from the Indochina War*, Rand Corporation (Santa Monica, Calif., May 1967), 168–72.

14. Trinquier, *The Indochina Underground*, 52.

15. Edward Geary Lansdale, *In the Midst of Wars: An American's Mission to Southeast Asia*, Harper & Row (New York, 1972), 112–13.

16. Trinquier, *The Indochina Underground*, 86, 99–101.

17. Alfred W. McCoy, *The Politics of Heroin in Southeast Asia*, Harper & Row (New York, 1972), 92–6.

18. When one surveys the unorthodox career of this decidedly unorthodox general, then Salan's interest in the maquis is hardly surprising. A native of the Tarn in southwestern France, Salan inherited in full the left-wing politics of his region and his family. His brother was a communist, while his close connections with the French Socialist Party and with the Masons earned him the reputation as a *militaire de gauche*—left-wing general—a somewhat ironic status given his career finale as patron of the April 1961 Algiers putsch against de Gaulle and subsequently chief of the OAS, the extreme right-wing terrorist organization. A stolid, almost bland appearance beneath a kepi tilted slightly back on his head belied a taste for risk and intrigue which had drawn Salan naturally to intelligence and special operations. His long service in Indochina combined with the air of serious reserve which marked his personality to earn for him the nickname of "the Mandarin."

Salan had joined the French army in the waning years of World War I. In 1924, he began an eight-year tour in Indochina which was spent largely in intelligence-gathering missions. In 1937, he returned to Paris and was assigned to the military staff of the Colonial Ministry. The following year, the Minister of the Colonies, Georges Mandel, created the Service de Renseignement Intercolonial. In view of his impeccable left-wing credentials and colonial intelligence experience, Captain Salan was an obvious choice as its first director. Salan's main duties were to furnish arguments based on intelligence to his minister, a hard-line antifascist, to use in cabinet debates against the appeasers. Between 1938 and 1940, Salan also directed an operation remarkably similar in concept to the Indochina underground. Disguised as a reporter for the French daily *Le Temps*, Salan recruited Spanish Republicans in French refugee camps and infiltrated them into Ethiopia to build up a resistance whose goal was to produce an uprising. With Italian forces diverted to internal police duties, the French reasoned, too few men would be left over to invade the French enclave at Djibouti. Unfortunately for Salan, the results of his mission foreshadowed those of the Indochina maquis, and for many of the same reasons. Nevertheless, the French could claim subsequently that their pioneering efforts in Ethiopia helped to pave the way for the success of the British-led Gedion Force in May 1940. For this little-known episode, see Hervé Desplanches, "Les Français face à l'Afrique Orientale Italienne: 1938–1940. L'Action subversive en Pays Abyssin," Maîtrise d'Histoire Contemporaine, Université de Provence, 1991.

19. McCoy, *The Politics of Heroin*, 102. Roger Faligot and Pascal Krop print an interview with the SDECE chief in Saigon in 1953 which suggests that Salan's attitude toward the opium connection was the ambiguous one that he knew of it but did not want to become involved in any scandal. *La Piscine: The French Secret Services Since 1944*, Basil Blackwell (Oxford, 1989), 94–5.

20. Raoul Salan, *Mémoires: Fin d'un empire*, Vol. II, *Le Viêt-Minh mon adversaire*, Presses de la Cité (Paris, 1971), 225.

21. Yves Gras, *Histoire de la guerre d'Indochine*, Plon (Paris, 1978), 478, on Salan's views.

22. SHAT, 10H 338, 2e trimestre 1953.

23. Trinquier, *The Indochina Underground*, 82–3, 107–12, 126–7. In many essential respects, the career of Henri Navarre paralleled that of his predecessor. Like Salan, Navarre had joined the army as the last shots of World War I echoed across the battlefields of northern France. After several troop commands and two years at the prestigious *école de guerre*, a rite of passage for future French senior officers, Navarre was assigned in 1937 to the French army's Deuxième Bureau as chief of the German desk. Navarre's association with French intelligence and subsequently with the clandestine life of the French Resistance in World War II seemed to have defined his character. Variously described as aloof, secretive, icy, cerebral, even feline, Navarre appeared to distance himself from his surroundings, while at the same time constantly observing, analyzing, or interpreting them. Nothing he could do as commander of the 5th Spahi Regiment in Marshal Jean de Lattre de Tassigny's French First Army in the tough winter campaign of 1944–45, or subsequently as leader of the French 5th Armored Division in Germany—where his American counterparts thought him gloriously second-rate—could dissipate the lingering impression of detachment and intrigue. Even when he arrived in Saigon in May 1953 as the seventh commander-in-chief since France's reoccupation of Indochina in 1946, the result of a

particularly warm recommendation by Marshal Alphonse Juin to Prime Minister René Mayer, Navarre remained the "intelligence officer" for his subordinates.

24. Croizat, *Lessons*, 157 and note 2.

25. In fact, the requirement for Giap to build up supply depots along the projected lines of advance severely limited the ability of Vietminh forces to react quickly to French initiatives.

26. SHAT, 10H 338, Comité d'Orientation de l'Action.

27. SHAT, 10H 338, "Rapport du Lt.-col. Trinquier," 19.

28. Croizat, *Lessons*, quotes an unnamed officer objecting that "the loss of [the outlying areas] would engender such political and psychological repercussions that the French would have either to commit additional forces there under unfavorable conditions . . . or to suffer the adverse effects which would arise from their inability to defend them" (pp. 145–6).

29. SHAT, 10H 338, "Rapport du Lt.-col. Trinquier," 18.

30. Bodard, *L'Enlisement*, 356–61. Vo Nguyen Giap, *People's Army, People's War*, Foreign Languages Publishing House (Hanoi, 1961), 183; quoted in McCoy, *The Politics of Heroin*, 106.

31. The Editorial Group for the History of Chinese Military Advisers in Vietnam, eds., *Zhongguo junshi guwentuan yuanyue kangfa douzheng shishi (A Factual Account of the Participation of the Chinese Military Advisory Group in the Struggle of Assisting Vietnam and Resisting France)*, People's Liberation Army Press, (Beijing, 1990), 88–90; quoted in Chen Jian, "China and the First Indo-China War, 1950–54," *China Quarterly*, No. 133 (March 1993), 99–100. Also Qiang Zhai, "Transplanting the Chinese Model: Chinese Military Advisers and the First Vietnam War, 1950–1954," *Journal of Military History*, No. 57 (October 1993), 708.

32. SHAT, 10H 273, "Situation militaire en Indochine: 11 septembre 1953."

33. Henri Navarre, *Le Temps des vérités*, Plon (Paris, 1979), 300–1 and note.

34. SHAT, 10H 1160. Italics added.

35. SHAT, 10H 1161, 8 November 1963.

14. DIEN BIEN PHU: THE INTELLIGENCE DIMENSION

1. Henri Navarre, *Le Temps des vérités*, Plon (Paris, 1979), 257–9.

2. Vo Nguyen Giap, *Dien Bien Phu*, Foreign Languages Publishing House (Hanoi, 1964), 54–5. See also Philip B. Davidson, *Vietnam at War: The History, 1946–1975*, Presidio Press (Novato, Calif., 1988), 178–80.

3. Davidson, *Vietnam at War*, 189. Italics in original.

4. V. J. Croizat, *Lessons from the Indochina War*, Rand Corporation (Santa Monica, Calif., May 1967), 153–5.

5. Henri Navarre, *Agonie de l'Indochine, 1953–1954*, Plon (Paris, 1956), 196–8.

6. Howard R. Simpson, *Tiger in the Barbed Wire: An American in Vietnam, 1952–1991*, Brassey's (U.S.), (Washington, D.C., and New York, 1992), 101–2.

7. Croizat, *Lessons*, 157, 159. This rather undermines the contention of Yves Gras that the maquis "caused some real anxiety in the Vietminh high command." *Histoire de la guerre d'Indochine*, Plon (Paris, 1978), 515.

8. Roger Trinquier, *The Indochina Underground*, Foreign Technology Division, Air Force Systems Command (1984), 131–3, 186–7. Trinquier complained that Cogny did not place great faith in maquis effectiveness. See also Croizat, *Lessons*, 157–8, for lack of support for the maquis.

9. Trinquier, *The Indochina Underground*, 182–3.

10. Alfred W. McCoy, *The Politics of Heroin in Southeast Asia*, Harper & Row (New York, 1972), 106.

11. Navarre, *Le Temps des vérités*, Plon (Paris, 1979), 275–86, 301–3. See also Navarre, *Agonie de l'Indochine*, 163, 196–9. Navarre's view is supported by Henri Jacquin, *Guerre secrète en Indochine*, Olivier Orban (Paris, 1979), who argues that Giap's strategy was based on a thorough knowledge of Navarre's plans leaked by several sources (pp. 224, 229–34). "To deprive himself of Dien Bien Phu meant for Giap a renunciation of his campaign . . . against Laos," Jacquin concludes.

12. Chen Jian, "China and the First Indo-China War, 1950–54," *China Quarterly*, No. 133 (March 1993), 100–1.

13. Croizat, *Lessons*, 145–6.

14. Service Historique de l'Armée de Terre (SHAT), 10H 273, "Procès-verbal de réunion d'information et de coordination des renseignements," 23 September, 22 October, 13 November, 7 December 1953.

15. SHAT, 10H 1161, 2e Bureau FTNV, Fiche of 28 November 1953.

16. Gras, *Histoire de la guerre d'Indochine*, 523. Davidson, *Vietnam at War*, 189.

17. Gras, *Histoire de la guerre d'Indochine*, cites an undated Deuxième Bureau document which concluded that, despite massive troop movements away from the delta in late November 1953, "nothing permits the affirmation that reinforcements will be sent toward the northwest and what will be their importance" (p. 523). Another (undated) document cited claimed that the Vietminh could not sustain more than two divisions, 20,000 coolies, and enough artillery and ammunition for seven days of combat at Dien Bien Phu (p. 524). Gras argues that Navarre's decision in early December to hold fast at Dien Bien Phu was based on the belief that he would confront only a

portion of Giap's *corps de bataille* there (p. 523). As Gras's otherwise excellent history fails to cite sources, this author could not locate these documents at Vincennes. But the ones he did consult speak of entire Vietminh divisions, not portions of divisions, massing at Dien Bien Phu. See, for instance, SHAT 10H 273, 4 January 1954.

18. SHAT, 10H 614, 2e bureau, 27 December 1953. Yves Gras agrees that Giap had decided to attack Dien Bien Phu in December, well before the French had agreed to the Geneva Conference on 18 February. *Histoire de la guerre d'Indochine*, 524. Also 10H 614, "Note sur l'évolution de la situation militaire," 7 October 1953.

19. SHAT, 10H 1160, 22 December 1953.

20. Qiang Zhai, "Transplanting the Chinese Model: Chinese Military Advisers and the First Vietnam War, 1950–1954," *Journal of Military History*, No. 57 (October 1993), 709.

21. SHAT, 10H 1160, Messages Postalisés.

22. Zhai, "Transplanting the Chinese Model," 711; Jian, "China and the First Indo-China War," 102–5.

23. SHAT, 10 614.

24. SHAT, 10H 1161, "Situation Viêt-Minh en Indochine du Nord: Caractéristiques d'Ensemble, 10 février 1954," CFTNV, Deuxième bureau.

25. Navarre, *Le Temps des vérités*, 255.

26. SHAT, 10H 1161, "Situation."

27. SHAT, 10H 614, 2e bureau, 27 December 1953.

28. SHAT, 10H 273, 1952, and 12 November 1953.

29. Jian, "China and the First Indo-China War," 106–9.

30. William J. Lederer and Eugene Burdick, *The Ugly American*, Norton (New York, 1958), 110–14.

31. Graham Greene's *Quiet American* is so soft-spoken that one must lean forward to catch his words. Alas, Pyle is inevitably in the midst of another irritating monologue about the righteousness of United States policy in the Far East, of which he is at once the custodian and the redeemer. A synthesis of ruthlessness and primordial innocence in almost equal measure, Greene's version of Lansdale, even allowing for artistic license, is at once disarming, bewildering, and, finally, terrifying.

32. Simpson, *Tiger in the Barbed Wire*, 145.

33. Edward Geary Lansdale, *In the Midst of Wars: An American's Mission to Southeast Asia*, Harper & Row (New York, 1972), 316. Alfred W. McCoy, *The Politics of Heroin in Southeast Asia*, Harper & Row (New York, 1972), 116–26. Stanley Karnow, *Vietnam: A History*, Penguin (London, 1984), 220–3.

15. THE ALGERIAN WAR

1. Philippe Bernert, *Roger Wybot et la bataille pour la DST*, Presses de la Cité (Paris, 1975), 444–6.

2. Jean-Charles Jauffret, *La Guerre d'Algérie par les documents*, Vol. I: *L'Avertissement, 1943–1946*, Service Historique de l'Armée de Terre (SHAT) (Vincennes, 1990), 39, 41, 99–100, 173.

3. Alistair Horne, *A Savage War of Peace: Algeria 1954–1962*, Macmillan (London, 1977), 27. Official French reports placed the number of dead at between 1,020 and 1,300. Cairo radio claimed 45,000. Another French expert, Robert Aron, advanced a figure of 6,000. The figure of 3,000 is suggested by Jauffret.

4. Jauffret, *La Guerre d'Algérie*, I, 306–9.

5. Jean-Charles Jauffret, "Les Débuts de la guerre d'Algérie: De l'absence d'une doctrine aux premières solutions spécifiques, mai 1945–août 1956," unpublished paper, 2. I am grateful to Professor Jauffret for his generous permission to use his research, which was to be part of a general series of documents on the Algerian War published by SHAT. For the moment, access to many of the documents which Professor Jauffret has consulted has been suspended, as has publication of the series.

6. Yves Courrière, *Les Fils de la toussaint*, Fayard (Paris, 1968), 183.

7. *Baraka*, often translated as "luck," more accurately means "the gift" from God. The revolutionaries used news of the defeat to convince Muslims that the French army had been completely annihilated and therefore no longer existed. Horne, *A Savage War of Peace*, 79.

8. Courrière, *Les Fils*, 101, 104–5, 215.

9. Courrière, *Les Fils*, 369.

10. "Les Débuts de la guerre d'Algérie," 1–4, 11–12.

11. Bernert, *Roger Wybot*, 446.

12. Courrière, *Les Fils*, 239–40, 272, 273–6, 283, 341.

13. Horne, *A Savage War of Peace*, 98–9.

14. Philippe Thyraud de Vosjoli, *Lamia*, Little, Brown (Boston and Toronto, 1970), 228–30, 246–8.

15. Philippe Bernert, *S.D.E.C.E. Service 7*, Presses de la Cité (Paris, 1980), 150–68. See also a novel written by Monique and Thyraud de Vosjoli based on this episode and on Le Roy's subsequent career, *Le Comité*, Editions de l'homme (Brussels, 1975).

16. Bernert, *S.D.E.C.E. Service 7*, 269–75.

17. Roger Faligot and Pascal Krop, *La Piscine: Les Services secrets français, 1944–1984*, Seuil (Paris, 1984), 153–4.

18. Bernert, *Roger Wybot*, 443, 449, 451–2.

19. Horne, *A Savage War of Peace*, 237–8.

20. Faligot and Krop, *La Piscine*, 142, quote a French officer who claims that the SDECE infiltrated the crew of the *Athos* and had tracked it since its departure from Beirut to Alexandria. However, Ian Black and Benny Morris believe that the original tip came from the Mossad. *Israel's Secret Wars: A History of Israel's Intelligence Services*, Grove Weidenfeld (New York, 1992), 173. French intelligence officer Henri Jacquin insists that Israeli intelligence gathered through North Africa's large Jewish population and passed on to the French was often "fresher" than the SDECE's. Cooperation between the services was ended by de Gaulle in 1961. Henri Jacquin, *La Guerre secrète en Algérie*, Olivier Orban (Paris, 1977), 164.

21. Faligot and Krop, *La Piscine*, 151.

22. Faligot and Krop, *La Piscine*, 151–2.

23. Jacquin, *La Guerre secrète en Algérie*, 177–8; Bernert, *S.D.E.C.E. Service 7*, 210.

24. Bernert, *S.D.E.C.E. Service 7*, 215.

25. Bernert, *S.D.E.C.E. Service 7*, 176–200; Horne, *A Savage War of Peace*, 261–3.

26. Horne, *A Savage War of Peace*, 129. Bernert, *S.D.E.C.E. Service 7*, 207–8 says that it was the invention of an "occasional agent."

27. Bernert, *S.D.E.C.E. Service 7*, 210.

28. Thyraud de Vosjoli, *Lamia*, 277.

29. Faligot and Krop report that Mattei was under surveillance, but that the SDECE had issued no orders to kill him. Besides, they no longer had a motive for doing so in October 1962, as the Algerian War was over. The authors repeat charges that Mattei was murdered by the mafia working under contract for the CIA. *La Piscine*, 218–19. Thyraud de Vosjoli offers Mattei's death as evidence of how far Jacques Foccart, de Gaulle's *éminence grise* in intelligence matters, was prepared to carry his vengeance even when it no longer served any political purpose.

30. Howard R. Simpson, *Tiger in the Barbed Wire: An American in Vietnam, 1952–1991*, Brassey's (U.S.) (Washington, D.C., and New York, 1992), 9.

31. Black and Morris, *Israel's Secret Wars*, 173; Jacquin, *La Guerre secrète en Algérie*, 140.

32. One version suggests that the French cabinet split when the possibility of intercepting Ben Bella was presented to them, with Premier Guy Mollet and the Minister for Tunisian and Moroccan Affairs, Alain Savary, against. Unfortunately, for whatever reason, their opposition was insufficient to abort the operation. See Irwin M. Wall, "The United States, Algeria, and the Fall of the Fourth Republic," *Diplomatic History*, XVIII, No. 4 (Fall 1994), 493–4.

16. THE WAR WITHIN ALGERIA

1. Robert Thompson, *Defeating Communist Insurgency: Experiences from Malaya and Vietnam*, Macmillan (London, 1966), 84.

2. Alistair Horne, *A Savage War of Peace: Algeria 1954–1962*, Macmillan (London, 1977), 124.

3. Henri Jacquin, *La Guerre secrète en Algérie*, Olivier Orban (Paris, 1977), 123–4.

4. Horne, *A Savage War of Peace*, 122.

5. Henry Ainley, *In Order to Die: With the Foreign Legion in Indochina*, Burke (London, 1955), 30.

6. Simon Murray, *Legionnaire: My Five Years in the French Foreign Legion*, New York (Times Books, 1978), 158–9.

7. Horne, *A Savage War of Peace*, 124.

8. Jacques Massu, *La Vraie Bataille d'Alger*, Paris (Plon, 1971), 164.

9. Jean Planchais, *Une Histoire politique de l'armée*, Vol II: *1940–1962: De de Gaulle à de Gaulle*, Seuil (Paris, 1967), 302–3.

10. Ainley, *In Order to Die*, 30–1.

11. Service Historique de l'Armée de Terre (SHAT), 10H 266.

12. Henryk Szarek, *Five Flags to Freedom*, unpublished manuscript in possession of the author (pp. 202–4). Published as *Ein Soldatenleben*, Barett Verlag (Düsseldorf, 1988).

13. Jacquin, *La Guerre secrète en Algérie*, 133–4.

14. Horne, *A Savage War of Peace*, 198.

15. Yves Courrière, *Les Fils de la toussaint*, Fayard (Paris, 1968), 417.

16. Massu, *La Vraie Bataille d'Alger*, 165. Jacquin also defended the work of the DOPs in breaking up the FLN networks in Algeria, blaming their excesses on soldiers' frustrations over lenient justice for FLN suspects. The DOPs were disbanded in 1960. *La Guerre secrète en Algérie*, 135.

17. Thompson, *Defeating Communist Insurgency*, 85.

18. Roger Faligot and Pascal Krop, *La Piscine: Les Services secrets français, 1944–1984*, Seuil (Paris, 1985), 158–9.

19. Jean Lacouture, *De Gaulle: The Ruler, 1945–1970*, Norton (New York, 1992), 266–7.

20. Jacquin, *La Guerre secrète en Algérie*, 239–50, 295.

21. Horne, *A Savage War of Peace*, 258.

22. Philippe Bernert, *Roger Wybot et la bataille pour la DST*, Presses de la Cité (Paris, 1975), 450.

23. Faligot and Krop, *La Piscine*, 165–9.

24. Faligot and Krop, *La Piscine*, 209.

25. Quoted in Faligot and Krop, *La Piscine*, 160.

26. Jacquin, *La Guerre secrète en Algérie*, 203–17.

27. Horne, A *Savage War of Peace*, 257.

28. Bernert, *Roger Wybot*, 449–50. On the other hand, Wybot had little cause to boast, as the DST had little experience in running agents. Its "Manipulation" section for Algiers was considered remarkably incompetent, especially after its deputy chief turned out to be an FLN agent. Faligot and Krop, *La Piscine*, 154.

29. Horne, *Savage War of Peace*, 336.

30. Pierre Péan, *L'Homme de l'ombre: Eléments d'enquête autour de Jacques Foccart, l'homme le plus mystérieux et le plus puissant de la Ve République*, Fayard (Paris, 1990), 223.

31. Péan, *L'Homme de l'ombre*, 224, 226, 228–9.

32. Bernert, *Roger Wybot*, 453–70.

33. Péan, *L'Homme de l'ombre*, 227.

34. François Mitterrand, *Le Coup d'état permanent*, Plon (Paris, 1965).

35. Wybot claimed that de Gaulle believed that the DST had bugged the room in a Paris hotel where de Gaulle received visitors during his weekly trips to Paris between 1946 and 1958. Bernert, *Roger Wybot*, 484, 486–7.

36. The commander-in-chief in Algeria, General Fernand Gambiez, received a warning from the Sécurité Militaire that officers were preparing a coup, but he refused to believe it. Roger Faligot and Rémi Kauffer, *Les Résistants: De la guerre de l'ombre aux allées du pouvoir, 1944–1989*, Fayard (Paris, 1989), 397.

37. In that it suggested that the OAS planned, on the Maoist model, to swim like a fish in the friendly waters of *pied noir* quarters of Algiers. Horne, A *Savage War of Peace*, 486.

38. Faligot and Krop, *La Piscine*, 219–20; Jacquin, *La Guerre secrète en Algérie*, 239, 314; Jacques Harstrich and Fabrizio Calvi, *R.G.: 20 ans de police politique*, Calmann-Lévy (Paris, 1991), 31.

39. Apparently, the SDECE failed to carry out orders to make airports in the Paris area inoperable in the wake of the April 1961 Algiers putsch, when it was feared that airborne troops from Algeria would try to capture de Gaulle. Péan, *L'Homme de l'ombre*, 241.

40. Roussillat at the SA and Grossin at the SDECE took the position that the role of their services was to combat the FLN, and that to employ them in divisive operations like the struggle against the OAS threatened their cohesion. According to Pierre Péan, Roussillat refused Foccart's request to assassinate Godard. Roussillat and Grossin also flew OAS conspirator Colonel Antoine Argoud out of Algeria on an SDECE plane and allowed him to escape into exile. Péan, *L'Homme de l'ombre*, 247–8, 250–1, 257–8.

41. During the trial of the OAS members eventually arrested for this assassination attempt, it was charged, though never proven, that Foccart had staged the attack to convince de Gaulle to devote more energy to the struggle

against the OAS and to be more security-conscious. Péan, *L'Homme de l'ombre*, 255.

42. Faligot and Kauffer, *Les Résistants*, 407–8.

43. "Rapport de la commission d'enquête sur les activités du Service d'Action Civique," *Assemblée Nationale. Seconde session ordinaire de 1981–1982*, No. 955, Vol. I, Alain Moreau (Paris, 1982), 181, 190.

44. Horne, A *Savage War of Peace*, 492–3.

45. Philippe Thyraud de Vosjoli, Little, Brown (Boston and Toronto, 1970), *Lamia*, 267.

46. "Rapport," 187.

47. It is more likely that the BDL was the source of intelligence on the OAS rather than the *barbouzes* as Horne suggests. A *Savage War of Peace*, 493–4. Harstrich and Calvi, R.G., 20–5.

48. Horne, A *Savage War of Peace*, 495.

49. Faligot and Kauffer, *Les Résistants*, 411.

50. Thyraud de Vosjoli argues that the purpose of *les spéciaux* was to carry out atrocities which would then be blamed on the OAS. *Lamia*, 268–9.

51. Horne blames Degueldre for the explosion. A *Savage War of Peace*, 494. Thyraud de Vosjoli says that Lemarchand sent it because the *barbouzes* had become a nuisance and had refused to cease their activities. *Lamia*, 269.

52. Horne, A *Savage War of Peace*, 495.

53. Horne, A *Savage War of Peace*, 503.

54. It is possible that the tip which led to Salan's arrest came from an anti-FLN Muslim group financed by the SA. See Péan, *L'Homme de l'ombre*, 249–50.

55. Péan, *L'Homme de l'ombre*, 257–9, repeats the accusation made by Argoud in *La Décadence, l'imposture et la tragédie*, Fayard (Paris, 1974). The parliamentary committee insisted that the Sécurité Militaire had been responsible. "Rapport," 188.

17. INTELLIGENCE IN DE GAULLE'S REPUBLIC

1. Jean Guisnel and Bernard Violet, *Services secrets: Le Pouvoir et les services de renseignements sous François Mitterrand*, Editions la Découverte (Paris, 1988), 107–8. These remarks apply specifically to the DST. But, as will be seen, they can be applied equally to the SDECE, RG, and Sécurité Militaire.

2. Wybot attributed his dismissal to a "disquieting" conversation between two diplomats, recorded by a DST microphone secreted in an ambassadorial desk. In the estimation of the DST director, the transcript of this conversation, forwarded to de Gaulle through the Minister of the Interior, confirmed in

the General's mind that the microphones discovered under the table at the Hotel Lapérouse in Paris, to which during his powerless "Desert Years" de Gaulle had traveled almost weekly from Colombey-les-Deux-Eglises to receive visitors, were a DST installation. "All secret police have bad habits, that's well known," de Gaulle was alleged to have said. What the General found "indigestible," however, was that the bug had been placed by a "Companion of the Liberation." He promptly terminated Wybot's fifteen-year tenure as chief of the DST. Philippe Bernert, *Roger Wybot et la bataille pour la DST*, Presses de la Cité (Paris, 1975), 475, 486.

3. Pierre Marion, *La Mission impossible: A la tête des services secrets*, Calmann-Lévy (Paris, 1991), 115–16.

4. Nicolas Fournier and Edmond Legrand, *E . . . comme espionnage*, Alain Moreau (Paris, 1978), 54.

5. Fournier and Legrand, *E . . . comme espionnage*, 110.

6. Marion, *La Mission impossible*, 116. Also Pierre Marion, *Pouvoir sans visage*, Calmann-Lévy (Paris, 1990), 109.

7. Christine Ockrent and Alexandre de Marenches, *Dans le secret des princes*, Stock (Paris, 1986), 121. Also Marenches and David A. Andelman, *The Fourth World War: Diplomacy and Espionage in the Age of Terrorism*, Morrow (New York, 1992), 80–2, 85–6.

8. Pierre Favier and Michel Martin-Roland, *La Décennie Mitterrand*, Vol. I: *Les Ruptures, 1981–1984*, Seuil (Paris, 1990), 513.

9. Roger Faligot and Pascal Krop, *La Piscine: The French Secret Services Since 1944*, Basil Blackwell (Oxford, 1989), 135–6.

10. Marion, *La Mission impossible*, 116, complains that Giscard refused to spy on allies. Faligot and Krop, *La Piscine*, 257.

11. Fournier and Legrand, *E . . . comme espionnage*, 126. Faligot and Krop, *La Piscine*, 270.

12. Favier and Martin-Roland, *La Décennie Mitterrand*, I, 513.

13. Ezra N. Suleiman, *Politics, Power, and Bureaucracy in France: The Administrative Elite*, Princeton University Press (Princeton, N.J., 1974), 370–1.

14. Faligot and Krop, *La Piscine: Les Services secrets français, 1944–1984*, Seuil (Paris, 1985), 416. Quoting an SDECE document.

15. Philippe Thyraud de Vosjoli, *Lamia*, Little, Brown (Boston and Toronto, 1970), 285, 294–6.

16. Interview with George Allen, ex-CIA employee, 4 February 1993. Faligot and Krop, *La Piscine: The French Secret Services*, 221, question whether Thyraud de Vosjoli ever ran an agent network in Cuba or was merely passing on to Paris information given him by the CIA.

17. Michael R. Beschloss, *The Crisis Years: Kennedy and Khrushchev 1960–1963*, Edward Burlingame Books (New York, 1991), 412–13, 423–25.

The CIA reckoned that of 200 agent reports of Cuban missiles received, only six were accurate. The solid intelligence was supplied by air reconnaissance photographs.

18. A. W. DePorte, "The Fifth Republic in Europe," in William G. Andrews and Stanley Hoffman, eds., *The Fifth Republic at Twenty*, SUNY Press (Albany, N.Y., 1981), 401.

19. Fournier and Legrand, *E . . . comme espionnage*, 60–1. Angelo Codevilla, *Informing Statecraft: Intelligence for a New Century*, Free Press (New York, 1992), 152.

20. Thierry Wolton, *Le Grand Recrutement*, Grasset (Paris, 1993), 235.

21. For accounts of the Sapphire episode, see Tom Mangold, *Cold Warrior. James Jesus Angleton: The CIA's Master Spy Hunter*, Simon & Schuster (New York, 1991), Ch. 9. Thyraud de Vosjoli, *Lamia*, 298–328. Faligot and Krop, *La Picine*, (Oxford, 1989), 210–20.

22. Phillip Knightley, *The Second Oldest Profession: Spies and Spying in the Twentieth Century*, Norton (New York, 1987), 253, 258–9, 263–6.

23. Christopher Andrew and Oleg Gordievsky, *KGB: The Inside Story*, HarperCollins (New York, 1990), 444.

24. John Lewis Gaddis, "The Intelligence Revolution's Impact on Postwar Diplomacy," in Lieutenant Colonel Walter T. Hitchcock, ed., *The Intelligence Revolution: A Historical Perspective*, Proceedings of the Thirteenth Military History Symposium, U.S. Air Force Academy, Colorado Springs, Colorado, 12–14 October 1988, Office of Air Force History (Washington, D.C., 1991), 258–61.

25. Knightley, *The Second Oldest Profession*, 343.

26. Andrew and Gordievsky, *KGB*, 7.

27. Andrew and Gordievsky, *KGB*, 444–5.

28. Pierre Péan, *L'Homme de l'ombre: Eléments d'enquête autour de Jacques Foccart, l'homme le plus mystérieux et le plus puissant de la Ve République*, Fayard (Paris, 1990), 388.

29. André Labarthe, Moullec, and Maurice Dejean. Wolton, *Le Grand Recrutement*, 241–2.

30. French specialist Thierry Wolton dismisses the generally accepted version that Dejean was forced into a compromising situation by the Soviets in the late 1950s and then blackmailed into spying. Rather, he believes that the compromising situation was arranged to force Dejean to continue to spy after he wanted to sever his contacts with the KGB once he became ambassador. Labarthe was arrested by the DST in 1964 as the result of the VENONA intercepts, suffered a heart attack, and died during interrogation. *Le Grand Recrutement*, 238–9, 241.

31. Peter Wright, *Spy Catcher*, Dell (New York, 1988), 301–5.

32. Mangold, *Cold Warrior*, 346, note 21. Péan, *L'Homme de l'ombre*,

518–20. Suspicion also fell on two senior French diplomats who had served in Eastern Europe.

33. Interview with author, 8 July 1991.

34. Ockrent and Marenches, *Dans le secret des princes*, 147.

35. Marion, *La Mission impossible*, 54.

36. Péan, *L'Homme de l'ombre*, 518–20.

37. Jean Lacouture, *De Gaulle: The Ruler, 1945–1970*, Norton (New York, 1992), 510–11.

38. Patrice Chairoff, *Dossier B . . . comme barbouzes: Une France parallèle celle des basses-oeuvres du pouvoir en France*, Alain Moreau (Paris, 1975), Ch. 12.

39. On the Ben Barka affair: Lacouture, *De Gaulle: The Ruler*, 509–13, 519–22; the French edition, *De Gaulle, Vol. III: Le Souverain, 1959–1970*, Seuil (Paris, 1986), 628–32, 647–52, has a slightly fuller version. Faligot and Krop, *La Piscine* (Oxford, 1989), 231–8; Philippe Bernert, *S.D.E.C.E. Service 7*, Presses de la Cité (Paris, 1980), 319–405, for Le Roy's claim that he was the scapegoat for a higher cover-up.

40. Lacouture, *De Gaulle: Le Souverain*, 632.

41. Lacouture, *De Gaulle: The Ruler*, 512–13, 521–2.

42. Tad Szulc, *The Secret Alliance: The Extraordinary Story of the Rescue of the Jews Since World War II*, Farrar, Straus & Giroux (New York, 1991), 98–9. Ian Black and Benny Morris, *Israel's Secret Wars: A History of Israel's Intelligence Services*, Grove Weidenfeld (New York, 1991), 46–7, 73–5, 171–82; Michael Bar-Zohar, *Spies in the Promised Land: Iser Harel and the Israeli Secret Service*, Houghton Mifflin (Boston, 1972), 225–30.

43. Black and Morris, *Israel's Secret Wars*, 203–4; Dan Raviv and Yossi Melman, *Every Spy a Prince: The Complete History of Israel's Intelligence Community*, Houghton Mifflin (Boston, 1990), 158–9.

44. Black and Morris, *Israel's Secret Wars*, 234–5.

45. Jacques Harstrich and Fabrizio Calvi, *R.G.: 20 ans de police politique*, Calmann-Lévy (Paris, 1991), 142, 208–9.

46. Faligot and Krop, *La Piscine*, (Oxford, 1989), 238.

47. Bernert, *S.D.E.C.E. Service 7*, 405.

48. Harstrich and Calvi, *R.G.*, 131. Bernert, *S.D.E.C.E. Service 7*, 277, 298–300.

49. Gaddis, "The Intelligence Revolution's Impact on Postwar Diplomacy," 265.

18. TERRORISTS, PARALLEL NETWORKS, AND
MONSIEUR PASQUA'S LUNCHEONS

1. *Libération*, 9 December 1992, pp. 21–2.

2. Jean Dolent and Thomas Daquin, *La Sécurité militaire*, Editions du Cerf (Paris, 1981), 24, 46.

3. The criticism has been that polls are conducted too far in advance to measure shifts in public opinion before elections. RG offices, especially in the provinces, are understaffed, so that they may be forced to rely on journalists for information on a meeting or demonstration they were unable to attend. Reports may be inadequately researched or the conclusions may be modified by subordinates unwilling to forward a report which may evoke ministerial displeasure. Alain Hamon and Jean-Charles Marchand, *P . . . comme police*, Alain Moreau (Paris, 1983), 168, 172.

4. Pierre Favier and Michel Martin-Roland, *La Décennie Mitterrand*, Vol. II: *Les Epreuves*, Seuil (Paris, 1991), 175. A recent report has insisted that, despite public statements to the contrary, the quality of RG reports has been compromised by fragmentation, lack of focus, poor recruitment, and low morale in the service, to the point that French politicians prefer to create their own intelligence cells or black chambers. Jean Guisnel and Bernard Violet, *Services secrets: Le Pouvoir et les services de renseignements sous François Mitterrand*, Editions la Découverte (Paris, 1988), 75.

5. *Libération*, 9 December 1992, p. 22.

6. Jacques Harstrich and Fabrizio Calvi, *R.G.: 20 ans de police politique*, Calmann-Lévy (Paris, 1991), 256.

7. Hamon and Marchand, *P . . . comme police*, 168–9.

8. Guisnel and Violet, *Services secrets*, 74–5. As the author can attest, foreigners marrying French nationals in France also undergo a background check. Fortunately, my future in-laws were told that there was nothing in my RG file which would disqualify me for family membership.

9. Guisnel and Violet, *Services secrets*, 70.

10. *Foreign Information Broadcast Service* (FBIS—*Western Europe*), 7 May 1986.

11. Georges Moréas, *Ecoutes et espionnage*, Stock (Paris 1990), 40–2.

12. John Hess, "CIA, Satire and Scandal: Why 'Le Canard' Endorses Domestic Intelligence," *Politicks & Other Human Interests*, I (14 March 1978), p. 30.

13. Guisnel and Violet, *Services secret*, 279.

14. See *The New York Times*, 5 March 1993, for accusations by journalist Edwy Plenel of *Libération* that his phone was tapped by the Elysée during his investigations of the *Rainbow Warrior* fiasco in 1986. Also Pierre Favier

and Michel Martin-Roland, *La Décennie Mitterrand*, Vol. I: *Les Ruptures*, *1981–1984*, Seuil (Paris, 1990), 516.

15. Moréas, *Ecoutes et espionnage*, 59, 27–8. Guisnel and Violet estimate that no more than 2,500 lines are monitored in France by the GIC, and not all of them simultaneously. *Services secrets*, 274–5.

16. Harstrich and Calvi, *R.G.*, 119–21.

17. Laurent Gally, *L'Agent noir: Une Taupe dans l'affaire Abdallah*, Laffont (Paris, 1987), 251.

18. For instance, investigation of the widely publicized murder of aristocratic industrialist Jean de Broglie in December 1976 revealed that the crime might have been prevented had the various police agencies involved coordinated the results of their taps. Moréas, *Ecoutes et espionnage*, 33.

19. Daniel Burdan, *DST: Neuf ans à la division antiterroriste*, Laffont (Paris, 1990), 83.

20. Harstrich and Calvi, *R.G.*, 127–39, 155–81.

21. The experience of this author, which admittedly is only anecdotal, would indicate that these files served to ensure that male students did their military service, sometimes in elite regiments, rather than allow them the alternative of civilian *coopération*.

22. Guisnel and Violet, *Services secrets*, 103.

23. Jean Rochet, head of the DST, claims that the RG insisted to de Gaulle that the CIA and Mossad were behind the May '68 disturbances. While the DST was able to disprove this, Rochet claims that he was able to stiffen Marcellin's backbone by demonstrating to him that the troubles were a product of the machinations of (unnamed) foreign intelligence services. *5 ans à la tête de la DST, 1967–1972: La Mission impossible*, Plon (Paris, 1985), 94–5.

24. Hamon and Marchand, *P . . . comme police*, 181.

25. Harstrich and Calvi, *R.G.*, 222–6; Hess, "CIA, Satire and Scandal," 27.

26. Harstrich and Calvi, *R.G.*, 154–65.

27. Hamon and Marchand, *P . . . comme police*, 165.

28. Jean-Marc Dufourg, *Section manipulation: De l'antiterrorisme à l'affaire Doucé*, Michel Lafon (Paris, 1991), 80–1, 108–18, 122–3.

29. *Libération*, 9 December 1992, pp. 21–2.

30. *Libération*, 20–21 March 1993, p. 8.

31. "Political Espionage in France Is a Cause Célèbre (Again)," *The New York Times*, 11 July 1994; "Les RG changeront d'orientation à la rentrée," *Libération*, 15 July 1994, p. 13; *Le Monde*, 13 July 1994, p. 26.

32. Favier and Martin-Roland, *La Décennie Mitterrand*, II, 423.

33. See *Le Monde*, 6–7 April 1986. Daniel Burdan of the DST's antiterrorist group recounted the story that a group of Palestinians wanted for a

bank robbery in Denmark were released by the DST because they threatened to unleash a bomb attack in France if they were extradited. Burdan, *DST*, 99–101.

34. Favier and Martin-Roland, *La Décennie Mitterrand*, II, 19–20.

35. Pierre Marion, *La Mission impossible: A la tête des services secrets*, Calmann-Lévy (Paris, 1991), 225.

36. It was the belief that the Basque ETA had been behind Audran's assassination which allegedly encouraged the Elysée to sanction the release of information to Spanish police on ETA refugees in France, who were subsequently assassinated. See below. Dufourg, *Section manipulation*, 80.

37. Pierre Péan, *La Menace*, Fayard (Paris, 1987), 132.

38. Pierre Marion, *Le Pouvoir sans visage*, Calmann-Lévy (Paris, 1990), 240–1.

39. Favier and Martin-Roland, *La Décennie Mitterrand*, II, 687–8.

40. Roger Faligot and Pascal Krop, *La Piscine: Les Services secrets français, 1944–1984*, Seuil (Paris, 1985), 328–9.

41. Marion, *Pouvoir*, 103.

42. Favier and Martin-Roland, *La Décennie Mitterrand*, II, 31–7.

43. Favier and Martin-Roland, *La Décennie Mitterrand*, II, 434.

44. Hamon and Marchand, *P . . . comme police*, 186–8.

45. See David Yallop, *Tracking the Jackal: The Search for Carlos, the World's Most Wanted Man*, Random House (New York, 1992).

46. Harstrich and Calvi, *R.G.*, 235.

47. Paul Barril, *Missions très spéciales*, Presses de la Cité (Paris, 1984), 241.

48. Favier and Martin-Roland, *La Décennie Mitterrand*, II, 18–20.

49. Guisnel & Violet, *Services secrets*, 215.

50. Marion, *La Mission impossible*, 74, 117, 124–5, 151–79.

51. Philippe Thyraud de Vosjoli, *Lamia*, Little, Brown (Boston and Toronto, 1970), 252–3.

52. The number of SAC members was never firmly established. The parliamentary committee convened to investigate SAC following the socialist victory of 1981 speculated that SAC hit its membership peak during the May '68 troubles, when it might have counted as many as 30,000 members. In 1981, the president of SAC claimed 10,000 adherents. The RG put SAC numbers at around 5,000. The committee counted 4,555, but not all departments are listed. An estimated 10 to 15 percent were in the police. Opportunists, gangsters, and men with extreme right-wing views were also well represented. "Rapport de la commission d'enquête sur les activités du Service d'Action Civique," *Assemblée Nationale. Seconde session ordinaire de 1981–1982*, No. 955, Alain Moreau (Paris, 1982), I, 67–73.

53. These tasks continued into the 1970s, and included the use of police

dogs, nightsticks, and even firearms by SAC members against opponents who appeared at rallies or tried to tear town political posters. They also moved to break up opposition campaign headquarters and disrupt their political rallies. "Rapport," 128–36.

54. "Rapport," 62.

55. Pierre Péan, *L'Homme de l'ombre: Eléments d'enquête autour de Jacques Foccart, l'homme le plus mystérieux et le plus puissant de la Ve République*, Fayard (Paris, 1990), 225.

56. "Rapport," I, 42–5.

57. "Rapport," I, 23–4, 143, 151, 156–8, 163–71.

58. "Rapport," 64.

59. "Rapport," 46–7; Guisnel and Violet, *Services secrets*, 190; Péan, *L'Homme de l'ombre*, 354–65.

60. "Rapport," 54–5; Francis Terry McNamara, *France in Black Africa*, National Defense University (Washington, D.C., 1989), 187.

61. McNamara, *France in Black Africa*, 80.

62. "Good Life in Gabon Comes at a Heavy Price," *The New York Times*, 4 June 1993, p. A10.

63. McNamara, *France in Black Africa*, 176, 182.

64. Péan, *L'Homme de l'ombre*, 290.

65. Jean Lacouture, *De Gaulle*, Vol. III: *Le Souverain*, 413.

66. Roger Faligot and Pascal Krop, *La Piscine: The French Secret Services Since 1944*, Basil Blackwell (Oxford, 1989), 193–6.

67. The assassin, named William Bechtel, was later arrested in Belgium and extradited to Switzerland to stand trial for murder. However, he was acquitted in 1980 because of insufficient evidence and, it is alleged, after substantial diplomatic pressure from France. Guisnel and Violet, *Services secrets*, 286–90.

68. Péan, *L'Homme de l'ombre*, 290–2, 304–9; Pierre Péan, *Affaires Africaines*, Fayard (Paris, 1983), 94–127.

69. *The New York Times*, 25 April 1993.

70. Bruce D. Porter, *The USSR in Third World Conflicts: Soviet Arms and Diplomacy in Local Wars, 1945–1980*, Cambridge University Press (Cambridge, Eng., 1987), Ch. 6.

71. Péan, *Affaires Africaines*, 71–92; Péan, *L'Homme de l'ombre*, 320–9; McNamara, *France in Black Africa*, 180.

72. Jean Lacouture, *De Gaulle: The Ruler, 1945–1970*, Norton (New York, 1992), 567–70.

73. Péan, *L'Homme de l'ombre*, 351–2.

74. Christine Ockrent and Alexandre de Marenches, *Dans le secret des princes*, Stock (Paris, 1986), 184–6.

75. Péan, *L'Homme de l'ombre*, 445–79.

76. Guisnel and Violet, *Services secrets*, 191.
77. Guisnel and Violet, *Services secrets*, 42.
78. Favier and Martin-Roland, *La Décennie Mitterrand*, I, 271–2.
79. Favier and Martin-Roland, *La Décennie Mitterrand*, I, 96, 99, 513–14.
80. Marion, *La Mission impossible*, 95–6, 99–104, 109–14.
81. Favier and Martin-Roland, *La Décennie Mitterrand*, I, 345.
82. Guisnel and Violet, *Services secrets*, 195.
83. Marion, *La Mission impossible*, 41.
84. According to Faligot and Krop, the circumstances surrounding this episode "remain obscure." *La Piscine* (Paris, 1985), 347. Alexandre de Marenches, SDECE chief during the Mecca incident, insisted that the French only served in an advisory capacity and supplied some equipment, and that they had not entered the Islamic sanctuary. Ockrent and Marenches, *Dans le secret des princes*, 273–5. One story given general currency was that the cellars of the mosque where the terrorists had taken refuge were pumped full of tear gas and they were shot as they came out.
85. Guisnel and Violet, *Services secrets*, 79.
86. Possibly because Prouteau had been particularly useful in digging up compromising documents on some of Mitterrand's political opponents. Favier and Martin-Roland, *La Décennie Mitterrand*, I, 516, 728.
87. Guisnel and Violet, *Services secrets*, 81–6.
88. Favier & Martin-Roland, *La Décennie Mitterrand*, II, 442–5.
89. Burdan, *DST*, 10–11.
90. Favier and Martin-Roland, *La Décennie Mitterrand*, II, 681.
91. Favier and Martin-Roland, *La Décennie Mitterrand*, II, 431–5, 592–3.
92. *Le Monde*, 31 July 1987.
93. Guisnel and Violet, *Services secrets*, 204.
94. Favier and Martin-Roland, *La Décennie Mitterrand*, II, 669–72.
95. Favier and Martin-Roland, *La Décennie Mitterrand*, II, 672–88, 741–5.

19. *L'AFFAIRE RAINBOW WARRIOR*

1. John le Carré, "Tinpots, Saviors, Lawyers, Spies," *The New York Times*, 4 May 1993.
2. Bengt Danielsson and Marie-Thérèse Danielsson, *Poisoned Reign: French Nuclear Colonialism in the Pacific*, Penguin (London, 1986), 277–319.
3. John Dyson, *Sink the Rainbow Warrior! An Enquiry into the "Greenpeace Affair*,*"* Victor Gollancz (London, 1986), 92; Pierre Favier and Michel

Martin-Roland, *La Décennie Mitterrand*, Vol. II: *Les Epreuves*, Seuil (Paris, 1991), 330.

4. For a general discussion of these issues, see Uri Bar-Joseph, *Out of Control: Intelligence Intervention in Politics in the USA, Britain and Israel*, Ph.D. dissertation, Stanford University, 1990, 563, 570–2.

5. *Libération*, 6 November 1981; quoted in Danielsson and Danielsson, *Poisoned Reign*, 285. Dyson, *Sink the Rainbow Warrior!*, 93, 159–60.

6. Dyson, *Sink the Rainbow Warrior!*, 84–5.

7. Ray Cline, an experienced CIA agent who became Director of State Department Intelligence, claimed that CIA "covert operations" which drew most criticism were invariably ordered by higher authority. "In most of these cases, [the CIA] was following White House orders, perhaps too obediently, but not irresponsibly," Cline insisted. Lieutenant Colonel Walter T. Hitchcock, ed., *The Intelligence Revolution: A Historical Perspective*, Office of Air Force History (Washington, D.C., 1991), 304.

8. Dyson, *Sink the Rainbow Warrior!*, 93–5. On the issue of "plausible deniability," see Bar-Joseph, *Out of Control*, 31–2, 85–6.

9. *FBIS—Western Europe*, 26 September 1985, speaks of journalistic speculation on Mitterrand's role. Favier and Martin-Roland quote Lacoste as saying that he informed both Mitterrand and armed forces chief of staff and ex-SDECE chief Jeannou Lacaze. However, the authors suggest that, as it was expected that there would be no loss of life, neither Mitterrand nor the Prime Minister, Laurent Fabius, need have been consulted. *La Décennie Mitterrand*, II, 331–2, 335. On the other hand, the cost of the operation was such that it had to be paid for out of the Prime Minister's personal budget, which required an authorization from Mitterrand's chief of staff, General Jean Saulnier (p. 336).

10. Bar-Joseph, *Out of Control*, 587.

11. Jean Guisnel and Bernard Violet, *Services secrets: Le Pouvoir et les services de renseignements sous François Mitterrand*, Editions la Découverte (Paris, 1988), 160; Pierre Marion, *Le Pouvoir sans visage*, Calmann-Lévy (Paris, 1990), 96, says Action was keen to carry out the operation. Favier and Martin-Roland, *La Décennie Mitterrand*, II, 32, for the last interpretation.

12. Dyson, *Sink the Rainbow Warrior!*, 95.

13. Michael King, *Death of the Rainbow Warrior*, Penguin (Harmondsworth, 1986), 191.

14. Pierre Joxe insisted that the DST took their time verifying the phone numbers to protect the DGSE and the agents. Favier and Martin-Roland, *La Décennie Mitterrand*, II, 338.

15. *Foreign Information Broadcast Service (FBIS—Western Europe)*, 8 August 1985, K1.

16. *FBIS—Western Europe*, 4 September 1985, p. K1; 5 September 1985, p. K5.

17. Favier and Martin-Roland, *La Décennie Mitterrand*, II, 341–2.

18. Favier and Martin-Roland, *La Décennie Mitterrand*, II, 333, 340. It also appears as if Fabius oscillated between the wildly opposing solutions of avowing everything and offering to resign, and taking refuge behind the *secret défense*, (p. 341).

19. *FBIS—Western Europe*, 29 August 1985, p. K6.

20. King, *Death of the Rainbow Warrior*, 198–9; Favier and Martin-Roland insist that Tricot did not intentionally deceive, but accepted the arguments of Lacoste and Hernu that their people were only on an "intelligence" mission and had not planted bombs. *La Décennie Mitterrand*, II, 344–5.

21. Favier and Martin-Roland, *La Décennie Mitterrand*, II, 357.

22. Favier and Martin-Roland, *La Décennie Mitterrand*, II, 370.

23. *FBIS—Western Europe*, 30 September 1985, p. K3.

24. Knowing full well that the affair would last as long as the leaks to the press, Imbot ordered the arrest of four DGSE officers, including the deputy chief of counterintelligence, and of the ubiquitous gendarme Paul Barril, all of whom he accused of leaking information to the press about the affair to embarrass the socialist government. The officers offered the rather ingenious defense that they had leaked the information because they knew their superiors were lying to the government. *FBIS—Western Europe*, 24, 25, and 26 September, 8 October 1985.

25. Dyson, *Sink the Rainbow Warrior!*, 184.

26. King, *Death of the Rainbow Warrior*. Roger Faligot and Pascal Krop, *La Piscine: Les Services secrets français, 1944–1984*, Seuil (Paris, 1984), 288–96.

27. *FBIS—Western Europe*, 30 September 1985, p. K3.

28. Dyson, *Sink the Rainbow Warrior!*, 179.

29. Favier and Martin-Roland, *Le Décennie Mitterrand*, II, 340, 357.

30. Guisnel and Violet, *Services secrets*, 281.

31. Pierre Favier and Michel Martin-Roland, *La Décennie Mitterrand*, Vol. I: *Les Ruptures, 1981–1984*, Seuil (Paris, 1990), 514.

32. *FBIS—Western Europe*, 28 August 1985, p. K3; Favier and Martin-Roland, *La Décennie Mitterrand*, II, 353.

33. In the United States, congressional control of the intelligence services rests on the notion that, in the words of the Church committee, "the intelligence agencies carry out their missions in accord with constitutional process." The CIA director under Jimmy Carter, Stansfield Turner, also felt that CIA behavior should be guided by "honesty, openness, and respect for the rights of the individual," because the American public expects and will tolerate

nothing less. For Turner, the advantages of congressional oversight are many: They guarantee public confidence in the credibility of the CIA, strengthen the hand of the director when his staff engages in a cover-up, and ensures that the calculations of risks versus gains are carefully weighed before undertaking a mission. A congressional committee also becomes a vehicle through which the intelligence services "keep in touch with national views," all of which, in Turner's opinion, outweigh the disadvantages of possible security leaks or indiscretions. The greatest enemy of intelligence is loose or nonexistent controls which invite rogue operations. Stansfield Turner, *Secrecy and Democracy: The CIA in Transition*, Houghton Mifflin (Boston, 1985), 145, 149–53.

34. Harold C. Deutsch, "A Retrospect on the Symposium," in Hitchcock, *The Intelligence Revolution*, 327.

35. Marenches argued that, even in Washington, increased congressional scrutiny introduced under Carter and Turner had brought about the "self-destruction of the American services," a view echoed by some CIA veterans. Christine Ockrent and Alexandre de Marenches, *Dans le secret des princes*, Stock (Paris, 1986), 360–5.

36. Guisnel and Violet, *Services secrets*, 281–92.

37. Hitchcock, *The Intelligence Revolution*, 303.

38. Ockrent and Marenches, *Dans le secret des princes*, 368–9.

39. Pierre Marion, *La Mission impossible: A la tête des services secrets*, Calmann-Lévy (Paris, 1991), 256–7, 253.

40. But the roles quickly became reversed, and it was the State Department which sought a role in defense policy. Ernest R. May, "Intelligence: Backing into the Future," *Foreign Affairs*, LXXI, No. 3 (Summer 1992), 65.

41. Turner, *Secrecy and Democracy*, 269–70.

42. Guisnel and Violet, *Services secrets*, 162.

43. Marion, *La Mission impossible*, 253.

20. CONCLUSION

1. Thomas Powers, "The Truth About the CIA," *The New York Review of Books*, XI, No. 9 (13 May 1993), 54.

2. Powers, "The Truth About the CIA," 55. Among the CIA failures, Powers lists failure to predict the first Soviet atomic bomb, the North Korean and Chinese invasions in Korea, the Hungarian revolt, Fidel Castro's victory and Khrushchev's placement of missiles in Cuba, the Soviet invasions of Czechoslovakia and Afghanistan.

3. See the chapter "The Politics of Intelligence," in Michael Handel, ed., *War, Strategy, and Intelligence*, Frank Cass (London, 1989). See also

Michael Handel, ed., *Leaders and Intelligence*, Frank Cass (London, 1989), 5.

4. For a discussion of these issues, see Westley K. Wark, "Introduction: The Study of Espionage: Past, Present, Future?" in *Intelligence and National Security*, VIII, No. 3 (July 1993), 1–13.

5. Richard Betts, "Analysis, War and Decision: Why Intelligence Failures Are Inevitable," *World Politics*, XXXI, No. 1 (1978), 961–88.

6. Handel, *War, Strategy, and Intelligence*, 217.

7. Wark, "Introduction," 5.

8. J. L. Granatstein and David Stafford, *Spy Wars: Espionage and Canada from Gouzenko to Glasnost*, Key Porter Books (Toronto, 1990), 200–10.

9. For a discussion of multiple advocacy in the context of American foreign policy formulation, see Alexander George, "The Case for Multiple Advocacy in the Making of Foreign Policy," *American Political Science Review*, LXVI, No. 3 (September 1972), 751–90.

10. Phillip Knightley, *The Second Oldest Profession: Spies and Spying in the Twentieth Century*, Norton (New York, 1987), 4–7, 47–9.

11. George, "Multiple Advocacy," 779.

12. Handel, *War, Strategy, and Intelligence*, 266–9.

13. George, "Multiple Advocacy," 758.

14. *L'Express*, 30 May 1991, pp. 105, 107.

15. Handel, *War, Strategy, and Intelligence*, 206–10.

16. Interview with the author.

17. General Jean Pichot-Duclos, "L'Evolution actuelle des services de renseignement français," *Bulletin de AASSDN*, II, No. 158 (1993), 13. See also his "Vers un culture de renseignement," *Défense nationale*, May 1992.

18. Handel, *War, Strategy, and Intelligence*, 189.

19. Roger Faligot and Pascal Krop, *La Piscine: The French Secret Services Since 1944*, Basil Blackwell (Oxford, 1989), 272–3.

20. *Le Monde*, 20 January 1994, p. 2.

21. *Le Monde*, 17 June 1993.

22. Roger Faligot and Pascal Krop, *La Piscine: Les Services secrets français, 1944–1984*, Seuil (Paris, 1984), 345.

23. *FBIS—Western Europe*, 15 September 1993, p. 39.

24. Pierre Marion, *La Mission impossible: A la tête des services secrets*, Calmann-Lévy (Paris, 1991), 127.

25. Harold C. Deutsch, "A Retrospect on the Symposium," in Lieutenant Colonel Walter T. Hitchcock, ed., *The Intelligence Revolution: A Historical Perspective*, Office of Air Force History (Washington, D.C., 1991), 327.

26. Wark, "Introduction," 7.

27. Hsi-Hue Liang, *The Rise of Modern Police and the European State System from Metternich to the Second World War*, Cambridge University Press (Cambridge, Eng., 1992), 45–6.

28. Raymond Marcellin, *La Guerre politique*, Plon (Paris, 1985), 46–51.

29. Marcellin, *La Guerre politique*, 127–9.

30. Thierry Wolton, *Le KGB en France*, Grasset (Paris, 1986), 131–2, 142.

31. Marion, *La Mission impossible*, 50.

32. Alain Hamon and Jean-Charles Marchand, *P . . . comme police*, Alain Moreau (Paris, 1983), 186.

33. Marcellin, *La Guerre politique*, 130, 181.

34. At the time of writing, the DST was operating against Algerian fundamentalists in France. See *Le Point*, 18–24 September 1993, p. 21; *Le Quotidien de Paris*, 5 November 1993, p. 1; *Libération*, 10 November 1993, p. 3.

35. *Libération*, 12 April 1994, p. 12; *Le Figaro*, 12 April 1994, p. 10.

36. *Le Figaro*, 4 January 1994, p. 9. See also editorial by Gérard Dupuy in *Libération*, 1–2 January 1994. *FBIS—Western Europe*, 10 January 199, p. 27.

37. See "Algerian Militant Base Uncovered in France," *The New York Times*, 7 April 1994. Also, French security agents were dispatched to Algeria in the wake of the Christmas 1994 hijacking of an Air France jet by Islamic militants to work with Algerian authorities: *FBIS—Western Europe*, 5 January 1995, p. 13. A defense agreement signed with the United Arab Emirates included provisions for the exchange of intelligence: *Libération*, 19 January 1995, p. 13.

38. *Libération*, 11 August 1994, p. 3.

39. *Le Figaro*, 26–27 June 1993, p. 7.

40. *Le Monde*, 31 January 1989, pp. 1, 15.

41. *The New York Times*, 30 April 1993.

42. *Le Figaro*, 24 May 1993, p. 5.

43. Knight-Ridder dispatch, 18 April 1993.

44. *Le Monde*, 6 July 1989, p. 13.

45. *Libération*, 18 June 1991, pp. 21–3.

46. *Le Monde*, 19 May 1990, p. 32.

47. "Evidence on French Spies Rocks the CIA," *Sunday Times*, 11 April 1993, p. 23.

48. Amy Borrus, "Should the CIA Start Spying for Corporate America?" *Business Week*, No. 3235 (14 October 1991), 96–100; Mitch Betts, "CIA Steps Up Foreign Technology Watch," *Computerworld*, XXVI, No. 16 (April 20, 1992), 121.

49. William Johnson, "Information Espionage: An Old Problem with a New Face," *Computerworld*, XXIII, No. 43 (23 October 1989), p. 85.

50. Daniel P. Scuro, "The Dangers of Openness," *Security Management*, XXXIV, No. 9 (September 1990), 93–5; Richard J. Heffernan, "And the SPI Survey Says . . ." *Security Management*, XXXV, No. 10 (October 1991), 39–40; Michael Gardner, "Searching for Safe Procedures," *Security Management*, XXXIII, No. 9 (September 1989), 179–82.

51. Jean Pichot-Duclos, *Défense nationale*, January 1994, pp. 73–85.

52. Jacques Isnard, *Le Monde*, 20 January 1994, p. 22.

53. *The New York Times*, 30 April 1993; Knight-Ridder dispatch, 18 April 1993; Michael J. Steadman, "Industrial Espionage: What You Don't Know Can Hurt You," *Business and Society Review*, No. 76 (Winter 1991), 25–32.

54. Interview with CIA agent, Bob.

55. *Le Monde*, 31 March 1993, p. 18.

56. *Le Monde*, 25 February 1993, p. 9.

57. Borrus, "Should the CIA Start Spying for Corporate America?"; *Le Monde*, 25 February 1993, p. 9. Henri Loizeau, *La Tribune DesFosses*, 29 November 1994, pp. 18–19.

58. *Le Monde*, 24 November 1993, p. 26.

59. *L'Evénement du Jeudi*, 24–30 August 1989, p. 33; *Libération*, 7 May 1991, p. 3.

60. *Libération*, 7 May 1991, p. 3.

61. Pierre Favier and Michel Martin-Roland, *La Décennie Mitterrand*, Vol. I: *Les Ruptures, 1981–1984*, Seuil (Paris, 1990), 513.

62. *Défense nationale*, July 1991, pp. 9–21; see also *FBIS—Western Europe*, 19 April 1991, 12.

63. *Le Monde*, 29 August 1990, p. 5.

64. *Défense nationale*, July 1991, pp. 9–21; *Le Figaro*, 20 August 1990, p. 5.

65. *Le Quotidien de Paris*, 6–7 July 1991, p. 7; see also *Le Figaro*, 20 August 1990, p. 5, for a fuller explanation of the panoply of French special operations forces.

66. James J. Cooke, *100 Miles from Baghdad: With the French in Desert Storm*, Praeger (Westport, Conn., 1993), 57–8, 60–1, 90.

67. *Libération*, 29 November 1993, p. 8; *Le Monde*, 26 September 1991, p. 12.

68. Cooke, *100 Miles from Baghdad*, 62.

69. "Intelligence Successes and Failures in Operations Desert Shield/ Storm," Report of the Oversight and Investigations Subcommittee of the Committee on Armed Services, House of Representatives, August 16, 1993, U.S. Government Printing Office (Washington, D.C., 1993), 1–29.

70. *Le Figaro*, 2 November 1993, p. 8.

71. *Le Figaro*, 30 June 1989, p. 2.

72. Jean Guisnel and Bernard Violet, *Services secrets: Le Pouvoir et les services de renseignements sous François Mitterrand*, Editions la Découverte (Paris, 1988), 352–3.

73. Wark, "Introduction," 6.

74. *Le Monde*, 31 March 1993, p. 18.

75. *Le Figaro*, 30 May 1990, p. 44; *Libération*, 18 June 1991, pp. 21–3.

76. *Le Monde*, 6 July 1989, p. 13; *Le Quotidien*, 4–5 August 1990, p. 24.

77. *Le Quotidien de Paris*, 6–7 July 1991, p. 7.

78. *Le Monde*, 31 October 1991, p. 11, and 11 March 1993, p. 26; *Libération*, 10–11 October 1992, p. 6.

79. *Le Journal du Dimanche*, 8 March 1992, p. 7; *Le Quotidien de Paris*, 14 August 1992, p. 14; *Le Monde*, 27 November 1993, p. 13; *Libération*, 29 November 1993, p. 8.

80. See, for instance, "La DGSE recrute," *Le Monde*, 17 April 1986, which points out that various schemes to improve the quality of recruitment have been launched since the war, with little success.

81. *Le Canard enchaîné*, 27 June 1990, p. 4.

82. *Le Monde*, 31 March 1993, p. 18.

83. *Le Figaro*, 2 November 1993, p. 8.

84. *Le Monde*, 24 November 1993, p. 26.

85. *Le Monde*, 25 February 1993, p. 6.

86. Ernest R. May, "Intelligence: Backing into the Future," *Foreign Affairs*, LXXI, No. 3 (Summer 1992), 69–71.

APPENDIX. ENCRYPTION/DECRYPTION

1. David Kahn, *The Codebreakers: The Story of Secret Writing*, Macmillan (New York, 1967), xiv.

2. For a detailed explanation, including examples, see ibid., 99–105.

3. Ibid., 100.

4. Ibid.

5. Ibid., 103.

6. Ibid., 104.

INDEX

Abbas, Ferhat, 360
Abwehr, vii, 231, 232, 242, 277
Achiary, André, 373
Action Directe, 433, 454
affaire des fuites, 291, 345, 447, 479
affaire Passy, 479
affaire Rainbow Warrior, 455–67
Africa: and Foccart, 440–44, 481–82;
    French neo-colonialism, 441–44;
    mercenaries in, 443, 480, 481–82,
    491; parallel intelligence operations,
    403, 442, 480–82; SDECE/DGSE
    in, 440, 441, 442, 443, 444, 491;
    special operations, 481–82
Agadir crisis, 44, 51, 53
Ainley, Henry, 302, 379, 381, 382
Air Command for Surveillance, Infor-
    mation, and Communication (CAS-
    SIC), 497
air reconnaissance: in Indochina, 303–
    4; in World War I, 55–56, 92–96;
    in World War II, 171–72
Alemeda, Capt., 88
Alexander, Martin, 138, 140, 147, 163,
    168
Alexander I (Czar), 16, 25
Alexandri, Marcel, 298

Algeria: external war against FLN, 358–
    76; and fall of French Fourth Repub-
    lic, 393–96; war within, 377–403;
    see also Front de Libération Natio-
    nale (FLN)
Algerian Provisional Government
    (GPRA), 386
Algérie française, 393, 395, 397, 401,
    409, 439
Algiers, Battle of, 381–85
Allal El Fassi, 368
Alliance (Resistance network), 187, 231
Allies: acceptance of de Gaulle, 225,
    396; and credibility of Free French,
    226; and Enigma codes, 141, 154–
    58, 162–63; and postwar intelligence
    services, 265, 279–80; and Ultra,
    227, 228, 251; view of wartime secret
    services, 201, 230, 250–51, 258, 273
ALN, *see* Armée de Libération Natio-
    nale (ALN)
Ambler, Eric, 131
Ambrose, Stephen, 247
Ames, Aldrich, 414
Amicale Action, 395
Andrew, Christopher, 20, 48, 53, 62,
    414

Mitterrand, François: and *affaire des fuites*, 289, 290–91; and Algerian insurrection, 358, 363, 364; attitude toward intelligence, 405, 406, 407; and Camp Beauregard, 283; co-existence with conservative Prime Minister, 475; and Gulf War, 492, 493; hires civilian to head SDECE, 479; intelligence services under, 416, 423, 427, 430, 433–34, 435, 436, 447–54, 480; and intelligence under de Gaulle, 397, 418; and *Rainbow Warrior* affair, 459, 461, 462, 463, 464–65; and Soviet Union, 447–48; as target of intelligence-inspired scandals, 479, 480
Moch, Jules, 395, 396
Mohammed V, 375
moles, 413–14, 415, 416
Mollet, Guy, 374, 385
Moltke, 66, 67, 75
Monde, Le, 431, 462
Mons, Jean, 290, 291
Monson, Sir Charles, 41
Montagnards, 306, 325, 326, 328, 329, 330, 331, 333, 339, 340, 341
Morand, Col., 287
Moravec, František, 137, 141, 146
Mordant, Eugène, 297
Morice Line, 376, 385, 391, 392
Morlière, Louis, 299
Moroccan Nationalist Party, 368
Morocco, 434
Mururoa atoll, 456, 457
Moser, Aspirant, 208
Mossad, 370, 420, 431, 434, 452, 491
Moulin, Jean: arrested by SD, 216–17, 239; background of, 209–11; communist question, 134, 210–11, 279, 415; and de Gaulle, 184, 211, 212–13; death of, 217, 232; as head of Conseil National de la Résistance (CNR), 214–15, 399; importance to de Gaulle's success, 225; "moral question" of French defense, 229, 262; as Resistance hero, 213, 215, 216; Rivet's view of, 220; view of Frenay, 230

Moumié, Felix, 441–42
Mouvement pour la Communauté (MPC), 400
Mouvement pour le Triomphe des Libertés Démocratiques (MTLA), 361
Mouvements Unis de Résistance (MUR), 214, 238
MPC, *see* Mouvement pour la Communauté (MPC)
MRP, *see* Christian Democratic Party
multiple advocacy, 474, 475
MUR, *see* Mouvements Unis de Résistance (MUR)
Muraille, Gen., 126
Murray, Simon, 379, 381
Muselier, Emile, 182–83, 224, 279, 415
Musse, Felix, 140
Mussolini, Benito, 141, 146, 166

Naccache, Anis, 432
Napoleon I: establishes Ministry of General Police, 8; royalist plot against his life, 7–8; and Russian campaign, 16; use of espionage by, 7–16; use of intelligence in campaigns, 10–16
Napoleon III, *see* Louis Napoleon
Na San, 307, 308, 327, 331, 332, 342, 350, 351
Nasser, Gamal Abdel, 366, 370
National Council of the Resistance, 415
National Security Council: proposed for France, 465–67, 494
National Security Council (U.S.), 459, 466, 495
Nationalist Chinese, 327, 334
NATO, 410, 412, 413, 415
Navarre, Henri, 382, 470, 473; beginning of Navarre Plan, 335, 337; justification of Dien Bien Phu, 339, 340; maquis significance, 331, 332, 338, 482; and Operation Castor, 318, 319, 320; strategic choices by, 342, 343, 344, 350, 353; takes command of French forces in Indochina, 303; and TR networks, 223, 230; view of *affaire des fuites*, 447; view of Geneva

Rassemblement du Peuple Français
(RPF), 275, 395, 397, 438, 439; see
also Service d'Action Civique (SAC)
Raymond, see Renault, Gilbert
Reagan administration, 447, 448; and
Iran-Contra episode, 459
Reinberger, Mr., 168–69
Reiss, Ignace, 133
Rejewski, Marian, 157, 161–62
Rémy, 187, 190, 199, 227, 233, 236,
239, 246
Renault, Gilbert, 180–81, 194
Renseignements Généraux (RG), 267,
268, 269, 284, 285, 361, 364, 383,
394, 399, 400, 401, 408, 422, 423,
424–25, 426, 428, 429, 430, 431,
432, 436, 439; defined, viii; statistical
and polling service within, 423–24
Renseignements Généraux de la Préfecture de Paris (RGPP), viii, 267, 268,
417, 418, 420, 423, 424
Renseignements Généraux Politique,
206
Resistance, 187, 199, 207, 225–64; and
action vs. intelligence gathering, 186,
278; beginning of, 175; carrying out
missions, 192–93; and civil war
among intelligence services, 218–24;
vs. collaboration, 275–76; communists in, 214–15, 278, 279; and de
Gaulle, 175, 406, 474; de Gaulle's
view of its role, 184–85, 225–26; divisions within, 187–88; as Gaullist
triumph, 217, 225; and German
STO, 209, 234, 238; and Giraud vs.
de Gaulle, 215–16; growth of, 209;
impact of, 257–58; Laval campaigns
against, 176; as model for organizing
secret services, 268; and Moulin,
210, 211–12, 213, 214–15; mystique
of, 226–29; not all networks Gaullist,
187–88; Passy's view of its role, 185–
90; as possible heir to French government, 204; and postwar intelligence
turf battles, 266; as prerequisite for
postwar intelligence work, 273–74;
purpose of, 225–26; secrecy in, 189;
shortcomings as intelligence model,
481; training for missions, 191–92;

unification of, 215–16; use of radio,
193–94, 240–45, 251
Resistance Myth, 226–29, 270, 329
Revers, Georges, 223, 285, 286, 287
Revers Plan, 309
Revolution of 1848, 18
Revolution of July 1830, 17–18
Rex, see Lemoine, Rudolphe
Reynaud, Paul, 148
RG, see Renseignements Généraux
(RG)
RGPP, see Renseignements Généraux
de la Préfecture de Paris (RGPP)
Rhodesia, 444
Ribière, Henri, 269, 271, 274, 286,
287, 288
Richard, Marthe, 129–30
Richelieu, Cardinal, 6
Richer, Henri, 130
Richer, Marthe Betenfeld, 130–31
Rif War, 122
Riquier, M., 127, 128
Rivet, Louis: boss of Paul Paillole, 142;
as Giraudist, 207, 218, 219, 221,
223, 224; head of SR, 141; and lead-
ers' refusal to listen to intelligence re-
ports, 142; leaves SR, 274; and
reorganization of intelligence, 267;
role in Giraud's escape from POW
camp, 202, 204; SR comes under
BCRA, 220; view of BCRA as politi-
cal intelligence service, 246; view of
leaders and intelligence, 141, 163;
view of SR as military intelligence
service, 206
Robert, Maurice, 441, 442
Robinson, Henri, 207, 210
Robinson, Peter, 248
Rocard, Michel, 431
Roccard, Yves, 250
Ronin, Georges, 174, 175, 176, 201,
204, 205, 207, 219, 225
Roosevelt, Franklin D., 184, 202, 203,
215, 219
Rosenberg, Julius and Ethel, 413
Ross, Steven, 141
Rougement, Jean-Louis du Temple de,
411
Roussillat, Col., 395

Tshombé, Moïse, 442, 443
Tunisia, 386, 434
Turenge, Alain, 460, 461
Turenge, Sophie, 460, 461
Turkish Airways, 432
Turpin, René, 290

"Ugly American," 355
Ultra, 227, 228, 251
United Nations, 363, 380, 385
Uris, Leon, 416
U.S. Army Security Agency, 279
U.S. National Security Council, 459, 466, 495
U.S. Office of Strategic Services (OSS), viii, 219, 231, 238, 248, 258, 261, 355
Uzdanski-Yelenski, Mr., 123

Valluy, Jean, 300, 305
Van Co, 286
Van Deman, Ralph H., 90
Vatican, 52
VENONA messages, 279
Vermeuil, Col., 274
Viaris, Gaetan de, 33, 35
Vichy government, 175, 204, 208, 209, 210, 224, 225, 254, 261, 266, 269, 276; Fourcaud contacts with, 194–95, 196–97; and French navy, 182, 183; leaders become collaborationists, 187; police (Milice), 232, 233, 236, 245, 255, 275, 278; role of intelligence, 175, 186; Service de Renseignements, 186, 188; and Vichy French in Indochina, 295; view of de Gaulle, 175; and Wybot, 268
Vidal, M., 237
Vietminh, 299, 301, 346–47; after French defeat, 354; Chinese support for, 294, 327, 335, 340, 341, 342, 345–46, 347, 348, 349–50, 351, 353; declare Democratic Republic of Vietnam, 298; defections by, 306–7; at Dien Bien Phu, 349, 350; failed

uprising in Hanoi, 300; finances of, 321, 323, 324; French need for alternative to, 294; Geneva negotiations, 289, 340, 345, 346, 353; growing power of, 335, 351, 353; and maquis, 327–28, 329, 344; and opium, 320, 330, 331; as resistance movement, 296; tactics of, 304–5; use of camouflage, 303–4; use of intelligence, 308–10, 311–12, 313; use of radio, 285, 299, 311, 313, 314–15
Vietnam, see Indochina
Vitasse, Maj., 394, 395
Viviani, René, 53
Voitot, Roger, 417, 420
von Bülow, Karl, 74
von der Marwitz, Gen. Georg, 74
Vo Nguyen Giap, 313, 318, 334, 343, 344, 470; attack on French in Hanoi, 298–99; Black River campaign, 327; at Cao Bang, 310, 311, 313; and Chinese communists, 341, 342, 346, 348, 349–50, 353; controls pace of war, 335; Laos offensive, 330, 331, 339; at Na San, 307, 313, 319, 327; and opium crop, 320, 330; view of Operation Castor, 347; viewed by French intelligence, 350–51
von Lancken (German ambassador), 51
von Stoffel, Baron Eugène Georges, 23
Vosjoli, Philippe Thyraud de, 234, 266, 269, 270, 274, 280, 281, 282, 285, 286, 288, 291, 292, 316, 366, 372, 373, 401, 409, 410, 412, 413, 416, 437, 488

Warin, Roger, 176, 189, 196–97; see also Wybot, Roger
Wark, Westley, 129, 145, 471
Watt, D. Cameron, 129
Weil-Curiel, André, 199
Weygand, Maxime, 148
wilaya: defined, ix